A QUESTION OF TRUST

A QUESTION OF TRUST

THE ORIGINS OF U.S.-SOVIET
DIPLOMATIC RELATIONS:
THE MEMOIRS OF
LOY W. HENDERSON

Edited, with an introduction, by
GEORGE W. BAER

HOOVER INSTITUTION PRESS

Stanford University, Stanford, California

Hoover Press Publication 333

First printing, 1986

Manufactured in the United States of America

90 89 88 87 86   9 8 7 6 5 4 3 2 1

Library of Congress Cataloging in Publication Data

Henderson, Loy W. (Loy Wesley), 1892-1986

  A question of trust.

  (Hoover archival documentaries)
  Includes index.
    1. Henderson, Loy W. (Loy Wesley), 1892-1986.
  2. Diplomats—United States—Biography. 3. United
  States—Foreign relations—Soviet Union. 4. Soviet
  Union—Foreign relations—United States. I. Baer,
  George W. II. Title. III. Series.
  E748.H412A36 1986   327.73047   86-7386
  ISBN 0-8179-8331-7 (alk. paper)

Design by P. Kelley Baker

Contents

Editor's Note

THE MANUSCRIPT OF LOY HENDERSON'S MEMOIRS in the Archives of the Hoover Institution is huge—1,519 typewritten pages. Nevertheless, it tells only part of the story of his service in the Department of State from 1922 to 1961, when he retired. He had hoped to recount his complete career, but illness in his family caused him to stop writing. The memoir, then, is incomplete, yet it has its own dramatic narrative structure, because it covers all his years in Eastern Europe from the end of World War I to the outbreak of World War II.

The present edition consists of 1,286 pages of the manuscript, taking the story up to 1939. It seemed unnecessary to include the final 300 or so pages, as they are largely drawn from records found in readily accessible official, published sources.

Also deleted are some lists of persons, verbatim memoranda that repeat points already made in the text, extraneous travelogues, and a few other repetitive or inconsequential passages. Some spelling and typographical errors were corrected and a few changes made for the sake of clarity. None of these changes alters in any way the memoir's tone or purpose, which is to record the opening chapters of Soviet-American relations from the perspective of an eyewitness.

PREFACE

THE HOOVER INSTITUTION ON WAR, REVOLUTION AND PEACE dates back to 1919 when Herbert Hoover gave Stanford University fifty thousand dollars to collect and preserve documents on the recently ended World War. Stanford sent a history professor to Europe to direct a team of young scholars who, at Hoover's request, were released from military service to become "historical sleuths." Their job was to search for official government reports and the records of private organizations, as well as for magazines, newspapers, and so-called ephemera (leaflets, tracts, broadsides, photographs, posters, and banners) that would provide scholars with the raw materials essential for their studies of the causes and consequences of the war. One of Stanford's scholar-sleuths, Dr. Frank A. Golder, was visiting Berlin in 1920 when he met Loy W. Henderson, who was serving as a member of the American Red Cross Commission. Golder secured Henderson's cooperation in locating documents on postwar famine relief efforts in Germany and Poland.

Mr. Henderson could not have foreseen that the Hoover War Library, as it was then called, would grow to be the world's largest private repository for documents on twentieth century history—the place to which scholars flock if they want to study the causes of war or the processes of peacemaking, revolutionary ideologies and movements, resistance to tyranny, or relief efforts on behalf of the victims of wars and famines. It is even less likely that Mr. Henderson could have imagined that 66 years later the Hoover Institution Press would be publishing his memoirs—the story of his long and distinguished career in the U.S. Foreign Service, including the central role he played in U.S.-Soviet relations between 1927 and the outbreak of World War II in September 1939.

A word or two about the genesis of these memoirs seems in order, as well as an explanation of how the manuscript came to be housed in the Hoover Institution Archives and why it is being published now, several years after we acquired it. When Mr. Henderson retired in 1961 he intended to write a full length autobiography, including his 37-year career as a diplomat. In October 1968 a representative of the Hoover Institution Archives visited Mr. Henderson in Washington, D.C., to inquire about the availability of his career papers and the memoirs he was known to be working on. Mr. Henderson replied that his writing, based on extensive research in the Library of Congress and the State Department's Archives, was progressing well. He had already filled ten binders with a total of 1,600 pages of unedited manuscript. He indicated that, in principle, he was favorably disposed to giving his memoirs to the Hoover Institution Archives someday and he expressed his hope that the Institution might be interested in publishing them. But he delayed making any firm commitment because he hoped to continue working on them, at least until he could bring his narrative up to the summer of 1943, when his activities shifted from Eastern Europe to the Near East, South Asia, and Africa.

Nine years later, when he was 85, Mr. Henderson reluctantly concluded that due to problems of ill-health and a lack of research and secretarial assistance, he was unable to complete his life story. He agreed to send the existing manuscript to the Hoover Archives, but he retained the right of publication because he still hoped to find time to edit and condense his memoirs. Several years passed before we heard from him again. In 1984, he wrote to us to say that he still hoped to see his memoirs published during his lifetime, but he realized that he could not do the necessary editing himself. He asked if a well qualified person was available to do the job.

By sheer serendipity, on the very day that Mr. Henderson's letter arrived here, someone was visiting the Hoover Institution who was an ideal candidate for the assignment. I asked Professor George W. Baer, a Harvard-trained historian and a recognized expert on twentieth century diplomatic history, if he would be willing to do the necessary editing and condensing. He took up the assignment with enthusiasm. After checking the manuscript for factual accuracy and verifying the quotations from the documents Mr. Henderson had used, Dr. Baer set out to condense the manuscript by several hundred pages. I believe the results speak well for his efforts. He has also written an introductory essay that ably sets the context for readers who have no prior knowledge of Mr. Henderson's career.

The editors and all who worked on this volume regret that Mr. Henderson did not live to hold the published work in his hands. He died on March 24, 1986, just three months short of his 94th birthday.

This volume is the ninth to be published in the Hoover Archival Documentaries, a series conceived by Milorad M. Drachkovitch. On behalf of Mr. Henderson, Dr. Baer, and myself, we want to thank Charles Palm, the Archivist of the Hoover Institution, for supporting and encouraging this publishing project, and Dr. John B. Dunlop, Associate Director of the Institution, for making time to review the edited manuscript. We are also indebted to Margot Johnston for typing the Introduction, to Julia Johnson for her conscientious copyediting, and to Patricia Baker for designing a handsome book and dust jacket.

Two other senior diplomats have previously published their eyewitness accounts of the early strained relations between the United States and the Soviet Union. To the essential list of readings that includes Charles E. Bohlen's *Witness to History* and George F. Kennan's *Memoirs, 1925–1950*, we are pleased to add Loy W. Henderson's *A Question of Trust*.

Robert Hessen
General Editor
Hoover Archival Documentaries

INTRODUCTION

George W. Baer

THESE MEMOIRS, written in the 1960s, describe Loy Henderson's career as a U.S. diplomat in Eastern Europe during the 1920s and 1930s. They are the report of a major participant in the formation of U.S. policy toward the Soviet Union. Henderson was one of the founders of the so-called Soviet Service in the Department of State. His work in the Baltic states during the early years of the Bolshevik regime, his service on the East European desk at the State Department in Washington, and his position as a leading member of the first two U.S. ambassadorial missions to the Soviet Union gave him an extraordinary vantage point on diplomatic relations with Moscow.

Henderson was a central figure in the bitter debate over whether the United States should grant diplomatic recognition to the communist regime, and his memoir gives readers a unique look at this controversy. The recognition decision, and all later dealings with the Soviet state, hinged on one crucial question: would the Soviet Union be a trustworthy member of the international community, or would its ideology and revolutionary goals lead it to flout the conventions of international relations?

How is one to judge Soviet actions and intentions? This is the main theme of the book as well as the central issue in U.S. foreign policy. The questions Henderson posed remain as relevant today as they were before World War II. Can the Soviets be trusted? Henderson's answer was "no."

> It was my belief that since leaders of the Kremlin eventually were intending to contribute to the violent overthrow of all the countries with which the Soviet Union maintained relations, they considered Soviet relations with every country to be of a temporary or transitional character, subject to change at any moment.

Therefore, in any dealings with the Soviets, Henderson advised that U.S. statesmen should concede nothing, get a quid pro quo for everything offered, and insist on ironclad guarantees for every agreement. This viewpoint, shared by Henderson and his colleagues in the 1920s, 1930s, and 1940s, constitutes the core of the tough U.S. policy of the Cold War era and the policy of containment that is followed to this day.

Henderson's engagement with political issues developed gradually. He was born in 1892, a minister's son, and spent his youth on what was still, in many ways, the American frontier. Reliable and hardworking, he was in training as a lawyer when the entry of the United States into the Great War awakened his interest in public service. He loved the law, predisposed to its demands for precision and its standards of order, but, as he writes, "by studying law in Denver while other young men were risking their lives on the battlefield, I was letting down not only my family but also my country." Unable to serve in the army because of an injury to his arm, he joined the American Red Cross just as the war ended.

Henderson's relief work in the Baltic states in 1919–1920 was an impressive example of American humanitarian service at its most demanding. His account conveys a rich sense of the enormous political and military turmoil in the region during the postwar era but tells too little of the forces and interests in conflict. Henderson's education in international politics was only just beginning. What confusion! The Russian civil war was raging; in the west, the "Volunteer Army" was pitted against the nascent Red Army. Tumultuous conflicts had arisen between local nationalist movements, regional soviets, and German military adventurists.[1] All this swirled about Henderson, who kept his head down and went on with his jobs of prisoner repatriation and humanitarian relief.

Henderson underplays the physical and mental effort his work must have involved. His biggest task, and the most successful, was the antityphus campaign in Estonia. The official report states the significance of this systematic sanitization: "Only in this drastic way could the entire country be protected from disease. . . Only in this energetic extension of intensive disinfection can the Baltic States and, through them, Western Europe and America be protected from the contagion now known to be raging in Soviet Russia." There is here an almost metaphorical foreshadowing of what was to be the central work of Henderson's diplomatic career: the prophylactic containment of the contagion of communism.

Henderson began his study of the Soviet Union in 1924 when, after a fondly remembered period of consular work in Ireland, he joined the State Department's Division of Eastern European Affairs. The department's position in the 1920s was that the United States should not recognize the new government of Russia as long as it seemed determined to interfere in America's internal affairs, failed to restore the confiscated property of American citizens, and repudiated debts incurred by the former Provisional Government of Alexander Kerensky. The State Department's stance was not fundamentally ideological. Instead, it was concerned mainly with traditional issues between nations and above all with standards of international law. These standards, for Henderson, were the necessary moral and political anchors of democracies in the otherwise anarchical, amoral world of international affairs.

Henderson was trained by the desk chief, Robert F. Kelley. As Charles E. Bohlen described him, "In no way was the tall, taciturn Kelly [*sic*] an anti-Soviet crusader. He had done exhaustive research on the Soviet Union in the 1920s and, as a result, insisted that because of the emotional controversy that surrounded the Soviet Union, the Eastern European Division should train its people not only to be objective but also to take special pains to make sure to verify every fact with substantial evidence."[2] When Henderson arrived at the State Department in 1924, the foundations of the U.S. position toward the Soviet Union were well established. This position was based on hardheaded caution, watchfulness, and a search for functional, formal agreements. There was no missionary opposition to the Soviet regime and little hope that it would change. This stance fit U.S. diplomatic tradition and the contemporary mood. Kelley and Secretary of State Charles Evans Hughes were deeply committed to international law and to abiding by one's contracts. This meant scrupulous attention to abiding by treaty agreements. Either the Soviet government would adhere to the accepted rules of international conduct or it would not. If it did adhere to the rules, then it could join the international community; if it didn't, then not. To have asked for a different approach in the years of Wilson, Harding, Coolidge, and Hoover would have been to ask for a different America.

Of course, the State Department's assessment of Soviet policy was made in light of an evaluation of the role that ideology played in the Soviet conduct of foreign affairs. In 1925, reading the department files, Henderson came to the conclusion that "the rulers in Moscow, although perhaps differing at times among themselves regarding the methods to be employed, were united in their determination to continue to promote chaos and revolution in the noncommunist world until they could achieve their ultimate objective of a communist world with headquarters in

Moscow...I did not see how anyone could reach a different conclusion after having gone through all the material I had examined on that tour in the Department and observing what the communists throughout the world were doing under Moscow's directions."

Perhaps this was an excessively narrow, ahistorical, and rigid position. Perhaps the State Department read too much into the Soviet government's revolutionary rhetoric or at least into its appetite for worldwide revolutionary upheavals. In the 1920s and 1930s too little note was taken of the Soviet regime's internal problems and its need for consolidation. However, the view that the Soviet Union was a political cause as well as an established country was the root of Henderson's—and the department's—outlook. It was not an ill-considered, knee-jerk response. It was a rational conclusion reached by people who evaluated the evidence and sought to protect an international order they valued.[3] This view of the Soviet Union as a political cause was shared by the State Department's Russian experts, notably George F. Kennan and Charles Bohlen. Commenting on the vigorous discussions among these men in the Moscow embassy in the 1930s, Henderson said: "While we all agreed what was the situation in the Soviet Union, the differences were about the extent to which we should allow the situation to affect relations between the U.S. and the USSR."[4]

Henderson was convinced that eventually the two states had to establish a workable diplomatic connection. But on what terms? After all, it was not simply the question of recognition that was at stake in the debates of the 1920s and the 1930s. At stake were the principles and the rules by which America conducted its affairs. The United States could not deal with a state if it could not be trusted to live up to its agreements or if its government actively endorsed the internal subversion of other states. Repeatedly, it was the matter of international conduct that was the core issue for Henderson.

In 1927 Henderson was posted to Riga, Latvia, which was the State Department's most important source of information on the Soviet Union. More specifically, in Henderson's words, the Riga legation was the only agency of the U.S. government "in a position to expose for the benefit of the Department the exaggerated nature of Soviet claims of accomplishments." This emphasis is important, for the staff thought it was not only Soviet propaganda they were combating but any misguided or mendacious reports by Western journalists and enthusiasts as well. "One of the main tasks of the Legation, therefore, was to try to bring more clearly into focus what it considered to be the true picture of the situation in the Soviet Union."[5]

Henderson's experience in Riga, including the studies he made for the State Department on Soviet agriculture, foreign trade, and the Soviet "world revolutionary program," confirmed the opinions he had brought from Washington. Until it was clear that the Soviet Union was trustworthy, until above all it would promise not to interfere in America's domestic political affairs, there was no point, indeed there would be only danger, in establishing a formal connection between the United States and the USSR. For Kelley, Henderson, and the Russian section in Riga there could be no recognition, no loans, and no commercial accords unless the Soviet leaders promised to prohibit revolutionary propaganda in the United States, to give assurances of civil and religious rights to U.S. citizens in Russia, and to settle government debts.

To the dismay of State Department professionals, President Roosevelt extended recognition to the Soviet state in 1933 without first obtaining clear commitments from Moscow. Henderson attributed the subsequent troubles in U.S.-Soviet relations to the president's lack of vigilance in his talks with Maxim Litvinov, the commisar for foreign affairs. In Henderson's view, the ensuing breakdown of negotiations on Soviet debts and U.S. claims was due to carelessness in formulating the recognition agreement. The rankling tone in this section of Henderson's memoirs reflects his irritation at having to cope with the confusion that followed recognition. Although he hardly mentions Secretary of State Cordell Hull's reticence in advancing the department's position during the recognition talks, Hull's behavior must have been frustrating. On the other hand, Henderson does not assess Roosevelt's broader political and international goals.

Above all, Henderson was appalled by the Soviet regime's refusal to live up to Litvinov's pledge to Roosevelt that it would be the "fixed policy" of the Soviet government not to harbor "any organization or group—and to prevent the activity on its territory of any organization or group—which has as an aim the overthrow or the preparation for the overthrow of, or the bringing about by force of a change in, the political or social orders of the whole or part of the United States, its territories or possessions."[6] Although this pledge did not mention the Communist International by name, it was clear to U.S. officials that this was the organization proscribed in the pledge. Thus, when the Congress of the Communist International met in Moscow in the summer of 1935 despite Ambassador William C. Bullitt's vehement protests, the State Department regarded it as a brazen reneging on the recognition agreement.

Henderson recalls that this breach of promise "did more . . . to damage relations between the United States and the Soviet Union during the period 1934–1938 than any other single factor." Certainly it destroyed Bullitt's hope of friendly relations, although Henderson notes that there were additional reasons for Bullitt's disillusionment: for instance, his exposure to the unexpected harshness of Soviet society. The honeymoon was over. It seemed by 1935 that the forebodings of the Foreign Service were borne out. Too much had been conceded too quickly. The Soviet government could not be trusted. This was the diplomatic lesson Henderson drew from the recognition controversy and its aftermath.

Henderson's descriptions of Bullitt and his successor, Ambassador Joseph E. Davies, are charitable and evenhanded. He was a friend of both men. Compared to Kennan's and Bohlen's assessment of Davies, Henderson's is positively benign. To the junior officers who shared the distrust and pessimism of Bullitt's final months, Davies seemed ignorant and naive. He was an embarrassment when he arrived in 1937. It was Henderson, as the senior career officer (he was first secretary when Bullitt left in June 1936), who silenced the grumbling and criticism and who kept the embassy on an even keel.

The contrast between the two ambassadors is indeed striking. Bullitt left full of bitter anguish; Davies arrived lighthearted and optimistic. Bullitt's premise for diplomacy was distrust; for Davies it was enthusiasm, a belief in the power of personal persuasion. One confronted hostile revolutionaries; the other anticipated stability and cordial agreement. The reports that Henderson himself sent from Moscow, even during the ebullient period of Davies's mission, consistently shared Bullitt's somber outlook.

But to what avail? In any discussion of U.S.-Soviet relations during this period, it is essential to remember that it was President Roosevelt, not the State Department, who set U.S. policy. Roosevelt was suspicious of the experts. He found their outlook restrictive and uncongenial. He shared Davies's optimism—and his ignorance—and it was by these lights that he set America's course. The president, not surprisingly, had only limited success in his effort to orient U.S. policy toward closer cooperation with the Soviet government. The unsettled debt question and the persistent warnings against trusting the Soviets, issues kept alive in the State Department, limited Roosevelt's capacity to make a fresh start.[7] He was further constrained in part by the strong isolationist and anti-Soviet mood of the United States and in part by the reluctance of the Soviets to cooperate.

In a valuable section of the memoirs Henderson gives an account of the Moscow purge trials of the late 1930s. He was the only official U.S. observer at the trial of Zinoviev and Kamenev, and his report presents an accurate picture of how the trials appeared to the diplomatic corps. Its members thought that the purpose of the trials was to purge Trotskyites who had challenged Stalin's leadership by accusing Stalin of moving away from communism in the direction of state capitalism. As the diplomats saw it, Stalin was doing away with his left-wing opponents, tarring them as pro-German, and blaming them for failures in his own economic and financial plans.

Thirty years later, while he was writing these memoirs, Henderson added a thought on one of the most intriguing aspects of these trials. Perhaps, he wrote, the astonishing willingness of the defendants to testify against themselves came not from any hope of winning clemency, but from an honest desire "to contribute to the unity of the Party and the strengthening of the Soviet State. They might have been persuaded that by their allegations of wrong-doing and by their praise of Stalin, they would be promoting the cause of international communism to which most of them, despite their differences, had dedicated their lives." Although this idea is familiar to readers of Arthur Koestler's *Darkness at Noon* and to modern students of the trials, it was not obvious to Henderson in the late 1930s.

Likewise, as he wrote his memoirs in the 1960s and reflected on the secret trials of top army officers, Henderson saw a dimension that he had missed originally. In his dispatches in June 1937, he argued that Stalin feared that the army was becoming independent of party leadership—that it was attempting to imitate the German model and stand above politics. Henderson's first view of the trials was that Stalin had decided to stretch the army officers' friendly feelings toward Germany into a charge of treason and to use the opportunity to destroy the army's independence and make it unconditionally loyal to himself.

In retrospect, Henderson concluded that there was a strategic dimension to this discord, involving fundamental disagreements on how a potential European war would be fought. Henderson proposes here that Marshal Mikhail Tukhachevsky and other members of the Soviet General Staff supported a strictly defensive strategy that would draw the Germans into Soviet territory on which, from strong defensive positions, the Russian soldier would fight more effectively and more willingly. Stalin, on the other hand, had vowed that if the Soviet Union went to war, the fighting would never take place on Russian soil. Henderson thinks Stalin had told the army, in the event of a war between Germany and France or England, to take quick action in Finland, the Baltic states, and portions of Poland and Romania, and to fortify these areas as buffer zones against possible German aggression. According to Henderson, the army opposed this strategy of forward deployment and defensive advances, and it lost confidence in Stalin's strategy and leadership abilities. The officers' attitude, in turn, provoked the dictator's wrath and triggered the purge of the disobedient or disgruntled members of the army staff. Behind it all was Stalin's passion for unquestioning loyalty and obedience coupled with his insistence on preserving the monolithic quality of the revolution and the totalitarian social controls of the Soviet state.

In 1938, as he ended his stay in the Soviet Union, Henderson wrote a *tour d'horizon* of Soviet policy. He stressed the unreliability of a U.S. alliance with Moscow since the Soviets would never resist a German attack on France or England. He noted that Russia's intentions and its cooperation were entirely tactical and, in the long run, contrary to American interests. He pointed to its long-term goals such as military buildup, territorial expansion, control of Europe, and world revolution. His premise in 1938 was that Russia was essentially a revolutionary state, and he never wavered from this position. But his four years of experience, and the new threats from Germany and Japan, showed him and other U.S. experts that Russia was also embroiled in traditional balance-of-power rivalries.

Henderson left Moscow in the summer of 1938 to take up a position in Washington, D.C, as assistant chief of the new Division of European Affairs, which absorbed the old Eastern European Division.[8] On July 22, 1939, Henderson wrote a memorandum outlining the future direction of Soviet policy. It began: "The present rulers of Russia are still dominated by a spirit of aggressiveness, that is, they have not departed from the ultimate aim to enlarge the Soviet Union and to include under the Soviet system additional peoples and territories." The Soviet government was not interested in collective security. Any agreement with the West, Henderson wrote, would "only be on a basis which will give them what amounts to hegemony over Eastern Europe and which will render impossible for at least many years to come a united Western Europe."[9] Thirty-two days after he made this prediction, the Soviet government signed a treaty with Nazi Germany. This nonaggression pact, with its secret protocol carving up Poland, threw Henderson into confusion. This agreement he had not expected. He asked if Stalin was "on the point of abandoning the struggle for what I had regarded for many years as his ultimate goal, i.e., a communist world?" He could not imagine the Soviet government jettisoning the goals of the Communist International, which a pact with the Nazis implied. In his earlier memorandum of July 22, stressing the Soviet Union's aggressive designs, he had set aside ideological considerations but only to suggest that tactical matters of power politics might also play a role in Soviet policy. The pact went far beyond any tactics he had imagined. As a result, he concluded that from a diplomatic perspective "there was no basis for predicting what [Stalin's] next moves would be."

Within weeks Henderson was back to his original position, convinced that the pact was merely a short-run expedient. When war came to Europe in September 1939, his concern was that the Soviet Union would wait until the noncommunist states of the West tore themselves to pieces while Russia was "strengthening itself internally, and preparing itself to become the master of Europe."

It is here, on September 1, 1939, that the tale of this volume ends. However, the following brief account of subsequent events and Henderson's later career should help to place this work in context.

With the outbreak of World War II, the immediate issues Henderson had to deal with involved U.S. responses to the westward march of the Red Army and its invasion of eastern Poland, the Baltic states, and Finland. Henderson and the Roosevelt administration took a cautious line. There was, after all, little the United States could do. The U.S. government did not want to alienate Stalin and open the possibility that, at a time when the West European states were under heavy Nazi threat, he would aid Hitler or seek some accommodation with Japan. On the other hand, the Roosevelt administration could hardly signal its approval of Stalin's conquests.

The U.S. government, therefore, did little, even though the invasion of Finland in particular shocked American opinion. Demands for aid to the Finns descended on Washington. Henderson wrote that "for the first time in many years the American people are really commencing to understand something about the Soviet Union and the result has been extremely helpful and cleansing." But the U.S. government turned aside the appeals for aid. Caution ruled. Henderson was perplexed, yet he never suggested using as a weapon the threat to withdraw recognition from Soviet Russia.[10]

The German invasion of the Soviet Union in June 1941 naturally changed the international constellation. Washington and Moscow were now de facto allies. Henderson supported Lend-Lease, although he lacked confidence in the way Roosevelt handled the negotiations. As ever, he opposed unilateral concessions. A leading scholar surmises that Henderson's mistrust of administration policy, and his pessimism about the capacity of the Red Army to repel a German assault, led Henderson to underestimate the strategic benefits to America from possible Soviet resistance.[11] Henderson did have a reputation as a hard-liner and, in some circles no doubt, an anti-Soviet. His views increasingly grated both on the government in Moscow, eager for U.S. assistance, and on members of Roosevelt's administration and entourage, eager to assist. Henderson had now been for four years the assistant chief of the Division of European Affairs, in charge of the East European section. He fully expected to continue. In 1942 he went on an inspection tour of U.S. embassies and missions in the Soviet Union and Iran, even serving temporarily as chargé in Moscow. While Henderson was in Moscow, the ambassador to the United States, Maxim Litvinov, told a U.S. official that there would never be good relations so long as Henderson was on the East European desk. Secretary Hull refused to be intimidated. In March 1943 Henderson was assigned back to his former job. However, the opposition to his appointment was too strong. Litvinov's remark had reached sympathetic ears in the White House. Henderson records the dismaying words of Cordell Hull: " 'The people over there,' he said with a gesture in the direction of the White House, 'want a change.' " There was nothing to be done. Henderson gave up the European desk and asked to be sent as minister to Iraq.[12]

He was in Baghdad for a year and a half, a relatively quiet time for him since Iraq was effectively under British control. In the spring of 1945, as the end of the war brought new concerns to the fore, he was called back to Washington as director of the Division of Near Eastern and African Affairs. In this position he played a central, and controversial, role in formulating U.S. policy toward the future of Palestine and the creation of the state of Israel. Also in this period, in February 1947, the British government notified him that Britain would end aid to Greece and Turkey six weeks hence. It is not an exaggeration to say that Henderson and the State Department saw at once, in the words of Joseph Jones, "that Great Britain had within the hour handed the job of world leadership, with all its burdens and all its glory, to the United States."[13]

For the next few weeks Henderson was at Under Secretary Dean Acheson's right hand. He chaired the Special Committee to Study Assistance to Greece and Turkey and coordinated the reports that were to be the basis of the U.S. response. Two days into the crisis, at Acheson's house, Henderson asked if they "were still working on papers bearing on the making of a decision or the execution of one." When Acheson replied "the latter," they raised a toast to the confusion of their enemies.[14] From these labors came the Truman Doctrine and the Marshall Plan and a radically new U.S. foreign policy. Containment, opposition to Soviet political and territorial expansion, efforts to keep Europe and Turkey out of the Soviet orbit—these policies flowed from the conclusions about U.S.-Soviet relations that Henderson and his colleagues had long held. To Henderson, the Cold War came as no surprise.

In 1948 Henderson was named ambassador to India and minister to Nepal, as India became a republic and showed its desperate need for technical and economic assistance. He was sent as ambassador to Teheran in 1951 to deal with the volatile problems associated with the Anglo-Iranian dispute; he held this post during the CIA-enhanced coup that overthrew the government of Premier Mohammed Mossadegh. In October 1954 he was given the State Department's Distinguished Service Award. Three months later he took on the excruciating job of under secretary of state for administration, and two years later he was named to the newly created rank of career ambassador, the highest position in the Foreign Service. In 1958 Henderson was among the first recipients of the President's Award for Distinguished Federal Service, and in 1967 his peers gave him the first Foreign Service Cup, afterward awarded annually.

The administrative reorganization of the State Department was Henderson's last major task. When he took it on, morale was at an all-time low due to the ravages of careless and ignorant "reforms," the politicization of appointments, and Senator Joseph McCarthy's sweeping accusations of disloyalty and incompetence. Henderson's administrative leadership, his professional authority, and his compassion turned morale around. To improve efficiency he directed the construction of a new building for the State Department, centralizing its activities at long last. His work was widely praised. When he retired he carried the sobriquet "Mr. Foreign Service." And, in recognition of his achievements, Secretary of State Henry Kissinger in 1976 dedicated a large hall in the new building in Henderson's name, the only career official ever so honored.

Throughout his years of service in the diplomatic corps, Henderson asked a fundamental question about our relations with the Soviet government: "Can the Soviets be trusted?" His answer, consistently, was "no." These memoirs reveal how Henderson came to this conclusion early on and how his subsequent experiences never forced him to change his answer. Hence the stern policies that he advocated during the Cold War era followed logically. To Henderson and many of his generation, two of the essential values of civilization were reliability and order, not merely domestically but within the world of international relations as well. Henderson upheld these values over the span of his service with the Department of State, and he held to them steadfastly. For those who want a consistent, firsthand account of what dealing with the Soviet Union involves, a reading of Loy Henderson's memoirs is essential.

NOTES

1. See Stanley W. Page, *The Formation of the Baltic States: A Study of the Effects of Great Power Politics Upon the Emergence of Lithuania, Latvia, and Estonia* (Cambridge, Mass.: Harvard University Press, 1959).

2. Charles E. Bohlen, *Witness to History, 1929–1969* (New York: Norton, 1973), p. 39. See also Frederic L. Propas, "Creating a Hard Line Toward Russia: The

Training of State Department Soviet Experts, 1927–1937," *Diplomatic History* 8, no. 3 (Summer 1984): 209–26.

3. This point is well made by Carolyn Eisenberg, "Reflections on a Toothless Revisionism," *Diplomatic History* 2, no. 3 (Summer 1978): 295–305.

4. Quoted in Daniel H. Yergin, *Shattered Peace, The Origins of the Cold War and the National Security State* (Boston: Houghton Mifflin, 1977), p. 29.

5. For the work of the Riga legation's Russian section see Natalie Grant, "The Russian Section, a Window on the Soviet Union," *Diplomatic History* 2, no. 1 (Winter 1978): 107–15, and George F. Kennan, *Memoirs, 1925–1950* (Boston: Little, Brown, 1967), p. 48. See also Kennan's vivid "Reflections," *The New Yorker* (February 25, 1985), pp. 56–57.

6. *Foreign Relations of the United States: Diplomatic Papers, The Soviet Union, 1933–1939* (Washington: Government Printing Office, 1952), pp. 28–29.

7. See Thomas R. Maddux, *Years of Estrangement: American Relations with the Soviet Union, 1933–1941* (Tallahassee: University Presses of Florida, 1980), pp. 81–101.

8. See Martin Weil, *A Pretty Good Club: The Founding Fathers of the U.S. Foreign Service* (New York: Norton, 1978), p. 93: Kennan, *Memoirs*, pp. 83–86: and Yergin, *Shattered Peace*, pp. 34–35.

9. *Foreign Relations of the United States, Diplomatic Papers, The Soviet Union, 1933–1939*, p. 774.

10. Cited by Thomas R. Maddux, "Loy W. Henderson and Soviet-American Relations: The Diplomacy of a Professional," in Kenneth Paul Jones, ed., *U.S. Diplomats in Europe, 1919–1941* (Santa Barbara: ABC-Clio, 1981), pp. 152–53.

11. Ibid., pp. 159–60. See also Richard H. Ullman, "The Davies Mission and the United States–Soviet Relations, 1937–1941," *World Politics* 9, no. 2 (January 1957): 239.

12. For details of this shake-up and the suspicion that behind Henderson's ouster were Mrs. Roosevelt and Sumner Welles, see Weil, *A Pretty Good Club*, pp. 134–41, and the Oral History Interview with Henderson conducted in 1973 by Richard D. McKinzie, on deposit at the Harry S. Truman Library, Independence, Missouri, pp. 23–28. Charles Bohlen wrote: "Henderson led the quiet struggle in administration against the soupy and syrupy attitude toward the Soviet Union. A man of the highest character, absolutely incorruptible, he always spoke his mind, a practice that did not make him popular. Overruled time after time, he asked in 1943 to be relieved of his duties as chief of the division, and I was appointed to succeed him. With the departure of Henderson, the Soviet field lost one of its founders, a man who probably did as much for the Foreign Service as any officer, living or dead" (*Witness to History*, p. 125).

13. Joseph Marion Jones, *The Fifteen Weeks, February 21–June 5, 1947* (New York: Viking, 1955), p. 7.

14. Dean Acheson, *Present at the Creation: My Years in the State Department* (New York: Norton, 1969), p. 291.

A QUESTION OF TRUST

PART I

PERSONAL BACKGROUND AND EDUCATION, JUNE 1892–NOVEMBER 1918

CHAPTER 1

MY EARLY YEARS

I WAS BORN IN THE EARLY AFTERNOON of June 28, 1892, in a small but well-constructed house of timber and clapboard overlooking a tumbling stream that twisted through the Ozark Mountains of northwestern Arkansas a few miles distant from the little town of Rogers. A brother of whom I was said to be a facsimile had preceded me by a few minutes.

Our father, who was studying for the Methodist ministry, was George Milton Henderson, a 22-year-old schoolteacher with heavy coal black hair, flashing black eyes, and a resonant persuasive voice. Our mother, born May Mary Davis, was a shy, slender girl a few months younger than her husband, with soft brown hair, blue-grey eyes, and a gentle sensitive face, who had been compelled to forsake schoolteaching as time approached for the arrival of her firstborn. The twins were given the names of Roy Wilmington and Loy Wesley. Wilmington was in honor of our paternal grandfather, Daniel Wilmington Henderson; Wesley in honor of our maternal grandfather, John Wesley Davis.

Although the grandfathers were neighbors and friends, they represented quite different generations and backgrounds. Grandfather Henderson was born in Maury County, Tennessee, in 1821. When still a young boy he had been taken by his father to southern Illinois, which at that time was still a part of the great American frontier. During his youth the tenor of his life, like that of many young men on the frontier, had been broken by a series of wars. Just as his father in Tennessee had participated in the wars of his youth under Andrew Jackson, so Daniel had participated in both the Mexican and Civil wars. Although he was 40 years of age when the Civil War began, he volunteered at once for service. As a member of the Fifty-Ninth Illinois Volunteer Infantry Regiment, he marched thousands of miles through Missouri, Arkansas, Kentucky, Tennessee, Mississippi, Alabama, and Georgia, participating in scores of skirmishes and in some of the great battles of that war. During his four years in the service, Daniel attained the rank of captain and earned the affection and respect of the others in his regiment. Since he was one of my boyhood heroes I was particularly pleased when, looking through the official records of the Civil War, I ran across the following passage from a report prepared on September 11, 1863, by Colonel Post, his commanding officer: "The soldierly bearing of Capt. D. W. Henderson, so conspicuously displayed on many of the battlefields in which the regiment has engaged throughout the several skirmishes and affairs of this campaign, demands special mention."

During March 6–8, 1862, one of the bloodiest of the minor battles of the war took place in the Ozark Mountains not more than twelve miles from the spot where I was born. This engagement, known as the Battle of Pea Ridge, was fought to determine whether the Union or the Confederacy would control Arkansas and the Southwest. The Confederate Army fought bravely, but it lost and retreated toward the southwest. Roving bands of guerrillas, however, continued to infest the area.

Following the battle, a detachment of Union soldiers found itself as evening approached in a broad grass-covered valley lying between a series of gently sloping hills. At the head of this valley was a low, richly forested plateau. From the base of this plateau, about a hundred yards apart, two streams of crystal-clear water came gushing out to join one another farther down the valley in the form of a Y.

The plateau seemed to be an ideal spot to spend the night, and the officer in charge ordered his men to bivouac under the protection of its trees. As he rested, wrapped in his blankets and listening to the night sounds of the wilderness, the officer fell in love with this peaceful valley and thought that if this dreadful war would ever end and if he were still alive, it would make the kind of home that he and his family would like.

The story of the Battle of Pea Ridge and of other battles in the war between the states, I heard many years later from this officer. I remember him in June 1901, at that time eighty years of age and an invalid, telling two eager-faced nine-year-old boys not only about these battles but also about many of the other experiences of his long and exciting life. This old man was, of course, our father's father, and the two boys were Roy and I.

We were spending our summer away from the heat of Little Rock with our Ozark relatives. We sat spellbound as he told us about his life, about his experiences in time of peace and war, and about the early frontier days of Tennessee, Illinois, and Kansas. He also shared some of the stories of even earlier frontier days that had come down to him from his father.

After his return home from the Civil War, Grandfather Henderson told us, he had become bored with the quiet, uneventful life on Illinois farms and was seized with a burning desire to strike out west as his own father had done. My grandmother, who was also descended from a line of pioneers, had a similar urge. My grandfather's mind had turned at first toward the valley of the two springs in the Ozarks, but he finally yielded to the entreaties of an older brother who wanted to join him in settling in a relatively wild area in central Kansas—a prairie region devoid of roads, bridges, and so forth. He described some of the dangers, diseases, and other hardships that he and his family had faced during the subsequent twelve years. Indian tribes roamed the prairies in search of opportunities to slaughter and pillage the newcomers. Prairie fires, droughts, blizzards, and the hot winds of summer took their tolls. The lack of medical and educational facilities and supplies, as well as difficulties in traveling to or even communicating with the outside world, added to the complexities of life. Nevertheless, the settlers banded together and organized a new county, which—in view of the fact that many of them had served in the Union army—they named Lincoln. My grandfather was one of a company of five who founded the county seat, which they also called Lincoln.

He said that he and my grandmother had enjoyed the challenge of the Kansas prairies. Nevertheless, as he attained the age of 60 and as his health—which had been undermined during his years of war service— deteriorated, the call of the Ozarks became too great to ignore. He took his family with him, therefore, to the milder climate of northwest Arkansas. There he and his son-in-law, James Travis, finally settled in the beautiful valley that he had seen so many years before and that he found to be unchanged.

It was rare for the old gentleman to open his heart as he did to us that day. He must have felt that his end was near and that he should leave us with some knowledge of the lives of our forebears that we could pass on to succeeding generations. He said that the United States would become a still greater country during our lifetime, and he hoped that it would be satisfying for his grandchildren and great-grandchildren to know that, although their ancestors had not amassed great fortunes or achieved national fame, they had helped to build up and protect their new and growing country. He also hoped that we would live up to the pioneering tradition of our forefathers.

My brother and I were deeply impressed. We felt honored by this attention from a patriarch whom we revered, and we tried to remember during the years to come what he had said. Without realizing it, we were listening to what amounted to his last will and testament. His condition steadily worsened, and a week later he died in his bedroom overlooking the plateau and the valley near which we had been born.

My grandfather Davis, after whom I was named, was born across the Ohio River in Kentucky in 1842, although he was a member of an Indiana family. He enlisted in the Sixth Regiment of Indiana Volunteers as a "musician" during the early days of the war. As he gained in experience and weight he was designated a sharpshooter. Even in his old age he was a crackshot. I can recall, for instance, seeing him, while looking for deer during the Thanksgiving season, bring down a wild turkey on the wing with a rifle. In those days guns played an important role in the lives of the inhabitants of the Ozarks. Shotguns or rifles ready for instant use were usually suspended on racks over both the front and back doors. When, during the day or night, the dogs would begin to bark, the farmers made it a practice to take down one of their guns before opening the door to learn the cause of the uproar.

During the course of his military campaigns, Grandfather Davis had also been attracted by the beauty of the Ozarks. A number of years after the war, therefore, he settled in a valley not far from that of the two springs. He, like Grandfather Henderson, was a frontiersman, descended from a line of frontiersmen. His family was among the early settlers of Indiana.

So far as I can ascertain, none of my ancestors came to the United States after 1800. Most, if not all, of them were pioneers who preferred hardships and risks to the secure, sedentary life of the cities and towns. Generation after generation had moved steadily and generally westward from the Carolinas and Virginia to Kentucky, Tennessee, and Illinois. I refer to my frontier heritage since there is no doubt that it has had an influence on my life—it has contributed to my outlook, interests, and even judgments.

In passing, I may remark that it is by no means rare for Americans with a heritage similar to mine to turn to the exciting frontier of international affairs, since the original American frontiers have dissolved in the great agricultural-industrial complex of the twentieth century.

The valley of the two springs has for me an additional significance. On an afternoon of that summer in 1901 in which my grandfather Henderson died, Roy and I decided to go down near the springs to play one of our favorite games: White Man and Indian. As I, in the role of an Indian, was scaling the wall of the stockade, which really was an old-fashioned rail fence, the rail rolled and I fell to the ground on my right arm. When I arose I found it was broken at the elbow. The local doctor failed to set it properly and as a result it became partially stiff. This accident, as will be noted later, changed the course of my whole future life.

My father was admitted to the ministry some three years after Roy and I were born. A year later, in 1896, he was appointed to a church in Little Rock. In 1904 we went to Jefferson, Ohio, to which father had been transferred. Our new home, Jefferson, was an attractive Western Reserve town with something of a New England atmosphere. We regretted leaving it two years later when father was assigned to a church in Youngstown. While in Youngstown Roy and I graduated from Rayon High School, the only high school in the city at the time. It was primarily a preparatory school with classical traditions, and on the advice of the principal and with the approval of our father we concentrated on Latin, Greek, English, and mathematics.

In view of modern concepts of education, I doubt that there exists in the United States today any public high school that is conducted as Rayon was in the first decade of this century. From the moment a student was enrolled as a freshman, he or she was treated as an adult and was expected to act like one. The teachers did not address members of the classes by their first names but uniformly used the title of Mister or Miss. The atmosphere that had been generated over the years was such that admonishment by the teacher for misbehavior or bad manners was a disgrace that could not easily be lived down. There were no social exchanges among the students in the classrooms, in the corridors, or on the stairs. The only organization connected with the school to which the students, other than seniors, were permitted to belong was the Literary Society, which met monthly. There were athletic heroes, of course, but students with the most prestige were those who excelled in scholarship. About 30 percent of the graduates went on to institutions of higher learning, an almost unheard-of proportion for that decade.

In 1911 father was assigned to a church in Winfield, Kansas; in 1913 he was transferred to one in Colorado, in which state he served for most of the remainder of his active life. Over the years our family had increased in number. A sister, Zella, was born in the Ozarks in 1894; another brother, George, was born in Little Rock in 1902; and a sister, Bernice, in Jefferson in 1905. The salary of a Methodist clergyman was small, and it was not easy for my father to support such a large family. This was particularly true since a pastor's family—exposed as it must be to the public gaze—could not resort to some of the small ways of economizing that were frequently practiced by families with a higher degree of privacy. The problem of finance, therefore, was always with us.

Our family was a firmly knit unit. One reason was the financial problems I just mentioned. As members of the family council, we children became aware of our problems at an early age, and as soon as we were old enough Roy and I found various ways of contributing to the family coffers. Another reason for our close family ties was, I suppose, the peripatetic character of our lives. There was no place we could look back upon as our "home town." Neighbors and friends were constantly changing. The family was the only common repository of recollections of shared experiences. We also shared ideas and viewpoints, and dinner-table conversations were both lively and enriching. Looking back now, after a lifetime in the Foreign Service, I recall that international affairs had always been one of the more frequent topics at these discussions.

As far back as I can remember Roy and I had been given to understand that some day we would go to college and that if we were to succeed in college we must master our lessons every day. At first we were not quite sure what college was, but we were convinced that if we should fail in it we would be a disgrace to our parents and a disappointment to our friends. During our years in grade school and high school, therefore, we were conscientious students, and we stood at or near the top of our classes.

Just as we were on the point of graduating from high school, a breakdown in our mother's health shattered our plans. We had been hoping that a way could be found for us to go to Harvard University, which was a mecca for many of our fellow students. The costs resulting from mother's illness placed such a drain on the family finances, however, that it became clear we would not be able to enter Harvard or, for that matter, to go away to any university.

One of the reasons that prompted father to decide upon Winfield, Kansas, when looking for a milder climate for mother was that in the outskirts of that town there was a small college, Southwestern, which Roy and I could attend while living at home. Thus we could go on with our education without subjecting the family to unbearable financial strain. I have never had reason to regret the years we spent at Southwestern and have always been grateful to the college for coming to our rescue.

Unfortunately, mother's health continued to deteriorate in Kansas and, in the spring of 1913, father obtained a transfer to a church in Colorado in the hope that her condition would improve in the higher altitude and drier air. His hope was not realized and she died in the latter part of that year. Her death was a grievous loss to all of us. With her gentle disposition and the sensitivity of her understanding, she had always exerted a constructive, quieting influence on a somewhat dynamic family and had been most helpful to father in his work.

Following mother's death, Roy and I entered Northwestern University in Evanston, Illinois, where we completed our undergraduate work and obtained our Bachelor of Arts degrees in 1915.

In high school Roy and I had decided to follow law as a profession. We had planned to enter law school upon completing our undergraduate studies and eventually to practice law as partners. Again, our plans went awry. Following our graduation from Northwestern we did not have the funds necessary for enrollment in law school. We had been for the most part self-supporting during our undergraduate days. Father had nevertheless made financial sacrifices on our behalf. He might have been able in some way or other to mobilize sufficient funds to enable us to go to law school, but this we could not let him do. From his comparatively small salary he had to maintain a household, including two small children. Our determination not to accept financial assistance from him was strengthened when we learned, just as we were graduating, that he was planning to remarry. His wife-to-be was the widow of a clergyman who had been one of his closest friends since Little Rock days. We were delighted to learn of these plans because we knew her to be a wonderful woman and we were confident that she would make a faithful wife and a good mother. Our confidence was not misplaced. She was both until her death almost 30 years later.

Lacking funds, we decided to do what father had done before us in preparing for the ministry, that was, to work and save enough money to enable us to pay for the beginning, at least, of a legal education. In our high school and college days we had helped with family finances in a great variety of ways. I had been a salesman in shops in Ohio, Kansas, New Mexico, and Colorado. I had worked in a rubber factory in Youngstown, in a steel mill in Pueblo, in a lumber mill in New Mexico, and in the harvest fields of Kansas. Now, armed with college degrees, my brother and I chose to enter the teaching profession.

In my spare time during my first year of teaching I prepared a group of pitbosses and firebosses to take (and pass) the newly required examinations for their licenses. We accepted principalships of schools in two small neighboring Colorado mining towns. We could not save enough during the first year to meet our law school needs, so we decided to stay in school work for another year.

In February of our second year, the United States became involved in the First World War. In keeping with our family tradition, Roy and I prepared at once to enter the military service. In early spring of 1917 we went to Colorado Springs to apply for admission to the First Officer's Training Camp at Fort Riley, Kansas. Roy was accepted; I with my crippled right arm was not.

My brother and I had rarely been separated since the day of our birth. We had attended the same classes in grade school, high school, and the university. We had been partners in both work and play. We had similar tastes. Our lives might have been replete with tensions if we had not learned in early childhood to determine by negotiation or by the drawing of lots who was to have that which both fancied but which was not divisible. We were accustomed to accept decisions of this kind with good grace. We had complete trust in each other.

The break in our close relationship, resulting from Roy's departure for Fort Riley, was a wrench for both of us. I had a feeling of humiliation, of being a misfit, and I sought desperately to obtain a waiver that would permit me also to engage in some kind of military service. Letters and telegrams to members of Congress and to various officials in Washington were of no avail. Finally I abandoned these efforts and decided that I would begin the study of law.

In the autumn of 1917 I enrolled in the law school of the University of Denver. I immediately developed a special interest in legal bibliography and spent such time as I could spare haunting the law library. The kindly, scholarly registrar-librarian of the law school, Charles Lincoln Andrews, noting my interest and being in need of an assistant, recommended me for the position. I was delighted. With the title of assistant registrar-librarian I could continue to work with law books and at the same time conserve my savings. I loved the study of law. Its clean-cut logic was for me a sort of intellectual refuge at a time when I was beginning to question many of the values that I had cherished. Here, at least, was something on which I could stand—something that had withstood the test of time and practice.

I enjoyed tracking down precedents through the labyrinth of systems and cross-systems of references. I relished the humor of understatement by the judges in their decisions. To me, the study of law was not work, it was an exhilarating sport, and I gave little thought to grades. Nevertheless, I could not help feeling a glow of satisfaction when I learned at the end of the freshman year that I had topped the class in scholarship.

In the spring of 1918, John A. Ewing, one of the leading lawyers of Colorado, invited me to work in his office in the First National Bank building of Denver. The arrangement would still permit me to attend classes in the law school, and I was glad to accept. He had the largest private law library in Colorado, and the numerous law firms with offices in the same building were permitted to use it. One of my jobs was to assist Mr. Ewing in preparing briefs and in looking up cases. At times I received some of his clients and prepared memoranda outlining their problems in order to save his time. Mr. Ewing's legal roots went back to the halcyon mining days of Leadville and Cripple Creek. Many of his clients were members of families whose fortunes were based on the gold and silver ore that had poured forth years before from the Colorado mountains.

I enjoyed my work in the law school and in the law office. Nevertheless, I was still uncomfortable. I had the feeling that I should be doing my part in the great drama that was unfolding in Europe and that by studying law in Denver while other young men were risking their lives in the battlefield, I was letting down not only my family but also my country. My frustration was especially acute because, as a minister's son, I had early developed a sense of responsibility to the public. For a time I was consoled by the fact that at least my brother was doing his part. But I lost even this consolation. While at the training camp, either as a result of strain or of an accident, Roy developed an ailment that resulted in the loss of one of his kidneys and in his medical discharge.

THE DECISION TO SERVE ABROAD WITH THE AMERICAN RED CROSS

In the summer of 1918 I learned from fellow students that the American Red Cross was planning to recruit for service in the war zones a number of young men who had been rejected for military service on medical grounds. I began to negotiate with the Red Cross and finally was informed in early October that I had been accepted for foreign service and would be expected to depart early in November. On the first of November, with deep regret, I withdrew from the law school, said farewell to Mr. Ewing and my other Denver friends, and proceeded to Greeley, Colorado, where my father was then serving, to tell my family good-bye. It was, I believe, near midday on November 6 that the members of my family lined up along the station platform to see me off on my long journey. In my father's face I could see affection and concern mingled with pride that one of his sons was to play at least some kind of a role in the great war. My brother's face registered anguish at being left behind and his look as we shook hands for the last time haunted me for years.

On the following day, as the train was speeding across the continent, the whistles in the towns through which we were passing began to blow and the bells in the churches to ring. We learned at one of the stations that the whole country was celebrating the signing of an armistice in France. Although I was happy that the war was over, my spirits sank at the thought that I was too late to contribute my share to the victory.

When we arrived in New York we discovered that the celebration was premature; no armistice had been signed; the fighting was still going on. At American Red Cross headquarters we were informed that even if an armistice should be signed, Red Cross workers would be needed in Europe more than ever. During the period between the cessation of hostilities and the departure for home, the morale of the troops, which had thus far been sustained by the challenge of warfare, was sure to sag dangerously, and Red Cross workers would be kept busy finding ways and means of combating discouragement and frustration.

The group of American Red Cross recruits of which I was a member was put through a week of training prior to embarkation. We were instructed about the general nature of our duties, our responsibilities and privileges, and our relationships with one another, with the officers and men of the armed forces of the United States and our allies, and with the civilians with whom we would come in contact. We were told from whom we were to receive orders, to whom we should report, and so forth. We learned that since the American Red Cross had been militarized in the war area we would not be permitted to take civilian clothing with us. We would be issued commissions signed by the secretary of war conferring assimilated ranks upon us, and we would be required to purchase uniforms that would be identical with those worn by United States Army officers except that rank would be indicated in the French manner by horizontal stripes on the cuffs rather than by shoulder insignia. I found that, like most other members of our group, I was to have the rank of first lieutenant.

While we were undergoing training the armistice was signed. Four days later we embarked along with a thousand or so other passengers aboard the former Cunard liner, the SS *Caronia*, which had been converted into a military transport.

PART II

WITH THE AMERICAN RED CROSS IN FRANCE AND GERMANY, NOVEMBER 1918–SEPTEMBER 1919

CHAPTER 2

SERVICE IN FRANCE

FROM NEW YORK TO FRANCE, NOVEMBER 1918

DURING THE VOYAGE the *Caronia* operated on a partial wartime basis: lights subdued, many conveniences lacking, and none of the gaiety that brightens a voyage during times of peace. The *Caronia's* passengers were a heterogeneous lot: officers and men of the different services; uniformed army nurses; Red Cross workers; important looking and acting American civilians; and a number of foreigners both in and out of uniforms. On the voyage hundreds became ill and scores died from the epidemic of Spanish influenza that was spreading over the world and was eventually to take some 10 million lives.

A happy contrast with the grim voyage was my first glimpse of Europe—the bright green hills of Ireland glistening in the sun. Although my family ties with Europe had been broken for at least 120 years, I must confess a feeling akin to nostalgia as I, the first of my family to return to the land of some of my ancestors, disembarked at Liverpool. After a brief stay in London I continued on to Paris, where I arrived on November 29. At Red Cross headquarters there I learned that I was to work for the Federal Board for Vocational Education department. Before I could begin work, however, I too came down with Spanish influenza and spent ten days in the hospital.

An Historic Day in Paris, December 14, 1918

I was released from the hospital in time to see President Woodrow Wilson's grand entry into Paris and was one of the thousands packed in the Place de la Concorde who cheered as the carriage in which he rode moved slowly between the lanes of soldiers standing rigidly at attention. I doubt that the prestige of the United States in Europe had ever been higher than it was on that day.

The thousands of U.S. soldiers who were on leave in Paris basked in the reflected glory of the President. They were literally mobbed by the enthusiastic French people. These spontaneous demonstrations of friendship did not last long, however. Within a matter of days the fondness for the Americans had worn thin, and the U.S. soldier on leave from the front who had been looking forward to several joyous days in Paris too frequently encountered coldness and rebuffs. There was a rising tide of resentment at what the French called the Americanization of the streets, the restaurants, and the cafés. In some of the better restaurants one could find every chair occupied by an American in uniform or by his female companion.

The unpopularity of the U.S. soldiers in Paris, once the fighting was over, made a lasting impression on me. The events I observed at that time in France caused me to believe that the stationing of U.S. armed forces in a friendly foreign country is almost certain to convert the friendliness of the people of that country to hostility unless our officers and soldiers have been thoroughly educated in advance with the importance of treating the local population with courtesy and consideration and unless they are subject to firm discipline while both on duty and on leave. Subsequent experiences over the years strengthened this belief.

Assignment to the American Hospital Center near Bordeaux, December 1918–March 1919

I was assigned to the Beau Desert American Hospital Center on the outskirts of Bordeaux. My task there was to try to raise the morale of the patients by telling them what the government was preparing to do for them following their return to the United States in the way of training and education.

The mission to Beau Desert was completed early in March 1919. Following my return to Paris I made a full report, my first report while in service abroad, to the American Red Cross headquarters in Paris. That report read in part as follows:

> From January 1st until March 10th we worked in this hospital center and saw many thousands of men. I myself personally talked before some 20,000 wounded or diseased soldiers and the girls also talked to them again and to others that I did not see. Our work was pleasant because the men were so delighted to hear of the opportunities which were being offered to them, and the surgeons were glad to have us talk...because they said that we encouraged the men and kept them from becoming morbid and discouraged...I found few men who were not...interested, and I felt rewarded for the many days spent walking through the hospitals in the rain and mud by the change of spirits which came over many of them after hearing what the Government was going to do for them. In addition...often I went with the serious cases on the hospital trains to the boats and on the way talked to them and gave them more information about the future which was being planned for them...
>
> The nurses told me that many men who were soured on the Army and on their country and who were hard to handle in the wards would change entirely after they had heard how they were to be cared for.

Several days after my return to Paris I was assigned to the American Red Cross commission in Berlin with the rank of captain as an inspector of prisoner-of-war camps. The commission was one of the components of the Interallied Commission for Repatriation of Prisoners of War. Other components of the Interallied Commission were the military missions of the Americans, British, French, and Italians. The Interallied Commission was charged with the task of looking after the welfare of the half-million Allied prisoners—mostly Russians—who had not yet been repatriated. It was the repatriation of these Russians that presented a major problem. A clipping I found among my papers, apparently taken from the *New York Times* of March 15, 1919, quotes from a report made to the Supreme War Council in Paris by Major General Harries, commander of the U.S. military mission in Berlin:

> The American forces in Germany, outside the occupied zone, consists of 80 officers and 600 men, a considerable part of the contingent being stationed at 20 camps at various places where 600,000 Russian prisoners are being cared for by the Americans...
>
> Thousands of Russian prisoners are clamoring to return home, but this would mean the sending of 600,000 Russians into the hands of the Bolsheviks. The latter are threatening the Polish front and have a powerful organization at Vilna, with unlimited funds for propaganda work...
>
> It is believed that a strong military zone in Berlin between Russia and

Germany, together with food relief, offers the surest means of holding back the Bolshevists' advance.

Under American care the Russian prisoners are in a reasonably good condition, with adequate food, and little sickness and mortality. Steps will probably be taken to return them to Russia by way of the Black Sea or by other routes so as to avoid forcing them into the Bolshevists' ranks.

CHAPTER 3

WITH THE INTERALLIED COMMISSION FOR THE REPATRIATION OF PRISONERS OF WAR IN BERLIN, MARCH–SEPTEMBER 1919

FROM PARIS TO BERLIN, MARCH 1919

IT SHOULD BE BORNE IN MIND THAT, in accordance with the terms of the armistice, the southern and southwestern portions of Germany during the first half of 1919 were under the control of Allied armies of occupation. Most of Germany, however, was unoccupied and was therefore under the control of the government of the newly established German republic. The only Allied forces stationed in unoccupied Germany were the members of the Interallied Commission for the Repatriation of Prisoners of War, which maintained headquarters in Berlin but had representatives stationed at a number of prisoner-of-war camps and various other points where they might be needed in connection with repatriation activities.

I left Paris by train on March 23 to go to Berlin by way of Brussels and Cologne in order to join the American Red Cross contingent of the Interallied Commission. Shortly after the train left Cologne, it entered unoccupied German territory. For most of the day it crept through Germany, making frequent stops. German civilians, laden with packages and bundles, gradually filled the corridors. The contrast was striking between them and the rosy-cheeked, smartly uniformed, and lively members of the Allied armed forces who had traveled with us as far as Cologne. The clothing of the Germans hung loosely over their emaciated bodies; the drooping flesh of their sallow faces also testified to loss of weight. Their thoughts apparently turned inward; they showed little interest in what was going on about them. This was the first time that I found myself among masses of human beings in various stages of undernourishment and starvation.

THE AMERICAN RED CROSS COMMISSION IN BERLIN

When the United States had become involved in the war in 1917, it had asked the Spanish government to represent our interests in Germany. Spanish officials had, therefore, taken over the chancery building of the U.S. embassy in Berlin. Since, in March 1919, the United States was still technically in a state of war with Germany, the Spanish officials looking after our interests continued to occupy several offices in our former embassy chancery. The remaining offices housed the headquarters of the American Red Cross mission. Both the chancery and the Kaiserhof Hotel, where we lived, were in the Kaiser Wilhelm Platz. The living quarters of the American Red Cross personnel, therefore, were only a hundred yards from their offices. The U.S. military mission segment of the Interallied Commission occupied the Adlon Hotel several blocks distant in the Pariser Platz at the foot of Unter den Linden.

The American Red Cross commissioner in Berlin was Lieutenant Colonel Carl Taylor, and his deputy was Lieutenant Colonel Edward W. Ryan. These two men were quite different in manner and outlook. I came to admire and respect both, however, during the next few months.

On the morning of March 25 I reported to Red Cross headquarters. Colonel Taylor and Colonel Ryan explained what my duties were to be as an inspector of prison camps. The work of inspection would involve some delicate problems, not the least of which would be to preserve the balance between the German and Allied officers who shared the responsibilities of the camps. German officers were responsible for supervising and maintaining law and order in the camps; Allied officers had the duty of watching out for the interests of the prisoners and looking after the stores of supplies in a way that would not undermine the authority of the German officers in charge. Another feature of the structure of these camps was the councils elected by the prisoners to represent them. Part of my task was to ascertain the situation in each camp with regard to morale, food, clothing, bedding, other supplies, health, recreation facilities, and so forth, and to report my findings to my Red Cross superiors. My role was to be that of an observer only; I was not to interfere in operations.

BERLIN, MARCH 1919

During the period that I was being prepared by headquarters to take up my new duties, I devoted my spare time to acquainting myself with the situation in Berlin and in the other areas of Germany where the camps I was to visit were located. Although more than four months had elapsed since the armistice, the Allies had continued to maintain a strict embargo upon the importation of foodstuffs into nonoccupied Germany. The population of the country, including Berlin, was, therefore, in various stages of undernourishment and starvation. The embargo also applied to other consumption goods such as soap, fats, oils of all kinds, wool, cotton, and leather. For the first time I realized the importance of soap to a civilized society. Its lack aggravated the already poor condition of the skin of most Germans that was the result of a scanty and ill-balanced diet. Wrinkled and aging skin brought out even more the gauntness of the faces of the people. German women, both young and old, were particularly conscious of the unattractiveness of their appearance. A bar of soap, not to mention a chocolate bar or a package of cigarettes, in the hands of the more irresponsible members of the Interallied Commission in Berlin was a powerful persuasive, and the sale of these items from the commission's commissary, as well as of other eagerly sought-for consumption goods, was rigidly rationed.

In the absence of textiles and leather, the Berlin shops were offering clothing made of specially processed paper and shoes of paper or wood. Because of the shortage of rubber, the tires of some of the automobiles were ungainly metal springs encircling the wheels. Relatively few automobiles were to be seen on the streets. The honk of the automobile horn had been replaced by the clatter of the hoofs of emaciated horses pulling delapidated droshkies.

The German people had more to worry about, however, than the hardships of the moment. They were concerned for the future of themselves and their children. The German soldier who had undergone years of suffering and hardship in Russia or in the trenches of the West now found himself without a job and with no assurance of a pension. The widows and children of soldiers who had been killed in the war did not know whether or not the impoverished government that had taken over would be able to give them aid for any length of time. German families that had lost members during the war did not have even the satisfaction of feeling that the sacrifice had been of benefit to their country. Some elements of the population had been dissatisfied with the old imperial regime and had felt relieved at its disappearance. Even to them, however, the future looked bleak.

Many of the Germans I met on the street seemed to be going about in a daze. Relatively few of them registered interest or curiosity at the sight of my uniform. Some did approach me with appeals of various kinds: food for sick children or aged parents, medicine, and assistance in obtaining the addresses of relatives or friends in the United States. One woman showed me the crooked legs of her child, a victim of rickets. There were no approaches of a hostile character, nor did I note any hostile glances.

Night clubs and cabarets were doing a flourishing business. Although they had little in the way of food to offer, they did have German champagne, wine, music, and demimondaines as drinking or dancing partners. The cynical atmosphere of these night spots, their clientele consisting mostly of profiteers (referred to in Germany as "shebas")—vultures who were preying on the poverty and miseries of the stricken people—was to me revolting.

The theaters and opera companies were making efforts to carry on. Since electricity was turned off at an early hour to conserve fuel, the performances started in the late afternoon. In the absence of heat the members of the audience sat bundled up in such clothing as they could muster. Between acts they slowly munched the sandwiches that they had brought with them.

Not all Berliners were looking to the future with resignation. There was ferment in some sections of the city, particularly in the working-class areas. Excited speakers could be seen in the squares and in the streets calling upon the people to rise up and take direct action. Parades of demonstrators were quickly formed and just as quickly dissolved. Sometimes these demonstrations grew large and resulted in pitched battles between the mobs and the police. It was rumored that much of this unrest was being stirred up by agents of the Russian Bolsheviks who were hoping for a German communist revolution that would unite a Soviet Germany with Soviet Russia. In any event, the revolutionaries, who called themselves Spartacists, were doing their utmost to convince the German people that their future should be entrusted to a German-Russian partnership under a red flag and that Germany could expect nothing but servitude at the hands of the West. The Spartacists made many converts and at times succeeded, though briefly, in gaining control of parts of the city.

Affected as the German people were both physically and psychologically by the humiliation of defeat, the revolutionary changes in their own country, the privations of the present, and the forebodings with regard to the future, it seemed to me remarkable that more of them did not follow the revolutionary banner.

INSPECTION OF PRISONER-OF-WAR CAMPS IN GERMANY

During the first half of April, I inspected five of the larger prison camps. In all of them I was received with courtesy by the German officers in charge, the U.S. officers stationed in them, and the Russian representatives of the prisoners. I found that in general the working relations between the German and U.S. officers were amicable. There was no fraternizing.

From my conversations with the U.S. officers and the Russian prisoners who spoke English, I tried to reconstruct a picture of what the camps might have been like during the period of active hostilities. Although the details varied from camp to camp, my general impression was that the Allied prisoners had not been treated as badly by the Germans as the American people had been led to believe. There seemed to have been many instances of brutality, depending on the behavior of the prisoners, the atmosphere of a particular camp, and the attitude of individual officers or guards. These instances, however, were not typical. Allied prisoners had sometimes been ill-fed. They had fared, however, at least as well as their captors. At times they had been confined in uncomfortable, unsanitary, and overcrowded quarters. It should be recalled, however, that during certain periods Germany had been literally swamped with prisoners. On the eastern front, for instance, tens of thousands of Russian prisoners had sometimes surrendered on a single day. Because there had not been enough barracks in the area to accommodate such masses of prisoners, many Russians had been placed temporarily in dugouts.

In some of the camps American Red Cross packages had been distributed regularly among the U.S. prisoners through the agency of the Danish Red Cross. The recipients of these packages had fared much better than their German guards from the point of view of food, tobacco, toilet articles, and so forth. During the course of my inspection it became clear to me that the Russian prisoners in the camps were, in respect to food, much better off than the Germans in charge of them. They were also quite well supplied with blankets and various articles of clothing. I found that most of the prison hospitals were in reasonably good condition although in need of various medicines and equipment. It should be borne in mind that for a period of almost two months before my inspection, the Allies had been providing supplementary food rations, blankets, clothing, and other supplies for the prisoners through the American Red Cross. In addition, the American Red Cross, representing the Allies, had been furnishing the prison hospitals with equipment and medicine under the supervision of medical officers.

With the coming of spring the prisoners at these camps became increasingly restless. They had little grounds for complaint, for they had fairly comfortable barracks, their food was better than they had received while in the Russian army, and in most camps they were permitted the freedom of frequent visits to the neighboring towns. In areas where, as a result of the war, there was a shortage of young men, some of them had left the camps and obtained jobs on German farms. Some had married Germans and had decided to remain in Germany. The great majority of prisoners, however, did not plan to remain there, and most of these were homesick. It was not easy to explain to them why nearly all of the Allied prisoners, except the Russians, had been repatriated.

During the month of March the Bolsheviks had been cleared out of certain areas of the eastern Baltic littoral, and plans were being laid to repatriate by boat to Baltic ports those prisoners whose homes were in the liberated areas. The pending departure of these prisoners added to the dissatisfaction of those who remained behind.

INTRODUCTION TO EASTERN EUROPE

On the morning of April 18 my inspection work was halted abruptly by a message from Colonel Taylor directing me to prepare at once to join a delegation of members of the Interallied Commission to Eastern Europe. Later in that day I received written orders amplifying Colonel Taylor's message. I was directed to go to Koschidary [Kaišiadorys], a town in the western area of the old Russian empire that was still under German occupation.

It will be recalled that, following the armistice, the Allies had not objected to the maintenance by the Germans of a line on the eastern front a hundred or so miles within former Russian territory for the purpose of preventing further Bolshevik advance toward East Prussia. To assist the Poles in pushing the Bolsheviks out of Poland, the Allies had also taken steps to strengthen the newly organized Polish armies. By these measures the Allies hoped to keep the Bolsheviks out of Central Europe. Bolshevik leaders, on their part, were hoping to take advantage of the instability in Germany resulting from the German revolution and of the chaos accompanying the dismemberment of the Austrian empire to spread communism through Central Europe. Fortunately for the West, the disorganized conditions in Central Europe were offset by an even worse state of confusion in the Soviet Union. The Bolsheviks were compelled to expend much of their strength and energy in combating several anti-Bolshevik armies that were gnawing at the vitals of the empire that they were in the process of taking over. The Bolsheviks lacked military supplies. Most of the great stores of Allied military supplies in the Arkhangelsk and Murmansk areas originally destined for the armies of Russia had been denied them. Also they found it difficult to find and mobilize the transport facilities needed to move their men and supplies. In addition, the rank and file of the Red

Army was not as eager as its leaders to extend the territories under communist control. Many members of the Red Army did not relish the idea of risking their lives to retain territory that the Bolsheviks had already taken.

The German-Soviet front, which sliced in a north-south direction the territory between the towns of Kovno (later known as Kaunas) and Vilna [Vilnius], was relatively quiet. The task of the Germans was merely that of holding the Bolsheviks back, and the Bolsheviks, in deep trouble because of the belligerent activity of the Polish armies, which were moving in the direction of Vilna, were not looking for a fight with the Germans.

Some of the Allies at the conference table in Paris had been insisting that the Russian prisoners in Germany be repatriated as soon as possible. They thought that it was not fair to detain prisoners in Germany merely because of the possibility that upon their return to Russia they might be drafted into the Red Army. Others argued that, to the contrary, it would be unfair to the Poles, who were engaging in a heroic struggle to re-establish their independence, to hand over tens of thousands of Russian prisoners to the Bolsheviks who were in need of husky, well-fed men to augment their armed forces. In particular, they objected to sending any prisoners to Russia through the German-Soviet front. That front was so near the Soviet-Polish battlefields that the Bolsheviks would be able, if they desired, to incorporate the newly repatriated prisoners in their front lines within a few days.

I realized that a decision must have been reached to begin the repatriation of the prisoners through the German-Soviet lines despite the objections that had been raised. I was told much later that one consideration responsible for the decision was that assurances had been received in Paris from the Bolsheviks, through informal but reasonably reliable channels, that they would facilitate the travel to their respective homes of all of the prisoners whom the Allies would repatriate through East Prussia.

Before the departure of our mission to Koschidary on the evening of April 19, the eve of Easter Sunday, I had an opportunity to exchange only a few words with Colonel Ryan. He told me that Major Thornburn, the head of the mission, had been thoroughly briefed and that I was to regard him as my chief while I was on the mission.

The German and American officers at Preussische-Holland [Pasłek] proved to be most cooperative. Early on Easter Sunday our special car was placed on a siding at that town where there was a large Russian prison camp. The German and American officers in charge of the camp escorted us through it. The thousands of Russian prisoners, hearing that we were working on their early repatriation, became quite excited. They gave us cheer after cheer and in the afternoon a choir of the prisoners entertained us with Easter anthems.

As we moved on the following morning between the fertile fields and broad meadows of East Prussia, I noted what I had observed elsewhere in Germany—the scarcity of domestic animals. Relatively few cattle, horses, and sheep were to be seen grazing in the extensive pasturelands. The lack of livestock strengthened my belief that Germany would have food problems for many years to come. I also noted, in the well-kept countryside and the neat villages, more and more houses in ruins as we approached the old German-Russian frontier—reminders of the Russian invasion of Germany in 1914.

When we crossed the frontier it was as though we were entering another world. The contrast between the German countryside and that across the border was striking. In place of well-ordered farms and woodlands, we found bleakness: village after village in ruins, gaunt chimneys surrounded by piles of rubble; in place of farmhouses were ragged forests and undrained land that had degenerated into marshes.

On our arrival in Kovno, which for several years had been under German occupation, we were met by several German officers who conducted us to the German commandant of the city. He informed us that arrangements had been made for us to stay in the Metropol Hotel to which we proceeded after the usual exchange of courtesies. As we entered the hotel I noticed that on each side of the door there were two sentries, one standing in front of the other. All four were in German uniforms. There were yellow stripes, however, on the lapels and caps of the two who stood in the rear. All four saluted stiffly as we passed. In the corridor beyond the sentinels we found ourselves facing a manned machine gun which had been placed on the landing of a stairway with its muzzle pointed at the entrance. As we stood in front of this gun a distinguished-looking man in formal clothes approached us courteously and bowed. Major Thornburn handed him his hat and coat. We did likewise and proceeded into the reception room. After disposing of our hats and coats the man followed us and bowed again. He said, in English, "As minister of supplies, I welcome you to my country." His words of greeting took us by surprise. Major Thornburn, after a few seconds of puzzlement, asked him politely the name of the country of which he was a minister. The reply was: "The Republic of Lithuania." The major immediately introduced himself and presented the members of the mission. Thus, my introduction to the field of diplomacy and my first contact with an official of a Baltic country, which I was to know well during the years to come, was inauspicious indeed.

The Unrecognized Republic of Lithuania, April 1919

So far as I am aware, no one in our mission realized when we crossed the old German-Russian frontier that we were entering the Republic of Lithuania—a state, the provisional government of which had not as yet been recognized by the Allied powers. It had been our understanding that we were visiting a portion of Russia still under German occupation. No one in Berlin, to my knowledge, had intimated that we would find in Kovno a Lithuanian government; our German contacts had not mentioned the existence of such a government; and the German commandant on whom we had just called had not referred to a Lithuania or to Lithuanians during our conversation. We had been under the impression that the only authorities whom we would meet while in German-occupied Russia would be the German military. I learned later that the exchange of information among the Interallied and Allied missions in Europe was never really effectively systematized. Consequently, there was a lack of coordination in the activities of these missions. This lack was undoubtedly responsible for our not being informed in advance that Kovno was regarded by the German occupying forces as the temporary capital of a Republic of Lithuania.

I suppose that the other members of our mission, like myself, had heard vaguely about Lithuania and the Lithuanians, just as we had been hearing about the Ruthenians, the Letts, the Estonians, and so forth. We had seen fragmentary reports to the effect that armed groups of Lithuanians, or Ukrainians, or perhaps Letts, were combating the Red Army. In 1919 new states were not being born on an almost monthly basis as they were some 40 years later. It had never occurred to me, therefore, that these fighting Lithuanians were in fact the armed forces of a new state.

It did not take long for our little mission to learn a great deal about Lithuania and its people. During the centuries of Polish and Russian rule, the light of Lithuanian nationalism had not been entirely extinguished. It began to burn more brightly in the early part of the twentieth century, and Lithuanian nationalists began to look for an opportunity to restore an independent Lithuania. As the Russian grip on the country progressively weakened during the war years, 1914–1917, groups of Lithuanians, some in exile, began to lay plans for the realization of their dream. Following the Bolshevik revolution of November 1917, Lithuanian leaders joined together, proclaimed the restoration of an independent Lithuania with its capital at Vilna, and took steps in the direction of setting up a shadow Lithuanian government. Most of Lithuania was under German occupation, however, and the Germans were not at that time prepared to recognize an independent Lithuanian state.

During the latter part of 1918, as reverses in the West gradually forced the Germans to abandon their hopes of winning the war, they apparently came to the conclusion that it might be advantageous to have a Lithuanian buffer state between East Prussia and Soviet Russia. In any event, they began to assist the shadow Lithuanian government to develop a governmental apparatus, located temporarily in Kovno, and to organize a Lithuanian army. They provided the army with light arms, uniforms, and other essential equipment. Although the Lithuanian armed forces maintained their own separate military organizations, they and the Germans cooperated in holding back the advancing Red Army. The Germans, apparently, were also cooperating at times with the Lithuanians in connection with the latter's attempts to drive the Bolsheviks out of the territory claimed by the Lithuanian government.

The government of Lithuania was eager to have what it considered to be its territory cleared of German, Bolshevik, and Polish troops. It had no especial fear of the Germans, since it was convinced that the occupation of its territory by a defeated Germany could be of only a temporary nature. Its main concern was Soviet Russia and Poland. It feared that both of these countries were determined not only to retain the portions of Lithuanian territory they were already occupying but also, later, to take over the areas occupied by the Germans. Soviet Russia had formerly been considered to be the most dangerous threat to an independent Lithuania, but the Lithuanians were beginning to feel that Poland represented an even greater danger. The Lithuanians believed that the Poles, imbued with a new chauvinism, were bent on taking over all the areas of the former Russian empire that had at one time or other belonged to historic Poland, including the territories to which the Lithuanians laid claim.

During the days that our mission was in Kovno, the Bolsheviks were being pushed back rapidly by the victorious Poles. The news that the Poles had taken Grodno and Vilna came as a shock to the Lithuanians. Would the Poles now claim these Lithuanian cities by right of conquest? How could the Poles be induced to turn over territory to Lithuania that they had taken from the Bolsheviks by force of arms? The Lithuanian army was full of fire and spirit and was straining at the leash. On several occasions it had met Bolshevik armed forces and had acquitted itself well. It did not, however, possess the armament and other equipment that would enable it to compete successfully in extensive and sustained operations with the Bolsheviks or the Poles.

Our new friend, the Lithuanian minister, told us that a cold buffet dinner had been spread on the tables in the dining room of the hotel and invited us, after we had stowed our bags in the rooms assigned to us, to join him there.

During this, our first dinner at the hotel, we discovered that the Lithuanian government was using the hotel as its headquarters and that a few days prior to our arrival several German soldiers, apparently on a drunken spree, had tried to force their way into the hotel and had killed one of the two Lithuanian sentries who had attempted to stop them. In order to prevent a repetition of an incident of this kind, the German commandant had placed a German guard at the door in front of each of the two Lithuanian sentries. Further, to discourage intruders, the Lithuanian government had planted the machine gun on the stairway overlooking the entrance. This information helped us to understand why there were four instead of two guards at the hotel entrance. Since the uniforms worn by the Lithuanian military were identical with those worn by the German military, the Lithuanians had added the yellow tags for purposes of identification.

At the buffet tables we were joined by several Swedish officers who had been brought into Lithuania to supervise the training of the Lithuanian army. Two French officers and two U.S. officers, who had arrived several days earlier as representatives of the American Relief Administration, also came in.

One of the U.S. officers told me during the course of the evening that the United States Food Commission had already shipped several consignments of food to Lithuania and that the first load was now moving on a boat up the Nieman [Neman] River from the Baltic port of Libau [Liepāja] and should be in Kovno within a day or two. He added that it was his understanding that plans were also underway to dispatch quantities of various kinds of surplus war materials to Lithuania, particularly blankets and clothing, for which the Lithuanian government had agreed eventually to pay.

This young officer seemed to have a considerable amount of experience in relief work and to know what was going on in Washington, Paris, and elsewhere. I met him from time to time in Washington years later when he was a member of Congress from Ohio, and I worked closely with him during the period 1955–1957, when he was in charge of our foreign aid program, that is, when he was director of the International Cooperation Administration. His name was John B. Hollister.

Among the Lithuanian officials who made their appearance while we were at the buffet dinner was Antanas Merkys, the minister of war, who invited us to be his guests at a dinner the following evening. He also asked whether or not we intended to call upon the president of Lithuania, Dr. Antanas Smetona. When Major Thornburn replied in the affirmative, the war minister said that he would make the necessary arrangements. Merkys, by the way, played a prominent role in Lithuania during the next twenty years, and I was to see him many times during that period. He served as prime minister in 1939 and 1940 during Lithuania's last days of independence.

We called upon President Smetona the following morning. A physician by profession, he was a scholarly appearing man who spoke slowly in a low voice as though he were choosing every word with care. He told us that he was pleased to welcome an Interallied mission to Kovno, that he hoped our mission would be the first of many such missions, and that one of his objectives was to promote the speedy development of friendly relations between Lithuania and the Allied nations. He emphasized that Kovno, or Kaunas as he referred to it, was only the temporary capital and that it was the hope of all Lithuanians that within a short period the government could move to Vilna, which was the historic capital.

In his reply Major Thornburn thanked the president for his courteous welcome and for the friendly hospitality that was being shown us by the Lithuanian government. He pointed out that our mission had come to Kovno for the purpose of exploring the practicability of repatriating Russian prisoners of war through the German-Bolshevik front. It was the opinion of the Western Allies that they owed it to the Russian prisoners who had been their comrades in arms to assist them in returning to their homes.

The president replied that he could understand the sentiments that prompted the efforts of the Western powers to repatriate the Russian prisoners. It was his opinion, however, that the situation at present in Eastern Europe was so complicated that repatriation of Russian prisoners through the German-Soviet front might become exceedingly difficult. We could be assured that, in spite of the difficulties involved, his government was prepared to do what it could to assist.

While the military members of the mission spent the afternoon of April 22 in a series of conversations with German officers regarding the problems of repatriation, I inspected several of the Lithuanian military and Red Cross hospitals and was appalled at the conditions that existed in them: for example, overcrowding and a lack of beds, bedding, medicine, and surgical apparatus and instruments. I also visited several charitable institutions, including one that housed war orphans, and found all of them in a pitiable condition. I was full of admiration, however, for the Lithuanian doctors, nurses, and caretakers who were carrying on so courageously in exceedingly difficult circumstances.

The Repatriation of the First Trainload of Russian Prisoners Through Lithuania

On April 23 we had a long talk about repatriation problems with the chief of the German staff. Our main concern was the apparent instability of the front. According to my recollection, the chief of staff was rather optimistic. He said that the German-Soviet front was still intact at the point where the exchanges were scheduled to take place near Koschidary and that, through existing channels for the exchange of information between his officers and the Bolsheviks, he had received assurance that the Soviet government was ready to begin receiving the returning prisoners and to send them on to their homes. He added that the first trainload of war prisoners was due in Kovno on the following day and should arrive at the repatriation point in the afternoon.

We decided, therefore, to proceed at once to Koschidary to acquaint ourselves with the situation there before the arrival of the Russian prisoners. Early in the afternoon our private railway car was attached to a locomotive that pulled us as far as Koschidary, where we changed to a flatcar that took us several miles east to the German front lines. All seemed quiet and the German officers who appeared from adjacent dugouts assured us that everything was ready for the morrow's repatriation drama. We returned to Koschidary in the evening and spent the night in our railway car. That town, like all the other towns east of Kovno through which we passed, was in complete ruins.

The train containing the Russian prisoners arrived on the following day, paused to have our car attached, and moved on to the repatriation area. The prisoners emerged in groups from the cars and lined themselves in an orderly fashion on a road parallel to the railroad tracks. Each group was headed by a Russian officer or noncommissioned officer. A Russian colonel who had been in charge of the train was their leader. A bag containing provisions calculated to take care of their needs for twelve days was issued to each man.

The members of our mission and the German officers who had been assisting in the repatriation arrangements took a position on a mound at the side of the road. The Russian colonel addressed the prisoners. I understood that he was trying to assure them that they had nothing to fear and that they should conduct themselves as they entered Russian-controlled territory as men who had been honorably serving their country. He then turned toward us and thanked Russia's former allies, through us, for the assistance that had made repatriation possible. Addressing himself to the German officers and members of the train crew who were present, he expressed appreciation for the help that they had given the convoy. After leading the prisoners in a cheer for us he saluted smartly, picked up his two bags—one containing the food rations and the other his personal effects—and took his position at the head of the column. One of the prisoners carrying a large white flag took his place beside him. The colonel gave a sharp command and the column moved up the road.

As prisoners passed by us I was struck by the differences in their facial expressions. Although laden with their bags, some were marching as though on dress parade with chins high and faces rigid; some made no attempt to hide their joy at the thought of returning after so many years to their families and homes; the faces of many of them, however, registered concern at what might be awaiting them on the other side of the hill ahead. Slowly the column went over the hill—not a man looking back— and disappeared. Only the crew of the train, the German officers, and our own little group remained. With subdued comments we returned to our car and the empty train backed us to Koschidary. Thence we were shuttled back to Kovno, where we spent the night again at the Metropol.

Because the advance of the Poles on Vilna might eventually make it difficult, if not impossible, to continue repatriation through Koschidary, our mission decided to look for alternate routes, particularly a route to the north of Kovno. During the next two days, therefore, pulled by a locomotive that the German military had placed at our disposal, we visited various towns in northern Lithuania. All of these towns were in the same dilapidated state: ruins everywhere; the inhabitants dressed in rags and bark, living in cellars like animals, and coming out to beg for food whenever we stopped; sick people, surrounded by their families, lying on station platforms hoping to obtain rides on passing troop trains to places where they could receive treatment; and frightened children peeping at us from behind piles of debris.

AN INCIDENT AT TILSIT

After our mission was completed, we began our journey back to Berlin. Our car was picked up during the night of April 26 by a German troop train at the Lithuanian town of Schaulen [Šiauliai] and dropped off in the early morning of Sunday, April 27, at Tilsit [Sovetsk] in East Prussia. There we were told that the next train moving in the direction of Berlin would not depart until late in the afternoon. We took advantage of the stopover to get a change from the tinned food on which we had been subsisting by having Sunday lunch at the hotel in the middle of the town. On our way to the hotel, the crowds coming out of the churches looked with surprise at our Allied uniforms. Herr Thiefes, our German liaison officer, told us we were the first Western Allied officers to visit Tilsit since the outbreak of the war. Both adults and children began to follow us, apparently to learn who we were and where we were going. The crowd swelled in numbers and we began to feel self-conscious as the clomp of wooden shoes on the cobblestones broke the quiet of a Sunday noon.

When we arrived at the hotel, Herr Thiefes introduced us to the manager and we were ushered into the dining room. Here an unpleasant incident took place. The German general in command of the troops in East Prussia was having his lunch there. In our hearing he loudly protested our presence to the hotel manager. The manager refused to order us to leave. The general stalked out, casting angry glances at us and muttering. We had to restrain the fiery Captain Mario, a member of the British military mission, who considered himself insulted and insisted that his honor required that he challenge the general to a duel. The hotel manager was embarrassed and he and the waiters made special efforts during the remainder of our stay to show us hospitality.

The attitude of this German general illustrated the difference in atmosphere between eastern Germany and the rest of the country. The revolution in the West had removed many of the old-line professional German officers from their commands and had replaced them by nonprofessional officers. In East Prussia, however, the revolution's effect had been much less sweeping. There the traditional ascetic army officers continued to set the tone of the German army and to influence the civilian population. The German armies in the East had not been defeated during the war and the officers and men of those armies refused to conduct themselves like a defeated people. The professional German officers in the East were highly sensitive about the position of Germany and about their own personal status. They were inclined to be correct and scrupulously polite to the Allied officers with whom they had to deal, but they were also quick to take offense if not given the kind of recognition that in their opinion was due their rank and uniform. I do not know just what caused the German general to act as he did in the hotel dining room. We may have failed in some way when we entered the room to give the kind of recognition of his presence that would be in keeping with strict Prussian military protocol.

We arrived in Berlin on the morning of April 28. Colonel Ryan sent word for me to report to him at once. After hearing my summary of our experiences, he asked me to prepare a report of the conditions that I had found to exist in Lithuania, so that he could take it to Paris within the next few days.

The report produced results immediately. The American Red Cross began shipping needed drugs and hospital equipment and supplies to Lithuania within five or six weeks. Our Red Cross mission in Berlin sent one of its doctors to Kovno to supervise the distribution of these supplies and he was able to report, two or three months later, considerable improvement in the medical and health situation in Lithuania. In the meantime, organizations headed by Herbert Hoover also expedited the dispatch of foodstuffs and war surpluses of various kinds, including uniforms and other clothing, into Lithuania. Although this assistance alleviated the conditions to a certain extent, the need was still great when I next visited Lithuania in December 1919.

REPATRIATING RUSSIAN PRISONERS OF WAR FROM MARIENBURG IN WESTPREUSSEN, APRIL–JULY 1919

The day after I submitted my report on Lithuania, I was given another surprise assignment. I was ordered to go to Marienburg [Malbork], a small town on the eastern fringe of West Prussia that had been selected instead of Preussische-Holland as the jumping-off place for the Russian prisoners who were to be repatriated through East Prussia. In Marienburg I was to ask the commandant of the town to place at the disposal of the Red Cross a warehouse and other facilities for storing the provisions the prisoners were to take with them into Russia. I was to employ local labor to repack these provisions in bags, each of which would contain one man's rations. These packed bags would then be placed in special cars at Marienburg. One of these special cars would be attached to each train and the provisions would be distributed to the prisoners as they left the train in order to pass through the German lines.

I was told by Colonel Taylor that when all preparations for the repatriation had been completed several U.S. Army officers and noncommissioned officers would be assigned to Marienburg to accompany the trains to the scene of repatriation. Two officers would be placed on each train. After supervising the distribution of rations, these officers were to make sure that the prisoners passed safely through the German front. A military physician was also to be assigned to Marienburg, not only to look after prisoners who might become ill but also to make health inspections of the train.

Because of the urgency of my mission I was on my way to Marienburg within three days after I had received my orders. When I arrived there in the small hours of the morning, I found the station deserted. I was able eventually to find a stray railway worker who for a consideration carried one of my two heavy bags and conducted me to the Hotel Koenig von Preussen, located in the center of the town. After much banging on the doors I awakened a porter, but I was not admitted and given a room until I had shown my papers from the German War Ministry calling upon all German citizens to give me such assistance as might be necessary. For the next two months the Koenig von Preussen was to be my place of residence.

The hotel was maintained on a wartime basis, but the director and the staff did their utmost to make me and the other Americans who arrived later as comfortable as possible. Because of the shortage of fuel the daily ration of hot water was about a quart, delivered early each morning. Since the town's electric works no longer operated, each guest was issued about an inch and a half of candle daily. The little milk available was reserved for children. There was, of course, no butter. The coffee was ersatz—apparently made from a combination of roasted potato peelings and grass seed. Our meat was usually balls of horse meat floating in some kind of stew. The bread, such as it was, was strictly rationed. The flour in it had been mixed with some kind of grain substitute that reminded me of sawdust. However, following the arrival two weeks later of Red Cross food boxes from Berlin, we began to fare much better than the Germans. Indeed, I was ashamed to eat our food in the presence of our German fellow diners, and at my insistence the American table was placed on the dining terrace where we could have our meals behind a screen.

The morning of my arrival I called upon the German commandant, Captain von Kummer, who had just received a delayed telegram announcing my pending arrival. He expressed regret that no one had met me at the station and said that he hoped I had not suffered too much inconvenience. He promised to find a warehouse for me and to give me such aid as I might require.

The warehouse that Captain von Kummer found for us was secure and well equipped but was located some distance from the railroad station. It was therefore necessary to transport through the town, in public view and under armed German guard, the food destined for the Russian prisoners. This was unfortunate, because food was scarce in Marienburg. The children in particular were not merely hungry, they were desperately hungry. When the stores of food destined for use by the Russian prisoners began to arrive, the burgomaster made a call on me. With tears in his eyes he told me that he had put aside his German pride in order to come and make an appeal on behalf of the children. Could I not allocate for their use a little of the food that we were storing in the warehouse for later distribution among the Russian prisoners? He was asking nothing for the adult population. His conscience would not rest, however, until he had made every effort to obtain food for the children. It was terribly difficult for me to turn down his request but I had to escort him empty-handed to the door.

After I had been in Marienburg for two or three weeks, trainloads of Russian prisoners began to arrive en route to the German front. Most of them were in a festive mood. Their railway cars had been decorated with pine boughs and other kinds of evergreen and the prisoners themselves wore wildflowers on their caps or shirts. While the trains were waiting at the station for the cars of prepacked rations to be attached and for the completion of other formalities there was much laughter and singing. Rival groups competed with one another in singing and dancing. There seemed to be none of the trepidation about what might await them on the other side of the frontier that had been so noticeable among the prisoners at Koschidary.

In June I was called upon to perform an exceedingly painful task. The Polish army had succeeded in driving a military wedge between the retreating Bolsheviks and the German lines. Shortly after the returning Russian prisoners had passed through the German lines, therefore, they found themselves facing not the Bolshevik but the Polish lines. The Poles refused to permit them to proceed to Russia across the Polish-occupied territory. The prisoners turned back to the German lines only to learn that the Germans had orders not to let them re-enter German-occupied Lithuania. The Russian prisoners, therefore, found themselves trapped between the lines. I was instructed by headquarters in Berlin to turn back a train loaded with prisoners that was due in Marienburg within an hour or so and to let no more trains come through. I immediately informed Captain von Kummer of the situation and asked that a squad of soldiers be sent to the station to assist in the event that disorder should break out.

When the train rolled in with the rejoicing prisoners I approached the Russian colonel in charge and told him what the situation was. How should we go about breaking the dismal news to the prisoners? We decided to call the leaders of the various groups together. We told them that as a result of an unanticipated shift in the military situation on the eastern front it had become necessary to postpone—we hoped temporarily—any further repatriation and that they must, therefore, return to the camps from which they had come. We sought the leaders' support in comforting the prisoners and in preserving order. It was the consensus that the announcement should be made by the colonel while the station-master and I stood beside him. The colonel's brief statement was greeted for a moment by dead silence. Then the storm broke. Weeping prisoners fell on their knees before us, imploring that we let them go on, come what may. Others beat their breasts and sobbed. Some merely went back to the train and sat in stunned silence. There was, however, no violence. After an hour or so the train, still bedecked with green boughs, turned back toward the West. Thus ended for many months the repatriation of Russian prisoners through East Prussia. According to Colonel Taylor's "Historical Report of the Commission," before our work was thus interrupted 24,753 Russians had been repatriated. This number, the report noted, did not include the 9,970 Lithuanians who had been repatriated through East Prussia and the 1,758 Estonians and 1,500 Letts who had gone home by sea.

REACTION IN MARIENBURG TO THE ANNOUNCEMENT OF THE SIGNING OF THE TREATY OF VERSAILLES, JUNE 28, 1919

Our group remained in Marienburg for another two or three weeks, hoping that arrangements could be made for further repatriation. While we were awaiting developments, my birthday, June 28, approached. In order to raise morale I invited the other Americans in Marienburg—there were by that time about eight of us—to a birthday dinner in the hotel.

By giving some of our tinned rations to the hotel chef in return for fresh food I was able to arrange an exceptionally good dinner. While we were enjoying our after-dinner coffee—not ersatz but the real thing that had come in one of our food boxes—a newsboy came rushing in to sell "extras" of the Marienburg *Nogat–Zeitung*. Because of the shortage of paper, the extra was limited to a single sheet about nine by ten inches in size. Under a big headline "Unterzeichnet" (in English, "Signed") were three lines that in translation read as follows: "Versailles, June 28. The Peace Treaty, as anticipated, was signed this afternoon at 3 o'clock." Among my papers recently I found that historic sheet of paper. My birthday party became one of rejoicing.

There was no rejoicing that evening among the Germans in Marienburg. A newsflash had come out of Paris to the effect that the town was to be given to Poland. As this news spread, crowds began to assemble outside the hotel. Hundreds of people demonstrated angrily against what they called the "inhuman decision," but there was no violence.

The next morning Marienburg learned that it had not been awarded to Poland. The Nogat River was to form the eastern boundary of the new Polish Corridor, and the future of the Marienverder District in which Marienburg was situated was to be decided by a plebiscite. The plebiscite took place in 1920 after I had left Marienburg. The people voted about nine to one in favor of Germany. History was not to favor their choice. Following World War II the Soviet Union turned Marienburg and the

Marienverder District over to Poland. The historic old castle of the Teutonic Knights, I understand, has again fallen into ruins.

REPATRIATION OF RUSSIAN PRISONERS OF WAR FROM
HAMBURG TO BLACK SEA PORTS, JULY–AUGUST 1919

In early July I was sent on a new assignment, this time to Hamburg. I was to assist in repatriating Russian prisoners whose homes were in the liberated areas of the Caucasus. During the war a number of merchant vessels belonging to Germany's ally, Turkey, had been trapped in German ports. These ships were being made seaworthy for their return to Turkey. On their way back they were to transport as many prisoners as they could safely carry to the Black Sea and discharge them at the Caucasian ports of Batum and Poti. My job was to assist in checking the prisoners' papers, to see that the food provided for them had been put aboard, and in general to look out for their welfare. Upon checking the food supply I found that a large proportion of it was dehydrated and I became concerned about the prisoners' health during the voyage. I was assured, however, that supplementary fresh food would be taken aboard at Gibraltar or elsewhere en route. During the several weeks I was in Hamburg we were able to dispatch to the Black Sea area some seventeen or eighteen hundred prisoners.

AN EXPLORATORY TRIP TO RIGA,
AUGUST–SEPTEMBER 1919

In the latter part of August 1919 I was called back to American Red Cross headquarters in Berlin to carry out still another assignment. Colonel Ryan informed me that since large areas of Finland and the three Baltic states—Estonia, Latvia, and Lithuania—had been liberated from the Bolsheviks, the American Red Cross was considering sending a commission to undertake relief work in those countries. The headquarters of the commission would be established in Riga. I was to go to Riga as soon as the necessary travel permits could be obtained in order to see if the idea had merit. This would involve, on the one hand, informal discussions with the various Allied representatives and, on the other hand, consultation with Latvian authorities to learn whether they would welcome such a commission in Riga. For their part, the Latvian authorities would have to assure the commission and its personnel freedom of operation, as well as customs immunities and the like. While in Riga I was also to collect as much information as I could about the current situation in Latvia and ascertain the most critical needs of the Latvian people. If I should come to the opinion that there would be no serious obstacle to the dispatch of a commission, I should try to persuade the Latvian authorities to send a vessel to the German port of Stettin [Szczecin] to pick up some valuable American Red Cross medical and hospital supplies stored there and to transport them, together with the two Red Cross officers who were looking after them, to Riga, where they could be available for distribution upon the arrival in Riga of the commission.

The colonel added that conditions in the territory between East Prussia and Riga were chaotic. I might, therefore, run into travel and other difficulties, particularly in going from Mitau [Jelgava], the provincial capital of Courland, to Riga. He did not give me any instructions or advice about this but left it to me to solve problems of this kind as they arose.

I left Riga on the evening of August 29. At Tilsit, with the aid of the stationmaster, I was able to board what appeared to be a troop train that was going north in the direction of Mitau. In the compartment with me on that train were a number of Germans in field uniform. They looked at me in a friendly manner, showing neither antipathy nor reticence at the sight of my American uniform. They seemed to be in high spirits at the thought of what lay ahead of them. They explained that they were going into Courland as volunteers in the "free army" composed of Germans and Russian ex-prisoners of war. They had been promised that if Courland should become an autonomous state each of the soldiers who had served in the "free army" would be given a small farm. They had also been assured that while in this volunteer army they would be well paid and well fed. When I asked what the German government thought of this "free army," they laughed. They did not care what the present German government thought; real Germans had no respect for it. Growing expansive, they added that in the not-distant future the present German government would be replaced by a monarchy, the only type of a government that the German people would respect. After the monarchy had reconstructed Germany, the Germans together with the Russian monarchists would work together to restore the Russian empire. The soldiers talked and acted like light-hearted, irresponsible schoolboys.

Two young soldiers in new uniforms stood in the corridor of the train somewhat apart from the others. I learned from them that they were members of families that had furnished officers to the Prussian army for generations. The father of one of them, a colonel, had been killed during the last few days of the war. The father of the other, a major, had been removed from his command by his noncommissioned officers during the course of the German revolution. The boys had been too young to serve in the war. They seemed to feel that the revolution and the ensuing armistice had cheated them out of the military role that every self-respecting young German man should play. They were convinced that the present German regime was completing the destruction of the kind of Germany they had known and been taught to love. These convictions had moved them to run away from home to join the volunteer army in Courland, which seemed to them to offer the only hope for the future of their country.

When we arrived at the German border the train stopped; the locomotive was detached and switched to a siding. The passengers got out to stretch. They walked up and down beside the train or talked in little groups. After half an hour a German officer came out of the station, mounted a truck, and proceeded to read a document in a loud voice. I could not understand all that he said but apparently he was quoting a governmental order forbidding the train and its passengers to go any further. His statement was greeted with uproarious laughter. The soldiers went back into their cars; in a few minutes another locomotive appeared from across the border and attached itself to our train. As we crossed the border, the soldiers waved to the official who had read the proclamation and who seemed undisturbed at this contemptuous flouting of the government's order.

THE WESTERN VOLUNTEER ARMY IN MITAU

I arrived in Mitau on the evening of August 30. The ancient town was crowded with officers and men wearing a variety of uniforms. The uniform most often seen was that of the old German Iron Division with its death's-head insignia and the inevitable iron cross on the breast. Some of the other uniforms were smarter and more resplendent than any that I had seen since my arrival in Europe: boots shining like mirrors, jackets and trousers of bright hues. The wearers of these uniforms, I was told, were officers of the "free army," which a German officer with whom I had become acquainted on the train referred to as the "Western Volunteer Army." This German officer also explained that allied with this Western Volunteer Army were the Iron Division, several regiments of Landeswehr composed of Baltic Germans, and several other German units. He also suggested that a German mission that had been established in Mitau and that performed services similar to those usually performed by German consulates might give me advice regarding how I might obtain the travel documents that I would need to go on to Riga.

On the morning of August 31, I called on the head of the German mission and exhibited to one of its members my credentials from the German War Ministry. He told me I should apply to the representative of Latvia in Mitau for a permit to enter the territory under the control of the Latvian government and to the headquarters of the Western Volunteer Army for papers that would permit me to leave the territory under the control of that army.

The Latvian representative readily gave me the desired permit and advised me that the only way for me to travel from Mitau to Riga was by boat down the Aa [Lielupe] River, then through a canal that connected the Aa and the Dvina [Daugava] River, then up the Dvina to Riga.

It looked for a time as though the officers at the headquarters of the Western Volunteer Army would not grant me a permit to leave Mitau for Riga. When, however, several German officers at the headquarters intervened on my behalf, the permit was reluctantly issued. By early afternoon I was on a small cargo vessel heading down the Aa River. Although the boat was overloaded with passengers and cargo we made good headway and arrived in Riga in the middle of the night. While on board I made the acquaintance of a smartly dressed young officer. He handed me a card indicating that he was a Baltic nobleman who had served as a first lieutenant in a tsarist imperial guards regiment. He told me that he was returning from a mission to Mitau in order to rejoin his Landeswehr regiment in Riga. He explained that his regiment was composed entirely of "gentlemen" and that most of the officers and men in it were members of the old Baltic German nobility who were willing to serve either in the ranks or as officers to prevent the country from being taken over by the Bolsheviks or by the Letts. He seemed to see little difference between the Letts and the Bolsheviks. One of their common objectives, he pointed out, was to break up the landed estates and to confiscate the property of the well-to-do classes. Of the two, however, he expressed some preference for the Bolsheviks because the Letts, he said, were vengeful in their attitude toward the Baltic barons.

The morning after my arrival in Riga I called at the headquarters of the U.S. military mission, headed by Lieutenant Colonel Warwick. The next day, an appointment having been made for me by the U.S. officers, I called on Karlis Ulmanis, the Latvian prime minister, a man with whom I was to become well acquainted in later years. Although not a demonstrative person, he was quite cordial. He said his government would welcome an American Red Cross mission and would take all the necessary steps to facilitate its operation, including the granting of permission to move its supplies across the frontiers of the country without being subject to restrictions or duties. He spent more than an hour describing the political situation of the country from the Latvian point of view. He indicated that he found it difficult to understand the policy being pursued by the U.S. government, which on the one hand seemed eager to apply the doctrine of self-determination to the nations formerly under Austrian and German domination, but on the other showed little or no sympathy for the aspirations of peoples who had suffered even more under the Russian empire.

In referring to the United States the prime minister, who considered the United States as his second home, spoke with the frankness of one American talking to another. He had been involved in the Baltic uprisings against the tsarist government in 1905 and had subsequently gone to the United States as a refugee. While there he had studied agriculture and had eventually become an instructor in animal husbandry at the University of Nebraska. When he heard that Latvia was again striving for independence he had hurried back and, in view of his demonstrated abilities, had been elected prime minister shortly after his return.

RETURN FROM LIBAU TO STETTIN BY BOAT

I discussed with the prime minister the need of the American Red Cross for a vessel to transport medical and hospital supplies from Stettin to Riga. He said he would refer the matter to his minister for transport and suggested that I call on that minister on the following day. When I did so, I was told that there was a small 100-ton ship in Libau that could be sent at once to Stettin for the Red Cross supplies if the British, who were blockading the harbor of Libau, would permit its departure. I took this matter up at once with the members of the British military mission. They assured me they would not object to the departure of the ship. They also told me that a British destroyer was leaving for Libau on the following day and that I could travel on it if I desired. The destroyer was a beautiful ship, clean and speedy, and I enjoyed my short voyage on it to Libau, the first leg on my return voyage to Berlin.

In Libau I spent the night as the guest of the Earl of Caledon, the chief of the British military mission and the older brother of Colonel Harold Alexander who, I had learned in Riga, had just been appointed commander of the Baltic Landeswehr and whom I was to meet later in Riga on a number of occasions. One of the tasks of the colonel as commander of the Landeswehr was to see that the regiments under him would concentrate on holding back the Bolsheviks on the eastern front of Latvia and not become involved in trying to undermine the Latvian armed forces in the Riga area.

More than 30 years later, at a dinner given by our ambassador in the

U.S. embassy in London, I found myself sitting by a distinguished-looking man whose face was vaguely familiar. From his place card I noted that he was "Lord Alexander of Tunis." He turned out to be the Colonel Alexander whom I had known in Riga. He was still interested in Baltic affairs and asked me many questions about the fate of some of his old associates in Latvia.

The British not only gave permission for the little Latvian cargo vessel to leave Libau but also supplied it with coal, a scarce commodity, for the voyage. During the two-day voyage to Stettin the weather was excellent and the sea calm, but I was by no means comfortable. I was compelled to carry on a constant battle against the lice and bedbugs that infested the ship. In my efforts to avoid them I tried sleeping on a leather-covered bench in one of the cabins, but they managed to find me wherever I went.

Before the war the captain had had considerable experience navigating the Baltic. He had not ventured to cross it, however, since the outbreak of the war. Ordinary navigation maps were of little help because the regular sea routes had been so heavily mined that they could not be used, and the vessel was without the needed navigational instruments. This meant we had to stay quite close to the coast during most of our trip, and from time to time the captain would hail fishing vessels to inquire about the safest routes. Upon my arrival in Stettin I insisted that, before the Red Cross supplies were stored on board, the ship be thoroughly fumigated and disinfected. I also took appropriate measures to have similar treatment administered to myself.

MY REPORT TO COLONEL RYAN REGARDING THE BALTIC TRIP

After my arrival by train in Berlin from Stettin on September 8, I reported to Colonel Ryan. The Latvian government, I stated, was eager to have an American Red Cross commission in Riga. Lithuania and Estonia also would welcome Red Cross assistance. The mere presence of the American Red Cross in these countries, I said, would help to strengthen the morale of the people. The conditions in the Baltic countries were so appalling, however, that whatever aid the Red Cross, with its limited funds and facilities, could give, would barely scratch the surface of the need. I cautioned, therefore, that unless the Baltic governments and people would understand this fact in advance, their expectations might be too high.

I also warned the colonel that because of the political, military, and economic conditions in the area, the commission would undoubtedly encounter unusual difficulties in establishing itself and in operating. My report on the complex political situation, based as it was on a short visit and, to some extent, on hearsay, was rather sketchy. I described some of the various groups: the Baltic German aristocracy known as the "Baltic barons," who tended to equate Baltic nationalism with Bolshevism; the advocates of a great Russia, who urged that efforts be made to restore the empire; the Poles, who insisted that future European security demanded a powerful Poland wedged in between Russia and Germany; and of course the Bolsheviks, who though weakened militarily at the time were looking for opportunities to take advantage of dissensions and conflicts among their East European neighbors.

So far as the military situation was concerned, I said that the German forces, which apparently had broken away from Reich control,* together with troops composed largely of Russian ex-prisoners of war whom they controlled, seemed determined at an appropriate moment to seize control of the territories of Latvia that had been liberated from the Bolsheviks and to use the Baltic area as a base for an eventual move against Moscow or Leningrad. The German Baltic aristocracy in Courland, fearful of what a republic dominated by the Latvians would do to them, were sympathetic to the aspirations of these German-Baltic forces and had contributed officers to their ranks. Many of the young Baltic

---

* I did not learn until much later that on September 5, while I was still on my Riga mission, the Reich government had ordered the German Eastern Command to withdraw all German troops from Courland; that General von der Golz, the commander of the German troops in the Baltic, who was conniving with the German and Russian monarchists, did not obey the order; and that on September 25, the German government finally issued instructions relieving the general of his command. The general, however, who had been tipped off that such instructions were about to be issued, had transferred his men, before the instructions could reach him, to the so-called Free or Volunteer Army in the Baltic—an army that considered itself an independent military unit. In the latter part of September, therefore, when the Council of Five in Paris demanded the complete withdrawal of German forces from the Baltic by October 20, the German government was compelled to point out that those forces were no longer under its control. Although von der Golz had transferred the command of these troops it was generally believed that he continued indirectly to exercise control over them so long as they remained in the Baltic.

It should not be assumed that the Weimar government was guilty of duplicity in this matter. It was clearly not strong enough, however, in the autumn of 1919 to take the stern measures that would have been necessary to bring the military in East Prussia and certain elements in the War Ministry under its control.

Germans, however, were serving in the Landeswehr under Colonel Alexander and were being kept busy fighting the Bolsheviks in the eastern part of Latvia, far away from the intrigues centered in Mitau. To add to the complications, a White Russian army in the north led by a General Yudenich was using eastern Estonia as a base in its efforts to capture Leningrad. It seemed to me obvious that the situation in the Mitau-Riga area was particularly tense. I thought it quite possible that fighting in that area could break out at any time.

My Decision to Become a Member of the American Red Cross Commission to Western Russia and the Baltic States

Colonel Ryan was particularly pleased that I had been successful in obtaining the small vessel to move the supplies from Stettin to Riga. He did not appear deeply concerned about the complications and uncertainties existing in the area. He was the kind of person who liked to work in difficult and even dangerous situations, and it was he who was to head the commission when it was established. The American Red Cross headquarters in Paris was awaiting word from him about when the commission should be actually organized and, following our conversation, he sent a message to Paris that the time had arrived. He told me that he hoped I would serve on such a commission and, when I hesitated in replying, he asked me to think the matter over. Regardless of what my decision might be, he said that he would like me to accompany him to Paris to assist in organizing it.

The colonel also told me that the Red Cross commission in Germany was being liquidated. It was no longer needed. The Treaty of Peace had been signed; foodstuffs and other necessities of life were beginning to enter Germany; furthermore, a decision had been made in Paris that the responsibility for the care and repatriation of the Russian prisoners should in the future rest on the German government. Colonel Taylor was planning to return to the United States while a few of the members of the Berlin mission would be selected to serve as a nucleus for the new commission to the Baltic states.

I was torn between the feeling that I should return immediately to the United States to resume my law studies and a desire to join the commission that Colonel Ryan was to head. Awaiting me in Berlin had been a letter from my twin brother informing me that he was entering the Harvard Law School and urging me to join him there. On the other hand, I had become interested in the Baltic and in the fate of the people in that area who were displaying admirable courage in the face of almost unendurable hardship and suffering. I simply could not turn down the opportunity to participate in relief work in the area under an inspiring leader like Colonel Ryan. My decision to accept the colonel's invitation represented one of the turning points of my life. From it flowed more than 40 years of work in the foreign field.

Part III

With the American Red Cross Commission to Western Russia and the Baltic States, October 1919–September 1921

CHAPTER 4

WITH THE AMERICAN
RED CROSS IN LATVIA,
OCTOBER–DECEMBER 1919

THE JOURNEY OF THE COMMISSION TO RIGA
FROM BERLIN, OCTOBER 1919

IN MID-SEPTEMBER I went to Paris from Berlin to assist Colonel Ryan in organizing "The American Red Cross Commission to Western Russia and the Baltic States," as the new commission was to be called. For two weeks I interviewed personnel, procured supplies the commission would need, arranged transport, and so forth. I then returned to Berlin. While I was in Paris the staff members who were to be transferred from our Berlin mission to the new commission had been busy. The mission's stores, supplies, and automobiles had been turned over to the commission and, together with additional supplies and equipment, had been prepared for shipment. A major problem was that of transport to Riga. Since no vessels were available we could not go by sea. Instead, commission personnel, supplies, equipment, and automobiles were to go by train as far as Mitau and then overland by automobile from Mitau to Riga. If the Mitau road was impassable, we would try to complete our journey by riverboat as I had done in September.

On Friday evening, October 3, 1919, a train that had been placed at our disposal by the German government left Berlin for Mitau. Behind the locomotive and two sleeping cars for the 25 members of the commission were boxcars containing food, gasoline, and personal luggage, and in the rear there was a long line of flatcars loaded with the automobiles. The food, most of which was for the use of the members during the coming winter, was in hundreds of small wooden boxes that had originally been packed in the United States for distribution by the Danish Red Cross to American prisoners of war in Germany and had been turned over to the American Red Cross mission in Germany after the American prisoners had been repatriated. During our journey, members of the commission took turns guarding the food since the danger of pilferage was great.

With the American members on the train was a German national, Fritz Beer. A former banker, who before the war had spent several years with the Guaranty Trust Company in New York in order to study U.S. banking procedures, Beer had been the liaison officer between the American Red Cross mission in Berlin and the German War Ministry. We had urged him to accompany us to Riga to help us deal with the German authorities en route, particularly in Mitau. He had served in the German army during the war on both the eastern and western fronts. He was acquainted with German military procedures and was expert in negotiating with the German civilian officials. He proved to be almost invaluable both in expediting the movement of the train and in assisting us in obtaining the necessary travel permits in Mitau. After we became established in Riga, Mr. Beer returned to Berlin and continued to serve as a consultant with the small office the American Red Cross maintained there. When I took charge of that office in the spring of 1920 he was still there, and we worked closely together during the remainder of my service with the American Red Cross. We developed a warm friendship that has continued through the years.

The German civil authorities had told Colonel Ryan that the situation between Mitau and Riga was tense. As I have mentioned, the German forces in Courland, of which Mitau was the capital, were mostly members of the Iron Division that had broken with the German government. These troops had joined with Russian forces to form an army of irregulars under the command of a former tsarist colonel by the name of Prince Aveloff Bermondt. This army was preparing an attack on Riga that might be launched at any time. Colonel Ryan urged us, therefore, to get our supplies to Riga as soon as possible, and he warned that we should not become separated during the journey.

On our return trip to Mitau we shared the narrow ragged road with an unending line of soldiers both mounted and unmounted, trucks, horsedrawn vehicles, and artillery, heading in the opposite direction, toward the front. At one point we were ordered to turn around and fall in behind the artillery. After we had gone back toward Riga for a time, we were again turned toward Mitau. At another point, passing German soldiers discovered that some of our trucks were loaded with food and began gleefully to help themselves. It was with difficulty that I persuaded them to keep their hands off. During all this time we could hear the bellow of artillery and see flashes in the direction of Riga. In the small hours of the morning we again entered the streets of Mitau.

Mitau under Aveloff Bermondt

Soldiers of the Iron Division with whom we had chatted during our return to Moscow had assured us that we would be detained in Mitau by the fighting for only a short time. They were confident that they would be in Riga within 24 hours and that there would be no more fighting in the territory between the two towns. "The Latvians will run," they said, "at the sight of an Iron Division uniform." Our informants turned out to be wrong. Although many of the Latvian troops were undisciplined young boys or old men mobilized from the rural districts, the backbone of their fighting force was composed of the vigorous and experienced survivors of the regiments known during the war as the Lettish Rifles—regiments that were among the crack units of the old Russian Imperial Army. Not even the famous Iron Division had a fighting record more brilliant than that of the Lettish Rifles, which had successfully defended Riga against almost continuous German onslaughts for many months.

Since the Latvians had practically no artillery they had to fall back to Thorenberg, a small town on the south bank of the Dvina opposite Riga. Their retreat was accomplished slowly and in good order in the face of German artillery and machine gun fire. At Thorenberg the bulk of the Latvian forces crossed the half-mile long steel railroad bridge over the Dvina into Riga. The Bermondt troops proceeded to occupy Thorenberg, expecting to pursue disorderly retreating Latvians across the bridge into Riga. The Latvians, however, barricaded the great bridge, opened it by lifting the drawbridge near the Riga side, and heavily fortified the Riga end. The rest of the Latvian troops, instead of crossing the Dvina, had retreated toward the sea along its left bank for some ten or twelve miles and established headquarters at a village called Bolderaa [Bolderaja] near its mouth. At Bolderaa these forces were protected by the guns of the British and French warships anchored in the estuary. Because these guns had a longer range and were more powerful than any of the artillery the Bermondt troops possessed, Bolderaa was comparatively safe from attack. The attackers were stopped cold since the terrain along the river made an approach from that direction almost impossible. For several weeks there was a deadlock. The Bermondt forces were not entirely idle, however. They bombarded Riga intermittently, particularly the portions near the bridgehead, and made excursions from time to time against the troops still on the southern banks in the direction of Bolderaa. They also arrested any Latvians in the area under their control who had been denounced by their Baltic-German allies as persons who might later be dangerous opponents.

Although the Iron Division could be depended upon to give an excellent account of itself when fighting as a unit of the German army, its members were not particularly eager to risk their lives battling the tough foe the Latvians had turned out to be merely to assist the Russians in capturing Riga and the Baltic barons in getting rid of a troublesome army.

Members of this division and the other German volunteers who had come into Courland for adventure and loot eventually became disillusioned and bitter. Some in their bitterness turned to pillaging and ravaging the countryside. Various stories of their atrocities that reached us in Mitau were undoubtedly exaggerated, but enough of them were true to account for the aroused feelings on the Latvian farms and in the villages throughout Courland. Cruel guerrilla-type fighting soon developed during which the rules of civilized warfare were disregarded by both sides.

While the situation I have described was developing we were penned up in Mitau. On the second day of our enforced stay in Mitau, Major Hugh R. Griffin arrived. A wise and benign man in his sixties and an old friend of Colonel Ryan, he had been sent from Paris apparently to counterbalance the impetuous and impulsive colonel. Unfortunately his health was not good and, though the members of the mission tried to protect him from undue exposure and overwork, he refused to be treated as an invalid and continued to face hardships difficult for a person of his age to endure.

Shortly after Major Griffin's arrival, Colonel Ryan, knowing that Riga would be bombarded, decided he should hurry back to that city to look after the safety of our men and supplies. He also hoped to arrange an armistice that would permit passage with our supplies. In Colonel Ryan's absence Major Griffin, who had had no experience in field work, was to be in charge. The next ranking officer was Major Malcom, in charge of supplies, who also had had no field experience.

Since a trip through the fighting lines, particularly crossing the bridge, would be extremely dangerous, Mr. Beer and I tried to persuade the colonel not to undertake it. He refused to be discouraged either by our arguments or by the difficulties put in his way by both the Bermondt and Latvian sides. Finally on October 11 he reached the river and, accompanied by a Russian officer bearing a large white flag, he walked as far as the chasm created by the uplifted drawbridge. A Latvian officer on the Riga side lowered a ladder and Colonel Ryan climbed to the top of the draw. Accompanied by the Latvian officer he completed his journey, while the courageous Russian who had accompanied him returned safely to Thorenberg.

A day or two after Colonel Ryan's departure we learned that Prince Aveloff Bermondt would welcome a call from the leader of our party. It was decided that a call should be made because the prince, after all, was at least nominally the commander of the Western Volunteer Army, and without his good will our difficulties might become greater. Arrangements were made for Major Griffin and me to call upon him. When we arrived at the army's headquarters, we were passed with heel-clicking and arms-presenting from one set of impressively arrayed guards to another until we found ourselves in a great baronial hall with a highly polished floor and enormous chandeliers. Officers in a variety of colorful uniforms stood elegantly about in groups, engaging one another in conversation. As we entered in our simple khaki uniforms, I felt that by some weird mistake we had suddenly been catapulted into a scene from a Viennese operetta. We stood in this hall only a few moments before a handsome young man who spoke beautiful English ushered us into a long inner room. At the far end of the room the prince, who was seated at a huge desk, arose as we entered. He came forward to meet us, graciously waved us to one of the divans that lined the wall, and placed himself opposite us in a luxuriously upholstered armchair. He was a handsome man, perhaps 35 or 40, of medium height, with expressive eyes and well-groomed mustaches, olive skin, and finely cut features. His heavy black hair, swept back from a high forehead, added drama to his face. He wore the uniform of a Caucasian colonel, replete with cartridge accouterment and rows of military decorations, to complete the picture of a dashing, romantic figure.

After an exchange of amenities he opened the conversation by expressing regret that we had been detained in Mitau. He said it was unfortunate that we had arrived just at the time when his army was moving forward in its continuing struggle to liberate Russia from the Bolsheviks. He hoped we would not be delayed too long. He would like to have us with him in Riga. He was concerned, however, about the attitude of the Allies toward him. They apparently failed to understand that his objectives and theirs were similar. Both desired a restored Russia, friendly toward the Western world.

Major Griffin explained that we were not in Mitau on a political mission and were, therefore, not in a position to discuss political matters. He stressed that our mission was of a strictly humanitarian nature and that it was our hope that arrangements could be made in the not too distant future that would permit us to proceed to Riga to carry it out. The major added that if we could be of assistance while in Mitau in relieving the human suffering that we saw on every side, we would be most pleased. The prince accepted this reply with good grace. He said he understood that our activities were not of a political character; he had mentioned what seemed to be the attitude of the Allies toward him merely because it was causing him deep concern. There was considerable suffering both among the civilian and military populations, he added, and perhaps arrangements might be made for our group to engage while in Mitau in the kind of activities for which the American Red Cross was so well known.

Shortly after our interview with Bermondt, our group was asked if we could send some of our ambulances to Thorenberg and other villages on the southern bank of the river to remove the sick and wounded, both civilians and military, who were badly in need of medical attention. During the remainder of our stay in Mitau our ambulances carried many of these people from the river area to the civilian or military hospitals in Mitau.

In the meantime, Colonel Ryan was active on the Riga side of the river. He had learned that the food supplies of the inhabitants of Thorenberg and the adjacent villages on the south side of the river, which normally came from Riga, had been exhausted and that the area was threatened with starvation. As a result of a series of radio exchanges between him and Bermondt headquarters carried on through Copenhagen, arrangements were made for several armistices of five or six hours each, during which boats crossed from the Riga side to the Thorenberg side laden with food furnished by the American Relief Administration. Our automobiles met these boats and transported the food to hastily organized food kitchens. Hundreds of hungry people in the river area, particularly children, were fed at these kitchens during the next two weeks. We took advantage of the trips of these vessels to send back large quantities of our supplies that were badly needed in Riga.

THE LATVIAN MOVE AGAINST MITAU, OCTOBER–NOVEMBER 1919

Within a few days after my arrival in Riga, Colonel Ryan asked me to recross the river and establish myself at the headquarters of the Latvian Third Division in Bolderaa. He said he would send with me two ambulances manned by competent Latvian drivers who had had experience as medical corpsmen. The Third Division lacked facilities to move its wounded to the river front where boats could take them over to the Riga side. It was Colonel Ryan's idea that I should attach myself to Third

Division headquarters and, if it should move elsewhere, I was to go with it. Since the Latvians were planning an offensive in the near future, it was entirely possible that I might be going toward Mitau, the town to which I had already been assigned.

The next morning I went with the two ambulances to a point several miles below Riga. Here the ambulances were loaded on a barge that was to be towed by a small tugboat downriver and across to Bolderaa. The Third Division staff there made me welcome and invited me to join their mess, which was headed by the commander, Colonel Janis Berkis. In the mess hall I was treated as a fellow officer and, from time to time, one of the officers who could speak English would sit by me and interpret the conversation of the other officers. The atmosphere of the mess was quite different from that of the messes one reads about, where airmen on the western front would leave the table with a gallant jest on their lips to keep a rendezvous with death. The Latvian officers were deadly serious in discussing the developments of the day and were businesslike and matter-of-fact when departing on dangerous missions. They were unashamedly patriotic and possessed an unwavering determination to drive the Russo-Germans out of their country, freeing it once and for all from the oppression it had endured since its conquest by the knightly orders of German warrior-monks in the thirteenth century. There was no bombast or heroics, no boasting of the day's accomplishments, and a minimum of banter. Usually Latvian was spoken, although on occasion the officers would drift into the use of German or Russian. Most seemed able to converse easily in any of these three languages. Their facility with Russian came from serving as officers in the Russian army. They did not dislike the Russians as a people because under the tsars they had usually received better treatment while serving in Russia than in the Baltic states, where the German Balts had worked systematically for centuries to keep the local population subservient.

Almost every day one or more officers would fail to show up. Their fellow officers would tell me with grief whether they had been killed or wounded. There was no talk of anyone having been taken prisoner, for by then tempers on both sides had been so aroused that neither side was taking prisoners. Each side circulated stories to the effect that the enemy was torturing the wounded prisoners before killing them. My own impression, obtained from viewing scores of dead on the battlefield and in the city streets, was that most of the wounded were put out of their misery quickly and mercifully.

Sometimes I learned at first hand what had become of the occupants of the now-empty chairs, for I had the sad duty of transporting a number of members of the mess who had been wounded from the front lines to the hospital boats. Most of the days, and some of the nights, I spent responding to calls from sections of the front for vehicles to transfer the wounded. The cold weather continued and from time to time there was snow. Our ambulances had high axles and, being relatively light, were able to negotiate roads over which heavier vehicles could not travel. Since we were not permitted to use lights at night we welcomed snow if it were not too deep, because the reflected light made it easier to find our way through the forests.

I admired the Latvian soldiers we met slogging doggedly through the forests or along the roads. Many were clad in rags, animal skins, and pieces of bark. Their footwear was often made of the soft inner bark of trees, undressed skins, or other makeshift wrappings secured with leather thongs. This lack of clothing, particularly boots, contributed a goulish note to the war. Before the bodies of the dead had become cold there was a scramble for their clothing. Practically all of the bodies that were strewn in the open fields, the meadows, and the forests had been stripped.

The bearing of some of the soldiers showed that they had had no military training. Many, moreover, were young boys—some not more than fifteen or sixteen years of age—who clearly could not have had previous military service. I remember one badly wounded boy who could not have been more than fourteen. He was in a state of semishock and, when I lifted him into the ambulance, he wrapped his arms around my neck and cried like a child upon my shoulder.

I did not try to keep count of the number of wounded brought in by our ambulances, but I know there was not a day when we did not arrive several times at the riverside with both ambulances loaded to capacity. Once, as we were placing a couple of wounded Latvians into an ambulance at a front-line dressing station, I saw a young German boy lying nearby who had been shot through the thigh. I asked the first aid people to dress his wound so that I could take him along. They said they had orders not to touch wounded enemies until an officer appeared. I ordered them to dress the wound and said I would not leave the station until they did. They at once picked up the boy, cleaned and dressed his wound with as much care as if he had been one of their own, and helped me put him into the ambulance. I had the impression they were glad to have an excuse to disobey orders, since they too seemed sorry for the poor fellow. On the way to the boat one of the Latvian wounded attempted to push the German out of the car. The other Latvian called upon us to interfere. I had to remain in the back of the ambulance during the rest of our journey to maintain order. The attendants on the hospital boat assured me the young German would be well taken care of. I nevertheless sent a note to the Red

Cross officer on the other side of the river asking him to keep an eye on the prisoner. This boy, like a number of other German wounded we had picked up, was regarded as a ward of the American Red Cross and was sent back to Germany after the cessation of hostilities.

As the days went by, it became clear that the Bermondt troops were in deep trouble. The Allied warships had moved up the river and were shelling not only the Bermondt frontal positions but also the roads vital to the maintenance of their communications, including the highway between Riga and Mitau. Our ambulances were compelled to go greater and greater distances to pick up the wounded. More and more Latvian troops were crossing the river. Furthermore, the Russian-Germans found themselves harassed from the rear. Latvian troops and irregulars moving in from the direction of Libau were interfering with their supplies. Both officers and men began to be haunted by the fear that they might at any time find themselves surrounded and cut off from possible retreat into East Prussia. One day in late November—I think it was the twentieth—the strain became too great, and the Russian-Germans began a withdrawal that in some areas degenerated into a rout. That evening the few officers who took time to enter the mess hall told me that the Bermondt troops were on the run and that the Latvians hoped to reach Mitau the next day before the retreating enemy had enough time to do much damage to the town.

In view of these developments I was not surprised when Colonel Ryan drove up the next morning to the headquarters of the Third Division. He was planning to follow the Latvians, who might well be in Mitau before nightfall, and he suggested I follow in one of the ambulances. The Bermondt retreat had been so rapid that we were able to push on toward Mitau just as fast as the condition of the roads permitted. The guns of Allied ships had done a thorough job of pitting the road between Thorenberg and Mitau, and the Bermondt troops had further contributed to our difficulties by destroying the temporary bridges after passing over them. Nevertheless, with the aid of Latvian soldiers who were erecting new temporary bridges and who helped our cars—sometimes lifting them up bodily—to get across the tough places, we were able to reach Mitau in the middle of the afternoon. As we crossed the hastily repaired bridges over the Aa, I was shocked to see the beautiful and historic castle, the home of the dukes of Courland for almost 200 years, in flames. Thick clouds of smoke over other sections of the city showed that, despite their haste to leave, the Bermondt troops had engaged in considerable destruction. I was told later by some of the German Balts that this destruction was not wanton; the only buildings burned were those that housed confidential records, which the Bermondt troops had had no time to move.

MITAU UNDER THE LATVIANS, NOVEMBER–DECEMBER 1919

As we entered Mitau we could hear shooting. Dead bodies, most of them stripped, lay in the streets. In the great square the Commandatur (the headquarters of the military commander of the town) was still burning and we could hear shots and screams from the buildings adjoining it. We went at once to the Latvian Red Cross hospital and asked if Mr. Beer was still there. When he was brought out of his hiding place he made no secret of his relief in seeing us. Someone had informed Latvian intelligence that a German spy was concealed in the hospital and several search parties had been looking for him. We arranged for Beer to return with Colonel Ryan in the evening to Riga. The atmosphere in Mitau was so tense that any German known to have had contact with Bermondt was in mortal danger.

I accompanied Colonel Ryan on an inspection trip through the military and civilian hospitals in Mitau for the purpose of determining their needs. Before leaving the Latvian Red Cross hospital, we arranged with a Latvian officer who had been attached to the colonel in a liaison capacity to have a guard stationed there to protect the staff, Mr. Beer, and their property. Colonel Ryan departed at nightfall for Riga with Mr. Beer, leaving me behind to obtain living quarters for several officers and office space for the Mitau branch of our commission.

The members of the skeleton staff of the Latvian Red Cross hospital were tense. They huddled together and winced at the sound of every rifle shot. Despite the presence of the armed guards they felt unsafe. They told me that house-to-house searches were being made for all persons known to have collaborated with the Bermondt forces. Most collaborators had fled with the departing troops, but those who remained were being dealt with summarily. Some were found in their homes and shot on the spot; others were shot in the streets while trying to escape; still others were taken to a small park not far from the hospital where they were lined up and shot. The bodies were usually left where they fell. Since many Baltic Germans were believed to have been in sympathy with Bermondt and had to an extent cooperated with the Baltic Germans serving under him, all Baltic Germans were suspect and in danger.

After dark two weeping women, an elderly woman with her daughter, appeared at the hospital and insisted on seeing me. They were quite incoherent but finally I was able to understand that the husband and father had been shot in the afternoon. They pleaded with me to take them in my ambulance to the place of execution to pick up the body, transport it to the Baltic-German cemetery, and there help them to lay it in the family burial plot. The dead man had apparently been on the list of those charged with collaborating with the Bermondt officials. The driver, the two women, and I went to the little park where the executions were taking place. There we discovered that a soft snow had covered the stripped bodies, and we had to brush snow from a number of faces before the women were able to identify the man for whom we were searching. The driver and I placed the body in the ambulance and, directed by the women, we went to a graveyard where we deposited it on a plot that they designated. At their request we left the women alone with the body in the dark, snowmantled cemetery.

Upon my return to the hospital I decided to walk the short distance to the officers' mess, to which I had been invited for dinner by a friend from the Third Division staff. This was a mistake. I had not walked for more than three or four minutes before I was stopped by two ragged soldiers who questioned me in Latvian. I attempted to explain in the few Russian words I had learned, who I was. I then tried my German. They still did not understand. They knew, however, that I was addressing them in German. Smiles lit their faces. They had caught a German officer trying to escape! With manifest pleasure they indicated to me by light prodding with their bayonets that I was to turn and go in the direction of the fateful little park. As I marched in front of them I continued desperately to try to explain that I was not a German, that I was an American. Their interest, however, was on my overcoat with its fur collar, on my shoes and puttees, and on my gloves. I could see that they had not had military training. My guess was that they were young farm laborers who had never attended school or been more than a few miles from the land they worked before they had become members of one of the community–recruited Latvian detachments.

As we neared the park I began to lose hope, especially since I was still unable to establish communication with them. I could see the park before us when a door in a house across the narrow street opened and a Latvian officer appeared in it. Before he moved out of the light I was able to see his face long enough to recognize him as one of the officers of the Bolderaa mess. I called to him and he came over at once. After exchanging a few words with my captors, he understood the situation and dismissed them. They left, casting last regretful glances at my warm clothing and shoes.

The officer accompanied me to the mess where we had a quiet dinner. Most of those present were just as tired as I. I felt that they were unhappy at what was going on throughout the town and were a little ashamed of, for instance, the incident in which I had just been involved. I told them I was concerned lest innocent people might be suffering. They admitted this might be the case, but pointed out that it was difficult to control troops at a time like this. Many of the soldiers were irregulars who had no real discipline or understanding of the rules of war. Furthermore, feelings were running high, especially since the Bermondt forces, before retreating, had executed a number of Latvians whom they had jailed as potential troublemakers. I was witnessing more than the military occupation of a town that had been in the hands of the enemy; Mitau was in the throes of a social revolution. The Latvians were determined, once and for all, to destroy the power of the Baltic-German aristocracy that had been centered in this historic capital of Courland. The Latvian officers assured me, however, that stringent steps were being taken to restore law and order.

During the next two weeks, working closely with our headquarters in Riga, with the newly established Latvian civilian authorities in Mitau, and with the Latvian military, we tried to alleviate the suffering that we found on every side. Special attention was given to the children, the aged, and the sick. Representatives of the Hoover Relief Administration came to Mitau and with our help set up food kitchens for the children in Mitau and throughout the countryside, particularly in the areas that had been the scene of the sharpest fighting. With the aid of various Latvian and other organizations we distributed tons of clothing. The Latvians who worked with us shared our view that aid should be given impartially, without regard to ethnic origin, religion, or politics. Latvians, Russians, Germans, Jews, and all others were given equal treatment. In a surprisingly short time the spirit of revenge, so painfully noticeable during the first 24 hours after the capture of Mitau, evaporated and was replaced by what seemed to be a universal desire to repair the ravages of war and to engage in reconstruction.

I had been in Mitau only two busy weeks when I received a message from Colonel Ryan to the effect that a Red Cross office was to be established in Lithuania at Kaunas (by that time we had decided to call Kovno by its Lithuanian name) and that I was to open it and take charge of it. The message indicated that he would be making a visit to Kaunas within a few days and that I should prepare to accompany him.

I was pleased at the thought of returning to Kaunas, since I had had a sympathetic interest in Lithuania dating from my visit there the preceding April and I had been trying to keep abreast of events that might affect that little country. I knew that although the Lithuanians had failed to attain their cherished objective of establishing their national capital in Vilna, which was firmly in the possession of Poland, they had managed to retain their independence.

When the Latvian officials in Mitau and Latvian charitable organizations with whom we had been working learned that I was being transferred to Lithuania, they sent word to me that they would like, before my departure, to show their appreciation of the work that the American Red Cross had been doing in Courland. They indicated that they would like to send a delegation to American Red Cross headquarters to express their gratitude and asked if I would be willing to receive such a delegation. I agreed with the understanding that Colonel Ryan would also be present. It was arranged, therefore, for Colonel Ryan to have luncheon with me in Mitau on the day before our departure for Kaunas so that he could join me in receiving the delegation. When the colonel and I stepped out of our office quarters, we found ourselves facing not a delegation but a demonstration. More than a thousand people were assembled in front of our headquarters, a band played the U.S. and Latvian anthems, and speeches of appreciation were made by civilian and military officials and by the heads of various charitable organizations.

Two months later I received a letter, which I still possess, from the Latvian official who, following the withdrawal of the Bermondt forces, had been chief of the province of High-Courland. I would like to quote the English translation, which was on the reverse side of the letter:

> To the Chief of the American Red Cross
> Commission, Mitau
> Captain L. Henderson
>
> Liquidating to-day the post of the Chief of High-Courland and considering my done work in the mentioned country, I can state with great pleasure, that the American Red Cross not equal to any one else, and especially through your honorable personality, dear Captain, who being the first organisator of High-Courland, has so most largely provided with victuals and clothes the country inhabitants and their children. These good actions have greatly dried the bitter tears of their faded cheeks and have many of them saved from famine and agony; they have as well largely helped me in maintaining regulation and peace in the country.
>
> According to the hitherto blessed doings, I and the country's inhabitants beg the American Red Cross and you, dear Captain, to accept our most sincerely thanks and the assurance, that we will never forget this great kindness of the U. S. of America at the present hard time.

I realized that this letter was not intended to honor me as a person but as the representative of the American people who by their contributions had alleviated so much suffering through our little Mitau office.

CHAPTER 5

WITH THE AMERICAN RED CROSS IN LITHUANIA, DECEMBER 1919–FEBRUARY 1920

THE JOURNEY FROM MITAU TO KAUNAS, DECEMBER 1919

THE DIRECT DISTANCE from Mitau to Kaunas is about 130 miles. After allowing for the condition of bridges and roads that necessitated frequent detours, for punctures and mechanical troubles, and for delays arising from inspections of our travel permits, Colonel Ryan and I estimated that we would be fortunate if we could complete the journey in ten hours. We left Mitau in the early morning of the day following the demonstration with a Latvian driver who could speak the local languages and who was an excellent mechanic.

The first part of our journey was uneventful. It was not until nearly noon that our troubles began with a light snow that gradually became heavier and began to stick to our windshield. Since in those days there were no automatic windshield wipers I had to get out and clear the windshield every mile or so. Our difficulties were compounded when we began to overtake long lines of German troops—the remnants of the German armies that had occupied the Baltic and were now on their way back to East Prussia. The soldiers were on foot but with each group were horse-drawn sledges or carts laden with their effects and loot. The puncture of one of our tires by a horseshoe nail also slowed us up. While the tire was being repaired we heard a horn behind us, and through the falling snow a heavy passenger car loomed up flying a large U.S. flag. It paused alongside and one of its passengers asked if we were in need of assistance. When assured that a puncture was our only problem, the passenger waved and his car went on. The passenger in question, the colonel told me, was the new U.S. commissioner to the Baltic states.

Since the United States had not as yet recognized the independence of the three Baltic states of Estonia, Latvia, and Lithuania, it had not sent ministers to them. Nevertheless, in the autumn of 1919, it had appointed John Gade, a former American businessman who, during the latter part of the war, had been serving as naval attaché in Copenhagen in the diplomatic capacity of U.S. commissioner to the Baltic states. Gade had arrived in Riga in November and had set up his office in that city. The members of the former U.S. military mission in Riga were then assigned to him as military attachés. Gade was now on his way to Lithuania to make his first official visit to that country.

After our tire had been repaired we again pushed along slowly as the snowdrifts piled higher. It soon became obvious that we could not get through the snow to Kaunas and we began to look for a suitable place to spend the night. As darkness fell we saw a large dark object in the road ahead of us. It was the commissioner's car firmly stuck in a snowbank. The commissioner, another passenger, and the chauffeur were doing their best to push the car out of the deep rut in which it had sunk. Our own chauffeur, Colonel Ryan, and I got out to lend a hand. The heavy car, however, would not budge. When the colonel introduced me to the commissioner and his companion I learned that the latter, whose name was John Lehrs, was assisting Gade during his journey as an aide and interpreter. Lehrs, a U.S. citizen born in Russia, could speak both Russian and German fluently. In later years he and I were to serve as friendly colleagues in our legation in Riga.

So far as I could recall, Gade was the first U.S. diplomat whom I had met. He was understandably not in the best of humor and such remarks as he made reflected the state of his feelings. My experience that evening caused me to believe that even the most gracious diplomats may sometimes lose a certain amount of their amiability when stranded in a strange country on a cold dark night in the middle of a snowstorm. The German columns that we had earlier regarded as a nuisance would at this juncture have been welcomed as a blessing, but they were many miles to the north and all peasant traffic had ceased. Colonel Ryan could not persuade the commissioner to go with us to the next farmhouse or village where we might find people who could assist in freeing his car. We decided, therefore, to go ahead without him and to arrange for a rescue party to go back to him.

We managed to get around the larger car and went on. After several miles of struggling through the snow we came upon a railway track. A railway worker told us that there was a station a mile or so distant. When we reached the station, with its lone caretaker, we explained our problem, and in a short time a party made up of a group of workers and several horses set out to follow our driver back to the commissioner's car. Colonel Ryan went to work on the stationmaster who, luckily, understood German. After cranking the decrepit telephone for what seemed an interminable time, and after engaging in a number of telephone conversations, he told us that a train would come to take us to Kaunas the following morning. He also arranged for us to have dinner and a place to sleep.

The cars appeared an hour or so later, the commissioner's being drawn by horses. At the same time the stationmaster's assistant arrived in a sleigh, which carried us to a huge stone house situated on a hill overlooking the snowy countryside. It was the palace of a great Lithuanian nobleman who, we were told, was the owner of thousands of the surrounding acres of arable and forest lands and the master of hundreds of peasants who eked out a living on them. No one knew of his whereabouts. If he were still alive he might be almost anywhere—in the Polish army, in Paris lobbying against the recognition of Lithuania by the Allies, or on the Riviera where, we were told, he customarily spent his winters. In any event, he was not likely to return to his estate as long as it was under Lithuanian rule because the great landowners of this area, while insisting on certain privileges and rights as members of the Lithuanian nobility had, so far as their tenants were concerned, become Poles. For hundreds of years they had sent their children to be educated in Poland. They spoke Polish among themselves and knew only enough Lithuanian to issue instructions during the brief period that they occupied their manors.

The house was unfurnished and unheated. The only inhabitants were caretakers who lived in the kitchen. They prepared a meal for us, found some makeshift mattresses, and even unearthed some khaki U.S. Army blankets that undoubtedly had entered the country as a part of the surplus war material the Hoover Relief Administration had allocated to Lithuania.

The train to take us and our automobiles to Kaunas was at the station the next morning. It had a passenger coach and a flatcar that could carry our two cars. Shortly before noon we arrived at the station in Kaunas, where a swarm of dignitaries had collected to greet the first diplomatic representative of the United States to come to Lithuania. Several representatives of the Lithuanian Red Cross and of various Lithuanian ministries detached themselves from the throng at the station to welcome Colonel Ryan. This was the U.S. commissioner's day, however, so the colonel and I slipped away unobtrusively to the Metropol Hotel.

The American Red Cross Office in Kaunas

The next morning Colonel Ryan and I made brief informal calls on the prime minister, the minister of war, and Dr. R. Sliupas, president of the Lithuanian Red Cross, who accompanied us on an inspection trip of the various hospitals. Early that same evening we were received with great courtesy by President Smetona, who told us of Lithuania's gratitude to the American Red Cross and his willingness to be of assistance to us.

Colonel Ryan left the following morning after having given me a number of final directions particularly with regard to the establishment of an office and the procurement of living quarters for myself and two assistants who were to join me in January. The hectic schedule the colonel followed was the only way he could keep up with what might be described as a many-ringed circus. Our American Red Cross commission had offices in several critical regions in Latvia in addition to its newly established office in Mitau. Offices had been, or were being, opened in Tallinn [Reval], Narva, and elsewhere in Estonia. A branch had been established in Helsinki and sub-branches in other Finnish cities and towns. The commission was also responsible for maintaining the office in Berlin, which served a number of other commissions. In order to maintain communication among the offices and to assist in making decisions in rapidly changing situations, the colonel was compelled to keep almost continuously on the move. For instance, his stay in Lithuania was brief because urgent problems awaited him in Estonia.

It was difficult to find living and office quarters in Kaunas. Hundreds of peope had flocked into the city from the devastated towns and villages and the city, as the temporary capital, was crammed with civilian and military officials. Many houses had been destroyed as armies had moved in and out during the war years. The houses that were still standing had been stripped by soldiers who had been billeted in them so that they were almost uninhabitable. Inner doors had been used for fuel. Electric wiring, doorknobs, locks, and other hardware—even nails and screws—had been removed and added to the booty that the soldiers had either sent or taken home with them. Most of the furniture had been sent out as loot or used as fuel. Kaunas was surrounded by forests, but because of the shortage of transport there was not enough wood for the stoves that were built into the walls of most of the houses.

I finally obtained an unfurnished house with enough bedrooms to accommodate several officers. From our Red Cross supplies I drew enough army blankets to curtain the inner doors, to hang over the broken windows, and to cover some of the empty wooden boxes we used as chairs. We also obtained mattresses and cots from our supplies. The minister of war furnished us with the needed cooking and other utensils. I also succeeded in obtaining an office large enough to accommodate our group: three Red Cross officers, the Lithuanian liaison officer whom the minister of war had attached to our office, a clerk, and a messenger. When I finally succeeded in getting a telephone, we were ready for business.

My work was to keep in touch with the hospitals and other charitable institutions and determine what we should give them from the limited supplies we had on hand and what additional supplies we should requisition. I also had close contact with the Lithuanian Red Cross and with the sanitary or medical branch of the Lithuanian army, which, with supplies received from the American Red Cross, was combating typhus and smallpox. The work was hampered by the lack of transportation, for the mission had no vehicles; public transportation, consisting of horse-drawn streetcars and a few dilapidated droshkies, was slow and irregular. The assistance we gave the Lithuanians was desperately needed and helped tide them over extremely difficult times. Although they were grateful, I had the feeling that they thought we should do more.

In the absence of diplomatic or consular representation—Commissioner Gade and Mr. Lehrs had remained in Kaunas for only a couple of days—I found my office engaging not only in the usual Red Cross activities but also in the kind of welfare work customarily performed by U.S. consular offices. Lithuanian nationals visited us or wrote letters requesting assistance in getting in touch with relatives in the United States, and letters streamed in from U.S. citizens of Lithuanian origin inquiring about the whereabouts and welfare of relatives in Lithuania. People claiming to be U.S. citizens appeared at our office asking for assistance. Some of them turned out to be what consular offices usually refer to as "protection cases," that is, persons in need of the protection of their government. I handled these matters as well as I could, hoping fervently that a U.S. consulate would soon be established in Kaunas.

The British had become deeply interested in Lithuania and maintained three missions in Kaunas—one military, one economic, and one political—which engaged in intelligence activities. A French mission also watched political and military developments, particularly those that might affect Lithuanian-Polish relations. The Lithuanians believed that much of the information the French were able to glean found its way to Warsaw, but paradoxically, the French officers attached to the mission were personally popular among the higher Lithuanian officials and their wives. The relations between our Red Cross mission and the various Allied missions were friendly, but I could sense that some members of these missions were wondering what the Americans were really up to. They found it difficult to believe that our relief activities did not shield activities of another character.

Shortly after my arrival in Kaunas I heard that an "American-Lithuanian Legion" was being organized in the United States and was to come to Lithuania to assist militarily in establishing and maintaining the independence of the country. The rank and file of this legion was to be composed mostly of U.S. citizens of Lithuanian origin or extraction, but the officers were to be selected for their military excellence without regard to ethnic origin. General Crozier, chief of the British military mission, seemed particularly intrigued by reports of this legion and on several occasions asked what information I had about it. I tried to convince him that I knew even less about it than he. General Crozier, by the way, was the British officer who a year or so later became famous as the commander of the British forces in Ireland.

In early January 1920 two officers, wearing U.S. uniforms bearing Lithuanian insignia, came to my office. The older one, who was perhaps in his midforties, introduced himself as Colonel Isabel, chief of staff of the American-Lithuanian Legion, and he presented the younger officer as his aide. The colonel was a powerfully built man with dark skin and heavy black hair. His carefully trimmed mustache and small pointed beard gave him the appearance of a Spanish conquistador. The colonel explained that they were the advance guard of the legion, which would soon begin to arrive. General Swarthout, who was to command the legion, was expected within a couple of days accompanied by a number of staff officers. Colonel Isabel was a professional soldier of fortune, an adventurer who had taken part in a number of Latin-American revolutions and had been in command of an American tank battalion during the World War. The young officer with him, the colonel said, was not only his aide but also his adopted son who had served with him in Latin America in the World War.

Before coming to my office the colonel had called on General Crozier. In talking to me he seemed nettled by the attitude he thought the general and his officers had displayed toward him and the American-Lithuanian Legion. He felt he would have to convince the British and the Lithuanians that the officers and men of the legion were a tough and seasoned group of fighters to be taken seriously. General Crozier had invited him to a dinner the following evening, to which I was also invited. The colonel expressed to me his hope that during the dinner he would have an opportunity to give the guests, particularly the British, an idea of the kind of men they might expect to find in the legion.

The dinner was held in the dining room of the Metropol Hotel. Colonel Isabel, as the guest of honor, sat on Mrs. Crozier's left and the minister of war on her right. Around the table were a number of other high-ranking civilians, Lithuanian military officers and their wives, and members of the Allied missions. The colonel was both gallant and animated and during most of dinner recounted tales of his various adventures. When coffee was served, General Crozier arose. After making a few gracious remarks about traditional British-American friendship and expressing pleasure at the arrival of the advance guard of the American-Lithuanian Legion, he proposed a toast to the success of the legion and to that of Colonel Isabel, its chief of staff.

Colonel Isabel then rose but, before beginning his response, took from his pocket a leather-colored shrunken human head that was about the size of an orange. As he placed it on the table before him he remarked that he usually carried this good-luck talisman with him and was accustomed to looking at it in times of danger, adding that he always felt himself in danger when he had to make a speech. He begged his table companions' forgiveness for putting it on the table. He explained that it was the head of a South American Indian that had been reduced in size by a process known only to a tribe of headhunters. Mrs. Crozier could hardly keep her eyes from this head with its long eyelashes and drooping mustache, one end of which rested in the colonel's saucer. Despite this bizarre beginning, the colonel's speech was appropriate to the occasion. He thanked General Crozier for his kind words and the general and his wife for their hospitality. He said that the American-Lithuanian Legion was determined to assist Lithuania in establishing its independence. He and the officers who were en route to join him looked forward with pleasure to close cooperation with the other Allied officers in Lithuania. He proposed a toast to American-British-Lithuanian cooperation. After the toast had been drunk, he remained standing. Turning to the waiters he called for a refilling of the glasses; he had another toast to propose. When the glasses were filled he asked everyone to stand and join him in drinking to the health of their charming hostess, Mrs. Crozier. He emptied his glass with a flourish and turning to Mrs. Crozier, he said, "It is not my custom when drinking to a beautiful lady to leave off merely because the glass is empty." Thereupon he proceeded, to the horror of those assembled, to devour the glass down to the stem. As we listened to the crunching of glass between the colonel's teeth, General Crozier leaped up and asked if the Colonel knew what he was doing. "Of course," the colonel said soothingly. "Don't be alarmed. I do this frequently. It will do me no harm. As an American soldier I have hardened myself so that I can eat almost everything and can endure all kinds of pain without flinching." To back up his words, he produced a long hatpin—hatpins were still used in those days—and thrust it through one cheek until it protruded through the other. Jerking it out he ran it through the upper part of each arm. With that he sat down. The dinner broke up shortly thereafter.

The next morning the colonel came to my office. "Well," he said, "after last night I hope our British friends will understand that the American officers of the American-Lithuanian Legion are not a group of softies." I asked him what his secret was. He said there was no secret; he had discovered that if he chewed thin glass thoroughly it would do him no harm. As for the hatpin, he had thrust it through places in his cheeks and arms where there were practically no nerves or blood vessels. Whether he was telling me the truth or whether he had performed a feat of legerdemain I do not know.

A number of other officers of the American-Lithuanian Legion, including General Swarthout, arrived several days later, but the rank and file never did show up. These officers proved valuable in training the Lithuanian armed forces to use different kinds of American weapons, and at least one of them was killed while helping the Lithuanians put down a communist–inspired military revolt. The colonel was an expert in handling tanks, and later the Lithuanians lent him for several months to the Latvians, who used him to help them train their newly organized tank forces. I heard that at a military dinner in Riga he again performed his glass-eating and cheek-piercing stunts. It is my understanding that Colonel Isabel, after becoming bored with service in Lithuania, left Eastern Europe in search of new adventures and later lost his life while participating in a civil war in China.

One morning in late January an American Red Cross officer with whom I had worked in Riga came to my office. He wore civilian clothes and was laden with pouches. He threw the pouches on the floor and said, "The government of the United States has arrived." He explained that he had just been made a noncareer vice consul and had been sent to Kaunas to open a consular office. That was good news. At last we would have an official of the U.S. government who could answer some of the difficult questions that were being put to us so frequently. Since Jay Walker, the new vice consul, had had no consular experience and had been given no training, he was at first less well equipped than we to cope with the problems that we passed along to him. Gradually, with our help and the help of the consular regulations that, together with a consular seal and stationery, were in his pouches, he learned what he might or might not do in various circumstances. Interesting enough, when I arrived at the U.S.

embassy in New Delhi 29 years later, I found Walker in charge of the consular section of that embassy.

THE JOURNEY FROM KAUNAS TO RIGA, FEBRUARY 1920

In late January 1920 rumors began to reach us of a ghastly epidemic of spotted typhus in Estonia. The disease had reportedly been brought there by General Yudenich's White Russian army, which, after having been defeated at the gates of Leningrad, had fallen back into Estonia. The substance of these rumors was confirmed when we received a circular from the American Red Cross in Paris asking for volunteers to work in the typhus areas. Now that our mission in Kaunas was well staffed and we had been able to turn over many of its problems to the newly opened consular office, it could, I was convinced, carry on quite satisfactorily without me. It seemed to me that I might be more useful in the typhus regions than in Lithuania, and therefore, I sent a message to Colonel Ryan volunteering for service in Estonia. Colonel Ryan replied by ordering me to report immediately to Riga in order to prepare for an assignment to Narva, on the Estonian-Russian border.

At noon on the third day we reached the Latvian frontier. The chief of the Latvian frontier guard provided me at once with a sleigh and sent a message by telephone to his superiors in Mitau requesting them to inform our Red Cross mission that we were proceeding up the road toward that city. Shortly before nightfall we met our Mitau ambulance, which picked me up and took me along with my bags to Mitau. I spent the night with my Red Cross associates in Mitau and went on to Riga the following day.

CHAPTER 6

THE ANTITYPHUS CAMPAIGN IN NARVA, ESTONIA, FEBRUARY–MARCH 1920

COLONEL RYAN DESCRIBES THE SITUATION IN NARVA

WHEN I REPORTED TO COLONEL RYAN he told me that I was urgently needed to relieve Captain Allen Campbell Robinson as head of the American Red Cross station in Narva. He then described the situation. The bulk of the defeated Yudenich White Russian army, twenty-five or thirty thousand men, had been interned either in or around Narva and of these at least eight or ten thousand were ill. In the absence of physicians, diagnosis was difficult, but it was obvious even to a layperson that many had spotted typhus. The disease was also spreading among the armed forces and civilians in Estonia, particularly in Narva and Tallinn (the name the Estonians used in referring to their capital, which the Russians and Germans had called Reval).

Under the leadership of the American Red Cross a systematic campaign against the epidemic had begun and was to be extended throughout Estonia. A number of factors had made the organization of the campaign difficult. One factor was the low morale of the officers of the Yudenich army. The overriding desire of most of them was to get out of Eastern Europe as soon as possible. They were more interested in getting hold of funds that would enable them to travel than they were in the welfare of their men. Officers so motivated could not be depended upon to assist in organizing the campaign.

Another factor was the friction that had developed between the more responsible leaders of the Yudenich army and the Estonian government. These leaders had taken the position that they should bear the responsibility for the discipline and the welfare of their officers and men who had taken refuge in Estonia. They did not like the idea of their officers, most of whom were moving about the country freely, or of their men, most of whom were in detention camps, taking orders from the Estonians. The Estonians had insisted that since these soldiers were on Estonian soil they must be subject to Estonian law and under the control of the Estonian authorities.

Still another factor was the lack of doctors, nurses, hospital space, and virtually every kind of hospital equipment, medical supplies, and transportation facilities. The only food available for the interned soldiers was bread and a soup made mostly of dried vegetables with a bit of dried fish or meat added from time to time.

The colonel had made a recent trip to Estonia and had found that some of these difficulties were in part being overcome. The Russian leaders had at last agreed that the Estonians were to have responsibility for, and the necessary authority over, the Russian officers and men. The Estonian government in turn had agreed to look to the American Red Cross to organize and conduct the campaign against the typhus. Both Russians and Estonians would also do their utmost to mobilize the staff and equipment needed in the campaign. The American Red Cross would furnish what medical officers and staff it could muster; it would try to enlist a number of the Russian doctors and nurses then serving elsewhere in the Baltic states and in Germany; and it would also try to bring from Western Europe as soon as possible some of the most urgently needed hospital and medical equipment and supplies.

CONDITIONS IN NARVA, FEBRUARY–MARCH 1920

The colonel told me that my job was to lay the groundwork for the campaign in Narva. I stopped in Tallinn for several days to observe how the campaign against typhus was being carried on there. When the train—on the broad, Russian-gauge tracks—pulled into Narva near the middle of February, Captain Robinson met me at the station in a droshky. As we slid through the streets between high banks of dirty snow he told me how glad he was to see me. We spent several days going through the buildings that housed the sick soldiers and the barracks where those who had not been stricken were living, looking over the buildings that were being converted into baths and delousing sheds, and checking the few supplies we had on hand. He also introduced me to the Estonian and Russian authorities who were to cooperate with the American Red Cross.

While reviewing with Captain Robinson the activities of the Red Cross in Narva I learned that, in addition to conducting the fight against typhus, it was also extending a limited amount of relief, particularly in the form of warm clothing and blankets, to the ragged and half-starved refugees who were continually streaming in from Russia.

The first makeshift hospital that Captain Robinson and I visited had been a textile mill before the war. The Bolsheviks, before withdrawing from Narva, had sent all the looms and other machinery to Russia, leaving an empty shell. Although I had visited hospitals in Tallinn full of typhus patients, I was not prepared for what I found in the central room of this large mill. Lying on the floor in disorderly rows were several hundred men clothed in remnants of old uniforms, tattered overcoats, or merely piles of rags. Some were lying on, or were wrapped in, dirty pieces of blankets. Through the long hair that covered their heads and faces we could see their eyes, frequently bright with fever, peering at us, some angrily, some pleadingly, some without any emotion at all. Next to most of the patients was a rusty and usually unwashed tin utensil—a small pail, a cup, or a bowl. These precious utensils, I subsequently learned, were zealously guarded against theft.

The sight of these miserable creatures was shocking, but even worse was the stench that filled the high-ceilinged, chilly room. Captain Robinson and I threaded our way carefully through the sick, trying to avoid stepping in the filth that covered the floors. Portions of the hair and beards of many of the patients were of a bluish gray color and on closer examination I found that these areas so colored were in motion. I felt nauseated when I discovered that the color and motion were due to closely packed colonies of lice and lice nits. Captain Robinson paused and pointed at a bluish gray column that was moving slowly along the floor toward a patient who was either asleep or unconscious. This column was leaving the beard and hair of a man who I saw was dead. These insects would not remain on a dead person. When a man died, therefore, they usually began their march toward the nearest living person, leaving their nits behind. Here and there I noted a number of other lifeless bodies, and I asked a Russian military doctor why they were allowed to remain among the living. He explained that the group of men responsible for the disposal of the dead went through the hospitals every few hours to remove those who had died and that the bodies we had seen were apparently those of persons who had died since the last visit of the corpse-removal squad.

Several of the patients tried to talk to us in Russian as we neared them. The Russian doctor who served as our translator told us that they were asking us to help them get out of this dreadful place and that they were begging to be bathed and given clean clothing and to receive medical attention. Some, instead of pleading, were cursing us, calling us names that the doctor refused to translate. Several men clawed lice from their heads and beards and threw them at us.

While we were there a corpsman went up and down the rows distributing chunks of bread. Some of the patients were too ill to be interested in food, but others greedily seized the chunks thrown to them and at the same time kept their eyes on the chunks lying beside their unconscious or semi-conscious neighbors. The doctor explained that soup would be brought later in the day and that some of the men would save their bread to eat with the soup.

This doctor was one of the few Russian medical men who continued to have an interest in the fate of these sick men. He told me I should not judge too harshly his colleagues who had gone off and left the sick. The doctors had found that without medicines, instruments, and other supplies and facilities they were unable to do much to help and that they could not endure the strain of standing helpless in the face of so much suffering. In their frustration and despair most of them had stopped trying to do anything. Some had fled the typhus area entirely.

We left the mill by the rear door. Near it, on a loading platform, neatly arranged, was a stack of frozen bodies awaiting the sledges that were to haul them like so much cordwood into the forest. During the days that followed I frequently saw sledges piled high with corpses moving along the streets. Sometimes the corpses were covered so that only the head and feet were visible; at other times there was no covering whatsoever. They were being taken to places in the nearby forests and piled up. There were not enough hands available to dig so many graves in the frozen ground, but I was assured that all of the bodies would be buried before the thaws set in.

Captain Robinson and I visited about a dozen of these so-called hospitals. Conditions in most were similar to those in the textile mill. Altogether there were perhaps fifteen or twenty buildings in the town that were being used to house the sick Russians. The old Swedish and Russian forts on the Narva River, for instance, were filled. No one, of course, knew whether a sick person had typhus, typhoid fever, pneumonia, or some other disease. One thing that all had in common, however, was lice.

In the afternoon Captain Robinson and I stopped at a tearoom where we hoped that a cup of tea and a little music might help us forget— at least for the moment—our experiences of the day. Even here, there was no complete escape. As I sat at a table I saw a louse moving on the cloth toward me. Later, returning to the hotel in a droshky, I noticed several crawling up the blanket with which the driver had tucked us in. At the hotel I found in my room a three-gallon bottle of liquid. Captain Robinson explained that this had been sent to me with the compliments of the First Division of the Estonian army, that the contents were pure potato alcohol, and that I was advised to sponge myself with this alcohol from head to toe at least twice a day. I was diligent in taking these sponge baths during the time I stayed at the hotel. The hotel had no running water and such water as was available for washing was in large earthenware pitchers, which, with earthenware bowls, were a part of the furnishings of each room.

THE ANTITYPHUS CAMPAIGN
GETS INTO FULL SWING, MARCH 1920

The staff of our Red Cross group in Narva was augmented by several American officers who had volunteered for work in the typhus area. Among them were Captain Wilbur F. Howell, Lieutenant Clifford Blanton, and Lieutenant George Winfield. Winfield, who was in his early forties, seemed to suffer throes of conscience at having been away from his wife and home so long. Blanton was not more than twenty, was full of animal energy, liked to play jokes, and seemed to derive real joy from his work; yet he, too, was homesick and was among the first to line up for the mail when the pouch would come in from Tallinn. Howell, who was in his late twenties, was quiet and hardworking. He carefully analyzed the problems confronting us and made many helpful suggestions. These three men, like myself, were field officers—not medical men. They worked almost day and night preparing for the coming campaign. They never spared themselves and did not allow the depressing scenes, which they were constantly encountering, to lower their morale.

With the effective cooperation of the Estonian Sanitary Corps and of a growing number of Russians, our preparations for the campaign moved forward rapidly. It was particularly heartening to see the change in attitude of the Russian doctors. Some of them who had abandoned all hope of being able to accomplish anything awoke from their apathy, joined us, and became enthusiastic workers. In addition to the local doctors, Russian doctors from nearby areas, upon learning what was taking place, also came to Narva.

While we were concentrating on completing preparations in Narva, the American Red Cross, Estonian officials, and groups of responsible Russians were busy in Tallinn, Riga, Germany, and elsewhere mobilizing doctors, nurses, and hospital attendants. A special effort was made to recruit those who had had spotted typhus and were, therefore, immune. Many of the Russian and Estonian volunteers, however, like the American Red Cross personnel, were not immune. In 1920 there was no effective serum against spotted typhus. To protect the workers and to minimize the further spread of the disease, team members were required to wear long rubber coats with rubber hoods, which the Red Cross had been able to procure.

In the second week of March we inaugurated the campaign and within a few days it was in full swing. Each day hundreds of clean beds were being filled by bathed, shaven patients. No patient, however sick, could be moved into the clean rooms until he had been completely deloused; otherwise, a new infection might develop. The delousing was a rather trying process. Some could not endure it and died in the trucks or in the baths. Within twenty days after the campaign had been inaugurated, the backbone of the epidemic had been broken. Practically all of the sick were in clean beds in disinfected rooms. The American and other doctors were examining and diagnosing their illnesses. Those with infectious diseases were segregated. Even the badly needed medicines that had been in short supply were on the way to Estonia. The morale of the Russians, sick and well alike, and of the whole Estonian community had been raised. The interned Russians who had not been hospitalized began to awaken from their fatalistic lethargy. Under the guidance of Russian doctors and medical corpsmen, and with the encouragement and assistance of the Estonians, they organized their own groups to clean the internment camps and to engage in massive delousing. The Estonian Sanitary Corps, supplemented by the Estonian Red Cross, mobilized thousands of volunteers who worked tirelessly in combating the spread of the plague-spreading insects in schools, churches, and private homes. Also, a number of sanitary stations were set up on the Russian border to inspect and delouse the refugees coming in from Russia.

A report published in the summer of 1920 in the bulletin of the American Red Cross Commission to Western Russia and the Baltic States may assist in giving the reader an idea of the dimensions of this campaign. Following are excerpts from this report:

It is in its work against the typhus epidemic that the Commission performed its greatest service. This service did not mean the impersonal distribution of supplies. It did mean the actual delousing of more than 9,000 persons; the disinfecting of 80 hospitals, and the organization and maintenance of a sanitary cordon between the district of Narva in the northeast of Esthonia, seventy miles from Petrograd, and the rest of Esthonia. Only in this drastic way could the entire country be protected from disease. This move was the foundation of the sanitary cordon of delousing stations and contagious hospitals which the Commission founded and either operates or supplies or both from Finland to the German-Lithuanian frontier. Only in this energetic extension of intensive disinfection can the Baltic States and, through them, Western Europe and America be protected from the contagion now known to be raging in Soviet Russia.

The greatest force, materially and morally, in this typhus clean-up campaign were the mobile sanitary squads which the Commission organized and operated. There were six teams of fifty men each, under the personal command of an American Red Cross officer. The men were Russians, mobilized by the Esthonian Sanitary Service and specially chosen from those soldiers who had had typhus. The Esthonian Government adopted the mobile sanitary squad idea and has put 80 groups of 4,000 men in the field. They work in the small towns and villages where the danger of typhus brought by individual refugees crossing over from Soviet Russia is a standing menace. These outfits work with supplies furnished by the American Red Cross Commission...

In less than two months the Commission has lowered the mortality from fifteen percent to less than one-half of one percent.

THE RED CROSS GROUP IN NARVA ENCOUNTERS TRAGEDY, MARCH 1920

The satisfaction we felt as we saw the plans for the campaign being realized was marred not only by the tragic memories it left with us but also by a more personal sorrow. One morning when the campaign was at its height, Blanton and Winfield failed to appear for breakfast in the hotel dining room. When I went up to their rooms to look for them I discovered that both were suffering from pains and aches and appeared feverish. The Estonian doctor who had been charged with looking after us arranged for them to be taken at once to the Estonian Hospital, which was the best in Narva. The following day I awoke with similar symptoms and was also taken to the hospital. That afternoon Howell, the fourth member of our original group, was brought in. Since I was the only one of us who could speak German, our language of communication with the Estonian doctors, the four of us were placed in the same room so that I could act as interpreter.

After examining us the doctors expressed the tentative opinion that all of us were suffering from spotted typhus. This did not come to us as a surprise, as we had been exposed daily for nearly three weeks. We refused to worry for we knew we would have the best care available, though some of the drugs that might be useful, such as digitalis, had not yet arrived. Although we felt miserable, our morale remained high. We were comforted by the thought that we had held out until the success of the campaign seemed assured. For the first few days we exchanged jokes and tried to look on the brighter side of things. Then my fever flared up and I began to lose consciousness. In my delirium I thought that I was dying, that I was bidding farewell to my twin brother. I could even feel his hand on my shoulder. I was surprised when, as my consciousness gradually returned a day or two later, I realized that I was alive. I was deeply troubled, however, because the farewell scene had seemed so real. Although I knew it was foolish, I began to worry about my brother. I had never believed—nor do I believe now—in mental telepathy and I tried to convince myself that the frightful experience of recent weeks and my high fever had unsettled my mind and were responsible for my forebodings.

My concern for my comrades soon crowded out these melancholy thoughts. I found that they also were having periods of unconsciousness or semiconsciousness. All three of them showed the telltale red spots of spotted typhus that I had seen on so many sick Russians. I examined my arms and my body. There were no spots. The doctors were puzzled about my case. Some were convinced that I did have typhus but that I was one of the rare persons who had an inborn resistance to that disease—a resistance that prevented the breakdown of the blood vessels, which was the cause of the spots. Others thought I had had some unknown disease complicated by pneumonia. Whatever the cause of my illness, I began to recover but I had been so weakened by fever that I was not allowed to leave my bed.

On the afternoon of March 26 the doctors told me that Blanton's heart was weakening under the strain of his fever and they feared he could not survive the night. They moved my bed close to his so that I could talk with him if he should regain consciousness. He did become conscious long enough to exchange a few words with me. I do not believe that he knew his end was approaching. He soon lapsed into a coma and died at about eight o'clock that evening. Shortly after midnight the next day the doctors moved my bed alongside Winfield's. At about four in the morning he too awoke briefly and was able to speak to me. He may have known that death was near for he asked me, in case he should not survive, to convey his love to his wife. He died just at daybreak.

Howell, the fourth occupant of the room, had been extremely ill but his heart withstood the fever. He gradually began to recover and was able to carry on brief snatches of conversation by the time I left the hospital.

EVACUATION TO RIGA, APRIL 1920

During the early days of my illness, Colonel Ryan had passed through Narva en route to Leningrad. Since he was the guest of the Estonian peace delegation, which was traveling in a special train that stopped only for a few minutes in Narva, he was not able to visit the hospital. He had sent word to us, however, that as soon as we were able to travel we should return to Tallinn and recuperate.

The special train carrying the Estonian peace delegation and Colonel Ryan returned through Narva on April 2 and, in pursuance of a telegram I had received from the colonel from Russia, I boarded it. It was on this train that I had my first meeting with Soviet diplomats, several of whom were on the train as guests of the Estonian delegation.

As we neared Tallinn I was again haunted by forebodings about my brother. Our exchange of farewells during my delirium had seemed so final. He had never fully recovered from the loss of one of his kidneys in 1918. I tried to comfort myself by recalling that the last letter I had received from him had been encouraging and by the thought that if anything had happened to him while I was ill I would already have received word.

When I arrived at the American Red Cross residence in Tallinn, I was relieved to learn that there was no mail for me. Late that evening, as several of us were listening to Colonel Ryan's description of his experiences in the Soviet Union, one of the men who had been working late in the office entered the room with an envelope in his hand. He said to me, "The Riga pouch has just brought this telegram for you." I said I was so fearful of its contents that I dreaded to open it. Colonel Ryan offered to do so. He glanced at it, folded it, and said nothing. He did not need to. He knew I had read the expression on his face. The telegram, dated March 21, had been sent by my father. It told me that Roy had died on the evening of March 18. Only a person who has been closely associated with an identical twin during most of his life can understand what this message meant to me. Two weeks later I received from my father several letters giving the details about my brother's death. It was plain from these letters that to the grief he felt at the loss of a son was added a deep concern over the effect the news would have on me. In one of his letters, written from my brother's room at 10 Oxford Street, Cambridge, Massachusetts, he urged me to stand up under the blow. "Life," he wrote, "is full of responsibilities...you must come home in time for school this fall. You must be doubly as good a man as you had ever planned to be. Plan to be home by September first and finish your school...Don't let this awful loss discourage you."

On the day after our arrival in Tallinn, Colonel Ryan asked me if I would be willing to take charge of the American Red Cross office in Berlin. It was important, he said, that the officer in charge of that office be someone on whom he could rely and who had had experience in the Baltic area. Although the office was under his jurisdiction as head of the Commission to Western Russia and the Baltic States, it also had responsibilities that were not related to the work of the commission. It was frequently called upon to perform tasks for the American Red Cross European headquarters in Paris and for the American Red Cross commissions in Poland and southeastern Europe. It was in effect the liaison office between the American Red Cross in Europe and the German government.

I agreed without hesitation to go to Berlin on condition that I be relieved near the end of the summer so I could return to the United States. I welcomed the Berlin assignment for several reasons. I thought that the work at Narva had reached such a stage that in the future it should be under the direction of physicians experienced in the field of public health rather than under that of a field officer. I also thought that with my previous experience in Germany and with the knowledge that I had acquired of the situation in the Baltic states, I might be of more value to the Red Cross in Berlin than in one of the East European offices. Furthermore, I thought that a residence of several months in one of the great cities of Europe before my return to the United States might be culturally enriching.

CHAPTER 7

REPRESENTATIVE OF THE AMERICAN RED CROSS IN GERMANY, APRIL 1920–AUGUST 1921

ACTIVITIES AND LIFE IN BERLIN

I ARRIVED IN BERLIN during the second week in April 1920 and assumed charge of the office there some two weeks later. The office in Berlin was in a suite of rooms over a bank at Unter den Linden 77. The location was excellent. One window of my corner room overlooked Wilhelmstrasse; the other the broad *Allee* of Unter den Linden. The Adlon Hotel was almost directly across Unter den Linden from the office, and a hundred yards distant was the Pariser Platz, where the French embassy was situated and to which years later our own embassy chancery was moved.

The office staff consisted of an excellent secretary, a German chauffeur, and Fritz Beer who had been with me in Mitau and who had been retained by the Red Cross on a part-time basis as an adviser on German affairs and as a liaison officer with the German authorities.

Our Red Cross office engaged in no direct relief work. It was primarily a negotiating and servicing station. It dealt with the appropriate agencies of the German government with regard to all matters in which the interests or activities of the American Red Cross might come in contact with those of that government. It was the transportation and communication hub of the American Red Cross in Central Europe. Routings and travel reservations were made through it, and missions in the Baltic states, Poland, Czechoslovakia, and the Balkans looked to it to expedite shipments of supplies destined for their use. It also kept track of the amounts that it spent on behalf of the Red Cross for transportation of relief supplies across German territory and, pursuant to an agreement between the German government and the Red Cross, collected rebates equaling half of these amounts.

In addition to carrying on activities of a relatively routine nature, our office in Berlin was frequently required to perform special services. I was, for instance, sent to Holland on one occasion to negotiate the purchase of additional delousing equipment for use in Estonia. I also negotiated purchases of equipment and supplies for other Red Cross commissions in Silesia, Austria, Saxony, and so forth. Another task of a rather delicate nature was assigned to me by Colonel Robert Olds, later one of my chiefs in the Department of State, who at the time was the American Red Cross commissioner for Europe with headquarters in Paris. This involved the inspection of a camp in Westphalia in which members of the Polish armed forces who had fled into Germany to escape encircling Soviet troops had been interned. Members of the Polish embassy in Paris had complained to the Conference of Ambassadors that the internees were being mistreated, a charge that the German government had vigorously denied. The American Red Cross had been requested to investigate. After spending several days in Westphalia in close consultation with the camp authorities and with the representatives of the internees, I was able to make a report that was factually agreed to by all concerned.

During the summer of 1920 I reminded Colonel Ryan several times of our understanding that he would be looking for someone to replace me so that I could be back in the United States by September. In July I went so far as to make reservations on a steamer scheduled to sail in the latter part of August. In early August, however, the colonel urged me as a personal favor to remain several months longer, explaining that the uncertain political situation in Eastern Europe might require the presence in Berlin of someone acquainted with the Baltic region and with the problems and activities of his commission. I found myself faced, therefore, with making an important decision. If I intended to go on with the study of law I should return immediately to the United States. I had already lost, so to speak, too many years so far as law was concerned. Many men of my age were already successful lawyers. Did I really want to bury myself in a law school for two more years in order to be admitted to the bar at the age of 30? Furthermore, my desire to practice law had become less keen following the death of my brother, who had been my prospective partner.

The decision that I finally made was that instead of resuming my law studies I should try to take up some kind of work in which I could make use of my past studies and of my recent experiences abroad. My first preference was public service in the field of foreign affairs. I doubted that I could be successful in business; I could work with enthusiasm in the interest of the public but did not believe I was so constituted that I could enjoy engaging in the rough-and-tumble of business in order to make profit for myself or for a private firm. I did not, however, know of any public service for which I could qualify. Hugh Wilson and Fred Dolbeare, two career diplomats attached to the United States commission to Germany, had advised me that it would be foolish for a person without private means to try to enter the Diplomatic Service. I was also informed by consular officers on duty in the commission that the examinations for the Consular Service, in those days separate from the Diplomatic Service, were extremely difficult and could not be passed without extensive and concentrated study.

In view of my uncertainties regarding what I should do upon my return to the United States, I took, I am ashamed to say, the course of least resistance and told Colonel Ryan that I would remain in Berlin several months longer. To assuage my conscience I tried to convince myself that my decision was based in part on Colonel Ryan's insistence that I was really needed in Berlin. I reproached myself many times during the ensuing twelve months for having made such a decision and resolved, regardless of what might be in store for me upon my return to the United States, that I would arrive there before the end of the summer of 1921.

During the winter of 1920–1921 I received a telegram from Colonel Ryan stating that a Mrs. Evan E. Young and her young daughter would be coming to Berlin and suggesting that I make hotel reservations for them and render them any other assistance of which they might be in need. Mrs. Young and her daughter happened to arrive in Berlin while one of the general strikes that had been plaguing that city was in progress. It turned out, therefore, that they were in need of much assistance, which I was happy to give them. I learned from Mrs. Young that her husband was the new U.S. commissioner to the Baltic states and a senior member of the U.S. Consular Service. Mrs. Young and her daughter were exceedingly grateful for such assistance as I had been able to render them while they were stranded in Berlin as the result of the strike, and I received a warm letter of thanks from Mr. Young.

During the late winter and spring of 1921 Mr. Young visited Berlin on several occasions and a friendship developed between us. When, during the course of one of his visits, he learned that I was undecided about what I should do after my return to the United States he urged me to consider the Consular Service. He said that it offered an opportunity for a satisfying public career and that, during the years to come, as the United States would be drawn more and more into international life, these opportunities would broaden. He admitted that the examinations for entrance were highly competitive and that some of them required detailed knowledge of difficult subjects. He insisted, however, that after preparatory study I should be able to pass them. I listened with awakening interest to his stories of his experiences in the Consular Service and of his adventures as U.S. minister to Ecuador during a revolutionary period.* It seemed to me that a service that could attract and hold a person like Mr. Young was worthy of consideration. Following my return to the United States I wrote Mr. Young that I had decided to take the consular examinations, and he wrote what I understand was a strong letter supporting my candidacy to Mr. Wilbur Carr, the director of the Consular Service. I shall describe later the manner in which an action taken by Mr. Young affected my whole future career in the Foreign Service.

DEPARTURE FROM BERLIN, AUGUST 1921

When Colonel Ryan passed through Berlin in July 1921, he insisted that before my departure for the United States I should take a short vacation in Europe. Although I had spent several weekends at German beaches on the Baltic and in small mountain or lake resorts in the neighborhood of Berlin, I had had no real vacation since my arrival in Europe in 1918. Some of my Berlin friends had leased a floor in a hotel in Garmisch in the Bavarian Alps during the month of August 1921 and had invited me to join them. Garmisch then had only a few hotels and had not as yet become part of the great vacation resort of Garmisch–Partenkirchen that later developed. The two weeks I spent in Garmisch were among the happiest of my life. I was the only American in a party composed of Germans, Romanians, and Austrians of various ages. We were provided with peasant costumes of the Bavarian Tyrol—costumes that in themselves inspired informality and gaiety. We climbed mountains, danced, motored, took walks, swam in the nearby lakes, and had song fests. Such carefree days have been rare in my life.

From the Bavarian mountains I went to Paris and several days later was on board the Dutch-American steamer *Ryndam*, en route to the United States.

---

* Mr. Young had been appointed minister to Ecuador by President Taft under whom he had served in the Philippines. He had obtained a leave of absence from the Consular Service in order to accept the appointment.

PART IV

AN INTERIM IN THE UNITED STATES, SEPTEMBER 1921–SEPTEMBER 1922

CHAPTER 8

READJUSTMENT TO A CHANGED UNITED STATES

THE VOYAGE HOME AFTER 34 MONTHS IN EUROPE

I SAILED FROM CHERBOURG on the Dutch steamer *Ryndam* in the latter part of August 1921. The ship was jam-packed with summer vacationists and their numerous progeny returning in time for the opening of school, college students who had been enjoying the summer in Europe, and the usual run of globe-trotters, businessmen, and fond mothers who had been escorting their young daughters on a cultural tour of Europe. Life on deck and in the salons was dominated by teenagers and would-be teenagers. They seemed oblivious of the other passengers. I detected a stridency in their voices and an insensitivity in their behavior that I had not previously noted in American youth. There was a gap between them and me greater, in my opinion, than could be explained by differences in age. I did not like to feel that my experiences during the last three years had changed me to such an extent that I was no longer at ease with my young fellow compatriots. I later learned that I was merely being exposed, without proper preparation, to the beginning of a new era in American life, an era that was to go down in our cultural history as the Roaring Twenties.

I shall not attempt to describe this era as it developed in intensity until its quenching during the depression seven or eight years later. In my opinion, the irresponsibility and grossness in behavior of this era, as well as the lack of consideration for others that its exponents displayed, left an imprint on American life that remained for decades. Despite the uproar and confusion I enjoyed the voyage. After nearly three years of dining "à la ration card," the food was a revelation. I had good company in the dining salon and was lucky in my deck chair neighbors. In fact I was regretful when, on a steaming hot Labor Day, we docked in New York. While on board I had been able to thrust aside oppressive thoughts about my uncertain future, but they came back as I traveled through the hot streets strewn with Labor Day litter to a Manhattan hotel.

A VISIT TO COLORADO

I had decided to spend several weeks with my family in Colorado before trying to make any decisions about my future. My father did not then have a pulpit. He was what the Methodists call a district superinten- dent. His jurisdiction included much of central Colorado and his resi- dence was in Colorado Springs. The five weeks that I spent in Colorado were memorable ones. Never again was I to remain for so long a period with the members of my family. My younger brother and sister were at the time with my father and stepmother, and my sister Zella and her two small sons, who were living in Trinidad in the southeastern corner of Colorado, came up to spend a week with us. The whole family drove to Pueblo to lay flowers on the graves of my mother and twin brother. We went on picnics into the mountains, one of which included a dinner on the top of Pike's Peak. My brother George, who was an ardent fisherman, and I made several fishing expeditions. My father and I spent several days on a shooting trip during which we traveled on horseback through wild areas of the Colorado mountains. I also accompanied my father during the last week of my stay on a number of his visits to churches in the mountainous areas of his district. The opportunities that we thus had to be together meant a great deal to both of us.

IMPRESSIONS OF NEW YORK CITY, OCTOBER 1921

I returned to New York in the middle of October. My brother George, who had never been east of Ohio, came with me. My father thought that it might be a good experience for George to spend several months with me in New York City. We took two rooms in the large West Eighty-fourth Street apartment of a kindly widow who, with her three young daugh- ters, occupied the rest of the apartment.

Our adjustment to New York life was not easy. New York was at first more foreign to me than London, Paris, or Berlin had been. The people in the restaurants and on the subway or elevated trains, and those who jostled me in the streets or pushed in front of me in the shops, seemed to have little in common with me.

Illustrative of the experiences that caused me at times to believe that the newest immigrant could not feel less at home in New York than I, was a scene that I witnessed in late October. More than half a century had passed since the end of the Civil War and the surviving veterans of both the North and South had, therefore, begun to age. I had been accustomed from childhood to treat these veterans with respect. One day on the elevated train I was sitting behind a group of loud-talking, gum-chewing young people, whose accents indicated that they might be foreign-born Brooklynites, when four old men in bemedaled blue uniforms took seats nearby. From their dress, their bearing, and the remarks that they were exchanging, I could see that they were members of the Grand Army of the Republic who had come to the city to attend one of the old soldiers' conventions. It gave me a touch of nostalgia to see the familiar old uniforms and the bearded, weathered faces. A young woman in the group in front of me stared at them and said to her companion in a voice audible to all in the car, including the veterans, "Hey! Take a look at those funny old guys! What country do you suppose they have come from?"

Although my initial impressions of New York were rather dismal, I realized that I was looking at its seamy side. There were beauty and glamor and glitter if one went to the right places and moved in the right circles; there was also a culture just as deep as any to be found in the capitals of Europe. During my first few months in New York, however, I had neither the time nor the desire to search for glamor or culture. My first task was to establish myself, to lay the basis for my future life. During my first five weeks in New York I talked with personnel directors and officers of a variety of firms that were engaged in international operations: oil companies, shipping companies, banks, and importing and exporting companies. I did this entirely on my own; I did not wish to bother persons living in New York with whom I had worked or whom I had met while abroad. I was received everywhere with consideration and a number of tentative offers were made to me, some of which from a pecuniary point of view had a certain amount of appeal. None of them, however, represented the kind of an opening for which I was looking. I did not, therefore, accept any of them, because I was determined not to embark on a career to which I could not wholeheartedly devote my life.

CHAPTER 9

ENTRY INTO THE
CONSULAR SERVICE, 1921–1922

MY DECISION TO TRY TO ENTER THE CONSULAR SERVICE

THE MORE I DISCUSSED business openings with prospective employers, the more I became conscious that my real interests lay in serving the United States in the foreign field. I could not forget the conversations about the Consular Service that I had had with Commissioner Young in Berlin. In early November, therefore, I wrote to Washington requesting information about the Consular Service and inquiring with regard to the date and nature of the next consular examinations. About two weeks later I received a reply from Wilbur J. Carr, director of the Consular Service, informing me that the next examinations would be held in Washington, D.C. on January 16, 1922. Mr. Carr also stated that suitable candidates for the positions of consul for economic investigation work, consul, vice consul of career, consular assistant, and student interpreter would be admitted to these examinations. He enclosed a pamphlet that furnished detailed information regarding the Consular Service and described the kind of examinations that candidates should be prepared to take.

The Consular Service as described in the pamphlet had greater appeal for me than any of the business careers that I had been considering. The examinations, however, presented a formidable barrier, since they covered subjects—such as international, maritime, and commercial law; political and commercial geography; and the natural, industrial, and commercial resources of the United States—that I had never studied, as well as a number of topics regarding which my knowledge was only fragmentary. Furthermore, the language requirements included the ability to write as well as to converse in French, German, or Spanish. I had learned to read the kind of German that one finds in newspapers and to speak German almost fluently, but I had no confidence in my ability to write in that language. Furthermore, the material that the examinations required to be translated from one language to another was full of technical commercial expressions, the exact meaning of which, even in English, was not entirely clear to me. It appeared that no matter how hard I might study my language I would receive a poor grade in it.

The week following the receipt of Mr. Carr's letter I again went through the throes of decisionmaking. If I were to try to enter the Consular Service there was no time to lose. I should submit my application at once and begin to study. If I should decide not to attempt to pass the consular examinations, I should give more serious consideration to the opportunities that had been offered me in private enterprise.

It was on Thanksgiving evening, while having dinner with my brother in a Manhattan restaurant, that I made my decision. I told him that I had decided to drop everything else and begin to prepare for the consular examinations. That very evening I sat up late filling out the application forms.

Preparing for the Consular Examinations

During the next two days I visited the book shops that served Columbia University and New York University in search of books that would most nearly fill my study needs. I purchased fourteen books and a secondhand typewriter. Luckily I was also able to find a good German teacher who lived in our neighborhood.

Every day, including Sundays, from Thanksgiving until January 15, I studied for at least twelve hours. My schedule, up to the first of January, was as follows: 6:00 to 7:30 A.M. study of German; 7:30 to 8:00 morning toilet and exercises; 8:00 to 8:30 breakfast; 8:30 to 9:30 a German lesson; 9:45 to 1:00 P.M. typing the summary of a book (I had learned touch-typing during the summer of 1911); 1:00 to 1:30 lunch; 1:30 to 2:00 walk through nearby Central Park; 2:00 to 6:00 more summary typing of books; 6:00 to 6:30 supper; 6:30 to 7:00 walk; 7:00 to 10:00 more typing of summaries. I marked particular excerpts of my summaries for subsequent memorization. I breathed a sigh of relief when at the end of the first week of January I completed the summary of what I regarded as the pertinent portions of all fourteen books.

What kind of books did I summarize? I outlined a book on each of the following subjects: international law, maritime law, commercial law, political geography, commercial geography, elements of accounting, economic history of the United States, resources of the United States, basic economics, American history, American government and institutions, history of Europe since 1850, history of South America since 1850, history of the Far East since 1850. Thank heaven we did not then, as we do during the latter part of this century, have diplomatic relations with more than 120 countries and were not members of more than 30 international organizations. Also, there were not then more than 50 departments and agencies in the executive branch of our government. Had there been more, my list of books to be summarized would have been much longer. As it was, even my fourteen books did not contain answers to all the questions that I thought might be asked, so I supplemented them with a number of reference books, among which were a good atlas, an almanac containing quantities of statistics, and a congressional directory.

It would have been lonesome work plugging along day after day on matters most of which were new and strange to me had it not been for the stimulating plaudits of my young brother. Sometimes I felt like a long-distance runner who could hear the voice of a loyal family member urging him to keep up his pace each time that he came loping by the grandstand.

It had taken several weeks to assemble all of the information necessary for the completion of my application. It was not until mid-December that F. M. Dearing, one of the assistant secretaries of state, informed me that I would be examined on January 16.

THE CONSULAR EXAMINATIONS, JANUARY 1922

It is amazing how full of facts and figures one can stuff oneself in seven weeks of concentrated study. In the early part of January I began to feel like a living encyclopedia, crammed so full that I would explode unless I could have an opportunity to release some of my pent-up knowledge. I was, therefore, eager to get into the examination rooms when, on the morning of January 15, my brother saw me off at Pennsylvania Station with many pats on the back and exhortations of "Let 'em have it."

Half an hour before the appointed nine o'clock on the morning of January 16, 1922, at the Civil Service Commission examination rooms in Washington, D.C., I found the corridor full of candidates, some clearly in a state of nervous tension and some apparently reeking with confidence. I noted a group, the members of which seemed to be well acquainted with one another and to have a tendency to hang together. They appeared to be looking on the unattached strangers who were filing into the room with a certain amount of condescending interest. I learned that the members of this relatively nonchalant group had been attending a "cram school" in Washington, which during recent years had achieved considerable success in assisting candidates to pass the consular examinations. I found their suggestions on how to impress the examiners during the oral examinations interesting and, in some instances, amusing.

After we had entered the large examination hall and each candidate had taken a seat behind a desk, I estimated the number of candidates as 150. Not all of them were taking the same examination. Some were candidates for consul class 7 and for vice consul of career, others for the lower positions of student interpreter and consular assistant. All four categories took essentially the same examination. Those aspiring to be student interpreters and consular assistants, however, were not required to answer all the questions. The written examinations for the candidates for consul class 7 and vice consul of career were identical. The Department of States reserved the right, however, to determine whether or not a successful candidate would be commissioned as a consul or vice consul. In view of my age and experience I had applied to take the examination for the position of consul.

The candidates were not permitted to take any papers or books into the examination room. Each desk had been supplied with notepaper. Supervision to prevent cheating was rigorous. Monitors continually walked up and down the aisles; others sat at desks commanding a good view of the room. As we entered, each of us was assigned a number. This number, instead of the name of the candidate, was placed on all papers prepared during the examinations.

I have sometimes wondered if competitive examinations are the best method of selecting personnel for government or other services. I believe that some persons possess a temperament that enables them to do better in examinations, both written and oral, than others whose qualifications may be as high, if not higher. So far, however, no better method seems to have been devised. I have no reason to complain regarding the practice of making selections on the basis of competitive examinations. I happen to be one of those persons who are usually at their best under examination stress. Although I was nervous before entering the examination hall, I was calm, collected, and relaxed as I picked up the first list of questions and began to answer them. Luck always plays a role in examinations of this kind, and as I went through the various lists of questions I was convinced that luck was with me on January 16 and 17. Scarcely a question was asked the answer to which was not to be found in the summaries that I had prepared and studied.

The arithmetic examination was not difficult in itself. It did call, however, for a considerable amount of figuring and I was out of practice in shuffling figures. As a result two of the three hours that had been set aside for the two examinations had elapsed before I could turn my attention to German.

The foreign language had been given a weight of only 5 percent in the computation of the total score of the written examinations. I was, therefore, sufficiently optimistic when I left the examination hall to send my brother a postcard telling him I thought I had survived the written examinations.

The oral examinations, which began on the morning of January 18, were of a strictly formal character. The five examiners sat in a row behind a long table regarding with expressionless faces the wretched candidates who were ranged four at a time in straight-back chairs in front of them. No effort was made to put the victims at their ease. There was an oppressive air of solemnity about the whole procedure.

The members of the examining panel were the chairman, F. M. Dearing; Herbert Hengstler, chief of the consular bureau; a member of the Civil Service Commission; one of the senior consuls general; and Wilbur Carr. As the group of four to which I had been assigned filed in to take our seats before this august panel I had difficulty, in spite of the solemnity of the occasion, in restraining a smile as I recalled the argument that had taken place in the corridor regarding whether during the interrogation we could cross our legs or should keep both feet planted firmly on the floor. The procedure was for each candidate to be grilled in turn. At any time, however, while one of us was under fire, the examiners were at liberty to direct surprise questions to any one of the other three. The questions followed a certain pattern. The candidate was first invited to give an outline of his background, education, and experience. He was asked why he wanted to enter the service and what kind of work he would like to do while in it. He was asked what books he had read during the preceding three years and was requested to discuss one of them. He was asked about his hobbies and military experience. At some point the panel would question him in detail on a subject about which, from his education or experience, he should have acquired special knowledge.

I was asked about the Baltic states: the ethnic background and language of the people, which ports were ice-free, what the main products were, and whether opportunities for trade with them might develop in the years to come. They also questioned me about my experience in postwar Germany. They then switched to the United States. I was asked to describe some of the great irrigation projects of recent years, to discuss U.S. trade with various countries of Latin America, and to state whom I considered to be the greatest of American poets and why. No more than fifteen or twenty minutes were allotted to any candidate. Our group of four went through the gauntlet of the panel in 45 minutes. When I left the room I had no idea what kind of a decision the panel would take with respect to me.

SUCCESS IN PASSING THE CONSULAR EXAMINATIONS

Following my return to New York from Washington, I had tried to think as little as possible about the examinations and the likelihood of entering the Consular Service. I did not want to be too deeply disappointed if I should be informed that I had failed. One evening in late March, upon returning to our rooms, I found my brother waiting for me with a sealed envelope in his hand. He gave it to me. "There it is," he said, "that is what you have been waiting for. It is from the Department of State. I have not dared to open it." In the envelope was a letter from the chairman of the examination panel. It read as follows:

Sir:

It gives me pleasure to inform you that in the recent consular service entrance examinations you passed with the rating of 86.25 percent, and that your name has been placed on the list of those eligible for appointment to the grade of Vice Consul *de carrière*.

If you are appointed you will receive due notification from the Department.

My pleasure at having passed the examination was dimmed by the discouraging "if" in the last sentence and by the fact that, although I had successfully passed the examinations as a candidate for a position as a consul of class 7, I had been declared eligible only for a position as vice consul *de carrière*. It will be recalled that in view of my age and experience I had applied for an appointment as consul. I may add that the titles vice consul *de carrière* and vice consul of career were being used interchangeably by the Department of State at that time. They both connoted that the bearers of these titles were vice consuls who had entered the Consular Service on a career basis after competitive examinations and that they were eligible, in case they demonstrated that they had the necessary qualifications, to be promoted over the years to the top grade of that service without taking any additional examinations.

Since it was important for me to know whether or not I was likely to receive an appointment in the near future, I wrote to Mr. Carr inquiring about the possibilities. In his letter of reply dated March 30, he told me that twenty-four persons were at present eligible for appointment as officers in the Consular Service, that eleven men had passed the examinations that I had taken, and that I ranked third in the eleven.

NOTIFICATION OF APPOINTMENT AS
VICE CONSUL OF CAREER

The next letter addressed to me by the State Department, which was dated July 22, informed me that I had been appointed vice consul *de carrière*, class 3. I discovered later that my commission had been signed on May 26 by Charles Evans Hughes. I never did learn why after its signing I had been kept on tenterhooks for two months. The letter of July 22 instructed me to be prepared on two weeks' notice to report to the State Department. Attached was an oath of office form, which I was to execute in New York on the day of my departure for Washington.

In early August I received the letter for which I had been waiting so long. It was dated August 2 and signed by Mr. Carr, instructing me to report to Room 113 in the Department of State at ten o'clock on the morning of August 17, 1922, for an instruction period not to exceed 30 days. It stated that at the end of the instruction period I should be prepared to go to the post to which I would be assigned. I at once notified the bank—where I had been working—of my appointment and submitted to it my resignation. I also began to prepare for my departure from the United States to an unknown destination. It was arranged that my brother would return to Colorado Springs to continue his education there.

INSTRUCTION PERIOD IN THE
DEPARTMENT OF STATE, AUGUST 1922

On August 16 I took my oath of office in New York and arrived in Washington on the evening of the same day. On the following morning, in accordance with my instructions, I reported to Room 113 of the State Department. The State Department was then, as it had been for over 60 years, housed in the rear of the State, War, and Navy Building on the west side of the White House. The portion of the building facing Pennsylvania Avenue was the headquarters of the armed forces.

I found in this room ten other young men, of whom eight had

passed the examinations with me. Only one of the new vice consuls was married. The exception was the youngest member, Charles Derry of Macon, Georgia, aged 21, whose marriage had taken place on the eve of his departure for Washington. Probably not more than one out of ten men entering the diplomatic and consular services in those days had a wife. Young men without private means at that time were not accustomed to marry unless they were so established that they could support a family without the aid of their parents. Furthermore, junior diplomatic secretaries were considered to be more useful when not encumbered by families.

In charge of our class was one of the outstanding consuls general of the service, Ralph J. Totten. Herbert Hengstler, chief of the consular bureau, also attended our opening session. Consul General Totten and Mr. Hengstler told us that our instruction period would last about two weeks, at the end of which we would be informed about the posts to which we were to be assigned. They also provided us with lists of the lectures to which we would be exposed while undergoing instruction and with a quantity of literature, including the consular regulations, which we were to study or to use for reference purposes in preparing for our lecture sessions.

I noted from an examination of these documents that our instruction was to be of a practical character. We were to be informed regarding the kind of duties that we would be called upon to perform as vice consuls and to learn as much as we could during our two weeks of instruction about the techniques employed in the performance of such duties.

During one of our sessions we were requested to complete forms indicating our post preferences. It was explained that it was rare that vacancies in the service should match post preferences and that we should not be disappointed, therefore, if our assignment should not be one of these posts. I expressed preference for posts where I might learn French or improve my German and indicated that eventually I would like to serve in Eastern Europe. On August 29, when our assignments were announced, I learned that I had drawn Dublin. I was a little disappointed because I had hoped to be able at my first post to remedy my foreign-language deficiency. Nevertheless, I preferred Dublin where, judging from the newspapers, there were likely to be problems and therefore challenges, to relatively quiet posts such as Birmingham, England, and Santa Marta, Colombia, to which other members of our group were being assigned.

PART V

U.S. VICE CONSUL IN DUBLIN AND QUEENSTOWN (COBH), AUGUST 1922–DECEMBER 1924

CHAPTER 10

VICE CONSUL IN DUBLIN, 1922–1923

THE JOURNEY FROM THE UNITED STATES TO DUBLIN

THE SS *LACONIA* raised its gangway at noon on September 7, 1922. Standing at the rail waving farewell to relatives and friends were four newly commissioned vice consuls going to their first foreign posts. They were Thomas H. Robinson, en route to Birmingham; Charles A. Amsden, en route to Marseilles; Albert M. Doyle, en route to Amsterdam; and Loy W. Henderson, en route to Dublin. When I could no longer see my brother, who had been waving at me from the pier, I joined my three colleagues in the smoking room in the stern where we could have a last look at the American continent. During the voyage a friendship developed among the four of us that lasted throughout all our years in the service. Both Robinson and Doyle remained in the service for more than 30 years. Robinson held a series of important consular posts in Europe, Asia, Africa, North America, and South America. Doyle also had an interesting career; among his later assignments, I believe, were those of consul general to Amsterdam and consul general to Frankfurt. Amsden, the young vice consul from New Mexico, who had both charm and brilliance, contracted tuberculosis within three or four years subsequent to his entry into the service and died shortly thereafter.

In the afternoon of what my Dublin friends would have called a "fine soft day," we dropped anchor in Queenstown (Cobh) harbor. In the chilly drizzle the shores of southern Ireland, which can be so beautiful in the sunlight, looked dreary and unwelcoming. When the tender came alongside I stood by, not knowing whether to disembark or go on to Liverpool. One of the ship's officers using a megaphone told a little group on the tender that the new U.S. vice consul to Dublin was aboard and would like to know whether there was any way of getting there from Queenstown. They answered that a packet for Dublin would be leaving Cork, a few miles up river from Queenstown, on the following afternoon.

On the morning of Sunday, September 17, I was deposited with my luggage on the Dublin docks. A telegram from Queenstown telling the consulate of the time of my arrival had failed to come through. No one, therefore, was at the docks to meet me. Leaving my trunks with the customs authorities I proceeded with my handbags to the Shelbourne Hotel where I was fortunate enough to obtain a room. I learned from the porter that our senior vice consul, Mr. Charles Bay, was living in the hotel. At dinner that evening Bay outlined the political situation in Ireland as he saw it and also some of the problems that the consulate was facing.

THE CONSULATE AT DUBLIN AND ITS MEMBERS, SEPTEMBER 1922

The consulate was located on the second floor of a rather shabby building on O'Connell Street not far from the monument to Daniel O'Connell. There Bay introduced me to Miss Johnston, a middle-aged Irish woman, who was serving as the consul's secretary; to Harold M. Collins, the other career vice consul; to Richard R. Willey, the noncareer vice consul; and to Lucius Hartwell Johnson, the sole American clerk.

Dr. Charles M. Hathaway, the consul, who had been paying a call at the Foreign Office, appeared at the consulate in the middle of the morning. When Bay ushered me into his office I found there a tall, scholarly looking man of about fifty with iron-gray hair and mustache. He was indeed a scholar who seemed to be almost as much at home in Greek, Latin, and Anglo-Saxon as in English. Before Dublin his posts had included Hull, Bombay, and Budapest. He possessed a pungent dry humor and it was possible to detect now and then through his silver-rimmed glasses a glint of mischief in his tired blue eyes.

INTRODUCTION TO CONSULAR ACTIVITIES, SEPTEMBER–OCTOBER 1922

Dr. Hathaway asked me if I would be willing as my first task to undertake a job that should have been done years ago. In the attic of the building that the consulate occupied there were great piles of bound consular records, some dating back almost a hundred years. For several years the State Department had been urging the consulate to sort them, make an inventory of them, and pack them for shipment to Washington where they could be stored in the archives. The job had never been done in view of the understaffing of the consulate. Would I mind carrying out the departmental instructions? He would like to place the whole matter in my hands.

Before leaving the consulate I went into the attic to look over the archives that were to be sorted and packed. The records were covered with a layer of dust so heavy that many of them were not even visible.

During the next two weeks I saw little of the consular office. I spent the days in the attic sorting out and making inventories of records. Many of the archives were extremely interesting, particularly those pertaining to the problems imposed upon the consulate during the American Civil War. It took considerable restraint to resist interrupting my work to pore over these old records. But because I did have to read some of the records, what seemed a routine task in fact gave me the background that enabled me to understand better the problems encountered during my two years in Ireland. I also gained a wider and firmer grasp of the nature of consular work than I could have obtained from reading any number of textbooks.

After the archives had been prepared for shipment, Dr. Hathaway assigned me a second task that he said was routine. It had to do with consular forms, of which the office carried over fifty different kinds. Every consular office was required by regulation to report each year to the State Department the number of each kind of form it had on hand and to accompany the report with a requisition for any forms it might need during the ensuing year. Our consulate had been so overburdened with work in the past few years that it had not been able to comply with this regulation. This had made it necessary to borrow forms on an emergency basis from neighboring consulates. My job was to remedy this situation. In performing this new task I found it necessary to burrow into all phases of consular activity, to read scores of regulations and amendments applicable to the forms, and to determine the number of each kind of form used in preceding years. I had then, and still have, an intense dislike for forms but this dislike contributed to the fierceness with which I set out to combat them. I grappled with their mysteries day and night for three weeks until finally I had the feeling that I had conquered them. During the rest of my comparatively short consular career I was looked upon by my colleagues as an authority on consular forms. Furthermore, in my efforts to master forms I had the acquired knowledge of regulations governing the performance of more than forty different kinds of consular services.

Although Dr. Hathaway had apologized for assigning me seemingly routine tasks during my first five weeks, he had in fact done me a service by giving me an opportunity to acquire a vast amount of basic knowledge about the theories and procedures of consular practice.

"GENERALIST" IN THE CONSULATE, OCTOBER 1922

The completion of the special tasks assigned to me by Dr. Hathaway coincided with the departure of Mr. Bay for his new post, Casablanca. Dr. Hathaway, therefore, asked me to assume responsibility for what he called the general work of the office. Dr. Hathaway had reserved for himself the political work of the consulate; Collins, now the senior vice consul, was to continue in charge of the economic, commercial, and trade promotion work; Johnson, who in the meantime had been commissioned as a noncareer vice consul, was to handle the visa and passport work; Willey was to be responsible for the certification of consular invoices and for services to ships, shipping, and seamen. Most of the other activities of the consulate fell to me: notarial services; the protection of the interests and welfare of U.S. citizens; assisting veterans of the Civil, Spanish, and World wars—of whom there were a surprising number in the Dublin consular district; taking care of visitors at the consulate whose needs did not fall within the jurisdiction of the other vice consuls; and helping my fellow officers when they became overburdened. I also maintained the record books, prepared fiscal and other reports to the State Department, and was responsible for the general administration.

THE POLITICAL SITUATION IN IRELAND, 1922–1923, AND PROBLEMS FOR THE CONSULATE ARISING THEREFROM

Dr. Hathaway found himself with a serious problem. Many American citizens of Irish origin were among the guerrillas terrorizing the countryside. If any were shot without the trial procedures customary in the United States, the effect could be disastrous. However, the Free State government could not appear to have one procedure for the punishment of Irish nationals and another for U.S. nationals guilty of the same crime. After protracted discussions, the Foreign Office and Dr. Hathaway agreed that any Americans who were captured with arms in their possession were to be held in jail or in a detention camp without trial until the cessation of Republican armed activities, at which time decisions could be made as to how they would be dealt with. This informal agreement was to be kept secret because, if it should become known that U.S. nationals were being given special treatment, the Irish Republicans and their American sympathizers would have protested.

One of my duties was to receive the numerous Americans who came to the consulate to make inquiries about American relatives or friends being detained and give such assistance as I properly could. Some of these visitors were genuinely concerned about what might happen to these detainees. To quiet their fears I told them that, based on our previous experience, we did not think the American prisoners would be executed. I even went so far at times as to indicate that when order had been restored in Ireland the prisoners would probably be allowed to return home, although I could not refer to, or even hint at, the informal understanding we had with the Free State authorities. Other visitors, however, were more interested in promoting the cause of the Irish Republic than in the fate of the Americans under arrest. Some of them may have thought that the summary execution of a number of Americans caught bearing arms might not be such a bad thing, since the repercussions in the United States might help the cause of the Irish Republic.

The agreement about American prisoners worked well and, so far as I know, no U.S. nationals caught with firearms were executed. With the cessation of guerrilla warfare most, if not all, of them were released and either deported or permitted to return to the United States. The observance of this agreement did leave the consulate open to attack by the more vigorous American sympathizers with the Republican movement. Letters were published in the U.S. press criticizing the consulate for failing to insist that the arrested Americans be either released or brought to trial. Members of Congress, pressed by their constituents, wrote critical letters to the Department of State, which forwarded them to the consulate, which continued to ignore them.

In late 1922 the Free State government was occupied with the preparation of its constitution and frequently consulted regarding its provisions with Dr. Hathaway. I had the valuable experience of attending with Dr. Hathaway many of the sessions of the Dail where the proposed constitution was debated.

Immediately after adopting the constitution in the first week of December 1922, the Dail set about selecting the members of the senate, which was to be the second legislative body. At this point the bitterness of the Republican opponents overflowed, and attempts were made to assassinate several members of the Dail on their way to one of its meetings. At least one deputy was killed and another was wounded. The Free State authorities, to discourage further assassinations, executed several of the Republican leaders who were under arrest, including a prominent guerrilla leader by the name of Rory O'Connor. Another spasm of terrorist acts followed, including numerous skirmishes on the Dublin streets during the winter of 1922–1923. Often at night I would be awakened by the rattle of machine guns or the firing of rifles. O'Connell Street, on which the consulate was situated, was one of the focal points of these disorders and we sometimes found it advisable to approach it by way of side streets. We could not, however, avoid O'Connell Street for the last hundred yards, and more than once the members of the staff, like others with business on that street, could be seen reporting for work on all fours.

In the fall of 1922, Eamon De Valera went into hiding after directing his Republican followers to resume the fighting. The authorities searched intensively for him for months. Vice Consul Willey, who had a tall, gangling figure and who wore heavily rimmed glasses, was picked up several times by the vigilant police who were convinced that they had found the rebel leader in disguise. De Valera was finally apprehended in Dublin in the spring of 1923. Shortly after his arrest I had an occasion to see him.

As background I should explain that to finance the Republican cause, De Valera and several other Republican leaders had sold several million dollars worth of Irish Republican bonds in the United States during the years 1919–1921. The bonds were placed in a New York bank, subject to withdrawal upon presentation of an order signed by De Valera and two other specified persons. After the Free State was established a dispute arose over the ownership of these bonds. The Free State government maintained that as the successor of the Irish Republican movement, the funds should be turned over to it. The dissident Republicans insisted that they were the true representatives of the Irish Republic and hence the sole owners of the funds. One of the men whose signature was required for a withdrawal was a supporter of the Free State, and the other two were Republicans. Since the signatures of all three on the same withdrawal order could not be obtained, several million dollars remained untouched in the bank. A suit had been instituted in a U.S. court for the purpose of determining to whom these funds belonged, the Irish Free State or the Irish Republic. The presiding judge requested the consulate to take testimony from the three persons whose signatures were needed for withdrawal. Vice Consul Collins, as senior vice consul and the member of the consulate most experienced in taking testimony, was given the task, and I went along with him to assist and to gain experience. There was nothing about De Valera's manner or well-groomed appearance that suggested he was being confined in a jail. He was composed and gave his answers without hesitation. After the testimony had been taken he shook hands with us and departed as though he had important business elsewhere.

VISA OFFICER AND
ADMINISTRATIVE OFFICER OF THE CONSULATE

In early 1923 I took over the visa work and also continued to be responsible for the general administration of the office. The visa work occupied more and more of my time since Irish emigration to the United States became heavier as warm weather approached. Although some members of the service feel that visa work is tedious and routine and that the experience derived from it is of little value in developing an officer for higher positions in the service, I disagree. The decisions the young visa officer must make daily are not routine unless he treats them as such. Decisions that can deeply affect the lives of others are never trivial and decisions as to whether or not a person should be given a visa require no less careful consideration than that which a judge gives to his rulings in a court proceeding. The impressions obtained by the trembling visa applicant as he or she sits before the consul or vice consul can color the applicant's views about the United States for years to come. Conscientious young officers assigned to visa work can learn to say "no" when necessary; they can also learn when to be tolerant and when to be firm.

I found the visa section challenging and refreshing even though, with the inadequate facilities at my disposal, I was frequently required to put in a working day of ten to twelve hours to meet its demands. The consulate did not have the staff that would enable it to carry on the correspondence that would be entailed by an appointment system. In the absence of such a system we could never be sure of the number of visa applicants who might appear on a given day. Because most of the emigrant-carrying ships left Liverpool and Queenstown on Saturday evening or Sunday morning and most emigrants applied for their visas en route to the ship, we were sure to face long lines during the latter part of the week. I often issued more than a hundred visas in a single day. Each visa entailed asking a number of questions required by law, an additional amount of interrogation if the answers should raise doubts, a literacy test, affixing of visa and fee stamps, notes on each emigrant for the immigration officials in the United States (this was done by inserting above the visa a series of cabalistic numbers), dating and signing of the visa, an entry in the fee book, and collection of the fee.

In spite of their anxiety, many emigrants retained a sense of humor and relaxed if I interjected a bit of badinage into the proceedings. Nevertheless, the work was of a serious character and I am troubled to this day at the despair registered on the faces of some of those applicants whom I found to be ineligible for entry into the United States.

LIFE IN DUBLIN

My life outside office hours in Dublin was quite pleasant. I had a small furnished flat on the second floor of an old residence on Fitzwilliam Square consisting of a large drawing room elaborately furnished with rather shabby antiques, including a huge locked china closet full of specimens of old English china too valuable to be touched, a dressing room, and a bedroom.

Social life in Dublin was necessarily limited. There was a strictly observed curfew and although we, as officers of the consulate, were given passes, we tried so far as our duties permitted to observe curfew rules. Anyone on the streets after curfew was certain to be challenged and the challengers were inclined to be trigger-happy. They had good reason, since many of the police had been shot without warning by innocent-appearing pedestrians whom they were preparing to challenge. One evening as I was returning late from the consulate, I was challenged. As I was showing my credentials, an automobile sped by. The sentry turned and fired. There was a smashing of glass but the car sped on. I asked the sentry if he had any idea who might be in the car; his answer was a shrug of the shoulders. In just this way a governor of the Bank of Ireland was killed when his driver failed to hear the command to halt.

I spent many of my weekends on long walks through the beautiful country surrounding Dublin. For instance, early on a Sunday morning I would take a train to the little town of Bray, 40 minutes from Dublin. There I would take a sidecar to the foothills of the Wicklow Mountains and would walk through them to some point where in the evening I could get a train back to Dublin. There was nothing more restful and satisfying after a nerve-racking week in the consulate than to sit near the top of a mountain in a spot so sheltered that wild flowers contrived to bloom in it all winter. Through the slow-moving clouds one could see the blue waters of the Irish Sea in one direction; in the other, neat whitewashed cottages dotted green meadows that were bordered by low hills covered with golden clumps of gorse.

During periods when the curfew was not in force and I could go out in the evening I had an opportunity to meet various interesting Dublin people. Among those whose friendship I prized most was the writer and artist George Russell, who was perhaps better known in the United States by his pseudonym of AE. He had an open house every Sunday evening to which Vice Consul Willey and I had standing invitations. On these evenings Willey and I met some of the leaders in Dublin's world of literature, art, and theater. The pressure of work at the consulate and the complex political situation that interfered with all normal social life made it impossible for these acquaintanceships to be developed into lasting friendships.

In July 1923, when I was beginning to feel at home in Dublin, I learned that I was to be transferred to Queenstown. Just after my instructions arrived I also received a letter from John A. Gamon, our consul there, saying he hoped I would report for duty as soon as possible. He and his family were planning a leave on the continent and would be able to get away only after I was there to take charge.

I realize now even more than I did then how fortunate I was to have as my first chief a man of Dr. Hathaway's breadth of understanding and knowledge. He remained in Dublin until 1927 when an American legation was established in that city. In that year the new legation relieved the consulate general, as the consulate had become, of the diplomatic responsibilities it had been carrying, and Dr. Hathaway was appointed consul general in Munich. He served for ten years in Munich prior to his retirement.

CHAPTER 11

VICE CONSUL IN QUEENSTOWN, AUGUST 1923–DECEMBER 1924

QUEENSTOWN, THE HARBOR OF CORK

IN THE MIDDLE OF AUGUST 1923, I assumed the duties of senior vice consul in Queenstown. For several hundred years that little port had been known as the Cove of Cork. When, however, in 1849 Queen Victoria landed there to make her first visit to Ireland, it was given in her honor the name of Queenstown. In 1922 its name had been changed by the government of the Irish Free State, in a burst of Irish nationalism, back to Cobh (the Gaelic way of spelling Cove). At the same time the name of Dublin had been changed to Baile Atha Cliath, but rarely did I hear anyone refer to that city by that name. Queenstown, however, became Cobh to most of the local inhabitants in a surprisingly short time. Shortly after my arrival there, the State Department took cognizance of its change of name and, therefore, in referring to it hereafter I shall use its most recent name.

If the roads between Cobh and Cork had been in better condition and if there had been more automobiles in the area, Cobh could well have been merely a suburb of Cork. For many years the U.S. consulate in southern Ireland had been located in Cork. It had been moved to Cobh primarily for the convenience of transatlantic travelers. Passenger ships usually anchored for an hour or so in the outer harbor, where they were served by tenders from Cobh. Since the Cobh docks could not accommodate seagoing vessels, freighters usually discharged and took on cargo at the commodious Cork docks up the river.

In spring and summer emigrants and tourists bound for the United States or elsewhere were accustomed to flock into Cobh by the hundreds. Also liners from the United States would disgorge their passengers, most of whom were of Irish origin, into the Cobh lighters. From the window of my living quarters overlooking the docks I could see the emotion that animated so many of these visitors as they planted their feet again on Irish soil. It was not unusual to see some of them fall sobbing on their knees to kiss the ground.

THE CONSULATE IN COBH AND ITS MEMBERS, AUGUST 1923

The consular quarters in Cobh were no credit to the United States, consisting as they did of several rooms over a saloon. The office was reached by a long narrow flight of stairs that was frequently packed with a line of emigrants. When I first saw these quarters I was shocked and made up my mind that it would be one of my tasks while in Cobh to persuade the State Department to authorize the consulate to move into suitable offices. My efforts were successful and the following year increased appropriations enabled the consulate to lease an attractive house with a garden that had been the residence of a leading banker of Cork.

The consulate staff consisted of the consul, Mr. Gamon; two vice consuls, one usually a career vice consul; several Irish clerical employees; a U.S. public health physician to inspect the ships and look over the emigrants; and a messenger.

Shortly after my arrival in Cobh the Gamons went on leave, and I had my first experience of being in charge of an office since 1921 when I was in charge of the American Red Cross office in Berlin. I felt a glow of pride as telegrams began to go to the State Department over my name even though they were of a routine nature.

INTRODUCTION TO ECONOMIC-COMMERCIAL WORK, OCTOBER 1923–MAY 1924

During the late fall and winter of 1923–1924 I devoted a considerable part of my time to economic and commercial work, which was the kind of work in which Mr. Gamon was particularly interested. I enjoyed preparing reports on economic developments and trends in southern Ireland and writing letters to American firms about the possibilities of markets for their products. I did not mind preparing some of the reports regarding opportunities for the sale of various commodities called for by ambitious heads of sections in the Department of Commerce.

The kind of commercial activities that I found disagreeable were those of searching out potential customers for specific American products and preparing "trade directory reports" on them. The more reliable firms in Cork had had business connections with firms in Great Britain and elsewhere for many years, and they tended to resent the aggressive commercial campaign in which the consulate was compelled by departmental instructions to engage on behalf of the Department of Commerce. My objection to barging into business houses in Cork in order to interest them in purchasing American goods stemmed in part from my belief that the interjection of the consulate in this way into the business world of southern Ireland was not an effective method of increasing the sale of American goods in the area. Also, I was convinced that by engaging in such competitive commercial activity, the consulate would soon lose much of its prestige, particularly among members of the business community, and that its representatives would no longer be welcome and honored callers. Perhaps the more useful results of my trade-promotion activities were the knowledge I acquired of some of the practical aspects of foreign trade and the friendships that I succeeded in forming with members of the Cork business community.

INSPECTION BY CONSUL GENERAL–AT–LARGE AND THE PASSAGE OF THE FOREIGN SERVICE ACT OF 1924 (THE SO-CALLED ROGERS ACT)

In May 1924 Robert Frazer, the consul general–at–large for Europe whom I had met in 1922 on the ship bound for Ireland, arrived in Cobh to inspect the consulate. These periodic inspections are rather important events in diplomatic and consular offices. The inspector examines in detail all of the activities of an office. He studies the records, closely questions the officers and staff, and tries tactfully to learn the standing of the office and its individual members in the community. He sends a detailed report on each office and staff member to the State Department. This report becomes a permanent part of that officer's personnel file and may affect promotions and assignments for years to come. Finally, the inspector is expected to make suggestions for the improvement of procedures and to note procedures adopted by one office that might be used advantageously by others. We did our utmost to make a good impression upon Mr. Frazer and apparently we did.

It was during Frazer's inspection that we learned that the Rogers Act had become law. The passage of that bill revolutionized the service. It provided among other things that the Diplomatic and Consular Services were to be merged into a single service, the Foreign Service of the United States. The officers of both services were to be issued new commissions as Foreign Service officers and could, thereafter, be assigned to positions in diplomatic missions, consular offices, or the Department of State. A new schedule of salaries would mean increases in pay for almost every officer. The greatest increases were to be in the diplomatic corps where the salaries, particularly in the middle and upper brackets, had been much lower than those of consular officers of corresponding rank. Eliminating the disparity would make it easier for officers without private means to accept diplomatic posts. Another provision authorized the granting of entertainment allowances to diplomatic missions and to consular offices in cities in which there were no diplomatic missions. Such allowances, if generous enough, might enable officers without private means to aspire to the rank of minister or ambassador.

The new legislation also provided for retirement annuities for both diplomatic and consular officers and stipulated that those over 65 should be retired immediately. This meant that many elderly consular officers— several over 80 years of age—whom the department had retained in the service because it had not had the heart to turn them out penniless in their old age, would be retired on a decent income.

The idea of merging the Diplomatic and Consular Services was not new. I had heard senior officers say while I was on my orientation detail in the State Department that they thought a merger was inevitable and that there was no longer any logical reason to maintain two separate services in the kind of international community that was developing. A merger would mean that the Foreign Service officers would, by serving in both diplomatic missions and consular offices, acquire a broader experience and outlook and a greater degree of professional competence. For my own part, I welcomed the thought that I might be given the opportunity to receive a diplomatic assignment, which would carry with it the possibility of engaging in more work of a political character. While assisting Dr. Hathaway in Dublin I had had an opportunity to get a taste of political work, and in Cobh Mr. Gamon had assigned me the task of preparing the fortnightly report on political developments in southern Ireland for the benefit of our embassy in London. I had found this kind of work particularly appealing.

When the Foreign Service Act of 1924, as the Rogers bill was formally entitled, went into effect on July 1, 1924, the career officers in the consulate at Cobh, like many others around the globe, took their new oath of office as Foreign Service officers. It was, by and large, a happy event. Inevitably, however, the sweeping revision of the rank and salary structure of the two former services produced some inequities. My own case is a small illustration. While the new legislation had broadened my opportunities, its immediate effect was to put me still further behind men of my age in the service. For instance, officers eight or nine years younger than me who had entered the Diplomatic Service only a few weeks prior to the passage of the Rogers Act had been placed in the Foreign Service two or more classes above me. Another problem was that of salary. The only active officers in the new service who received no salary increase were the vice consuls, of which I was one. In fact, reductions in order to build up a retirement fund had reduced our pay by 5 percent. My income reduction was offset several weeks later, however, when I received a promotion, my second in nine months. (I had been promoted to vice consul of career, class 2, in November 1923, the equivalent to Foreign Service officer, unclassified, grade B.) My new rank was Foreign Service officer, unclassified, grade A, although my title continued to be that of vice consul.

EFFECT OF THE IMMIGRATION ACT OF 1924 ON VISA WORK IN THE CONSULATE

Another piece of legislation was enacted while I was on duty in Cobh that had an important effect on the work of our consulate. I refer to the Immigration Act of 1924. This act, which went into effect on July 1, 1924, differentiated between immigration and nonimmigration visas. It established three categories of immigration visas—quota, nonquota preferred, and plain nonquota—and several categories of nonimmigration visas. Complex regulations implemented the new law. Visa applicants were required to furnish evidence that would enable the consulate to determine the kind of visa, if any, they might be entitled to. This legislation and the regulations based on it made it necessary to reorganize our consulate in Cobh and other consular offices situated in areas where immigration to the United States was heavy. Immigrants were no longer able to stop by the consulate on the way to the ship to get their visas. No longer could a consular officer assisted by several clerks grant visas at the rate of ten or twelve an hour.

With the passage of this law the consulates in Dublin and Cobh were flooded with inquiries. These came from would-be immigrants, from Irish nationals who had already emigrated to the United States and who were back in Ireland on a temporary visit, from representatives of steamship companies, and from travel agencies. At first the consulates had neither the staff nor the information to handle the inquiries. As soon as the new regulations arrived, Dr. Hathaway and Mr. Gamon asked me to head a group to study the new law and regulations, evolve a plan of operation, and draft documents that we would need in carrying out the new procedures.

When the documents had been prepared and printed, they were distributed among the steamship lines and travel agencies throughout the Irish Free State. The consulate in Belfast also became interested in our system and adopted it for Northern Ireland.

An interesting aspect of our visa work was the intense rivalry among the steamship lines that catered to the immigrant traffic. Each line jealously watched relations between our consular office and rival lines. The consulates took care not to appear to favor the passengers of one line over those of another. The subagents of some of the American lines working in the back country sometimes dropped vague hints to the effect that American consular offices might give special consideration to their clients. This, of course, infuriated the agents of the other lines.

To forestall charges of unequal treatment, the two U.S. consulates in the Free State refused to give consideration to any applications for visas to be given under the Immigration Act until the day after it came into effect. The consulates also informed all inquirers that they would accept only applications received by mail and would consider applications in the order the envelopes containing them were opened by the consulates. Representatives of the steamship companies in Cobh assembled their clients' applications in bags, which were turned over to the post office before the day the act became effective. The post office worked valiantly and on July 1, 1924, the sacks of mail containing more than five thousand applications were delivered to our office. Fortunately, the State Department had authorized us to triple our clerical staff and had sent additional vice consuls and an American clerk to help us.

Representatives of the steamship lines were invited to be present while we opened all the mail bags, scrambled their contents into great piles on the floor and began to draw out and number the envelopes. While the consulate struggled to master the mountain of applications, its other activities, other than those of an urgent nature, came to a standstill. We had prepared in advance ten or twelve form letters requesting additional information or documents from the applicants, informing them of the procedures they should follow, or giving them appointments to appear in person. Within ten days a steady stream of visa applicants was pouring into the consulate in an orderly way and we were quite proud of ourselves.

GUERRILLA WARFARE, 1924

Although life in Cobh was more peaceful than it had been in Dublin, guerrillas still operated there. The agreement that gave birth to the Irish Free State provided that the Cobh harbor defenses were to be maintained by the British, and that certain mooring buoys were to be retained for the use of His Majesty's ships. The British military forces that manned these defenses were stationed on Spike Island, the heavy fortifications of which dominated the entrance to the inner harbor. The officers and men made frequent trips on shore leave to Cobh where they were welcome visitors. They, of course, came unarmed, were well behaved, and were liberal spenders. One day, while the launch from Spike Island was discharging passengers and 20 or 25 Britishers were standing on the pier, several automobiles full of men armed with machine guns came speeding down the road from the direction of Cork. They paused just long enough to sweep the pier with machine gun fire and then sped back toward Cork. They were Republican guerrillas. No one knew where they came from or where they went. They simply disappeared, leaving the pier littered with dead and wounded men.

The townspeople were panic-stricken. They feared that in retaliation the guns from Spike Island might be turned on Cobh. The members of the urban council appealed to Mr. Gamon and to the local clergy, Catholic and Protestant, to approach the officers in command of Spike Island on their behalf and to point out that the citizens of Cobh were not responsible for the attack and were deeply grieved and shamed that it had taken place.

A funeral was held on the island for those who had been killed. It was attended by representatives of the government of the Irish Free State, which had expressed its formal regrets at the attack, and by representatives of the towns of Cork and Cobh. Mr. Gamon and I also attended. No further shore leave was permitted until the Irish authorities were able to convince the British commander that adequate preventive measures had been taken.

During the latter part of my tour in Cobh, law and order were well enough restored to permit us to make trips in the consular district and acquaint ourselves with its towns, enterprises, and people.* I found the

---

* The Irish Free State had been divided by the Department of State for purposes of consular responsibility into two districts. The northern counties were assigned to the Dublin consular district and the southern to that of Cobh.

southern portion of Ireland to be just as beautiful and in some ways even more beautiful than the countryside around Dublin. The Killarney and Bantry Bay areas, so well known to many Americans, were within the Cobh district as was the charming little seaport of Tralee in County Kerry, and the historic town of Limerick. Blarney Castle, only a few miles distant from Cork, was the destination of several weekend outings with visiting Americans. I not only kissed the Blarney Stone but also became adept at sitting on the legs of my guests while they hung head down over the ramparts in order to do the same.

Return to the United States on Leave

Foreign Service officers at that time were entitled to home leave of two months at their own expense after they had served abroad for two years. In October 1924, soon after I became eligible for leave, I boarded the SS *Republic* bound for New York. It was not until the ship had lifted anchor and begun to move out to sea that I realized I was very tired. During my 25 months in Ireland I had not had a single day of leave. My deck chair looked inviting and I was quite content to lie back and let that part of the world represented by several hundred fellow passengers go by. After several days of relaxation, however, I began to take an interest in what was going on around me, and during the remainder of the voyage I enjoyed mixing with the other passengers.

Following my arrival in New York I went immediately to Washington for the three days of consultation that were usually required of officers returning to the United States on leave. The purpose of these consultations was to give the desk-bound officers and the officers coming in from the foreign field an opportunity to become personally acquainted with one another and discuss problems or topics of mutual interest. It was customary for consular officers to pay their first call on Herbert Hengstler who, until July 1, 1924, had been chief of the Consular Bureau but who, following the establishment of the Foreign Service, had become chief of the newly created Division of Foreign Service Administration. In his new position, although operating under the general direction of Wilbur Carr, who had been elevated to the rank of assistant secretary, Mr. Hengstler continued to exercise a tremendous amount of authority over officers acting in a consular capacity.

Assignment to the Division of Eastern European Affairs, December 1924

As I was coming out of Mr. Carr's office where, at Mr. Hengstler's suggestion, I had left my card, I met Evan E. Young, the former U.S.

commissioner to the Baltic states, who had urged me while I was in charge of the American Red Cross office in Berlin in 1921 to give consideration to the Consular Service as a career. Mr. Young told me that he was at the time chief of the Division of Eastern European Affairs and suggested that I accompany him to his office for a talk. During the talk he asked if I would be willing to take a desk in his office. He said he needed a junior officer who had had some acquaintance with Eastern Europe. I told him that Mr. Hengstler had informed me that the plan was for me to return to Cobh but that if he would like to have me in his division and if the State Department approved, I would be glad to work under him.

Perhaps two weeks later, while I was in Colorado Springs visiting my father, I received a personal letter from Mr. Young informing me that I was being detailed to his division. The formal instruction transferring me to the Department of State arrived several days later.

PART VI

MEMBER OF THE DIVISION OF EASTERN EUROPEAN AFFAIRS, DEPARTMENT OF STATE, WASHINGTON, D.C., DECEMBER 1924–JULY 1927

CHAPTER 12

THE DEPARTMENT OF STATE
IN THE MID–1920S

THE TWO AND A HALF YEARS that comprised my first tour in the Department of State were of particular importance to me from the point of view of training obtained and knowledge acquired. It was during that tour that I learned both from observation and from participation what the Department of State was trying to do and how it was trying to do it. Since I was a member of the department rather than a disinterested observer, some of my comments may rightfully be considered to be of a subjective character. Nevertheless, I shall try faithfully to set forth what I observed, learned, and felt as I struggled to improve my understanding of our foreign policies and of the instruments through which these policies were being conducted.

When I entered the old State, War, and Navy Building in the latter part of December 1924, I found myself again moving into a new and unfamiliar world. The only persons in the department at that time who might possibly have recognized me by name were Herbert Hengstler, the chief of the Division of Foreign Service Administration; Consul General William Dawson, one of the instructors of our class of vice consuls; three or four officers on whom I had paid calls during my three days of consultation; Evan E. Young, under whom I was to work in the Division of Eastern European Affairs; and Charles Derry, the youngest and the only married member of our vice consular class. Derry had been assigned in

1923 to the department as a consular assistant when the health of his wife had broken down in Santa Marta, Colombia. I had met William Castle, the chief of the Division of Eastern European Affairs, in Paris in 1918, and Hugh Wilson, chief of the Division of Current Information, in Berlin in 1920. I do not believe that either of them knew me well enough to recognize me. I did not know, as I took over my new desk, what the various divisions and offices of the department were doing and what their relations might be with one another.

I had learned enough about the State Department, however, to know that before going to the Eastern European Division I should register my arrival in the book maintained by the Division of Foreign Service Administration for the signing in of Foreign Service officers reporting to the department. While I was registering, I had an opportunity to discuss my new assignment with Hengstler. In response to the questions that I put to him, he told me that he feared I would not learn much in one of the "political divisions on the third floor" that would raise my qualifications as a consular officer. Sensing my disappointment he said I should realize that, although the factors of training and development were important and were, therefore, given consideration in the making of assignments, other factors, such as the needs of the service and the officer's background and qualifications, could not be ignored. He added that apparently the decision to assign me to the State Department had been based primarily on the fact that I was acquainted with Eastern Europe as a result of my service there with the Red Cross. I should not permit myself, he said consolingly, to be discouraged. Perhaps after a year a transfer might be arranged for me to a foreign post or to another office in the department where I could obtain experience of a more practical nature.

In spite of Hengstler's injunction not to allow myself to be discouraged, my morale was sagging as I climbed the stairs to the third floor to report to the Division of Eastern European Affairs. My spirits rose, however, at the cordial manner in which I was greeted by Young and the other members of the division. After thanking me for curtailing my leave, Young introduced me to the newly appointed assistant chief of the division, Robert F. Kelley, whom I had met briefly in Riga in the spring of 1920 where he was serving as military observer in the office of the American commissioner to the Baltic provinces.

Kelley escorted me through the various rooms housing the division and introduced me to its members. The division at that time, in addition to Young and Kelley, consisted of Alexander Magruder, a veteran diplomatic officer on temporary detail who was preparing to depart for his new post as counselor of legation in Stockholm; Preston Kumler, a drafting officer; four clerical employees; and a messenger. Kelley told me that Earl

L. Packer, a Foreign Service officer who had formerly served in the division and who was on detail in the legation at Riga as a vice consul with the rank of third secretary, would be returning to the division within a few weeks as its third ranking officer. Since I was to work in close cooperation with Kelley and Packer for a number of years it might be helpful for me at this point to introduce them.

Kelley at 31 was at the time the youngest assistant chief of a political division in the department. It was unusual for an officer so junior to be appointed to such a responsible position. I found that an exception had been made partly because Young, under whom Kelley had worked in Riga, had insisted that the latter be his first assistant, and partly because during the year that Kelley had served in the division he had displayed both marked ability and stamina.

When Young was appointed minister to the Dominican Republic in the autumn of 1925, Kelley, who was considered to be too junior by the administrators of the department to succeed him as chief of the division, was made acting chief. As acting chief he made such a favorable impression upon Secretary Frank B. Kellogg that the latter in 1926 insisted that he be elevated to the chiefship. Kelley continued to serve as chief of the division for the next eleven years and came to be regarded as the "Mr. Eastern Europe" of the department.

By temperament, education, and background Kelley was well fitted to serve in the Eastern European Division. While still a student in a Boston high school—he was not, as were so many members of the department in those days, the product of an exclusive Eastern private preparatory school—he had displayed an interest in international affairs, particularly in matters relating to Russia. His high school record won him a scholarship to Harvard. After earning his A.B. degree *magna cum laude* and his A.M. degree, he was given a year's fellowship at Paris. During the course of his studies he had specialized in Russian studies and had succeeded in mastering the Russian language.

He was working for his doctorate as an instructor at Harvard when the United States entered the First World War. He left to join the armed forces and after undergoing officer training was given a commission in the regular army. He was kept in the United States training other officers during most of the war. Early in 1920 he was assigned to the Baltic states as a military observer with the rank of captain. It was there that he met Mr. Young, who was so impressed with his character and ability that Young urged him to take the consular examinations. Kelley followed Young's advice, passed the examinations, resigned from the army, and was assigned to Calcutta as vice consul. He had been in India only a few months when Young, who had become chief of the Eastern European Division, requested his services in that division. Since prior to the Rogers Act a vice consul could not be assigned to the department, Kelley resigned his consular commission and entered the department as a drafting officer. He was recommissioned, however, a few months later when the Rogers Act went into force, as a Foreign Service officer class 8 and a consul.

Following the abolishment of the Division of Eastern European Affairs in 1937, upon which I shall dwell later, Kelley was assigned to Ankara as counselor of embassy where he served several years. His retirement from the service in 1945 represented, in my opinion, a distinct loss to the service and to the United States.

Earl Packer, who in the spring of 1945 became the third ranking officer of the division, came to Washington from Utah in 1915 in order to accept a position in the Bureau of Insular Affairs in the War Department. Early in 1917 he was transferred to the U.S. embassy in Petrograd [Leningrad], and when the United States entered the war shortly after his transfer, he was given a commission as first lieutenant and the title of assistant military attaché. Following the Bolshevik revolution he accompanied the embassy when it was transferred to Arkhangelsk.

Packer was brought back to the United States in early 1920 and, in view of the knowledge that he had acquired of the situation in Russia and of the Russian language, was made a member of what was then the Division of Russian Affairs of the Department of State. While serving in that division he passed the consular examinations and in 1922 was admitted to the Consular Service and assigned as vice consul to Riga.

While previously on duty in Washington, by studying in the evenings and over the weekends, he had earned an A.B. degree from George Washington University. When he returned to the department in 1925 he undertook the study of law at the same university. He eventually received his law degree and was admitted to the bar of the District of Columbia.

Following the appointment of Kelley as acting chief of the division in 1925, Packer took over the assistant chiefship and continued to serve in that capacity until his reassignment to the legation in Riga in 1936—this time as first secretary of legation. As chargé d'affaires he had the sad duty of closing the legation when the Baltic states lost their independence in 1940. He subsequently served as consul in Dresden, first secretary in Ankara, consul general and chargé d'affaires in Rangoon, and consul general in Tunis. He retired in 1950 after having rendered his country 35 years of distinguished service.

I shared an office during most of my first State Department assignment with Preston (Pete) Kumler, a drafting officer. Pete was a quiet, reserved man in his late forties. After graduating from Yale Law School, where he had been editor of the *Yale Law Journal*, he had taken up the practice of law in Chicago. His efforts to bring about various reforms in that graft-ridden city brought him considerable prominence. When the war came he gave up a lucrative practice to enter the army. After the war he had gone to Russia as a member of the American Relief Administration under Hoover. He became so interested in Eastern Europe that upon his return to the United States he accepted a desk in the Division of Eastern European Affairs instead of resuming his practice in Chicago. Kumler's death in the late 1920s as the result of an automobile accident brought grief to his many friends in Washington, particularly those in the State Department and in legal circles.

As I have already indicated, the State Department was housed in the rear half of the great grey structure to the west of the White House, then known as the State, War, and Navy Building. The front half of the building was occupied by the top echelons of the Departments of War and Navy. The building extended north and south for more than two city blocks. At the time of its completion in the 1870s it was said to have been the largest granite office building in the world. Its exterior was enlivened by numerous small balustrades, enclosed balconies, and stone columns. The corridors, floored by worn black-and-white marble tiles and flanked by rows of fluted ornamental columns, traversed the whole length of each of three of its five floors. The long corridors were connected at intervals by short cross corridors. The outside rooms on the sides of the building overlooked either the White House and its gardens or Seventeenth Street. The inside rooms faced inner courts. Broad marble winding stairways, embellished with heavy marble or bronze railings, connected the floors as did manually-operated, leisurely-moving elevators. Along the corridors swinging louvered doors only partially covered each doorway and gave a degree of privacy to the occupants of the offices without depriving them of ventilation. During the long hot summers these doors and the drone of hundreds of electric fans in the lofty corridors and offices helped to create a drowsy tropical atmosphere.

The ground floor of that portion of the building assigned to the State Department housed offices of a kind that were not likely to be visited by distinguished callers—visa offices, mail and supply rooms, a cafeteria, a shoeshine room, and so forth. In the cavernous cellar under the ground floor were the furnaces and other mechanical equipment. During the winter months there was, it seemed to me, an almost constant stream of trucks discharging coal down chutes into the cellar amid showers of dust that drifted into the windows opening on the inner courts.

On the first floor were a series of offices of an administrative character, including the Division of Foreign Service Administration, the Passport Division, the Office of Foreign Personnel, the Stenographic Section, and the newly established Foreign Service School.

It did not take long for me to realize that the seat of authority in the State Department was the second floor. On it were not only the offices of the secretary and the under secretary but also those of the four assistant secretaries, the solicitor (later the legal adviser) of the department, and the chief clerk. This floor also housed the Division of Current Information and the Office of Coordination and Review. On the third floor were the so-called political divisions, which in the years to come developed into what became known as the Geographical Bureaus. Each of these political divisions had special responsibilities for handling relations between the United States and the countries of a specified area of the world and for conducting or coordinating State Department correspondence relating to these countries.

The Division of Eastern European Affairs occupied six rooms along the east corridor between the Division of Western European Affairs, which was at the end of the corridor adjacent to the library, and that of Far Eastern Affairs. Three of these rooms were on the outside overlooking the executive offices of the White House, and the other three faced a noisy inner court. During most of this my first tour in the State Department (December 1924–July 1927), I occupied various rooms, some on the outside and some on the court. As a junior officer, however, I usually sat in one of the inner rooms.

Members of the division whose windows overlooked the White House grounds sometimes found it difficult not to notice the activities of the presidents. It was the custom for various religious, professional, political, and other groups to ask to visit the White House and have photographs taken with the president. Mr. Coolidge apparently found it difficult to refuse these requests. Hardly a week went by that a group did not assemble on the lawns for these exercises. When the visitors had been arranged, a message would be sent to the president. Mr. Coolidge, wearing a hat, would emerge from the executive offices, walk briskly to the spot reserved for him, remove his hat while the camera clicked, replace it, and hurry back to his office, often without speaking to anyone. The results, however, seemed to be quite satisfactory to most visitors. I have no doubt that even today thousands of people throughout the United States treasure photographs showing a family member in the company of President Coolidge. President Hoover only occasionally posed for photographs, but when he did so he usually remained for a few minutes to speak to the group. President Roosevelt, probably because of his infirmity, did not make a practice of joining convention delegates in the White

House gardens. On pleasant days, however, he could sometimes be seen sitting on the back lawn with co-workers and friends.

During the course of the next twenty-two years I spent more than eleven years in this old building as I alternated between departmental and foreign assignments. Like many other Foreign Service officers I came to regard it as my American home and to love it. When the Departments of War and Navy in the 1930s moved to more commodious quarters we hoped that the Department of State, which had already overflowed into several other buildings, could take over the whole building. Our hopes, however, were not realized. The Executive Offices of the White House expanded into the vacated space and continued to eat into the building until finally, in 1947, President Truman decided that the offices attached directly to him should occupy the whole building, which has since become formally known as the Executive Office Building. The central elements of the Department of State were banished to a relatively new monstrosity in Foggy Bottom that had been built and then outgrown and discarded by the War Department; other elements were distributed throughout the city. For more than twelve years the department's library was not in its main building and was almost inaccessible to members of the department. By 1955 the department was trying to operate in some 27 different buildings in the District of Columbia and Virginia.

It has become quite modish for lovers of contemporary design to ridicule the old State, War, and Navy Building as an ugly, antiquated eyesore that should be replaced by a more "tasteful" modern structure. When I hear these critical remarks I feel as though a dear old aunt is being ridiculed because she does not wear the latest fashions or do the newest dances. I do not agree that it is hideous. To me the old building is entitled to permanence as an authentic relic of an era that should not be forgotten.

During my first assignment in Washington, bearing in mind the advice given me by Hengstler, I continued to make a special effort to learn as much as I could about the State Department from my vantage point on "the third floor." I was interested in the building in which it was housed and in its organizational structure, but much more so in the human beings that made it a living organism. What were their outlooks and backgrounds? What were their motivations? What were their aspirations so far as concerned the welfare of the United States, of the Department of State, and of the Foreign Service? To what extent were they dedicated—I use the word "dedicated," overworked as it is, because I can find no acceptable substitute for it—to the service of the public, and to what extent were they self-serving?

An atmosphere of old-world courtesy permeated the State Department. In general, its members, regardless of rank, treated one another with consideration and respect. Displays of pettiness were rare. There were in the department and in the Foreign Service during the period of my first assignment to Washington individuals who, on the grounds of wealth, family connections, educational institutions (particularly preparatory schools) attended, social backgrounds, and so forth, considered themselves to be superior to the common run and who conducted themselves accordingly. Such people are to be found, however, in almost every society, particularly among circles that are bent on acquiring what they consider to be a higher social status or on protecting the special status they believe themselves to possess. Demonstrations of snobbishness did take place from time to time. They were in general frowned on in the department. They also created hostile feelings toward the department and the Foreign Service, particularly in congressional and journalistic circles and among other governmental agencies. The members of the Diplomatic Service on duty in the department or abroad had for years been favorite targets for attack on the ground of snobbishness. During his testimony in support of the Rogers bill before the Foreign Affairs Committee on January 17, 1924, Ambassador Gibson, one of the more distinguished products of the Diplomatic Service, defended that service as follows:

> It is regrettable that the American people do not know more of what the diplomatic service is doing. It is regrettable that public interest in the service is generally concentrated on foolish articles in the papers and magazines depicting the more or less imaginary antics of a few young secretaries and representing these as typical American diplomats. As a matter of fact, we have a service to be proud of, and the so-called white spatter is of no importance beyond the fact that he is obnoxious...
>
> Now I have no hesitation in saying that the diplomatic service is not snobbish. We have perhaps a few specimens of this sort of undesirables, but no larger proportion than can be found in any group of men. We have no use for them, and every self-respecting member of the service would be delighted if they were thrown out neck and crop.
>
> Reproaches of snobbishness in the diplomatic service are almost always aimed at the young secretaries. There is another form of snobbishness that is seldom referred to, but which is far more offensive than that of immature young men. I mean that form of snobbishness that leads grown-up Americans to seek appointments as minister or ambassador to gratify their desire to shine in the society of European Courts. The fact that this is often done to satisfy the social ambitions of their wives doesn't make it any better...

When the ambassador at this point was interrupted by one of the members of the committee who pointed out that he seemed now to be referring to political appointees, he continued as follows:

> I am willing to admit that. The pathetic part is that they rarely do shine because everybody sees through them and they only make themselves ridiculous. The unfortunate thing is that they usually contrive to make America ridiculous in the process, and to create the belief, which is very prevalent abroad, that this sort of shoddy display is really representative American. It doesn't take long experience in the foreign service to learn that no American is going to dazzle a European court. If an American representative wants to make a hit in a foreign capital, the easiest way is to be perfectly simple, natural, and unostentatious. The flashy people are soon forgotten . . .

I am quoting Mr. Gibson's remarks here for two reasons: first, to show how the senior, responsible members of the Diplomatic Service in 1924 felt about snobbishness in their service; and second, because the ambassador's remarks are just as pertinent now as they were when they were made. In my opinion, they should be required reading for all U.S. nationals and their spouses who are going abroad to represent the U.S. government. I should add, however, that in recent years the number of persons who successfully seek ambassadorships because of the social ambitions of themselves or their spouses has sharply declined.

As of January 1, 1925, the personnel of the Department of State, including Secretary Hughes at the top and the humblest worker at the bottom, numbered approximately 650, of which 62 were Foreign Service officers "on detail," that is, subject to being sent to a foreign post at any moment. The remainder were presidential appointees at an under or assistant secretary level, civil service officers, clerks, messengers, laborers, and so forth, who represented what was usually referred to as "departmental personnel." Many of them were members of the Civil Service; others possessed a sort of temporary Civil Service status; still others were serving on a temporary basis with no Civil Service coverage.

The responsibility for the management of the nation's foreign affairs at the time rested on Secretary Hughes and his colleagues, subject of course to supervision by the president. Although the secretary meticulously made his foreign policy decisions in a framework approved by the White House, President Coolidge rarely intervened in foreign affairs matters. The authority of the secretary, however, was limited by the existence of a network of laws and Executive Orders that prevented him from acting on impulse in matters involving, for example, the expenditure of funds, changes in the fundamental organization of the department, and treatment of personnel.

Joseph C. Grew, the under secretary and alter ego of the secretary, was charged with the general direction of the work of the State Department and of the Foreign Service. He was also chairman of the Foreign Service Personnel Board. Leland Harrison, one of the assistant secretaries, was charged with handling matters pertaining to foreign commercial policy, commercial treaties, and so forth. He also supervised the work of the Office of the Economic Adviser. J. Butler Wright was the assistant secretary charged with the administration of the department, administrative matters concerning international conferences, and ceremonial and protocol matters. Among the entities under his supervision were the Office of the Chief Clerk, the Division of Publications, the Bureau of Accounts, and the Bureau of Indexes and Archives. He was also one of the three members on the Foreign Service Personnel Board. Wilbur J. Carr, the assistant secretary who had risen to that position through the Civil Service, was charged with the direction of the Consular Service and all consular activities in connection with the work of the several bureaus and divisions of the department. His office was also responsible for the censoring, grading, and criticizing of commercial and economic reports and for the distribution of commercial and economic reports to other agencies of the government. As budget officer of the State Department he was required to be thoroughly acquainted with its innermost workings. The fourth assistant secretary was John Van A. MacMurray, who was charged with dealing with Far Eastern questions and supervising the Division of Passport Control.

The legal adviser of the State Department, who had the rank of assistant secretary, was the solicitor, Charles Cheney Hyde, one of the great international jurists of the day. He left the department shortly after my arrival and was succeeded by one of his assistants, Green H. Hackworth, also a famous international jurist.

At a lower level were the six political divisions. The Western European Division, headed by William R. Castle, formerly an assistant dean of Harvard and a departmental officer; the Division of Far Eastern Affairs, headed by Frank P. Lockhart, a veteran departmental officer; the Division of Near Eastern Affairs, headed by Allen W. Dulles, a Foreign Service officer; the Division of Latin American Affairs, headed by Francis White, a Foreign Service officer; the Division of Mexican Affairs, headed by Franklin Mott Gunther, a Foreign Service officer; and the Division of Eastern European Affairs, with Evan E. Young at its head.

The offices of the secretary, the under secretary, the assistant secretaries, and the chiefs of political divisions were modest in size. The secretary of state, for instance, had only a private secretary, two clerks, and three messengers in his office; the under secretary only two assistants, one of whom was the "agent" (that is, chief investigator) of the department, a private secretary, five clerks, and three messengers. Officers of secretarial rank rarely had more than five or six assistants in their immediate offices. Between ten and twelve persons—a mixture of Foreign Service and State Department personnel—staffed each of the six political divisions. The bulk of the personnel of the department was on duty in the offices charged with different phases of administration—for instance, personnel, administering of funds, accounting, and budget preparation—and the supervision of the performance of passport, visa, and miscellaneous consular services. The largest offices in the department were the Passport Division and the Bureau of Indexes and Archives. The latter was responsible for maintaining the central files of the department, for receiving, indexing, and distributing reports from the foreign field, and for decoding and encoding telegrams. The Division of Foreign Service Administration also employed a large staff in connection with its work of administering the U.S. diplomatic and consular establishments, preparing budgets for those establishments, and controlling and allocating funds for the use of the Foreign Service.

During the mid-1920s the working relations among members of the State Department, which was not much more than a tenth of the size of the department some forty years later, partook of a personal character. The clerks who decoded the telegrams of particular interest to our division and who frequently brought incoming telegrams to us by hand; those who maintained in the central archives the files of documents pertaining to Eastern Europe; the legal advisers who interpreted U.S. and international law for us; the passport and visa personnel who helped us when we ran into problems arising from the absence of diplomatic relations with Russia; the administrative personnel to whom we turned when we encountered personnel problems in our missions and consulates in Eastern Europe and who assisted us in extricating ourselves from administrative entanglements; and personnel in other offices with whom we worked; these people were not merely voices on the telephone or initials on memoranda. They were fellow members of the departmental family. The permanent personnel in the department went out of their way to be helpful to the Foreign Service officers who were with them on detail. They developed a personal interest in us that followed when we left for foreign posts. While we were abroad they read communications coming in from us or relating to us. When we came back on leave or on a fresh detail, they welcomed us warmly. For this reason the department became the "home town" of many Foreign Service officers and the place where we could renew old associations and make new ones.

CHAPTER 13

THE ROGERS ACT OF 1924 AND THE ESTABLISHMENT OF THE FOREIGN SERVICE OF THE UNITED STATES

FROM TIME TO TIME, in order to cope with changes in the internal or international situation or because of the desire of a new administration for "reform," the Department of State goes through the agonies of a reorganization. Sometimes these reorganizations strengthen its effectiveness. They nearly always, however, create new problems and leave scars that can last for years. Any meaningful reorganization of a bureaucratic, highly sensitive institution such as the Department of State is usually to the personal advantage of some of its members or some of its candidates for membership, and it usually has a harmful effect upon the position, status, or opportunities for development and advancement of some of its other members. Although most members of the department realize that organizational changes are sometimes desirable, they hope that the changes can be made without resorting to drastic measures.

At the time that I took over a desk in the Division of Eastern European Affairs in January 1925, the department was going through the throes of a major reorganization. It was in the process of merging the former Diplomatic and Consular Services into a single service in accordance with the provisions of the Rogers Act of 1924.

In reporting on the bill, which became the Foreign Service Act on May 24, 1924, Congressman Rogers, chairman of the Foreign Affairs

Committee, stated on February 5, 1924, on the House floor that it included four fundamental proposals. They were as follows:

1. The adoption of a new and uniform salary scale with a modest increase in the average rate of compensation.
2. An amalgamation of the Diplomatic and Consular Services into one foreign service on an interchangeable basis.
3. Representation allowances for the purpose of eliminating, or at least lessening, the demands on the private means of ambassadors and ministers.
4. A retirement system based upon the principles of the Civil Service Retirement and Disability Act of May 22, 1920, but administered entirely separately therefrom.

The passage of the bill was welcomed by most members of the Consular Service for the following reasons:

1. The adoption of a uniform salary scale for all officers serving in the same class in the new Foreign Service, regardless of whether they were serving as diplomatic secretaries or consular officers, would render it financially possible for consular officers without private means to be detailed from time to time to embassies or legations. The salaries that had been paid in the past to diplomatic officers had been so low (the top salary, for instance, in the Diplomatic Service had been only $4,000 per year as compared to $8,000* in the Consular Service) that persons without private means could not perform effectively in that service. The provisions of the bill that greatly increased the salaries of persons holding diplomatic positions were, therefore, welcomed by consular officers.

2. The amalgamation of the two services into one foreign service on an interchangeable basis made it at least theoretically possible for persons who were at the time in the Consular Service to engage eventually in all kinds of foreign service work, gave them the opportunity to compete for presidential appointment positions such as ambassador, minister, and assistant secretary of state, and,

---

* The salaries of the consuls general in London and Paris were $12,000 per year, the same as that of the secretary of state and higher than that of most ministers.

if implemented as they assumed it would be, should raise the status of officers on duty in consular offices. Many of the consular officers felt that they had the ability to participate in what was called political work but that they had heretofore been bureaucratically barred from engaging in it. Consular officers in the past, with the exception of Evan E. Young,* had not been elevated to presidential appointment positions. The rank of consul general, therefore, had been the highest to which a consular officer could aspire. Many diplomatic officers, particularly the junior officers, believing themselves to be members of a more elite service, had in the past assumed a patronizing and superior attitude when dealing with consular officers. Consular officers hoped that the merging of the two services would result in the growth of a feeling of solidarity and harmony among all the members of the new Foreign Service and that the demarcation line between officers serving in diplomatic missions and those on duty in consular offices would gradually disappear.

    3. The retirement system provided for in the Rogers Act meant much to the consular officers. Most of them had entered the service with the intention of making it their life's career. Many of them were without private means. Their salaries were not large enough to enable them to prepare financially for old age; the more distant future, therefore, was murky. The passage of this bill enabled them to look forward with confidence to a retirement on a decent annuity (they did not foresee at that time the future decline of the purchasing power of the dollar). Furthermore, by enabling the State Department to retire more than 35 senior officers, the retirement provisions opened the way for a series of long-delayed promotions.

The members of the Diplomatic Service regarded the passage of the Rogers Act with mixed feelings. Some of them were opposed to it in its entirety; others welcomed certain of its provisions; most of them, however, had apprehensions about what it might mean for their personal future and for the future of the Diplomatic Service. Their reactions, as I understood them, to the various provisions of the bill were as follows:

    1. They were, in general, pleased with the clauses that increased their salaries, although a number were fearful that the

---

* Mr. Young had been appointed as a minister by President Taft on a personal basis, not as a promotion for a member of the Consular Service.

increase might result in an influx of persons into the Diplomatic Service without private means and without the "background" that private means render possible. They were particularly concerned lest officers in the Consular Service who previously could not afford to occupy diplomatic positions might now begin to compete for such positions.

2. Most of the members of the Diplomatic Service regarded with apprehension the proposals providing for the amalgamation of the two services into one Foreign Service on an interchangeable basis. They had forebodings that this might result eventually in the extinguishment of the Diplomatic Service as an identifiable entity. They were proud of what with considerable justification they regarded as an elite service, and they did not relish the possibility that they might find themselves submerged in a sea of Foreign Service officers, most of whom would be holding consular positions. Few, if any, diplomatic officers desired to serve in a consular capacity. The word "interchangeable," therefore, sounded ominous. The junior officers also feared that, in an amalgamated service, promotions would come less rapidly. In view of the large turnover in the Diplomatic Service, as a result of the fact that relatively few of its members spent their whole active lives in it, newcomers could reasonably expect that they would reach the top of that service within twelve or thirteen years. It usually required, however, between twenty and twenty-five years for consular officers to attain the top of their service. An amalgamation of the two services, therefore, might well result in a slowing of promotions of officers occupying diplomatic positions.

3. A few senior diplomatic officers welcomed the provisions authorizing representation allowances. Since, however, most of them realized that an authorization for such allowances was worth little unless Congress should later provide funds for such purposes, they were not deeply impressed. They had doubts that the funds in any appreciable amount would be provided in the foreseeable future.

4. A number of officers in the Diplomatic Service were pleased at the incorporation of the retirement provisions. These provisions, however, did not by any means impress all of them. A large proportion of the young officers in the Diplomatic Service had no intention of remaining in it until they reached retirement age. Many of them planned to spend several interesting years moving in international circles in the world's capitals and then return to private life. Since they had plenty of private means, retirement

annuities were of little significance. Furthermore, there was also a concern among some of them that the retirement provisions, like those calling for an increase in diplomatic salaries, might encourage competition from persons who had no private means.

Following the passage of the Rogers Act, the under secretary and the three assistant secretaries of the State Department, all of whom had come from the Diplomatic Service and who were concerned about the future, devised a plan for carrying it out. According to this plan the Foreign Service was to be set up with two distinct branches: a diplomatic branch and a consular branch. These branches were to be administered as though they were two distinct services. The whole Foreign Service was to be under the general supervision of the Foreign Service Personnel Board, to be composed of the under secretary as chairman and two assistant secretaries. Under this board was to be an executive committee of three Foreign Service officers: one to serve as committee chairman, one to represent the diplomatic branch, and one the consular branch.

When this plan was put into effect, the under secretary, a former member of the old Diplomatic Service, was appointed chairman of the personnel board. The other two members were the senior assistant secretary, also a former member of the old Diplomatic Service, and Mr. Carr, a member of the Civil Service, who became an assistant secretary on July 1, 1924, in accordance with the provisions of the Rogers Act.

Charles C. Eberhardt, the grand old man of the Consular Service, was appointed chairman of the executive committee. The other two members were Hugh Wilson and Edward J. Norton. The former had been a member of the old Diplomatic Service and was to be consulted about diplomatic appointments and promotions and other matters affecting the interests of the diplomatic branch. Norton, a former member of the old Consular Service, was to represent the interests of the consular branch.

This form of organization helped maintain the separate identities of the two formerly separate services. The 121 former members of the Diplomatic Service would continue to compete with one another for assignments to diplomatic positions and for promotions and need not compete with the members of the consular branch. Similarly, the officers in the consular branch would continue to compete with one another for consular assignments and promotions. Interchangeability would thus be held to a minimum. In an exceptional case, if a consular officer with the appropriate background demonstrated ability that would make him a useful member of the diplomatic branch, he might be given a diplomatic position and even become a member of that branch. Similarly, a diplomatic officer found unsuitable for diplomatic work could be transferred to the consular branch. During the two and a half years following the creation of the Foreign Service, fewer than a dozen consular officers were assigned to diplomatic positions, and fewer than six diplomatic officers were transferred to consular posts. Several diplomatic officers did resign, however, when it was suggested to them that their talents might best be used in a consular assignment.

One of the first problems the Foreign Service Personnel Board had to face was how to determine the branch to which new Foreign Service officers—those entering the service after July 1, 1924—should be assigned. They had taken the new examinations prescribed for Foreign Service candidates and were entering as members of the Foreign Service Officer Corps, not as diplomatic or consular officers. After much debate it was decided that all of them should be commissioned vice consuls and brought initially into the consular branch. If, after one or two tours of service, an officer should be found to have qualifications for work in the diplomatic branch, he could then be given a commission as a diplomatic secretary and assigned to a diplomatic position.

The young officers who entered the Foreign Service following the merger of the two former services did not go into the field innocent of the ways of the department and of the service as I had. Instead of being sent abroad after a couple of weeks of orientation in the department, they were given several months of concentrated training in the newly established Foreign Service School. The experiment was also tried of immediately detailing some of them as vice consuls at posts not too distant from Washington to give them several months of field experience before bringing them back to the department for formal training.

During their months of formal training these neophytes were given the opportunity of coming into contact with officers in the department "who knew their way around." Among the bits of knowledge that they had picked up from these "sophisticates" was that the diplomatic career ladder was shorter and less arduous than the consular. It was not surprising, therefore, that most of them left for their first consular assignment in the hope that if they served this apprenticeship period satisfactorily they would be tapped by the diplomatic branch.

The morale of many consular officers had begun to sag by the latter part of 1926, particularly the morale of those on duty in the department who could observe developments firsthand. They felt that the Rogers Act was being implemented in a way that tended to lower the prestige of the consular branch. In the past they had been proud of their connection with a service possessing long and honorable traditions, with its members universally respected both at home and abroad. It seemed to them that the Consular Service was now being reduced to a second-rate branch of the newly established Foreign Service, and as such was likely to become a dumping ground for unwanted members of the diplomatic branch. The fear was growing that in the future the more promising young officers, following their period of vice-consular apprenticeship, would invariably be selected for the diplomatic branch and that those not so selected would be left with a feeling of inferiority. Furthermore, study of the promotion lists that had appeared following the passage of the Rogers Act revealed that members of the diplomatic branch were being promoted much more rapidly than consular officers.

In the latter part of 1926 and the early part of 1927, a number of unhappy consular officers expressed their concern to the congressmen who had supported the Rogers bill. Some of the congressmen thus approached became disturbed and began agitating for a congressional investigation. On February 16, 1927, the House of Representatives passed a resolution calling upon the State Department to furnish certain information regarding the manner in which the Rogers Act was being carried out. Secretary Kellogg had been so deeply immersed in substantive matters that he had not been concerning himself with career personnel problems. When the rumblings of congressional dissatisfaction reached him he undertook a personal investigation of the situation. He was unhappy at what he found and immediately began to take steps to make changes in the Foreign Service personnel structure and procedures. The two-branch structure was junked and the promotion system revamped.

Foundations were laid for a uniform Foreign Service, the officers of which could be assigned to diplomatic or consular positions as the exigencies of the service might require. There was no longer to be one set of officers wearing a diplomatic label and another a consular. The artificial barriers that had been erected between diplomatic officers and consular officers were gradually to disappear.

While Kellogg was supervising the revamping of the structure of the Foreign Service, he was also shuffling some of the top diplomatic assignments. The under secretary was appointed ambassador to Turkey and the other two assistant secretaries, who had been struggling to protect what they regarded as the integrity of the Diplomatic Service, were named ministers to attractive posts in Europe. Their departure placed Carr, the assistant secretary who had been an advocate of a unified service, in a more advantageous position to carry out what Kellogg considered to have been the intent of Congress in passing the Rogers bill.

The elimination of the two-branch approach to the problems of a single Foreign Service was a blow to the morale of the former Diplomatic Service. Its senior members were unhappy at the loss of identity of a service of which they had been proud; its junior members could foresee that the tone of a single, branchless Foreign Service would be quite different from that of the service they had entered, that competition for diplomatic positions would be more intense, and that promotions would come much more slowly. Some members of the former Consular Service, who had been proud of that historic service, also regretted the complete merging of the services.

For a number of years there was a lack of harmony in the Foreign Service. Fortunately, as the years went by, these divisive loyalties gradually disappeared and Foreign Service officers began to judge one another on the basis of character, personality, and accomplishment, rather than on the service from which they had come.

CHAPTER 14

FOREIGN POLICIES OF THE UNITED STATES AND POLITICAL ACTIVITIES OF THE DEPARTMENT OF STATE IN THE MID-1920S

THE FOREIGN POLICIES of the U.S. government seemed to me to be a reflection of its internal policies. Our general policies might best be epitomized by the words "minimum of involvement at home and abroad." Internally, the government was following a policy of restraint in concerning itself with what it regarded as local affairs. In the field of foreign affairs it was moving with caution lest it become enmeshed in some of the intrigues in which it believed various European nations to be engaging.

In his State of the Union message, delivered on December 8, 1925, President Coolidge set forth his philosophy, which was widely shared at the time. With regard to internal policies he said:

> The age of perfection is still in the somewhat distant future, but it is more in danger of being retarded by mistaken government activity than it is from lack of legislation. We are by far the most likely to accomplish permanent good if we proceed with moderation.
>
> In our country the people are sovereign and independent, and must accept the resulting responsibilities. It is their duty to support themselves and support the government. That is the business of the nation, whatever the charity of the nation may require. The functions which the Congress are to discharge are not those of local government but of national government. The greatest solicitude should be exercised to prevent any encroachment upon the rights of the states or their various

political subdivisions. Local self-government is one of our most precious possessions. It is the greatest contributing factor to the stability, strength, liberty, and progress of the nation. It ought not to be infringed by assault or undermined by purchase. It ought not to abdicate its power through weakness or resign its authority through favor. It does not at all follow that because abuses exist it is the concern of the federal government to attempt their reform.

Society is in much more danger from encumbering the national government beyond its wisdom to comprehend, or its ability to administer, than from leaving the local communities to bear their own burdens and remedy their own evils. Our local habit and custom is so strong, our variety of race and creed is so great, the federal authority is so tenuous, that the area within which it can function successfully is very limited. The wiser policy is to leave the localities, so far as we can, possessed of their own sources of revenue and charged with their own obligations.

Carried over into the international field, this philosophy found its expression in the determination of the Coolidge administration, overwhelmingly supported by Congress, to limit its participation in European affairs primarily to encouraging the nations of Western and Central Europe to solve their problems among themselves. The United States, if asked, might give a word of advice, but it was not prepared to become a participant in the various disputes that were taking place in Europe.

In the State of the Union message from which I have just quoted, the president in discussing our foreign relations said:

The Locarno agreements were made by the European countries directly interested without any formal intervention of America, although on July 3 I publicly advocated such agreements in an address made in Massachusetts. We have consistently refrained from interfering except when our help has been sought and we have felt it could be effectively given, as in the settlement of reparations and the London conference. These recent Locarno agreements represent the success of this policy which we have been insisting ought to be adopted of having European countries settle their own political problems without involving this country. This beginning seems to demonstrate that this policy is sound.

Some of the members of the department who were working closely with Secretary of State Hughes expressed privately the opinion that he felt frustrated at times at our policy of noninvolvement in Europe. He was by nature an activist. Possessed of a tremendous amount of intellectual vigor and deeply interested in international developments, he was not the sort of person who relished standing on the sidelines awaiting a request for advice. There was a belief among some of my colleagues that he would have liked to try to find a way whereby the United States could cooperate more closely with the League of Nations instead of boycotting it. Whether there were any factual grounds for this belief, I did not know.

The secretary, with his judicial background and his dedication to law and order, understandably turned his energies to promoting the concept of world peace through law. He devoted himself to the cause of disarmament and arms control and to the problem of strengthening the tribunals, such as the Permanent Court of International Justice (also known as the World Court), to which international disputes could be submitted. The secretary played a more active role in Latin America. He did not hesitate to give advice—even when unsolicited—to the nations of the western hemisphere, nor did he hesitate to bring pressure on them to submit their differences to mediation or arbitration. During the period of my first assignment to the State Department, the United States was playing in Latin America the role of a friendly neighbor endeavoring to promote harmony and law and order throughout the neighborhood. The role, although friendly, was not lacking in an element of firmness that manifested itself in an insistence that the countries in this hemisphere conduct themselves in accordance with what was generally considered at the time to be the precepts of international law.

It is understandable, in view of the atmosphere in which the Department of State was operating, that much of its energies during the years of my first assignment to it were devoted to participation in various conferences for the limitation and control of armaments, to endeavors to establish greater respect for the tenets of international law in the western hemisphere, to efforts to find a solution of such Latin American problems as the Tacna-Arica dispute, to negotiations with Mexico regarding our claims arising from the confiscation of United States–owned property in that country, to search for ways that would enable the United States to participate in the World Court, and to the promotion and protection of U.S. foreign trade. Problems connected with the civil wars that were producing chaos in parts of China and threatening the lives and property of U.S. citizens in the Far East also added to the department's burdens.

Much of the time of members of the State Department and of our diplomatic and consular establishments abroad was taken up by observing and reporting on trends, events, and developments that might have international repercussions. The department was eager to know what was taking place in all parts of the world even though the United States was unable to participate in some of the arenas in which important international decisions were being made. It was in such a setting that the Division of Eastern European Affairs was working to carry out the functions assigned to it.

CHAPTER 15

THE RESPONSIBILITIES, PROBLEMS, AND ACTIVITIES OF THE DIVISION OF EASTERN EUROPEAN AFFAIRS

ACCORDING TO THE REGISTER of the State Department, the Division of Eastern European Affairs was charged with "General supervision, under the secretaries, of matters pertaining to Russia (including Siberia) and of relations, diplomatic and consular, political and economic, with Esthonia, Finland, Latvia, Lithuania, and Poland."*

As I began to read the communications coming in and going out of the division, I realized that until I had deepened my knowledge of the U.S. policies with regard to Eastern Europe, the considerations on which those policies were based, the historical and current internal and international problems of the countries in the area, and the procedures of the State Department, my contributions to the general supervision of matters pertaining to the area would be feeble. After discussing my concern in this respect with Kelley, I set out systematically to study the files of the department and to read such books and other publications relating to the area as he recommended to me. I studied the histories of the countries and peoples of Eastern Europe and tried to gain an understanding of the attitude of the United States toward them and their problems. For in-

---

* "Poland" was interpreted as including Danzig [Gdańsk] and the Danzig corridor.

stance, I read and reread the files relating to the Polish Corridor and Poland's relations with the Soviet Union, Germany, and Lithuania. I also acquainted myself with the struggle of the Finnish people for their independence. The subjects that I found most intriguing were our policies with regard to the Soviet Union, in particular the basis for our policy of nonrecognition of the Soviet regime and our policies relating to the recognition of the independence of the three Baltic states.

The Policies of the United States with Respect to the Soviet Union During the Early and Mid–1920s

A study of the "Russian Policy Book," a binder maintained in the division that contained copies of the basic policy decisions, pronouncements, and other documents of a significant character relating to Soviet Russia, made it clear to me that the policies of the Harding-Coolidge administration with regard to Russia were really quite similar to those of the Wilson administration. President Wilson's strong belief in the principles of self-determination had led him to emphasize that the Soviet regime had seized power through trickery and was ruling without the consent and against the wishes of the Russian people. Secretary Hughes, perhaps because of his interest in strengthening international law, tended to stress that the Soviet Union by its systematic interference in the internal affairs of the United States, by its refusal to recognize the obligations to the United States of the former Russian governments, and by its confiscation without compensation of the property of U.S. citizens, was not acting in accord with accepted principles governing international intercourse. He did not believe that any useful purpose could be served by maintaining diplomatic relations with such a regime.

The U.S. government took the position that it could not recognize or negotiate with the Soviet regime until the latter had complied with three demands: First, that it stop trying to bring about the overthrow of American institutions, including the U.S. government, through propaganda and instigations to revolution. The United States would not have relations with a regime that was systematically interfering in its internal affairs. Second, that it restore the confiscated property of U.S. citizens or make effective compensation for losses resulting from the confiscation. Third, that it repeal its decrees repudiating Russia's obligations to the United States (that is, debts contracted by former Russian governments).

The Soviet Union took the following positions: First, that it was not engaging in efforts to overthrow American institutions, including the U.S. government, that the U.S. government was apparently confusing the activities of the Communist International with those of the Soviet government and was failing to realize that the Soviet government and the Communist International were distinct entities, and that the Soviet government on the basis of reciprocity was quite willing to undertake not to interfere in the internal affairs of the United States but it would make no commitments on behalf of the Communist International.

Second, the Soviet Union stated that it was prepared to negotiate on the basis of reciprocity a settlement of the claims of the U.S. government and of U.S. citizens and that the negotiations should include consideration of its own claims against the United States arising from damages inflicted on Soviet property and on the persons of Soviet citizens by American armed forces in northern Russia and Siberia.

Third, the Soviet Union said it was ready to do all that was consonant with its own dignity and interest to bring about the desired end of a renewal of friendship with the United States.

The counterposition of the U.S. government was: First, that it had ample evidence that the Soviet regime was systematically interfering in the internal affairs of the United States and was endeavoring to stir up revolution-minded groups in the United States to bring about the overthrow of U.S. institutions and the U.S. government and that the U.S. government was not at all confused regarding the relationship between the so-called Soviet government and the Communist International. U.S. officials believed that the real rulers of Soviet Russia were a small group of leaders of the Communist Party and that these rulers were employing various instruments in carrying out their program of world revolution. Among these were the so-called Soviet government, the Communist International, and the Red International of Labor Unions (Profintern). There were also other instruments. The leaders of the Communist Party of Soviet Russia through interlocking directorates controlled all of these instruments. They—not the so-called Soviet government—governed Russia and were completely responsible for the interference in the internal affairs of the United States by the Communist International as well as for the activities of the so-called Soviet government.

Second, U.S. leaders said that such claims as the Soviet regime might present to the U.S. government for damages accruing from U.S. occupation of areas in northern Russia and Siberia should not be connected with consideration of the claims of the U.S. government and citizens arising out of Soviet acts of confiscation and repudiation.

Finally, the United States could see no reason, so long as the Soviet regime maintained its present position, for negotiations. If the Soviet authorities were sincerely ready to restore the confiscated property of U.S. citizens or to make effective compensation, they could do so without negotiations. If they were ready to repeal their decrees repudiating Russia's obligations to the United States and to recognize such obligations, they could do so. If they were prepared to cease their continued propaganda and their attempts to effect the overthrow of the institutions of the United States, they could say so and do so. The U.S. government could not enter into negotiations until activities of this kind directed from Moscow were abandoned.

Since the Soviet regime was unwilling to meet the conditions for negotiations laid down by the United States, a deadlock ensued.

Unable to budge Secretary Hughes by a frontal assault, the Soviets resorted to an indirect approach in their efforts to obtain recognition from the United States. They held out before the American business community the possibility of an enormous amount of Soviet-American trade. They found a powerful ally in the person of Senator William E. Borah, the chairman of the Senate Foreign Relations Committee.

As early as the spring of 1923 Senator Borah had attacked the State Department because of the failure of the United States to recognize the Soviet government and to establish relations with it. His criticisms were directed against the department, not the president or Secretary Hughes. I had not been in the service long before I learned that when a member of Congress who belongs to the party in power criticizes our current foreign policies, he rarely attacks the president. Occasionally he may criticize the secretary of state but usually his target is the State Department, or the "underlings" or "career boys" in the department.

The senator insisted that the United States should recognize a regime that during its five-year existence had managed to gain control over most of the country. In May 1923 he introduced a resolution: "Resolved, that the Senate of the United States favor the recognition of the present Soviet Government of Russia." That resolution was not acted upon. The following December, however, he reintroduced it. The senator's position was that the Soviet government and the Communist International were separate and distinct organizations, that the Soviet Government itself was not engaging in subversive activities in the United States, and that it should not be held responsible for the actions of the Communist International. He also intimated that the increase in trade with Soviet Russia, which could follow the establishment of normal relations, would be advantageous to American business. Hearings on the resolution were scheduled for January 1924.

Secretary Hughes was quite prepared to meet this challenge. He sent Young and Kelley to lay before the Senate Foreign Relations Committee some of the information the department had collected regarding the ties between the Soviet government and the Communist International

and the extent to which the Soviet government could be depended upon
to abide by any commitments it might make to cease interfering in our
internal affairs. I do not see how anyone who studies the hearings can fail
to admire Kelley's pluck and ability when, as a junior officer in the
department, he appeared before one of the great orators and debaters of
our time. The pontifical senator, backed up by a flock of research assistants, was apparently expecting to make mincemeat of the State Department witnesses. Kelley played the role of David before Goliath. He
stood his ground and carried out, with deference to the senator, his
mission of presenting the views of the department and the information
upon which they were based. He did not hesitate to correct some of the
misapprehensions of the senator, who considered himself an expert on
matters pertaining to diplomatic intercourse. When, for instance, the
senator inquired whether or not any country that had recognized the
Soviet government had withdrawn recognition because of Soviet failure
to live up to its commitments to discontinue interference in the country's
internal affairs, Kelley pointed out to the senator that recognition, once
granted, could not be withdrawn. The senator, nettled at such an answer
from a junior officer of the State Department, indicated that in referring to
the withdrawal of recognition he had in mind the severance of diplomatic
relations. Was not the severance of diplomatic relations really the same
thing as the withdrawal of recognition? To the senator's discomfort,
Kelley explained why they were not the same. Borah apparently had not
realized that the granting of recognition to a government gave it a status in
international law and in domestic courts that could not be taken away by
the severance of relations.

The evidence submitted and interpreted by Kelley before the Senate
was so overwhelming that not only Senator Borah but many of the
Americans who were sympathetic to the Soviet experiment and who had
been criticizing our policies toward Soviet Russia found it difficult to deny
the existence of organic ties between the so-called Soviet government and
the Communist International.

In answer to the argument that the establishment of normal relations with the Soviet government might result in the strengthening of
Soviet-American trade to the advantage of the U.S. economy, Hughes
took the position that the principles on which the United States based its
international intercourse were not for sale. He also continued to stress
that without the assistance of long-term credits, Soviet Russia would not
be able to make the heavy purchases in the United States that many
American businesses seemed to envisage. He pointed out that, in view of
the Soviet refusal to recognize its international obligations and its failure
to compensate for property that it had confiscated, it had lost its credit

standing, and the mere granting of recognition would not itself result in the extension of the needed long-term credits. He emphasized that U.S. nationals or firms were free to engage in trade with Soviet Russia or to work within that country but should understand that they were acting at their own risk. They might well learn from actual experience the difficulties involved in dealing with the regime in control in Russia.

The U.S. government made it clear, however, that it was not prepared to permit U.S. nationals or firms to learn from actual experience the risks involved in advancing long-term credits or in extending loans to the Soviet Union. This policy was clearly set forth in a letter drafted by Mr. Kelley after consultation with the president and the secretaries of state, treasury, and commerce. The letter, signed by Under Secretary Olds on November 28, 1927, read in part as follows:

> It is hardly necessary, I believe, for me to say that the Department is fully aware of the potentialities of Russia as a market for American products and of the interest of American manufacturers in establishing connections with that country, even under the present regime. Accordingly, while the Government of the United States has not granted recognition to the regime now functioning in Russia, no restrictions were imposed upon the carrying on of trade and commerce with that country or with the Soviet regime, and no objections had been raised to the financing of ordinary current commercial intercourse; it being understood of course, that individuals and corporations availing themselves of the opportunity to engage in such trade do so upon their own responsibility and at their own risk. The Department has objected, however, to financial projects involving the flotation of loans in the American market, and to banking arrangements not incidental to the sale of American commodities to Russia, that have amounted to proposals for making advances to the Soviet regime which, as you know, had repudiated the obligations of Russia to the United States and its citizens, and confiscated the property of American citizens in Russia.

Since the Soviet Union had little to export, American-Soviet trade in the absence of loans or long-term credits continued to remain relatively insignificant. Both the United States and the Soviet Union continued to adhere to their respective positions for many years. It was not until 1933 that the deadlock was broken when, at the invitation of President Roosevelt, Litvinov came to the United States to negotiate conditions for the establishment of relations between the two countries.

It became apparent to me during my studies that our policies toward the Soviet Union were not based on feelings of antagonism toward Russia and the Russian people. There were strong sentiments in the United

States, particularly among our foreign-policy makers, favoring the maintenance of a strong Russia. It seemed to me that Secretary Hughes himself had a sort of sentimental attachment to Russia as a country and to the Russian people. Like President Wilson and many other Americans, he looked upon Russia as an ally, which, while weakened by war, had fallen victim to a gang of well-organized, cruel conspirators. Although Hughes was unprepared to recognize the regime set up by these conspirators as the government of Russia, he agreed with President Wilson that out of loyalty to our former ally we should try to prevent Russia from being broken up while in its weakened condition. Just as for many years we had espoused the cause of an integral China, so we were now pursuing that of an integral Russia. Our devotion to the cause of maintaining a Great Russia had been so intense that we had opposed most projects that might have led to Russian fragmentation. Although we had committed ourselves to an independent Poland, we had pressed Poland in 1920, after it had defeated the Red Army, to show restraint in extending its boundaries to the east. Although we had granted de facto recognition to the Republic of Armenia, we had taken no action when the short life of that little republic had been snuffed out by the Red Army. For the same reason, one of the chief purposes of our expedition to Siberia following the First World War had been to prevent Japan from taking advantage of Russia's weakness to annex portions of Siberia.

Another manifestation of this attitude was our reluctance to recognize the independence of the Baltic states. Our recognition was accorded nearly two years after they had been recognized by other great Western powers and had become members in good standing of the League of Nations.

The Problem of Extending Recognition to the Three Baltic States of Estonia, Latvia, and Lithuania

For more than fifteen years following my entry into the Division of Eastern European Affairs of the Department of State, I was engaged in work that brought me into close contact with the Baltic countries of Estonia, Latvia, and Lithuania. In connection with my efforts to become acquainted with our past and present policies with regard to the countries with which the division was concerned, I spent many hours poring over old documents in the files of the department in order to ascertain just what our attitude had been toward the Baltic states from the time of their proclamations of independence to the date of our extension of recognition to them as independent countries.

My studies convinced me that we had little interest in the Baltic states during the months immediately following the announcement of their independence. While we seemed to be pleased that some of the armed forces of these so-called states were assisting in holding back or driving out the Bolsheviks, we nevertheless tended to regard the Baltic area as a part of the Russian empire and were looking forward to the time when it would be included in a great democratic Russia. Our early military observers in the area were not, in general, sympathetic with the national aspirations of the Baltic peoples. They, like President Wilson and his international advisers, thought it would be a mistake to adopt an attitude that might encourage other submerged peoples in Russia to demand independence.

I found it interesting that Wilson's doctrine of self-determination was apparently being reserved for peoples who had been under the domination of our defeated enemies. Although the ethnic, cultural, social, and religious differences among the peoples who had been bound together in the old Russian empire were in some instances more pronounced than those that had existed among the peoples who had composed the former Austrian empire, this doctrine was not being applied to the former.

Some of the members of the department who assisted in the formulation of our policies with regard to Russia during the last years of the Wilson administration and the early years of the Harding-Coolidge administration had served in St. Petersburg [Leningrad] or Moscow during the First World War when Russia was our ally. In Russia they had met many attractive, sensitive, and friendly Russians. They had studied Russian, attended theaters, opera, and ballet, and read the great Russian classics. They had been charmed by the exotic and beautiful culture of this ancient country. There was something impressive, romantic, and even nostalgic about the grandeur of the old Russian empire with its majestic sweep of steppes, forests, tundras, deserts, and mountains, its great winding rivers, its teeming cities, and its many thousands of picturesque villages built around quaint and colorful churches and connected with one another during the long winters by snow-covered roads enlivened by jingling troikas and slow-moving sledges. It was only natural that members of the State Department whose interests had been centered on Russia should have been influenced, to an extent at least, by their experiences and associations in that country, that they should have tended to look at Eastern Europe from the point of view of St. Petersburg or Moscow, and that they should have little sympathy for the nationalistic aspirations of comparatively small ethnic groups who seemed to prefer devoting their energies to the setting up of their own governments to attempting to restore this imagination-capturing empire on a more democratic basis.

In Moscow and St. Petersburg these Americans had undoubtedly met people from the Baltic states—mostly German Balts or Polish aristocrats who moved in the social circles of those cities. The German Balts were accustomed to ridicule the idea of an independent Latvia or Estonia, and the Poles were certainly not enthusiastic about the establishment of an independent Lithuania. Furthermore, the Russians who had managed to migrate from Russia were inclined to be bitterly critical of the Estonians, Latvians, and Lithuanians for deserting Mother Russia in its hour of weakness.

In view of the strong pro-Great Russia atmosphere that prevailed in the White House and the State Department, suggestions from members of the department or from our missions abroad that we give consideration to the recognition of the independence of the Baltic states were slow in coming.

From a study of the files of the department I learned that one of the first officials of our government who had ventured to suggest that the United States recognize the independence of the Baltic states was Evan E. Young, who at the time was our commissioner to those states. On January 31, 1921, he repeated his suggestion of six months previous and presented in considerable detail the reasoning on which it was based. In his memorandum he pointed out that:

> In each of the three so-called states the governments now in power represent the great majority of the people. Elections have been held openly and have been carried out in a manner which has assured to the electorate a free and unrestriced voice at the polls. The authorities now in office unquestionably govern by and with the consent of the people, and in connection therewith it is both important and interesting to note that unmistakable evidences toward conservatism are apparent among the people and also on the part of the government in their conduct of affairs.

He then almost apologetically suggested that *de jure* recognition be extended to these countries:

> If I may venture a suggestion as to what form our policy should take, if any change in our policy is or may be contemplated, it would be that we extend without further delay *de jure* recognition to Esthonia, Latvia, and Lithuania, coupled with a frank statement that we leave to the future the determination of the relationship which shall exist between the so-called Baltic States and a new, orderly and stable Russia . . .
> I feel quite confident of my statement that the world at large little

appreciates the real danger and menace of Bolshevism and Communism as exemplified in Soviet Russia to our civilization. In extending *de jure* recognition to these states we are assisting to some extent at least those governments which are as bitterly opposed to Bolshevism and to Communism as is our own. The question as to whether the Bolsheviks will be successful in bringing about a world revolution and with it the destruction of everything for which civilization stands today is to my mind of more pressing importance than the question as to the relationship which shall in the future exist between the Baltic provinces and the new Russia.

Judging from what I found in the files, Young's dispatch gave rise to considerable discussion in the department. The "old Russian hands"—none of whom had ever, so far as I am aware, visited the Baltic states—were unanimously opposed to recognition. Apparently no one in the department was prepared at that time to support Young's suggestion.

Norman H. Davis, a financier who recently resigned from a high State Department post, presented a memorandum dated March 23, 1921, which read in part as follows:

Any good will that might be obtained from the inhabitants of these Baltic States would not by any means compensate for the loss of good will on the part of the Russian people as a whole, which would undoubtedly happen if we in any way encourage the dismemberment of Russia. There is really no well-founded national movement for independence on the part of the inhabitants of these districts. They declared their independence because they were hostile to the Soviet Government, and they have been able to maintain their apparent independent existence because the Bolsheviks have been willing to have them do so and thus act as buffers or agents for the Bolshevist Government, and these states could not maintain their independence against the will of Russia unless supported by the principal powers. By extending recognition we would assume a moral responsibility for their protection and would merely play into the hands of England and other countries who are in favor of dismemberment.

One of the proponents of a Great Russia, who had resided in St. Petersburg during the war and who at the time was on detail in the Office of the Trade Adviser, wrote a memorandum dated April 2, 1921, which contained the following:

The formation of the independent Baltic States is a direct consequence of the Bolshevist regime in Russia, and not due to legitimate national aspirations of the people of these territories...

The Baltic States are a part of Russia's entity, and are natural economic outlets. International European Acts created these states...

America is interested in the restoration of a strong and unified Russia...

Our selfish commercial interests are not in any wise concerned with commerce in the Baltics. Recognition thereof would interpose a difficult obstacle between our direct trade with Russia...

The policy of safeguarding Russian patrimony is but a deed of justice toward a people whose sufferings are the result of strain and sacrifice given to the common cause in the first years of the war. No other course could be justified toward an ally. However, through this policy the United States has advanced a new principle of international law of the greatest importance—the necessity for a community of nations to protect the patrimony of a nation temporarily disabled...

America has nothing to fear but all to gain politically from a strong and reunited Russia. The countries have no ax to grind. On the contrary, their interests are closely akin, both in so far as European peace is aspired to and stability in the Far East is concerned. A sick and dismembered Russia means Balkanization of Europe, anarchy in Asia and perpetuation of contest and disturbance throughout the world...

As a result of the Allied victory, German imperialism has been destroyed and the whole country brought to a condition of infinite weakness and disability. There is all reason to believe that if surrounded by proper political environment the people of Germany will embark into an era of peaceful and productive development. Germany, however, might return to the old paths if an opportunity presented itself. The key lies in Russia... German domination of Russia is possible only if indiscriminate policies of western Europe will thrust the great Slav nation into German hands against the will of the Russians.

The debate within the U.S. government continued through the year and into the spring of 1922. Young, who remained convinced that our policy with regard to the Baltic states should be subject to review, sent a second dispatch dated April 6, 1922, to the State Department urging recognition. After advancing various arguments in favor of recognition he endeavored to disarm those in the department who he knew would balk at the thought of a dismemberment of Russia by closing his dispatch as follows:

It is idle at this time to discuss the question as to whether the Letts, the Esthonians, and the Lithuanians were morally justified in proclaiming their independence in the hour of Russia's weakness. The simple fact is that these nationalities, though unquestionably animated by nationalistic aspirations, preferred the creation and establishment of what may be termed modern civilized governments to their existence either as a part of Soviet Russia under a communistic regime or with the status of autonomous soviet republics. Whatever their future may be, it is certain that their action in proclaiming their independence has resulted in the maintenance of at least this part of the former Russian Empire free from the ravages and destruction of communism and bolshevism. . .

It is entirely possible, or even probable, that some time in the indefinite future these so-called States may once again become an integral part of Russia. It seems most probable, however, that until that time comes they will be able to maintain their political stability, and with that their independence. Further, it seems most probable that for much time to come these nationalities will exercise a predominating influence on this fringe of territory. Admitting that, from our viewpoint, a strong Russia is greatly to be desired, it is still difficult for an observer here to suggest any course of action other than the immediate recognition of these States. Personally, I am not of the opinion that the recognition which has been accorded to these States by the European powers tends in any way to retard the restoration of a strong and stable Russian Government. Rather does it seem that through a certain measure of encouragement to the so-called States one may make certain that this part of Russia will remain free from the ravages of the present Moscow regime. Later, it is not improbable that through the operation of fundamental economic laws these countries will become a part of a federated Russia or will retain autonomous powers, but will be linked with the Russian Government through close economic and political treaties and agreements. While our policy has been consistent, I am not at all certain that a continuaton of this policy in the future would be either wise from the viewpoint of our own interests or helpful as regards the restoration of Russia.

Young's second plea for recognition of the Baltic states fell on more fertile soil. By the spring of 1922 the prospects of the restoration of a stable Russia with which the United States could have mutually beneficial relations had grown dim. The three Baltic states had demonstrated an ability to survive that was beginning to elicit respect even from the "old Russian hands." On May 1, 1922, Under Secretary Phillips sent the following note to Secretary Hughes:

Here is a report of considerable interest from the Commissioner at Riga. He reaches the conclusion that recognition *de jure* of Esthonia and Latvia would be wise, and also the recognition *de jure* of Lithuania as soon as its frontiers are definitely delimited. I share his conclusions and think that we ought to give recognition as soon as the situation in Genoa will permit.

Four months later, on July 24, 1922, the secretary sent a letter that had been drafted by DeWitt C. Poole, chief of the Russian Division, to the

White House seeking the president's approval of the recognition of the three Baltic republics. It read in part:

> I believe the time has now come to grant recognition to the so-called Baltic States—Esthonia, Latvia, and Lithuania.
>
> The Esthonian, Latvian, and Lithuanian Governments have been in continuous existence since 1919 and have brought about stable economic and political conditions within their respective jurisdictions. We have maintained informal intercourse with these governments for two years or more, an American Commissioner being stationed at Riga and American consuls at Riga, Reval and Kovno, while unofficial representatives of the Baltic Governments have been received informally in this country.
>
> These governments have been recognized by all the important governments of the world except the United States.
>
> Recognition by the United States has been delayed by considerations connected with the whole Russian problem, especially the need which existed at one time for combating a tendency on the part of certain European governments to encourage a breakup of the Russian state; it was felt that the interest of the United States required for the future a strong and united as well as democratic Russia. Now, however, the Russian situation has so developed and the policy of the United States has won such wide approval that we can, I believe, deal with the Baltic question on its own merits, extend recognition to the Baltic Governments and have this action accord with our general Russian policy.
>
> I propose making the following announcement, if you approve:
>
> The Government of the United States recognizes the Governments of Esthonia, Latvia and Lithuania . . .

Attached to the draft announcement sent to the White House was the following explanatory statement to be published with it:

> The Governments of Esthonia, Latvia and Lithuania have been recognized either *de jure* or *de facto* by the principal Governments of Europe and have entered into treaty relations with their neighbors.
>
> In extending to them recognition on its part, the Government of the United States takes cognizance of the actual existence of these Governments during a considerable period of time and of the successful maintenance within their borders of political and economic stability.
>
> The United States has consistently maintained that the disturbed condition of Russian affairs may not be made the occasion for the alienation of Russian territory, and this principle is not deemed to be infringed by the recognition at this time of the Governments of Esthonia, Latvia and Lithuania which have been set up and maintained by an indigenous population.

The president, in his reply also dated July 24, agreed with these suggestions and on July 28, 1922, the United States extended full recognition to the Baltic states as independent countries and sent a telegram to the interested U.S. diplomatic missions and consular offices to that effect.

There was a striking contrast between our attitude in the early 1920s and that in the decades subsequent to the Second World War toward the admission of new members into the community of nations. We granted recognition to the Baltic states only after more than two years of hesitation and debate. Yet during the 1950s and 1960s we have been almost automatically recognizing as independent countries and as responsible members of the community of nations dozens of new states, without making any attempt to determine the degree of their viability, the wishes of their people, or the intention of their governments to adhere to the principles upon which orderly international intercourse is based.

During my years in the Foreign Service I found that the debates regarding the advisability of recognizing the Baltic states were typical of most discussions that take place in the State Department when a controversial foreign policy decision is under consideration. Both those favoring and those opposing such a decision usually advance principles of international intercourse favoring their respective points of view. When no recognized principle supporting the position can be found, neither side hesitates to formulate and cite new principles. The policymakers, therefore, frequently find it necessary to choose between principles in making their decisions.

Each side is also almost certain to put forward considerations of national interest or security in support of its position. Again the policymakers must determine which of these considerations are overriding. Furthermore, the two sides may disagree with regard to certain sets of facts that should not be ignored by the policymakers and the latter must decide which set to accept. During the discussions about the recognition of the Baltic states, for instance, Young stated that the peoples of those states were "unquestionably animated by nationalistic aspirations," whereas some of the members of the department argued that "there is no well-founded national movement for independence on the part of the inhabitants of these districts." The policymaker, therefore, should be a person of courage and experience with an understanding of international affairs.

Following the recognition of the Baltic states there was a gradual change in the division that was handling East European affairs. The name of the division was changed from Russian Affairs to that of Eastern European Affairs, and Poole, former U.S. consul in Moscow and a staunch advocate of an integral Great Russia, was replaced by Young, the former commissioner to the Baltic states. Young brought into the division Kelley, Packer, and me, all of whom, while deeply interested in Russia, Poland, and Finland, also had a knowledge based on personal experience of the people and problems of the Baltic states.

CHAPTER 16

APPRENTICESHIP IN THE DEPARTMENT OF STATE

IN VIEW OF THE WORLD SITUATION and the policies of Hughes and Kellogg, the Division of Eastern European Affairs could not be said to be working in the mainstream of the department's many activities. The Divisions of Latin American and Mexican Affairs were immersed in the problems of this hemisphere; the Division of Far Eastern Affairs likewise was busy with China and disarmament. The Western European Division bore the main burdens of such peace movements as disarmament, arms control, and the World Court.

Nevertheless, our division, although not facing so many active current problems as some of the others, did not find it easy with its limited staff to carry out its varied responsibilities. Some of the work of the division—for example, the conduct of relations with Poland (which at that time was handling the foreign affairs of the free city of Danzig), Finland, and the three Baltic states—did not place an inordinate burden on us. In support of the State Department's policy of promoting world peace, the division was involved in a constant exchange of notes with these countries regarding the problems of arms, the World Court, and so forth. It assisted in the negotiation of treaties of friendship, commerce, and consular rights and in a variety of agreements of a more technical character relating, for instance, to ships and shipping.

In the area of trade promotion the division effected exchanges of notes with the countries of Eastern Europe (other than Russia) accorded most-favored-nation treatment. In cooperation with offices in the Department of Commerce it kept in close touch with the trade promotion work of our consular offices in Eastern Europe that were keeping the U.S. government informed about trade barriers and opportunities and other matters relating to trade in which American business might be interested.

The president and Congress were particularly eager to reach agreements with other countries for the settlement of debts incurred during and immediately after the war. The Division of Eastern European Affairs, therefore, facilitated debt negotiations with the countries for which it had responsibility. Among the early debt-funding agreements to be signed were those with the free countries of our area.

Through our three legations in Eastern Europe—in Warsaw, Riga, and Helsinki—as well as our consular offices in Tallinn, Kaunas, and Danzig, we were kept fully informed of all internal and international developments in that area that might be of interest. Like our colleagues in the Division of Western European Affairs, we were usually prohibited from taking any action that might be construed as intervention in purely European affairs. Illustrative of our policy of noninvolvement was an exchange of telegrams in August and September of 1922 between the State Department and our chargé in Paris. Our chargé had asked what views he might express about the disposition of the Memel territory [Klaipėda] and about the Lithuanian interpretation of its obligations with regard to the internationalization of the Niemen River in case these matters should come up at one of the meetings of the Conference of Ambassadors. The department's reply, dated September 25, 1922, read in part as follows:

> It is felt that the subjects in question are primarily matters of European concern, in the settlement of which this Government is not necessarily called upon to participate. You should refrain from any expression of views and keep the Department fully informed regarding any discussions which might take place, reporting by cable in the event of decisions which might seem to be contrary to the interests of the United States.

Most of the time and energy of the Eastern European Affairs Division was devoted to matters relating to Russia. Trade between Russia and the United States was slowly increasing. Information poured into the State Department about developments within Russia and about other events involving Russia. There were numerous communications relating to Russia from other executive agencies of the government, from members of Congress, and from private U.S. citizens or firms. The division also assisted the legal adviser's office in its efforts to compile the numerous claims of U.S. nationals arising from Soviet acts of renunciation and confiscation and in its work of furnishing U.S. courts with information needed in connection with a variety of legal suits involving Russia. One of the division's most time-consuming activities was to observe developments in Soviet Russia's internal and foreign policies and practices that might justify a reconsideration of our policy of nonrecognition. If changes were taking place that could give ground for belief that the Soviet Union might be prepared to meet the conditions that our government had laid down as a prerequisite for recognition, it was important that the department should be the first to note them in order to move in the direction of recognition without having to be pushed in that direction by critics in Congress.

Many of the multilateral activities of other divisions were complicated by the absence of diplomatic relations between Russia and the United States. Young and his successor, Kelley, were frequently called upon for advice on how we might attain certain international objectives without taking action that might be construed as recognition of the Soviet government. Under what conditions, for instance, could representatives of the United States and the Soviet Union sign the same multilateral treaty without implying that we had accorded de facto or *de jure* recognition to the Soviet Union? During the early years the department was extremely conservative about matters of that kind. As late as 1925, for instance, the department found it necessary to object to the adherence of the Soviet government to the Spitsbergen treaty.* When it was clearly in the interest of the United States that we and the Soviet Union sign the same multilateral document, we followed the practice of insisting that a caveat be attached indicating that our act of signing did not constitute recognition. Eventually, however, the division, with the aid of the Office of the Legal Adviser, worked out a formula that eased our difficulties. That formula, in effect, was that no action by the United States should be construed as the recognition of a government that we had not as yet recognized unless the action had been taken with the explicit intent to accord recognition. That formula has subsequently proved useful in a number of comparable situations in which the Soviet Union was not involved.

When I began to draft replies to incoming letters, to prepare memo-

---

* The multilateral treaty of 1925 recognizing Norwegian sovereignty over Spitsbergen and neighboring islands. The United States later withdrew its objections and the Soviet Union adhered to it.

randa on various subjects, and eventually to draft instructions to the field and notes for transmission through our missions abroad to foreign offices or for delivery by the State Department to diplomatic missions in Washington, I ran into difficulty. The department had a style and terminology to which it required drafting officers strictly to adhere. It demanded clarity and precision of expression, except in those instances where clarity and precision were not desired, and the avoidance of sweeping unqualified statements or of statements that might cause embarrassment if quoted out of context. It insisted on the kind of phrasing that would be just as understandable a hundred years hence as it was on the day that it was written. The drafter of documents in the department was required to bear in mind that he was not writing for purposes of entertainment or of impressing the reader with his wit, erudition, or sophistication. It was the writer's task to state views or to record events and situations not only for the audience of the day but also for posterity. A little humor now and then was tolerated but unnecessary literary flourishes or attempts at what is currently called "creative writing" were frowned upon. Efforts to brighten documents by the turning of neat phrases or the introduction of picturesque language, "creative" though they might be, could be dangerous. They might tempt one unconsciously to sacrifice accuracy for the sake of being clever. One should use words and expressions the meaning of which has been firmly established and not experiment with innovations.

Although it was exceedingly difficult to satisfy the perfectionists in the department, I was encouraged after a number of months to find that my drafts were frequently going without too much mutilation through the mill that processed outgoing correspondence.

One of my early responsibilities in the division was to help in keeping the State Department informed of the activities of communist-controlled organizations in the United States and the extent to which they were directed, managed, and at times financed by the rulers of the Soviet Union. There was then no federal agency charged with observing the activities of subversive organizations in the United States. We obtained much of our information through the publications of such organizations as the Workers' Party, as the overt arm of the Communist International Party in the United States called itself; of united-front organizations in the United States such as the Trade Union Educational League; of the Communist International; and of the Red International of Trade Unions. The fact that Moscow was directing and assisting the communist movement in the United States was not difficult to prove, but we were also charged with ascertaining the degree of Moscow's control. We were assisted in our work by Robert Bannerman, who as the agent of the department was attached to the office of the under secretary as its chief investigator. Through his contacts with the state and municipal police he and his assistant were able to obtain certain information for us. The Army and Navy Intelligence were cooperative and helpful. Our diplomatic and consular officers throughout the world also sent in information about communist activities in the countries where they were stationed and about the relationship, if any, between these countries and Moscow. Our representatives in countries that had recognized the Soviet Union also kept us informed of the experiences of the diplomatic missions of those countries in Moscow and of the impressions that the members of these missions were obtaining of developments in the Soviet Union.

Our most important source of information was the U.S. legation in Riga. Even before our recognition of the Baltic states the department had established in its Riga office of the U.S. commissioner to the Baltic states a section charged with collecting information on Soviet Russia. That section was staffed with officers who had served in Russia, most of whom could speak and read Russian. Assisting them in research and translation work were a number of local employees. The legation, which succeeded the Office of the Commissioner, had been successful in acquiring for its library and for that of the Eastern European Division a mass of Soviet books, pamphlets, newspapers, and other periodicals that was almost without parallel outside the Soviet Union. Both libraries, for instance, had complete sets of Soviet laws and decrees as well as numerous legal treaties, most issues of *Izvestiia* and *Pravda* dating back to the early days of the Bolshevik revolution, and files of other newspapers published in Moscow, Leningrad, and the capitals of many of the constituent republics of the Soviet Union. The legation at Riga was attempting to acquire by direct purchase from Mezhdunarodnaya Kniga (International Book), a state company set up in the Commissariat for Foreign Trade for exporting Soviet publications, additional material that might shed light on all phases of Soviet activities and life. During the mid-1920s, for instance, the legation subscribed to more than 50 different newspapers and other periodicals. Among publications on the shelves of the libraries in the legation and in the Eastern European Division were books, brochures, and sets of periodicals relating to the programs, decisions, and proceedings of the organs of the Communist International and its affiliated organizations. Of special interest were the detailed instructions from the headquarters in Moscow of these international organizations to the communist parties and communist-manipulated organizations in other countries.

The Soviet newspapers and periodicals usually arrived in Riga by train within 36 hours after their publication in Moscow, although at times there were unexplained delays. The legation telegraphed summaries of or excerpts from articles that it thought should be brought to the immediate attention of the State Department. Details and less urgent information were sent by diplomatic pouch. During the mid-1920s the legation did not have a large enough staff to make many analytical studies of developments in the Soviet Union. From time to time, nevertheless, it prepared memoranda, some of which were quite exhaustive.

Soviet publications were not the legation's sole source of information. To Riga from Moscow and elsewhere in the Soviet Union came diplomats of friendly countries, newspaper reporters, businessmen, and technicians for a breath of fresh air. These visitors usually had no hesitation in discussing privately with members of the legation their experiences in the Soviet Union and in giving their views on the developments and trends in that country. Officials in the foreign offices of the Baltic states and Baltic diplomats on leave from duty in Moscow seemed to be particularly well informed with regard to the Soviet Union. In general, the governments of these three countries were trying to maintain good relations with the Soviet government, and their officials, while at times critical of Soviet practices, were inclined to lean backward in their endeavors to understand and rationalize Soviet actions that seemed shocking to many observers from Western Europe.

Since in those days the United States had no intelligence service other than that of the armed forces, the legation also arranged to obtain information from the secret services of several friendly countries. Some of the information thus acquired was useful; some of it, however, was not considered sufficiently trustworthy by the Eastern European Division to justify its use as a basis for the formulation of policy or for the taking of action.

In view of the limited space allotted them by the Soviet government for living and working quarters, the lack of other facilities, and the manner in which they were spied upon and quarantined, the diplomatic missions in Moscow found it almost impossible to prepare reports of the kind the department was receiving from Riga.

The mass of information on the Soviet Union that we received showed that, in spite of our lack of representation in that country, we were as well informed regarding developments and trends there as the foreign offices of any other country with the possible exception of Germany and the Baltic states. It was unfortunate that because the division was understaffed and had other responsibilities the material it was accumulating could not be utilized to maximum advantage.

As a result of the constant criticism that the State Department was receiving from the Department of Commerce, it was endeavoring during the 1920s to stimulate a deeper interest among our consulates throughout the world in the promotion of U.S. exports. Our consular officers were informed that records were being maintained of their economic and commercial reports and that these records would be consulted in the preparation of promotion lists. Each geographic division was required to grade every economic and commercial report received from the consular offices in the area under its jurisdiction. These reports, with the grades affixed to them, were sent to the Consular Commercial Office of the department, which credited the author with the report and its grade. Most Foreign Service officers disapproved of the practice of grading. They felt that it was placing them in the category of schoolboys. Nevertheless, it did encourage our consulates to devote more attention to commercial work. One of the tasks delegated to me was that of grading the economic and commercial reports coming in from our consulates in Eastern Europe—a task that I did not relish, since it seemed incongruous for me to be grading the work of officers who were senior in rank to myself.

Much of my time was devoted to work of a research character. One project was a study of treaties and international agreements to which the Soviet Union was a party for the purpose of learning the kind of international commitments that the Soviet Union was prepared to assume and the extent to which it was accustomed to live up to them. This work formed the basis for a much more detailed study in 1933 when the Division of Eastern European Affairs was preparing for the negotiations with the Soviets that was to lead to recognition. Of particular interest to the division was the development of relations between Germany and the Soviet Union. We studied the background that gave rise to the German-Soviet Treaty of Rapallo in 1922 and closely followed Germany's efforts to strengthen its relations with the West without departing too far from "the spirit of Rapallo." We were hopeful that the acceptance of the Dawes Plan and the conclusion of the Locarno Pact in the latter part of 1925 including the four great Western powers (Great Britain, France, Italy, and Germany) would herald a new era in Western Europe, an era of wholehearted cooperation.

The most sweeping concessions that the Soviet government had made up to that time to any noncommunist country were to be found in a series of agreements—a treaty of commerce and consular rights, a railway convention, a navigation convention, and an agreement on taxation— entered into between Germany and the Soviet Union on October 12, 1925, just four days before Germany signed the Locarno Pact. We hoped that these agreements might signify a turning point in Soviet policies toward the noncommunist world. Our hopes, however, were short-lived. They died when the Soviet press and Soviet officials began several days later to denounce Germany for signing the Locarno Pact on the ground that the pact was incompatible with "the spirit of Rapallo." German arguments that improving its relations with the countries of Western Europe did not necessarily represent a weakening of its friendship with the Soviet Union did not satisfy Moscow.

To propitiate the Soviet Union, the Germans signed a treaty of neutrality with it shortly after having entered into the Locarno Pact. This treaty provided that neither state would allow itself to become a party to an attack or an economic or financial boycott of the other. Although the commitments Germany made in this treaty were not inconsistent with the terms of the Locarno Pact, they did mean that Germany had no intention of wholeheartedly cooperating with the West. The signing of this treaty, therefore, served to destroy the effects of the Locarno Pact and to dispel the hopes we had begun to have of a united Western Europe.

It seemed to me that although the United States preferred not to become involved in European affairs, we nevertheless had a vital interest in what was taking place on that continent, and it would be in accord with our efforts to promote peace for us to advocate close and friendly cooperation among the great powers of Western Europe. In fact, we had been involving ourselves in their affairs in a half-hearted way. We had, for instance, indirectly supported the Dawes Plan, the acceptance of which might have been a basis for West European unity and, as I have already pointed out, President Coolidge in July 1924 publicly expressed his approval of the Locarno agreements.

It was clear to me that in the mid-1920s the Soviet Union was pursuing the policy of trying to keep the countries of Western Europe at loggerheads, while we were hoping that these countries could eventually bury their old feuds and work together. The Soviet Union was working feverishly to secure the success of its policy, while we were doing little to back ours. With the aid of the German militarists the Soviet policy eventually prevailed. Whether a more dynamic policy on our part would have brought about different results is, of course, open to question.

As a result of my studies and experiences in the Eastern European Affairs Division I became convinced that the rulers in Moscow, although perhaps differing at times among themselves regarding the methods to be employed, were united in their determination to promote chaos and revolution in the noncommunist world until they could achieve their ultimate objective of a communist world with headquarters in Moscow. Even at that time it was fashionable among groups of so-called intellectuals to scoff at convictions of this kind, to intimate that those holding them were naively paying attention to slogans and exhortations rather than to actions. Nevertheless, I did not see how anyone could reach a different conclusion after having gone through all the material I had examined while on that tour in the department and observing what communists throughout the world were doing under Moscow's directions.

RECOMMENDATIONS FOR GIVING MEMBERS OF THE FOREIGN SERVICE OPPORTUNITIES FOR SYSTEMATIC PROFESSIONAL TRAINING

While in the State Department I was able to observe many energetic, ambitious young men who were just entering the Foreign Service. Their attitudes contrasted sharply with those of officers who were visiting the department after years in the foreign fields. Many of the veterans, though enriched by experiences, seemed to have lost a certain amount of initiative; some of them who had been serving in more remote areas or in positions where they were bogged down in routine, appeared to have lost contact with world trends and to have become outmoded or jaded. It seemed to me that it would be advantageous to these officers and to the service for them to be subjected from time to time to activities that would rekindle them mentally, shake them out of their lethargy, and reawaken their enthusiasm.

Shortly before leaving the department for my next foreign assignment, therefore, I had the temerity to write a memorandum to Assistant Secretary Carr suggesting that he give consideration to recommending to the Budget Bureau and Congress that a sabbatical-year system be established for Foreign Service officers and that they be given an opportunity to engage in studies of a kind to be agreed upon between them and the department during the course of one year out of every seven. I pointed out that teachers, physicians, and lawyers find it necessary now and then to take refresher courses. Certainly it should be no less important that officers who are working on international affairs in a changing world, sometimes in remote spots abroad, be given a similar opportunity. Carr sent for me, thanked me for the memorandum, and agreed that it made sense but said there was not the slightest chance Congress would accept a recommendation that would so materially increase the cost of maintaining the Foreign Service.

My experiences in later years, when the country was more interested in having a stronger Foreign Service than it was in the latter 1920s, convinced me that Carr was right. Nevertheless, I continued through the years to agitate for systematic training for mid-career and senior officers. It was not until 1946 that a Foreign Service Institute, charged with training officers of all grades, was established. That institute languished, however, for another ten years because of the reluctance of Congress to provide appropriations for its support.

In the mid-1950s, as the result of the findings of a committee that had been appointed by Secretary Dulles to make recommendations for the strengthening of the Foreign Service and was headed by Henry Wriston, former president of Brown University, foundations were laid for a Foreign Service Institute worthy of the name. It fell upon me during the mid- and late 1950s to carry on the struggle with Congress for the appropriations needed to carry out the Wriston recommendations for raising the potentials of personnel already in the service by systematic training. Since the mid-1950s the department has been assigning scores of Foreign Service officers and staff personnel to the Foreign Service Institute, the War College, and institutions of higher learning throughout the country for systematic study. In my opinion, as international problems continue to change rapidly in substance and in importance, still more training for the Foreign Service is needed. If I could have been given some of the training of the kind for which I had been agitating, I am convinced that my value to the service would have been greater. During my 39 years in the service my systematic training was limited to the two-week period of orientation following my entry into it.

My belief in the importance of professional training for Foreign Service personnel caused me to join Kelley and Packer in drawing up plans for the development of a corps of East European specialists. The department had already developed small corps of specialists for the Far East and the Near East. These specialists were being given the opportunity to study the languages, customs, and histories of the areas in which they were working. We were convinced that the Eastern Europe of the future promised to be sufficiently important to justify the training of specialists in that area. Carr was sympathetic to the idea and agreed to take steps toward the training of a corps of East European specialists.

ASSIGNMENT TO THE LEGATION AT RIGA

In April 1927, while the details for the development of a corps of Foreign Service East European specialists were still being worked out by the administrative area of the State Department, Kelley sent for me to show me a memorandum drafted by him for Carr which, he said, he did not wish to sign without consulting me. The memorandum suggested that during the early summer I be assigned to Riga to fill a need in our legation to the Baltic states for a third secretary. Kelley asked if I would like to serve in the Riga legation. I replied that I had been hoping for an assignment of this kind. After serving in consular offices and in a political division of the department I felt the need of experience in a diplomatic capacity. While in the department I had increased my knowledge of the East European area and had learned a great deal about Soviet Russia and the strategy of its rulers. Still more important, I had attained what I considered to be an understanding of our policies toward Eastern Europe and of the type of information in which the department was most likely to be interested.

Several days after my talk with Kelley the Senate approved my nomination as a diplomatic secretary and I was commissioned as a secretary in the Diplomatic Service. On May 12 I was appointed third secretary of legation to Estonia, Latvia, and Lithuania; in the second week of July I embarked on the S.S. *George Washington* for my new post.

FAREWELL TO SECRETARY KELLOGG

Just as I was preparing to leave Washington Secretary Kellogg, busy as he was, sent for me to say good-bye and wish me well. I had had little opportunity to meet him while I was on duty in the department. The only times that I had talked with him had been when he wished to consult someone in the division and Kelley and Packer were not readily available. That he should have taken the time to call me to his office was illustrative of the considerate attitude that he was accustomed to show to those serving under him. In my opinion history has not dealt kindly with Kellogg. He assumed the secretaryship at a difficult time. It would not have been easy for anyone to succeed Hughes, who had a particularly strong and impressive personality and who was the personification of integrity and courage tempered by kindness. Kellogg, like Hughes, was also a man of integrity, possessed of the kind of courage that, in my opinion, every secretary of state should have. He did not always, however, cut an impressive figure. He was short, somewhat gnarled in appearance, and obviously high-strung. He was, like Hughes, an activist and at times he displayed feelings of frustration at his inability, in view of our policy of noninvolvement, to pursue courses that in his opinion would have been in the national interest. His quick, incisive mind enabled him sometimes to perceive pitfalls that had escaped the attention of his subordinates. Some of his projects, such as the so-called Kellogg-Briand Pact [Pact of Paris, 1928], failed to yield the hoped-for results. Nevertheless, most of them gave the American people the feeling that the United States, in spite of its policy of noninvolvement, was contributing its share to the maintenance of world peace.

PART VII

SECRETARY OF LEGATION IN THE U.S. LEGATION AT RIGA TO ESTONIA, LATVIA, AND LITHUANIA, SEPTEMBER 1927–DECEMBER 1930

CHAPTER 17

FROM WASHINGTON TO RIGA AND EARLY IMPRESSIONS OF RIGA

BEFORE LEAVING FOR MY NEW POST as secretary of our legation at Riga, I obtained the approval of the Department of State to take en route some of the unused leave that I had earned during the preceding two years. I had learned from my previous experiences in the Baltic states that a good command of German would be extremely helpful in Eastern Europe, particularly in Latvia and Estonia. It was my plan, therefore, to spend my vacation at some place in Germany where I would have the opportunity to improve my German, which I had not used for more than five years, and at the same time enjoy sunshine and the seashore.

When I landed in Germany in the middle of July 1927, I informed our consul in Bremen, Leslie Reed, of my plan and asked him to recommend the kind of place that I had in mind. Upon his recommendation I went to Travemuende, a small sea resort near the ancient Hanseatic city of Lübeck. In a comfortable pension in that quiet resort I spent more than five weeks. My room had a balcony overlooking the Baltic Sea on which I devoted the hours from six to twelve every morning to a concentrated study of German. My breakfast was served on the balcony and I had my luncheons and dinners in the dining room. Foreigners were rare in Travemuende at that time and my fellow guests, all of whom were German, seemed pleased to have me with them to join in their conversations. The afternoons I usually spent swimming, lying on the beach, playing tennis, or visiting the neighboring countryside.

I found that Berlin, which I visited as I continued my journey to Riga, had improved remarkably since I had left it in 1921. Despite the difficult times through which Germany had passed during the intervening six-year period, the city was much brighter and more cheerful. I spent two pleasant weeks in Berlin, enjoying the theaters and concerts and renewing old friendships.

While in Berlin I made a number of calls at our embassy where for the first time I met DeWitt C. Poole, the counselor, and John C. Wiley, the first secretary, both of whom were keenly interested in Eastern Europe. It will be recalled that Poole, after having served as consul in Moscow during the time of the Bolshevik revolution, had been assigned to the Department of State where he had organized the Division of Eastern European Affairs, of which he was the first chief. Wiley, despite his comparatively youthful age, was already a veteran diplomat. I was later to have the opportunity to work closely with both of them.

Introduction to the Riga Legation, September 1927

My trip from Berlin to Riga in a comfortable sleeping car was in marked contrast with my journey between the same two cities in August 1919, when I had traveled by German troop train as far as Mitau and thence had proceeded to Riga by riverboat. I was met at the railway station in Riga by Louis Sussdorff, the counselor of legation; John A. Lehrs, Attaché (later special assistant to the minister); and Walter McKinney, the chief clerk of the legation.

As we moved along in Sussdorff's car from the station to the apartment where I had been invited to stay until I could find suitable living quarters, I looked with interest at the city that, when I had left it in the spring of 1920, had been showing the scars of war. The leaves of thousands of trees that lined the boulevards and shaded the chain of parks that extended through the center of the city were beginning to turn, and there was a touch of autumn in the air. The sun was shining brightly; swans were gliding over the lakes and streams in the parks; the early autumn flowers were glowing. When I later became acquainted with the picturesque buildings in the ancient squares that dated back to the era of the Hanseatic League, with the Opera House, with the steepled Gothic churches, and with the magnificent views across the broad Dvina River, I could understand why the Baltic Germans loved Riga and why they had been so determined to remain masters of it.

In the evening I was taken in Sussdorff's car to his villa in one of the forest suburbs of Riga. Both Louis and his wife Flores were most hospitable and, while discussing the activities and problems of the legation, took me completely into their confidence. From that evening until the date of my departure from Riga more than three years later, I was made to feel that I was a member of the Sussdorff family.

In spite of the warmth of the welcome given me by both the American and the non-American members of the legation, my visit to the chancery the following morning left me rather depressed. I had served in what seemed to me to be inadequate offices both in Dublin and in Cobh, and it looked as though I might again spend several years in an office that was certainly no credit to the United States. The chancery was in a former residence of a wealthy Riga merchant. It had been allowed to fall into disrepair during the war years and had finally been leased by the merchant's widow to the legation. Although it was well situated and had an imposing façade, its interior was not suitable for an office.

Minister Frederic W. B. Coleman, Sussdorff, and I had a conference during which they outlined the role in the legation that they contemplated for me. The minister produced instructions that he had received from the State Department. In part they read:

> In assigning Mr. Henderson to the Legation, the Department has taken into consideration the experience . . . he has gained, during his detail in the Division of European Affairs, of the Department's needs with respect to information relative to Russian and Baltic matters, and it feels that his services will be particularly useful to the Legation in connection with the study of the Russian situation.
>
> The Department has also in mind the desire of Mr. Henderson to prepare himself for possible future service in Russia, and, accordingly, it expects insofar as it is practical, he will be afforded the opportunity to equip himself in this regard, especially to increase his knowledge of the Russian language. The Department, however, necessarily leaves to your judgment, within the general limits of its instructions, the precise duties which are to be assigned to Mr. Henderson.

The minister and Sussdorff told me they sympathized with my desire to prepare for possible service in Russia, but they were sure I would understand that the urgent needs of the legation must take priority over the training and development of the members of its staff. They said that the organization of the legation needed to be overhauled; there was a lack of coordination among its various sections. In addition, more personnel were required if it was to meet the department's demands and there should be more office space to accommodate the larger staff. In view of the situation, they had decided that my primary duty for the time being should be to try to improve the effectiveness of the organization of the legation and simultaneously to prepare dispatches to the department urging that the mission be provided with needed additional personnel and funds. They said that, in addition to my administrative responsibilities, they expected me to assist in the negotiations of several treaties and agreements that were pending between the United States and the three Baltic states, particularly in the negotiation of a treaty of friendship, commerce, and consular rights with Latvia. They added that they hoped I would also find time to do some reporting on developments in Latvia. The consulates in Tallinn and Kaunas, they thought, were keeping the department fairly well informed with regard to Estonia and Lithuania. The reports from Riga regarding Latvia, however, needed strengthening. Although the three Baltic states were not playing a major role in international affairs, their position on the flank of the Soviet Union might at any time bring them into prominence. The reports on them, therefore, should not be neglected.

Coleman and Sussdorff indicated that David Macgowan, the first secretary, assisted by John Lehrs, would continue to be responsible for reporting on the Soviet Union, which was of course the most important activity of the legation. It would be advisable, however, for me to keep in touch with the Russian section and to study its reports. I might even, with the approval of Macgowan, try my hand from time to time at preparing reports on the Soviet Union but should not allow such reporting to interfere with my other work.

I was convinced that eventually the United States and the Soviet Union would establish diplomatic relations, and I had been hoping that I would be given work in the legation at Riga that would prepare me for service in the Soviet Union and that I would also be given time to study the Russian language. I was, therefore, somewhat disappointed to learn that I was not to be detailed immediately to the Russian section. Nevertheless, it seemed to me that the minister and Sussdorff were right in their decision that I should work where my services were most urgently needed.

DESIGNATION AS A MEMBER OF THE
NEWLY ORGANIZED CORPS OF EAST EUROPEAN SPECIALISTS

My desire to qualify as a specialist on Eastern Europe was quickened by instructions from the State Department, dated October 24, 1927, informing me that the project of developing a corps of officers trained for work in Eastern Europe had taken form and inquiring whether or not I would welcome designation to that corps. The instructions indicated that the number of officers to be assigned to it would in all probability not be more than ten. I replied that I would consider it an honor to be among the original group of officers selected for regional assignment and would accept such a designation with pleasure.

Instructions from the department, dated February 27, 1928, informed me that I had been designated as an "East European regional specialist." Although I was pleased at the designation, I was beginning to wonder whether or not it would have any real meaning so far as I was concerned. Letters from friends in the department had intimated that only young officers still in the unclassified grades in the service were to be assigned to formal study of the Soviet Union and the Russian language, and that the officers in the higher grades would be expected to acquire the qualifications expected of specialists while on assignments to East European posts or to the Division of Eastern European Affairs. The question in my mind was whether I, as a member of the new corps, was to be given an opportunity to benefit from formal training or whether I was to be charged with holding the fort, so to speak, while only junior officers new to the field were to be given the opportunity for study that I had so ardently hoped to have. Several years elapsed before I had a definite answer to that question.

CHAPTER 18

DUTIES AS A MEMBER OF THE LEGATION AT RIGA, SEPTEMBER 1927–NOVEMBER 1928

ADMINISTRATION

FROM SEPTEMBER 1927 TO NOVEMBER 1928 a considerable portion of my time was taken up by efforts to improve the working conditions and effectiveness of the legation. We were able to effect some improvements by delineating more clearly the duties and responsibilities of members of the staff, by replacing several local employees whose work was unsatisfactory, and by rearranging our working space. I found it difficult, however, to accomplish much in the way of strengthening the legation so long as the chancery occupied its unsuitable quarters and our budget was so sharply restricted.

During the Coolidge administration economy was the watchword. Both the administration and Congress were apparently of the opinion that during the war years the governmental bureaucracy had become addicted to extravagance and that it was incumbent upon them to reduce the costs of government to levels approaching those that had prevailed before the war. Although Mr. Carr understood the needs of the State Department and the Foreign Service, he was prevented by the ever-watchful Bureau of the Budget from presenting them to Congress. In fact, he was required to describe each year what the department had been doing to reduce the costs of operation.

The administration required all government agencies to make periodic reports of the specific steps they were taking to effect savings. Each office in the Department of State and each diplomatic and consular office abroad was, therefore, under instructions to keep the department informed of what it was doing to cut costs of operation. While I was serving in the department, it had been one of my duties as "savings officer" of the Division of Eastern European Affairs to prepare periodic reports showing the division's contribution to the economy campaign. After I had exhausted lists of our savings in the field of postage, telegrams, stationery, and so forth, I was at a loss as to what next to report. Finally, not wishing to let the division down, I prepared for Kelley's signature a memorandum directing the staff to turn off electric fans and lights whenever they left their rooms even if their absence were to be for only a short time.

Shortly after my arrival at Riga I discovered that the legation was reporting economies in the consumption of carbon paper. Instead of discarding worn carbons, the economy squad of the legation was holding them over a lighted candle until the ink on them had been redistributed and they could again be put to use. Recalling how I had strained my eyes in the department while attempting to read some of the carbon copies of reports from Riga, I put a stop to this particular economy effort.

The month of March 1928 marked one of the turning points in the affairs not only of the legation but also of the State Department and the Foreign Service as a whole. Early in that month I discovered a new brick building under construction on a quiet square facing the beautiful old Kaiser Garten Park, not more than 200 yards from the Dvina River. The owner-builder was prepared, if satisfactory terms could be worked out, to alter his plans for the interior so that it would suit the needs of the chancery and to lease the building to the legation.

The minister, Sussdorff, Macgowan, and I developed a floor plan that seemed almost ideal for a chancery, and we began negotiations with the owner. Within a week we came to an agreement, subject to the approval of the department, for leasing the building for three years with options for renewal. The annual rent would total about $3,000, of which $600 would be paid by the military attaché who would be provided with a suite of rooms on the second floor. Nevertheless, I was worried because the department's share of the rent would be perhaps two or three hundred dollars more than what we had been paying.

I discovered later that by coincidence our telegram had arrived in Washington at the very time that the State Department was in the process of making some radical changes in its outlook with regard to its own needs and those of the Foreign Service for adequate personnel and facilities and of adopting a more aggressive approach when presenting these needs to the Bureau of the Budget and the appropriations subcommittees. I have never been able to learn just what chain of events resulted in these changes. I am inclined to believe that the accumulation of dismal stories pouring into the department from our diplomatic missions and consular offices in all parts of the world regarding the conditions under which they were trying to operate so depressed Carr that he finally presented the situation in all its bleakness to Olds, the under secretary; that Olds, shocked at the picture painted by Carr, took the matter up with Secretary Kellogg; and that the secretary went directly to the president. Kellogg was not a man to hesitate when convinced that energetic action was called for, and it seems probable that he persuaded the president to take a less uncompromising attitude with respect to the needs of the department and the Foreign Service.

However it came about, on March 16, 1928, the department sent to all U.S. diplomatic and consular officers rather startling instructions entitled "Conditions of Finances and Estimates of Needs." These instructions were revolutionary because, rather than preaching further economies, they actually encouraged our diplomatic missions and consular offices to inform the department of their needs for additional personnel and facilities. It was in harmony with the spirit of these instructions that the department, ten days after they were issued, authorized the legation to lease the new chancery in Riga. The agreement was entered into on March 31.

We now had quarters capable of housing a much-needed larger staff. We believed, as did the members of the Division of Eastern European Affairs, that additional staff was necessary if the State Department was to receive the information that it should have about the Soviet Union. I continued to do my best to persuade the administrative and personnel departments of this.

I prepared my first appeal, incorporated in a dispatch dated September 14, 1928, shortly after we had moved into the new chancery. I emphasized, in particular, the needs of the Russian section for competent, well-educated translators and also for personnel capable of editing translations and checking their accuracy.

The State Department's reply to this and later dispatches was an apparently regretful "no funds available." The time and effort spent in preparing these dispatches were not wasted, however, since they gave the administrative officers of the department a better understanding of what the legation was trying to do and of the necessity that its work be carried out with accuracy.

REPORTING ON LATVIA

The knowledge of Latvian politics that I gained in the preparation of reports to the State Department proved of particular value to me during the subsequent years that I served in the East European area. The political mosaic of Latvia no longer represented the confusing puzzle that I had previously found it to be. I profited also in a larger sense. A concentrated study of the political interplay in a small country can have significant educational value. I had observed the turmoil in Ireland as that country was painfully developing into a free independent nation, in the Baltic states as small peoples long deprived of their freedom struggled to establish stable, viable, and relatively prosperous republics, and still later in Iraq as a semifeudal, semitribal society endeavored to convert itself into a modern nation-state. These experiences taught me much about people as political animals, about the frailty of human institutions, and also about the sometimes unsuspected capacities of such institutions for survival.

One of the conclusions that I have drawn in observing the efforts of small nations to survive and develop in this century of rapid change and clashing ideologies and aspirations, is that only too frequently some of the most valued precepts of freedom—precepts that seem democratic and fair as theories—can sometimes lead to disorder, chaos, and misery when practiced. For instance, the concept of "one man, one vote," though appealing in theory, can benefit only a society in which the average person has the capability of understanding the issues to be voted on, forming a reasonably intelligent opinion of what is good for the society as a whole, and taking this opinion into consideration when casting a vote. Similarly, proportional representation may seem fair in theory, in that it provides minority groups with representation in the legislative forum. In practice, however, such a system can undermine the stability and impede the development of a state if the minority groups are numerous and are so intent upon promoting their own narrow interests that they have little or no regard for what the effect of their activities may be upon the country as a whole.

The events in Latvia during the latter 1920s and early 1930s illustrate the manner in which minorities can misuse the special privileges that have been accorded them. In Latvia some 85 percent of the people considered themselves to be Latvian ethnologically, although over the centuries a certain amount of Scandinavian, Polish, Estonian, and Russian blood had been mingled with Latvian. Approximately 15 percent of the people of the country regarded themselves as members of ethnic minorities. Among these the Germans, although divided among themselves, were the most active and skillful politically. While I was serving in Riga, German members of the Saeima were able over a protracted period to persuade representatives of several minority groups to unite into a tight legislative bloc of thirteen members. Since the parties that did not rest on an ethnological basis were almost evenly divided on many of the outstanding issues of the day, this little bloc of thirteen, which was relatively indifferent to issues other than those that might promote the narrow short-term interests of its members, was at times in a position to bring about the overthrow of a government that was unwilling to meet its demands. On occasions the demands of the minority bloc were so excessive that the rival national parties would join forces in rejecting them. Such occasions, however, were rare, and the minority coalitions succeeded for many years in playing a large role in the maintenance or overthrow of various governments.

Latvia had serious internal problems other than those caused by the activities of the ethnic minorities. Although the Communists were not permitted to have a party of their own, energetic and intelligent groups of Latvian Communists, trained in and directed from Moscow, did their utmost to keep alive and to fan such antagonisms as are usually the aftermath of the establishment of a new state, particularly when the establishment is accompanied by basic social reforms. In the area of agriculture, for instance, the Communists did their utmost to promote friction between the new farmers who had received pieces of land when the great estates had been broken up and the prewar farmers whose farms had been so small that they had not been affected by the land reform legislation. In the cities and towns, where there were housing shortages, they strove to stir up animosities between tenants and landlords. In the armed forces they attempted to create misunderstandings between the senior and junior officers and between the junior and noncommissioned officers. They tried also to convince the government employees, particularly the teachers, that they were underpaid and that life for them would be happier under a Soviet regime. They were active among the industrial workers whom they made special efforts to win over by promises of the opportunities they would have, not only for gainful employment but also for wielding political power if the country should become a Soviet republic.

As I studied Latvia's problems it became more and more amazing to me how, in the face of all its difficulties, this country was succeeding not only in surviving but also in developing its resources and in raising its cultural and living standards.

Reporting on the Soviet Union

As I have already indicated, David Macgowan, chief of the legation's Russian section, was responsible for reporting on the Soviet Union. From personal observations while in Russia and from years of study he had gained a thorough understanding of the basic objectives of the small group of International Communists who were in control of the apparatus that called itself the government of the Union of Soviet Socialist Republics. He knew that the same group was also in control of the All-Union Communist Party, the Communist International, the Red International of Trade Unions, the orthodox communist parties, and a myriad of united-front and communist-dominated organizations in other countries. He also understood that no organization, regardless of character, was permitted to exist in the Soviet Union unless it was under the direct or indirect control of this small group. In short, he was under no illusions regarding the purposes and the nature of the regime that was governing what was once the Russian empire.

Macgowan was a prolific writer. The number of dispatches he prepared for the State Department during a month's time was staggering. Many of these dispatches served merely as transmittal covers for translations of Soviet press articles, statements of Soviet leaders, decrees, and so forth. Others contained comments on the material that was being transmitted. A few of them were analytical but, because of the broad field that he was expected to cover, he had little time for analysis. Some of the scholars who in later years have examined these reports have criticized them for superficiality and for what they regarded as a tendency to emphasize Soviet shortcomings and belittle Soviet accomplishments. In defense of Macgowan and the Russian section I would like to point out that, although the material published in the Soviet Union did at times include self-criticism for the purpose of spurring the Soviet officials and people to even greater efforts, most of it was boastful propaganda. There was at the time no U.S. government agency, other than the legation, in a position to expose for the benefit of the State Department the exaggerated nature of Soviet claims of accomplishments. Furthermore, dispatches by foreign journalists residing in the Soviet Union were subject to strict censorship. Many of the American so-called intellectuals admitted to the Soviet Union had been carefully handpicked by the Soviets. Many of these intellectuals, as well as some of the American journalists, who had reservations with respect to what they found in the Soviet Union, were unwilling upon their return to the United States to make their true feelings public for fear of injuring their future relations with Soviet officials or of giving offense to the particular sections of the American public to which they were linked by common bonds of sympathy for the "Soviet experiment." One of the tasks of the legation, therefore, was to try to bring more nearly into focus what it considered to be the true picture of the situation in the Soviet Union.

My reporting on the Soviet Union before the legation moved into its new chancery was limited. From time to time I did prepare monographs on Soviet activities or developments in which I believed the State Department would be particularly interested.

When David Macgowan was absent from Riga or ill I took over his job and did what I could to maintain the flow of dispatches to the department. The administrative load under which I was laboring and the pressures of my work connected with the Baltic states made this extra task particularly difficult.

After the legation had settled in its new quarters, the administrative problems began to diminish and the minister decided that I should devote at least half of my time to work in the Russian section. The hard-pressed Macgowan was pleased to have me. I was charged with keeping the department informed on Soviet foreign economic developments, including the structure and activities of the Soviet foreign trade monopoly and the institutions through which this monopoly was being exercised, Soviet concessions to foreigners, and the manner in which the foreign concessions fared. In addition, I was asked to prepare a series of reports on how the leaders of the All-Union Communist Party were planning to accomplish their avowed aims of world revolution. Of particular interest to me at the time was the increasing emphasis that was being placed upon the Soviet state as the future base for the support of the revolutionary movement in other countries and upon the Red Army as a future instrument in promoting world revolution.

It was already possible to detect the pragmatic mind of Stalin at work. If he had ever had any confidence in the effectiveness of propaganda unsupported by power in bringing about a communist-controlled world, it appeared to me that he had lost it; he had apparently become convinced that, although propaganda might be useful at times, it was not likely to play a decisive role unless backed by physical power. His first objective, therefore, had become the building up of a powerful Soviet state. Once an impregnable, highly industrialized Soviet state possessing mighty armed forces could be achieved, its rulers could then seriously begin to carry out their world revolutionary program. Stalin, of course, did not foresee that, at the very moment the Soviets had achieved success in removing the main barriers to Soviet expansion, the appearance of atomic weapons in the international arena would render it impossible for any state, regardless of its monolithic character and of the iron will of its rulers, to achieve impregnability.

During the autumn of 1928 I became more and more immersed in the work of the Russian section. I rejoiced in the opportunity to study the drama that was unfolding in the huge expanses stretching from the borders of the Baltic states to the waters of the Pacific. I realized that what was going on was certain to have profound influence on the world of the future. Unfortunately, that realization was shared at that time by only a comparatively few members of the Department of State and by a small section of the American public.

Chapter 19

Duties as a Member
of the Legation at Riga,
April 1929–November 1930

Assignment to the Russian Section

IN SPITE OF MY FEVER on returning from six-months sick leave in Davos, my morale began to go up as the train passed through West Prussia, the Polish Corridor, East Prussia, Lithuania, and Courland. After we had pulled out of the Mitau station, I raised the window blinds in my compartment. The view in other circumstances might not have been particularly inspiring—leaden skies, soggy meadows, and rows of leafless trees along muddy roads. The Baltic countryside is not at its best between the disappearance of the winter snows and the fresh green of spring. I was so pleased, nevertheless, at the thought that I was only minutes away from my post that what I saw looked much grander to me than the snow-clad mountains of Switzerland.

As the train passed over the long bridge that connected Thorenberg and Riga I noticed that the Dvina River was choked with great chunks of ice that seemed to vie with one another, like so many lemurs, in a mad rush to sure destruction in the sea. The breaking up of the ice was a sign that spring was around the corner. Following my return to Riga the minister and Sussdorff told me that they had decided I was to be relieved of administrative responsibilities except those relating to personnel, that I was to be assigned to the Russian section to assist Macgowan and Lehrs, and that as a health precaution I could decline all invitations for a period of at least six months. They added that they hoped George Kennan, a member of the new corps of East European specialists on a temporary language assignment in Tallinn, could be brought down from Estonia to assist in the Baltic area until the autumn, when he was scheduled to attend the University of Berlin for Russian language and East European area study. Their plans, subject also to the department's approval, envisaged that after the departure of Kennan for Germany, Landreth Harrison, a Foreign Service officer who had been serving as a vice consul in the Riga consulate, would be transferred to the legation.

This was good news. I was eager to be able to devote more of my time and energy to the Soviet Union. My temporary release from representational activities meant that I could carry my share of the load in the chancery without overtiring myself. The thought of working with Kennan and Harrison, both of whom I liked and admired, was also most agreeable.

Spring in the Baltic area, once winter's stubborn grip has been broken, usually comes on with a rush. By mid-May the weather had become so mild that I moved from the minister's residence, where I had been staying, to Priedine, a cluster of summer villas in a pine forest near the Baltic Sea. During that summer I commuted daily from my village home to the legation in Riga. At first I spent no more than five or six hours daily in the legation. Later, as I again became accustomed to sitting at a desk, my workday gradually lengthened.

The department's demands on the Russian section had increased so that eventually I began to take work home in the evenings. The fact that I was not required to participate in social activities made a tremendous difference. That summer was the last for more than 30 years during which I was able to live a fairly normal nondiplomatic life. When my train would come into Priedine at 6:30 in the evening (the commuting time was about 35 minutes), I could stroll through the forest to my cottage where an elderly housekeeper would have dinner awaiting me. Since during most of the summer it remained light until nearly eleven o'clock, I would still have a long evening ahead. I enjoyed the commute because it gave me a chance to meet and chat with a wide variety of fellow passengers with whom I would not have otherwise come in contact.

In September I took a small furnished apartment not far from the legation. After my troublesome tonsils had been removed in late summer my health had improved and I again began to participate in the social life. Profiting from my experience, however, I tried to keep my social engagements within reasonable bounds. Gradually my concern about my health disappeared, and by the end of 1930 the nightmare of Davos had become merely a disagreeable memory. Although I have conscientiously tried to conserve my energies during the years that have since elapsed, there have been times when it was necessary for me to work under great strain for long periods and to forgo leave for years in succession. Despite this not one of my dozens of physical examinations since Davos have even suggested the presence of the dread disease that seemed to have been threatening me on what Thomas Mann called "the Magic Mountain."

During my months in Davos, Herbert Hoover had replaced Coolidge and Henry Stimson had become secretary of state. President Hoover, perhaps because of the many years he had devoted to activities in the international field, seemed inclined to ascribe more importance than President Coolidge had to our foreign relations. As head of the Department of Commerce, Hoover had taken a personal interest in the development of a strong Foreign Service for that department; similarly, as president, he did not hesitate to stress the need for strengthening the machinery for the conduct of our national foreign policies.

It is true that in late 1927 and throughout 1928 the Coolidge administration, partly as a result of the prodding of Secretaries Kellogg and Hoover, was beginning to realize that more funds should be appropriated for the State Department and the Foreign Service. The increases, however, were not by any means sufficient to meet the basic needs.

Those of us in the Foreign Service who, as a result of the lack of funds, had been unable to accomplish tasks that should have been carried out were encouraged when the new president in his State of the Union message, delivered on December 3, 1929, stated:

> The Congress has by numerous wise and foresighted acts in the past few years greatly strengthened the character of our representation abroad. It has made liberal provision for the establishment of suitable quarters for our foreign service staffs in the different countries. In order, however, that we may further develop the most effective force in this, one of the most responsible functions of our Government, I shall recommend to the Congress more liberal appropriations for the work of the State Department. I know of no expenditure of public money from which a greater economic and moral return can come to us than by assuring the most effective conduct of our foreign relations.

Unfortunately that message was delivered when the United States had already fallen under the shadow of the Great Depression. On October 24, 1929, the crash in the New York stock market heralded the beginning of an era of economic crises that, with variations, was to continue up to the beginning of the Second World War. The State Department and the Foreign Service, which had been treated as institutions of second-rate importance during the prosperity of the mid–1920s, were to be faced with even more distressing financial problems during the depression years.

Secretary Stimson was a member of a rather closely knit fraternity of socially prominent Eastern business and professional leaders who, after graduating from exclusive preparatory schools and well-known universities and becoming affiliated with business or professional firms composed of people with similar backgrounds, tended to enter politics as liberals or progressives. After serving for a number of years in Elihu Root's law firm, Stimson had become district attorney of New York while still young and had earned his spurs as a progressive by assisting Theodore Roosevelt in the latter's "trust-busting" activities. Later, as secretary of war, he had served in the cabinet of President Taft. In 1927 he again came into national prominence when President Coolidge sent him as a special commissioner to mediate between the warring factions in Nicaragua. His success there increased his prestige and led to his appointment as governor of the Philippines. Hoover's decision to appoint him secretary of state was a popular one. Stimson brought into the department as his top assistants a group of bright young men from Harvard, Yale, and Princeton—men with the proper background and the urge to enter public service at a high level. During his years as secretary, relations between the State Department and prominent business and professional men of the cities of the East were extremely close.

STALIN BECOMES VIRTUAL DICTATOR, NOVEMBER 1929

In connection with my assignment to report on the Soviet Union, I wrote a series of reports regarding internal developments in the Soviet Union during the latter part of 1929 and all of 1930. It seemed to me that Stalin was carrying on a determined struggle to eliminate, or at least to silence, his opponents and to gain absolute control of the country. The results of this struggle were, in my opinion, certain to have a profound effect on Soviet policies for years to come. Stalin classified most of his opponents as "right-wingers" or "left-wingers" while he and his supporters maintained that they represented the central truly Leninist stream of the party. Stalin seemed to believe that he had considerable justification in thus classifying his opponents. In fact he was occupying a central position between, on the one hand, those elements of the party that were insisting that regardless of obstacles and possible dangers the party should press for the immediate realization of communist ideals in the Soviet Union and for quick social revolutions abroad under communist leadership, and, on the other hand, those elements that believed that the success of the party's world revolutionary program was so dependent on the development of a powerful and impregnable Soviet Union that the party in making basic policy decisions should give primary consideration to the security and strengthening of the Soviet state.

Although the differences within the All-Union Communist Party were largely those of strategy, personal factors were also involved. Among Stalin's opponents were a number of old Bolsheviks who had played leading roles in the early revolutionary period. Some of them who, as a result of their past contributions, felt that they had a sort of proprietary interest in the party and in the Soviet state resented Stalin's efforts to make himself the leader with dictatorial powers of the world revolutionary movement. Although the leaders of the right and left wings had opposing views regarding the policies that the party should pursue, they shared concern and resentment at Stalin's growing personal power and at the ruthless manner in which he was using it.

Details of this struggle within the party during 1929 and 1930 are so complicated that it would require volumes to describe them accurately. Suffice it to say that, at a meeting of the Central Committee of the Communist Party that took place in November 1929, Stalin won a victory that crushed his opponents temporarily and had a permanent effect on the internal and foreign policies of the Soviet Union. His overwhelming victory was reflected in the Soviet press on December 21, 1929, when the whole country joined in celebrating his fiftieth birthday. The praise of him by the press on this occasion approached adoration. Some of the language used was of the kind customarily reserved for a deity. The obsequious tone of the press seemed so rampant that I wrote a dispatch on the subject to the State Department. It contained quotations from the organs of the party, the government, the Communist International, and the trade unions hailing him as their leader. An excerpt from this dispatch dated January 3, 1930, reads:

> I have the honor to report that the fiftieth birthday of J. V. Stalin, the Secretary General of the All-Union Communist Party of Bolsheviks, which took place on December 21, was treated as an event of national and even of world-wide importance by the Soviet Press. It is doubtful if Lenin in the height of his power and popularity was ever given so much acclaim and praise as that accorded to the present leader of the Party. The Soviet newspapers of December 21 were almost entirely devoted to Stalin. Numerous portraits and photographs of him, as well as congratulatory messages addressed to him from communist organizations in practically all parts of the world, were the features of the leading newspapers. But little effort was made to disguise the fact that as chief of the All-Union Communist Party Stalin is also in fact the dictator of Soviet

Russia and the controlling director of such international organizations as the Communist International and the Red International of Labor Unions. "The whole world is thinking of Stalin," wrote Ordzhonikidze, Stalin's fellow Georgian and personal friend, in an article appearing in the Moscow *Izvestiia*, "his enemies with hatred, his friends with love"... This concept of unified leadership does not tend to confirm Soviet contentions that the Party, the State, and the Communist International, are separate and independent organizations.

The State Department was so deeply impressed by the position that these tributes showed Stalin to have created for himself that it established in its Index Bureau (the central files of the department) a special dossier devoted to him (861.44 Stalin, J. V.), in which my dispatch was the first enclosure. This dossier was to become exceedingly fat in the years to come.

Socialization of Agriculture

Following the reduction of his opponents to a state of impotency, Stalin began energetically early in 1930 to put into effect some of the policies he had advocated at the November meeting of the Central Committee of the party. In his opinion, apparently, the solution of the vexatious problems in the field of Soviet agriculture should have primary attention. During the first half of 1930, therefore, while not neglecting other problems on the home front or those connected with foreign affairs, he concentrated on agriculture, clearly the weakest sector of the Soviet economy. Most Soviet leaders had been in agreement that, if the Soviet Union was to succeed in its efforts to develop quickly into a world power, it must be able to carry out its grandiose plans for rapid industrialization. The execution of these plans, however, had been frequently retarded by the inability of the responsible Soviet organs to supply technicians, skilled and unskilled laborers, food, raw materials, and transport.

The Soviet government had taken and was continuing to take energetic measures for solving the problem of the shortage of technicians and of skilled and unskilled laborers. While Soviet technicians were in training, thousands of foreign technicians were being brought in from Europe and the United States. With the aid of special organizations created for the purpose, both skilled and unskilled labor had been organized into great flexible corps. Soviet workers were no longer allowed to decide for themselves the kind of work in which to engage or the places where they were to work. By judicious exercise of its control over food, other articles

of consumption, travel, and housing, the Soviet government had gradually been able to reduce labor to a state of relative tractability. The Soviet
labor union system had been developed in such a manner that it, as well
as the Soviet police system, was a helpful adjunct in meeting the Soviet
labor problem. Considerable progress had also been achieved by the end
of 1929 in increasing the output of the extractive industries and in improving transport facilities. Similar successes, however, had not been achieved
in agriculture.

Stalin believed that one of the reasons for the sluggishness of agriculture had been the failure of the leaders of the Communist Party to
agree upon the manner in which it should be organized over the long term
and upon the direction that it should take. The agricultural policies of the
party had been shifting to meet the urgent needs of the moment. He was
convinced that the time had come to meet the problems of agriculture
head on and bring the Soviet farmer into the socialized sector of Soviet
economy.

THE COLLECTIVIZATION CAMPAIGN OF 1930

When it had become apparent early in 1930 that the year was to be an
eventful one for Soviet agriculture, David Macgowan had asked me to
assume responsibility for keeping the State Department informed about
what was taking place in that field. After preparing several agriculture
reports, I came to the conclusion that I could not write truly compre-
hensible reports on current agricultural developments unless there existed a basic historical and analytical study of Soviet agriculture to which I
could refer from time to time. Over the years the legation had not had the
personnel available for such a study. Although I was by no means an
agricultural economist, I volunteered to undertake such a study based
primarily on Soviet sources—a study that would cover Soviet agricultural
developments from 1917 to the spring of 1930. Macgowan accepted my
offer and assigned several of our more experienced translators and typists
to assist me. For more than eight weeks I worked almost feverishly on
this project. The translators and typists became so interested in our
joint undertaking that they voluntarily contributed many hours of over-
time to it.

The report was completed on May 3, 1930. It took the form of five
interrelated dispatches each bearing that date. The major dispatch,
number 6941, was devoted to a discussion of Soviet agricultural policies
and developments, past and present, supported by references to more
than 200 decrees, resolutions, and statements that had appeared in Soviet

publications. Translations of many of the documents referred to were appended as enclosures. Dispatches numbers 6942, 6943, 6944, and 6945 served as supplements to the major dispatch. One of them presented statistics based on Soviet sources regarding agricultural developments over the years. Another transmitted comments and explanations, translations, and summaries of articles that had appeared in Soviet publications during the twelve-month period ending in November 1929 (the month in which the Central Committee of the party had approved Stalin's policy decision with regard to agriculture). Another dealt entirely with Soviet policies in the field of agricultural taxation, and the last dispatch analyzed the resolutions of the Central Executive Committee of the Union of Soviet Socialist Republics providing for the reorganization of the village soviets. These dispatches with their enclosures were put into neat volumes by an expert Riga bookbinder—a member of a guild that went back to Hanseatic days. Each volume consisted of more than 600 typewritten pages. Several of these volumes were sent to the State Department for distribution among its various divisions and among other interested governmental agencies. One of them, which was placed in the central archives of the department, now rests in peace among thousands of other rarely read reports in the National Archives.

I do not know how useful my report was to the personnel of the State Department and other agencies. I have since wondered how many of the department's harassed personnel, whose desks were usually piled high with material to be studied, found the time to wade through a volume of this kind. I have derived some comfort from the fact that for a number of years the volumes, for me at least, were a valuable source of reference while I was serving in the legation at Riga, in the department, and in our embassy in Moscow. I am sure that I was the chief beneficiary of the study. I learned much in preparing it, not only about Soviet agriculture but also about the direct and indirect methods that a dictatorial or semidictatorial power can employ in bringing about fundamental changes in the society under its control wtihout concerning itself too deeply with the effects that such changes might have on the members of that society. I have since observed the employment of similar methods in Nazi Germany, in Communist China, in East European countries, in Cuba, and to a lesser degree in some of the emerging countries of the Middle East and Africa.

After the completion of my study of Soviet agriculture I continued, during the remainder of my tour in Riga, to write reports on Soviet internal and external policies and developments. Among them were several on the outcome of the sowing and harvesting campaigns of 1930.

Unrealized Hope for a Language Assignment

Following my return to Riga from Davos, I had been so immersed in my reporting work that I had had little time to devote to the study of the Russian language. I had found it impossible to do justice to my reporting assignments and at the same time to concentrate on language study. It was my belief that an East European specialist worthy of the name should be proficient in Russian. I was confident that, if I could be freed from other activities for a year or even for six months so that I could work full time on Russian, I would learn more during that period than I could during many years on a part-time basis. In May 1930, I therefore wrote a dispatch to the State Department expressing hope that it could detail me for a year to Russian language study. Robert Kelley, who was still the chief of the Division of Eastern European Affairs, replied to my dispatch in a personal letter in which he said that the department was following the policy of assigning only junior officers in the unclassified grades to Russian language study. He added that perhaps when some of these officers had completed their studies and were ready to take up their work on the firing line, some kind of an arrangement could be made that would permit me to concentrate on the Russian language.

An Experiment in Cooperative Living

In June 1930 I left the little apartment in which I had been living since my return to Riga from Priedine in September 1929 and moved into a large apartment across the square from the legation chancery. Sharing with me in an enterprise in cooperative living were Lee Morse, the commercial attaché; Landreth Harrison, third secretary; and Norris Chipman, who had succeeded Harrison as vice consul.

Lee Morse was a genial and likeable person devoted to hunting and fishing. The success of his forays in the forests and meadows and along the fast-moving streams of the Baltic countryside was frequently reflected in the dishes that appeared on our dining table.

Landreth Harrison had not, like so many of his colleagues, entered the service a year or so after graduating from a university. At the outbreak of the First World War he had left the University of Minnesota in order to enter the embryo U.S. Air Force. He had seen considerable combat service in France before being shot down with a bullet in his spine. His wound compelled him to spend a year or two in military hospitals but as soon as he was able he resumed his studies in Minnesota, where he earned A.B. and M.A. degrees. Following two years of study in Paris and a short stint as a member of the Minnesota faculty, he took the examinations and entered the Foreign Service. Although Riga was his first post, his maturity resulted in his being entrusted with highly responsible duties. In future years our paths crossed frequently. From Riga he was sent to the Eastern European Division of the State Department. In 1936 he was assigned as second secretary to our embassy in Warsaw and was on duty there when the Germans invaded Poland. The courage and ability he displayed in rounding up U.S. nationals in Poland and conducting them in a long caravan to Bucharest earned the commendation of the department. He later served in Berlin, Berne, London, and Paris. He was on duty in the department when, as a senior Foreign Service officer, he retired in the late 1950s. He undoubtedly possessed the qualifications that would have enabled him to hold the highest positions in the service had he been willing to sacrifice some of his varied and broad interests in order to concentrate upon service activities. In my opinion, officers like him who have a wide range of interests contribute much to the richness and attractiveness of the service.

Norris Chipman, the son of a Washington stockbroker, entered the service in 1928 shortly after his graduation from Dartmouth. His interests, like mine, were concentrated on Eastern Europe and he was delighted during the summer of 1930 to be detailed to Paris for Russian language study. He and I kept in close touch with each other during the succeeding years. We served together in the Eastern European Division of the department and in our embassy in Moscow. He was never to acquire renown as a Russian specialist, but the views that he ably expressed of current and future developments in the Soviet Union have turned out to be astonishingly accurate. He left the East European field to serve in a variety of posts but returned to it during the latter part of his career. He died in the late 1950s in Switzerland while on sick leave from his post in Belgrade, where he was serving as counselor of embassy.

When Chipman left Riga for language study in Paris he was replaced as vice consul by Bernard Gufler, a young Kansan who had been educated at Princeton and Harvard. Gufler was keen to raise his qualifications as a Foreign Service officer and concentrated on his work in the consulate. He was a warm-hearted, friendly person with a keen sense of humor, and we were glad to have him with us. He had no ambition to become an East European specialist. His interests lay primarily in Central Europe and he spent several hours each day studying German. Gufler, like Harrison, performed outstanding service during the early days of the Second World War. As chargé d'affaires in Kaunas in 1940, when the Soviets seized control of Lithuania, he acted with courage and cool judgment in an extremely difficult situation. He served in our embassy in Berlin during the early part of the Second World War. After the war he was stationed again in that city in the capacity of assistant chief of the U.S. mission to Germany with the rank of minister. Subsequently he served as ambassador, first to Ceylon and then to Finland.

CHAPTER 20

CHANGE IN MARITAL STATUS AND TRANSFER TO THE STATE DEPARTMENT, DECEMBER 1930

IN 1921 when I resolved to devote my life to serving the United States in the foreign field, I simultaneously abandoned all thought of marriage. From what I had observed and heard during my Red Cross tour in Europe, it seemed to me that the life of a family in the Foreign Service without private means, particularly if the head of that family was in the middle or lower ranks of the service, was likely to be bleak. I had come to believe that it would not be fair to any woman to invite her to share such a life. Furthermore, I could not think of having children who would be subject to the worries and privations that members of my family had undergone in attempting to obtain an education. During the eight years I had been in the service I had at times felt the lack of a family to share my woes and my minor successes, but second thoughts of what this entailed had always triumphed. Such second thoughts failed to deter me, however, in the middle of June 1930. If I suffered any qualms at the time they were dissipated in the presence of a sweet young face, expressive and somewhat sorrowful gray-blue eyes, a lovely soft voice, and a gracious and charming presence.

I met Elise first at a charity ball given at the Latvian Officer's Club. She was sitting at a table with a group of young Latvians, including junior officers of the armed forces and Foreign Office. At my request the wife of one of my friends from the Foreign Office introduced me to her and I invited her to dance. As was my custom on meeting strangers at affairs of this kind in Riga, I spoke to her in German. She answered in Latvian. When I apologetically told her that I could not speak Latvian, she replied that since we were in Latvia she preferred to carry on the conversation in the language of the country. She was under the impression that I was a Baltic German who was unwilling to speak Latvian, but after I had made my peace by explaining that I was a foreigner we carried on our conversation in German, which we found to be our best common language. When I saw her at balls or other affairs I danced or talked with her and eventually summoned the courage to invite her to the opera. After that we saw each other more and more frequently and our acquaintanceship developed into an understanding friendship. Her company was a welcome change— a pleasant escape from the more staid diplomatic functions that I considered myself obligated to attend. Although our backgrounds were strikingly dissimilar, we seemed to have much in common.

Elise had been born in Courland, not far from the Latvian port of Windau [Ventspils]. She had spent her early childhood uneventfully in the beautiful Courland countryside, which in atmosphere and appearance was more like southern Sweden than like the Russian empire of which it was then a part. Shortly after she had entered an elementary school, the even tenor of Courland was rudely interrupted. War had broken out between Russia and Germany, and Russia was mobilizing. Most of the able-bodied men in the area were called up. Russian columns with flags and pennants flying and bands playing, led by smartly uniformed officers, passed through the towns and villages on the way to East Prussia. Not many months later, however, remnants of these Russian forces came streaming back, broken and dejected, bringing thousands of their wounded with them. Behind them the victorious German forces were advancing in the face of rear-guard resistance. Many of the civilians, fearing what might happen when the Germans arrived, packed their most precious effects and fled eastward. Village after village became miniature battlefields; in many places the Germans, enraged at the sniping, shot on sight all adult males. Even young boys barely old enough to bear arms were among the victims of this savagery. In fact, several boys who had sought refuge in her father's garden were shot before Elise's eyes.

For five years her father's house was occupied by uniformed men — Russians, Germans, and Bolsheviks. It was not until late 1919 that a Latvian government took over and restored order. The suffering of the civilian population under occupation had been intense. Although during the period of German occupation many Germans had been kind and considerate, others had been overbearing and brutal. Much of the food that this relatively rich farming area had been able to produce had been requisitioned for the use of the occupying forces or for export to starving Germany. The local civilians had suffered from the lack not only of food but also of medicine, clothing, and other consumer goods. Weakened by undernourishment and hardship thousands died, including Elise's mother. Peace found a formerly prosperous people in a desperate condition. Their savings disappeared with the collapse of the Russian empire. Much of their personal property had been appropriated by retreating armies.

Fortunately for many of the children, as the result of Herbert Hoover's foresight and genius for organization, kitchens were opened in 1919 and 1920 in many of the towns and villages. These kitchens dispensed soup, cocoa, and other kinds of food that growing children need, until with the new crops the food shortage became less acute and the kitchens were closed. Many years passed before the wounds of war finally healed. The scars, however, never entirely disappeared. In her girlhood Elise had seen so much shooting and bloodshed that she never afterward could tolerate, even in the theater or the cinema, scenes of violence or the sound of shooting.

Elise had been gifted with a beautiful voice and had come to Riga for training. If she had not met me she might have become a talented singer. She felt so strongly her need to learn English that she decided in the spring of 1930, with the consent of her aged father, to drop her music studies temporarily and go to England where, for six months, she would be able to concentrate on the study of English. On the eve of her departure in the middle of June, realizing how much she had come to mean to me, I somewhat timidly suggested marriage to her. I thought it only fair to tell her that it might not be easy to adjust to life in the United States and that if I should remain in the Foreign Service the fact that she was of foreign origin might add somewhat to the problems of diplomatic life. She was, however, young and courageous and not at all daunted by my warnings. We became engaged.

Mr. Westmanis, the Latvian minister in London, and his wife knew from mutual friends that Elise would be in England and they invited her to stay with them in the legation during the summer. Shortly after her arrival they told her they would like to present her and another young Latvian to the court at a levée that the king was giving in July. They said that other embassies and legations were presenting young women from the countries they represented and they would like to present a couple of Latvians. Elise wrote me asking whether I could see any objection to her being introduced at court. I replied that the experience to be gained by such an introduction might be useful, so within several weeks after her arrival in London she was presented at the court of St. James.

It was the State Department's practice—one with which I thoroughly agreed—not to station a Foreign Service officer in a country of which his wife was a national. According to U.S. law, a year must elapse before Elise, after marriage to me, could become a U.S. citizen. I therefore wrote Kelley in the department telling him that, since it was my intention to marry a Latvian national at the end of the year, the department might care to transfer me at that time to another post. I added that it would be advantageous if my next post were in an English-speaking country so that my future wife would be able to improve her English. Kelley replied asking whether I would be willing to accept another detail to the Division of Eastern European Affairs. Since such an assignment would permit me to continue to work on Eastern Europe and would make it possible for Elise to improve her English and acquire U.S. citizenship, I replied that I would welcome it. Early in October I received the telegram assigning me to the department and suggesting that I plan to report there for duty in January 1931.

I left Riga on November 30, 1930, for Washington via London. Elise, now a radiant, quite sophisticated-appearing Londoner, met me at the railway station in London, and during the next 36 hours I rushed around making calls and acquiring the necessary papers. We were married on December 3 in St. Jude's Church in the Earl's Court section of London. The wedding was an informal affair attended by only a few of our friends who happened to be in the city. In the absence of the Latvian minister and his wife, who were on leave in Latvia, Mr. Seya, the Latvian consul general in London whom I had previously known as the Latvian minister in Washington, gave the bride away. The American consul general, Mr. Halstead, who had insisted on taking the morning off in order to attend, acted as my best man. Charles A. Broy, the senior consul with whom I had become acquainted while on duty in the department, and Mrs. Broy gave a small reception for us at their home following the ceremony. That evening we flew to Paris and the next morning we boarded a train for Menton, on the French Riviera, where we spent our honeymoon.

PART VIII

MEMBER OF THE DIVISION OF EASTERN EUROPEAN AFFAIRS, DEPARTMENT OF STATE, WASHINGTON, D.C., JANUARY 1931–FEBRUARY 1934

CHAPTER 21

THE DEPARTMENT OF STATE DURING THE LATER YEARS OF THE HOOVER ADMINISTRATION, JANUARY 1931–FEBRUARY 1933

IT WAS ON THE MORNING of January 27, 1931, that I entered the Department of State to begin my second tour of duty in the Division of Eastern European Affairs.

After 45 days of leave in southern France, my bride and I had embarked on January 15 on the steamship *President Roosevelt* and had arrived in New York some 9 days later. The voyage had been peaceful and restful — quite different from that which I had experienced in the latter part of the summer of 1921. Notably absent were the rowdiness and shrillness that in 1921 had introduced me to the United States of the Roaring Twenties. Although there were many young persons aboard, they gave evidence of a maturity that was quite unfashionable among the youth of the early and middle 1920s.

Following my arrival in the United States after the absence of three and a half years, I found that a change had also taken place in the attitude of the American people in general. The atmosphere both in New York and Washington, for instance, seemed to me to be more like that which had prevailed in the United States during the days of my youth. Two years of depression had apparently served to mute the raucousness that had dominated the era of prosperity. The dollar had lost some of its prestige; it was no longer so widely accepted as the measuring rod for determining the status of an individual or that person's value to society. I sensed a feeling of human kindliness and of consideration for one another that had not been so noticeable during my previous tour in the United States.

Now that I was married I was particularly interested in finding a suitable place to live. In spite of the depression and of the fact that there were numerous empty houses in Washington, the cost of rental for pleasant living quarters had not gone down. I had long held the belief that it would not be easy for a fairly low-ranking Foreign Service officer with a family to live on his salary in Washington, and this was speedily confirmed. I use the term "fairly low-ranking" because it continued to be applicable to me. After three and a half years in class 8 I had been promoted to class 7 in May 1929. In the latter part of February 1931, a month after my return to Washington, I had gone up to class 6. The financial benefits of this promotion were soon to be offset, however, by an economy measure requiring all employees of the government to take a month's leave without pay. Since the department was extremely short-handed, many of its members, including myself, met the situation by working without pay during the month of fictitious leave. Somewhat later the lowering of salaries was regularized by a so-called temporary measure, which reduced everyone's salary by 15 percent.

As a further measure of economy, admission of new members into the Foreign Service was suspended from January 1932 until March 1933, and promotions were suspended between July 1931 and July 1934. The plight of the members of the service on duty abroad became grave during the period that elapsed between the sudden devaluation of the dollar in 1933 and the enactment of relief legislation. Partly as the result of the economy measures, my net annual salary in February 1934—when I left Washington to take my next foreign post—was only a few hundred dollars more than that which I had been receiving as a vice consul ten years previously. I had fared no worse, however, than my colleagues. Since July 1, 1924, the date of the establishment of the Foreign Service, no one had passed me by in the marathon climb up the Foreign Service ladder. The slowness of promotions in the lower echelons of the service was due in part to the depression, in part to the attitude of the Bureau of the Budget and of Congress, and in part to a traffic jam among the rungs of the promotion ladder above us. This jam was to delay promotions for the officers at my level for years to come. It was not until October 1935, for instance, when I was already 43 years of age and had been 13 years in the service, that I went to class 5. I am not dwelling on the slowness of promotions during my early years in the service in a complaining spirit. I am referring to promotions because they, or the lack of them, are features too important to be ignored in the career of a Foreign Service officer. Furthermore, junior officers who in the years to come may be discouraged over the slowness of their travel toward the higher levels of the service may take heart after reading of my own tortoise-like progress.

My wife and I eventually found a little apartment that seemed to meet our needs on the top floor of an old apartment building then known as Florence Courts, situated on California Street at Twenty-second Street, Northwest.

It was customary in those days for a Foreign Service officer, who, like myself, was beginning a tour of the State Department, to pay calls upon the officers of the department with whom he would be likely to work most closely during the period of his assignment. Protocol demanded that he leave cards in the offices of the secretary, the under secretary, and all officers of assistant secretary rank. It was also incumbent upon him and his wife to leave their cards at the White House and with the members of the cabinet and their wives, with the dean of the diplomatic corps and his wife, with the chiefs of diplomatic missions with whom he was most likely to deal and their wives, and with the principal officers of the State Department and their wives.

I had few contacts with Secretary Stimson during the two years that I served under him. Only on rare occasions did I see him in his office or participate in conferences that he attended. It was my impression that he was not particularly interested in the work of the Eastern European Division or for that matter in problems relating to the Soviet Union. I had the feeling that he had no strong views with respect to the advantages or disadvantages of recognition of the USSR by the United States. The fact that he was a close friend and admirer of Felix Frankfurter and frequently turned to the latter for advice tended to confirm my belief that he personally was not strongly opposed to the establishment of diplomatic relations with the Soviet Union; Frankfurter had been for many years a strong advocate of recognition. Stimson also appeared to be particularly fond of Senator William Borah, who had never abandoned advocacy of recognition. On several of the rare occasions when he found it necessary to talk with Robert Kelley of the Eastern European Division on matters relating to the Soviet Union, Stimson had indicated that he hoped at some time to be able to bring the senator and Kelley together for a long talk. In New York in 1931–1933, there were a number of prominent and successful professional men with a background similar to that possessed by Stimson—men of integrity accustomed to deal with other men of integrity—who sincerely believed that if "one would treat the Bolsheviks as gentlemen worthy of trust the Bolsheviks would respond as gentlemen."

In my opinion, Stimson might well have tried to prevail upon the president to permit him to explore the possibilities of coming to an understanding with the Soviet Union—an understanding that would justify the establishment of diplomatic relations—were it not for his concern lest the recognition of a government that openly flouted the principles of international intercourse might endanger the success of his policies in the Far East. Stimson's concern in this respect was set forth in a letter that he wrote to Senator Borah on September 8, 1932. To this letter he attached a copy of a memorandum of the pros and cons of recognition, which, he said, had been prepared in the spring of 1932 at his request by the Division of Far Eastern Affairs. That memorandum had "reached conclusions which were dependent upon the situation as it then existed." The wording of the letter was of such nature as to give the senator to understand that the views expressed in the memorandum were those of the Far Eastern Division—not necessarily Stimson's own. The letter read in part:

> In the Far Eastern situation the United States was making a fight of world-wide importance for the integrity of international obligations. We were trying to buttress the great peace treaties which had been negotiated since the end of the war by developing in behalf of them an international sentiment throughout the world in support of good faith and the sacredness of keeping international promises. We were doing this solely by pacific means, endeavoring to enlist behind our movement the support of a world opinion and avoiding anything which approached force or political alliance.
>
> If under these circumstances and in this emergency we recognized Russia in disregard of her very bad reputation respecting international obligations and in disregard of our previous emphasis upon that aspect of her history, the whole world, and particularly Japan, would jump to the conclusion that our action had been dictated solely by political expedience and as a maneuver to bring forceful pressure upon Japan. We should thereby lose the moral standing which we had heretofore held in the controversy with Japan. She would regard us as merely an opportunist nation, seeking to enforce a selfish anti-Japanese policy against her by the usual maneuvers of international policies. I felt that this loss of moral standing would be so important that we could not afford to take the risk of it. However innocent our motives might be, they would certainly be misunderstood by the world at large and particularly by Japan, and that misunderstanding would destroy much of the influence of the moral pressure which we have been endeavoring to exert.

I might add that Stimson during 1931 and 1932 was so immersed in problems relating to the Manchurian crisis, to other Japanese encroachments in the Far East, and to disarmament, war debts, reparations, and various crises in the western hemisphere that he had little time to devote to thoughts about Eastern Europe, the Near East, and Africa.

One of the first persons in the State Department upon whom I called was Wilbur Carr, who continued to hold the thankless job of assistant secretary for administration. My conversation with him, like many of my later talks with this harried officer, was interrupted again and again by telephone calls. He nevertheless displayed what was to me a surprising knowledge of what I had been doing during the previous three years and of some of the problems that the legation was facing in Riga. He made no secret during our conversation of his disappointment at not being able to use funds already appropriated for maintaining the department and the Foreign Service at levels that the needs of the United States demanded. He told me that Mr. Hoover personally realized that more funds were needed but that, in view of the depressed economic conditions of the country, the president considered it necessary to effect economies in all government agencies.

My talk with Carr confirmed my belief that he thought the staff of our legation at Riga was unduly large in comparison with the staffs of other U.S. diplomatic missions throughout the world. I did my best to explain why I considered it important that the legation be provided with able officers interested in Eastern Europe, particularly in the Soviet Union, and that these officers be furnished competent translators and clerical assistants. He listened patiently but I could see that he was not convinced. He told me several years later, following his retirement as minister to Czechoslovakia, that two years in the Foreign Service abroad had given him an understanding of many of the problems of the service that he had been unable to obtain during 40 years in the department. He said he was particularly pleased that he had been succeeded by a Foreign Service officer who had served in the foreign field.* He added that as a result of his own experience he considered it to be of the utmost impor- tance that the chief administrator of the department be a career officer with extensive years of service both in the department and abroad. He thought that no experience as an administrator in government or in private life and no study of textbooks could qualify a person who had not gone through the Foreign Service mill, both at home and abroad, to administer the complex, far-flung, dual institution that he referred to as the "State Department–Foreign Service." He added that some of his own decisions, attitudes, and approaches to Congress would have been differ- ent if he had had a few years of substantive as well as administrative experience at a foreign post.

---

* Henderson held the post of deputy under secretary of state for administration from 1955 to 1961 (ed.).

CHAPTER 22

THE EFFECT OF THE DEPRESSION ON THE INTERNATIONAL SITUATION, JANUARY 1931–MARCH 1933

THE INTERNATIONAL SITUATION from January 1931 up to the end of the Hoover administration in March 1933 was gloomy. The depression hung like an immovable dark cloud not only over the United States but over most of the world. In Europe, Latin America, and the Far East the wheels of industry were moving more and more slowly. As a result, the demands for raw materials decreased. Scores of millions of persons found themselves without means of livelihood. Debtors could not pay their creditors. Banks closed. Firm after firm went into bankruptcy. The peoples of many countries, including the United States, tended to blame their governments and, in many instances, the system of private enterprise for their plight. Revolutions broke out in many parts of the world. There was a worldwide decline of confidence in democracy as a workable form of government. Many former advocates of democracy came to believe that their only hope for the future lay in the establishment of a dictatorship. Some of them favored the so-called proletarian dictatorships; others, repelled by the excesses that had cost millions of lives in the Soviet Union, preferred what might be called "middle-class dictatorships" and fell easy victims to the harangues of Fascist and Nazi demagogues. Still others thought that military dictatorships represented the best antidote to decadent democracy.

Many countries, particularly in Europe, were heavily indebted to the United States. Since the United States displayed no willingness to cancel their debts in spite of the patent inability of the debtors to pay, the United States was branded as an "Uncle Shylock" and anti-Americanism developed on a wide scale.

In the United States the politicians opposed to the administration in power insisted that its leaders were responsible for the situation. President Hoover, who had come into office at a time when the country seemed assured of continued prosperity, was the particular object of attack. The president tried valiantly to meet the internal and external economic crises that seemed to arise almost daily. The problems, both in complexity and in magnitude, were of a kind that the United States had never previously encountered. Our institutions were not adequately prepared to cope with them. Eventually, when it became clear that steps of an unprecedented character must be taken, the president found himself handicapped by an uncooperative and unsympathetic Congress. Although most of the career members of the department were apolitical—that is, they were committed to serving the administration that happened to be in power, regardless of its party complexion—they were nevertheless conscious of the past accomplishments of the president, his integrity, and his great ability. They admired the patience, courage, and dignity with which he bore the attacks upon him and could not but be moved by what they regarded as the unfairness of his being treated as a whipping boy both at home and abroad.

The worldwide depression had a less harmful effect upon the Soviet Union than it had had upon the more highly developed areas of the world. This was partly because Soviet economy was more independent of the international environment than that of the other great powers and partly because the scale of living in the Soviet Union was so low that even a depression could not push it much farther down. Nevertheless, the depression did curtail the markets abroad for Soviet raw materials and this resulted in a slowdown of Soviet economic development. Furthermore, the credits that the Soviet Union had been receiving from Germany began to taper off as the Nazis tightened their control over their country.

In fact, the depression brought certain political advantages to the Soviet Union in connection with its efforts to promote communism internationally. Hundreds of millions of persons were impressed by the insistence of Soviet agents that the depression clearly demonstrated "the bankruptcy of capitalism and its partner, imperialism." Soviet leaders were not particularly disturbed by the appearance of fascism and nazism in some countries of Central and southern Europe, even though such appearance temporarily rendered it more difficult for them to obtain foreign credits. In my opinion, the Soviets honestly believed their tenet that fascism and nazism were the garments in which capitalism could be expected to array itself in its last days; they were genuinely convinced at the time that nonproletarian dictatorships would help to prepare the way for the final victory of international communism. In their opinion it would be much easier for communism to take over countries in which the people were already accustomed to dictatorships than for it to tighten its control over countries in which the people were accustomed to democratic processes. They were, however, disturbed at the progress of militarism in Japan since they feared that a military dictatorship there might undertake adventures in the Far East that could be harmful to Soviet interests.

The depression resulted in some interesting changes in the attitude of big business corporations in the United States with respect to the Soviet Union. Although during the years of prosperity these businesses were prepared to deal with the Soviet Union on a cash basis, they nevertheless regarded that country with suspicion and were not eager for the United States to enter into political relations with it. Since 1921 the U.S. government, it will be recalled, had not opposed the development of trade between the United States and the USSR provided such trade did not involve financial or long-term credits. The U.S. government had from time to time even taken steps to facilitate such trade. It had, for instance, issued regulations that made it possible for Soviet officials engaged in buying and selling to visit and reside in the United States. It had also adopted procedures that made it possible for U.S. businessmen and technicians to enter and reside in the Soviet Union with the understanding, of course, that if they should get into trouble with the Soviet authorities the U.S. government would not be in a position to protect them. In order to facilitate further Soviet-American trade, the United States had permitted the Soviet Union to establish an agency, incorporated in the State of New York, under the name of Amtorg Trading Corporation. Using Amtorg as a base, Soviet officials had been successful in establishing business and personal contacts with important financing institutions and firms not only in New York but throughout the United States. The influential Chase National Bank, which was serving as the principal banker and financial adviser of Amtorg, other financial institutions and businesses that were profiting or hoping to profit from trade or economic relations with the Soviet Union, and a group of Soviet officials attached to Amtorg had cooperated in organizing an American-Russian Chamber of Commerce. This chamber had been joined by scores of U.S. manufacturers, exporters and importers, engineering firms, and industrial establishments, before whom the Soviet agents connected with Amtorg were dangling glittering possibilities of lucrative trade between the United States and the Soviet Union. These agents were insisting that the Soviet markets for U.S. products were almost unlimited and that Soviet orders could cause the wheels to turn in many factories and plants that had become idle. Manufacturers, such as those engaged in making machine tools, were indulging in dreams of turning out hundreds of millions of dollars worth of machinery to satisfy the needs of the growing Soviet industry.

The Soviet agents were also maintaining that the artificial dam that was preventing a free flow of trade between the two countries could not be broken down in the absence of diplomatic relations, and that if Soviet orders for U.S. products, technical assistance, and so forth were to prove a stimulus to the U.S. economy, diplomatic relations between the two countries must be established. The agents failed, however, to stress a fact that was apparent to all of us who had been closely observing developments in the Soviet Union: unless recognition were accompanied by the advance of tremendous amounts of credit, Soviet purchases in the United States would not be likely to increase materially since the Soviet Union had few excess commodities to offer in exchange for foreign products.

The American-Russian Chamber of Commerce, spurred on by its Amtorg members, began to take the lead in demanding the establishment of diplomatic relations with the Soviet Union. Some of the members of the chamber went so far as to employ influential public relations firms to assist in carrying on the campaign for recognition.

Business concerns were not alone in pressing for recognition. Many of the leading intellectuals and so-called liberals, as well as numerous communist-controlled united-front organizations, participated in the campaign. In Washington, Boris Skvirsky, a Soviet official who had been permitted by the U.S. government to establish an informal and unrecognized Soviet Information Bureau, was carrying on his own campaign for recognition among his numerous contacts, which represented many left-wing journalists, academicians, and even a number of U.S. government officials.

In addition to the pressure groups that were prompted by such considerations as monetary gain or kinship of ideology to support recognition of the Soviet Union, there were many persons and groups throughout the country who, although repelled by what they regarded as the inhumanity of the Soviet regime and unimpressed by arguments relating to the prospects of the development of a huge American-Soviet trade, believed nevertheless that the establishment of diplomatic relations between the United States and the Soviet Union would strengthen the United States internationally and would be in the interest of world peace.

Interesting enough, among the more active opponents of recognition was the American Federation of Labor, which through the years had been carrying on a battle to prevent the infiltration of Communists and communist sympathizers into its ranks and which feared that recognition might give international communism a respectability that would render trade unions and other organizations of workers more vulnerable to communist infiltration.

CHAPTER 23

THE DIVISION OF
EASTERN EUROPEAN AFFAIRS,
JANUARY 1931–MARCH 1933

THE DIVISION OF EASTERN EUROPEAN AFFAIRS had undergone a number of changes during my absence in the Baltic states. Robert Kelley continued to be chief and Earl Packer assistant chief. The desk formerly filled by Kumler, who had been killed in an automobile accident, had been taken over by Raymond E. Murphy, a permanent member of the department. Murphy, after obtaining his A.B. degree from Bates College, had entered the Department of State as a clerical employee in 1920. While in the department he had studied law at night and had received a law degree from Georgetown University. In the latter 1920s he had been assigned to the Division of Eastern European Affairs as an assistant analyst. In the division he had been charged with observing the communist movement in the United States from the point of view of its subservience to Moscow. In connection with his work over the years he had accumulated in his files a valuable collection of documents relating not only to the activities of international communism in the United States but also to U.S. nationals implicated in such activities. His files became one of the primary sources of our government's information regarding the efforts of international communism to promote revolutionary activities in the United States and to penetrate governmental departments, and Murphy developed into one of the outstanding authorities in the United States on communist personnel intrigues. Again and again he was successful in foiling communist plots to obtain footholds in the department and other government agencies. In so doing he incurred the hostility not only of the American Communists and fellow travelers but also of many so-called liberals who were not communist in sympathy but who were inclined to ridicule the idea that the United States might be endangered by communist activities and infiltration. I can recall one instance in which several members of the Division of Western European Affairs of the Department of State instituted a personal boycott against Murphy because he had prevented, on security grounds, a popular member of that division from being appointed to an extremely delicate governmental position. They refused to speak to him or take a seat at a table where he might be sitting. They were quite sheepish several years later when the popular officer in question took refuge in a communist–controlled East European country in order to escape prosecution by the U.S. government as the agent of a foreign power.

During periods of the years to come Ray Murphy was to work under my direction. I admired him for his courage, ingenuity, and tenacity and sympathized with him for the martyrdom to which he was sometimes subjected. When he died in the early 1960s I considered it a privilege to participate in the preparation of a tribute to him for the services that he had rendered to the United States—a tribute that was presented in the U.S. Senate.

Another addition to the division was Orsen Nielsen, a Foreign Service officer, who had entered the service as a clerical employee in the consulate general in Moscow in the latter part of 1916. He had been promoted to vice consul while still in Moscow in 1918 and had subsequently served at Stockholm, Berlin, Dublin, and Tehran. Since he was a Foreign Service officer of class 5 he outranked me. I was, therefore, for a time fourth ranking officer of the division. Subsequently, as a result of the appointment of Nielsen as first secretary of our embassy at Warsaw and his replacement by Landreth Harrison from Riga, I again became the third ranking officer. Nielsen and I occupied the same room in the State Department for over a year and he proved to be a genial and agreeable colleague. He was a subtle drafting officer and some of the hints I received from him proved helpful during both this particular period and ensuing years in rendering as palatable as circumstances might warrant diplomatic notes the contents of which were certain to be displeasing to the addressee.

My activities in the Eastern European Division during the two years under Stimson were in general similar to those that I had performed during the latter part of my first assignment. I resumed the work of grading and supervising the distribution of dispatches and reports coming into the department from our posts in Eastern Europe, of preparing memoranda regarding matters in which the division was particularly interested, and of drafting notes, instructions, telegrams, and miscellaneous correspondence relating to East European affairs. It was also a part of my duties to establish friendly relations with the personnel of the embassies and legations of Eastern Europe in Washington and to receive the junior officers of those missions when they called at the department on official matters.

As the campaign for the recognition of the Soviet Union increased in intensity during the last year of the Hoover administration, the Division of Eastern European Affairs began to devote more and more time preparing to meet various problems that in our opinion would arise in case the United States should decide to reconsider any of its policies in regard to the Soviet Union. These preparations were of a two-fold nature. They involved the assembly of material for possible use by the administration in power in defending the continuation of the policy of nonrecognition and also of material that in our opinion would be useful in the course of negotiations leading to recognition.

Each of the officers of the division was made responsible for the assembly of material and the preparation of documents relating to specific subjects that would probably be considered during a reexamination of our Russian policies in the light of the world situation. I was, for instance, assigned by Kelley to the task of assembling the international commitments entered into by the Soviet Union that might conceivably be of interest to the administration in connection with negotiations looking toward the establishment of diplomatic relations with the Soviet Union and of arranging them according to subject matter and country in a manner that would make them convenient as a reference source.

Although over the years the division had been making a careful study of the more important treaties to which the Soviet Union was a party, my assignment, nevertheless, meant much work. In some instances we found it necessary to ask our embassies abroad to assist us in obtaining copies of agreements to which we found references but of which we had no copies. The most important source for the material that I needed was the massive files of the Eastern European Division. The file clerks spent many hours tracking down needed documents. Also most helpful in this work was a new arrival in the division, Virginia James, who subsequently devoted almost 30 years to the field of American-Soviet relations. Prior to her retirement at the end of 1965 she maintained a desk in the office of Soviet Union Affairs where, in addition to her other work, she served as a source of information to young officers entering that office regarding the problems that had arisen in the years gone by in relations between the United States and the Soviet Union.

My next task was to assemble such information as might be available regarding the attitude that the Soviet government had displayed toward its treaty commitments. Since the division had been engaged for many years in collecting documents on this subject, my task consisted primarily of getting these documents together, having them edited and retyped, and attaching the copies thus produced to the specific treaty commitments to which they related. When this assignment was completed the possessors of these compilations could ascertain with a minimum of difficulty which international commitments the Soviet regime had been willing to give in the past and the extent to which it had lived up to them.

I may have gone into rather tiresome detail in describing these particular tasks because they illustrate the kind of work in which some of the divisions of the State Department engaged in the years gone by— work unknown to the public or to the academicians who have sometimes unfairly accused the department of failing to prepare itself adequately for possible eventualities. I realize that the filing systems employed in those days are now becoming outmoded and that the time is quickly approaching when information on almost every conceivable subject in the field of international affairs will be snugly stored in rows of computers, so that at the mere pressure of a button the particular data desired will come gushing out of the maws of a machine. I am confident that if members of the Department of State during the computer age should happen to read my description of the kind of amateur research in which the Division of Eastern European Affairs, with its limited facilities, engaged during the early 1930s, they will smile condescendingly, just as many of us were inclined to do when reading accounts of the work in the department prior to the advent of the typewriter.

The members of the division under the supervision of both Kelley and Packer also undertook to assemble and analyze documents relating to subjects that in their opinion were likely to play important roles in such relations as might develop between the United States and the Soviet Union. Among these subjects might be mentioned the practice of the rulers of the Soviet Union of interfering in the affairs of other countries, in particular, their endeavors to bring about the overthrow by violence of noncommunist governments; also of concern was the attitude of the Soviet regime toward the payment of international debts incurred by previous governments in Russia and toward the compensation of foreign governments and foreign nationals for damages resulting from Soviet acts of nationalization and confiscation. There were also the problems of Soviet claims against the United States for alleged damages resulting from the dispatch of U.S. troops to northern Russia and Siberia during the latter part of the war and the possibility that, following recognition, the Soviet government might lay claim to funds or property in the United States that belonged to previous Russian governments. Among the other subjects studied were the treatment of foreigners by the Soviet regime in the Soviet Union, the rights of foreign diplomatic and consular officers in the Soviet Union—in particular, the extent to which they might have access to and assist their nationals visiting or residing in the country who might be in trouble, the kind of legal processes to which foreigners in the Soviet Union might be subjected, and the extent to which foreigners might enjoy freedom of worship.

We collected in quickly accessible form documents dealing with problems experienced in the Soviet Union by diplomatic and consular representatives of other countries that had established diplomatic relations with the Soviet Union. Among these problems were the difficulties encountered by these representatives in obtaining living and working quarters, the lack of contact between them and Soviet nationals, the unwillingness of the Soviet authorities to furnish them with the kind of information usually exchanged between friendly governments, the restrictions placed upon their movements and travel, the shortage of nearly all kinds of articles of consumption in the Soviet Union, difficulties arising from the exchange rates established by the Soviet government, the dearth of drugs and medical facilities, the inadequacy of local transportation facilities, and the ever-present danger of arrest of subordinate diplomatic and consular personnel by the Soviet police.

CHAPTER 24

THE DEPARTMENT OF STATE
DURING THE FIRST YEAR
OF THE ROOSEVELT ADMINISTRATION,
MARCH 1933–FEBRUARY 1934

WHILE THE EASTERN EUROPEAN DIVISION was engaged in making studies for use in case our government should reexamine our policies with regard to the Soviet Union, the cruel election campaign of the fall of 1932 was grinding to a halt with an overwhelming victory for the Democrats. The period between the November elections and the inauguration on March 4, 1933, was trying for most members of the State Department. The president-elect and the president in power had little contact. It was our understanding that Roosevelt was not acting the part of a generous or chivalrous victor and that he was unwilling to confer with Hoover regarding either short-term or long-term foreign policy problems on the alleged ground that he did not wish to share in the responsibility for such decisions as might be made while Hoover was still president. Although early in 1933 conversations of a limited character did take place between Roosevelt and Stimson regarding international problems involving far-reaching decisions that could not be postponed until March 4, the substance of these conversations was not imparted to the personnel of the State Department.

The members of the Eastern European Division had no idea what the attitude of the new administration was likely to be with regard to the recognition of the Soviet Union. Persons said to be close to Roosevelt issued from time to time public statements ridiculing the failure of the

U.S. government to recognize a government that had successfully ruled one of the great countries of the world for fifteen years. No one knew, however, whether these statements reflected the views of the president. There were stories in the press indicating that the president-elect in Hyde Park was being inundated with the petitions from individuals and groups favoring recognition. Walter Duranty, the well-known correspondent of the *New York Times* in Moscow who had long favored recognition and who was said to be in the confidence of some of the Soviet leaders, after accepting an invitation to visit the president at Hyde Park, dropped hints that he was in possession of an important secret and had been entrusted by the president with a mysterious mission.

As March 4 approached, regret deepened among the career personnel of the State Department at the impending departure of Stimson and his able group of noncareer advisers. Stimson, while uniformly courteous during his term of secretaryship, had tended to remain withdrawn and aloof from those members of the Foreign and Civil Services who did not belong to the small circle with which he was closely working. He had not shown any high degree of interest in the administration of the department and of the Foreign Service and had taken no energetic measures for the purpose of strengthening them or adding to their effectiveness. It is true that during his first two years in office certain legislation had been enacted that was destined over a long period to strengthen the Foreign Service and that the appropriations for the Department of State had been materially increased. These steps forward were not, however, the result of actions taken by the secretary. The most important piece of legislation was a law that went into effect on June 26, 1930, authorizing Congress to appropriate funds for the payment of rent, heat, and light of the living quarters of U.S. employees abroad. In view of the economy measures that were adopted soon after the passage of this law, relatively small amounts were appropriated for this purpose during the remainder of the Hoover administration. Subsequently, however, this legislation was to prove helpful in enabling Foreign Service personnel without private means to serve at posts where costs of living were inordinately high.

The State Department had requested, and Congress had appropriated, 17.2 million dollars for the use of the department and the Foreign Service during the fiscal year beginning July 1, 1930, an unprecedented increase of almost 2.5 million dollars over the appropriations for the preceding year. Unfortunately for the department and the Foreign Service, as the result of the inauguration of economy measures, most of this increase, instead of being used for the purposes intended, was returned to the treasury.

Wilbur Carr, with the support of President Hoover, had been primarily responsible for the enactment of this legislation. The increases in the amounts appropriated for the State Department were the results of the pressures put on Kellogg and Coolidge by Under Secretary Robert Olds and Carr during the last days of the Coolidge administration— pressures that were eventually felt by both the Budget Bureau and the appropriations committees of Congress.

Regret at the impending departure of the secretary was mingled with concern regarding the kind of a person who might succeed him. Many in the department and the Foreign Service had not forgotten the dismal period twenty years previously when they had served under William Jennings Bryan. There was an almost unanimous sigh of relief when the announcement was made that Senator Cordell Hull had agreed to accept the secretaryship and that William Phillips, one of the able graduates of the old Diplomatic Service, was to be under secretary. The senator was known as a statesman type of politician and as a person in whom one could have confidence. We were pleased that Hull's alter ego was to be Phillips, who had already served a term of under secretary during 1922 and 1923. It was Phillips who in 1922, as a comparatively youthful under secretary, had signed in the capacity of acting secretary my first commission as vice consul *de carrière*.

Our pleasure at the appointment of Phillips was diluted by the retirement of William Castle, who had been one of the wheel horses of the department for many years. His retirement, however, came as no surprise since he had forfeited his noncareer status by campaigning vigorously for President Hoover. It was generally believed in the department that if Hoover had been reelected Castle would have become the next secretary of state.

During the first twelve months of the new administration there were a series of shifts in the assistant secretaryships. The president, although sometimes going through the rite of consulting Secretary Hull, had selected the latter's top assistants to suit himself. Unfortunately, his selections too frequently resulted in discord and the lowering of the general effectiveness of the State Department and the Foreign Service. The only assistant secretary of the Hoover administration who survived the first few months of the new administration was Carr. Several days after the inaugural, Raymond Moley and Harry F. Payer were appointed assistant secretaries to succeed James G. Rogers and Harvey H. Bundy. Moley was a forceful and articulate product of the academic world who had also maintained an interest in public affairs. It was manifest that he looked to the president rather than to Hull for guidance. In any event, the president encouraged him to bypass the secretary and to deal directly with the White House. The relations between Hull and Moley degenerated so rapidly that after a period of several months the latter tendered his resignation.

Payer was a successful lawyer from Cleveland, Ohio, who in addition to practicing law had found time to dabble in politics and to engage in writing and lecturing. He had been a strong supporter of Roosevelt both before and during the election campaign and was appointed apparently as a reward for services rendered since he had no outstanding qualifications for a top position in the Department of State. With his flamboyancy and his flair for the dramatic he enlivened the department during the period that he was connected with it. His gaudy gold-plated automobile with its ornate mellifluous siren was an object of awe to many of the tourists who, in spite of the depression, flooded Washington during the late spring months. His tenure in the department was also of short duration.

Francis White was appointed minister to Czechoslovakia shortly after the new administration took over. Jefferson Caffery, also a veteran of the old Diplomatic Service, took over the assistant secretaryship for Latin American Affairs long enough to permit Sumner Welles, who was slated for that position, to serve for several months as ambassador to Cuba. In the latter part of 1933 Caffery and Welles exchanged posts as had been planned. Welles was a tall, austere man in his early forties when he became assistant secretary for Latin American Affairs. Like the president, a graduate of Groton and Harvard, he had for many years been a friend both of the president and Mrs. Roosevelt. Extremely able and ambitious, he was impatient with any person or thing that might restrict his activities or block his advancement. It was the impression of many in the department that he tended to regard Hull as an unsophisticated product of the backwoods of Tennessee. This impression was derived more from what seemed to be his general attitude toward the secretary than from specific words or action. Nevertheless, Hull clearly resented what he regarded as the condescending manner in which Welles treated him. He also objected to the practice of Welles—a practice encouraged by both the president and Mrs. Roosevelt—of making policy decisions or taking actions without consulting the secretary on the basis of conversations in the White House.

Moley and Payer were succeeded by Robert Walton Moore and Francis Bowes Sayre in September and November, respectively, of 1933. Judge Moore, as he was usually referred to in the department, was already 74 at the time of his appointment. He was, nevertheless, full of energy and, in view of his many acquaintances in Washington and contacts with personnel in the White House and with members of Congress, he soon made his presence felt in the department. His home was in Fairfax, Virginia, and he had been a member of Congress from that area from 1919 until 1931. While in Congress he had established close friendly relations with Hull. In view of Hull's confidence in Judge Moore's loyalty to him and of the care taken by Moore to keep the secretary informed of his activities, the secretary did not seem to resent the close relationships that Moore maintained with the White House. Since Moore was particularly interested in affairs pertaining to the Soviet Union, the members of the Division of Eastern European Affairs had frequent contacts with him during ensuing years.

Sayre, as assistant secretary, was charged with handling matters of an economic, financial, tariff, and general trade character. Like many of the top officials of the State Department of the New Deal era, he was a graduate of Harvard Law School and had engaged both in teaching and practicing law. He was a person of considerable influence in the Democratic party. His wife, who had died only a few months before he entered the department, had been a daughter of President Wilson. He had not, however, endeavored to exploit this relationship. While serving in the department he did not engage in any of the intrigues that made life complex during the early years of Roosevelt's presidency but limited his activities primarily to carrying out the duties assigned to him. He left the department in 1939 to accept the position of U.S. high commissioner in the Philippines, where he remained until the outbreak of the war with Japan. He subsequently engaged in missions of an international character for both the United States and other countries before his retirement as a highly respected statesman.

Another appointment to the State Department shortly after the beginning of the new administration was that of William C. Bullitt as special assistant to the secretary. I shall not undertake here to describe Bullitt's background, career, and personality in detail. Since, however, I was destined to work in close association with him for several years, and since I shall have occasion to refer to him frequently during subsequent portions of my narration, it might be helpful for me to devote a few descriptive words to him at this point.

If, in a democratic country like the United States, it is permissible to use the term "patrician," it might be said that Bullitt was a member of one of the great patrician families of the United States. Some of his ancestors had played leading roles in the building of the colony of Virginia and subsequently in establishing America's independence. One of them had moved from his estate in eastern Virginia in the latter part of the eighteenth century to what became the state of Kentucky in order to establish a new residence about eight miles distant from Louisville. That residence is still regarded by members of the Bullitt family as their family headquarters. Bullitt's grandfather, John C. Bullitt, married into a distinguished

Virginia family (his wife was Theresa Langhorne), set up a law office in Philadelphia, and became one of the civic leaders there; his statue now stands in the center of Philadelphia to commemorate his successful efforts to procure a charter for that city.

Bullitt had an excellent education in private preparatory schools and at Yale. In his youth he traveled abroad extensively and was given ample opportunities, of which he took full advantage, to learn both French and German and to become accustomed to European ways of thinking and living. While at Yale he became interested in journalism. After graduating from Yale, at the urging of his family, he put aside his journalistic ambitions and enrolled in Harvard Law School. He found law so boring, however, that following the death of his father he abandoned the study of it.

In the summer of 1914 the youthful Bullitt made one of his trips to Europe. It included visits to England, France, Germany, the Scandinavian countries, and Russia. He was still in Moscow when the First World War began. He was fond of Europe and of the Europeans and was enraged at the thought that the people of that enlightened continent, whom he had regarded as intelligent, should be so stupid as to resort to war in order to resolve their differences. He decided at once to devote himself to the kind of work in which he had for years been interested—to pursue journalism as a career. As a journalist he would have, he thought, opportunities to express his views regarding war and peace and many other matters that concerned him to wide audiences. He therefore returned to the United States and concentrated for several months on mastering stenography and touch-typing. Following these studies he accepted a position on one of the great newspapers in Philadelphia, the *Public Ledger*.

Bullitt had been only a short time with the *Ledger* when its editor asked him to go to Europe with the Ford Peace Ship in order to report on the activities of its passengers. It will be recalled that Henry Ford, as a dramatic gesture in the interest of peace, had chartered a vessel, filled it with idealistic pacifists, and was sending it to Europe where he hoped that the passengers could promote peace among the warring nations. Bullitt sent back a series of amusing descriptions of what was transpiring on the vessel during the voyage. His reports on the antics of some of the more naive, as well as some of the more sophisticated, passengers were published in newspapers throughout the world. Almost overnight he became one of the best-known American correspondents. Subsequently he was sent by his newspaper to Germany where his reports regarding the wartime situation in that country were also widely read. He then came back to the United States to become associate editor of the *Public Ledger*.

In 1917, as the United States was being drawn into the war, Bullitt became a member of the Department of State where he served as the chief of a section dealing particularly with information regarding Germany, Austria, Hungary, and Belgium. Woodrow Wilson took particular notice of this promising, rather brash young man and arranged for him to become a member of the U.S. peace delegation to Paris, which was to participate in the negotiation of the Treaty of Peace. On that delegation Bullitt had the title of chief of current intelligence summaries.

In 1919 Colonel House, on behalf of the president, asked Bullitt to go to Moscow on an informal mission. In later years, after I had become a close friend of Bullitt, he told me that the purpose of this mission was to explore the possibilities of an end being put to the numerous wars that were then taking place on the territory of the former Russian empire— wars that might well develop into new major international conflicts. While in Russia he had become convinced that the Bolsheviks would remain in power for an indefinite period of years and that it would be in the interest of world peace for relations to be established between the victorious powers of the West and the Soviet regime.

Upon his return with the draft of a detailed agreement, which the Soviet leaders had assured him of their willingness to accept, for bringing about the cessation of fighting on Russian territory, he found that a change had taken place in the atmosphere of the U.S. delegation to the peace conference. President Wilson had apparently lost confidence in Colonel House and was under the influence of persons who had little experience in handling foreign affairs. There was a minimum of interest in the circle then around the president in matters pertaining to Russia and no action was taken with regard to the papers that Bullitt had brought back with him.

As the peace conference dragged along Bullitt, who was by nature a humanitarian with instinctive feelings of sympathy where human suffering was involved, was stirred by what he regarded as the brutal attitude of the Allies in refusing to permit food to go into Germany, particularly to the starving children, until the Germans would agree to a victor-imposed treaty. He endeavored to persuade his young colleagues on the mission to join in protesting the use of starvation as an instrument of diplomacy. Although some of his co-workers agreed that this kind of policy was not compatible with Western civilization, they were unwilling to join in his protests. Revolted by the food blockade and concerned that the kind of a treaty being imposed upon Germany would lead to protracted tensions and possibly to another European war, he eventually resigned in protest from the peace mission and returned to the United States in order to use his talents in opposing the ratification of the treaty by the Senate.

His prophetic testimony before the Senate Foreign Relations Committee against the Treaty of Versailles still makes interesting reading.

Between 1919 and 1933 Bullitt devoted himself to writing, traveling, and the study of international affairs. He maintained friendly relations with intellectuals, writers, and political leaders both in the United States and abroad. During his travels he became acquainted with many of the outstanding statesmen of Europe. Bullitt was an articulate and witty conversationalist. When he turned on his charm he could be almost irresistible. His sarcasm, when he made use of it, could also be devastating. It was understandable that President Roosevelt, who loathed people that bored him and who admired brilliance, should become extremely fond of Bullitt, whom he had met while serving as assistant secretary of navy, and should desire to make use of Bullitt's abilities.

Bullitt had continued to follow events in Russia since his visit there in 1919. During the interim between the elections in November and the inauguration of the president in March, he had again visited Russia and upon his return had reported his findings to the president. His report to the president was not made public. Bullitt, however, told me many years later that while he was making his report the president and he had agreed that it would be in the interest of the United States to establish diplomatic relations with the Soviet Union. The president had pointed to a map of Europe and Asia that hung on the wall and said, "It is ridiculous that the United States is not on speaking terms with that big hunk of territory." As a result of that conversation and of many others that he had with the president on the same subject, Bullitt was convinced that the president had made up his mind even before taking his oath of office to establish diplomatic relations with the Soviet Union just as soon as conditions, in his opinion, would be favorable to such a development in both the Soviet Union and the United States.

In view of Bullitt's interest in the Soviet Union and of his personal acquaintance with Soviet leaders, the president, in appointing him special assistant to the secretary of state, undoubtedly had in mind making use of him in matters pertaining to the Soviet Union. Although Bullitt owed his appointment to the president rather than to Hull and was frequently invited to the White House to confer with the president, he got along surprisingly well with the secretary. The relations between the two were always correct and sometimes cordial. Bullitt's closest friend and confidant in the department, however, was Judge Moore, who had been a lifelong friend of Bullitt's father—a friendship established when the two men had been fellow students in the University of Virginia.

The early days of March 1933 were memorable for members of the

Department of State. We said farewell to Stimson and his coterie of top assistants and were looking forward to meeting the new group who, under President Roosevelt, were to be responsible for the conduct of our foreign relations. As nonpolitical civil servants we desired to serve them just as loyally as we had tried to serve their predecessors.

I had been on duty in Washington when Coolidge had been sworn in for his second term as president in March 1925. There was comparatively little excitement in the department at that time. Although Kellogg was to replace Hughes as secretary of state and several changes were contemplated among the top personnel of the department, no upheaval had been anticipated. It was generally understood in 1933, however, that Roosevelt intended to make sweeping changes in both the foreign and domestic policies of the United States and to replace, to the extent that the Civil Service and other regulations would permit, personnel who had come into the government during the twelve years of Republican administration. According to apparently inspired press reports there was to be a complete new deal. Moth-eaten bureaucrats and unimaginative personnel were to be replaced by bright, shining, forward-looking activists.

Criticism of the State Department by pro-New Deal columnists and editorial writers was particularly severe. There were insistent demands that the reactionaries be rooted out and replaced by persons who could be depended upon to carry out enlightened New Deal policies.

The results of the anticipated purge of the department were highly unsatisfactory to many Democrats, particularly to the New Dealers hungry for jobs. It was not easy to create vacancies in a department of approximately 800 members when about 700 of them had either Civil Service or Foreign Service status. Similarly, the officer positions in our diplomatic and consular offices abroad, other than those occupied by chiefs of missions, were filled by members of the Foreign Service or by officers of the Department of Commerce and of the armed services. There were, however, a number of ambassadorships and ministerships that could be bestowed upon deserving Democrats. Furthermore, there were quite a number of unfilled nonofficer positions in our embassies, legations, and consular offices.

The appetite for jobs in the State Department was so strong that in the middle of March 1933 a special team was sent in to examine the situation. We did not know whence the members of this team derived their authority, whether they were working for the White House, the Bureau of the Budget, or the Democratic party. In any event they systematically entered every office in the department in their search for fugitive bureaucrats not protected by Civil Service or Foreign Service legislation. A young man, perhaps 30 years of age, had apparently been assigned to explore the bureaucratic jungle on the third floor. We observed him with notebook in hand going from office to office. Eventually he barged into the room occupied by Orsen Nielsen and myself. Not troubling to introduce himself he ordered Nielsen and me to give him our names and our status and to describe our activities. Ignoring his overbearing attitude we gave our names, told him we were Foreign Service officers, and added that we were working on matters relating to Eastern Europe. "What," he said with a mixture of disgust and contempt in his voice, "more of these Foreign Service officers! Oh Hell!" He snapped shut his notebook, turned on his heel, and left the office as abruptly as he had entered.

This team was successful in unearthing a few members of the State Department who had neither Civil Service nor Foreign Service status. Most of them were replaced almost immediately by deserving Democrats or friends of deserving Democrats. Some of the new appointees were so clearly unfitted for the work assigned to them that they did not remain long in the department. Some, glorying in the fact that they were participants in the New Deal and were, therefore, close to the seat of power, assumed at first a patronizing attitude toward the permanent personnel. As the more capable New Deal infiltrators became immersed in the work and as they discovered that the permanent personnel sincerely wanted to help them, the dividing line between them and the career personnel of the department tended to disappear. Some of the new arrivals were clearly persons of ability—not mere job hunters—who desired to engage in public service. They soon earned the respect of the permanent members. In fact, some of them over the years attained career status.

Carr, as the chief administrator of the department, fought manfully to protect the career people and the Foreign Service from eager job hunters. If a person of less stamina and prestige had occupied his position the Foreign Service would probably have been torn to shreds and the protective cover would have been entirely removed from the Civil Service employees. Even the secretary, under pressure from the White House, the politically minded Budget Bureau, and some members of Congress, insisted that Carr take more energetic measures to separate officers and clerks from their respective positions so that vacancies could be created for New Deal Democrats. By the middle of summer approximately 70 officers and nearly 150 clerical employees who had been serving in our offices abroad had been removed from their positions and slightly over 20 officers and 60 clerical employees of the department had been released. Carr refused to accept suggestions from the Budget Bureau that he "unblanket" appointments of a "political" character that had been covered by the Civil Service during the previous administration. He maintained that political appointments had not been given career cover in the department during previous years. He was compelled, however, during the latter part of 1933 under direct orders from Hull, to effect a fictitious type of reorganization that would justify the release of a limited number of the permanent members and permit the filling of the newly created positions by friends of members of the administration.

In spite of the attitude of indifference—at times almost approaching contempt—that President Roosevelt manifested toward the State Department and the Foreign Service and of the sustained campaign of villification carried on against these two institutions by the left wing of the New Deal, both the department and the Foreign Service weathered the change of administration surprisingly well.

The Department of Commerce and its Foreign Service, however, fared badly. For eight years that department had been of prime interest to Hoover. As secretary of commerce he had expanded its activities in the United States and had instituted its own Foreign Service. Some of the members of the Department of Commerce and of its Foreign Service had served previously under Hoover in various capacities during the period of the First World War and immediately thereafter. The White House insisted that these two institutions were riddled with Hoover appointees who had been given Civil Service or Commerce Foreign Service cover and that these appointees be unblanketed and dismissed. The cowed Civil Service Commission agreed and the Department of Commerce and its Foreign Service were fragmented. On short notice many members of the Commerce Foreign Service who had entered it with the impression that they were embarking upon a lifetime career were brought back from their posts abroad, fired, and replaced by persons on the administration's list of applicants. The unanticipated loss of their positions represented stark tragedy for many of those who had been serving abroad. They had lost contact with their home communities and had little hope of finding new positions during depression times. Some of them, unwilling to join the lines of the unemployed, committed suicide on the way home or shortly after their return.

CHAPTER 25

PREPARATIONS FOR POSSIBLE NEGOTIATIONS WITH THE SOVIET UNION, MARCH–NOVEMBER 1933

IT BECAME APPARENT to the Eastern European Division during the spring of 1933 that within the next four months the new administration would undertake a review of our Russian policies. The pressure groups that had been advocating recognition during the Hoover administration were growing stronger and more strident and were being reinforced by left-wing elements of the New Deal. Several of the new appointees in the department were quite frank in stating their belief that we should recognize the Soviet Union. There was a growing feeling, furthermore, throughout the country that, although the rulers of Soviet Russia might be pursuing policies and engaging in practices that were repugnant to the American people, it was nevertheless important that the United States and the Soviet Union be at least on speaking terms, in view of the complicated and dangerous situation in the Far East.

We in the division concentrated upon assembling in an orderly fashion the documents that we had been collecting over the years and upon preparing or bringing up to date memoranda based on these documents. In these memoranda we endeavored to set forth clearly the differences in points of view and in practices between the United States and Soviet Russia that had prompted the administrations under Wilson, Harding, Coolidge, and Hoover to refrain from recognizing the Soviet Union. Basing our arguments on the experiences of other countries, we offered suggestions regarding the conditions under which, in our opinion, recognition could be most advantageously accorded. We indicated in some of the memoranda that in the absence of clear-cut understandings with the Soviet Union in respect to the points at issue between it and the United States, our relations with the Soviet government after recognition might well be more unpleasant than they had been in the past.

We tried to drive the point home that, unless prior to the accordance of recognition the United States could come to agreements with the Soviet Union that would not only eliminate certain differences that already existed between it and us but would also prevent the development of additional differences after recognition that other countries had encountered, our future relations with the Soviet Union would almost certainly be stormy. In preparing the memoranda we were careful not to give the impression that if the Soviet government gave the commitments we were suggesting this would in itself guarantee the smoothness of future Soviet-American relations. The documents in our possession showed only too clearly that the Soviet government had been consistently unwilling to interpret commitments it had given to other countries as obligations on its part to cease acting in consonance with its principles of militant communism.

The members of the Eastern European Division believed that regardless of such commitments as the emissaries of the Soviet government might make in Washington or elsewhere, the rulers of the Soviet Union would continue their efforts through the Communist International or other instruments at their disposal to bring about the overthrow—if necessary, by force—of the U.S. government and other noncommunist governments and would not take any action that would involve recognition of any obligation on their part to compensate the U.S. government or nationals for losses resulting from Soviet acts of repudiation or confiscation. I myself did not see how any intelligent person who, over a period of years, had observed the sacrifices that the Bolshevik leaders had been willing to make for the sake of their revolutionary principles and of the artifices to which they had resorted in order to survive in an unsympathetic world while still adhering to those principles, could have believed otherwise.

We did not endeavor to conceal our beliefs from the members of the administration who were charged with making policy decisions with regard to the Soviet Union. We did not, however, try to press our views upon them. To an extent we were handicapped by the fact that we represented the division that had provided much of the ammunition used by preceding administrations in defending their policies of nonrecognition. Until we had earned the confidence of the new top policymakers there was a limit to the extent to which we could go in giving them unsolicited advice.

Although we were convinced that, regardless of any commitments that the Soviet leaders might give the United States, the relations between the Soviet Union and the United States following recognition would not be smooth, we were not opposing recognition for that reason. Indeed, we realized that in certain situations it might prove advantageous for the United States, even though its relations with the Soviet Union were far from good, to be able to exchange views with it. We also believed that in its future dealings with the Soviet Union the United States would be in a stronger position if, at the time of recognition, it had obtained certain commitments even though those commitments would not be kept.

During his discussions with the secretary, the under secretary, and Bullitt, Kelley had informed them of the studies in which we were engaged and they had expressed an interest in them. We, therefore, began passing the results of our work to them in the month of May 1933. One of the first memoranda sent by Kelley to the second floor was devoted to the "Soviet Attitude and Policy with Respect to the Repudiation and Confiscation of Property." This memorandum was based on provisions of Soviet law, statements made by responsible Soviet leaders, official accounts of the experiences of the United States and other countries in connection with efforts to obtain compensation for losses, and so forth.

In the latter part of July Kelley submitted to William Phillips, the acting secretary in the absence of Hull, another memorandum prepared in the division entitled "Problems Pertaining to Russian-American Relations Which, in the Interests of Friendly Relations Between the United States and Russia, Should Be Settled Prior to the Recognition of the Soviet Government." This memorandum, a copy of which was sent by Phillips to the president on July 27, opened with the following paragraph:

> In order that the United States may derive from the recognition of the Soviet Government the benefits which normally follow the recognition of a foreign government, the recognition of the Soviet Government should involve the establishment of relations with Russia on a basis which would render possible the maintenance of friendly cooperation between the Governments of the United States and Russia and the development of trade and intercourse between the two countries. The experience of countries which have extended recognition to the Soviet Government has shown pretty conclusively, it is believed, that there are serious obstacles in the way of the establishment of relations with Russia on such a basis, and that so long as these obstacles remain, official relations, established as a result of recognition, tend to become, in view of the extraordinary nature of these obstacles, the source of friction and

ill will rather than the mainspring of cooperation and good will. It would seem essential, therefore, that every endeavor should be made to remove these obstacles prior to the extension of recognition. Until a substantial basis of mutual understanding and common principles and purposes has been established, official intercourse, with its increased contacts, is bound to lead to friction and rancor. Formal diplomatic relations may be established, but the substance of a useful relationship will be lacking, as much for the Russians as for ourselves, unless and until we have cleared up the existing difficulties through mutual agreement and worked out a *modus vivendi* for the future.

The first problem discussed in this memorandum was that relating to communist world revolutionary activities. Since later developments served to emphasize the prescience demonstrated in the treatment of that problem, I quote in full the paragraph relating to it:

The fundamental obstacle in the way of the establishment with Russia of the relations usual between nations in diplomatic intercourse is the world revolutionary aims and practices of the rulers of that country. It is obvious that, so long as the Communist regime continues to carry on in other countries activities designed to bring about ultimately the overthrow of the Government and institutions of these countries, the establishment of genuine friendly relations between Russia and those countries is out of the question. Even when these activities do not constitute a present menace to the established order, the systematic interference of a foreign power in the domestic affairs of a country constitutes *ipso facto* a source of deep resentment and unavoidable friction. The persistence of such interference after diplomatic relations have been established leads inevitably to the rupture of relations—as has taken place in the case of England, China, and Mexico—or to serious tension and the reduction of the existing diplomatic relations to a barren, meaningless relationship—as has taken place at times in the case of France, Germany, Poland, et cetera. It would seem, therefore, that an essential prerequisite to the establishment of harmonious and trustful relations with the Soviet Government is the abandonment by the present rulers of Russia of their world revolutionary aims and the discontinuance of their activities designed to bring about the realization of such aims. More specifically and with particular regard to the United States, this prerequisite involves the abandonment by Moscow of direction, supervision, control, financing, et cetera, through every agency utilized for the purpose, of communist and other related activities in the United States.

The second problem treated in the memorandum was the question of repudiated debts and confiscated property. In view of the important role that this problem was to play in future relations between the United States and the Soviet Union, I quote below excerpts from the passages of the memorandum relating to it:

> Another serious difficulty in the way of the establishment of mutually advantageous relations with the Soviet Government is the unwillingness of that Government to observe certain generally accepted principles governing the conduct of nations toward each other. Among these principles is the duty of a State to respect the rights of citizens of other States which have been acquired within its jurisdiction in accordance with its laws, and the duty of a Government to honor the financial obligations contracted by a State under preceding Governments. The Soviet Government has confiscated the property of foreign nationals in Russia and has repudiated the contractual obligations of Russia to foreign governments and foreign nationals. It is to be noted that through these acts not only has damage been done to the interests of foreign States, but what is more important, the Soviet Government has rejected international obligations which the experience of mankind has demonstrated are vital to the satisfactory development and maintenance of commerce and friendly intercourse between nations. These acts have severely handicapped the development of commercial relations between Russia and foreign countries, since they have practically destroyed the basis of ordinary credit to the Soviet Government or Soviet organizations. Any substantial improvement of Russian credit would appear to be unlikely until a settlement has been reached with respect to repudiated bonds and confiscated property, and until Russia has furnished adequate evidence of its purpose to maintain its international relations in accordance with recognized standards...
>
> It is to the interest of the United States to obtain a settlement of the question of repudiated bonds and confiscated property on the basis of accepted international practices, not only on account of the material losses involved, but especially in view of the fact, as indicated above, that the settlement of these matters is of great importance for the establishment of a sound basis for trade between the United States and Russia. Moreover, it is to be noted that the Government of the United States has a profound interest in the maintenance of the sanctity of international obligations, not only in view of the worldwide activities of its citizens, but even more in consequence of its earnest desire to see strengthened those forces making for the promotion of peace and international good will...
>
> It is to be especially emphasized that if the questions of repudiated debts and confiscated property are not settled prior to recognition, there is little likelihood that subsequent negotiations would result in a mutually satisfactory settlement. Evidence of this is to be found in the fruitlessness of the long-drawn-out negotiations in regard to these questions

conducted by France and Great Britain subsequent to their recognition of the Soviet Government.

The third problem discussed in the memorandum, that of bridging the differences between the economic and social structure of the United States and Russia, was of a more general character. Since the paragraphs devoted to this problem describe with accuracy some of the difficulties that every U.S. official assisting in the conduct of relations between the United States and the Soviet Union has since encountered, I quote them in full:

A third major problem requiring solution in the interest of the establishment of harmonious and mutually beneficial relations between the United States and Russia is the difficulties arising out of the profound differences between the economic and social structure of the two countries. Reference is made here specially to the State monopoly of foreign trade in Russia and to the class character of the Soviet State.

Commercial relations between a country with a State monopoly of foreign trade and a country with its foreign trade carried on by private individuals cannot be conducted on the same basis as trade between two countries of the latter category. None of the accepted principles governing international commercial relations, such as most-favored-nation treatment, national treatment, etc., is applicable to trade between Russia and other countries. Those countries which have concluded trade agreements with Russia on a most-favored-nation basis, such as Germany, Great Britain, etc., have learned to their cost that the application of the most-favored-nation principle in treaties with Russia is, as the British Minister for Foreign Affairs recently said, "distorted and ridiculous." Furthermore, a government monopoly of foreign trade, in carrying on commerce with foreign countries, has a natural advantage over individual business concerns in such countries. In practically every country trading with Russia endeavors have been made, usually with little success, to find ways and means of putting trade relations on an equal footing and removing the disadvantages under which the individual businessman labors in dealing with the Soviet monopoly of foreign trade. Finally, it is to be noted that the existence of this monopoly has given rise to difficulties and misunderstandings in the case of several countries that have recognized the Soviet Government in connection with the determination of the status of Soviet Trade Delegations, the extent of the responsibility of the Soviet Government for acts of Soviet commercial organizations, the right of Soviet organizations to participate in retail trade, etc.

Another question which has led to serious friction between Russia and foreign countries, especially Germany and Great Britain, is the treatment to which foreigners in Russia are subject under Soviet laws and practices. While it is a principle of international law that aliens are amenable to the laws of the country in which they are residing, the system of justice existing in Russia is so far removed from that maintained in the countries of Western Europe, and the Communist conception of justice is so alien to that held in such countries, that foreign countries have been obliged at times to take vigorous measures of reprisal in connection with the application to their nationals of Soviet judicial procedure and certain Soviet criminal laws to which Soviet nationals are subjected. For example, the Soviet conception of espionage, especially economic espionage, is of such a broad nature that almost every foreigner in Russia commits acts which may readily be interpreted as violating the laws on this subject. Soviet practices with regard to arrest and incarceration of foreign nationals constantly lead to friction with foreign States. Matters such as these, involving the question of the protection of life and property of American citizens in Russia, should be settled by agreement in order to create a satisfactory basis for intercourse with Russia.

To assist the reader of the memorandum in ascertaining the magnitude of the claims of the United States against the Soviet Union resulting from "the Soviet policies of repudiation and confiscation," Kelley listed them according to categories. The total was approximately 628 million dollars, not a large amount when one considers the size of governmental transactions during the years to come, but a significant sum in the early 1930s. The memorandum emphasized, moreover, that considerations other than money were involved—for example, considerations relating to the creation of confidence of the U.S. business community in the credit of the Soviet government and those relating to "the maintenance of the sanctity of international obligations."

During most of the month of May 1933 the new secretary was immersed in matters relating to disarmament and to the coming Monetary and Economic Conference in London. He sailed for England to attend the conference on May 31 and did not return until nearly the middle of August. Shortly after his return he discussed problems connected with the Soviet Union at some length with Kelley, who provided him with an assortment of documents that the division had prepared on the subject. We had the impression at the time that Hull had so many other problems facing him on his return from London, particularly in the Far East and in Latin America, that he was not eager to add to them by becoming involved in the controversial and complex problem of Russian recognition.

Although Henry Morgenthau, the acting secretary of the treasury, and other New Dealers close to the president appeared to be impatient at the slowness with which the administration was allowing itself to be seized of this problem, the secretary apparently did not wish to be pushed. Nevertheless, specific problems relating to the Soviet Union were constantly arising that could not be satisfactorily dealt with in the absence of decisions regarding what our policies toward that country were to be. One of these problems involved the extent to which the administration should go in assisting U.S. businessmen to increase their exports to Russia. Several of the advisers to the president were urging that the appropriate agencies of the U.S. government extend loans or credits to facilitate Russian purchases in the United States.

Following several conversations with Kelley regarding this problem, the secretary sent a memorandum to the president on September 21, 1933, in which he dwelt on certain factors that he believed should not be overlooked in the making of decisions involving the extension of loans or credits by agencies of the U.S. government for the purpose of facilitating Russian purchases in the United States.

In referring to problems that had contributed to decisions of previous administrations not to establish diplomatic relations with the Soviet Union, the secretary stated:

> I think that there is no question that until these fundamental problems have been settled through agreement in a manner satisfactory to the United States, there will be lacking any sound basis for friendly cooperation between the Governments of Russia and the United States and for the development of mutually beneficial trade and intercourse between the two countries.

He pointed out that the Soviet government was eager to obtain two things from the government of the United States, namely, credits or loans, and recognition, and he stated:

> I am convinced, from the experience of other countries, that unless we utilize every available means of exerting pressure on the Soviet Government in order to obtain a settlement of outstanding problems, there is little likelihood that such problems can be satisfactorily solved. It is evident that if loans of any considerable amount should be extended to the Soviet Government except as part of an agreement involving a satisfactory settlement of such problems, one of our most effective weapons would be taken from our hands—possibly the most effective—since the Soviets, it is believed, prefer at the moment credits to recognition.
>
> It would seem, therefore, highly undesirable that any loans should be extended to facilitate purchases by the Soviet Government in the United States except as part and parcel of a general settlement of our relations with Russia.

Although the secretary in his memorandum referred to a "general settlement of our relations with Russia," he did not include in it suggestions regarding steps that might be taken in the direction of achieving such a settlement.

I have always had deep respect and real affection for Secretary Hull. Again and again, during the many years that he was head of the Department of State, in his quiet way he prevented the president and some of the impulsive advisers around the president from taking actions that, in my opinion, would have been harmful to the United States. Like all of us, however, he had certain weaknesses. It is no secret, for instance, that he disliked participating in decisions of a highly controversial character. He was inclined to postpone from day to day the making of difficult decisions on matters that demanded action. One might gather the impression from reading the secretary's memoirs that he acted decisively with respect to problems connected with the recognition of the Soviet Union. Such, however, was not the case. He preferred that the decisions be taken by the president not upon his advice but upon that of his subordinates.

In the latter part of September 1933 word trickled down to Kelley that the president was considering the advisability of sending a personal message to the head of the Soviet Union suggesting conversations looking toward the establishment of diplomatic relations. Kelley, who had assisted in the preparation of the secretary's memorandum to the president of September 21, was not sure that the memorandum had actually come to the attention of the president. Concerned lest the president take some action that would weaken the position of the United States in the absence of a general settlement, Kelley sent a memorandum on September 25 to Phillips recommending that the secretary bring to the president's attention "along the lines contained in the letter which it was proposed to be sent to the President last week (i.e., the Secretary's memorandum to the President of September 21 regarding loans and recognition), the desirability of retaining in our hands one of the most effective weapons we have to obtain from the Soviet Government some measure of conciliation in reaching a solution of outstanding problems, namely, government financial assistance, in the form of loans or credits, to facilitate American exports to Russia."

It was on October 5, two weeks after he had sent the memorandum of September 21 to the president, that Secretary Hull made a definite move of his own in the direction of establishing relations with the Soviet Union—a move that, in my opinion, indicated that he still preferred not to become too personally involved in decisions with regard to Russia. This move consisted of a note to the president, dated October 5, 1933, which read as follows:

My dear Mr. President:

I requested Judge Walton Moore and William Bullitt each to prepare a memorandum on the more important conditions and understandings that might be considered significant in connection with the development of plans for the recognition of the Russian Government. These two memoranda are attached hereto for whatever the information may be worth.

The respective memoranda of Moore and Bullitt attached to the note presented some of their views regarding steps that might be taken in the direction of recognition. If the secretary had any views of his own at that time regarding this matter other than those advanced in his memorandum to the president of September 21, he did not, so far as I know, put them in writing. I think that the secretary's mind was more at ease on the matter now that he had a team of this caliber in the State Department to work on it. Judge Moore with his vast experience and canniness, and Bullitt with his brilliance and drive, made a combination that should have been quite capable of holding its own in councils in which people like Morgenthau, who was emotional in his advocacy of Russian recognition, would participate. Bullitt was as close to the president as Morgenthau; furthermore, at the London Economic Conference Bullitt had proved his loyalty to the secretary. Behind both Moore and Bullitt stood Kelley, laden with documents on almost every conceivable subject that might come up during the course of negotiations with the Russians. Backstopping Kelley were the members of the Division of Eastern European Affairs, who were prepared on short notice to produce such additional memoranda or notes as might be needed. Despite the briefness of their acquaintance with Kelley, it was clear to me that both Moore and Bullitt had begun to depend on him for precise, unprejudiced information and helpful suggestions.

In his memorandum dated October 4, the cautious Judge Moore took the position that recognition should be accorded only after agreements had been reached with the Soviet government covering a number of questions. He apparently was not in favor of over-hasty action.

Bullitt, in his memorandum of October 4, was more specific. Since during the ensuing three years he was to be deeply concerned regarding the extent to which the Soviet government was to live up to the commitments given by it at the time of recognition, it is interesting to note what his views were prior to recognition. I therefore quote his memorandum in full:

Whatever method may be used to enter into negotiations with the Soviet Government, it seems essential that formal recognition should not be accorded except as the final act of an agreement covering a number of questions in dispute. Before recognition and before loans, we shall find the Soviet Government relatively amenable. After recognition or loans, we should find the Soviet Government adamant. Among the chief agreements which, in my opinion, must be reached before recognition are the following:

1. Prohibition of communist propaganda in the United States by the Soviet Government and by the Comintern.

2. Protection of the civil and religious rights of Americans in Russia which are inadequately protected under current Russian practice (e.g., "economic espionage").

3. Agreement by the Soviet Government that the act of recognition shall not be retroactive to the foundation of that government (which is the usual practice), but shall take effect only from the day on which it may be accorded. This is essential to protect both our Government and many citizens and corporations from suits for damages.

By negotiation before recognition, we should also attempt to obtain an agreement in regard to the repayment of the loans of the Government of the United States to the Kerensky Government, a waiver of Russian counterclaims based upon our Vladivostok, Archangel and Murmansk expeditions; also some sort of provision for the settlement of claims of American nationals and corporations for property, goods and cash seized by the Soviet Government.

There are, of course, scores of other questions involved in resuming normal relations with Russia. Our position would be strongest, I believe, if all these questions, whether of a legal, economic or financial nature, should be handled as a unit in one global negotiation, the end of which would be signature of the agreements and simultaneous recognition.

Within a few days after the dispatch of Hull's note to the president, Kelley was called down to the second floor to talk with Judge Moore and Bullitt. There he was told that the president had made up his mind regarding the approach that he desired to have made to the Soviets. The president had requested that a message for his signature be drafted at once to Mikhail Kalinin who, as president of the Soviet All-Union Central Executive Committee, was nominally the head of the Soviet state, inviting the latter to send representatives to explore with him personally all questions outstanding between the United States and the Soviet Union.

It would appear that the president had decided that an attempt to draw up a treaty disposing of all such questions would be time-consuming and perhaps even self-defeating. Furthermore, it would be necessary

for a treaty to be ratified by the U.S. Senate. No one could foresee what
might take place in the Senate if such a treaty should be laid before it. An
exchange of notes, the president thought, would serve our purpose just
as well as a formal treaty. The president seemed to believe that commitments entered into by the Soviet Union through notes of this kind would
be no less binding on it than commitments contained in a complicated
treaty. He was apparently confident that, if the Russians understood that
he personally would engage in the negotiations, they would send a
person of high rank to represent them—a person who would not find it
necessary to obtain instructions from Moscow in respect to every detail.
The president seemed to be convinced that with both sides desiring to see
friendly relations established, he and a Soviet representative possessed of
authority to make decisions could come to agreements rather quickly with
regard to most problems that had muddled relations between the Soviet
Union and other countries that had entered into relations with it.

Kelley was informed that his immediate task was to prepare for the
president a message to Kalinin couched in such language that Kalinin
would find it difficult not to send a high-ranking person, such as Litvinov,
the commissar for foreign affairs, to Washington to represent the Soviet
government. The message was drafted hurriedly. It read as follows:

> Dear Mr. President:
>
> Since the beginning of my Administration, I have contemplated the
> desirability of an effort to end the present abnormal relations between
> the hundred and twenty-five million people of the United States and the
> hundred and sixty million people of Russia.
>
> It is most regrettable that these great peoples, between whom a happy
> tradition of friendship existed for more than a century to their mutual
> advantage, should now be without a practical method of communicating
> directly with each other.
>
> The difficulties that have created this anomalous situation are serious
> but not, in my opinion, insoluble; and difficulties between great nations
> can be removed only by frank, friendly conversations. If you are of a
> similar mind, I should be glad to receive any representative you may
> designate to explore with me personally all questions outstanding be-
> tween our countries.
>
> Participation in such a discussion would, of course, not commit either
> nation to any future course of action, but would indicate a sincere desire
> to reach a satisfactory solution of the problems involved. It is my hope
> that such conversations might result in good to the people of both
> countries.

Before this letter was sent it was informally discussed with Boris

Skvirsky who had been permitted to reside in Washington as the head of the unrecognized yet useful Soviet Information Bureau and who was in constant touch with his principals in Moscow. We in the division did not know what took place during the consultation with Skvirsky, who talked with him, whether or not he was shown a copy of the proposed note to Kalinin, or what his comments were. In any event, it was our understanding that his comments were favorable, and the note was sent on October 10.

Kalinin replied on October 17. As the president had hoped, he stated that the Soviet government would send Litvinov to Washington to "discuss with you questions of interest to our countries. . . at a time to be mutually agreed upon." Upon receipt of this reply interested personnel in the White House and certain sections of the State Department began to clear their desks for action. The confrontation between the Soviet Union and the United States, for which the Eastern European Division had been preparing for so many years, was at hand.

I was unable, however, during the month of October to be of much assistance to Kelley and Packer in preparing the U.S. negotiators for the coming Litvinov visit. My desk was littered at the time with documents and books of statistics. In late September I had been given a task that was proving onerous and time-consuming. That task was the urgent preparation of a memorandum that would estimate the maximum value of goods produced in the Soviet Union that the United States might be able to absorb in its economy annually over the next few years. The State Department required such an estimate in order to evaluate more accurately the claims of Soviet commercial representatives and overoptimistic American businessmen that, following the establishment of diplomatic relations, trade between the two countries could approach hundreds of millions of dollars annually and that Soviet purchases in the United States could make important contributions to the dispersion of the depression.

Such an estimate would also be of value to the department in determining the ability of the Soviet Union to discharge within five or ten years such indebtedness as might be created by the United States granting it loans or long-term credits. The secretary, in particular, was conscious of what had happened in Europe in the late 1920s when some European countries had found themselves unable to repay loans that had been granted to them by the United States primarily to enable them to buy American goods. He was determined that the United States should not be stampeded by enthusiastic U.S. exporters into extending to the Soviet Union loans in amounts that the latter could not reasonably be expected to pay on the due dates.

Landreth Harrison, who had served with me in Riga and who had been detailed to the Division of Eastern European Affairs; Bertel Eric Kuniholm, a Foreign Service officer who had just completed his Russian language studies in Paris; and several other junior officers were assigned to assist me in preparing this memorandum. We decided that the first step to take in approaching this problem was to select the Russian products that experience had shown could be marketed in the United States. We then tried to determine the maximum amount of each of these products that the United States might be able to import annually. We discovered that 82 to 91 percent of Soviet imports during recent years comprised 23 items. Interesting enough, 12 of these items accounted for 79 percent of U.S. imports from Russia in 1913.

Our second step was to make a careful study of each of these items. This study included an estimate of the amount of the items that the Soviet Union would be able to produce during the next decade, the amount that it would require for home consumption, and the amount that the United States could absorb. There were, of course, some additional factors to be considered. For instance, to what extent would the Soviet Union consider it essential in protecting its foreign trade with other countries to sell to them some of its surplus commodities instead of to the United States? To what extent should the United States curtail its purchases from other friendly countries in order to buy from the Soviet Union? Should we reduce our purchases of anthracite from the United Kingdom and elsewhere so that we could increase our imports of Soviet anthracite? Should we transfer our purchases of asbestos, pulpwood, and timber from Canada to the Soviet Union? Since our terms of reference called for the "maximum value of possible annual imports," we did not hesitate in making our estimates to take into account the possibility that the Soviet Union would give us preferential treatment in connection with the export of its products and that we would give it preference over other countries in the matter of purchases.

Our third step was to examine Soviet statistics and plans in order to ascertain whether there would be items in addition to the 23 that the Soviet Union might be in a position to sell to the United States and that the United States might need. In preparing our estimates we called for assistance on other government agencies. The Bureau of Mines, the Bureau of Fisheries, the Bureau of Foreign and Domestic Commerce, the Department of Agriculture, and the Tariff Commission placed competent experts at our disposal. We completed this task on November 1, just six days before the arrival of Litvinov in the United States. What were the final figures? In our master tables we estimated that the "maximum value of possible imports into the United States of merchandise of Russian origin," was 88.87 million dollars annually, of which 9.3 million dollars were accounted for by items other than the 23. The value of our imports from Russia in 1913 (that is, from the whole of the Russian empire as it then existed) had been 29.3 million dollars; in 1930 24.2 million dollars; and in 1932 9.7 million dollars.

Our memorandum met with a mixed reception. A few of its readers in other agencies, who had been optimistically talking of the possibilities of U.S.-Soviet trade in terms of hundreds of millions of dollars annually, maintained that we had been too conservative in estimating the maximum value of possible U.S. imports from Russia. Most readers agreed with us, however, in our view that 88.87 million dollars was an exceedingly liberal estimate. Our position was later strengthened by Bullitt in a dispatch to the State Department dated January 4, 1934, written on board the SS *Washington*. In that dispatch Bullitt stated that Litvinov had expressed the opinion to him on December 21, 1933, "that the United States could not take more than $60,000,000 worth of goods from the Soviet Union in any one year, and that if we wanted an export trade with the Soviet Union of more than this amount we would have to extend long-term credits."

It seems hardly necessary to point out that the Soviet Union might have been able to draw from sources other than the proceeds of its sales to the United States in order to meet its indebtedness arising from the extension to it of long-term loans and credits. It might, for instance, have paid certain amounts in gold held or mined in the Soviet Union or from favorable balances achieved in its trade with other countries. No one knew at the time, however, the amount of gold that the Soviet Union had at its disposal or the value of the amount being mined annually. Furthermore, if the Soviet Union was to give the United States preference in allocating its exports, there would be exceedingly few countries that would be buying more from it than they were selling to it. It should also be borne in mind that the Soviet Union was directly indebted to several other countries that had granted it long-term credits.

President Roosevelt and his advisers had apparently already come to the conclusion that it would be impossible during the course of the coming conversations to iron out all the problems that might complicate or becloud our future relations with the Soviet Union. There were several problems, however, so important that they could not be ignored. Their importance was derived not only from the effect that they might have on the future of Soviet-American relations but also from the interest of Congress and the American people in them. The president, before making a decision in the area of foreign affairs, was usually careful to consider how such a decision might affect his personal popularity and public support for his foreign policies, as well as the effect that it might have on the welfare of the United States. Among the problems that the president and his advisers decided must be dealt with during the discussions with Litvinov were:

1. The practice of the rulers of Soviet Russia of systematically interfering in the internal affairs of the United States.
2. The right of U.S. nationals residing in or visiting the Soviet Union to worship in accordance with their conscience and to engage in rites of a religious nature.
3. The right of U.S. nationals who might be arrested while visiting or residing in the Soviet Union to have a speedy public and fair trial and to consult with a U.S. diplomatic or consular officer.
4. The danger that U.S. nationals visiting or residing in the Soviet Union might be arrested at any time on charges of engaging in economic espionage.
5. The possibility that, following recognition, the Soviet Union might use the U.S. courts in order to acquire title to property and funds of previous Russian governments in the United States.
6. The claims of the Soviet government against the United States arising from the U.S. military expeditions into northern Russia and Siberia.
7. The claims of the United States and of U.S. nationals against the Soviet Union arising from Soviet acts of confiscation, nationalization, and repudiation.

Word was passed along to us that so far as possible such commitments as Litvinov might be requested to make should be couched in language similar to commitments that the Soviet government had previously made to other countries. It was quite sensibly the belief of the negotiators that it would be easier to persuade Litvinov to agree to a commitment if it could be shown to him that his government had in the past given commitments of a similar nature to other countries.

In view of the analyses that I had made in 1932 of Soviet treaties—particularly of those sections that might be of interest to the United States in connection with the establishment of diplomatic relations with the Soviet Union—I was asked by Kelley to assist in the drafting of commitments relating to problems (1) and (3) listed above. In the course of the next two weeks I prepared a series of drafts of a commitment that would obligate the Soviet Union not to interfere in our internal affairs. Each of these drafts was the subject of a conference with Kelley and Packer, during which it was cut to pieces—pieces that it was my job to reassemble with somewhat different wording and sequences. Our object was to produce a commitment that (1) would on its face seem so reasonable that it would be difficult for Litvinov to refuse without leaving an inference that it was not the sincere intention of the Soviet Union to try to maintain genuinely friendly relations with the United States; (2) would unmistakably obligate the Soviet government to not interfere in our internal affairs as well as to not permit the Communist International and kindred international subversive organizations to continue to operate on Soviet territory; and (3) would be heavily interlarded with sentences and phrases borrowed from Soviet commitments to other countries.

Kelley had a double task, that of coming to an agreement with Packer and me regarding the form and content of the various papers, and that of prevailing upon the negotiators on the second floor to accept them. The negotiators had the additional tasks of satisfying the president of the agreements' reasonableness and of finding ways to persuade Litvinov to accept them in their original or in a negotiated form.

While we were engaged in drafting and redrafting documents and in submitting them to the negotiators, Litvinov on the SS *Berengaria* was approaching the United States in a blaze of publicity. Litvinov, as I learned later, possessed an inordinate amount of vanity. He must, therefore, have found those days in the early part of November most satisfying. His fellow passengers on the huge vessel as it made its way across the Atlantic looked on him with awe. The press throughout the world was interested in every word he might utter and every move he might make. Hundreds of newspaper reporters in the United States were eagerly looking forward to the opportunity of seeing him and exchanging a word with him. In Washington the president and other high officials were awaiting his arrival. If Litvinov had concern lest his mission result in failure there was nothing in his bearing to indicate it. He informed interviewers en route that he could come to an agreement with President Roosevelt in half an hour. Upon his arrival in New York he told the press that the question of recognition would be the only one that he would discuss with the president and that the discussion of other questions could be taken up at a later date.

CHAPTER 26

THE ROOSEVELT-LITVINOV NEGOTIATIONS OF NOVEMBER 1933 RESULTING IN THE ESTABLISHMENT OF DIPLOMATIC RELATIONS BETWEEN THE UNITED STATES AND THE SOVIET UNION

LITVINOV WAS MET IN NEW YORK on November 7 with due ceremony by the protocol officers of the Department of State, by representatives of the state of New York and New York City, by mobs of journalists, and by hundreds of cheering admirers. On November 8 he was escorted by the protocol officers to Secretary Hull's office. Hull had two long conversations with him on November 8 and another on the following morning. During these conversations the secretary informed Litvinov that there were a number of topics to be discussed and agreements to be reached before diplomatic relations could be established. On November 9 Hull turned Litvinov over to the negotiating team of Judge Moore and Bullitt and began to make final preparations for his own departure on November 11 to Montevideo where he was scheduled to attend a Pan American conference.

Judge Moore and Bullitt lost no time letting the commissar know what was expected of him by outlining the kind of commitments that were required as a prerequisite for recognition. Although at times during these early conversations Litvinov seemed to lose some of his hauteur, he nevertheless appeared to hope that in view of the distance the U.S. government had gone in the direction of recognition, it would be reluctant to retreat and that if he would remain firm, he might be able to obtain recognition without making commitments of a character that would be displeasing to his superiors in Moscow.

After a series of talks in the State Department, arrangements were made for the commissar to talk with the president personally on November 10. Apparently his conversation with the president convinced Litvinov that there was no escape from making at least several commitments. His problem, therefore, was to find a way of giving promises that would not involve loss of face to himself and to the Soviet Union and of so wording them that they would satisfy the president and yet be tolerable to his own government. The president and the negotiating team were prepared to cooperate with the commissar in solving these problems.

The negotiations went on for several days. The president played the role of moderator. If concessions were to be made by the United States, it was he that would make them. In doing so he usually indicated that he expected a responsive, flexible attitude on the part of Litvinov.

Bullitt proved to be a tough negotiator. Nevertheless, the tactics he employed were such that in spite of his seeming intransigence his personal relations with Litvinov continued to be pleasant and he emerged from the negotiations as a sort of hero in the Soviet Union. It was his practice to continually impress upon the commissar that his insistence on certain commitments was not based on any personal distrust of the Soviet Union but on his conviction that if the Soviet Union would not agree to them and would not live up to them, it would be difficult for the United States and the Soviet Union to maintain friendly and truly advantageous relations.

On November 16, 1933, the negotiations were finally terminated and a communiqué was released to the public setting forth the series of letters and statements, all bearing that date, that in their aggregate comprised the establishment of diplomatic relations and the commitments made on the part of the Soviet Union and the United States. This collection might be called "the recognition documents."

Since Litvinov had been publicly insisting that recognition should be given unconditionally and that any agreements entered into should be negotiated only after the establishment of diplomatic relations, the sequence of the several exchanges was important from the point of view of saving face. In the communiqué, therefore, the first exchange consisted of letters registering the establishment of diplomatic relations between the two governments. Litvinov's commitments were set forth in subsequent exchanges. The exchange establishing relations read as follows:

> The White House
> Washington, November 16, 1933

My dear Mr. Litvinov:

> I am very happy to inform you as a result of our conversations the Government of the United States has decided to establish normal diplo-

matic relations with the Government of the Union of Soviet Socialist Republics and to exchange ambassadors.

I trust that the relations now established between our peoples may forever remain normal and friendly, and that our nations henceforth may cooperate for their mutual benefit and for the preservation of the peace of the world.

I am, my dear Mr. Litvinov,

Very sincerely yours,

Franklin D. Roosevelt

Mr. Maxim M. Litvinov
People's Commissar for Foreign Affairs
Union of Soviet Socialist Republics

* * *

Washington, November 16, 1933

My dear Mr. President:

I am very happy to inform you that the Government of the Union of Soviet Socialist Republics is glad to establish normal diplomatic relations with the Government of the United States and to exchange ambassadors.

I, too, share the hope that the relations now established between our peoples may forever remain normal and friendly, and that our nations henceforth may cooperate for their mutual benefit and for the preservation of the peace of the world.

I am, my dear Mr. President,

Very sincerely yours,

Maxim Litvinov
People's Commissar for Foreign Affairs
Union of Soviet Socialist Republics

Mr. Franklin D. Roosevelt
President of the United States
The White House

The second exchange in the communiqué consisted of the letters relating to noninterference in internal affairs. Litvinov's letter containing this commitment was almost identical with the draft that had been prepared in the State Department. He had been particularly reluctant to sign this commitment and did so only when he realized that otherwise the negotiations would break down. Litvinov's letter read as follows:

I have the honor to inform you that coincident with the establishment of diplomatic relations between our two Governments it will be the fixed policy of the Government of the Union of Soviet Socialist Republics:

1. To respect scrupulously the indisputable right of the United States to order its own life within its own jurisdiction in its own way and to refrain from interfering in any manner in the internal affairs of the United States, its territories or possessions.

2. To refrain, and to restrain all persons in government service and all organizations of the Government or under its direct or indirect control, including the organizations in receipt of any financial assistance from it, from any act overt or covert liable in any way whatsoever to injure the tranquility, prosperity, order, or security of the whole or any part of the United States, its territories or possessions, and in particular, from any act tending to incite or encourage armed intervention, or any agitation or propaganda having as an aim, the violation of the territorial integrity of the United States, its territories or possessions, or the bringing about by force of a change in the political or social order of the whole or any part of the United States, its territories or possessions.

3. Not to permit the formation or residence on its territory of any organization or group—and to prevent the activity on its territory of any organization or group, or of representatives or officials of any organization or group—which makes claim to be the Government of, or makes attempt upon the territorial integrity of, the United States, its territories or possessions; not to form, subsidize, support or permit on its territory military organizations or groups having the aim of armed struggle against the United States, its territories or possessions, and to prevent any recruiting on behalf of such organizations and groups.

4. Not to permit the formation or residence on its territory of any organization or group—and to prevent the activity on its territory of any organization or group, or of representatives or officials of any organization or group—which has as an aim the overthrow or the preparation for the overthrow of, or the bringing about by force of a change in, the political or social order of the whole or any part of the United States, its territories or possessions.

In order to make this commitment more palatable to Litvinov, the president in his letter of reply stated, after quoting from Litvinov's letter: "It will be the fixed policy of the Executive of the United States within the limits of the powers conferred by the Constitution and Laws of the United States, to adhere reciprocally to the engagements above expressed."

The Division of Eastern European Affairs had comparatively little to do with Litvinov's third commitment—that pertaining to the freedom of worship of U.S. nationals. Our main contribution was to bring to the attention of the negotiators the kind of commitment that the Soviets had made in this regard in the German-Soviet treaty of October 12, 1925. Article 9 of that treaty read as follows:

> Nationals of each of the Contracting Parties. . . shall be entitled to hold religious services in churches, houses or other buildings, rented according to the laws of the country, in their national language or in any other language which is customary in their religion. They shall be entitled to bury their dead in accordance with their religious practice in burial grounds established and maintained by them with the approval of the competent authorities, so long as they comply with the police regulations of the other Party in respect of buildings and public health.

We could see no reason why Litvinov could not give to the United States a commitment regarding the freedom of worship of U.S. nationals in the Soviet Union at least as liberal as that he had given to Germany. The president was particularly interested in this article. It was his hope that Litvinov would give a commitment of a nature that would allay the opposition of church members, particularly the Roman Catholics, to the establishment of relations with a regime that was widely regarded as being antireligious. In giving the commitment Litvinov, in his letter to the president, did his part to assist in dispelling the belief that the Soviet government was antireligious by quoting at length Soviet laws, which on their face showed extreme religious tolerance.

The members of the Eastern European Division considered it important that as strong a commitment as possible relating to the legal protection of U.S. nationals be obtained from the Soviet Union. In our files were many documents describing how nationals of countries maintaining relations with the Soviet Union had disappeared while visiting or residing in that country. Although it was assumed that they had been arrested, it had not been possible in many instances to learn what had happened to them. A number of U.S. nationals in the Soviet Union had also dropped mysteriously out of sight. Some of them, after serving long sentences in Siberia or elsewhere following secret trials, had been released and permitted to leave the country. The fate of some of the others was unknown. In view of the Soviet practice of arresting and subjecting both their own nationals and nationals of other countries to secret trials, we believed it might assist our diplomatic and consular personnel in the Soviet Union in protecting U.S. nationals if the United States would have a commitment from the Soviet government that the appropriate U.S. diplomatic or consular officers would be promptly informed in case of the arrest of a U.S. national, that they would have the right to visit the detained person, and that the person under arrest would have the right to a fair, public, and speedy trial and access to legal counsel.

Our difficulty in drafting a commitment to extend all of these rights was that the Soviet Union thus far had not been willing to give such a commitment to any country. The farthest that it had gone in this respect was in the German-Soviet treaty of October 12, 1925. The pertinent excerpt of that treaty reads as follows:

Ad Article 11

> 1. The consul shall be notified either by a communication from the person arrested or by the authorities themselves direct. Such communications shall be made within a period not exceeding seven times twenty-four hours, and in large towns, including capitals of districts, within a period not exceeding three times twenty-four hours.
> 2. In places of detention of all kinds, requests made by consular representatives to visit nationals of their country under arrest, or to have them visited by their representatives, shall be granted without delay. The consular representative shall not be entitled to require officials of the courts or prisons to withdraw during his interview with the person under arrest.

We, nevertheless, prepared a draft of a commitment that contained all the clauses we considered essential if U.S. nationals in the Soviet Union were, in our opinion, to have a sense of security. For good measure we incorporated in our draft the excerpt quoted above from the German-Soviet treaty. Litvinov, according to our understanding, balked at giving any assurances in a delicate legal matter of this kind other than those contained in that treaty. This difficulty was overcome by the fourth exchange of letters between Litvinov and President Roosevelt. Litvinov in his letter stated:

> The Soviet Government is prepared to include in a consular convention to be negotiated immediately following the establishment of relations between our two countries provisions in which nationals of the United States shall be granted rights with reference to legal protection which shall not be less favorable than those enjoyed in the Union of Soviet Socialist Republics by the nation most favored in this respect. Furthermore, I desire to state that such rights will be granted to American nationals immediately upon the establishment of relations between our two countries.

He concluded his letter by quoting the excerpt from the German-Soviet treaty that I have set forth above.

The president in his reply thanked Litvinov for his letter and then added:

> I have noted the provisions of the treaty and protocol concluded between Germany and the Union of Soviet Socialist Republics on October 12, 1925.
>
> I am glad that nationals of the United States will enjoy the protection afforded by these instruments immediately upon the establishment of relations between our countries and I am fully prepared to negotiate a consular convention covering these subjects as soon as practicable. Let me add that American diplomatic and consular officers in the Soviet Union will be zealous in guarding the rights of American nationals, particularly the right to a fair, public, and speedy trial and the right to be represented by counsel of their choice. We shall expect that the nearest American diplomatic or consular officer shall be notified immediately of the arrest or detention of an American national, and that he shall promptly be afforded the opportunity to communicate and converse with such national.

Thus Litvinov in his letter stated the specific rights that U.S. nationals in the Soviet Union would enjoy in the matter of legal protection and rights of U.S. consular officers to learn of the arrests of such nationals and to visit them in prison. The president, after thanking him for this commitment, set forth the additional rights including those of fair and speedy trials, which the United States expected its nationals arrested in the Soviet Union to enjoy. Although this statement on the part of the president did not place additional obligations on the Soviet government, it did nevertheless serve as a basis for intervention on the part of U.S. diplomatic and consular officers in the future on behalf of American citizens under detention in the Soviet Union.

It will be noted in connection with this exchange that although Litvinov on behalf of the Soviet Union undertook to grant to U.S. nationals immediately upon the establishment of relations the rights extended to German nationals in the German-Soviet treaty, the president did not specifically grant the same rights on the basis of reciprocity to Soviet nationals in the United States. Since the commitments given by the Soviet government in the German-Soviet treaty were of a reciprocal nature, however, I took the position in later years that the United States was at least morally obligated to give to Soviet citizens under detention in the United States the same rights, so far as visits to them of Soviet diplomatic and consular officers were concerned, as the Soviet government had committed itself to extend to U.S. nationals in the Soviet Union.

The problem of the concern on the part of the U.S. government lest American citizens in the Soviet Union who had not consciously violated Soviet law might nevertheless find themselves charged with economic espionage was not one that lent itself to solution by an exchange of letters. The Soviet laws regarding economic espionage were of such a general and hazy character that foreign visitors and residents who had engaged in what seemed to them to be innocent conversations regarding the state of some sector or other of Soviet economy too frequently found themselves under arrest as economic spies. The president discussed at length this concern with Litvinov who insisted that there was no valid reason for it. It was finally decided to meet this problem by a statement on the part of Litvinov to be included among the documents to be published following the negotiations. This statement read as follows:

> The widespread opinion that the dissemination of economic information from the Union of Soviet Socialist Republics is allowed only in so far as this information has been published in newspapers or magazines, is erroneous. The right to obtain economic information is limited in the Union of Soviet Socialist Republics, as in other countries, only in the case of business and production secrets and in the case of the employment of forbidden methods (bribery, theft, fraud, etc.) to obtain such information. The category of business and production secrets naturally includes the official economic plans, in so far as they have not been made public, but not individual reports concerning the production conditions and the general conditions of individual enterprises.
>
> The Union of Soviet Socialist Republics has also no reason to compli-cate or hinder the critical examination of its economic organization. It naturally follows from this that everyone has the right to talk about economic matters or to receive information about such matters in the Union, in so far as the information for which he has asked or which has been imparted to him is not such as may not, on the basis of special regulations issued by responsible officials or by the appropriate state enterprises, be made known to outsiders. (This principle applies pri-marily to information concerning economic trends and tendencies.)

The description in this statement of what constituted "economic espionage" was so vague that it later proved to be of little help to U.S. nationals in the Soviet Union in determining how far they could go in discussing Soviet economic developments among themselves or with Soviet nationals without being guilty of violating Soviet law. The problem of the extent to which our embassy in Moscow could go in obtaining and passing along to the State Department or to visiting American busi-nessmen information relating to Soviet economic developments without making itself and those with whom it communicated vulnerable to charges of economic espionage plagued the members of the embassy and of the department for many years. A similar problem troubled foreign correspondents in the Soviet Union, particularly those whose dispatches were irritating to the Soviet government.

The fifth exchange between the president and Litvinov related to the problem of assets in the United States to which the Soviet government, following recognition, might be able to lay claim in U.S. courts. The U.S. government would be subjected to sharp public criticism if it would let a situation develop in which the Soviet government, while failing to reimburse the U.S. government and U.S. nationals for losses resulting from Soviet acts of confiscation, nationalization, and repudiation, would be able through U.S. courts to obtain possession of millions of dollars worth of the assets left in the United States by previous Russian governments, by representatives of former Russian corporations, or by Russian nationals, and would also be able to press claims arising from pre-revolutionary transactions against U.S. firms and citizens.

In order to surmount this problem the United States negotiators suggested that the Soviet government assign to the U.S. government such claims as it or Soviet nationals might have to funds and property in the United States. The assets that might derive from such an assignment could then be considered as part payment by the Soviet government of the claims that the U.S. government and nationals had against the Soviet Union.

Litvinov recognized the force of the representations made to him in this matter by our negotiators and addressed the following letter to the president on November 16, 1933:

> Following our conversations I have the honor to inform you that the Government of the Union of Soviet Socialist Republics agrees that, preparatory to a final settlement of the claims and counter claims between the Governments of the Union of Soviet Socialist Republics and the United States of America and the claims of their nationals, the Government of the Union of Soviet Socialist Republics will not take any steps to enforce any decisions of courts or initiate any new litigations for the amounts admitted to be due or that may be found to be due as the successor of prior Governments of Russia, or otherwise, from American nationals, including corporations, companies, partnerships, or associations, and also the claim against the United States of the Russian Volunteer Fleet, now in litigation in the United States Court of Claims, and will not object to such amounts being assigned and does hereby release and assign all such amounts to the Government of the United States, the Government of the Union of Soviet Socialist Republics to be duly notified

in each case of any amount realized by the Government of the United States from such release and assignment.

The Government of the Union of Soviet Socialist Republics further agrees, preparatory to the settlement referred to above not to make any claim with respect to:

(a)   judgments rendered or that may be rendered by American courts in so far as they relate to property, or rights, or interests therein, in which the Union of Soviet Socialist Republics or its nationals may have had or may claim to have an interest; or,

(b)   acts done or settlements made by or with the Government of the United States, or public officials in the United States, or its nationals, relating to property, credits, or obligations of any Government of Russia or nationals thereof.

In his reply the president added:

I am glad to have these undertakings by your Government and I shall be pleased to notify your Government in each case of any amount realized by the Government of the United States from the release and assignment to it of the amounts admitted to be due, or that may be found to be due, the Government of the Union of Soviet Socialist Republics, and of the amount that may be found to be due on the claim of the Russian Volunteer Fleet.

Efforts to prevail upon Litvinov to waive on behalf of his government claims for damages inflicted by U.S. military expeditions in 1918, 1919, and 1921 to northern Russia and Siberia achieved only partial success. A mass of documents presented to him apparently convinced him that our expedition to Siberia had as its purpose the preservation of the integrity, rather than the partitioning, of Russia. In any event, he addressed a letter to the president that stated in part:

The Government of the Union of Soviet Socialist Republics agrees that it will waive any and all claims of whatsoever character arising out of activities of military forces of the United States in Siberia, or assistance to military forces in Siberia, subsequent to January 1, 1918, and that such claims shall be regarded as finally settled and disposed of by this agreement.

Litvinov refused categorically, however, to waive on behalf of his government Soviet claims against the United States arising from the Arkhangelsk and Murmansk expeditions. These claims thus developed into one of the minor, though permanent, discordant notes that served to mar the harmony of future Soviet-American relations.

It was in respect to the problem of debts and claims that the negotiators on both sides ran into almost inextricable difficulties. Litvinov adamantly refused to make any statement that might indicate Soviet responsibility for losses incurred by the U.S. government or nationals as a result of Soviet acts of confiscation, nationalization, or repudiation. When it appeared that Judge Moore and William Bullitt were not able to work out a solution of this problem with the commissar, the president asked Henry Morgenthau, the acting secretary of the treasury, who was emotionally involved and obsessed by the fear that the State Department would find some way of sabotaging the negotiations, to participate in the discussions relating to debts and claims.

One method of approaching the problem that was explored by Moore, Bullitt, and Litvinov, and that for a time seemed to be promising, was for the United States and the Soviet Union to come to an understanding on the global amount that the Soviet Union would undertake to pay the United States in order to extinguish all claims of the U.S. government and nationals against the Soviet Union and nationals. After this amount had been determined the United States would undertake huge long-term loans or credits to the Soviet Union at rates of interest higher than normal. The excess interest received by the United States would then be used to liquidate the amount of indebtedness to which the Soviets had agreed.

The wording of the agreement under exploration would refer only to the "Kerensky debt"; nevertheless, the United States would be free to decide for itself how the amounts received from the Soviet government in the form of excess interest payments would be distributed among the U.S. creditors. Litvinov had insisted that reference to U.S. claims against the Soviet Union would be limited in the wording of the agreement to the "Kerensky debt" because the United States was the only country that had any claims against the Soviet government arising from funds or supplies furnished by it or its nationals to the Kerensky government. Since the Soviet government had committed itself to extend most-favored-nation treatment to several other governments in the matter of debts and claims, Litvinov considered it important that the Soviet government should not acknowledge even by inference the validity of any U.S. claims that might belong to the same category as the claims of those other governments.

During his conversations with Litvinov regarding the problem of debts and claims, Bullitt sought to impress upon the commissar the importance of the solution of that problem to the future of Soviet-American trade. He told Litvinov that pending before Congress was a bill, known as the Johnson bill, which prohibited the purchase or sale of bonds, securities, or other obligations of any foreign government or of making a loan to such government while it was in default in the payment of its obligations to the United States. He indicated to the commissar that in his opinion that bill would become law and that if it did, in the absence of a settlement of the debts and claims problem, the Soviet Union would not be able to obtain financial credits in the United States. Litvinov refused, however, to allow this threat to Soviet-American trade to disturb him. I may add in passing that this bill did become law on April 13, 1934— a law that contributed to blocking U.S. financial credits and loans to the Soviet government for many years.

In spite of Litvinov's intransigence there was hope until the afternoon of November 15 that some kind of an arrangement could be worked out. The president and Litvinov could not, however, come to an agreement with regard to the global amount owed by the Soviet government. Litvinov took the position that he would recommend to his government a sum no larger than 75 million dollars. He did not believe that he could justify a larger amount. The president on his part did not believe that he could persuade Congress to accept an amount less than 150 million dollars. Furthermore, there were other details to be negotiated in reaching a definite agreement of the kind under consideration. For instance, decisions must first be reached regarding the size of the loans or credits, the conditions under which they were to be extended, and the normal and excess rates of interest to be charged. Decisions of this kind could not well be made by the president without reference to Congress or by Litvinov without reference to his government. This would involve a considerable amount of time, and both the president and Litvinov were eager to bring the negotiations to a close and to be able to announce the establishment of diplomatic relations.

The president apparently came to the conclusion that, unless recognition was to be deferred for an indefinite period of time, it must be extended before a precise agreement in the matter of debts and claims could be reached. Apparently it seemed to him that, since the procedure for solving the problems of debts and claims had been informally worked out and since it should not be too difficult to come to an understanding regarding the details following recognition, it would be preferable not to delay the establishment of diplomatic relations. He and Litvinov, therefore, agreed that the lack of agreement with regard to debts and loans would be bridged temporarily by a joint statement to be made public along with the other documents relating to the establishment of diplomatic relations. This joint statement read as follows:

In addition to the agreements which we have signed today, there has taken place an exchange of views with regard to methods of settling all outstanding questions of indebtedness and claims that permits us to hope for a speedy and satisfactory solution to these questions which both our Governments desire to have out of the way as soon as possible.

Mr. Litvinov will remain in Washington for several days for further discussions.

The communiqué of November 16, 1933, announcing that the United States and the Soviet Union had established diplomatic relations, although not unexpected, made headlines in newspapers throughout the world. The two documents that excited the most interest were the exchange of letters relating to noninterference in internal affairs and the joint statement in respect to debts and claims. Did the exchange of these letters mean that the Soviet government had finally agreed that it would not permit the Communist International and kindred communist organizations to continue to use Soviet territory as a base for carrying out their international revolutionary activities? Most press editorials took the position that in view of the careful wording of the letter relating to interference it would be difficult for the Soviet government to argue that its commitments did not extend to the Communist International. Official spokesmen both for the United States and the Soviet Union refrained from interpreting the commitments contained in the press release. Publicly they took the attitude that it was preferable to let the documents speak for themselves.

Some of the commentators wondered why the Communist International was not specifically referred to in these letters. Why did not the U.S. negotiators insist that the words "such as, for instance, the Communist International" be inserted in the fourth paragraph of the letter relating to noninterference? The answer was that Litvinov had made it clear at the very beginning of the discussions that he could not enter into any commitment that specifically mentioned the Communist International. Furthermore, even if the Communist International had been referred to by name, it would always have been possible for that organization to continue to function under another name if the rulers of the Soviet Union should be determined to continue to carry on international revolutionary activities.

Although for almost two years official spokesmen for the Soviet government were careful not to state frankly that Litvinov's pledge of noninterference did not cover the activities of the Communist International, the communist-controlled press was not so reticent. Within a week after the announcement of the establishment of diplomatic relations the *Daily Worker* of New York City, for instance, which was under the control of the Communist International, insisted that "every attempt to claim that Article 4 of the Litvinov pact applies to the Communist International will meet with defeat."

CHAPTER 27

PREPARATIONS FOR THE EXCHANGE OF DIPLOMATIC AND CONSULAR REPRESENTATIVES BETWEEN THE UNITED STATES AND THE SOVIET UNION, NOVEMBER 1933–FEBRUARY 1934

ON THE DAY following the establishment of diplomatic relations the president announced that he was naming William Bullitt as the first U.S. ambassador to the Soviet Union. Two days later the announcement was made that Alexander A. Troyanovsky, former Soviet ambassador to Japan, was to be the first Soviet ambassador to the United States, and that Boris Skvirsky who, as I have already pointed out, had been acting as the head of the Soviet Information Bureau in Washington, was to be the counselor of the newly established Soviet embassy and to act as chargé d'affaires pending the arrival in the United States of Mr. Troyanovsky.

PLANNING FOR THE ESTABLISHMENT OF A U.S. EMBASSY IN MOSCOW

Another task that faced the Division of Eastern European Affairs as the result of the establishment of relations was that of assisting in the planning of a U.S. embassy in Moscow. I was charged with drawing up an organizational chart for the new embassy. In frequent consultation with Kelley, Packer, and other members of the division, and in close cooperation with the office of Mr. Carr, assistant secretary for administration, I developed an organizational chart of an embassy that in my opinion would meet our representational needs in Moscow. In doing so I hoped that the embassy in Moscow could also serve as an organizational model for our embassies throughout the world.

For many years I, like many other Foreign Service officers, had been of the opinion that the practice of maintaining a separate consular office in a capital city where we had a diplomatic mission was completely outmoded. I therefore welcomed the opportunity to draw up an organizational chart for our embassy in Moscow. The chart was not at all complex. It provided for only one U.S. government establishment in Moscow—an establishment to be headed by an ambassador and his chief assistant and alter ego, the counselor of embassy. The embassy, according to the chart, would comprise four major sections, each headed by an experienced Foreign Service officer: (1) an administrative section, (2) a political section, (3) an economic section, and (4) a consular section. Attached to the executive head of the embassy, that is, the ambassador and his counselor, would be the military and naval attachés. There would be no commercial attaché unless one of the officers in the economic section would be given such a designation.

Although they were aware that the establishment of a consular section in our embassy would create a storm in certain areas of the State Department, both Kelley and Carr approved my organizational chart. In order to soften opposition, however, they suggested that the section be referred to as the "consulate general" instead of as the "consular section." They also decided, wisely as it turned out, that it would be preferable not to try to determine precisely what the relationship between the officers in that section and the embassy should be or what status these officers should have until after the mission had been set up and the ambassador had had an opportunity to discuss the matter with the Soviet authorities.

Ambassador Bullitt had decided to leave Washington in the early part of December for Moscow in order to present his credentials and to engage in frank conversations with top Soviet officials while they were still in fairly good humor in view of the success of the Litvinov visit. We were hopeful that the ambassador would take advantage of the exceptional popularity that he was enjoying at the time among the Soviet leaders in order to obtain from them concessions, particularly in the matter of working and living quarters.

It was not until the middle of January 1934, when Keith Merrill, the State Department's assistant for foreign buildings, returned to Washington, that we learned for the first time that instead of the approximately 280 rooms we had requested, we would have only 72. This news came as a shock to those of us who had been hoping that our representation in

Moscow would not be faced with the housing problems that had been plaguing the representations of other countries.

When I expressed my disappointment to Merrill he said that in his opinion our mission would be in a much better position in the matter of housing than most of the other diplomatic missions in Moscow. The ambassador would have a residence second to none and the space made available for the working and living quarters of the staff would be larger than that which the Soviets had made available to the members of most of the other countries. Furthermore, he pointed out, during the ambassador's short sojourn in Moscow he had obtained from Stalin personally a promise that the United States could erect its own embassy building in the immediate future. The new embassy, when completed, would be large enough to satisfy all of our building needs.

While in Moscow Merrill had been aided in his search for living and working quarters by George Kennan, whom Bullitt had taken with him on his advance trip. Kennan had completed his two years of Russian language studies following his detail to our legation in Riga and had subsequently been reassigned to the legation for service in its Russian section. He had been in Washington on a temporary visit in November 1933 and had been invited by Bullitt to accompany him to Moscow. It was decided that Kennan should remain in Moscow, following the ambassador and Merrill's return to the United States, in order to look after some of the numerous details connected with our housing problems.

In view of the limited amount of space that would be available for the mission it was necessary to revise sharply our plans for Moscow. Although the outline of the organizational chart was not altered, deep cuts were made in the number of U.S. personnel to be assigned to the mission. Such a reduction meant, of course, a curtailment both quantitatively and qualitatively in the activities of the mission. It became clear, for instance, that with its relatively small staff the mission would not be able to engage in the type of reporting that required research in depth. This meant that the Russian section of our legation in Riga would continue to prepare most of the time-consuming studies of developments within the Soviet Union. It was also decided that for the time being the Soviet visa work would continue to be performed by the legation at Riga.

When Bullitt learned of our housing crisis he ruled that temporarily, at least, wives and other dependents should not accompany members of his staff to Moscow and that in the selection of personnel preference should be given to those who were not married. In order to render it easier to house several clerks in one small apartment, he also decided that all clerical employees, including stenographers and typists, were to be male. Those of us in the department who were acquainted with conditions in the Soviet Union were concerned at this tendency in the direction of an all-male mission. We did not think that in the atmosphere that prevailed in Moscow an establishment composed entirely of unmarried men or married men without family could carry on for any length of time without running into difficulties. The members of the staff would eventually feel the need for female companionship and we were convinced that no Russian girl would dare to be seen with a member of the U.S. embassy without the advance approval of the OGPU—an approval that signified, in effect, that she had become an agent for the secret police. Nevertheless, we realized that until the members of the embassy could move out of the Savoy Hotel and the limited space available for housing had been distributed, it would be preferable for the mission to operate on a military-like basis without dependents.

When the State Department had a definite knowledge of the amount of space that would be available, it began seriously to approach the task of selecting personnel. At the time that Bullitt had agreed to go to Moscow as the first U.S. ambassador to the Soviet Union, an understanding had been reached between the president and him that he personally could select the members of his staff. Among the early selections that he had made was that of John C. Wiley as his counselor and deputy. Wiley, although comparatively young in years, was a veteran member of the former Diplomatic Service. Subsequent to his entry into the Foreign Service in 1915 he had been stationed in no less than eleven different diplomatic missions in Europe and Latin America. Since he had served as counselor of embassy in both Warsaw and Berlin, where he had had unique opportunities to acquaint himself with some of the problems of Eastern Europe, he seemed to be particularly well qualified for the Moscow assignment. Furthermore, he had worked closely and harmoniously with Bullitt during the London Monetary and Economic Conference in the spring of 1933. The fact that Wiley was unmarried was another factor in his favor.

Among the other early selections made by Bullitt were three junior Foreign Service officers who had been given special training by the department for work in the Russian field: George Kennan, who had studied at the University of Berlin, and Charles E. Bohlen and Bertel Kuniholm, who had been pursuing Russian language studies in the School of Oriental Languages at the University of Paris. Kennan was the only one of the three with a wife. Before leaving Washington for his short visit to Moscow, Bullitt had had several conferences with these junior Russian language officers and was enthusiastic at the thought of having them with him. He had made it clear at that time that he preferred to have his staff composed of young men who had not as yet been shaped into the "typical Foreign Service officer mold." He wanted dash, brilliance, imagination, and enthusiasm unchecked and undimmed by years of servitude in the straitjacket of government service. He regarded Wiley, with his Bohemian tendencies and keen sense of humor, as an exception in that the latter had not developed into a run-of-the-mill senior Foreign Service officer.

Another senior Foreign Service officer who was one of the early selections was our consul general at Harbin, George C. Hanson, another bachelor. Hanson was known throughout the Far East as a competent officer, a delightful host, and a bon vivant. He spoke both Russian and Chinese fluently and, in spite of the fact that the United States and the Soviet Union, up to the date of recognition, were not supposed to have been on speaking terms, had managed to make many friends among the numerous Soviet officials in Harbin. He was a kindly and good-natured man in his early fifties with the physique that had made him a famous oarsman during his undergraduate days at Cornell. Will Rogers had been so impressed with him during a visit to the Far East that he had dubbed him the "uncrowned King of Manchuria," a title that stuck. Soviet officials both in Washington and Moscow in talking with Bullitt had spoken highly of Hanson. When, therefore, the Division of Foreign Service Personnel recommended him for the consul generalship, Bullitt included him on his list.

My Unexpected Assignment to Moscow

Since both Judge Moore and Robert Kelley insisted that there be on the embassy staff at least one Foreign Service officer with extensive Russian experience, Bullitt agreed to take Earl Packer along as first secretary. Packer had served as assistant military attaché in St. Petersburg and later in Arkhangelsk during the First World War. Since February 1920 he had been working continuously in the department or in the Baltic states on matters pertaining to Russia. He had been assistant chief of the Eastern European Division since October 1928. In accepting the assistant chiefship he had resigned his Foreign Service commission with the understanding that if and when he should be needed again in the field he would be recommissioned. Packer spoke Russian fluently and could read it without difficulty.

Kelley told me that when Packer left for Moscow he would like me to take his place as assistant chief of the division. That was agreeable to me. I had long looked forward to the time when, after working so many years on matters pertaining to the Soviet Union, I might assist in opening our embassy in Moscow. I was of the opinion, however, that since my command of the Russian language was not nearly as good as that of Packer, and since Packer had already spent almost three years in Russia, he would be more valuable to Bullitt than I. Furthermore, I was convinced that an assignment in Moscow under existing conditions could be for me a humiliating experience. It was my understanding that the ambassador did not care to have with him older and more experienced officers. If he had had an awareness of my existence he had not demonstrated it. He had not asked to see me or otherwise shown the slightest interest in me. I would have liked to meet him and talk to him, but I was unwilling to go to his office for what might seem to be the purpose of attracting attention to myself. It seemed to me that my presence in Moscow not only was not needed but was not desired. I had, therefore, come to the conclusion that it would be preferable for me to remain in the Division of Eastern European Affairs until January 1935, at which time my four years of assignment to the State Department (four years represented the maximum length of an assignment of a Foreign Service officer to the department) would expire, and then to suggest that I be assigned to a post outside the field of Eastern Europe. I was distressed at the thought of leaving that field after having invested so many hours over so many years in it. Nevertheless, I managed to comfort myself to some extent by thinking that what I had learned during those years would be useful in other areas.

The Divison of Foreign Service Personnel had prepared a long list of Foreign Service officers and clerical employees who might be available for service in the Soviet Union and submitted it to Bullitt following his return from Moscow. Although the ambassador accepted some of the officers included in this list, he decided to choose his clerical assistants without reference to the Division of Foreign Service Personnel. In doing so he offended some of the members of that division to such an extent that they took the position that they could not share any further responsibility for the composition of the embassy. Their irritation with Bullitt broadened to include other members of the department who were trying to cooperate with him, in particular the members of the Division of Eastern European Affairs. As a result both the embassy in Moscow and the Eastern European Division were for a number of years in the black books of the personnel and administrative areas of the State Department.

One of the first noncooperative decisions taken by the Division of Foreign Service Personnel with respect to our embassy personnel problems was destined to have far-reaching effect on me. When Packer discussed with that division the matter of his reinstatement into the Foreign Service so that he could accompany the mission to Moscow, he was informed that he could be readmitted only at the lowest grade of class 5, a rank that would make him a second secretary rather than first secretary. Since a number of Foreign Service officers who had entered the service subsequent to Packer were already in higher classes, and since his salary in the department was equivalent to that of an officer in the middle of class 4, his acceptance of a commission at the bottom of class 5 would have represented a demotion both in rank and salary. Packer, therefore, stated that he did not wish to be reinstated in the Foreign Service under such circumstances. The Division of Foreign Service Personnel also refused to budge.

As a result of the ensuing deadlock, Kelley asked me if I would be willing to go to Moscow in place of Packer. He said that he regretted making a suggestion of this kind so near the time of sailing. He was doing so only because he considered it important that either Packer or I go, and he could not expect Packer, who had worked so hard and effectively for many years in the division, to go at the personal sacrifice demanded by the Personnel Department. I replied that I was at the disposal of the State Department. I added that I doubted I could be of any great value in Moscow since the idea seemed to be that experience was a handicap rather than an advantage. Kelley said he would discuss the matter with Bullitt.

A few hours after my conversation with Kelley, Bullitt sent for me. On the desk before him lay my dossier. He said, far from cordially, "It is my understanding that you wish to go with my mission to Moscow. Is that correct?" I replied that I was not advancing myself as a candidate for a position in the embassy, that I was a Foreign Service officer prepared to go to any post that the department might select for me, and that if the department and he would like me to be a member of his mission, I would be glad to go with him. He then asked, "Am I to understand that you are not eager to go?" My reply was that the suggestion that I go to Moscow had not come from me; nevertheless, I would be glad to go if the department and he thought I could be of use there; if I went I would do my best loyally and effectively to serve him and the United States. He replied, "Well, I shall look into the matter. I prefer to have with me people who are looking forward to the challenge with enthusiasm." That terminated our interview. I left Bullitt in the belief that he would tell Kelley that he did not want me.

On the following day the chief of the Division of Foreign Service Personnel informed me that I was being designated second secretary of embassy at Moscow and that I was being instructed to proceed to Moscow on the SS *Washington* sailing from New York on February 15. He said he was processing my written instructions and that they would reach me in due course. I suggested that he check in order to make sure that there was no misunderstanding. I then described my conversation on the previous day with Bullitt and said that I had left his office with the impression that he would prefer that I not be a member of his mission. I added that during my more than eleven years in the service I had never gone to a post where I felt that I was not wanted and that, in my opinion, it would be a mistake to send anyone to Moscow whom the ambassador would not welcome as a member of his staff. The chief's reply was that he had in his hands the request, bearing Bullitt's initials, that the appointment be made. I should go, therefore, and do the best I could. If I should find the situation unbearably humiliating I should drop him a line. I should, however, try to stick it out for at least a year. My written instructions, dated February 8, reached me on February 9.

Shortly after my conversation with the chief of Foreign Service Personnel, Judge Moore sent for me. He told me he was pleased at my willingness to go to Moscow and he agreed with Kelley that there should be at least one member of the mission with a considerable depth of knowledge regarding Soviet leaders, institutions, practices, and so forth. He hoped that as a member of Bullitt's staff I would not be too diffident. I should not wait until asked to express my opinion on matters that I might consider to be important. I would not be performing my duty or be living up to my responsibilities if I should remain silent when decisions were being made that might affect the work of the embassy or the interests of the United States.

Bullitt's Warm Welcome in Moscow

Bullitt had returned from his visit to Moscow glowing with enthusiasm. He had been given the warmest welcome ever accorded in the Soviet Union to an ambassador. He had been vodkaed and dined by the highest officials of the Soviet Union and the All-Union Communist Party. At functions in his honor given by the great revolutionary leaders, toasts of a most friendly character had been offered both to the president and to him. At a dinner given by General Kliment Y. Voroshilov, for instance, which had been attended by what Litvinov referred to as the "inside directorate of the Soviet Union," Stalin himself had offered a toast to the president and had later stated that "President Roosevelt is today, in spite of being the leader of a capitalist nation, one of the most popular men in the Soviet Union."

Following the presentation of his credentials to President Kalinin on December 13, the latter had requested the ambassador to say to President Roosevelt that "he and everyone else in Russia considered the President completely out of the class of the leaders of the capitalistic states; that it was clear to them all that the President really cared about the welfare of the laboring men and the farmers and that he was not engaged in protecting the vested rights of property."

Kalinin had also informed the ambassador that he hoped the latter would travel in every part of the Soviet Union. When Bullitt suggested that in order to see the country it would be useful for him to have a plane of his own in Moscow Kalinin had gone so far as to assure him that there would be no restrictions whatsoever upon the latter's movements. He added that since Lenin had referred in a friendly manner to Bullitt on a number of occasions he had the feeling that he was welcoming someone whom he had known for a long time.

Bullitt's report to the State Department, written aboard the SS *Washington* on January 4, 1934, was read with astonishment by the members of the department, particularly by those of us in the Eastern European Division who had been following for many years developments in the Soviet Union. The treatment given our new ambassador, the statements made to him, and the promises that he had obtained made us wonder whether the newspaper commentators who had been maintaining that the Soviet Union was undergoing profound changes and that the Soviet leaders were preparing to convert Soviet Russia into a society that could maintain genuinely friendly relations with noncommunist countries, had not after all known what they were talking about.

Bullitt had brought back with him assurances that he could have his own plane in the Soviet Union and that he would not be subject to restrictions in using it to travel around the country. He had been promised by Stalin himself that Sparrow Hills, the name of which was being changed to Lenin Hills, the beautiful bluff across the Moscow River overlooking Moscow, would be presented to the U.S. government as a site for a new U.S. embassy building. Grinko, the people's commissar for finance, had promised that he would make a private arrangement whereby members of the U.S. diplomatic and consular staffs in Moscow could obtain through Bullitt an adequate number of rubles for minor expenses at a fair rate so that they would not, like members of other diplomatic missions, be compelled to buy their rubles in the black market. The chief of the Central Administration of Economic and Social Statistics had agreed that he would place at the disposal of the embassy staff all the statistics available in his department as well as the complete library of his department.

Unfortunately, the Soviet leaders had failed to make the needed commitment with regard to housing for the chancery of the embassy or for the living quarters of the staff. They had, however, not hesitated to talk with apparent frankness regarding the international situation, in particular about the situation in the Far East, which seemed to concern some of them.

Bullitt's successes were by no means limited to Moscow. He also achieved a number of "firsts" in his relations with U.S. officialdom. His personal charm, his articulate persuasiveness, and the aura, derived from the backing of the president, that enveloped him, enabled him to break through many administrative practices that had been hallowed by tradition. For instance, he was able to obtain from the Department of State a ruling that all the American members of his staff from the counselor down to the lowest ranking clerical employee be armed with diplomatic passports. He prevailed upon the Navy Department to provide his residence with the silver service and the other accouterment customarily reserved for a battleship carrying a high-ranking admiral. He also obtained from the armed services for use in our embassy a great quantity of bedding and other equipment, including a supply of medicines, generally used in military hospitals. The War Department promised to make available to him a plane replete with pilot, crew, and medicines. The Public Health Service agreed to provide the embassy with one of its best physicians. He persuaded the office of the State Department charged with the furnishing of embassies to purchase and expedite the shipment of furniture, kitchen equipment, and so forth needed to complete the furnishing of his residence, which was being rented partly furnished.

The success of Bullitt's visit to Moscow introduced a note of optimism in the State Department and in the White House. There was a growing feeling that perhaps he and his mission really would be able to make valuable contributions to the cause of promoting international good will and peace. Perhaps the Soviets would keep their promises in the matter of noninterference in internal affairs. Perhaps they would agree to a debts and claims settlement that would justify the extension to them of the long-term credits in amounts that would enable them to make sizable purchases of U.S. products.

It was in such an atmosphere that my wife and I, after bidding farewell to our friends, left Washington on the afternoon of St. Valentine's Day in 1934 in order to board the SS *Washington* on the following day, together with other members of the little group that was to establish in Moscow an embassy of the United States to the Union of Soviet Socialist Republics. I was bound for Moscow and she for Riga where she was to wait until arrangements could be effected for wives in Moscow.

PART IX

SECOND SECRETARY, FIRST SECRETARY, CHARGÉ D'AFFAIRES, U.S. EMBASSY IN MOSCOW, FEBRUARY 1934–JULY 1938

CHAPTER 28

FROM WASHINGTON TO MOSCOW, FEBRUARY 15–MARCH 1, 1934

ACCORDING TO MY RECOLLECTION, the members of the mission on that ship numbered 25. They included Ambassador Bullitt and four Foreign Service officers: John Wiley, the counselor; Dana Hodgson, former chief of the Visa Division of the State Department who, it was planned, would eventually be in charge of the visa work in Moscow but who would establish himself temporarily in the consulate at Riga until the visa activities could be transferred to Moscow; Bertel Kuniholm, one of the secretaries; myself, with the title of second secretary; and my wife. There were also from the State Department nine clerical employees, including two noncareer vice consuls.

The armed services were represented on board by Lieutenant Thomas D. White, assistant military attaché for air and acting military attaché; Captain David R. Nimmer of the Marine Corps, naval attaché, and Mrs. Nimmer; six noncommissioned officers of the marines; and from the navy a chief pharmacist mate and an electrician mate, first class.

In addition to the members of the mission there was another person on board the vessel who was en route to Moscow. I refer to Father Leopold Braun, a young Roman Catholic priest who was to act informally as the spiritual adviser of the Catholic members of the American community in Moscow. This modest and dedicated priest, by his good works and kindly disposition, was, during the next nine years, to earn the respect and affection of all members of our mission, Catholic and non-Catholic alike.

The president, in order to forestall charges that the members of our mission were without the benefit of clergy, had persuaded the Catholic church to send a priest to Moscow with us. Father Braun had been the selection of the church. He began to carry out his new duties immediately by holding religious services on Sunday morning for the benefit of the Catholic members of the mission and for others on board who might care to attend.

It was, I believe, on our third day out that the ambassador called the first meeting of all members of the mission who were aboard. After a brief social session he gave an informal talk setting forth the administrative and other policies and practices that he intended to follow and indicating what some of his expectations were with respect to the attitudes and conduct of his staff. According to my recollection he emphasized that he did not desire his mission to resemble the U.S. embassies that he had visited during his many trips abroad. In the first place, he was opposed to diplomatic missions being operated on a hierarchical basis. So far as he was concerned, every member of his mission from top to bottom would have equal status. He would not recognize or tolerate any distinctions between officers and clerks. He would be equally accessible to all members of his staff regardless of the category into which the State Department, through its bureaucratic machinery, might have assigned them. He wished, in particular, to impress upon those who were entering the service of the United States abroad for the first time that they should not feel handicapped because of the lack of Foreign Service experience. In his opinion, previous experience in the State Department and in the Foreign Service might well prove to be a handicap rather than an asset to members of a diplomatic mission operating in the Soviet Union.

The ambassador devoted a few words to the treatment accorded to him during his recent visit to Moscow. He indicated that the special consideration shown him caused him to believe that the Soviet leaders sincerely hoped for the development of friendly relations and even close collaboration between the Soviet Union and the United States. It was important, therefore, that the members of his mission enter the Soviet Union in a spirit of friendliness and that although they should constantly bear in mind that their first duty was that of endeavoring to promote the interests of the United States and the welfare of the American people, they should also try to create goodwill for the United States among Soviet officials and among the Russian people in general. It was his sincere belief that friendly relations and, in appropriate circumstances, friendly cooperation between the United States and the Soviet Union would be in the interest of the United States and of world peace. Every member of the mission, therefore, should do his part to make sure that if friendly relations and cooperation with the Soviet Union should fail to develop, the failure would not be due to shortcomings of the mission but rather to Soviet attitudes and policies.

During the course of this voyage I was subjected to conflicting hopes and doubts. I hoped that the ambassador with the support of the members of his mission would achieve success in his efforts to create a friendly and cooperative relationship between the United States and the Soviet Union on a stable and lasting basis. Success, in my opinion, would mean much to a world in which I had assumed I still had many years to live. But it seemed to me that success would also mean that the Soviet Union would cease its efforts to bring about the overthrow of the government of the United States and all other noncommunist governments and that it would accept and live up to the principles that must be adhered to if there is to be sincerely friendly intercourse among members of the family of nations.

Was it possible, I asked myself, that the Soviet leaders would decide that it would be to the advantage of the Soviet Union and its people for them to endeavor to cooperate in a friendly way with noncommunist nations instead of trying to produce revolution and chaos? Did the treatment that they had extended to Ambassador Bullitt signify that a fundamental change was taking place in Soviet policies and practices? I tried to convince myself that the answer to these questions might well be in the affirmative. Nevertheless, nagging doubts could not be dismissed. Recollections of the stubbornness with which Litvinov had fought against making definite commitments, which if lived up to would indicate a cessation of the Soviet practices that had resulted in setting the Soviet Union apart from the rest of the world, tended to strengthen my doubts. Furthermore, the Soviet press since the establishment of relations seemed to be as hostile as ever to the noncommunist world. The question that only time could answer was: Were the courtesies shown and the compliments paid to Ambassador Bullitt during the course of his visit sincere expressions of friendly feelings, or did they represent merely so much flattery cynically extended in the hope that the ambassador as an influential friend of the president might persuade the latter to extend to the Soviet Union, on terms acceptable to it, the loans and credits that it needed and to cooperate with the Soviet Union in the field of international policies, even though no changes in Soviet policies and practices were taking place? I sensed that questions of a similar character might also be worrying the ambassador.

It was, I believe, on February 17 that the ambassador asked me to come to his stateroom. He said that he had decided to disembark in Le Havre and thence to proceed to the Soviet Union through Paris, Berlin, and Warsaw. He thought it might be useful for him, before opening the embassy in Moscow, to exchange views with members of our embassies and with officials of the Foreign Offices in those cities. He also thought that it would be a good idea to take with him Wiley, Kuniholm, White, and the Nimmers, as well as one of the clerks to act as his secretary. He wondered whether I would be willing to take the other eight clerks and the noncommissioned marine and naval officers directly on to Moscow and, with their assistance and that of George Kennan, who was already in Moscow, prepare the embassy for opening as soon as possible after his arrival. I, of course, agreed. The ambassador and his group, therefore, disembarked at Le Havre and our party was reduced to Father Braun, Dana Hodgson, my wife and me, eight of the clerks, and the eight naval and marine noncommissioned officers. We landed at Hamburg on the evening of February 23 and thence proceeded by train to Berlin.

In Berlin I was informed that the embassy had obtained railway reservations that would render it possible for our Moscow-bound group to leave on the morning of February 28. On February 27 I put my wife on a train bound for Riga, where it was planned she should stay until accommodations could be arranged in Moscow for the wives of members of the mission. Dana Hodgson had decided to remain in Berlin until the arrival of Ambassador Bullitt before proceeding to Riga. Arrangements had been made for Father Braun, who was not sure of the kind of treatment that he would receive from the Soviet authorities at the frontier, to proceed to Moscow with us.

I learned that it was not easy to conduct sixteen active young men, some of whom had never been abroad before and were eager to see the world, across Europe, particularly when we were encumbered with an enormous amount of personal baggage and hand luggage, including sealed bags of material that must be continuously under guard. The members of the naval and marine contingent were not difficult to handle. Captain Nimmer on board the ship had given them explicit orders in writing that, pending his arrival in Moscow, they were to "accept and execute such orders as may be given by Mr. Loy W. Henderson, member of the Diplomatic Mission."

A leathery marine gunnery sergeant, Philip Odien, who at the advanced age of 43 was deferentially referred to by the other noncommissioned officers as "Pop," was in charge of them and made sure that they were continuously on the alert. These members of the armed forces had no doubts about their status and were quick to obey orders. Several of our clerical employees, however, seemed to feel that they were tourists on a sightseeing expedition. They tended to take photographs, buy postcards, and scatter in various directions at times when it was important that we remain in a group. On several occasions I had difficulty in making them understand that even though the ambassador had stressed that he would regard all members of his staff as equals, they were under my personal orders until the ambassador would join us in Moscow.

Although during my almost thirteen years in the service I had become accustomed to international travel, I felt a thrill when, early on the morning of March 1, we crossed the Polish-Soviet border and found ourselves in the Soviet Union. I had been working on matters pertaining to the Soviet Union for more than nine years and had been constantly hoping that some day I might enter that exciting country and see for myself what it was like and what was taking place in it.

Our party was treated with courtesy by the Soviet authorities at the border, although our passports and hand luggage were carefully examined. Questions were raised, however, with regard to Father Braun's effects. Since he had no diplomatic passport the Soviet officials went carefully through his baggage and made inventories of its contents. They regarded with suspicion his vestments, books, and the other belongings that he needed in connection with his religious duties. When I explained to the chief customs officer that Braun was to serve as the chaplain to some of the members of Ambassador Bullitt's mission, that officer decided not to confiscate what he clearly regarded as subversive material or to demand the payment of customs duties.

Soviet railways are several inches wider than the standard gauge railways in Western Europe. It was, therefore, necessary for railway passengers entering the Soviet Union from Poland to be transferred at the frontier with all their effects to a broad–gauge Soviet train.

After we had transferred we found attached to our new train a commodious dining car in which breakfast was being served. By the time that the train was in motion the members of our party were enjoying their first meal in the Soviet Union. It was at this breakfast that I received my first lesson in the importance of restraining my inquisitive tendencies. Among the dishes set before us were some appetizing stewed pears. I complimented the chef on them and asked how they had been prepared. He froze at my question, hesitated a moment, and then replied stiffly that the manner of their preparation was a secret, which he was not prepared to divulge.

As the train glided toward Moscow most of us kept our eyes glued to the windows. It was in the dead of winter and the landscape was almost exactly as I had pictured it would be. Snow covered the plains broken from time to time by white-blanketed forests, rather dreary towns, and small villages composed of wooden unpainted houses ornamented with lacy wood carvings. Some of the small towns and villages were huddled around churches. In others there appeared to be no buildings of consequence. In place of dashing troikas there were sledges drawn by plodding shabby horses, and pedestrians bundled up against the cold were trudging through the snow.

CHAPTER 29

PREPARATIONS FOR THE ARRIVAL OF THE AMBASSADOR IN MOSCOW AND THE INITIAL CONFERENCES BETWEEN HIM AND OFFICERS OF HIS MISSION

AT THE STATION IN MOSCOW we were greeted by George Kennan and Charlie Thayer, a young West Point graduate from Philadelphia whom Mr. Bullitt had met during his recent Moscow trip and had invited with the department's approval to join our staff. Also at the station was an expert on U.S. foreign buildings by the name of Daves, whom the State Department had sent to Moscow to assist in preparing the ambassador's residence and the chancery for occupancy. All three were so deeply buried in their high fur collars and fur caps that it was difficult to see their faces. Others in the welcoming group were several American journalists; Spencer Williams, chief of the Moscow office of the Russian-American Chamber of Commerce; and a number of junior members of the Commissariat for Foreign Affairs. It was a cold windy day and we in our American hats with ears and faces exposed looked with envy upon the Moscow veterans on the platform in their winter-defying clothing.

Kennan and Thayer had arranged for automobiles to convey the members of our party with their luggage to the Savoy Hotel in which rooms had already been assigned in advance to each of us. While we were en route to the hotel, Kennan and Thayer outlined for my benefit some of the problems that they were encountering. The most urgent of which, as I had foreseen, was the problem of the ruble.

THE RUBLE CRISIS

Since the complicated ruble problem was an enduring one that in some form or other plagued the embassy during most of the period of my service in Moscow, I shall at this point try to explain some of its ramifications. The ruble in common circulation in the Soviet Union was usually referred to by foreigners as the "paper ruble." If purchased at the legal foreign exchange rate from a Soviet institution, it would cost 88 cents. Paper rubles could, however, be bought in Moscow in the open market, as the black market was euphemistically called, or in the money markets of Eastern and Western Europe at between 30 or 40 for a dollar. The purchasing power in the Soviet Union of a paper ruble was reckoned by foreign residents in Moscow to be generally equal to that of 3 or 4 cents in the United States or Western Europe. If a foreign resident in Moscow would pay 88 cents for rubles that would have a purchasing power of only 3 or 4 cents, his living and operating expenses would be fantastically high. Foreign residents in Moscow, including diplomatic personnel, journalists, and businessmen, who had foreign currency at their disposal, were accustomed, therefore, to buy such paper rubles as they needed in the open Moscow market or to import them from abroad. It was, of course, illegal to buy rubles on the open market or to import them, but the Soviet government, apparently realizing that the legal exchange rate was unrealistic, preferred winking at these illegal practices to introducing more reasonable rates.

In addition to the paper ruble the Soviet government made use of what it called a "gold ruble." The gold ruble did not exist physically. It was in fact merely an exchange figure used in statistics of various kinds and in certain transactions with foreigners visiting or resident in the Soviet Union. The legal exchange rate for the gold ruble was also 88 cents. Since there were no gold rubles in circulation, Soviet practice required that all bills in such rubles be paid in U.S. dollars or in the equivalent of dollars in some other acceptable foreign currency.

Intourist, the Soviet agency responsible for looking after foreign visitors in the Soviet Union, charged them in gold rubles for hotel rooms, meals, local transportation, and so forth. Gold ruble prices were only a fraction of the paper ruble prices established for similar things or services. A registered American tourist, for instance, in one of the hotels operated by Intourist, might be charged six gold rubles for a meal for which an American journalist resident in Moscow sitting at the same table and eating a similar meal might be charged 160 paper rubles, the amount that a Soviet national would also have been required to pay. The American tourist would pay the bill in dollars. It would amount to $5.28. The journalist would pay in paper rubles that had been bought in the open market at the exchange rate of, let us say, 30 for a dollar. The rubles that the journalist paid for the meal would have cost, therefore, $5.17. If, however, the journalist had bought paper rubles at the legal rate, the meal would have cost $148.80.

There was another agency that dealt primarily with foreigners in gold rubles. I refer to Torgsin, which maintained several shops in Moscow and other cities in the Soviet Union. One of the purposes of Torgsin, which priced all of its merchandise in gold rubles, was to obtain badly needed foreign currency from foreign visitors and residents by selling them limited varieties of foodstuffs and other commodities not otherwise available in the Soviet Union, such as pseudo-antiques. Most members of the diplomatic corps were accustomed to supplementing such foodstuffs as they imported or were able to buy with paper rubles by purchases paid for in dollars or other acceptable currency at Torgsin. Tourists looking for souvenirs and antiques also made extensive purchases in foreign currency at Torgsin shops.

Neither the Department of State nor Ambassador Bullitt had liked the idea of our embassy or its personnel violating Soviet law in order to obtain paper rubles. Ambassador Bullitt, while visiting Moscow in December 1933, had discussed this matter with Litvinov and Grinko, the people's commissar for finance, and both of these responsible officials had promised that the Soviet government would work out a method for satisfying the embassy's needs for local currency by selling it paper rubles at reasonable prices. Following the ambassador's return to Washington, the department with the ambassador's approval had issued instructions strictly forbidding the purchase of paper rubles by any member of the embassy or the consulate general.

Since at the time of my arrival in Moscow no arrangement had been worked out that would enable the embassy to buy paper rubles from the Soviet government at reasonable prices, since we had been forbidden to buy such rubles illegally, and since we hesitated to buy paper rubles at Soviet institutions at the exorbitant legal rate, Kennan and Thayer were in a quandary. They pointed out that if they had been compelled to pay for the transportation of our party from the station to the hotel in paper rubles purchased at the official rate, the cost would have amounted to several hundred dollars. Fortunately they had been able to obtain the use of automobiles through the Intourist hotel, at which Kennan was staying, on a gold-ruble basis.

Kennan and Thayer said they had thus far been able to carry on in the framework of the instructions not to purchase rubles on the open market. However, now that there were twenty instead of three members of the staff in Moscow and that a variety of expenditures must be made at once in local currency, it was necessary without further delay to face up to the ruble problem. A shipment of furniture and other equipment for the use of the embassy had arrived and was in the railway yards. Arrangements must be made to transfer part of this shipment and other shipments expected soon to the ambassador's residence and to store the remainder until the Mokhovaya Building was ready for occupancy. The transport and storage must be paid for in paper rubles. How were we to obtain these rubles? It would be ridiculous to buy them at official rates.

The thought occurred to me that we might solve our difficulties on a temporary basis by borrowing paper rubles from the Soviet State Bank pending the arrival of the ambassador. Both Kennan and Thayer approved this idea. On the following morning, therefore, Kennan introduced me to a member of the Third Western Division of the Commissariat for Foreign Affairs, which was handling relations with the United States. I presented our problem to this young diplomat and asked him to arrange for us to meet an appropriate official of the State Bank. When we met that official on the following day it was evident that he had been informed in advance of the purpose of our visit. I told him that we had come to request a loan on behalf of the U.S. embassy. He asked who would be responsible for repayment. I replied that I was seeking the loan in the name of the government of the United States, which at the moment I was representing, and that the government would guarantee repayment. How, he then inquired, would the embassy obtain the rubles needed to repay the loan? I replied that that was a matter for the ambassador, following his arrival in Moscow, to work out with the Soviet Union. After further discussion it was agreed that he would open an account in the bank in the name of the U.S. embassy from which we could begin to draw rubles. I forget the amount of credit placed at our disposal but I believe it amounted to approximately 10,000 rubles. Although we were extremely frugal in the expenditures of such rubles that I withdrew, the embassy owed the State Bank thousands of rubles by the time the ambassador arrived in Moscow several days later. The ambassador approved our transactions and proceeded to borrow additional funds from the State Bank in order to cover the ruble expenses of the embassy pending an arrangement that would permit the embassy to purchase rubles at a tolerable rate.

Our advance group, reinforced by Kennan, Thayer, and Daves, set to work immediately to make preparations that would enable the embassy to begin conducting business at the earliest possible date after the arrival of the ambassador. Since the ambassador's residence had been rented partly furnished, it would be possible for him, although with considerable discomfort, to begin living in it at once. We decided that it would be convenient for him if his personal secretary and several other members of the staff would also stay temporarily in the residence. It seemed to us that it would also be wise for the ambassador to maintain an office in the chancery as well as in the residence when the Mokhovaya Building was ready for occupancy. A portion of the embassy work, particularly that of a highly confidential nature, could be performed in the residence, and the remainder, including work of a routine, administrative, and consular character, in the Savoy Hotel. Several rooms in the Savoy had been set apart by Kennan for office purposes. The typewriters, stationery, seals, code books, and so forth that we had brought with us were unpacked. All documents and articles both of an unclassified and classified character were guarded by members of the marine contingent on a 24-hour basis.

By March 7, the date on which the ambassador arrived, the mission, excluding the consulate general, was prepared to conduct business. It would have been impossible to have accomplished this had it not been for the effective work carried on by George Kennan, Charlie Thayer, and representatives of the Foreign Buildings Office of the State Department during the preceding months. They and a Soviet assistant, whom they had hired as a messenger and interpreter and who was the fortunate possessor of a motorcycle, were particularly helpful to us during those seven trying days.

PROBLEMS DISCUSSED AT INITIAL EMBASSY STAFF MEETINGS

The ambassador lost no time following his arrival in Moscow in summoning to his residence various members of the embassy, including George Kennan and myself; Wiley, who as the counselor served as the ambassador's alter ego, participated in most of these discussions.

Among the more urgent problems that we outlined to the ambassador were:

The Use of Rubles. I explained that we had been satisfying our ruble needs by borrowing from the State Bank and stressed that we could not continue to operate on borrowed rubles indefinitely. The ambassador agreed and said he would at once remind Litvinov and Grinko of their assurances to him that the Soviet government was prepared to enter into arrangements that would enable the embassy to satisfy its ruble needs by purchases from the Soviet government at reasonable prices.

Transportation. We emphasized the urgent need of the embassy for several automobiles for the transport both of personnel and of goods. The distance between the new chancery and the ambassador's residence was more than a mile. As more personnel, furniture, and supplies arrived the cost of transport would continue to mount. Our problem was complicated because Congress was not willing to appropriate funds that would enable the State Department to provide automobiles to diplomatic missions and consular offices. The War and Navy Departments had appropriations, however, that enabled them to furnish automobiles to armed forces attachés abroad. In view of the exorbitant cost of hiring automobiles in Moscow it seemed to us that our problem of transportation deserved special consideration. The ambassador said he would send an urgent telegram on the subject at once to the State Department and added that, if the reply of the department were negative, he would present the problem to the president and urge him to use his influence with the State Department, the Budget Bureau, and Congress in prevailing on them to drop the outmoded ban.

Employment by the Mission of Soviet Personnel. We said that we were severely handicapped in establishing an effectively operating mission because of our inability to approach most Soviet institutions except through the Third Western Division of Narkomindel (the People's Commissariat for Foreign Affairs, as the Soviet Foreign Office was called). It was almost impossible without advance authority of Narkomindel to gain admittance to such institutions. If by chance or oversight we should be admitted, the Soviet officials in them would be afraid to talk with us. Burobin, the Soviet institution charged with renting properties to foreigners, was of course authorized to deal with us, but we had many problems to solve that could be met only by having some kind of access to other Soviet agencies. If, with the approval of Narkomindel, we could employ qualified Soviet personnel, some of them might be able to go into areas that were closed to us. We realized, of course, that Narkomindel could not authorize the employment by us of any Soviet national unless he or she had been approved by the OGPU (as the Soviet secret police were called at the time), and that all of our Soviet employees would be required to report regularly to OGPU. Nevertheless, in our opinion Soviet personnel would be essential to the effective conduct of our mission, not only to serve as a channel of communication in Soviet institutions but also to assist in translating, typing in the Russian language, making purchases, and running errands. It would be up to us to prevent classified material or information from falling into their hands. We believed this need to be urgent. The ambassador agreed and promised to request the department to authorize us to begin employing the needed Soviet personnel.

Preparation of a List of the Officer Personnel of the Embassy for Presentation to the Protocol Office of Narkomindel.   We said that the Protocol Office was requesting a list of officers of the embassy so that it could issue the appropriate identification cards and include it in the new Soviet Diplomatic List. We were aware that the ambassador did not like the idea of a distinction being drawn between the officers and nonofficers of the embassy. It was, however, the universally recognized practice of all governments to request each diplomatic mission accredited to them to submit the names and titles of each of its diplomatic officers so that they could be included in the officially issued Diplomatic List. The ambassador authorized us to draw up such a list for his approval. We then asked whether or not the Foreign Service officers who were being assigned to consular duties should be included, pointing out that their names could not go into the list unless they were given diplomatic titles such as counselor, or first, second, or third secretaries of the embassy. If they were not included they would to a degree be isolated. In all except one* of the other diplomatic missions in Moscow, career officers performing consular functions were listed as diplomatic officers and treated as such by Narkomindel and other members of the diplomatic corps. If our Foreign Service officers performing consular work were not to have diplomatic rank they could not conduct business with Narkomindel, would not be included in functions of a diplomatic character, would rank at the bottom of the totem pole when attending social affairs in which diplomatic personnel would be present, and would not be entitled to immunities of a diplomatic character. Upon the advice of Wiley, who, as a former member of the old Diplomatic Service, was opposed to consular work being performed in an embassy, the ambassador decided that for the time being no diplomatic titles would be given to the officers assigned to the consulate general and that the list we were to draw up should not include their names.

During our discussions with the ambassador and Wiley we also mentioned the following less urgent, nevertheless important, problems:

Establishment of U.S. Consular Offices in the Soviet Union.   We recalled that, in informal conversations, responsible Soviet officials had indicated that they would welcome the establishment, by the United States, on a

---

*The Soviet lists of foreign consular officers in Moscow contained only one name, that of a British consul.

reciprocal basis, of consular offices in several cities of the Soviet Union. Should we prepare to begin negotiating at once with the Soviet government for the purpose of obtaining its formal consent to the establishment of such offices? If so, in which cities should we seek permission to establish them—in Leningrad, Vladivostok, Tiflis [Tbilisi], Kiev, or perhaps other places? While in Washington Litvinov had hinted at the possible conclusion of a consular convention between the United States and the Soviet Union. Should we also prepare to negotiate such a convention in connection with arrangements for the establishing of consular offices? The ambassador and Wiley took the position that as soon as we could dispose of our more urgent problems we could explore the advisability of establishing a number of consular offices. The ambassador expressed the opinion that, after the opening of a consular office in Moscow, first priority should be given to establishing offices in Leningrad and Vladivostok and that the opening of offices in those cities would match what was understood to be the desire of the Soviet government to establish consular offices in New York and San Francisco.

The Proposed Building of a U.S. Embassy on Lenin Hills overlooking Moscow. We pointed out that although the Soviet government informally had agreed to the erection of an embassy building on a beautiful site among these hills, no details had as yet been worked out. It seemed important, therefore, that no time should be lost in the construction of an embassy of our own. The ambassador agreed. He said he had already made arrangements for a prominent American architect to come to Moscow to complete the designs of the proposed embassy buildings and added that it was his intention to push this matter personally.

In addition to the problems referred to above and other problems of what might be called an administrative character there was considerable discussion during our meetings with the ambassador of several problems that were clearly basic to the maintenance of genuinely friendly relations between the United States and the Soviet Union. Foremost among these problems were the question of U.S. claims against the Soviet Union and the damages to it and to the U.S. citizens resulting from Soviet acts of repudiation, nationalization, and expropriation; the conditions under which the United States might grant credits to the Soviet Union; the extent to which the Soviet Union would be disposed to respect its pledges not to interfere in the internal affairs of the United States; and the conditions under which there might develop at least some degree of collaboration between the United States and the Soviet Union in matters affecting world peace.

Another matter to which we devoted considerable discussion related to the kind of treatment that the Soviet government would accord in the future to U.S. citizens in the Soviet Union. During the days preceding the arrival of the ambassador a number of persons who maintained that they were U.S. citizens had called on us in the Savoy Hotel for the purpose of eliciting our aid in obtaining permission from the Soviet authorities to leave the country. The stories that several of them told us of the treatment they and other U.S. citizens had been encountering were disturbing. Among the questions that caused us concern was whether, now that the United States had an embassy and consulate general in Moscow, the Soviet authorities would treat U.S. citizens differently from the way they had treated them in the past and would live strictly up to the commitments that Litvinov had given to the president relating to the treatment and privileges to be accorded these citizens. The failure of the Soviet government to live up to the Litvinov commitments could, in our opinion, be a serious impediment to the development of truly cordial relations.

Following our discussions with him the ambassador instructed me to keep in touch with Narkomindel at the Third Western Division level with regard to our current administrative and organizational problems.

Before I undertake to discuss the efforts of the mission to deal with the administrative and substantive problems referred to above, as well as with unforeseen problems that arose during my tour in Moscow, I shall attempt to give some of my impressions of Moscow and of its people as I found them in the mid-1930s, to depict what life in Moscow was like during those years, and to describe some of my fellow members of the mission who shared with me the frustrating yet challenging and interesting experiences of the first four and one half years of the existence of a U.S. embassy in the Soviet Union.

CHAPTER 30

MOSCOW: IMPRESSIONS OF THE CITY AND LIFE IN IT, 1934–1938

DURING THE FIRST SIX WEEKS after my arrival in the Soviet Union I spent a considerable amount of time wandering through different sections of Moscow in order to become acquainted as rapidly as possible with the city and its inhabitants. When the weather and the pressures of work in the embassy permitted I continued during the remainder of my stay in Moscow to explore the city and its environs. I also visited the opera and the theaters, the Park of Culture and Rest, and three or four comparatively large department stores that existed at the time, and a number of the myriad of smaller shops—all owned and controlled by the state. I stood in the long lines waiting to travel in crowded buses and streetcars and took walks through both the center of the city and its outskirts.

The center of the city was usually so crowded that I found myself being jostled off the narrow sidewalks onto the cobblestoned streets. The people with whom I competed for sidewalk space showed even less consideration for their fellows than the people on the sidewalks of New York City. The polite words and little acts of courtesy to which a Westerner was accustomed were completely lacking. The words in Russian for "please," "thank you," "I'm sorry," "after you," and so forth seemed to have been forgotten. I discovered that courtesy and politeness were considered hypocritical, bourgeoise manifestations. When, for instance, in entering a shop I would hold a door open to permit an aged woman to go ahead of me, a whole stream of customers would go rushing through, apparently oblivious of the fact that I was holding the door.

I could walk blocks through the crowds without hearing a laugh or seeing a smile. Most of the women and girls who were pushing through the throngs wore drab shawls or scarfs to cover their unkempt short-cut hair and to protect themselves from the piercing cold winds. The men and boys wore fur or cloth caps. Full beards were rare among the men but most of their faces were covered with stubble. A cleanly shaven face, it seemed, might create the impression that its possessor had bourgeois tendencies. Men, women, and children during the cold days of March and of early April were bundled up in bulky, shabby overcoats or were protected from the wind by nondescript pieces of cloth held together by thread or pieces of string. Frequently the outer clothing was reinforced by layers of newspapers. It was rare indeed to meet anyone with a good pair of leather shoes. Many of them wore boots or shoes of heavy felt with rubber, leather, or what seemed to be thatched soles. Here and there a necktie or a hat would indicate the presence of a foreigner.

I may add that during my first year in Moscow I visited a number of what might be called modernistic theaters in which beauty and grace were notably absent. Even the Bolshoi Theater had in its repertoire a number of ballets and opera that were designed to promote the theme of world revolution and victory of the worker over the exploiter. In some of the modernistic theaters scenery or stage setting were entirely lacking; in others the actions and gestures of the performers as well as the settings had no relevance to the words being uttered. Stalin, however, was a classicist so far as the theater and art were concerned and in 1934 he began to take steps to discourage the extreme "contemporary." In 1934 and 1935 the opera, ballet, and theater, therefore, gradually dropped many of their modernistic and politically inspired performances in favor of the conventional and traditional, much to the disgust of many advance–guard American visitors who had come to the Soviet Union in search of fresh approaches to the performing arts. Nevertheless the theaters, and even the opera, continued at intervals to give performances of a novel character. New ideas in music were also encouraged in a mild way.

The incidence of lice and bedbugs was so common in Moscow that I disliked having my overcoat and fur cap piled up in the cloakrooms with the garments of the other spectators. The rule that all outer wraps must be checked was, however, strictly enforced. I soon learned that this rule was sensible. In the absence of dry cleaning establishments in Moscow the odor of long-worn uncleaned clothing tended to distract from the enjoyment of the performance. If the members of the audience would have brought with them their outer garments the stench would have been even more offensive.

The public transportation facilities in Moscow and its environment contributed to the misery of the underfed and poorly housed and dressed people. Droshkies might be found at times in the center of the city. The gaunt horses that pulled them, however, could rarely move faster than a walk. Taxis were even more rare. The average worker, furthermore, could not afford to travel by droshky or taxi. In all kinds of weather, therefore, long lines would be found at streetcar and bus stops. After people had succeeded in pushing their ways into the overcrowded, slow-moving buses or streetcars they were certain to enounter difficulty in disentangling themselves when the time came for them to alight. The atmosphere in the streetcars and buses was not congenial. There was no joking or laughing among the passengers. An air of resignment to misery was prevalent. It was not uncommon for workers living in the city to devote four hours daily to travel between their homes and the places of their employment. Those who lived in the suburbs and made use of local trains frequently spent even more time in commuting.

When we arrived in Moscow a subway was under construction. The project had been given top priority and Moscow citizens were called upon to volunteer to work on it on their free days or after their regular working hours. Shortly after we had taken possession of our new chancery in the Mokhovaya Building next door to the Hotel National in the late spring of 1934, the row of old houses across the street from us, which had been obstructing our view of the Kremlin, was torn down in order to make place for the subway. From our windows we could observe the feverish operations that continued day and night. Mud-spattered men and women of all ages, including young boys and girls, could be seen emerging from the deep miry tunnels in which they had been working in order to stand in lines waiting for buses and streetcars. Many of the young workers of both sexes, who evidently were ardent young Communists working as volunteers, appeared to regard this underground work as an exciting adventure. There was no doubt that the subway project was popular among the rank and file of the population. The completion of the first section a number of months later was greeted enthusiastically by hundreds of thousands of Moscovites as an omen of the coming of a better life. As other sections were added, the transportation hardships in various parts of the city were greatly ameliorated. Nevertheless, up to the time of my departure in 1938, moving from one part of Moscow to another continued to present difficulties for most of its inhabitants.

It seemed to me that the builders of the subway deserved much credit not only for the speed with which they had constructed it but also for the beauty of their creation. Prior to the opening of the first section, the city was deluged with appeals to the people to cooperate in keeping their subway clean. These appeals, supplemented by strict police supervision, had astonishing results. Woe to the passenger who dropped a cigarette or a piece of paper on a subway platform or on the floor of a car. He was sure to be denounced loudly by his fellow passengers and, if police were in the vicinity, to be arrested. Apartment houses built for the use of the workers usually became filthy within a few days after occupancy; the old prewar railway stations were dirty and malodorous; but the subway continued to be a justifiable source of pride for the citizens of Moscow because of its beauty and cleanliness.

The center of Moscow, with its rows of gloomy small shops, was relieved at times by larger buildings also in need of repair, and housing and governmental and public institutions were shabby and depressing. The narrow side streets in the residential portion of the city were even more dismal. I noticed during my first walks through these streets that the relatively few pedestrians whom I met were accustomed to use the center of the street instead of the sidewalks. It did not take me long to learn why. The pieces of brick, stone, glass, and cement that were strewn over the sidewalks were the result of the crumbling of the fronts of old neglected buildings as the thaws began to break the grip of winter. Again and again I witnessed whole windowpanes, and at times the windows themselves, crashing to the sidewalks. Frequently overhanging eaves and loose facades contributed to the debris.

The fall of a windowpane or of the whole window represented a major catastrophe to the occupants of the apartments in these areas because replacement glass was not to be had. I may add that during the four and a half years that I was in Moscow many of the old buildings that were gradually disintegrating were repaired or replaced. By the time I departed in 1938, therefore, there were fewer accidents resulting from falling windowpanes and cornices.

I have referred to the shabby small shops and also to some of the large department stores. Many of the small shops contained used articles of clothing, bits of furniture, household utensils, and so forth. There were also a number of so-called antique shops, which sold merchandise on commission. A Soviet citizen could bring his more valuable possessions to some of these shops, which would sell them for him and retain a commission of 25 percent for themselves. If he should happen to have gold and silver articles he might be able to turn them in at one of the Torgsins that catered to foreigners and receive in return Torgsin coupons, which would enable him to purchase certain types of groceries and other merchandise that could not be bought with paper rubles.

There were a limited number of shops that had been renovated, equipped with bright lights and large windows, and it was generally believed that these shops had been reconstructed to impress visiting foreigners with the growing prosperity of the Soviet Union. Some of them specialized in foodstuffs and had most tempting cuts of meat in the show windows. It was rarely possible, however, to buy in these shops meat of the kind that was displayed in the windows. The fact was that many of the cuts on display were beautifully made of rubber.

During the first year that we were in Moscow, bread was rationed. It was usually of such an inferior quality that many members of the diplomatic corps purchased their bread with foreign currency from one of the Torgsins. Some of the diplomatic missions satisfied their needs for foodstuffs by importing them. A year or so after our arrival in the Soviet Union, following an improvement in the Soviet food supply and distribution system, bread tickets were abolished in Moscow and the quality of bread became better.

In season it was sometimes possible to buy in the government shops a limited amount of fresh vegetables and fruits from the Caucasus. During the winter months, however, there were no fruits or vegetables of any kind. Nevertheless, during the whole period that I was in the Soviet Union the situation in Moscow, so far as food was concerned, was much better than in other parts of the country. I recall that in the summer of 1934 during a trip that my wife and I were making through the Caucasus, we discovered that there were more Caucasian melons, fruits, and vegetables for sale in Moscow than in Tiflis. On the boat, buses, and trains by which we traveled we heard considerable grumbling by the local people that the choice foodstuffs grown in the area were being systematically gobbled up in Moscow. It was so well known throughout the Soviet Union that there was a higher level of living in Moscow than elsewhere in the country that in my opinion millions of people would have come rushing to Moscow if they had been permitted to do so. A Soviet citizen could not, however, come to Moscow even on a visit without obtaining permission in advance from the Soviet authorities. I was not critical of the Soviet government for making rules of this kind. Freedom to travel is in principle one of the more important freedoms. If, however, such a freedom had existed in the Soviet Union in the mid-1930s, there would have been, in my opinion, even more human misery than that which existed in the absence of such freedom.

One of the unpleasant features of life in Moscow was the artificial wall that had been erected between members of the diplomatic corps and the Soviet people. Such a wall was not entirely new in Russia. Under the tsars, up to the beginning of the eighteenth century, a similar wall had existed between foreigners and the Russian people. Beginning with the time of Peter the Great this wall had gradually weakened so that by the early part of the twentieth century communication between foreigners visiting or living in Russia and the Russian people had become comparatively free. Following the revolution a system similar to that under the tsars of the sixteenth and seventeenth centuries was reintroduced.

The police at the doors of the ambassador's residence and at the doors of the chancery building usually tried to prevent Soviet citizens from entering unless they could show that they had a good reason to do so. The ambassador and the members of his staff were never invited to the home of any Soviet citizen unless the citizen had received permission in advance to entertain them. The embassy on its part usually sent all invitations to its receptions through Narkomindel because it had learned from experience that Soviet citizens would be afraid to accept an invitation from the embassy that did not come to them through official channels.

Members of the diplomatic corps were not permitted to join any Soviet clubs, including sporting clubs. Golf was, of course, unknown in the Soviet Union. Frequently, new diplomats not acquainted with the situation arrived in Moscow imbued with the idea that they would please the Soviet government by trying to cultivate friends among the Soviet people. They soon learned, however, that by insisting on establishing social relations with Soviet citizens they would not only be embarrassing the latter but even endangering them. The Soviet authorities were likely to become suspicious of persons who, without special authorization, were receptive to friendly approaches from diplomatic missions.

In order to make sure that the newspapers and other publications that the embassy brought in from abroad would not fall into the hands of Soviet citizens we were required not to let any of them go out with the trash. The Soviet authorities insisted that those publications no longer needed be burned on the premises. A Soviet painter who, after doing some work in one of our apartments, used an old discarded American newspaper in order to wrap his working clothes, was arrested and subjected to weeks of interrogation before he could convince the Soviet authorities that he was not deliberately engaging in distributing propaganda obtained from the embassy.

To prevent members of diplomatic missions from surreptitiously forming friendships with Soviet nationals who had not received permission to associate with them, the Soviet police kept the officers and subordinate personnel for foreign missions under strict surveillance. Most of the ambassadors and ministers and also some of the counselors of embassy had assigned to them members of the OGPU who followed them everywhere. Lower-ranking members of the embassy, although not openly followed, were systematically shadowed. When I would step into a shop someone whom I was eventually able to identify as a member of the OGPU was almost sure to come in after me.

During my later years in Moscow, when I was acting intermittently as chargé d'affaires, I was honored by being given the treatment similar to that accorded to the ambassador. I was no longer followed surreptitiously. Nine OGPU men were openly assigned to look after me. They worked in three eight-hour shifts. Three men were responsible at all times of the day and night for observation of my movements. If I would take a walk one man driving a car would move slowly in the street parallel with me and two would walk close behind me. If I would go into a shop one of them would wait outside in the car and the other two would accompany me. If I should go to the theater, three of them in the car would follow my car; when I entered the theater one would remain outside with the car and the other two would politely request persons in the theater sitting immediately behind me to give them their seats so they could be breathing down my neck. Between the acts they would keep close to me in the lobbies in order to note whom I greeted and with whom I talked.

These police were apparently not allowed to establish social relations with the person to whom they were attached; nevertheless, in case I needed emergency assistance of any kind, they were always on hand. For instance, on one bitterly cold snowy night in November 1942, during the course of my second tour in Moscow, when I was crossing Red Square in order to keep a midnight appointment with Molotov, my car, which was a Soviet Ford, broke down. The OGPU men came gallantly to the rescue and by making room in their car for me enabled me to keep my appointment.

In order to make life easier both for my OGPU escort and for myself I eventually made arrangements through my Soviet chauffeur that worked out quite well. At the beginning of each day I would send through him to the members of the escort my exact schedule for the day. If I should find it necessary to change my schedule during the course of the day he would notify them. If, for instance, I was going to the theater my chauffeur would give them the number of my ticket so that they could make advance arrangements to sit behind me. I never once tried to outwit or escape from my escort. Although I believe that I eventually earned their confidence they never permitted themselves to relax their close surveillance of my activities. All night long these three men with their car stood in front of my living quarters prepared to accompany me if I should appear.

Some of the members of the embassy enjoyed playing a sort of game with their escorts. Ambassador Bullitt, for instance, who was a magnificent swimmer, swam out so far in the Black Sea near Odessa that the

OGPU man who was following him was not able to swim back and the ambassador was compelled to play the role of a lifesaver.

On another occasion, Angus Ward, the chief of the consular section of the embassy and an accomplished mechanical engineer, had built a motor boat for use on the Moscow River and took the ambassador with him on its maiden voyage. The members of the OGPU escort, who had not been notified in advance that the ambassador was going on a river cruise, stood disconsolately on the pier while the boat glided down the river. The ambassador and Ward chuckled at the thought that they had finally outmaneuvered the ambassador's escort. The resourceful OGPU men, as they saw their quarry disappear around a bend, rushed to telephones and within minutes a sleek police patrol boat with the three members of the escort on board was following Ward's boat.

During the critical time of the Great Purge, which I shall discuss later, the Soviet government apparently did not place full trust in its own officials. Beginning in the latter part of 1935 I noticed that when I engaged in a conversation with officials of Narkomindel they almost always asked me to sit at a small table in the office. When we were seated they would talk to me not as one human being to another but as a person talking for the record. I gradually realized that while at such a table I could not expect the give and take that usually softens diplomatic conversations and I, therefore, also began to choose my words with special care. I did not wish to say anything that might later embarrass the officer with whom I was talking or cause embarrassment to myself. I noted also that when an officer of Narkomindel would leave the conversation table and accompany me to the door, his closing remarks, which apparently were not being recorded, were in a lighter and more friendly vein.

The secret police had at their disposal a number of exceptionally well-groomed and intelligent young women who apparently had been assigned the task of making friends with both the married and unmarried members of the diplomatic missions and foreign correspondents. It was quite easy for those of us who were acquainted with Soviet intelligence techniques to spot the women who were serving the police. We knew enough about the Soviet system to realize that these young women would not be meeting foreigners or inviting them to their apartments unless they were authorized to do so. Some of them, in an effort to conceal the fact that they were working for the police, would pretend that they were in deadly fear that the OGPU would find out about their liaison activities. Others, after becoming well acquainted with their foreign friends, would frankly tell them that they were working for the police but had no intention of doing them any harm. In some instances the woman and her target would fall in love. Such a development usually spelled disaster for her and she would eventually disappear. There were a few instances, however, in which the Soviet authorities relaxed and allowed the woman to marry and leave the country. They sometimes tried by blackmail and threats to maintain a hold on the women whom they allowed to go abroad with their foreign husbands.

During the late spring, summer, and early autumn, members of our embassy, of other foreign diplomatic missions, and of the small foreign nondiplomatic, noncommunist community in Moscow sometimes went on picnics in rural areas adjacent to Moscow. The countryside, for the most part, was beautiful and unspoiled. We had to exercise care, however, in selecting the spot to visit and the route that we took in order not to find ourselves inadvertently in areas that were closed to the public. Some of the closed areas contained secret military establishments; in others were the summer homes, exclusive clubs, or "rest houses" of the new Soviet aristocracy, the members of which did not desire their privacy to be disturbed.

The social activities of the diplomatic corps in Moscow were by no means limited to excursions in the rural areas or visits to the theater, opera, and various other places of amusement. There were not in Moscow at the time restaurants or nightclubs worthy of the name. Nevertheless, our social life was hectic. The members of the diplomatic corps from the chief of mission down to third secretary, including the armed forces attachés, were almost incessantly giving luncheons, dinners, receptions, and dances. The guests at these affairs included not only diplomatic colleagues, foreign correspondents, and other foreigners residing or visiting Moscow, but also Soviet officials of varying rank and other Soviet citizens who had permission to mix with foreigners. The latter were few in number. Since members of the diplomatic corps liked to have Soviet faces at their parties, these few were deluged with invitations.

In no post in which I have served were members of the diplomatic corps more closely bound together in ties of real friendship than the diplomats in Moscow. We frequently likened ourselves to the passengers from a ship that had been wrecked on a desert island surrounded by a shark-infested sea.

Although the Soviet authorities in principle preferred that members of foreign diplomatic missions not try to travel extensively in the Soviet Union, they nevertheless did permit them to take trips along routes carefully worked out in advance. It will be recalled that Ambassador Bullitt had visions shortly after we had established relations of flying freely around the country in a U.S. Air Force plane. These visions were never realized. Most of his travels were by train. He crossed the Soviet Union, for instance, on the Trans-Siberian Railway. Later, Ambassador

Davies made several trips through the industrial areas of the Ukraine; he and Mrs. Davies usually made these trips in a private sleeping car. All of us visited Leningrad from time to time. We traveled almost uniformly on Soviet trains, planes, and vessels. Soviet roads, even in the environment of Moscow, were frequently almost impassable. The great highways, such as the historic road between Moscow and Leningrad, were so full of deep potholes that few ventured to use them. On several occasions I applied for permission to visit Central Asia but was informed by Narkomindel that that area was closed to foreign diplomats.

The steady flow of foreign tourists and other visitors to Moscow served to prevent the members of many of the diplomatic missions from becoming embedded in a comfortable social rut. Following the establishment of diplomatic relations a wave of starry-eyed, hopeful U.S. businessmen appeared on the scene, apparently convinced that they would be among those selected to assist in alleviating Soviet needs for capital and consumer goods. Nine out of ten of them went away empty-handed. Some tended to blame the embassy for not giving them sufficient assistance. Others, after a short stay, came to realize that unless they had come on the express invitation of the Soviet authorities, it was not easy to make sales.

Since during the first year and a half of my tour in Moscow I was in charge of the economic section of the mission, I came in close contact with U.S. businessmen. By 1934 the Soviets had been successful, with American and German technical assistance, in establishing a number of steel mills and machine tool establishments. Thus they were able to copy much of the manufacturing equipment being produced by countries of the West. Instead, therefore, of buying machine tools and machinery parts in quantity, they would purchase one or two as samples and copy them. During the mid-1930s many of these copies were far from durable. Although they might resemble the samples in appearance, the kind of metals used frequently did not possess the properties needed to resist stress and strain or heat and cold. Later, however, as Soviet technicians studying in the United States and Germany returned with improved knowledge of the processes of fusing and amalgamating, the quality of Soviet machine tools and machinery gradually improved.

When the Soviet government succeeded in making copies of a piece of machinery or of a machine tool, it was sometimes not satisfied with manufacturing them solely for the Soviet markets. On occasion it began to export them. This practice created considerable resentment among many U.S. manufacturers who, as might be anticipated, blamed the State Department for not prevailing upon the Soviet government to enter into treaties that would protect U.S. patent rights. The Soviet authorities, however, had no intention of permitting such capitalistic devices as patents and copyrights to slow up Soviet industrial and cultural development.

The American tourists* who came crowding into Moscow in the summer of 1934 and whose numbers increased during the next three years, might be said to fall into four categories: (1) the inveterate globetrotter and sightseer; (2) the seeker after knowledge who came to observe for himself what was going on in the Soviet Union; (3) the so-called liberal—I do not include a Communist in this category—who came to the Soviet Union in order to get a thrill from witnessing the results of the "Great Experiment"; and (4) the American "rugged individualist" who came primarily so that he might be able to tell his friends upon his return that, based on his own personal observations, communism was unworkable in practice and that the attempt of the Soviet leaders to make it work was causing suffering on a scale never equalled in the history of mankind. Some of those who came to the Soviet Union full of enthusiasm for what they had understood was being accomplished left the country disillusioned and unhappy, and some of the rugged individualists returned to the United States frightened at the strides that, in their opinion, the Soviet Union was making in the direction of becoming a world power with tremendous military potentials.

During the summers American visitors arrived in Leningrad by the hundreds on deluxe vessels that had been chartered for cruises. They poured into Moscow in possession of letters of introduction addressed to the ambassador from the secretary of state or members of Congress. Bearers of these letters were usually invited to an afternoon reception in the embassy.

In the summer of 1937, when Ambassador Davies was away and I was in charge of the embassy, over 80 letters of introduction were presented to me in one day by passengers from a single cruise ship. I invited the bearers of these letters to the embassy for an afternoon reception. To my consternation over three hundred guests showed up. Those with special letters had taken the liberty of inviting on my behalf fellow passengers, who possessed no letters, to accompany them to the reception.

The promoters of some of the cruises, noting the desire of passengers to visit the embassy, included in their advertising literature "re-

---

*I do not include among the tourists American Communists, fellow travelers, and businessmen who came to the Soviet Union for purposes not connected with tourism.

ception at the American embassy" as one of the attractions in Moscow. When we learned of this kind of advertising we protested and the State Department put a stop to it.

To add to our problems, groups of tourists frequently insisted that the ambassador or one of the members of his staff give them the "low down" on the Soviet Union. As a matter of courtesy we felt it necessary to talk to them and answer some of their questions. We did not, however, wish to mislead them regarding the validity of the claims of the Soviet government that it was providing a wonderful life for the Soviet people. Neither did we wish to take a position that would give the embassy the reputation of carrying on anti-Soviet propaganda. In nearly every group that approached us there were several fanatically pro-Soviet tourists who would become indignant if the embassy spokesman was not as fulsome in his praise of Soviet accomplishments as in their opinion he should be. Although we exercised moderation in discussing the Soviet Union and its accomplishments with tourists, we did not hesitate to point out to American businessmen the factors that they should consider when undertaking to do business with the Soviet Union.

During the first summer that we were in Moscow the Institute of International Education arranged through Professor Stephen Duggan of Princeton University to establish in Moscow a summer school for U.S. university students. The year 1934 was the "honeymoon year" of Soviet-American relations. Interest in the Soviet Union was so high that several hundred students, many of them from well–known American families, enrolled. The inquisitive proclivities of these students, particularly of those who had ample means to move about, was a source of considerable annoyance to the members of the Soviet secret police who were accustomed to look with jaundiced eyes upon the presence in the Soviet Union of any group of foreigners that, in their opinion, might well harbor spies.

Professor Duggan was a man of high ideals and of liberal views. It had been his hope that cultural exchanges between the Soviet Union and the United States would bring the American and Soviet people closer together. He, therefore, strove mightily to promote friendly relations between the student body and Soviet officialdom. The task that he had undertaken was not easy. The student body was far from homogeneous. Some of its members were so enamored with communism and the "Soviet experiment" that they tended to look at everything connected with the Soviet Union through rose-colored glasses and to resent remarks that might be disparaging of the result of Soviet efforts. Others who were inclined to be critical of conditions in the Soviet Union as they perceived them became critics of the method and content of the instruction that they were receiving on the ground that it seemed to them to be merely so much thinly disguised Soviet propaganda. Still others who were looking for excitement and adventure became bored and restive. The student body was, therefore, not a happy and contented family. The Soviet officials who had favored the establishment of the school were disappointed because of its failure to stimulate among the students the kind of enthusiasm over Soviet aims and accomplishments for which they had hoped. They tended to blame poor well-meaning Professor Duggan and his assistants for this failure.

In the latter part of the summer I was shocked when a high official of Narkomindel told me that his colleagues, in talking among themselves about the school, were accustomed to refer to the bearded Professor Duggan as "that old billy goat." Professor Duggan, who like many American liberals was convinced that his attitude of friendliness toward the Soviet Union was being duly appreciated by the Soviet authorities, had no idea that he was in fact an object of ridicule.

In spite of the difficulties experienced by the school, plans were made for a second session to be held in the summer of 1935. After many of the students for the second session had already arrived in the Soviet Union, the OGPU finally intervened. It insisted that plans for holding the session not be carried out. As usual, the views of the OGPU triumphed and the Soviet government announced that no session would be held. Intourist (the All-Union Corporation for Foreign Tourism) and Voks (the All-Union Society for Cultural Relations with Foreigners), which had sponsored the school, did what they could to smooth the ruffled feelings of the students by arranging for them to take a number of conducted tours in the Soviet Union, some of which were in areas that were usually closed to ordinary tourists. It seemed to me that there was less dissatisfaction among the students who went on these tours than there had been among those who had attended the school in 1934.

CHAPTER 31

MEMBERS OF THE U.S. EMBASSY IN MOSCOW, 1934–1938

No ACCOUNT OF MY EXPERIENCE in Moscow would be complete unless it contained a description of the personnel in our mission with whom I was privileged to work. Over the years I have frequently received inquiries from young men and women, who were considering the advisability of attempting to enter the Foreign Service, regarding the kind of a challenge and career that the service offers. Frequently my inquirers have had doubts regarding the opportunities in the service for persons who did not possess ample private means. In answering inquiries of this kind I have been accustomed to cite as an example the kind of careers that my fellow Foreign Service officers in Moscow, most of whom were living on the income that they received from the service, carved out for themselves.

As of July 1, 1934, the following Foreign Service officers and officers of the armed forces were on assignment to the U.S. embassy in Moscow:

John C. Wiley, counselor of embassy
Loy W. Henderson, second secretary
George F. Kennan, third secretary
Bertel E. Kuniholm, third secretary
Charles E. Bohlen, third secretary
Major Philip R. Faymonville, military attaché

First Lieutenant Thomas D. White, assistant military attaché and
  assistant military attaché for air
Captain David R. Nimmer, assistant naval attaché

Assigned to the consulate general on the same date were the following Foreign Service officers:

George C. Hanson, consul general
Harold Shantz, consul
Angus I. Ward, consul
Elbridge Durbrow, vice consul

As of possible interest to my readers I shall sketch the background
and future careers of several of these officers.

John C. Wiley.   Wiley was a Foreign Service officer with a tremendous amount of experience. He was born in Bordeaux, France, in 1893.
His father, a former member of Congress, was the U.S. consul in Bordeaux at the time of John's birth. His mother was an American artist
whom his father had met in Paris. The father died when Wiley was still a
child, and his mother took charge of his upbringing and education. She
placed him under a series of private tutors and took him from one
European country to another. When, therefore, Wiley went to the United
States for his secondary education, he was almost as much at home in
French, Spanish, and German as he was in English.

Wiley continued his studies in the United States at Union College
and Georgetown Law School. He took the examinations for the old
Diplomatic Service in 1916 and entered it in the same year as third
secretary of embassy in Paris.

Since he was unmarried and, therefore, exceptionally mobile, he
was rapidly transferred from post to post in Europe and Latin America for
a period of fifteen years. In 1930, as a Foreign Service officer class 2 he was
appointed counselor of embassy at Warsaw. In that capacity he also served
during the next three years successively in Berlin and Madrid. When he
arrived in Moscow as counselor he was regarded as one of the most
experienced officers in the Foreign Service.

As deputy chief of mission he had general supervisory control of the
embassy under the direction of Ambassador Bullitt. His main interest,
however, was in the political activities of the embassy. In addition to his
duties as deputy chief of mission he served as chief of the political section.
He selected as his assistants in that section the two junior officers who had
just completed their Russian language studies, George Kennan and

Charles Bohlen. In the spring of 1934 these three able officers began to supply the Department of State for the first time with information obtained on the spot regarding Soviet internal and international political developments.

Wiley, who was a large man physically, had a commanding presence and an exceptionally resonant voice. With his broad experience, his agreeable personality, and his linguistic accomplishments, he developed into one of the outstanding figures in the Moscow diplomatic corps.

In the late spring of 1934, Wiley went on leave to Western Europe in order to marry a charming young Polish artist whom he had met while serving in Warsaw. Irena, his bride, was also an accomplished linguist as well as a painter and sculptor.

In accord with its newly established policy of assuring that so far as possible every Foreign Service officer, before achieving the rank of minister or ambassador, should have a certain amount of consular experience, Wiley was transferred in the latter part of 1935 to Antwerp as consul general. In July 1937 he was assigned to Vienna where he served as chargé d'affaires during some of Austria's most tragic days. In July 1938 he was sent to Riga as minister to Estonia and Latvia, where he served until the freedom of the Baltic states was snuffed out by the Soviet Union in 1940. He subsequently served as ambassador to, respectively, Colombia, Portugal, Iran, and Panama, from which post he retired from the service in 1953 with the rank of career minister, the highest grade of the service at that time. He was one of few members of the embassy who possessed private means. Subsequent to his retirement he made his home in Washington, where I continued to see him frequently until his death in 1967.

Loy W. Henderson. In the spring of 1934 when the embassy was originally organized, I was appointed by Ambassador Bullitt as chief of the economic section. In addition to my work as chief of that section I was also charged with handling problems with Narkomindel that were not being taken up by the ambassador and Wiley. Subsequent to the transfer of Wiley to Antwerp, I was promoted to the rank of first secretary and succeeded him as deputy chief of mission. As deputy chief of mission I took over supervision of the work of the combined embassy and consulate general and served intermittently as chargé d'affaires for an aggregate period of approximately twenty months while Ambassador Bullitt and his successor, Ambassador Joseph E. Davies, were absent from the Soviet Union.

George F. Kennan. Kennan was born in Milwaukee, Wisconsin, in 1904. During his childhood his family resided for a time in Germany so that Kennan was able to attend grade school in Hamburg. He obtained his secondary education in the United States and received an A.B. degree from Princeton University in 1925. In 1926, at the age of 22, he was appointed a Foreign Service officer, unclassified, and assigned as vice consul to Geneva. He subsequently served as vice consul in Hamburg and Berlin. As a youthful East European specialist he was appointed third secretary of legation at Riga in the spring of 1929 and in the autumn of the same year he was assigned to Berlin for Russian language study. I have already pointed out that, in view of his ability to speak Russian, he accompanied Bullitt to Moscow in November of 1933 when the ambassador went there to present his credentials and that he remained in Moscow in order to assist in preparing living and working accommodations for the members of the mission. He was appointed third secretary to our embassy in Moscow on February 12, 1934. In January 1935, for health reasons, he was transferred temporarily to Vienna. He returned to Moscow in the fall of 1935 and continued to serve there until he was transferred to the State Department in 1937 where he was assigned to the Russian desk. In 1938 he was sent as second secretary in Prague, where he was serving when Hitler's troops took over the city. Following the closing of our embassy in Prague he was transferred to our embassy in Berlin, where he served until Germany declared war on the United States in 1941.

In 1942, after serving temporarily in the State Department, Kennan was assigned counselor of legation at Lisbon. In 1943 he was transferred to London to act as counselor of the U.S. delegation to the European Advisory Commission, which was working on matters pertaining to the postwar fate of Europe. In 1944 he was assigned to Moscow as counselor of embassy. It was while he was on duty in Moscow that he wrote his famous "Mr. X" report, advocating a policy of containment in meeting the Soviet challenge.

In 1946 he was brought back to the State Department and appointed deputy for foreign affairs in the National War College. In 1947 he became director of the newly organized Policy Planning Staff of the department. In August 1949 he was promoted to the position of counselor to the department—a position that carried with it the rank of assistant secretary. In March 1952 he was appointed ambassador to the Soviet Union. He retired from the Service in July 1953 with the rank of career minister and accepted a position as a faculty member of the Institute for Advanced Study in Princeton. He returned to the service in 1961 and was appointed by President Kennedy ambassador to Yugoslavia where he served until his final retirement in 1963. During the periods that he was not in the active service he wrote a number of books relating to foreign affairs, some of which are known to most American students of international relations. He has continued to write and to lecture since his retirement in 1963.

I first met Kennan in 1927 when as a young neophyte in the Foreign Service School of the State Department he visited the Eastern European Division for orientation purposes. I was favorably impressed by this young man. His attractive personality and intellectual approach to subjects under discussion convinced me that he had the qualifications that should carry him far in the service. My conviction was strengthened during the periods that we later served together in Riga, Moscow, and the Department of State.

Following the opening of the embassy and the establishment in it of a political section, Kennan devoted most of the time that he was in the embassy during my first tour in Moscow to work in that section.

George's wife was an attractive young Norwegian whom he had met and married during an early assignment to Berlin. She had accompanied him to Moscow before the ambassador's edict that Foreign Service wives should not accompany their husbands to Moscow until living quarters had been obtained for them. During the first few months following the establishment of the embassy, as the sole Foreign Service wife in Moscow, she was in much demand socially.

Bertel E. Kuniholm.   Kunni, as we were accustomed to call him, was born in Gardner, Massachusetts, in May 1901. After graduating from the U.S. Military Academy at West Point, he served in the U.S. Army for several years before entering the Foreign Service in 1928. At the time of his entry he indicated an interest in Eastern Europe. The department, therefore, sent him first to Kaunas, Lithuania, as vice consul, and thence to Paris in 1930 for Russian language study. Following the completion of his language studies in 1933 he served in the Division of Eastern European Affairs in the State Department for several months before being assigned on February 6, 1934, to Moscow as third secretary. In 1936 he was brought back to the Division of Eastern European Affairs in the department where he served for a year before being transferred to the Russian section of our legation in Riga. During the next three years he served successively in Switzerland, Iceland, the State Department, and Tabrīz. He was consul in Tabrīz during 1942 and a part of 1943 when Soviet troops were in occupation of Azerbaijan. His knowledge of the Russian language and techniques made it possible for him to keep the United States particularly well informed of the efforts of the Soviet authorities to convert the northwestern part of Iran into a communist entity that might be used later as a base for the communization of all Iran. The presence in Tabrīz of an American observer capable of understanding what they were trying to do was particularly painful to the Soviets and they insisted on his withdrawal in the early part of 1943. The department, therefore, transferred him to Tehran where he continued to report on Soviet activities in Iran. His subsequent posts were Quebec, Beirut, Seoul, and Ankara. At most of them his qualifications as an East European specialist were most useful. He left the service in the early 1950s to engage in nongovernmental work relating to the Soviet Union. While in Moscow in 1934, Kuniholm, like Wiley, took leave in Western Europe in order to marry and to bring back to Moscow a charming young wife whom he had met while studying Russian in Paris.

During most of his stay in Moscow Kuniholm engaged in administrative work connected with the establishment and operation of the embassy. He also found time, however, to prepare a number of interesting reports to the department.

Charles E. Bohlen. Chip, as we were accustomed to call Bohlen, was born in New York City in 1904 and received his A.B. from Harvard University in 1927. While still in the Foreign Service School in 1929 he had expressed a special interest in Eastern Europe. The State Department, therefore, assigned him as vice consul in Prague where he served for two years before being detailed to Paris for Russian language study. In February 1934 he was assigned to Moscow where he served under Wiley in the political section of the embassy.

In August 1935 he was ordered back to the State Department where he served for nearly two years as special assistant to William Phillips, the under secretary of state. He returned to the political section of the embassy in the summer of 1937 and remained in Moscow until the latter part of 1940 when the department, upon the insistence of Joseph Grew, at that time our ambassador to Japan, transferred him to our embassy in Tokyo. In December 1941, when Japan made war on the United States he, along with other members of our embassy staff in Tokyo, was interned for several months before an exchange of interned diplomats could be effected between the United States and Japan.

Upon his return to the United States in June 1942 Bohlen was assigned to the East European section of the Division of European Affairs in the Department of State, where he served as one of my assistants. In July of 1943 he succeeded me as head of that section. During the next six years while on duty in Washington he was assigned a series of positions of steadily increasing responsibility. In 1947 he was appointed counselor of the department; in 1948 he was promoted to the grade of career minister; in 1949 he was assigned as counselor of embassy in Paris. He returned to the department as counselor in 1951 in which capacity he served until appointed ambassador to the Soviet Union by President Eisenhower in 1953. Subsequently he served for two years as ambassador to the Philippines. In 1960 he was elevated to the permanent rank of career ambassador, the highest in the Foreign Service. In 1962 he was appointed by President Kennedy as ambassador to France. He returned to the department in 1968 to accept the position of deputy under secretary for political affairs. He retired in 1969. His book, *Witness to History, 1929–1969,* was written during his retirement and is, in my opinion, required reading for students of contemporary American history.

During my tour in Moscow Avis Thayer of Philadelphia came to the Soviet Union to visit her brother Charlie, who was sharing an apartment in the Mokhovaya with Bohlen. A romance ensued, which resulted in the acquisition by Bohlen of a wife who has been an asset over the years not only to him but also to the Foreign Service as a whole.

Bohlen was a well-liked member of the diplomatic corps in Moscow during the years that we served there together. He had a pleasing personality, a keen sense of humor, a gift for amusing conversation, and a certain amount of spontaneous joyousness, all of which added to his popularity. He had a particular talent for forming close friendly associations with members of the press. To the grief of those who had worked with him, Bohlen died on January 1, 1974.

Angus I. Ward. Ward was born in Canada in 1893 and became a U.S. citizen while still a young man. He studied at Valparaiso University in Indiana where he developed mechanical engineering skill of a high order. He served in the U.S. Army as a first lieutenant in the First World War. Subsequently he served with the American Relief Administration under Herbert Hoover in Finland and the Baltic states. I met him for the first time on a train in Estonia in 1920 near the town of Narva while I was serving with the American Red Cross in the typhus-stricken area of Estonia.

Ward entered the Foreign Service in 1925 as a vice consul and was assigned to several posts in the Far East, including Mukden and Tientsin. He was an accomplished linguist. As a boy he spoke Gaelic in a Scottish community in Canada. During the war he learned to speak not only French but also a certain amount of Spanish and Basque. While with the American Relief Administration he added Russian and Finnish to his treasury of languages. In Mukden he specialized in Chinese and Mongolian. One of his particular hobbies was Mongolian and while in Moscow he spent much time working on an English-Mongolian dictionary and in adding rare volumes to his rich collection of books in a variety of languages relating to Mongolia. His ability to carry on a conversation in Russian exceeded that of most of the Foreign Service officers who had spent two or three years of concentrated Russian study in Western Europe.

Subsequent to the establishment of the consular section in the embassy in 1935 he became its chief with the rank of second secretary.

The Wards had no children and were accustomed to lavish their affections on pets. I shall never forget the stir caused by their arrival in Moscow in the latter part of March after a ten-day journey on the Trans-Siberian Railway. The train, which I had planned to meet, was said to be 28 hours late. It made up some time, however, and when the Wards arrived at the station there was no one to meet them. They were resourceful travelers and succeeded eventually in obtaining a conveyance to the Savoy Hotel. I first learned of their arrival when I received a telephone call in my room in the hotel from the startled porter at the front door who requested me to come down immediately. There, talking to the porter, I found a tall, strongly-built man with a flaming red beard dressed in a heavy tan coat, shorts, and a pair of long woolen hose above which his knees were showing. On his head was a beret, which matched his coat. With him was a woman dressed in a smart-looking tan tailored suit. In her arm was a restive hen. Ward was carrying a cat and held a huge Alsatian dog on a leash.

Although I had not seen Ward for fourteen years, his beard did not prevent me from recognizing him. The porter did not quite know what to do about the pets since the hotel was not accustomed to house hens, dogs, or cats. Ward explained to me that he and his wife were fond of these animals and did not like to leave them behind. The hen, it seemed, was a cripple, which his wife had looked after from chickhood. He pointed out that he and his wife had a small country cottage in Finland near the Soviet border and it was their intention to leave the cat and hen in this cottage within the next few weeks. The porter weakened and I escorted the Wards and the animal members of their family to their room which, like all our rooms in the hotel, had a private bath. The animals dwelt happily in the bathroom until the cat and the hen could be taken to Finland. The hen, becoming accustomed to hotel life, began regularly to lay eggs in the bathtub. Its cackle from time to time gave a homely barnyard atmosphere to the otherwise dreary corridors of the hotel.

As consul in charge of the consular section, and later as second and first secretary, Ward was one of the mainstays of the embassy for a period of more than six years. His mastery of consular techniques, his valuable cooperation in the field of administration, and his readiness to undertake with enthusiasm any task, however disagreeable it might be, that was assigned to him, meant much to those of us who were responsible for the operation of the embassy.

In 1940, when the Soviet Union agreed to the opening of a U.S. consular office in Vladivostok, Ward was sent there as head of that office, in which capacity he served for nearly four years. His subsequent posts were counselor of embassy in Tehran; consul general in Mukden, where he was seized and imprisoned for several months by the Chinese Communists; consul general at Nairobi; and ambassador to Afghanistan, from which post he retired in the mid-1950s. In 1969 he died in Spain where he and his wife were living in retirement.

Elbridge Durbrow. Durby, as he was called by his colleagues in the embassy, was born in California in 1903. After graduating from Yale University with a Ph.B. in 1926, he continued his studies in France and the Netherlands. He entered the Foreign Service as vice consul and diplomatic secretary in 1930 and was assigned as vice consul at Warsaw in the same year and as vice consul at Bucharest two years later. He was transferred to Moscow as vice consul in March 1934 and was commissioned as third secretary in 1935. In 1937 he was assigned as consul to Naples where he served until 1939.

In the latter part of his stay in Moscow Durbrow relieved me as officer in charge of the economic section. He became so interested in economic work that after leaving Moscow he asked the State Department to give him an opportunity to specialize in economics. In 1939, therefore, he was detailed to the University of Chicago for a year of economic study. He made good use of what he learned in Chicago when he was attached to our representation to the Bretton Woods Conference in 1944. He was made chief of the Division of Eastern European Affairs in the department in 1944. In 1946 he was appointed counselor at Moscow and two years later was brought back to the department to serve as deputy for foreign affairs in the National War College. In 1950 he was made chief of the Division of Foreign Service Personnel in the department and two years later returned to Rome as minister-counselor. In 1955 he was assigned to Singapore as consul general with the rank of minister. In March 1957 he was appointed by President Eisenhower as ambassador to Vietnam. In 1961 he was assigned to Paris as deputy U.S. representative to NATO in which capacity he served for four years. In 1965 he was appointed deputy for foreign affairs at the Air War College at Maxwell Field from which assignment he retired in 1968.

Durbrow was one of the most amusing members of the diplomatic corps. He and Charlie Thayer were certain to promote gaiety in any social group in which they happened to be. In the chancery, however, Durbrow was an indefatigable worker. His political and economic judgment was outstanding. His judgment of people and ability to deal with them contributed to his success as chief of foreign service personnel.

Durby remained one of my closest friends over the years. When, in London in the summer of 1948, he married Emily Moore, a young American woman whom he had met in Moscow where she was visiting the daughter of Ambassador Davies, I was his best man. Chip Bohlen and I are also joint godfathers of his oldest son.

During my 52-month tour in Moscow several Foreign Service officers who were not in the list of those assigned to it as of July 1, 1934, served in our embassy in Moscow. The background and future career of several of these officers are sufficiently interesting to justify, in my opinion, a brief description of them. I refer to Edward Page, Norris Chipman, Charles Thayer, and Alexander Kirk.

Edward Page, Jr. Page was born in Ardmore, in the environs of Philadelphia, in 1905. He received his A.B. from Harvard in 1928 and subsequently studied at the universities of Grenoble and Heidelberg. When he entered the Foreign Service in 1929 he was given a temporary assignment to Montreal as vice consul. In the same year William Castle, to whom I have already referred as having been for many years chief of the Division of Western European Affairs, was appointed by President Hoover as ambassador to Japan. Castle had taken a fancy to the accomplished and darkly handsome young Harvard man and insisted on taking Page with him to Tokyo as one of his third secretaries of embassy. Although Page enjoyed his work in the Far East he did not lose interest in Eastern Europe, and he continued to hope for specialization in that area. In 1931 he was assigned to Paris for Russian study. Following the completion of his studies in the spring of 1934 he was sent, much to his disappointment, to the Russian section of our legation at Riga instead of to our embassy in Moscow.

In August 1935 he was given a temporary assignment of several months in Moscow, after which he returned to Riga. He was again sent in July 1937 to Moscow where he served for another nine months before going to the State Department to take over a desk in the East European section of the Division of European Affairs. In February 1942 he was assigned again to Moscow, where he served as a second and later first secretary during the remainder of the Second World War.

He returned to the department in the autumn of 1945 to serve again for a year in the East European area. His subsequent posts were Rome (first secretary and subsequently counselor); the National War College; Berlin; Paris (counselor of embassy); Munich (consul general); and Sofia, his last post prior to retirement, where he served as minister to Bulgaria.

Subsequent to his retirement in 1964 he made his home in Rome, where he died in 1965.

While on his second assignment to Moscow in the early 1940s he met an attractive Philadelphia girl who with a group of friends was touring the Soviet Union. A romance ensued and they were married a few months later. Terry, his wife, was with him in Rome at the time of his death.

Page served with me not only in Moscow but also for almost three years in the East European section of the Division of European Affairs in the Department of State. I have never had a more agreeable colleague. He had excellent political sense. Although he did not profess to be a Kremlinologist, no officer with whom I worked had, in my opinion, a better understanding than he of Soviet tactics and policies. He also had the courage, when called upon to do so, to state frankly his views even though they might not have been welcome during a period of euphoria when many U.S. officials seemed to believe that anyone who had doubts regarding the good faith of the Soviet leaders or who questioned Soviet motivations must be under the influence of Hitler.

Charles Wheeler Thayer. Thayer was born in Villa Nova, in the suburbs of Philadelphia, in 1910 and graduated from West Point near the top of his class in 1933. While studying at West Point he had become interested in international affairs and, believing that he would be happier working in the field of international relations than he would be if he remained with the armed forces, he managed to obtain his release from the army shortly after his graduation. In the summer of 1933, convinced that President Roosevelt intended to establish diplomatic relations with the Soviet Union, he went to Moscow to study the Russian language and to become acquainted with the situation in the Soviet Union. It was his hope that such knowledge as he might acquire would be useful to the future U.S. embassy in Moscow. When Ambassador Bullitt arrived in Moscow in the latter part of November in order to present his credentials, Thayer called upon him and offered to be of assistance to him. Thayer made a favorable impression on the ambassador and, upon the latter's recommendation to the State Department, Thayer was added to the staff of the embassy.

After serving for a few months as the ambassador's personal secretary, Thayer was assigned to the consulate general where he worked for a period in a clerical capacity. When I was chargé d'affaires in 1936 I transferred him to the political section of the embassy where he could make full use of his demonstrated ability as a writer. In 1937, after taking the examinations, he was commissioned as a Foreign Service officer and assigned as third secretary and vice consul to Berlin. Subsequently he served in Hamburg, again in Moscow, in Afghanistan, in London (attached to the European Advisory Commission), in Belgrade (on a special assignment connected with the Office of Strategic Services), in the State Department as head of the Voice of America (chief of the International Broadcasting Division), in our embassy in Bonn, and in Munich (consul general). He also spent a year attending the National War College. He resigned from the service in 1952 in order to devote himself almost entirely to writing. He is the author of a number of books, some of a whimsical character, such as *Hands Across the Caviar*, and several of such a serious nature that they are widely used in many American universities by students of international affairs.

Thayer's youthful exuberance, his ready wit, and his ingenious pranks brightened many of the days in the chancery. He was an adventurer by nature and was attracted by the new and the unconventional. I can remember that he timed one of his leaves to the United States so that he would be able to return to Europe on the first commercial trans-Atlantic flight made by a zeppelin.

Typical of Thayer's ingenuity was his success in prevailing upon the director of the Moscow Circus to permit several trained seals to perform at a Christmas party given by Irena and John Wiley in 1934 for the U.S. colony in Moscow. The seals, accompanied by their trainer, were to parade across the ballroom of the embassy balancing small lighted Christmas trees on their noses. This they did successfully amid the applause of the guests. When they reached a point near the top of a stairway that led to the basement, the odor of fish coming up from the embassy kitchen was too much for them. Breaking ranks they went slithering down the stairs with amazing speed and headed for the fish that the chef was preparing. The chef took one look at the charging seals, jumped on a table, and screamed for help. Thayer and the trainer by an impartial distribution of fish eventually got the seals under control and succeeded in mollifying the chef.

Thayer encountered additional difficulties in getting the seals back to the circus. They were placed in the back of the stationwagen-type covered truck of the embassy. The trainer and Thayer rode in the front seat with the driver. As they were going through a quiet narrow snow-covered street, Thayer heard a noise in the rear. He looked back in time to see one of the seals, which had climbed over the backboard, gliding along the snow into an alley. The car stopped and Thayer climbed out but could not catch the seal, which seemed to be quite at home on the snowy streets. He called to the trainer for assistance. The latter, however, overcome by too much celebrating, was wrapped in deep sleep. Finally Thayer and the driver succeeded in arousing the trainer and making him understand the seriousness of the situation. The trainer climbed out and staggered through the maze of alleys and narrow streets emitting a series of calls apparently calculated to deceive the seal into believing that fish were available. Eventually the enterprising seal responded to the call and the three men were able to heave it back into the truck.

Following his retirement Thayer and his wife—a daughter of James C. Dunn, a retired Foreign Service officer who was one of my chiefs during my 1938–1942 assignment to the State Department—spent a part of each year in their home in Villa Nova near Philadelphia and a part in their "hunting lodge" near Munich. Thayer devoted much of his time to study and writing. His death in the summer of 1969 was a blow to his friends and former associates to whom his blithe spirit had been an inspiration.

Norris Bowie Chipman. Chipman was born in Washington, D.C., in 1901, graduated from Dartmouth in 1927, and entered the Foreign Service as vice consul in 1928. While an undergraduate at Dartmouth he had become interested in Eastern Europe. Upon his entry into the service, therefore, he expressed a preference for specialization in that area. Accordingly, he was assigned to Riga as vice consul, where he served for a year before being detailed to Paris for Russian language study.

Following the completion of his studies in Paris he was assigned to the Russian section of the legation in Riga. In March 1934, instead of being ordered to the embassy in Moscow, as he had hoped he would be, he was transferred to the Division of Eastern European Affairs in the State Department. It was not, therefore, until the summer of 1936 that he was able to report to the embassy for duty. After three years in Moscow he was transferred to Cairo. Among the subsequent posts that he held were Paris (first secretary); Rome (counselor); Bonn (first secretary); London (first secretary); and Belgrade, where he was serving as counselor of embassy at the time of his death in 1957.

While a Russian language student in Paris, Chipman had met a young French painter whom he married before proceeding to Moscow.

I had met Chipman in Washington at various social affairs while he was still an undergraduate. Since I was working in the area of Eastern Europe at the time, the interest that he showed in that area served to create a bond between us. At the time of his assignment to Riga, I was second secretary in our legation in that city and was pleased to learn of that assignment. During the last months of my tour in Riga several members of the service, including Chipman and myself, shared a bachelors' apartment. I therefore had the opportunity to become closely acquainted with him. He wore well. The better I knew him, the more I liked him. In the service I always respected officers who gave truth, courage, and professional integrity precedence over ambition for rapid promotion and high position. Chipman was one such officer.

He and his wife arrived in Moscow, like so many young idealists, with the hope that by demonstrating sincere friendliness for the Soviet Union and for the Russian people they could break through the artificial barriers that placed members of the diplomatic corps under what amounted to a quarantine. His wife came with letters to wives of Soviet officials who were reputed to be interested in art and asked to call upon them. They continued for a period of several months to try to make friendly contacts with a number of Soviet nationals. When finally they discovered that the barriers could not be penetrated, they were bitterly disappointed. Since they regarded life in the Soviet Union as empty—devoid as it was of associations with the Soviet people—they were happy when they were transferred to Cairo.

While in Moscow Chipman served both in the consular and the economic sections of the embassy and rowed more than his weight in both.

In Paris, London, and Bonn he specialized in the activities of international communism. His death so soon after his assignment to Belgrade represented a loss to the United States since his background was enabling him to prepare valuable studies on the interplay between the Belgrade and the Moscow brands of communism.

Alexander Comstock Kirk.   Kirk was born in Chicago in 1888. He took his A.B. degree from Yale in 1909 and his LL.B. from Harvard Law School in 1914. Before entering the old Diplomatic Service in 1915 he also pursued studies in political science in Paris. When it was decided in March of 1938 that I was to be transferred to the State Department during the course of the coming summer, he was assigned to Moscow to succeed me as deputy chief of mission. He arrived in Moscow shortly before my departure in July 1938 and we were able to serve together for a number of weeks.

Kirk, like Wiley, had had an enormous amount of experience before his arrival in Moscow. In addition to a series of assignments to desks in the department he had served in positions of ascending importance at such posts as Berlin, The Hague, Paris (where he was attached to the Commission to Negotiate Peace in 1918–1919), Tokyo, Peking, Mexico City, and Rome (counselor of embassy).

Ambassador Davies left Moscow in order to take the position of ambassador to Belgium in June 1938; his successor, Ambassador Lawrence Steinhardt, did not arrive in Moscow until almost a year later.

During most of the interim Kirk was chargé d'affaires. He was transferred to Rome as counselor in 1939 shortly before the arrival of Ambassador Steinhardt. He was also chargé d'affaires during much of the period of his assignment in Berlin since, shortly after he reported there for duty, President Roosevelt, as a snub to Hitler, recalled Ambassador Hugh Wilson and did not appoint a successor.

When Germany provoked the Second World War by invading Poland in the late summer of 1939, it fell to the lot of Kirk as chargé d'affaires to look after the hundreds of U.S. citizens who were caught in Germany in the maelstrom of war and to assist them in getting home. In September 1940 he was sent back to Rome again to serve there as counselor. Italy at the time, as an ally of Germany, was already at war with France and Great Britain and, under Mussolini, its relations with the United States were far from friendly. In 1941 President Roosevelt appointed him minister to Egypt, in which capacity he served until his appointment in 1944 as ambassador to Italy. He resigned his ambassadorship and retired from the service in 1946. During his 31 years of service Kirk's experiences had been rich and varied. Following his retirement he settled in the mountains of Colorado where for a number of years he amused himself operating a ranch and raising cattle. Tiring of Colorado he went to Texas where he made his permanent home.

During the time that we were together in Moscow he spent hours questioning and cross-questioning me regarding problems that he would be likely to face regarding Soviet policies and practices, individual Soviet officials, members of the diplomatic corps, and so forth. He interrogated other officers of the embassy in a similar manner. When I left Moscow for Washington, I was convinced that under Kirk the embassy would be in good hands. In my opinion, the embassy never functioned better than it did during the nine months that he was in charge of it. Since I was on the other end of the line in Washington during that period, I was in a good position to judge.

Attachés of the Armed Services

Among the officers other than Foreign Service officers assigned to the embassy as of July 1, 1934, were Major Philip R. Faymonville, military attaché; First Lieutenant Thomas D. White, assistant military attaché and assistant military air corps attaché; and David R. Nimmer, captain in the Marine Corps, assistant naval attaché.

Philip R. Faymonville. Faymonville was born in San Francisco in

1888, graduated from West Point in 1912, and later, like many West Point graduates, engaged in graduate studies in several American universities. Although ordnance was his specialty, much of his career was devoted to intelligence work. He was, for instance, an intelligence officer under General Graves while the latter was in command of our expedition to Siberia during 1918–1920. In 1923 he was assigned to Tokyo, first as assistant military attaché and later as military attaché. Following the inauguration of President Roosevelt he was attached for a time to the White House in some capacity that was never quite clear to me. He might have been one of the junior attachés. In any event he became acquainted while there with Mrs. Roosevelt, who was intrigued by his views regarding the Soviet Union and who maintained thereafter a special interest in him. He was appointed military attaché in Moscow in February 1934 and reported to the embassy for duty in July of the same year.

He served as military attaché with the rank of major and later lieutenant colonel in Moscow until the late spring of 1939 when he was reassigned to a post not connected with foreign affairs in the United States. Following the entry of the Soviet Union into the Second World War he volunteered for further duty in the Soviet Union. With the aid of Mrs. Roosevelt and Harry Hopkins he obtained the appointment of chief of our Lend-Lease mission to the Soviet Union with headquarters in Moscow and was given the temporary rank of brigadier general. He continued to serve in this capacity until the spring of 1943 when he was reassigned to duties in the United States that had no connection with the Soviet Union.

While serving in Siberia, Faymonville, like his commander, General Graves, developed a distrust of the Department of State and of its members. General Graves's feelings in this respect were so strong that he voiced them in a book entitled *America's Siberian Adventure*, published in 1931, in which he insinuated that the Department of State was more deeply concerned about weakening the Soviet hold on Siberia than it was about countering Japanese ambitions to obtain control of the eastern seaboard of the Asian continent. At the time of Faymonville's appointment I was told that he had assisted the general in writing this book. I do not recall the source of this information and cannot vouch for its accuracy. Nevertheless, when on an occasion in Moscow I criticized this book, Faymonville, who was present, broke his rule of reticence and in an emotional manner defended the general and his book. I may add that in 1932 while on duty in the department I had participated in checking some of the statements and innuendos that were to be found in the book and found many of them had no basis in fact. In the same year the department incorporated most of the documents relating to the Siberian intervention into a volume, *Foreign Relations of the United States, 1918, Russia*, which served to discredit the charges of General Graves. These documents were so persuasive that Litvinov, in November 1933, after perusing them, dropped all claims for damages resulting from the presence of U.S. troops in Siberia.

While in the Far East Faymonville also developed a strong aversion to Japan and all things Japanese. His dislike of Japan and distrust of the career personnel of the State Department may have to an extent influenced his attitude toward the Soviet Union. During the 1920s he studied the Russian language and maintained unostentatious, friendly, and informal contacts with representatives of the Soviet Union who happened to be in the United States.

In view of his long–established friendly interest in the Soviet Union, his knowledge of the Russian language, the fact that he was *persona grata* to the Soviet government, and his support by Mrs. Roosevelt, it was almost inevitable that he should have been selected as our first military attaché to the Soviet Union.

Faymonville's attitude of distrust of the Department of State and of its members manifested itself almost immediately upon his arrival in the Soviet Union. He was, so to speak, a lone wolf. At embassy-staff meetings he rarely contributed to the discussions. In private conversations with other members of the embassy he showed an interest in eliciting their views with regard to the developments in Soviet-American relations and events that were taking place in the Soviet Union, but was reserved in expressing his own. He was careful at all times not to make any statements even to his closest colleagues in the embassy that might be considered as critical of Soviet policies and practices. He apparently wished to make it clear to the Soviet authorities and to American visitors that he should not be considered as a part of the embassy but as a military man who was remaining aloof from the numerous problems and differences that were casting gloomy shadows over U.S.-Soviet relations. Under standing instructions Faymonville, as military attaché, was obligated to show the chief or acting chief of the embassy such reports as he might make to the War Department. Although he had access to, and read with avid interest, the reports written by the other members of the embassy, it was rare that he let anyone, even Ambassador Bullitt, see what he was sending in. On several occasions when I was chargé d'affaires, I asked him to let me see what he had written on various subjects of military importance, he appeared to resent requests of this kind and at no time showed me any of his reports other than a few innocuous documents that could have been of little interest to the War Department or to the embassy.

Faymonville was highly secretive in his relations not only with his colleagues in the embassy and also with other military attachés in the diplomatic corps. From time to time the War Department expressed concern that it was not receiving military intelligence reports of value from him. When faced with such criticisms he usually took the position that it was more important that he not jeopardize his standing with the Soviet government than that he undertake to provide the War Department with the piffling detailed intelligence that it desired.

Following the departure from Moscow of Lieutenant White and Captain Nimmer in the early part of 1935, the War Department desired to send another officer to Moscow as an assistant to Faymonville. It hoped that the additional officer would obtain information of the kind that Faymonville was failing to supply. Although the relations between Faymonville and White had been agreeable, largely as a result of White's tact, Faymonville was not enthusiastic at the thought of having another assistant. Apparently he feared that the officer assigned might be someone whom he could not trust. Finally, however, in 1937 the War Department did send an assistant military attaché to Moscow. Faymonville did not take this assistant fully into his confidence. In fact, he became furious when the latter agreed to share a dacha (Russian country cottage) in a village in the environs of Moscow with two members of the embassy. Faymonville seemed to feel that the reputation of his office, so far as the Soviets were concerned, would be injured if his assistant maintained close friendly relations with representatives of the State Department.

For several weeks following the arrival of Faymonville in Moscow his relations with Ambassador Bullitt were quite close. When Faymonville perceived, however, that the ambassador was becoming disillusioned regarding the intentions of the Soviet government to live up to the promises that Litvinov had given at the time of the establishment of relations and that the personal relations between the ambassador and the top Soviet leaders were becoming strained, he adopted an attitude toward the ambassador that resulted in a cooling of the relationship between the two men.

When Ambassador Davies arrived in Moscow in early 1937, he and Faymonville greeted one another with enthusiasm. Friends of Faymonville in the United States had informed the ambassador that Faymonville had won the confidence of the Soviet authorities and urged the ambassador to work closely with him. Since Ambassador Davies was also eager to earn the goodwill of the Kremlin, he heeded this advice and during his tenure of office in Moscow continued to keep in close touch with Faymonville.

Thomas D. White. First lieutenant White, who was born in Minnesota in 1901, graduated from West Point near the top of his class in 1920.

Following his graduation he asked for service in the Air Corps. After earning his wings he studied both the Russian and Chinese languages in the United States. I first met White in 1925 when we were in the same Russian language class in Georgetown University. The pressures of my work in the department, however, made it necessary for me to drop out of the class but he was able to continue his studies for two years. In 1927 he was sent as language officer to Peiping [Beijing] where he continued to concentrate on those two languages for approximately four years. He was appointed assistant military attaché and assistant military air corps attaché in Moscow in January 1934 and served in that capacity until early in 1935, when following the breakdown of our negotiations with the Soviets relating to debts and claims, the position of assistant military air corps attaché was abolished and he was transferred to our embassy in Rome.

As acting military attaché from March to July 1934, White made a most favorable impression upon the Soviet military and upon the military attaché corps in Moscow. Shortly after the opening of the embassy, he gave a stag dinner in the National Hotel for the top officers of the Soviet army. They turned out in force headed by Voroshilov, who was at that time people's commissar for defense. The dinner was the liveliest party that I attended during my five years in Moscow. Most of the generals and admirals present apparently genuinely wanted to be friendly and they were uninhibited in their gaiety. One of the highlights of the evening was a series of Ukrainian and Caucasian dances put on by Voroshilov, Budenny, and others. Unfortunately, most of the top-ranking officers present were purged by Stalin during the next three or four years. Some were executed, others committed suicide, and others just disappeared.

White's relations with the nonmilitary members of the embassy were close during the ten months that he was with us. His apartment in the Mokhovaya Building was across the hall from mine and we therefore saw one another daily. He managed to get along quite well with his chief, Faymonville, but the latter never took him completely into his confidence.

We all regretted the departure early in 1935 of Captain David R. Nimmer, the naval attaché, and his charming wife. Nimmer had a distinguished record during the Second World War, following which he retired with the rank of brigadier general.

The U.S. staff personnel in our embassies are by no means mere faceless numbers. Most of them are highly individualistic persons who take pride in the responsible work that they are performing and are sensitive about their status. They expect to be treated with consideration as trusted employees of the U.S. government and with rare exceptions they merit and receive such consideration. Some of the veterans in the staff are more valuable in maintaining a cohesive, effectively operating embassy than are junior Foreign Service officers who are just beginning to earn their spurs.

It is one of the conventions of diplomacy that the clerical personnel are not included in the Diplomatic List and, therefore, do not as a rule participate actively in the social life of the diplomatic corps. This convention on occasion causes heartburn among the socially minded, ambitious wives of some of the staff members who are convinced—sometimes with reason—that they personally have the qualifications that would enable them to play a successful role in diplomatic society if given the opportunity. Although this convention is sometimes assailed as a relic of the days of feudalism, much can be said in its defense. The social life of the diplomatic community has purposes other than entertainment or amusement. Much of it is burdensome; some of it is boring. Diplomatic social life would be much more trying if diplomatic entertaining should be extended to include members of the clerical and technical staff, particularly in places where the numbers of members of the staff and their families of an embassy might reach into the hundreds.

In a closely knit mission where the officers and staff members live in the same compound, the artificial social distinction that is drawn between officers and nonofficers—particularly in cases where the nonofficers have had no previous service in diplomatic missions—can create situations of considerable delicacy that can be alleviated only by tact and understanding on the part of all.

During the early months of our embassy's existence there were no wives of staff members in Moscow. By the time women began to arrive, primarily as the result of marriages—single life in Moscow was rather trying—their husbands had become accustomed to the convention and were able to explain the situation to their wives. I may add, in passing, that it did not take Ambassador Bullitt long after his arrival in Moscow to understand that in the absence of the kind of hierarchy that he had denounced during his talk to us on the boat, an embassy could not function effectively. He, therefore, did not hesitate to delegate his authority down a chain of command.

CHAPTER 32

RESULTS OF THE EFFORTS OF THE U.S. EMBASSY IN MOSCOW TO COPE WITH PROBLEMS OF AN ORGANIZATIONAL OR ADMINISTRATIVE CHARACTER

PERSONAL AND ORGANIZATIONAL DIFFICULTIES PECULIAR TO SERVICE IN THE SOVIET UNION

THE ORGANIZATIONAL AND ADMINISTRATIVE PROBLEMS that the members of our embassy in Moscow faced as they sought to establish and organize their mission and to place it on an effective operating basis were formidable. They found themselves in an environment that was unfamiliar physically, morally, and spiritually. The absence of many things and services that they had learned to take for granted as a necessary part of urban life; the differences in the meaning of words, in concepts, and in precepts, which frequently rendered the exchange of ideas difficult; the sense of isolation from the people of the country; the almost complete dependence on the whims of a suspicious bureaucracy for many of the essentials for living; the absence of precedents to serve as a guide; and the difficulties in making Washington—particularly the officials in the administrative areas in the State Department who must explain all their decisions to unsympathetic congressional committees—understand the situation, were among the factors contributing to the difficulties encountered by the little band of Americans who, clustered on an island of diplomatic immunity in a stormy inhospitable sea, were trying to set up an institution that would serve to represent the United States in the Soviet Union.

The laws and the regulations of the State Department and other U.S. government agencies had not been framed to meet the kind of problems and situations that were presenting themselves daily in Moscow, and yet there were conscientious officials in the Department of State, the Bureau of the Budget, and the Office of the Comptroller General whose duties included the strict enforcement of laws and regulations governing U.S. establishments abroad. I shall not attempt here to describe how we tried to meet all the organizational and administrative problems that arose and the degree of success that we achieved in meeting them. I shall limit myself to a discussion of those that we regarded as most important at the time.

CHANGES IN STRUCTURE, ACTIVITIES, AND PERSONNEL OF THE EMBASSY

Changes in the nature of the structure, the activities, and the outlook of our embassy in Moscow were constantly taking place during the years 1934–1938. These changes were in part the result of a better knowledge—derived from experience—on the part of the embassy and the Department of State regarding the kind of an institution, activities, and attitudes that would be most effective in dealing with the Soviet government. They were also due in part to changes in the point of view of Washington regarding the kind of cooperation that could be expected from the Soviet government, and in part to changes in the number, interests, and qualifications of the personnel who composed the mission.

Although the embassy continued to maintain its four sections— political, economic, consular, and administrative—the officers and clerical personnel who staffed them were frequently shifted to meet new situations. There were, for instance, a series of changes in the political section. Wiley, who had acted as the head of that section in addition to performing the duties of deputy chief of mission, was transferred to Antwerp in the fall of 1935. Kennan and Bohlen, who had been assisting Wiley in that section, took turns in receiving assignments to the Department of State; and Chipman and Thayer helped to carry the burdens of the political section.

Hanson served as first secretary of the embassy for a few weeks before his final departure from Moscow in the late summer of 1934. Shantz left for Athens in December 1935, and Ward remained for several years as chief of the consular section.

In the early part of 1936, as a result of the departure of Wiley, Hanson, and Shantz, I became deputy chief of mission and, during the absences of the ambassador, chargé d'affaires. Durbrow succeeded me at that time as chief of the economic section. Following Durbrow's departure for Naples in 1938, Chipman became the head of that busy section.

The most important personnel change—one that was to have long-lasting ramifications—was the departure from the Soviet Union in April 1936 of Ambassador Bullitt and his subsequent appointment as ambassador to France, and the arrival in Moscow in January 1937 of his successor, Ambassador Joseph E. Davies.

During the nine months that elapsed between the departure of Ambassador Bullitt and the arrival of Ambassador Davies, I was responsible for the operation of the embassy. My duties as chargé d'affaires were primarily of a holding nature. I was under instructions to keep the ship steady, to make sure that it was following the course chartered by Ambassador Bullitt and the State Department, and to operate it in a manner that would facilitate its use by the new ambassador.

The line of approach followed by Ambassador Davies toward the internal and external problems of the embassy was quite different from that of Ambassador Bullitt. This difference, which I shall discuss in a subsequent chapter, had a marked effect upon the character of the work of the embassy.

Some of the problems that the embassy found itself facing when it opened in 1934 had either become less urgent or, having been found insoluble, had been placed, so to speak, in cold storage by the time Ambassador Davies arrived. Nevertheless, a number of problems continued actively to harass us during the ambassador's stay in Moscow, and even those that had been consigned to cold storage could not be entirely ignored.

Let us consider in some detail how the embassy sought to meet some of its more urgent organizational and administrative problems, including those relating to the ruble, to local transportation, to the employment of Soviet nationals in the mission, to the establishment of U.S. consular offices in the Soviet Union, and to the procurement of adequate housing for working and residential purposes. These problems were, of course, more acute during the first two years of the embassy's existence.

The Problem of the Ruble

Within several days after his arrival in Moscow, Ambassador Bullitt had begun to discuss the ruble problem with Litvinov, Divilkovsky, Grinko, and other top Soviet officials. Although these officials seemed to agree that it was necessary for the mission to be able to purchase a certain amount of rubles at reasonable rates, they appeared to be unable to advance precise suggestions regarding how this could be accomplished on a legal basis. In a conversation between Ambassador Bullitt and Litvinov in the latter part of March 1934, the latter admitted that the Soviet government was encountering difficulties in finding a method of providing rubles at a reasonable cost to the Americans without establishing a precedent. The commissar indicated during the conversation that the ambassador's insistence on being able to purchase rubles at a reasonable price from the Soviet government was causing embarrassment to that government and added that "if worse comes to worst you know we shall have no objection to your obtaining paper rubles in any way that you see fit."

On April 2, 1934, Bullitt reported to the State Department that there seemed to be no possibility of prevailing on the Soviet government to sell rubles to us at special prices. He pointed out that in his last conversation with Litvinov the latter had said "there is nothing for you to do except to buy rubles in the open market." The ambassador therefore reluctantly asked the State Department to authorize him to purchase abroad such rubles as might be required to satisfy the needs of the embassy and its personnel. The department also with reluctance gave the requested authorization. Thereafter, the ambassador or, in his absence, the officer in charge of the embassy proceeded methodically to purchase rubles abroad and to have them brought into Moscow in the diplomatic pouch.

In order that no Soviet nationals be involved in ruble transactions, no purchases were permitted in the Soviet Union. Strict regulations were drawn up to prevent members of the mission from taking an unfair advantage of their ability to obtain rubles at open market prices. For instance, the amount provided each officer and clerk was limited to what was judged sufficient to meet reasonable personal needs. Furthermore, members of the mission were strictly enjoined not to purchase rubles from anyone except the ambassador or the chargé d'affaires. Litvinov was made aware of our decision to purchase rubles in the open market in accordance with his suggestions. We were, therefore, importing rubles purchased abroad with the full knowledge of the Soviet government. Nevertheless, those of us who had been trained in the traditions of the Foreign Service were, like the ambassador, unhappy at this solution of the ruble problem. It went against the grain for us to participate in the violation of the laws of the country in which we were stationed even though we had been encouraged to do so by responsible officials of that country.

THE PROBLEM OF LOCAL TRANSPORTATION

Within a few hours after his arrival in Moscow Ambassador Bullitt had sent an urgent telegram to the State Department requesting it to furnish the embassy several automobiles and a motorcycle. We were not surprised when the department replied that it had no authorization from Congress to expend funds for the purchase of automotive equipment for the use of our diplomatic missions. The ambassador thereupon ordered several automobiles, including both sedans and trucks, from the representative of General Motors in Copenhagen. He also ordered an American motorcycle for the embassy messengers. In doing so he assumed personal responsibility for payment. When the cars and motorcycle arrived several weeks later, he turned them over to the embassy commissary, which proceeded to rent them to the embassy at Burobin prices.

The commissary used the funds that it received from the rental of the vehicles to pay for them. Eventually the ambassador persuaded the department to authorize the embassy to receive the automobiles as a gift. I do not recall the exact nature of these transactions but it seems to me that the ambassador paid such balances as were due for the purchase of these machines from his own pocket. As a result of his experiences in Moscow the ambassador became interested in the attitude of the government in regard to supplying our representatives abroad with automobiles. He, backed by Judge Moore in the State Department, questioned the wisdom of a policy of refusing to provide our diplomatic and consular establishments with automotive vehicles at posts where the possession of them would materially add to the effectiveness of operations. The president also took an active interest in the matter. As a result the Budget Bureau and Congress took a somewhat more lenient attitude and eventually began to authorize the purchase of automobiles at a limited number of posts where the need for them was particularly pressing.

Nevertheless, many years elapsed before it became an accepted practice of the State Department to furnish its offices abroad with automotive transport. During the intervening years the War and Navy Departments had no difficulty in obtaining funds for the purchase of automobiles for the use of their personnel attached to our diplomatic missions. The U.S. diplomatic and consular officers who did not own their own cars continued to make official visits or to proceed to official functions on foot or by cab at a time when diplomatic and consular officers of most other countries moved about in American-made automobiles furnished by their governments.

PROBLEMS CONNECTED WITH THE EMPLOYMENT OF
SOVIET NATIONALS BY THE U.S. MISSION IN MOSCOW

One of the ambassador's first moves after his arrival in Moscow had been to request the State Department for authority to employ a dozen Soviet nationals. That request was granted and we began immediately to build up our Soviet staff by hiring messengers, doormen, servants for the ambassador's residence, interpreters, typist-translators, and so forth. After our transfer from the Savoy Hotel in the early summer of 1934 to our new chancery in the Mokhovaya Building, he asked for and obtained authority to employ additional Soviet personnel. As the activities of the embassy broadened and deepened we gradually increased the number of Soviet employees to more than thirty. Our additional personnel included two librarian-typists, two switchboard operators, a foreign trade expert, a political scientist, an agricultural economist, a lawyer, and several "contact" men.

It was one of my duties during most of this assignment to Moscow to obtain the approval of Narkomindel before placing a Soviet national on the embassy's payroll. Some of our Soviet personnel came to us on the recommendation of officials in Narkomindel. Others applied direct and their employment was approved by Narkomindel after we had interviewed them. We, of course, carefully screened all applicants recommended by Narkomindel and rejected a number of them.

In general during the first two years of the existence of the embassy we found Narkomindel reasonably cooperative so far as the employment of Soviet personnel was concerned. It frequently assisted us in finding personnel with the qualifications we needed and rarely refused to approve the employment of those who had the temerity to apply to us direct. Since it was difficult for a Soviet national to pass through the gates of the compounds of either the Mokhovaya Building or the ambassador's residence without being interrogated by the Soviet police, we took it for granted that most applicants who applied at the embassy had come to us with the blessings of the Soviet government.

Our Soviet staff played such an important role in the operation of the embassy that any description of the embassy, its work, and its problems would in my opinion not be complete if it did not at least mention a number of our more highly qualified Soviet employees. Roman Bisk, the legal adviser; Philip Bender, the chief contact man and "troubleshooter"; Victor Shiffer, the foreign trade expert; Abraham Svyadoshch, the economist who later became a political research assistant; and Valentine Malitsky, the agricultural economist, were among those who, in my opinion, deserve special mention.

THE GREAT PURGE BEGINS TO AFFECT
OUR LOCAL EMPLOYEES

For approximately two and a half years after the establishment of the embassy, our Soviet employees performed their duties quietly and for the most part efficiently in an atmosphere apparently secure. Although we knew that they were reporting to the Soviet secret police and although they must have been aware of our knowledge, we gradually grew attached to most of them and the majority, in their turn, seemed to like us and, in my opinion, were just as loyal to us as the complicated situation permitted.

During the late summer and fall of 1936, as the great Soviet purge gradually claimed more and more victims, I began to sense a growing uneasiness among the Soviet members of our staff. In August I found one of our female Soviet employees hunched over her typewriter, sobbing. At first she refused to tell me the cause of her distress. Finally, however, she told me that she was so frightened that she could not sleep at night and was finding it difficult to keep her mind on her work. She feared that she and other members of her family might, like many of her friends and acquaintances, be arrested at any moment. She had not done anything that she considered to be wrong, nor had any members of her family. Nevertheless, for many years they had been corresponding with relatives living in Poland. The police were now arresting and interrogating Soviet citizens known to have been exchanging letters with persons living abroad. Since most Jews in the Soviet Union had relatives in Poland, in other countries of Eastern and Western Europe, or in the United States with whom they had been corresponding, they were being arrested in droves. Some of them, after interrogation, had been released; many of them, however, had simply disappeared without trace. Since Trotsky was a Jew, there was a tendency for the police to regard all Jews who were not in a position to prove their loyalty to the present Soviet regime as Trotskyists. The fact that her family was Jewish and had been corresponding with foreigners must inevitably place it under suspicion. Only recently one of her uncles and two of her cousins had disappeared. There was little that I could do to comfort this frightened woman. I suggested that she might care to take leave for several days but she said that she felt safer in the embassy than at home.

Several of our other Soviet employees, without being so outspoken as the typist, began also to hint by word or gesture concern for themselves and their families. It was my thought that there might have been a change in the attitude toward them of the police to whom they had been reporting; perhaps the police were beginning to show distrust of them. Whether or not this thought had any basis in fact I do not know.

The first embassy casualty among our local employees was Malitsky. One morning in September 1936 Mrs. Malitsky came to me in tears to tell me that during the preceding day the police had entered and searched their apartment and had taken her husband away with them. I immediately arranged for an interview with a member of the Third Western Division of Narkomindel, told him that Malitsky had been arrested, and said that the embassy would appreciate it if he could ascertain and let it know the cause of the arrest. The official answered that it was not the custom of Narkomindel to make inquiries regarding the arrest of a Soviet national; arrests of this kind did not pertain to the area of foreign affairs. I pointed out that the embassy thought that it had a legitimate interest in the case since Malitsky was one of its employees and the husband of a U.S. citizen. Although the official continued to insist that he was not authorized to discuss with a foreign diplomat the arrest of a Soviet citizen, he said that he would nevertheless look into the matter. He added that although he knew nothing about the case he personally was confident that the arrest was in no way connected with Malitsky's employment in the embassy.

The State Department was disturbed when it received my report of Malitsky's arrest and registered a protest with Alexander Troyanovsky, the Soviet ambassador to the United States.

For weeks Mrs. Malitsky haunted Soviet offices in unsuccessful efforts to find out what had happened to her husband. I also approached members of Narkomindel again and again on the subject. Simultaneously, top officials of the State Department were expressing their concern to the Soviet ambassador in Washington. Finally, in the middle of December 1936, the chief of the Third Western Division of Narkomindel told me that Malitsky had been tried secretly before a military court, had been found guilty after full confession of involvement in a terrorist plot, and had been sentenced to ten-years' imprisonment. He added that since Malitsky would probably be sent to a distant internment camp it would not be possible for his wife to be with him and that, although the Soviet authorities had nothing against his wife, they believed that for her own good she should return to the United States.

In spite of this advice, which I relayed to Mrs. Malitsky, and similar advice given by me she remained in the Soviet Union for many months in the unrealized hope that she could be of help to her husband in some way. She was convinced, as were the American members of the embassy who had worked with Malitsky, that he was innocent and that if he had confessed to any crime, he had done so, as had so many Soviet citizens during the era of the Great Purge, under some kind of compulsion.

I have never learned whether or not Malitsky survived his term of imprisonment, which was eventually reduced to seven years. Comparatively few prisoners in the forced labor camps of northern Russia or Siberia were able to keep alive in them for more than a few years.

The Malitsky case was unusual in that the embassy was finally informed of the nature of the charges against him and of his sentence. It was not able to ascertain the reason for the arrest of most of its other Soviet employees who became victims of the purge, or the kind of sentences they received. The Soviet authorities usually refused to go any further in discussing these arrests than to state that they had no connection with the employees' work in the embassy.

During the period 1936–1938 Mrs. Svyadoshch and Mrs. Bisk informed the embassy that the police had come to their homes in the middle of the night and taken away their husbands. Mrs. Svyadoshch was arrested shortly after the arrest of her husband. In early September 1939, more than a year after I had left Moscow, Ambassador Steinhardt reported that Shiffer had resigned partly because of his fear of being arrested if he should remain with the embassy. Shiffer's resignation did not help him, however, and he was arrested shortly after. Bender was arrested in the early 1940s. We never learned the fate of these two men. In the early 1940s the young typist whom I had found in tears also disappeared. The husbands and other members of the families of several of our other Soviet employees were also victims of the purge. In general, the chauffeurs, the messengers, and the janitors fared better than our employees who possessed higher qualifications.

Thus, much to my personal distress, our venture of making use of Soviet employees in the embassy ended in disaster for some of them. The need for employees with their qualifications to assist the embassy, particularly in the matter of research and contact with Soviet institutions, was urgent at the time. All kinds of misinformation were being peddled in the United States regarding the Soviet Union; the Communists, fellow travelers, and left-leaning "liberals" of the New Deal were painting the Soviet Union as a paradise, while many of the more conservative opponents of the New Deal were insisting that it was a living hell on the verge of extinction. No U.S. government agency other than the Eastern European Division of the State Department and our legation in Riga was attempting to make a serious study of Soviet policies and developments. The relatively few U.S. institutions and individuals who were engaged in research with regard to the Soviet Union were for the most part ideologically motivated.

As the years went by the need for members of our embassy in Moscow to engage in work of a research nature diminished. The Bureau of Research and Intelligence of the Department of State set up a section to study Soviet policies and developments. Other sections in the Central Intelligence Agency and other departments of the government established offices to study Soviet activities and developments of a kind in which the United States might be particularly interested, and a host of private institutions began to spend millions of dollars annually on Soviet studies. Furthermore, the U.S. government and people during later years knew much more about the Soviet Union than they did in the mid-1930s. Nevertheless, in my opinion, it is important that our representatives in the Soviet Union continue to keep themselves informed in depth regarding what is going on in that country and not succumb to the temptation to limit their assessment of Soviet activities and trends to superficial reports.

I believe the Soviet government made an error in judgment in arresting our Soviet employees. Most of those arrested were exceptionally able people of the kind who could have been useful to it. Furthermore, their arrest tended to strengthen the disgust in U.S. governmental circles at the senseless orgy of human destruction that went on in the Soviet Union during the period of the purges.

THE PROBLEM OF THE ESTABLISHMENT OF U.S. CONSULAR OFFICES IN THE SOVIET UNION

The problem of the establishment of U.S. consular offices in the Soviet Union proved to be so closely interrelated with that of the status of officers in the mission in Moscow that for purposes of discussion they can best be treated as a single problem.

Following the arrival in Moscow on March 21, 1934, of Consul General Hanson and the formal opening immediately after his arrival of the consulate general, the matter of the status of the Foreign Service officers on duty in the consulate general in Moscow, which had been answered on a temporary basis two weeks earlier, came up again for consideration. It seemed incongruous that a senior high-ranking officer like Hanson should be relegated to the Soviet consular list. Such a relegation would mean that he would have in Moscow only one foreign consular colleague, a British consular officer who was accustomed to perform certain consular services in the British embassy. As a consular officer with no diplomatic status, Hanson would not be able to discuss with Narkomindel or with other Soviet institutions problems of a consular character, such as those relating to the protection and welfare of U.S. citizens, to ships and shipping, and to visa services. Furthermore, since the economic section of the embassy was being charged with activities relating to economic matters, including trade, he would not, as consul general, be expected to prepare reports of a commercial nature or to assist U.S. businessmen interested in establishing trade relations with the Soviet Union. As consul general in Harbin and as chief of consular offices in other cities in the Far East, he had held positions of great responsibility and corresponding prestige. As consul general in Moscow he would be performing a limited number of consular services in an atmosphere of isolation.

When the consul general discovered what his position and status were to be, his morale, like that of our other Foreign Service officers assigned to the consulate general, began to sag. It went lower when shortly after his arrival he found it impossible to get in touch with the Soviet officials then on duty in various state organizations in Moscow whom he had befriended, and sometimes aided, while they were serving in Harbin. It became clear to him that regardless of the friendliness of the relations that he had enjoyed with some Soviet officials in Harbin, they did not dare to receive him in their offices or homes in Moscow, or even to meet him.

The position of the consulate general became even more difficult when the Soviet government took the position that the Moscow consular district must be limited to the City and Oblast (province) of Moscow. Although the Soviet authorities, as a concession, indicated that they would have no objection if the consulate general would perform consular services of a routine character for persons living in other oblasts, they insisted that problems relating to the protection and welfare of U.S. citizens outside the Moscow Oblast should be handled by the embassy.

As a result of my conversations with the officials of Narkomindel relating to our consular problems, I became more convinced than ever that the consulate general should be merged into the embassy as a consular section and my reports to the State Department reflected my views. Wiley, however, continued on the basis of precedent and of principle to oppose such a merger, and it was not until February 6, 1935, that the department in a telegram addressed to the embassy ordered the abolition of the consulate general and the establishment in the embassy of a consular section, which would consist of the organization and staff of the former consulate general and which in the future was to perform all consular services. In the same telegram the department stated that the two Foreign Service officers who were at the time on duty in the consulate general (that is, Ward and Durbrow) were being assigned to the embassy in the capacity of diplomatic secretaries and that one of them, Ward, should be made the chief of the new section. The telegram added: "Inasmuch as Ward and Durbrow will function in the eyes of this Government in both diplomatic and consular capacity they should sign all documents of a consular nature in their consular capacity. A consular seal should be used in performing technical consular services." Thus for the first time a U.S. consular office in a great world capital was transferred into a section of a U.S. embassy.

The closing of the consulate general, as I shall explain later, served two purposes. In the first place, it eliminated some of the difficulties that the United States had been experiencing in maintaining a separate consular office in Moscow. In the second place, the manner in which it was announced served as an indication to the Soviet government and, in fact, to all the world that the United States was taking such a grave view of the collapse of the negotiations in respect to debts and claims that it was beginning to believe that it would not be possible to maintain close friendly relations with the Soviet Union. The reaction of Soviet officials to this announcement was also of a dual nature. They were pleased at the decision to merge the consular office with the embassy and irritated at what they regarded as the pettish manner in which the decision was announced.

During the period that had elapsed between the opening of the consulate general in March 1934 and its absorption by the embassy in February 1935, steps had been taken to alleviate the situation so far as Hanson was concerned. In July 1934 he was transferred to the embassy with the rank of first secretary, and Harold Shantz, a consular officer who had just arrived in Moscow, was placed in charge of the truncated consulate general. Hanson, however, never fully recovered from the disappointment that he had suffered in Moscow. He had looked forward to occupying a position as consul general in which he could make full use of his experience and talents. Being a gregarious person he had anticipated that he would find himself in Moscow surrounded by friendly Russians. In September 1934 he left Moscow in order to take home leave in the United States. He was in a downcast mood when he bade us farewell. The State Department, believing that in the circumstances it would not be wise for him to return to the Soviet Union, assigned him to Addis Ababa as consul general and first secretary. While he was en route to this post his assignment was changed to that of consul general at Salonika. Broken in health and shattered in morale, he committed suicide following the receipt of his new instructions.

We had been in Moscow only a few weeks when both the State Department and Ambassador Bullitt agreed that, in view of what they regarded as the lack of a spirit of cooperation on the part of the Soviet government, it would be preferable for the time being to limit the establishment of consular offices outside of Moscow to a consulate in the city of Leningrad.

Protracted negotiations by the embassy with the Soviet government about the opening of a consulate in Leningrad had resulted in an impasse. The Soviet authorities had made us an offer of a building at a rental so fantastically high that if it had been accepted the maintenance of our consulate office in Leningrad would have rendered it one of the most costly of U.S. establishments abroad. When we asked for less expensive quarters we were informed that no other space was available. During the course of our negotiations we learned from conversations with the consular officers of other countries stationed in Leningrad that their contacts with the local authorities in Leningrad were extremely limited, that they had no contacts whatsoever with the local population, that their functions were primarily those of performing services for their nationals living in or visiting Leningrad, and that the society in which they moved was confined to the members of the consular corps and to foreigners in the area. Our difficulties in arranging for the opening of a consulate in Leningrad were still further compounded by intimations from the Soviet authorities that it might be difficult for the American members of the consular staff in that city to find living quarters. We finally abandoned all thoughts of opening a consular office in any city other than Moscow.

It was not until after the Soviet Union became involved in the Second World War that we established and maintained for a limited period a consular office in Vladivostok, which matched the Soviet consular office that had been opened several years previously in San Francisco. Thus the dreams of a U.S. embassy in Moscow supported by U.S. consular offices in perhaps a half dozen Soviet cities, all cooperating with the national and local Soviet authorities in strengthening friendly relations between our two countries, were abandoned. We had found that it was difficult enough to maintain the embassy with a consular section in Moscow.

The Problem of Living and Working Space

In an outburst of apparently friendly generosity, Stalin had promised Bullitt on December 20, 1933, that the United States could have as a site for its embassy building a piece of property on Lenin Hills (the name was changed from Sparrow Hills to Lenin Hills in 1934). Upon the ambassador's return to the United States in January, therefore, he urged the State Department to lose no time in taking advantage of Stalin's promise.

The State Department with the support of the Budget Bureau began immediately to make arrangements for the inclusion of a million dollars in its budget for use in the construction of an embassy compound at Lenin Hills that would provide suitable living and working quarters for our ambassador and the American members of a staff. A distinguished architect was commissioned to draw up plans for the compound, which was to be similar from an architectural point of view to the building complex of the University of Virginia. It was the hope of the department and of the ambassador that the new compound would be the answer to our Moscow housing problems.

Within a few days after his return to Moscow in early March 1934, the Ambassador began his endeavors to work out arrangements with the Soviet authorities that would provide a framework around which the State Department and the embassy could complete their building plans. He urged that the Soviet government at an early date submit to the embassy for transmission to the department a draft of a lease for the Lenin Hills property. He also inaugurated conversations of an exploratory nature with the Soviet authorities with the purpose of obtaining at least tentative answers to a number of questions, more formal answers to which we should have before entering into contractual arrangements. Among the numerous questions to which we needed answers were:

1. Would it be possible for the Soviet government to set up in its bureaucratic machinery a special agency with which the embassy could deal with respect to all matters relating to the construction of the new building? Such an agency would serve as a channel to the numerous state institutions, the cooperation of which would be necessary if the building program was to be carried out.

2. To what extent could the embassy rely upon the Soviet government to supply it with the building materials that would be needed for the construction of the new building? Building materials were in short supply in the Soviet Union.

3. Would the Soviet government be disposed to cooperate in the matter of supplying local skilled and unskilled labor and in permitting the embassy to import foreign architects, artisans, and so forth? Since no Soviet citizen would dare to work for

foreigners without the consent of the Soviet government and since foreign architects, artisans, engineers, and mechanics would be needed, this cooperation would be necessary.

4. Would the Soviet government permit the embassy to import, duty free, the kinds of materials and equipment that would be needed for the construction of a modern, representative embassy building?

5. How would the cost of Soviet workmen and the conditions of their employment be determined? Would the American architects and building contractors have the right to hire them, direct them, and fire them?

6. How would indebtedness to state institutions and to private Soviet nationals incurred for the furnishing of labor, materials, transport, and so forth be discharged? Would payment be in dollars or in rubles? If in rubles, at what exchange rate could they be purchased?

It did not take long for the ambassador to realize that the construction by the United States of an embassy compound in the Soviet Union under the conditions and in the atmosphere that prevailed at the time would not be a simple undertaking. Stalin and a few of the top Soviet leaders who had Stalin's confidence could afford to be friendly and generous on occasion in their dealings with foreigners. Soviet officials at lower levels, however, who dared to make friendly concessions to representatives of the imperialist camp, were incurring grave danger. It was their duty to extract all possible advantages from such representatives and to give as little as possible in return.

Within less than three weeks after his arrival in Moscow in March 1934, the ambassador began to run into difficulties of such magnitude in connection with his efforts to expedite the conclusion of arrangements that would permit us to go forward with our building program that he became discouraged. On March 28 he sent a dispatch to the State Department indicating that it had begun to appear to him that the Soviet government was not disposed to carry out its understanding with regard to Lenin Hills.

He said that it seemed that the Moscow Soviet in December 1933, until overruled by Stalin personally, had opposed the leasing of the Lenin Hills site to the U.S. government. It was his belief that the members of the Moscow Soviet, now that the honeymoon following the establishment of diplomatic relations was beginning to wane, were again trying to prevent the erection of a U.S. embassy on such a choice piece of Moscow land. The

Moscow Soviet, furthermore, was not without recourse to methods of obstructing our building plans. Those methods consisted primarily of delays, evasion, and negative attitudes.

It was not, however, merely the Moscow Soviet that assumed what seemed to the ambassador and his staff to be an uncooperative attitude. When members of the embassy undertook to discuss matters relating to the building project with Narkomindel and other Soviet institutions, they found the latter vague and evasive.

Finally, on September 19, 1935, the secretary of state sent a telegram to the ambassador that read in part as follows:

> As there would seem to be no immediate prospect of initiating Moscow construction, I would like your comments . . . as to the possible diversion of the fund that was proposed to be used at Moscow. I believe that if we subsequently find it practicable to proceed with Moscow buildings we will have ample time to make good by future appropriations whatever we may now use in Central America for the immediate protection of our officers.

The ambassador's reply of September 27 to Secretary Hull was brief: "I favor heartily transfer Moscow buildings fund to construction at unhealthy posts in Central America."

During the remaining years of my tour in Moscow I became convinced that by March 1934 Stalin had come to regret the promise that he had made on the spur of the moment to Ambassador Bullitt in December 1933, and that, not wishing to be placed in a position of failing to live up to a promise made by him personally, he had authorized his subordinates to resort to the obstructive and delaying tactics that caused the U.S. government eventually to drop its building plans.

On March 10, 1939, while I was on duty in the State Department, Constantine A. Oumansky, who at the time was Soviet chargé d'affaires in Washington, approached me on the subject of the Lenin Hills site. Was the United States still planning to build on the site? I told him that it would be necessary for me to consult the officials in the department who were carrying out our foreign buildings programs. I prepared a memorandum of our conversation and took it personally to George S. Messersmith, who in July 1937 had succeeded Carr as assistant secretary of state in charge of administration and who had responsibility for making decisions relating to foreign buildings.

After reading my memorandum, Messersmith said that in view of our experiences over the years in dealing with the Soviet Union in matters of an administrative and fiscal character, he was confident that a request made by him for an appropriation of a million dollars or more for the purpose of constructing an embassy compound in Moscow would serve no purpose other than to create doubt among members of the Budget Bureau and of Congress regarding the soundness of his judgment. During the five years that had elapsed since Congress had been receptive to Ambassador Bullitt's urging for appropriations that would enable us to build such a compound, many members of Congress had become disillusioned regarding the possibility of the development of close friendly relations between the Soviet Union and the United States.

Messersmith added that furthermore he was already facing so many problems of an administrative nature that he simply could not afford to devote the time and energy to what he was confident would be protracted and futile negotiations with the Soviet authorities. At the same time, he said, he disliked the idea of taking responsibility for a decision which he believed the Soviet government desired the United States to make, of abandoning such claims as we might have to the attractive Lenin Hills site. I told him that I would be grateful if he would give me a memorandum on the subject that I could use in framing a reply to Oumansky. He called in one of his secretaries and in my presence drafted a lengthy memorandum, dated March 10, 1939, for my use. I based my reply to Oumansky on the last two paragraphs of this memorandum. They read as follows:

> When we go ahead at Moscow with the erection of a Government building, it will have to be a considerable project and will run into a very considerable amount of money. I do not believe that the Congress will be disposed at this time to make available such a considerable sum of money for a project in Moscow and, in my opinion, it would not be advisable to seek such funds for Moscow . . .
>
> In my opinion, therefore, we may tell the Soviet Embassy that we appreciate the Soviet Government having held this site for us, that the Commission (the Foreign Service Building Commission) has no money available at the present time for proceeding with this project, which will involve a very considerable expenditure as we wish to do it on a proper scale when we do proceed, and that as they may have other use for the site we will quite understand their not continuing to hold it for us. As it is our intention to proceed with the erection of a building there as soon as we can, we would naturally be glad to have a site continuously available to us and the availability of such a good site as this would undoubtedly somewhat influence the time that we are able actually to go ahead.

Oumansky seemed pleased at my reply, which he apparently interpreted as a release by the United States of any claims that it might have with regard to the Lenin Hills property. His mission had been successful. He was in a position to report to his government that the Department of State had informed him that, since the U.S. government would not be able within the near future to make use of a site that the Soviet government had already held for more than five years, it would be understandable if the Soviet government should decide to make other use of it. In the circumstances no one would be in a position to accuse the Soviet authorities of going back on a promise made by Stalin. Thus ended Bullitt's dream of a U.S. embassy on Lenin Hills.

The Mokhovaya Building

Keith Merrill, who was in charge of the Foreign Building Office of the Department of State in 1934, had been sent to Moscow to obtain living and office quarters for Ambassador Bullitt and the members of the mission. He had estimated that in addition to a residence for the ambassador we would need no less than 40 rooms for the chancery and 220 rooms for living quarters for the American members of the mission. Those of us in the department who realized how important working and living space was for the effective functioning of the mission had been disappointed when we learned that Merrill had succeeded in obtaining a total of only 72 rooms for both the chancery and living quarters. Since the embassy compound was never constructed, the embassy in Moscow has been handicapped for more than 30 years by the lack of sufficient housing and working space.

The Mokhovaya Building was in an advantageous position. After the houses across the street from it had been razed in order to make room for the subway, the space in front of the building had been converted into a great plaza on the opposite side of which was a small park encircling the Kremlin. This plaza swung around to the right where it joined the great Red Square containing Lenin's tomb, adjacent to the platforms from which the leaders of the Soviet Union and members of the diplomatic corps reviewed parades on May 1 and November 7. The small park with its numerous benches under shade trees was a favorite spot for members of the embassy to sit outdoors during the summer months.

The seven-floor building presented an imposing appearance with its many windows and ornamental stonework. In the center was an arch two stories high through which automobiles could enter into a small walled court in the rear. The building was flanked on the right by Moscow University and on the left by the National Hotel, at that time the leading hotel in Moscow. In back of the rear court was one of the buildings of the

Medical School of Moscow University. The first three floors on the side of the building adjoining the National Hotel were devoted to the chancery of the embassy. The first three floors on the other side of the arch housed the offices of the consulate general, the office of the doctor, and the offices of the armed forces attachés. The U.S. personnel were allotted apartments on the upper four floors of the building.

Although the building had a long frontage it was only two rooms deep. Therefore, most of the apartments had windows overlooking the Kremlin. The building was steam heated and had running hot and cold water. The kitchens were equipped with gas stoves. Electric refrigerators were not in use at that time in the Soviet Union, but the State Department sent one for each of the apartments in the Mokhovaya Building and several for the ambassador's residence. They were regarded with envious curiousity by such Soviet nationals as had an opportunity to see them.

When I became deputy chief of mission, my wife and I moved from the fourth floor to the duplex apartment on the seventh floor that had been occupied by the Wileys. During the nearly two and a half years that we spent in that apartment we trudged up the six flights of stairs hundreds of times as the result of the elevator being out of order.

Three small apartments in the building had been reserved by the Soviet government for Soviet officials: L. M. Karakhan, assistant commissar for foreign affairs, who had formerly served as Soviet ambassador to China; D. T. Florinsky, chief of protocol in the Commissariat for Foreign Affairs; and P. L. Mikhailsky, a leading Soviet columnist who wrote under the pen name of "Lapinsky."

Florinsky was one of the few surviving officials who had served under the czarist regime. He had been retained in government service when the Ministry for Foreign Affairs had been converted into the Commissariat for Foreign Affairs because he had won the confidence of Chicherin, the first Commissar for Foreign Affairs who had also previously served in the czarist Ministry of Foreign Affairs. Florinsky was an accomplished linguist who had all the graces of a European protocol chief of the old school. Although he never discussed political or substantive matters, he was an interesting conversationalist at a diplomatic dinner table and was in general liked by members of the diplomatic corps.

On an evening in August 1934 while Florinsky was a dinner guest at the British embassy, one of the embassy servants entered the dining room and whispered in his ear. He murmured his apologies, left the table, and went to the front door where two men were awaiting him. He left the embassy with them and so far as I know was never seen again by any member of the diplomatic corps. A few days later it was announced that B. N. Barkov had been appointed chief of protocol. For many months no one knew what had happened to Florinsky. There were rumors that he had been shot, that he had been sent to a Siberian prison camp, or that he had been merely exiled. My recollection is that eventually word trickled down that he had been exiled and had been assigned a minor job in some remote village in Siberia or northern Russia. We liked Florinsky and regretted the disaster that had befallen him. That did not prevent us, however, from urging that his apartment be assigned to the embassy. After several months of bickering we finally succeeded in obtaining it.

Mikhailsky was a studious, quiet little man. Judging from the lights in his apartment he worked on his columns until the small hours of the morning. He always greeted us in a friendly manner when we encountered him in the halls or on the stairs of the Mokhovaya—he rarely used the elevator. One evening in the latter part of May 1937, while I was taking my daily walk around the Kremlin walls, I overtook Mikhailsky who was moving along slowly with the help of a cane. He greeted me and asked if I would not join him. I was astonished, since high-ranking members of the Communist Party as a rule did not like to be seen in the company of a member of a foreign embassy. I had taken a liking to the old man and was glad to accept his invitation. He spent most of the 40 minutes that we were together talking about his youth and his days in exile. We had been informed that he was one of the early Bolsheviks, that he had been a friend of Lenin, and that he had been on the famous sealed train that had carried Lenin across Germany from Switzerland to Finland just prior to the Bolshevik revolution. During our walk he made several references to Lenin, commenting on his subbornness and quick temper. I thought that I detected a note of nostalgia in his voice when he was discussing some of his youthful adventures. He said that the days he spent in exile in Prague were the most peaceful of his life. As a student he could go on a trip over the weekend in the mountains and never worry about what was happening while he was away. Now, he said, when he awakens in the morning he wonders with a sinking heart what might have taken place during the night.

It was only a few weeks later that Ward informed me that the seal of the NKVD* was on the door of Mikhailsky's apartment. Like Florinsky and dozens of Soviet officials whom we had known, poor old Mikhailsky, one of the veterans of the revolution, dropped out of sight. We heard later that he had been sentenced to seven years in a prison camp.

When it became clear that Mikhailsky was not coming back, we

---

* The initials "NKVD," standing for the People's Commissariat for Internal Affairs, were gradually replacing "OGPU" in referring to the Soviet secret police.

attempted to persuade the Soviet authorities to let us rent his apartment. For many months we received only evasive replies. At the beginning of an unusually warm weekend late in the following winter I was informed by members of the embassy who were occupying an apartment on the third floor immediately under that of Mikhailsky that a torrent of water was coming through their ceilings. I hurried over in time to see big chunks of the plaster falling over furniture and furnishings. A few moments later the water commenced to come through the ceilings of the office of the military attaché. It was also beginning to flood the corridors and the stairs. I asked Bender, our troubleshooter, to try to find some Soviet official who would have the authority to enter Mikhailsky's apartment and turn the water off. All offices were closed and no officials could be found. I realized that if the water were allowed to run for several hours at least half a dozen of our precious apartments would be damaged and would probably be unlivable for a protracted period. In my desperation I committed the sacrilege of breaking the NKVD seal. We had little difficulty in forcing the door. Leino, our American-Finnish handyman who accompanied me, turned the water off. It seemed that during the winter the water in the radiators and pipes had frozen in the unheated apartment and the pipes had burst. During the unseasonably warm weather the ice had melted and the flood was the result.

I prepared a note describing what I had done and why and delivered it personally to Weinberg of Narkomindel as soon as that commissariat was again open for business. Weinberg looked at me in terror. "You have committed a grievous crime," he said, "a diplomat can be declared *persona non grata* for less." I replied that if the Soviet government should decide that I had committed an unforgivable act, I was prepared to take the consequences; I had done what I did, however, because I did not think that it would be in the interest of either the Soviet or the U.S. government for me to stand idly by while water poured through our living and working quarters for a period of more than 36 hours. As I recall it, Weinberg suggested that I not leave my note with him. He preferred to handle the whole matter orally. The upshot was that he told me later that his government would not make an issue of what I had done but that in the future no one in the embassy should ever again tamper with the seal of the NKVD. Now that its seal was broken, representatives of the NKVD removed all the furniture and furnishings from the Mikhailsky apartment and Burobin (the Soviet organization charged with maintaining the premises rented to foreign diplomats) sent workers to repair the apartments that had been damaged by the flood. When all of the apartments had been repaired, the Soviet authorities relented and allowed us to rent the one Mikhailsky had occupied.

Karakhan left the Commissariat for Foreign Affairs a few months after our arrival in Moscow in order to go to Turkey as ambassador. During the two years of his assignment to Turkey he retained his Mokhovaya apartment although he rarely used it. Shortly after his return to Moscow in late 1937, he was arrested and in December of that year his execution was announced. His wife, a noted ballerina, performed with unusual brilliance on the evening of the day of the announcement. The embassy was also successful in obtaining the use of his apartment so that by the spring of 1938 we finally had the whole Mokhovaya Building to ourselves.

After members of the mission had settled themselves in their living quarters in the four upper floors of the Mokhovaya, the ambassador consented to permit those who had wives to join them. My wife arrived in early August 1934. During our first year in Moscow there were few children in the building. As time went on the unmarried personnel began to make changes in their status. Wiley was one of the first to introduce a bride to the embassy family in the building. During the next four years no less than fifteen other members of the mission followed his example, including Bohlen, Page, and Kuniholm. Following the marriages, babies began to arrive. Most of the mothers, however, went to Finland, Poland, or Latvia to have their children.

The appearance of the infants raised some problems of a religious nature. Father Braun could take care of baptisms in the Catholic families. There were, however, no American Protestant pastors in Moscow, and it was difficult to find a Protestant clergyman of any nationality. Finally the pastor of a small Latvian Lutheran church expressed willingness to perform the necessary baptismal rite. Most of the members of the mission and their families gathered in one of the apartments in the Mokhovaya for the impressive ceremony. A few days later we learned that the pastor, the last of the Lutheran clergy in Moscow, had disappeared. We never again tried to make use of a local clergyman to take care of our spiritual needs.

The addition of wives and babies to our community placed a still greater strain on our housing situation. After the embassy had made numerous requests, Narkomindel finally agreed to permit three or four of our clerical personnel to rent rooms or small apartments outside the Mokhovaya.

THE SPASO HOUSE

As I have already indicated, the ambassador was able to move into his residence, generally referred to as the Spaso House, immediately following his arrival in Moscow on March 7, 1934. The house derived its

name from the fact that it faced a short street known as the Spaso-
Peskovskaya, which in turn derived its name from that of a little church
which it served. Although the Soviet government had not been responsive to the needs of other members of the mission for living and working
quarters, it was generous in the matter of a residence for the ambassador.
Few of our ambassadors in the 1930s lived in residences that could compare with the Spaso House in size or magnificence. The house had been
built by a socially ambitious, rich Moscow merchant shortly before the
outbreak of the First World War. The builder, however, was apparently
more interested in producing an impressive rather than a convenient
dwelling. The vestibule, as I recall it, led into a beautiful, long but well-
shaped room with a large fireplace that served as a library. On the left side
of the vestibule were two large doors that opened on the huge ballroom
around which the house was built. This room, with its highly polished
floors, could easily accommodate two or three hundred dancing couples.
From the great dome that roofed the ballroom hung an enormous chan-
delier that was so strong and heavy that the workmen who cleaned it
periodically did not hesitate to climb around in it as though they were
squirrels in a tree.

Lofty galleries like balconies encircled the ballroom. On these galleries opened the rooms on the second floor, including the ambassador's
private offices and a number of sleeping apartments. When balls were
given, spectators lounging in these galleries could look down on the
dancers below.

Off one of the sides of the ballroom was a modest, though beautifully designed, dining room that could seat perhaps 18 persons. Shortly
after the ambassador moved in, however, the Soviet government built to
the rear of the ballroom a long annex opening on the garden that could be
used as a dining room capable of seating 60 guests or as an assembly room
for receptions. Between the ballroom and the annex was another room
that we converted into a small motion-picture theater capable of seating
perhaps 40 persons.

The U.S. government rented the Spaso House partly furnished. The
Soviet government provided antique furnishings for the lower floor, and
the State Department supplied most of the furnishings for the second
floor and for the commodious kitchen which, together with the sleeping
and living rooms for the servants, was in the basement.

The Spaso House continued for many years to serve as the residence
of our ambassadors in Moscow. When the ambassador was out of the
country the representational portions of it were usually placed at the
disposal of the chargé d'affaires for entertainment purposes. Over the
years many distinguished personages have been guests in the residence
and it has been the scene of many historical conferences and decisions.

CHAPTER 33

THE PROBLEMS OF DEBTS AND CLAIMS

IN A PREVIOUS CHAPTER I described some of the proceedings—from the point of view of a member of the Eastern European Division of the Department of State—that resulted in the establishment of diplomatic relations between the United States and the Soviet Union. I touched on the failure of President Roosevelt and of People's Commissar Litvinov to reach an agreement prior to recognition with regard to the problem of debts and claims. When it had become apparent that no agreement in respect to this problem could be reached during the limited period of Litvinov's stay in the United States, the president had found himself facing the choice of postponing recognition or of establishing relations with the Soviet Union prior to a debts and claims settlement, and he chose the latter alternative. The president, in order to soften the impact upon the American public of his failure to achieve an agreement in the matter of debts and claims, had included among the papers made public at the time a joint statement signed by himself and Litvinov to the effect that there "had taken place an exchange of views with regard to methods of settling all outstanding questions of indebtedness and claims that permit us to hope for a speedy and satisfactory solution of these questions which both of our Governments desired to have out of the way as soon as possible."

In addition to this joint statement, another document relating to debts and claims was signed by the president and the commissar prior to the establishment of relations. On November 15, the day preceding recognition, the debts and claims problem was discussed during the course of a conference in which President Roosevelt, Litvinov, Morgenthau (at that time acting secretary of treasury), and Bullitt participated. The participants in that conference came to the conclusion that this problem was so complex that it was not subject to speedy solution. Since considerable progress seemed to have been made in the direction of a solution, the president concurred in a suggestion that a memorandum to be signed by himself and Litvinov be drawn up in the form of a "gentlemen's agreement" that would record the understandings thus far attained and could be used as the basis for further negotiations. Litvinov expressed his willingness to sign such a memorandum provided that it meet his approval and that its existence remain secret. The president also was of the opinion that it would be preferable, at least for the time being, that the document be kept confidential.

It is my understanding, based on conversations that I had with Ambassador Bullitt a number of years later, that a memorandum agreeable to all four participants was hastily drawn up on the spot and that although Bullitt believed that as drafted it described fairly accurately the status of the negotiations, he had urged that in view of its possible future importance it be reviewed before signature by Judge Moore and other competent and experienced officers in the Department of State, including Green Hackworth, the legal adviser. Morgenthau, according to Bullitt, took the position, however, that since the document was only a "gentlemen's agreement" there was no need for its submission to bureaucrats in the Department of State. Since Litvinov was prepared to sign the memorandum as drafted, and since time was of the essence, the president was inclined to Morgenthau's point of view and both he and Litvinov signed it immediately.

This memorandum, which was not published until many years later, read as follows.

Memorandum by President Roosevelt and the
Soviet Commissar for Foreign Affairs (Litvinov)

Washington, November 15, 1933 - 2:45 p.m.

Mr. Litvinov, at a meeting with the President, the Acting Secretary of the Treasury, and Mr. Bullitt, made a "gentlemen's agreement" with the President that over and above all claims of the Soviet Government and its nationals against the Government of the United States and its nationals, the Soviet Government will pay to the Government of the United States on account of the Kerensky debt or otherwise the sum to be not less than $75,000,000 in the form of a percentage above the ordinary rate of interest on a loan to be granted to it by the Government of the United States or its nationals, all other claims of the Government of the United States or its nationals and of the Government of the Union of Soviet Socialist Republics or its nationals to be regarded as eliminated.

The President said that he believed confidently that he could persuade Congress to accept a sum of $150,000,000, but that he feared that Congress would not accept any smaller sum. Mr. Litvinov then said he could not on his own authority accept any such minimum, as his Government had already stated that it considered this sum excessive.

Mr. Litvinov said that he had entire confidence in the fair-mindedness of the President and felt sure that when the President had looked into the facts he would not feel that a sum greater than $75,000,000 was justified. So far as he personally was concerned, and without making any commitment, he would be inclined to advise his Government to accept $100,000,000 if the President should still consider such a sum fair.

Mr. Litvinov agreed to remain in Washington after resumption of relations and to discuss with Mr. Morgenthau and Mr. Bullitt the exact sum between the limits of $75,000,000 and $150,000,000 to be paid by the Soviet Government.

M[axim] L[itvinov]   F[ranklin] D. R[oosevelt]

Although during the subsequent confidential negotiations, which took place both in Moscow and in Washington while I was on duty in the embassy in Moscow, references were made from time to time to a memorandum of some kind, I was not aware of the circumstances in which it had been drawn up or of its contents until it was published in the 1950s.

A casual glance at the memorandum might give the impression that it created a basis for an agreement on the subject of debts and claims and that all that remained to be done to achieve a solution of the debts and claims problem would be working out a few details. When, however, in March 1934 Bullitt entered into conversations in Moscow with Litvinov regarding these details it became immediately clear that the two parties were still far apart.

The ambassador encountered his first shock during the course of a conversation on March 14 with Litvinov. In a telegram to the State Department dated March 15, 1934, the ambassador described a portion of this conversation as follows:

Litvinov took the surprising position that he had not agreed to pay any extra interest on any credits whatever but only on loans to be given to his Government to be used for purchases anywhere. I combated this assertion as vigorously as possible reminding him that we had long discussions of the possibility of using frozen American credits in Germany and emphasizing the fact that the President had never had any idea of a direct loan to the Soviet Government but only of a loan in the form of credits. I pointed out that no loan could possibly be made by the United States to any foreign country at the present time and that we had assumed that he was fully aware that a loan in the form of credits was the only possibility. He agreed that he had known that it would be extraordinarily difficult for the Government of the United States to make any loan to the Soviet Union but insisted that he had thought the President would find a way to do so. I feel sure that the President never envisaged a loan in any other form than that of a commercial credit to be expended in the United States. An instruction from the President stating his point of view in regard to this matter with vigor would be of great assistance to me in subsequent conversations with Litvinov.

In its reply to the ambassador's telegram, the department stated in a telegram on March 17, 1934: "You may inform Litvinoff that the President expressly states that he has never had any thought of a direct loan to the Soviet Government and that there is not the slightest possibility of such a loan being made."

In a subsequent conversation that the ambassador had with Litvinov on March 21 Litvinov softened somewhat with regard to the use that the Soviet government might make of the loan it was demanding. He indicated that it might agree to spend the entire proceeds of the loan in the United States. In view of the importance of this second conversation I quote excerpts from the ambassador's telegram of March 21 in which he reported it:

Litvinov, in another long conversation at the hospital today, reiterated his unwillingness to settle on the basis of credits saying "We shall never accept credits in place of a loan. We might agree to spend the entire proceeds of a loan in the United States but what we insist upon is a straight loan like the one the Swedish Government has just granted us so that we can pay for all our American purchases in cash."

I replied that the message I had received from the President was decisive, that no loan could or would be granted. I added that if his position should be unalterable I would wish to cable the President immediately so that the Export-Import Bank might be liquidated at once and all thought of trade with the Soviet Union abandoned. I then expressed the hope that in the absence of trade our relations might nevertheless remain friendly. Litvinov answered: "We could remain on friendly terms with the United States without mutual trade but I fear that the United States would not remain on friendly terms with the Soviet Union."

During the numerous subsequent conversations on the subject of debts and claims that took place both in Moscow and Washington, the U.S. negotiators adhered firmly to the position that the president in signing the memorandum of November 15, 1933, had in mind the granting of a loan to the Soviet Union in the form of controlled credits. They insisted that, during the discussions in Washington between the president and Litvinov, the terms "loans" and "credits" had been used synonymously and that in their opinion it had been clearly understood by all that such credits as might be granted would have certain strings attached to them. They indicated that they could not understand how Litvinov could possibly have derived the impression that the United States was considering the granting of an open direct loan to the Soviet Union.

Litvinov argued—sometimes vehemently—that the memorandum in referring to "interest on a loan" reflected his understanding and that the United States by attempting to interpret the word "loan" as controlled credits was backing out of the "gentlemen's agreement."

I am personally convinced that Litvinov was quite aware when he signed the memorandum that any "loan" that might be extended to the Soviet Union was to be in the form of credits to be controlled by the Export-Import Bank, which was being set up at the time for that purpose. My conviction is based on conversations of which I was cognizant that were taking place in the Department of State at the time, including exchanges between the Division of Eastern European Affairs, Hackworth, and Judge Moore, who were keeping in almost hourly touch with the development of negotiations. I am also confident that if Judge Moore and Hackworth had had an opportunity to review this memorandum they would have changed the word "loan" to "credits" in order to avoid any misunderstanding.

There is no doubt in my mind that Litvinov realized when he signed the memorandum that it would be extremely difficult, if not impossible, for the president to persuade Congress to approve an open loan to the Soviet Union. He was, in my opinion, quite aware that the American people were not in a mood to make loans to foreign governments in view of the fact that so many foreign governments were at the time almost cynically defaulting on their debts to the United States. I believe that it was his intention to make use of the imprecise wording of the hastily drafted memorandum in order to attempt to obtain sweeping concessions from the United States in the matter of debts and claims or in placing upon the United States the blame for the failure of a settlement in case the United States would not be prepared to come to an agreement that would be acceptable to the Soviet Union.

Although the issue of a loan versus credits was one of the most important stumbling blocks to reaching an agreement, other issues developed during the negotiations on debts and claims. There were, for instance, wide differences regarding the amount and the terms of the loan or credits to be granted, the amount of the lump sum to be paid by the Soviet Union, the rates of interest, and the wording of the drafts under consideration.

At times the Soviet negotiators indicated that in lieu of a loan they might be willing, if the United States would make specific concessions, to accept financial credits with no strings attached. The U.S. negotiators, however, were firm in their insistence that such credits as might be granted should be under the control of the Export-Import Bank.

During the course of the exchanges, Litvinov and other negotiators repeatedly expressed concern lest payments by the Soviet Union to the United States would cause other creditors, such as Great Britain and France, to revive their claims against the Soviet Union. In his talks with Ambassador Bullitt, Litvinov took the position he was unwilling to enter into any agreement with the United States that might give other creditor countries grounds to complain that the United States was being given preferred treatment.

When it began to become clear that no agreement regarding debts and claims was likely to be reached, Litvinov tried to play down the importance of the debts and claims problem. On June 16, 1934, for instance, he told Ambassador Bullitt during a heated conversation that he and "his Government were entirely ready to let the matter drop immediately and permanently, that the Soviet Government had not asked for any such agreement but had acceded to such an agreement at the request of the President, that the agreement was clear and the Soviet Government would not change its mind." When the ambassador indicated that he felt that "this attitude on his part might terminate any possibility of close collaboration between our two nations," Litvinov replied: "I do not take the matter so tragically. No nation today pays its debts. Great Britain has defaulted. Germany is defaulting. And no one will be able to make propaganda against the Soviet Union if we do not pay one dollar on a debt we did not contract."

Ambassador Bullitt's last conversation on October 10, 1934, on the subject of debts and claims was most unsatisfactory. It took place on the eve of the ambassador's departure to the United States for consultation with the president and the State Department. The depth of the ambassador's disappointment at his failure to reach an agreement with Litvinov is reflected in the former's telegram to the department reporting the conversation. The latter part of the telegram reads as follows:

> I called his attention to the fact that a loan was impossible, had always been impossible, and always would be impossible. He replied that the Soviet Government had no desire even for a loan except at a very low interest rate; that it desired to let the entire matter drop; that if the question of payment of debts and claims were settled in any way whatsoever he would have grave difficulties in his relations with England and France. I told him that it was indeed curious that he was in the habit of saying to me that there were no difficulties in the matter of debts and claims except his relations with England and France; that there were no difficulties in the question of our consular districts except his relations with Japan and Germany; that there were no difficulties with regard to the use of our airplane(s) except his relations with Germany, Poland, and England. I told him that I considered it deplorable that he should allow the relations between our two countries to be controlled by his relations with those countries which he considered to be his enemies.
>
> He finally said that he would make a final proposal through Troyanovsky and then would refuse to discuss the matter further. I replied that I deeply regretted that he seemed determined to kill all possibility of really close and friendly relations between our countries.
>
> I had the impression today that I was talking with the traditional bazaar bargainer of the Near East.

The following excerpts from a memorandum dated July 19, 1934, from Assistant Secretary Judge Moore to Assistant Secretary Sayre, reflect the impact that the attitude displayed by Litvinov during the course of the loan negotiations was making on the members of the Department of State who were backing Ambassador Bullitt:

> As you know, Mr. Litvinov left here with everything undetermined except recognition. When he and Mr. Bullitt got together in Moscow, he insisted that our Government should make a straight cash loan to the Soviet, to be expended as it might think proper, or as an alternative a straight, uncontrolled credit, enabling it to make purchases in this country at will, with all of the possible discrimination and confusion certain to result. Should either thing be done, it will of course be within the power of the Soviet to make use of the cash or credit for the purchase of war materials, or to place manufacturers of the same product in bitter competition with each other. Considerations of that character, coupled with the fact that the Export-Import Bank was organized for the very purpose

of controlling such credit as might be granted, led the President to say that a loan in either form, whether in cash or by pledging the credit of our Government, without the Government having any control, is unthinkable...

Litvinov now is really trying to shelve the debt question as he has done with England and other countries. One of his reasons for this is that he fears that other countries will contend that a payment to the United States is a recognition of the Kerensky debt, and that they should have similar treatment. But as you will notice on reading the paper marked "A," no mention is made of the Kerensky debt, it being stated generally that whatever amount is agreed on shall cover the balance due this country and its nationals, after taking into account all of our claims and all of the counter claims. I may tell you that in a conversation with Troyanovsky, at which I was present, Mr. Roosevelt clearly stated to him that in the event of an agreement Congress would be asked to allow nearly all of the amount received to be applied to the private claims instead of the Kerensky debt.

The formal breakdown of the debts and claims negotiations took place at a conference in Secretary Hull's office on January 31, 1935. Present, in addition to the secretary, were Ambassador Troyanovsky; Judge Moore, assistant secretary of state; Ambassador Bullitt; and Robert F. Kelley, chief of the Division of Eastern European Affairs. Since what occurred at that conference had a profound and protracted effect upon the state of relations between the United States and the Soviet Union, I quote below excerpts from a memorandum of the conference prepared by Kelley:

> After some hesitation the Soviet Ambassador, in response to an inquiry by the Secretary, stated that he had discussed at length with officials of his Government in Moscow the proposal made by the United States with regard to the settlement of the question of debts and claims... it was very hard for his Government to deal with this matter, since acceptance of the American proposal would make the relations of his country with other countries more difficult. Furthermore, he declared that other countries were now offering his Government much better terms than those contained in the American proposal. His Government, while desiring to have friendly relations with the United States, could not go beyond the proposal which he had presented to the Department prior to his departure.
>
> The Secretary stated that he was greatly disappointed at the attitude of the Soviet Government. With regard to the Ambassador's statement to the effect that a settlement of the question of debts and claims between the United States and the Soviet Union could not be reached because it

would make difficult the relations of the Soviet Union with other countries . . . that Mr. Litvinoff had not mentioned this consideration when he was in Washington. If he had . . . possibly there might have been a different story . . . he had sought in every way to cooperate with the Soviet Government, but had not met with much response. A settlement of the outstanding questions would have furnished a basis for cooperation in important matters of world significance. If the two Governments, however, could not deal in a statesmanlike way with what, after all, was a minor problem, there was little expectation of their being able to cooperate in larger matters.

The Ambassador stated that there was a big difference with regard to only one point. While there had been no agreement with regard to the amount of the indebtedness or the interest rates, the differences were not great. Furthermore, his Government was prepared to take half of the proposed financial assistance in the form suggested by the United States. But his Government could not but insist on the extension to it of a $100,000,000 loan.

The Secretary said again that he was profoundly disappointed. The United States had gone to the limit to which it could go and had made considerable concessions. In view of the position taken by the Soviet Government the negotiations would seem to have come to an end.

The Ambassador agreed and said he had no proposals to make.

Following the collapse of the debts and claims negotiations, the State Department took a number of steps for the purpose (1) of emphasizing for the benefit of the Soviet government the seriousness with which it viewed the failure of the Soviet Union to accept what it regarded as its generous proposals for solving the debts and claims problem, and (2) of apprising the American and the world public of its disillusionment with the Soviet Union.

One such step was the issuance of a statement to the press by Secretary Hull on the evening of January 31, 1935, announcing the breakdown of the negotiations. In this statement the secretary, after outlining his last proposal to the Soviet Union, said:

> We hoped confidently that this proposal would prove entirely acceptable to the Soviet Government and are deeply disappointed at its rejection. In view of the present attitude of the Soviet Government, I feel that we can not encourage the hope that any agreement is now possible. I say this regretfully because I am in sympathy with the desire of American manufacturers and agricultural producers to find a market for their goods in the Soviet Union and with the American claimants whose property has been confiscated. There seems to be scarcely any reason to doubt that the negotiations which seemed so promising at the start must now be regarded as having come to an end.

It will be for the Board of Trustees of the Export-Import Bank to determine whether or not there is any good reason for continuing the existence of the Bank.

A statement to the press a week later, on February 6, announced the withdrawal of the naval and air corps attachés from Moscow, the abolition of the consulate general, and the reduction in the personnel of the embassy in Moscow.

The tone of the secretary's press statement of January 31 drew a prompt reply from the Soviet government. On February 1 the Soviet press, after publishing the secretary's statement in full, appended a statement by Litvinov that read as follows:

The basic principles of the agreement for the liquidation of the mutual Soviet–American monetary claims were worked out during my personal negotiations with President Roosevelt about a year ago. These principles were in full accord with the reiterated statements of the Soviet Government of its readiness to discuss the question of old debts only provided its counter claims were recognized and a monetary loan was advanced to it. I therefore left Washington with the full confidence that the further negotiations would affect only the details of the agreement and would not therefore present any difficulties.

To our regret in the subsequent negotiations begun by Mr. Bullitt, American Ambassador, with me in Moscow and continued subsequently by the State Department with Comrade Troyanovski, one of the basic factors of the agreement reached in Washington, namely, that of a loan, was placed in doubt. The Soviet side in its proposals strictly remained within the confines of this agreement, making concessions to a point beyond which the whole of the Washington agreement would begin to be revised. We refused to enter this path which might have led to the complete annulment of the results secured in Washington and the necessity of new negotiations on the principles of the agreement. We naturally regret very much that the negotiations have so far failed to bring the desired results but, nevertheless, believe that this fact must not affect the relations between the two states including trade relations, the development of which has been rather hampered by the negotiations conducted up to this time. Besides the Soviet Union and the United States as other peace loving states are confronted with more serious general objects for which it is possible to work without injuring the material claims of this or that state. The difficulty of solving the problem of mutual monetary claims between states has now become a general phenomenon of international life but it does not interfere with international cooperation in the development of trade relations or in the preservation of peace.

In a conversation on February 5, 1935, with John Wiley, who had been left in charge of the Moscow embassy during Bullitt's absence,

Litvinov insisted that the breakdown was due to the failure of the United States to live up to the agreement that had been made while he was in Washington. Wiley's telegram to the State Department reporting this conversation read in part as follows:

> Litvinov said that he had long since accepted the rupture of the negotiations with the United States for a settlement of debts and claims as a foregone conclusion. That was why he had consented to have the negotiations transferred to Washington. He claimed that when the American Government decided to abandon the "letter of the agreement," namely a loan, he had "capitulated" just as far as possible. However, it was not possible for the Soviet Government to accept a settlement which involved the extension of credits to the manufacturers instead of direct to Soviet agencies. He added that he thought it was a good thing for the negotiations to be "put on ice" for a while. Perhaps at some later date they could be resumed with better chances of success. I asked what inspired his optimism. He replied that political conditions would change and might greatly influence matters. I answered that the possibility of any such political change in the United States was indeed remote. He explained he had Europe in mind; not the United States. He did not clarify his cryptic allusion.

The Soviet authorities, in my opinion, were not entirely unhappy at the prospect of the withdrawal of the naval and air corps attachés, the abolition of the consulate general, and a reduction in the staff of the embassy, although they were annoyed at the context in which these changes had been announced. Lieutenant White, assistant military air corps attaché, and Captain Nimmer, the naval attaché, were *persona grata* and were as popular as members of the armed forces of a capitalist state could be among the Soviet officers with whom they had come in contact. Voroshilov, the commissar for defense, took occasion in bidding them farewell to express regret at their impending departure. Nevertheless, I had the impression that the closing of the offices of White and Nimmer was welcomed by the Soviet government because it disposed of two vexatious problems: (1) the assurances given to Ambassador Bullitt when he had visited Moscow in December 1933 that our air corps attaché could bring a plane with him into the Soviet Union and could pilot the ambassador freely around the country in it; and (2) the promise made to Ambassador Bullitt that he could include on the staff of the naval attaché a number of marines to be used for internal guard and messenger duty.

When the air corps attaché's plane arrived in Moscow, several other chiefs of diplomatic missions in Moscow, not wishing to be outdone by Ambassador Bullitt, had asked that their missions also be allowed to bring in planes. A number of ambassadors and ministers had indicated that it might also be a good idea for them to use as internal guards and messengers the armed forces of the country that they represented.

The Soviet authorities responsible for preventing foreigners from learning what was going on in the country were outraged at the spectacle of a foreign diplomat flying around the country in a foreign plane piloted by a foreign attaché, and also at the thought that members of foreign armed forces were being admitted into the country to serve as guards in a foreign embassy. Narkomindel, therefore, under pressure from these authorities, had refused to permit other diplomatic missions from enjoying the privileges that high Soviet officials, in moments of exuberance at having obtained recognition from the United States on such favorable terms, had granted to the Americans. As a result, some members of the diplomatic corps had been acidly accusing the Soviet government of discriminating against them in favor of the Americans.

In June 1934 White's plane, while landing on the Leningrad airfield, had capsized in a swampy area and had been wrecked. Narkomindel, again under pressure from the internal authorities, had refused to permit the embassy to import another plane. Although Ambassador Bullitt had made a series of protests at what he regarded as the failure of the Soviet authorities to live up to the assurances that had been given him, Narkomindel had remained adamant.

The Soviet officials considered that Ambassador Bullitt would no longer have grounds for complaint since from their point of view the closing of the air corps attaché's office had released them from their promise to permit him to fly in the air corps attaché's plane. The were also pleased because the withdrawal of the naval attaché and his staff relieved them of the embarrassing presence of the marines.

The closing of the consulate general and the transfer of its functions to the consular section and other sections of the embassy also had their brighter sides so far as the Soviet authorities were concerned. The disappearance of the consulate general as an entity relieved both the Soviet government and the embassy of a number of complicated problems, in particular, those relating to the status of the consulate general and the privileges and exemptions to be accorded American personnel on duty in it.

Nor were the Soviet authorities depressed at the prospect of a reduction in the number of personnel on duty in the embassy. During the period of this, my first tour of duty in Moscow, they had had a tendency to regard all foreign diplomatic missions as nuisances to be tolerated since they were concomitants of the maintenance of diplomatic relations with capitalistic governments. On various occasions during those years, members of Narkomindel made a point of asking me why our embassy had so large a staff. "How," they would ask, "can you keep so many people busy?" "What are they doing?" "Is it necessary to have so large a staff merely for the purpose of maintaining diplomatic relations with us?"

If Narkomindel had had any hopes that following Mr. Hull's announcement the staff of the embassy would be sharply reduced, it was doomed to disappointment. A study by the State Department and the embassy of the tasks that Washington expected the embassy to perform and of the number of persons available for carrying them out, made it clear that any meaningful reduction would not be in the interest of the United States. The actual reduction, therefore, was limited to the departure of White and Nimmer and members of their staffs.

The collapse of our debts and claims negotiations might well be regarded as the formal termination of what sometimes has been referred to as the "Soviet-American honeymoon." Many Americans—including certain types of liberals, leading members of the academic world, other self-styled intellectuals, U.S. businessmen who had hoped to profit from an increase in Soviet-American trade, and a number of our foreign policymakers—were deeply disappointed at the breakdown. They had been hoping that the United States and the Soviet Union would be able to come to a series of agreements that would enable the two countries to collaborate in the future to their own mutual benefit and in the interest of world peace. The tone of the exchanges that accompanied the breakdown came, therefore, as a shock to these optimists. The acerbity of the exchanges did not, however, surprise the members of the State Department working on Soviet affairs or the staff of the embassy, who had known for a considerable length of time that the honeymoon was already in an eclipse. For almost a year they had been observing the growing tendency of the Soviet Union, regardless of promises that had been made either in writing or orally to U.S. officials prior to or immediately after the establishment of diplomatic relations, to accord the United States treatment no better than that which, in keeping with its principles, it had been giving other nations of the capitalistic world. Within three weeks after the opening of the embassy in Moscow in March 1934, Ambassador Bullitt had begun to sense that the Soviet government was reluctant to live up to the commitments made at the time of the establishment of diplomatic relations or shortly thereafter. As early as March 28, 1934, the ambassador wrote a dispatch on the subject to the secretary of state, which began with the following sentence: "I have the honor to report in regard to several instances in which the Soviet Government does not seem disposed to carry out understandings between it and the Government of the United States." In the same dispatch he stressed the failure of the Soviet government to abide by promises that had been made orally. In this connection he said:

> These three extraordinary incidents indicate clearly that the "misunderstandings" have been produced not so much by bad faith as by inefficiency. The members of the Soviet Government seem disposed to make promises without taking into consideration all the factors involved. There are several organs in the Soviet Government of negative authority which are in a position to prevent the carrying out of promises made by individual members of the commissariats.
>
> Whatever the source of these "misunderstandings," it seems to me that in every case understandings with the Soviet Government or representatives thereof should be made in writing or should be confirmed at a later date by a written document.

I agreed at the time with the ambassador that in making some of the promises that later were not lived up to, the Soviet authorities were not necessarily acting in bad faith. They were merely making commitments without taking into consideration all the factors involved. When they discovered later that the honoring of a commitment thus given by them either orally or in writing would represent a departure from principles that the Soviet government considered important, they did not hesitate to advance an excuse or a series of excuses for not living up to it. I am convinced, however, that Litvinov, in giving a number of commitments during the negotiations leading to recognition, knew quite well that his government would not live up to them and that this knowledge did not unduly disturb him since he had confidence in his ability to disembarrass both his government and himself when later faced with charges of violation of pledges.

During the interim between the breakdown of the debts and claims negotiations and the outbreak of World War II in 1939, the problem of debts and claims was brought up from time to time either by the Soviet or U.S. officials during discussions of Soviet-American relations. Formal negotiations, however, with regard to this problem have never been reopened. As a corollary the U.S. government for many years refused to approve loans or financial credits to the Soviet government or any of its agencies.

CHAPTER 34

THE PROBLEM OF MOSCOW'S INTERFERENCE IN THE INTERNAL AFFAIRS OF THE UNITED STATES

THE VIOLATION OF THE PLEDGE made by Litvinov to President Roosevelt on November 16, 1933, relating to Soviet interference in the internal affairs of the United States, did more, in my opinion, to damage relations between the United States and the Soviet Union during the period 1934–1938 than any other single factor. It will be recalled that although this pledge did not mention the Communist International by name, its provisions were of such a character that any reasonable person acquainted with the inter-locking relationships between the Communist International and the Soviet government and the activities and avowed aims of the Communist International could not fail to understand that it applied to that organization. In paragraph 4, for instance, the Soviet government stated that it would be its fixed policy

> Not to permit the formation or residence on its territory of any organiza-tion or group—and to prevent the activity on its territory of any organiza-tion or group—which has as an aim the overthrow or the preparation for the overthrow of, or the bringing about by force of a change in the political or social order of the whole or any part of the United States, its territories or possessions.

On October 5, 1934, as he was preparing to depart for Washington for consulation, the ambassador, troubled at the announcement that a congress of the Communist International was scheduled to be held in Moscow in January 1935, told Litvinov that if during such a congress "there should be attacks on the Government of the United States or indications that the Communist movement in the United States was being directed by Moscow the most serious consequences might result." Litvinov's answer was that he did not even know that such a congress was to meet and was not aware of any activities of this nature.

Several days later during a heated conversation between the ambassador and Litvinov on the subject of debts and claims, the ambassador again referred to the problem of the Communist International. He described as follows this exchange in a telegram dated October 10, 1934, to the State Department:

> I went on to say that if a negative attitude with regard to a settlement of debts and claims should be followed by activities of the Comintern directed against the United States our relations would become so difficult as to be almost impossible. He replied, "No nation ever starts talking about the activities of the Comintern unless it wishes to have as bad relations as possible with us. The activities of the Comintern are merely an excuse for breaking diplomatic relations." I told him that the people of the United States as well as the Government of the United States were extremely sensitive about any interference in our internal affairs and that he might expect the most drastic reaction in case the Comintern congress should take place and there should be evidence of interference in the internal affairs of the United States.

These two conversations were a prelude to numerous discussions on the subject of the Communist International during the ensuing eleven months in Moscow between the ambassador and Soviet officials, including Litvinov; between Wiley and Soviet officials; and in Washington between members of the Department of State and members of the Soviet embassy.

On the U.S. side there were strenuous efforts to impress on the Soviet government the seriousness with which the government and people of the United States would view the holding of a congress of the Communist International in Moscow, particularly if it would be attended by representatives of the American Communist Party and would engage in discussions of the activities of the American Communist Party in the United States and of programs to be carried out in foreign countries, including the United States. It was the hope of the ambassador and the U.S. government that such a congress would not be held and that if it should meet, discussions of the work of the American section of the Communist International would not take place.

During these conversations the Soviet officials with whom the ambassador talked adopted varying attitudes. Sometimes they were evasive, sometimes they pretended ignorance of Communist International plans for a congress, and sometimes they displayed irritation.

The postponement of the congress until the latter part of the summer of 1935 strengthened the hope of Ambassador Bullitt and members of the Department of State that it would not meet at all. These hopes were not realized. In spite of the vehement protests and warnings of Ambassador Bullitt, the Seventh All-World Congress of the Communist International met in Moscow on July 25 and continued in session until August 20. Representatives of the American Communist Party played a prominent role during the course of the proceedings.

Ambassador Bullitt was incensed that in spite of the solemn pledge given by Litvinov to the president, in spite of his warnings to Litvinov and his pleas to other Soviet leaders, the congress had been held, had been attended by leaders of the American Communist Party, had discussed revolutionary activities in the United States, and had even made suggestions regarding tactics to be employed in overthrowing the government of the United States. On the evening of August 20 the ambassador called a conference in his residence of a number of the Foreign Service officers who were on duty in the embassy at the time. He said that he wanted to obtain our individual and collective views regarding the actions that he should recommend the U.S. government take in the face of the violation by the Soviet government of its pledge not to interfere in the internal affairs of the United States.

After advancing arguments of his own for and against the severance of diplomatic relations, the ambassador asked each of the officers present to state whether in his opinion it would be in the interest of the United States to break relations. Of the five or six officers present, only one, a junior officer who took pride in being an activist, spoke in favor of breaking relations. The ambassador then asked each officer to state what actions in his opinion, short of severing relations, the U.S. government might appropriately take for the purpose of letting the Soviet government understand that it could not expect to have friendly cooperative relations with the United States so long as it continued systematically to interfere in the internal affairs of the United States.

The discussions that ensued lasted until after midnight. According to my recollection Wiley and I were inclined toward moderation. Wiley, tempered by many years of experience in the diplomatic service, had developed an attitude of philosophic calm in approaching the problems of the moment. I suppose that one of the reasons that caused me to counsel restraint that evening was that I was not at all surprised or shocked at the line the Soviet government was following. As a result of my years of study of Soviet attitudes and policies, it had seemed almost inevitable to me that Moscow would not abandon its international revolutionary activities merely for the sake of good Soviet-American relations. Furthermore, I could not think of any action that we could take other than that of making strong protests and of publicly denouncing the Soviet government for the breaking of its pledges that would not eventually result in injury to the United States as well as to the Soviet Union. Nevertheless, I had deep sympathy for the ambassador. He had favored the establishment of relations with the Soviet Union; he had worked hard in Washington during the period of the Roosevelt-Litvinov negotiations in order to find formulas that, if lived up to, would have rendered possible good relations between the United States and the Soviet Union; he had given of himself unsparingly as ambassador in trying to prevail upon the Soviet leaders to carry out the commitments that they had given. In spite of his efforts he had now found that the Soviets were pursuing the policies that the opponents of recognition had insisted they would follow.

I have known some ambassadors who, when faced with situations of this kind, would have attempted to cover up the fact that they had been deceived by those in whom they had placed trust; they would have tried to minimize the importance of the activities in which the Soviet government was engaging; they would have taken the position that, after all, during the course of the Comintern congress the participants had interfered more vigorously in the internal affairs of other countries with which they maintained relations than in those of the United States. Ambassador Bullitt, however, was too honest to try to hide from the president and the State Department his belief that the decision the Kremlin had made to continue to foment revolutions in other countries, including the United States, had smashed all hopes for sincerely friendly relations between the United States and the Soviet Union.

The ambassador spent most of the following day studying the notes made during our discussions and dictating and redictating one of the longest telegrams that he had sent to the State Department from Moscow. Some of the suggestions contained therein were the product of the conference of the preceding night. Others represented the personal views of the ambassador himself. I quote a few excerpts:

> The Congress of the Communist International which closed last night was a flagrant violation of Litvinov's pledge to the President.
> The mere holding of the Congress in Moscow under control of the Soviet Government would have constituted a technical breach of Litvinov's pledge. The violation, however, was far more serious.

The participation of American delegates in the Congress, the inclusion of Browder and Foster in the Presidium, together with Stalin, Manuilski and Pyatnitski, the inclusion of Americans in other committees of the Congress, the numerous speeches by American delegates in which Stalin was referred to as their leader, the numerous references to the United States in other addresses and the election at the last session of the Americans Browder, Green and Foster to the Executive Committee of the Communist International, place beyond the question of fact that the Government of the United States would be juridically and morally justified in severing diplomatic relations with the Soviet Government.

In mitigation the Soviet Government can plead only that attacks on the Government of the United States were less severe than attacks on other governments and that no direct attacks were made personally by members of the Soviet Government. There is, of course, no doubt concerning it, also no proof that the entire course of the Congress was dictated in advance by Stalin.

To break relations would satisfy the indignation we all feel and would be juridically correct; but in my opinion this question should be decided neither on emotional nor juridical grounds but on the basis of a cold appraisal of the wisest course to pursue to defend the American people from the efforts of the Soviet Government to produce bloody revolution in the United States.

If we should sever relations now on the ground that the Soviet Government has broken its pledged word to us and cannot be trusted, resumption of relations would be inordinately difficult and we should almost certainly not be able to reestablish relations with the Soviet Union during this decade. In this decade the Soviet Union either will be the center of attack from Europe and the Far East or will develop rapidly into one of the greatest physical forces in the world. In either event an official observation post of the United States Government in Moscow will be desirable, not only to gather information on conditions in the Soviet Union and relations of the Soviet Union with the nations of Europe and the Far East, but also, and more important, to inform the Government of the United States with regard to activities of the Soviet Government directed against the lives and interests of American citizens.

American diplomatic representatives in the Soviet Union are harassed and restricted; but there is no way in which a sense of reality with regard to the Soviet Union may be obtained and preserved except by the painful process of living within its confines. As the Soviet Union grows in strength it will grow in arrogance and aggressiveness and the maintenance of an organization in Moscow to measure and report on the increasingly noxious activities and breach of faith of the Soviet Union seems definitely in the interest of the American people.

Moreover, unless we should expel from the United States along with the Soviet diplomatic representatives all Soviet citizens including officials of such organizations as Amtorg and Intourist, the Soviet Government for all practical purposes would still have representation in the United States, while the Government of the United States would be without representation in the Soviet Union...

I believe that we should not now break relations with the Soviet Government.

I believe that we should not make a written protest to the Soviet Government. Such a protest would produce only a violent and insulting reply and a fruitless exchange of notes.

I believe that an oral protest to Troyanovsky and the Commissariat for Foreign Affairs in Moscow would be inadequate to meet the menace set forth in the new "united front" tactics of the Soviet Government and its servant the Comintern.

I believe that we should employ this occasion to make clear to the American people the aims of the Soviet Government which lie behind the mask labeled "united front against Fascism and war."

I believe we should revoke the exequaturs of all Soviet Consuls in New York and San Francisco, leaving only the consular section in the Soviet Embassy at Washington.

I believe that we should restrict to a minimum the granting of American visas to Soviet citizens...

I venture to suggest that henceforth the law excluding Communists from the United States should be applied rigidly and that you should instruct all American Missions to refuse visas to Soviet citizens unless they present entirely satisfactory evidence proving that they are not and have never been members of the Communist Party or Communist International and are not candidates for admission to the Communist Party or Communist International and are not members of the Profintern [Red International of Labor Unions].

The two steps canceling the exequaturs of the Soviet Consuls in the United States and rigorously enforcing the law with regard to visas to Communists should become an irreducible minimum...

The question of reducing to a skeleton the staff of the Embassy in Moscow is one which depends entirely on the amount of work that the Department of State and other departments of our Government intend to demand of this mission. I expect to return to the United States as usual to spend Christmas with my daughter and I feel that extremely radical reduction of the Embassy staff should be the subject of discussions at that time.

In the same telegram the ambassador also suggested that the president himself make a speech in which he would inform the American people of the failure of the Soviet government to live up to the Litvinov pledge, of the various ways in which Moscow through the American Communists was attempting to create unrest in the United States and to overthrow our government, and of the reasons responsible for the steps that the United States was taking in order to counter these subversive activities.

The president and the Department of State were apparently unwilling to take measures as strong as those recommended by the ambassador. The Soviet consular offices in the United States were not closed, the granting of U.S. visas to Soviet citizens was not reduced to a minimum, and the president did not make a speech. Instead, the State Department in a telegram dated August 23, 1935, sent the ambassador a draft of a note for delivery by him to the Soviet government protesting strongly "against the flagrant violation of the pledge given by the Government of the Union of Soviet Socialist Republics on November 16, 1933, with respect to noninterference in the internal affairs of the United States." The note, which was handed by the ambassador on August 25 to Nikolay Krestinsky, the acting commissar for foreign affairs in Litvinov's absence, closed with the following paragraph:

> The Government of the United States would be lacking in candor if it failed to state frankly that it anticipates the most serious consequences if the Government of the Union of Soviet Socialist Republics is unwilling, or unable, to take appropriate measures to prevent further acts in disregard of the solemn pledge given by it to the Government of the United States.

Krestinsky gave the ambassador the Soviet note of reply on August 27. The reply was relatively brief. This note stated that the Soviet government regarded "with the greatest respect all obligations which it has taken upon itself, including naturally the mutual obligation concerning noninterference in internal affairs, provided for in the exchange of notes of November 16, 1933, and discussed in detail in the conversations between the President of the United States of America, Mr. Roosevelt, and the People's Commissar, Litvinov," and added that "there are no facts of any kind in your note of August 25 which could be considered as a violation on the part of the Soviet Government of its obligations."

It should be noted that the inclusion of the phrase "and discussed in detail in the conversations between the President of the United States...and the People's Commissar, Litvinov," contained a hint that there might have been oral exchanges between the president and the commissar that the Soviet government regarded as part and parcel of the agreement.

The Soviet note did not attempt to explain why the proceedings of the Seventh All-World Congress of the Communist International did not in its opinion represent a violation of Litvinov's pledge. It did state, however, that: "It is certainly not new to the Government of the United States that the Government of the Union of Soviet Socialist Republics cannot take upon itself and has not taken upon itself obligations of any kind with regard to the Communist International."

Upon receipt of the Soviet note, Secretary Hull made public a strong statement setting forth in detail the reasons why the United States considered that the Soviet government was violating the pledge not to interfere in the internal affairs of the United States. In conclusion, the secretary stated that:

> If the Soviet Government pursues a policy of permitting activities on its territory involving interference in the internal affairs of the United States, instead of "preventing" such activities as its written pledge provides, the friendly and official relations between the two countries cannot but be seriously impaired. Whether such relations between these two great countries are thus unfortunately to be impaired and cooperative opportunities for vast good to be destroyed, will depend upon the attitude and action of the Soviet Government.

There were no more official exchanges between the two governments at the time on the subject of interference in internal affairs. The exchanges that had taken place served merely to clarify the positions of the two governments. Both governments continued to hold steadfastly to their respective positions and the Soviet Union continued to host international organizations under its control that were engaged in stirring up revolutionary activities in the United States—activities that continued to embitter relations between the two countries for the next six years.

It was not until several weeks after Litvinov's return to Moscow that we learned of the basis on which the Soviet government had been resting its insistence that it had not taken any obligations with regard to the Communist International.

Early in November 1935 Robert Kelley, chief of the Eastern European Division of the State Department, made his first visit to Moscow. On November 9, the ambassador, Kelley, and Litvinov had lunch together. During the luncheon conversation Litvinov brought up the subject of the Communist International and expressed regret that he had not been in Moscow when the exchanges with regard to his pledge to President Roosevelt had taken place.

The conversation as reported by Ambassador Bullitt in a telegram that he sent later in the day is so interesting that I shall quote from it:

> Litvinov said that he wished he had been in Moscow when I had presented our note of protest against the actions of the Third International.

He then asserted that he had an entirely clear conscience; that I must know that he had said to the President that he could not be responsible for the Third International; and that the President had replied that he would hold the Soviet Union to its pledge only in case of important injury to the interests of the United States.

I replied that my memory was entirely different; that I recalled that he had said he could make no promises about the Third International, but that the President had told him that he would hold him to strict accountability with regard to the Third International and he, Litvinov, had subsequently signed the pledge. He replied that he had made his statement to the President after signing the pledge.

As this statement made his position even weaker, and as the conversation was growing acrimonious, I suggested that a discussion of present relations might be more valuable than further remarks about the past. Litvinov then made it clear that the Soviet Government would not in any way restrain the activities of the Communist International in the United States or the Soviet Union, or of American Communists connected with the Communist International in the Soviet Union. He expressed with his customary cynicism the view that there was no such thing as friendship or "really friendly" relations between nations.

Both Kelley and I had told him that the United States had desired really friendly relations with the Soviet Union but now felt that the direction of the activities of the Communist International by Stalin was incompatible with really friendly relations. Litvinov then expressed his views in almost exactly the words reported in my despatch 980, October 26, saying that the truth about the United States was that we desire to remain aloof from all active interest in international affairs. He did not add aloud but implied that therefore really friendly relations with the United States were of small importance to the Soviet Union.

I have since discussed this matter with Ambassador Bullitt. The ambassador told me that the problem of the Communist International was so important that he had listened with the greatest attention to every word exchanged on the subject between the president and Litvinov, that Litvinov had at first taken the position that he could make no promises with respect to the Communist International, that the president in showing him the draft of the written pledge had pointed out that, although it did not mention the Communist International by name, it nevertheless was so worded as to include that organization and if Litvinov signed it the U.S. government would hold the Soviet government strictly accountable for the activities of the Communist International, and that Litvinov without any further argument had signed it.

It seems to me that if Litvinov had honestly believed that there was an oral understanding between himself and the president to the effect that in signing the pledge he was making no commitments so far as the Communist International was concerned, the commissar might have so informed Ambassador Bullitt instead of acting in an evasive or hypocritically innocent manner. The only other reason that I could think of for Litvinov's evasiveness might have been that he feared that if he would publicly assert that there was a tacit understanding between him and the president that his commitment did not include the Communist International and kindred organizations, he would in effect be accusing the president of having deceived the American public and he did not desire to offend the President.

CHAPTER 35

Problems in Connection with the Protection of U.S. Citizens in the Soviet Union

Among the more vexatious problems faced by our embassy in Moscow were those connected with our endeavor to extend protection to U.S. citizens. Difficulties in according protection to U.S. citizens residing in or traveling in the Soviet Union have continued to trouble our Moscow embassy and the Department of State up to the time of my retirement from the department and Foreign Service in January 1961. These difficulties were experienced even during those supposedly halcyon days when the United States and the Soviet Union were allies, at least in name, engaged in fighting Nazi Germany.

In a previous chapter I have already pointed out that the members of the Division of Eastern European Affairs of the Department of State, as the result of their studies of Soviet practices during the period before recognition, were fully aware at the time of the establishment of relations that the kind of treatment the Soviet authorities were accustomed to accord to Soviet citizens and to foreigners on Soviet soil was radically different from that which was being accorded by most countries to their own and foreign nationals. We were conscious of the fact that the Soviet authorities were accustomed secretly to arrest, to interrogate, to try, to sentence, and to carry out sentences on its own citizens and on citizens of other countries who happened to be in the Soviet Union.

The division had, therefore, recommended that among the pledges to be sought from Litvinov at the time of the establishment of relations there be a commitment relating to the legal protection of U.S. citizens in the Soviet Union. An examination by the division of the commitments with respect to legal protection that had been given by the Soviet Union to other countries showed that the pledge contained in the German-Soviet treaty of October 12, 1925, was the most far-reaching and specific. The division, therefore, had drafted a pledge for Litvinov to sign that would give U.S. citizens in the Soviet Union rights in the matter of legal protection that would be no less favorable than those that had been granted to German nationals. The pledge as drafted contained stipulations to the effect that the Soviet authorities would not only notify the appropriate U.S. consular officer promptly when a U.S. national was arrested and would permit a U.S. consular officer to visit the detained person in jail but would also give the arrested person a right not contained in the German-Soviet treaty: that is, the right to a fair, speedy, and public trial. Although Litvinov was prepared to promise that U.S. nationals would be entitled to treatment in the matter of legal protection no less favorable than that which the Soviet Union had promised to grant to German nationals, he was unwilling to make any commitment regarding the manner in which they would be tried in Soviet courts.

Among the specific rights accorded to U.S. nationals in the Soviet Union that were promised by Litvinov on the basis of the German-Soviet treaty were:

1. The American Consul shall be notified when an American citizen is arrested either by a communication from the person arrested or by the authorities themselves direct. Such communications shall be within a period not exceeding seven times twenty-four hours, and in large towns, including capitals of districts, within a period not exceeding three times twenty-four hours.

2. In places of detention of all kinds, requests made by consular representatives to visit nationals of their country under arrest, or to have them visited by their representatives, shall be granted without delay. The consular representative shall not be entitled to require officials of the courts or prisons to withdraw during his interview with the persons under arrest.

3. The same procedure shall apply if a prisoner is transferred from one place of detention to another.

Although we in the Division of Eastern European Affairs knew that the Soviet government was systematically failing to accord to German nationals the treatment that it had promised in the treaty of 1925 and that German nationals in the Soviet Union, in spite of the commitments that had been given, were disappearing mysteriously no less frequently than nationals of other countries, we nevertheless hoped that the pledge exacted by the president from Litvinov would provide at least legal basis on which U.S. diplomatic and consular officers could rest requests and protests made in connection with their efforts to protect U.S. citizens.

Immediately upon their arrival in Moscow, members of the embassy staff were besieged by U.S. citizens in distress who were requesting assistance. Even before we had had time formally to open the embassy and the consulate general for business some of these unfortunate people were importuning us in our hotel rooms. Many of those who claimed to be U.S. citizens came to us in the hope of obtaining documents that would enable them to return to the United States. Other visitors sought our aid on behalf of persons, allegedly U.S. citizens, who had disappeared and who had presumably been arrested. Still others, fearful of arrest, were eager to obtain from us documents that would serve as evidence of their U.S. citizenship. Letters also began to pour in from U.S. citizens in the United States urging us to find out what had happened to (allegedly) American relatives or friends who had dropped out of sight in the Soviet Union.

We soon learned that we were not to receive much cooperation from Narkomindel in connection with our efforts to obtain information regarding the status, whereabouts, or fate of persons alleged to be U.S. citizens who were among the missing. We noted that the officials of Narkomindel not only seemed to have no influence with the secret police and other officials of NKVD but seemed to be very much in fear of them.

When we inquired of officials of Narkomindel (members of the embassy were not permitted to approach other commissariats unless specifically authorized to do so by Narkomindel) regarding persons whom we believed to have claims to U.S. citizenship and who apparently were under arrest or missing, we were usually told by the officers of that commissariat that they had never heard of such persons but would make inquiries of the "appropriate authorities." Repeated requests for information on our part usually resulted in our being told either that no one had been able to find any trace of the missing persons or that the investigations had shown that the missing persons were Soviet citizens and that Soviet officials were not permitted to discuss with foreigners matters relating to citizens of the Soviet Union.

Many of the persons applying as U.S. citizens to the embassy in Moscow for protection or for assistance in getting back to the United States had become U.S. citizens through the naturalization of themselves or of their parents. At some time or other the depression years had created hardships for some of them and they had turned toward the Soviet Union as the land of opportunity and promise. Others had become converts to communism while in the United States and had come to the Soviet Union in order to live under communist rule.

Prior to recognition the United States did not issue passports good for entry into the Soviet Union. Most of these migrants, therefore, had proceeded on travel documents issued by Soviet authorities or the representatives of those authorities. During the process of obtaining Soviet visas a large proportion of them had signed documents that, according to Soviet law, made them Soviet citizens. Many of those who did so could still claim that they were U.S. citizens since generally they had not taken actions that would divest them of U.S. citizenship. The law of the country in which persons possessing dual citizenship happen to be is the law that prevails in citizenship cases. Since these persons were residing in the Soviet Union, the embassy was therefore not able to assist them.

Since prior to the merging of the consulate general into the embassy, members of the consulate general could not approach Narkomindel, it fell to my lot to take up with officials in that commissariat many cases involving the protection of U.S. citizens. One of the more tragic cases that I handled involved a girl who appeared to be about sixteen years of age. She visited the embassy in order to plead that we help her mother, her two younger sisters, and her to return to the United States. It seemed that several years previously her father, a naturalized U.S. citizen and a skilled mechanic, had migrated from the United States to the Soviet Union with his foreign-born wife and American-born children. Either before his departure from the United States or following his arrival in the Soviet Union, he had signed documents on the basis of which he had become a Soviet citizen. Several weeks before the opening of the embassy he had divorced his wife, had married a young Russian girl, and had brought her to live with him, his former wife, and three children in his one-room apartment. The new wife was eager to get rid of the divorced wife and three children and was treating them with almost unbearable arrogance. The first wife had been unable to obtain other living quarters. She had no means of support other than such meager funds as she was receiving for herself and her children from the divorced husband. They were, therefore, completely dependent upon him.

I discussed this case with officials in Narkomindel. After investigating the citizenship status of the mother and children they informed me that, according to Soviet law, the mother and children had become Soviet citizens and that, therefore, it would be inappropriate to discuss their problems with the embassy. My insistence that since the children were

American-born the embassy had a legitimate interest in them made no impression upon the Soviet officials with whom I talked. Following my conversations in Narkomindel the police who guarded the entrance to the embassy refused to permit the young girl to visit us again and we were never able to learn what eventually happened to her and to the other members of the family.

Failure of Soviet Authorities to Live Up to the Soviet Pledge to Notify U.S. Representatives of Arrest of U.S. Citizens

From time to time the embassy, acting on information that had come to it to the effect that a U.S. citizen had been arrested, would take steps to ascertain the facts. If our inquiries and investigations caused us to believe that a U.S. citizen had actually been arrested, we did what we could to be of assistance to him or her. I do not recall a single instance during the period of my assignment to Moscow in which the Soviet authorities, in conformity with the pledge given by Litvinov to the president, informed U.S. diplomatic or consular officers of the arrest of a U.S. citizen within time limits specified in the pledge. We usually learned of the arrest through letters received from the United States, through persons in the Soviet Union acquainted with the person under arrest, or from others who had met the arrested person in prison.

When we had reason to believe that a U.S. citizen had been arrested we pressed the Soviet authorities for details. In most instances we were compelled to write many notes and make numerous visits to Narkomindel before we could obtain any information whatsoever about the case in which we were interested. In only two or three instances, so far as I can recall, did the Soviet authorities consent to let U.S. diplomatic or consular officers visit U.S. nationals in prison. In these instances the permission was obtained only after vigorous and protracted representation on our part.

CHAPTER 36

TRADE RELATIONS BETWEEN THE UNITED STATES AND THE SOVIET UNION, 1934–1938

IT WILL BE RECALLED that certain American business circles in the United States, including some of the members of the Russian–American Chamber of Commerce, which was sponsored by a number of New York banks, had visions in 1933 of the Soviet Union buying hundreds of millions of dollars worth of U.S. goods following the establishment of diplomatic relations. Persons acquainted with the internal situation in the Soviet Union were quite well aware that these dreams, which for the most part had been based on propaganda and wishful thinking, were unrealistic. It had been of course possible that, if the establishment of relations had been followed by the extension on generous terms of large financial credits or loans to the Soviet government by the U.S. government or by private U.S. firms, there might have been an appreciable increase in Soviet purchases in the United States.

THE AMERICAN–SOVIET COMMERCIAL AGREEMENT OF 1935

When, following the breakdown of the debts and claims negotiations, the U.S. government took steps to prevent the extension by U.S. institutions and firms to the Soviet Union of financial credits and loans, hopes for any immediate spectacular increase in U.S. exports to the

Soviet Union collapsed. During these negotiations Litvinov on several occasions had hinted to Ambassador Bullitt that unless the Soviet Union could receive liberal financial credits or loans from the United States, trade between the two countries would languish.

For a couple of months after the collapse of the debts and claims negotiations in the early part of 1935, the governments of the two countries were so irritated with each other that neither was willing to display interest in the development of mutual trade. On March 27, 1935, however, the Department of State broke the ice by sending a telegram to Wiley, who was chargé d'affaires at the time, instructing him to ask Litvinov if the Soviet government would be interested in entering into an exchange of notes, which would provide that "if the Government of the United States generalized to the Soviet Union modifications of duties and other import restrictions, specified in trade agreements with other countries, such action on the part of the United States would be reciprocated on the part of the Soviet Government by a substantial increase in the purchase of products of the United States." Wiley, in carrying out this instruction, engaged in a preliminary conversation with Litvinov who gave the impression that he was only mildly interested. After a delay of several days, however, he informed Wiley that the Soviet government was prepared "in principle" to accept tariff concessions on a most-favored-nation basis but that it would be impossible for it to stipulate rigidly what the value of future Soviet purchases in the United States would be. In this connection, he pointed out that in 1935 the value of Soviet purchases would probably amount to $30 million, which would be approximately twice what they were in 1934.

Following protracted arguments between the ambassador and the commissar, during the course of which Litvinov at times was inclined to be rude and even overbearing, the Soviet government dropped its insistence upon being promised most-favored-nation treatment and contented itself for the time being with receiving only such tariff concessions as the United States had extended to or would extend to other countries, excepting Cuba, under the authority of the act of June 12, 1934 (entitled the "Act to Amend the Tariff Act of 1930"). The United States on its part dropped its insistence that the Soviet note should state how many dollars worth of goods the Soviet Union would purchase in the United States during the next twelve months. It agreed that in the text of the note the Soviet government would merely promise to take steps to increase substantially the amount of its purchases in the United States and that the exchange would be supplemented by a letter addressed by Litvinov to Bullitt stating that it was the intention of the Soviet government to buy in the United States during the next twelve months goods to the value of $30 million.

Since I was the chief of the economic section at the time and had had a certain amount of experience in connection with the negotiation of agreements relating to trade, I worked closely with the ambassador during his negotiations with Litvinov. One of my chores was to explain in detail to Boris Rosenblum, who at the time was director of the economic section of Narkomindel, and to Mark Plotkin, the acting director of the legal division, the reasons for the positions taken by the State Department. I found these two officials, in general, to be more understanding than Litvinov of our problems.

Although the conclusion of this agreement did little to remove the chill that had enveloped Soviet-American relations following the failure of the debts and claims negotiations and the consequent blocking by the U.S. government of the extension of U.S. financial credits to the Soviet Union, it nevertheless had a stabilizing effect on our commercial relations in that most Soviet products entering the United States were in fact subjected to treatment just as favorable as the goods of any other country except Cuba.

The United States had no reason to complain of failure on the part of the Soviet government to carry out its declared intention of purchasing $30 million worth of U.S. goods during the twelve-month period following July 13, 1935. In fact, its purchases of such goods during that period were approximately $37 million in value, more than double the value of its purchases in the United States during the preceding twelve months. It was my belief, however, that the increase was due primarily to the Soviet ability to buy the kind of goods that it needed more advantageously in the United States than elsewhere rather than to a deliberate policy on its part of giving preference to the United States in satisfying its needs.

The American–Soviet Commercial Agreement of 1936

When the question arose in June 1936 regarding an extension of the commercial agreement for another twelve-month period, I was chargé d'affaires in the absence of Ambassador Bullitt and carried on the negotiations for the embassy. In the absence of Litvinov the Soviet official in charge of Narkomindel was Nikolay Krestinsky, who at the time was assistant commissar for foreign affairs. Although he was a stubborn and skillful negotiator, Krestinsky was lacking in the arrogant slipperyness that Litvinov was accustomed to display from time to time, and such differences as developed between us during the negotiations were ironed out in a frank and friendly atmosphere. Most of my conversations in Narkomindel were carried on with the second echelon of its officialdom: Alexes F. Neymann, who had become chief of the Third Western Political Division that handled American affairs; A. N. Kaminsky, assistant chief of the Foreign Trade Policies Division; and Boris Rosenblum, director of the economic section.

The major issues that developed during our conversations were for the most part similar to those that had prolonged the negotiations of 1935. It was fortunate for me, therefore, that I had had the experience derived from those negotiations.

On June 7, 1936, in pursuance of instructions that I had received from the State Department, I called on Krestinsky to inquire about the total value of Soviet purchases in the United States since July 13, 1935, and about the intentions of the Soviet government with respect to such purchases during the ensuing twelve-month period. He replied that it was his understanding that Soviet purchases in the United States would probably reach $36 million in value during the twelve-month period and added that the Soviet government in his opinion would be willing to extend the agreement for another year on the basis of Soviet purchases to a value of $30 million provided the United States would cease to discriminate against Soviet coal.

I expressed surprise that the question of coal had again been raised. Both the State Department in Washington and the embassy in Moscow had repeatedly pointed out that the U.S. government could not in an executive agreement undertake to lift the tax on Soviet coal. Only in a formal treaty that had been approved by the Senate could a most-favored-nation clause relieve the U.S. importers of Soviet coal from paying duties.

I shall not bore my readers with the many oral and written exchanges that followed, particularly those relating to the inclusion of a most-favored-nation clause and the problem of the duties on Soviet coal. These exchanges eventually resulted in an exchange of notes on July 11, 1936, between Krestinsky, on behalf of the Soviet Union, and myself, on behalf of the United States, which served to extend the agreement of July 13, 1935, for another year. Supplementary to these notes Krestinsky addressed a letter to me stating that "the economic organizations of the Union of Soviet Socialist Republics intend in the course of the forthcoming year to buy in the United States of America goods in the amount of $30,000,000"; on my part, I addressed an informal letter to Neymann regarding the tax on Soviet coal in which I informed him for his "strictly confidential information that it is my understanding that the Department of State is considering at the present time the possibility of seeking the removal of at least the discriminatory features of the tax by legislative action at the next session of Congress." I added that "it is not possible, of course, to forecast what action Congress may take."

On July 17 I sent to the State Department a number of memoranda for reference purposes summarizing conversations that had taken place between Soviet officials and me. In this dispatch I made the following comment:

> The experiences of the Embassy in carrying on these negotiations is to an extent similar to the experiences, as related to members of this Mission, of the representatives of other Governments and of business firms in Moscow which have negotiated agreements with the Soviet Government or Soviet organizations. Soviet negotiators apparently make a practice of repeatedly advancing an argument in support of a point favored by themselves, regardless of the fact that the arguments may have been answered several times irrevocably. Persons experienced in dealing with Soviet officials take the view that these tactics can best be combated by patiently replying to each argument irrespective of the number of times it may have been advanced.

I may add that I took a liking to the Soviet officials with whom I negotiated this agreement. I felt that they were sincerely and conscientiously trying to get a good bargain for their government. I regretted that it was not possible for me to have social relations with them and to become better acquainted with them. During the ensuing year I had occasion to deal with them quite frequently and my good opinion of them was strengthened. I was sorry when, during the course of the next two years, three of them fell as victims of the Great Purge: Krestinsky was shot; according to our understanding Neymann was either shot or committed suicide; and Rosenblum disappeared.

During the year covered by the agreement of July 11, 1936, the value of the purchases of American goods in the United States again was approximately $37 million, $7 million in excess of the amount that Neymann had mentioned in his letter to me. The State Department, however, during that year was unable to effect a change in the law that was responsible for the levying of the tax on Soviet coal.

The American–Soviet Commercial Agreement of 1937

The negotiations of the commercial agreement of 1937 followed lines in general similar to those that resulted in the agreement of 1936. There were, however, certain differences in the participants, in the attitudes of the two governments, and in the points at issue.

The participants for the embassy were Ambassador Davies, Durbrow (who had become chief of the economic section of the embassy), and me. Litvinov, Neymann, Rosenblum, and Mark Plotkin, assistant chief of the legal division, did most of the negotiating for Narkomindel. Ambassador Davies and Litvinov met on perhaps two occasions for discussions regarding the progress of the negotiations but left the actual negotiating and most of the drafting to Neymann and me. I was careful, however, to keep the ambassador fully informed of what was going on and made a point of making no suggestions to the State Department during the periods that the ambassador was in Moscow without obtaining his concurrence. The ambassador at times inserted in our telegrams to the department suggestions that I did not personally approve. Our relations were such that I had no hesitation in arguing with him when we differed.

Our telegraphic reports to the State Department regarding the progress of the negotiations were rather formal during the periods when the ambassador was in Moscow since he preferred that no names other than those of Litvinov and himself be mentioned in them. If, for instance, Durbrow and I would have a talk with Neymann and Rosenblum, in our reports to the department we would refer to conversations between representatives of the Foreign Office and the embassy. Sometimes we would begin a telegram with a sentence like this: "From conference today with Foreign Office officials we obtained following impression."

As a preliminary to the opening of the negotiations in Moscow, a talk took place in Washington on May 14, 1937, between Troyanovsky, the Soviet ambassador, and Secretary Hull during the course of which Hull apologized for the inability of the department to eliminate the discriminatory tax on Soviet coal. The secretary in summarizing his conversation in a telegram addressed to the embassy, said:

> I told him [the Ambassador] that the discrimination against coal imports from the Soviet Union was opposed by me and others, much more strongly, if possible, than by the Soviet Government, for the reason that we feel that the success of our broad economic program should not be delayed or impeded by such "sore thumbs" as the discriminatory tax on Soviet coal. I said that I would be glad for his Government distinctly to understand that we were now striving in the most earnest manner, day by day and week by week, to get rid of the discriminatory coal tax complained of, and that we would continue so to strive. I emphasized that we have been fighting vigorously for many years against discriminations such as this in international trade practices and methods, whether carried on by this Government or other Governments.

The secretary added for the information of the embassy that the Executive Committee on Commercial Policy had been working for several months on the problem involved in removing the discrimination and that all interested governmental departments were agreed on the desirability of eliminating the tax.

In subsequent telegrams from the State Department we learned of the ingenious but risky plan that the State Department had worked out in conjunction with the Department of the Treasury to solve the problem. Probing had shown that vested interests opposed to the increase in imports of Soviet coal were so strongly entrenched on Capitol Hill that there was no possibility that the law responsible for the discrimination could be changed. Therefore, if the tax was to be removed, it must be done by executive action. The plan was to obtain an informal commitment in writing from the Soviet government to the effect that in case the tax should be eliminated, it would not export to the United States during the next twelve months more than 400,000 tons of coal (approximately the amount of coal that it had been exporting annually to the United States). If the Soviet Union would be prepared to make such a commitment, the United States on its part would be willing to incorporate in the exchange of notes a most-favored-nation clause to be followed by this reservation:

> It is understood that so long and insofar as existing law of the United States of America may otherwise require, the provisions of the foregoing paragraph, insofar as they would relate to duties, taxes or charges on coal, coke manufactured therefrom, or coal or coke briquettes, shall not apply to such products imported into the United States of America.

To enhance the status of the agreement the president would proclaim it in the same manner as he customarily proclaimed formal treaties.

Although the State Department was not in a position to give the Soviet government a solemn promise that the incorporation of such a provision in a commercial agreement would result in the elimination of the duty or tax on Soviet coal, since it could not be sure what the Customs Court would decide if the problem should come before it, it authorized the embassy to assure the Soviet negotiators that if they would accept the wording of the most-favored-nation clause as worked out in Washington and the reservation appended to it relating to coal, the Treasury Department authorities would hold that Soviet coal would be exempt from tax.

During our conversations we were compelled to admit to the Soviet officials with whom we were dealing that there was of course the possibility that the U.S. Customs Court could, if the matter should be submitted to it, overrule the treasury and decide that the coal was taxable. That was a risk, however, from which neither we nor they could escape.

After much debate, the Soviet negotiators decided to accept in principle this suggested solution of the coal problem. They nevertheless haggled over the wording of the clauses that had been sent the embassy by the State Department and introduced some new clauses of their own. They insisted, for instance, that the most-favored-nation clause be redrafted in such a way as to make it reciprocal, that is, so that the Soviet Union would also be obligated to extend most-favored-nation treatment to imports from the United States. The department, as I was sure it would, rejected this change partly on the ground that in view of the existence of the Soviet foreign trade monopoly such a commitment would be of no value to the United States, and partly for another reason that we did not divulge to the Soviet negotiators: in the future the Soviet government might well argue that since the most-favored-nation clause was reciprocal, there was no reason why the Soviet Union should make any additional concessions in return for receiving most-favored-nation treatment from the United States.

The Soviet negotiators also insisted on the insertion in the notes to be exchanged of a clause, similar to one contained in a recently concluded American–Dutch trade agreement, that would give the Soviet Union most-favored-nation treatment in the matter of exports of goods from the United States to the Soviet Union. The State Department was willing to insert such a clause provided it was accompanied by a number of reservations relating to the exportation of gold or silver, arms, ammunition, military supplies, and so forth. The Soviet Union objected to these commitments but, when the embassy under departmental instructions stood firm, they finally capitulated and agreed to these reservations.

The State Department took the position that, in view of the important concessions that it was making to the Soviet Union, the Soviet government should express the intention to buy from the United States during the next twelve months American goods in an amount of not less than $40 million. After many exchanges the Soviet negotiators finally agreed to this figure.

On July 31, in the absence of Ambassador Davies who had gone on a trip to the Scandinavian countries, I was finally able to telegraph the State Department that the embassy and Narkomindel had come to an agreement on all points and were prepared to sign the agreement on August 4. I then sent a message to the ambassador, who was eager to sign the exchange when an agreement had been reached, informing him that the documents were ready for signature and suggesting that he return temporarily in order to sign them. On August 4, therefore, the ambassador and Litvinov signed the notes that constituted the agreement and exchanged the letters supplementary to the agreement including the letter containing assurances that the Soviet Union would not export more than 400,000 tons of coal to the United States during the ensuing twelve months.

Our gratification that we had been able to complete successfully these complicated negotiations was dampened by the fact that on July 25, when I appeared at Narkomindel to keep an appointment with Neymann, I found the familiar NKVD seal on his door. We never had definite information regarding his fate. There were unconfirmed rumors that he had committed suicide. His wife, who I believe was a Belgian, and his children, we learned, had been evacuated from Moscow shortly after his disappearance. Neymann had served for a short time in Washington as first secretary of embassy under Ambassador Troyanovsky and had been well liked by members of the diplomatic corps and the U.S. officials with whom he dealt. We in the embassy also liked him. Even though the situation made it impossible for him to bend when talking to us in his office and he was obliged to say "nyet" many more times than he could acquiesce to our requests, we sensed that he had an understanding of our policies and our problems.

The Soviet government during the next twelve months lived up to the agreement contained in this exchange. It ordered more than $70 million worth of U.S. goods, although only slightly more than $40 million worth had left the United States by August 4, 1938. The advantages that the Soviet Union had expected to gain as a result of the elimination of the duties on coal were, however, disappointing. Instead of the 400,000 tons that it had planned to export to the United States during the twelve-month period it had exported only 200,000 tons. Furthermore, in spite of the fact that U.S. imports of coal from the Soviet Union were declining, U.S. producers of coal in the latter part of the twelve-month period had begun to take exception to the ruling of lifting the tax on Soviet coal imports; the Treasury Department, realizing that they were preparing to take the matter to the Customs Court, had been impelled to announce that if the right of importers to import Soviet coal tax free should be challenged it would leave it to the U.S. Customs Court to decide whether or not any coal brought into the country after May 21, 1938, should be taxed. U.S. importers of Soviet coal, therefore, did not know whether or not their purchases subsequent to that date would be subject to tax. This situation in itself discouraged the importation of Soviet coal.

AMERICAN–SOVIET COMMERCIAL AGREEMENTS OF 1938 AND 1939

I was on my way to Washington to begin another tour in the Department of State when Alexander Kirk, at that time our chargé d'affaires, negotiated with Narkomindel the commercial agreement of 1938, and I was on duty in the Department of State in July and early August when Stuart Grummon, who was chargé at the time, with the assistance of Norris Chipman, the chief of the economic section of the embassy, negotiated the agreement of 1939. I might say, however, that during the 1938 negotiations the Soviet spokesmen did not stress the coal problem. The fact was that the Soviet Union had found markets elsewhere for most of the coal that it did not need for its own developing industries. The negotiators emphasized, instead, the excess of Soviet imports from the United States over U.S. imports from the Soviet Union and insisted that measures be taken in the direction of effecting a balance of trade between the two countries.

On July 22, 1939, the embassy received from the Commissariat for Foreign Trade, which was taking over the negotiations on behalf of the Soviet government, a memorandum expressing its readiness to begin immediate negotiations in Moscow for the renewal of the commercial agreement. In that memorandum it was again suggested that in order to rectify the imbalance in Soviet-American trade, the United States reduce the rates of tariff duties on certain Soviet products and, furthermore, that the United States undertake to purchase 800,000 tons of Soviet manganese during the next four years. The memorandum added that if the United States would make concessions of this nature "in view of certain forthcoming naval orders in American shipyards concerning which there is agreement in principle between the two Governments," the Soviet Union would be willing to agree to "an increase of imports from the United States to the Soviet Union from $40,000,000 to $50,000,000 for the 1939–1940 treaty year."

Although we realized as early as 1937, when the Soviet negotiators objected to certain reservations contained in our clause granting it most-favored-nation treatment in the matter of U.S. exports, that the Soviet government was interested in assuring its ability to import freely armaments and other war material from the United States, the reference by the Commissariat for Foreign Trade to the "orders in American shipyards," which were for warships, was the first Soviet overt attempt to introduce the sale of implements of war into our commercial negotiations.

The position of the State Department was similar to that which it had taken in 1938, that is: that the United States in purchasing manganese could not display partiality toward any one country and its purchases must be made on a purely commercial basis; that the changing of tariff duties on specific commodities would require extensive hearings and ensuing delays; that if the Soviet government should desire to enter in trade agreement negotiations with the United States for the purpose of exploring the possibility of modifications being made in U.S. duties on certain items that the Soviet Union would be in a position to export, the United States was prepared to meet that desire; and that, in the meantime, notes should be exchanged that would prevent the lapse of the agreements in existence. The department also made a point that the Soviet negotiators were unable to refute: one reason for the smallness of U.S. imports from the Soviet Union was that the Soviet Union in reality was in a position to export only a limited amount of its products, and it was selling much of what it was able to spare to countries other than the United States.

The result of these negotiations was an exchange of notes and letters between Grummon and Anastas Mikoyan, the commissar for foreign trade, on the evening of August 2, 1939, that prolonged the commercial agreement for another twelve months on terms almost identical with the agreements of 1937 and 1938.

VOLUME OF SOVIET–AMERICAN TRADE, 1933–1939

The table set forth below presents statistics prepared by the U.S. Department of Commerce relating to Soviet-American trade during the years 1933–1939.

Year	Value of Exports to USSR (In Thousands of Dollars)	Percent of Total U.S. Exports	Value of Imports from USSR (In Thousands of Dollars)	Percent of Total U.S. Imports
1933	8,997	.5	12,114	.8
1934	15,011	.7	12,337	.7
1935	24,743	1.1	17,809	.9
1936	33,427	1.4	20,517	.8
1937	42,903	1.3	30,752	1.0
1938	69,691	2.3	24,064	1.2

In view of what might appear to be the relatively small amount of trade between the United States and the Soviet Union during these years, the reader may wonder why the U.S. government and people paid so much attention during that period to Soviet–American trade relations.

It should be borne in mind that during the depression and post-depression years the United States in general was foreign-trade minded. Both the Hoover and Roosevelt administrations believed that sharp increases in U.S. exports would assist in offsetting the ravages of the depression. Secretary Hull had a particular interest in the promotion of international trade, which he regarded as potentially, at least, one of the most powerful factors in the maintenance of world stability and peace.

Furthermore, the presence and activities in New York City of Amtorg served to keep alive and stimulate the hope among influential U.S. business circles that they would be able to realize huge profits from doing business with the Soviet Union. Amtorg, although incorporated in the United States, was owned and controlled by the Soviet government. As the leading Soviet buying and selling agency in the United States it continued after the establishment of diplomatic relations its former practice of dangling possibilities of hundreds of millions of dollars worth of business before the eyes of U.S. financiers, industrialists, importers, and exporters. It caused a number of them to hope that if they would bring pressure on the U.S. government to accede to Soviet demands they would be rewarded in the form of lucrative Soviet contracts. Some of the outstanding public relations firms in the United States were employed to broadcast the benefits that Soviet trade could yield to the United States provided credit was extended to the Soviets on attractive terms.

The Kremlin, which, in my opinion, sincerely believed that the U.S. government was being run by Wall Street, underestimated the integrity of most U.S. business leaders and overestimated the influence that certain important U.S. business houses working closely with Amtorg could exert on members of Congress and top officials of the U.S. government. Nevertheless, the propaganda stimulated by Amtorg and the American firms cooperating with Amtorg served to keep alive public interest in the status of Soviet-American trade.

Problems Connected with Soviet–American Trade, 1934–1938

Commercial relations between the United States and a number of the largest corporations in the United States developed during the 1930s in a mutually advantageous manner. The Soviet Union made a practice of including in many of its purchasing contracts with American firms clauses obligating these firms to extend technical assistance to it. In some instances these clauses provided that Soviet engineers and mechanics could be trained in U.S. plants. As a result hundreds of Soviet nationals were trained in U.S. automotive, electronic, chemical, metal, and other industries. American technical assistance made it possible, for instance, for Soviet technicians to make military use of radar almost simultaneously with the adoption of radar equipment by our own armed forces. During the 1930s Soviet institutions were not only using early types of American computers but also making copies of them.

Most of the contracts that large, experienced U.S. firms entered into with Amtorg in New York were carried out with a minimum of friction. Amtorg was governed by U.S. laws. Furthermore, its political role would have been weakened if it had not maintained a reputation for reliability. Firms that were planning to deal with Amtorg also had the advantage of being able to obtain advice from U.S. lawyers regarding liabilities and risks involved.

Our embassy in Moscow had comparatively little to do with contracts signed in the United States with Amtorg since most of them were carried out to the satisfaction of the parties concerned. It did, however, receive numerous complaints from firms that had signed either in the United States or in the Soviet Union contracts with representatives of Soviet organizations that were based in the Soviet Union. Some of these trading organizations maintained representatives in New York who, with the aid of Amtorg, made direct contact with U.S. manufacturers or exporters. Amtorg, however, was not always a party to the contracts that ensued.

Toward the latter part of the 1930s the Soviet government tended to encourage certain U.S. firms desiring to do business with it to conclude contracts in Moscow instead of in the United States. One of the reasons for this tendency was the insistence of the U.S. Internal Revenue authorities that Amtorg, like any other U.S. corporation, should pay income tax on many of its transactions. Another reason was that experience had shown that the Soviet government was likely to obtain better terms from contracts signed in Moscow. Yet another reason was that if disputes should arise in respect to contracts signed in the Soviet Union they would be subject to adjudication in Soviet courts or settled through an arbitration tribunal under Soviet control. I may add that no case ever came to my attention in which the Soviet court or arbitration tribunal decided a case in favor of the U.S. firm.

Many of the difficulties encountered by U.S. firms that were attempting to do business with the Soviet Union resulted from the fact that these firms were competing with one another for contracts with a monolithic foreign trade monopoly. As Mr. Kelley so well pointed out in his lengthy memorandum that had been submitted to the president on July 27, 1933, regarding differences between U.S. and Soviet economic and social structures:

a government monopoly of foreign trade, in carrying on commerce with foreign countries, has a natural advantage over individual business concerns in such countries. In practically every country trading with Russia endeavors have been made, usually with little success, to find ways and means of putting trade relations on an equal footing and removing the disadvantages under which the individual businessman labors in dealing with the Soviet monopoly of foreign trade.

Firms that hoped to have business relations with the Soviet Union frequently hesitated to give offense to the monopoly by indicating a lack of confidence in it or by appearing to be squeamish with regard to the wording of the form contracts that they might be handed to sign.

Representatives of U.S. firms who had come to the Soviet Union for the purpose of negotiating contracts frequently asked the advice of the embassy. Since there was no one else in Moscow in a position to give them frank advice the embassy did what it could to help them. We suggested to some of them that they might find it advantageous to sign such contracts as they might be successful in negotiating in Moscow with Amtorg in New York.

The Soviet authorities did not like the idea of U.S. businessmen in the Soviet Union turning to the embassy for advice but were not in a position to prevent them from doing so. At times, however, members of Amtorg in New York complained to their U.S. business contacts of the unfriendly attitude of the embassy toward Soviet institutions engaging in foreign trade. The fact was that the embassy did what it could, in keeping with the current policy of the U.S. government, to strengthen the economic intercourse between the United States and the Soviet Union but, nevertheless, took the position that it had the duty to assist U.S. businessmen who were not acquainted with the practices of the Soviet foreign monopoly.

Many of the complaints that came to the embassy from representatives of U.S. firms were of a minor character; some were more serious. The inability of representatives of a U.S. firm in Moscow to communicate with any assurance of privacy, either by letter or by telegram, with their superiors in the United States during the course of negotiations was one of the major complaints. As an exception to its general rule the embassy at times sent to the State Department by coded telegram or by courier pouch for transmission to the home offices of these businessmen messages that seemed to be of an urgent and confidential character. It also gave the businessmen in question the substance of the replies to these messages.

During the last two years of my stay in Moscow the Soviet government undertook to place large orders in the United States for war supplies and implements of war. It was particularly interested in purchasing a complete warship of the latest type—a warship that would be one of the most powerful in the world. It was successful in its efforts to buy various types of airplanes and an appreciable amount of military hardware.

Since most of the negotiations for Soviet military and naval purchases took place in the United States, the embassy had little to do with them. Nevertheless, from time to time Soviet officials, in the belief that Ambassador Davies was in sympathy with their desire to strengthen the Red Army and to build a navy "second to none," urged him to press Washington to be more helpful in the matter of letting them purchase U.S.-manufactured war supplies and implements.

As interest in the Soviet Union increased, more and more U.S. citizens, including businessmen, tourists, and scholars, began to call at the embassy to ask questions regarding Soviet conditions and practices. The number of letters from the United States containing inquiries regarding the Soviet Union also increased. Many of the questions raised deserved an answer, but the embassy with its limited staff was unable to respond to all of them on an individual basis. With the approval of the Department of State it, therefore, prepared a brochure entitled "General Information Regarding the Union of Soviet Socialist Republics." This brochure was carefully drafted in order to give American inquirers the information that they might need and at the same time not unduly to offend the Soviet authorities, who did not relish any information regarding the Soviet Union being dispensed in that country that had not been censored by them.

CHAPTER 37

THE PROBLEM OF OPERATING
A U.S. EMBASSY IN THE
CLOSED SOCIETY OF THE SOVIET UNION

MANY OF THE DIFFICULTIES that our embassy was constantly encountering in endeavoring to carry out the duties expected of it stemmed from the unusual and complex situation in which it was functioning.

Diplomatic missions in Moscow during the 1930s were not welcome guests. The presence in the Soviet Union of diplomatic missions representing noncommunist countries were so many painful thorns in the flesh of the Soviet body politic. These missions were particularly obnoxious when they represented great and prosperous countries and when their members insisted on receiving treatment of the kind that they had been accustomed to receive in other world capitals.

It was galling to the rulers in the Kremlin that there should be in the confines of their country institutions and persons over whom they could not exercise absolute control. Nevertheless, they realized that the presence of foreign embassies and legations in Moscow must be tolerated if the Soviet Union was to have diplomatic relations with other countries, and they were convinced that the maintenance of such relations was to their advantage. They also realized that, unless they were prepared to permit these foreigners to possess the facilities that would make life for them in the Soviet Union bearable and unless they were willing to extend to them at least some of the customary privileges and courtesies, the embassies and legations in Moscow might well be closed and the Soviet government might be requested to withdraw its diplomatic missions.

The concept of diplomatic immunities and privileges is based on millennia of experience in the conduct of relations between peoples and states. It has been recognized for hundreds of years that if diplomatic representatives are to be able fearlessly and freely to represent their governments, they should be in a position that would make it difficult for the authorities of the host country to bring direct or indirect pressures on them. They should not be required to pay taxes to the host government or be brought before its courts; they should have the facilities of secret communication by telegram or by letter with their governments; their persons, residences, offices, and baggage and other personal belongings should not be subject to search. The immunities that they enjoy should also be extended to the members of their households and in varying degrees to their entourages. Among the courtesies that the host country customarily extends to its guest diplomats are the arrangements that enable them to have appropriate living and working facilities, reasonable facilities for obtaining the necessities of life and the supplies needed in connection with their mission, and transport facilities. It also arranges for them to have ready access to its appropriate officials.

The diplomats on their part are expected to respect the laws of the host country and not to take unfair advantage of the immunities and the courtesies extended to them. If they should do so, they may be declared *personae non grata* and required to leave the country.

In a totalitarian country where most property and activities are under the control of the government, foreign diplomats must depend heavily upon the host government for the satisfaction of their needs. This is particularly true in a country where there is a scarcity of most of the necessities of modern life. The diplomats must depend on that government to enable them to buy local currency at a reasonable price and to obtain either by purchase or by duty-free import food, clothing, and other essentials. Only through agencies of the government can they obtain permission and tickets for travel and for admission to theaters and other places of entertainment, relaxation, or amusement; fuel for the heating of their houses and offices and for automobiles; permission to consult a physician or dentist; permits enabling them to bring into and take out of the country personal effects free of duty. I could go on almost indefinitely listing ways in which diplomats must depend on government officials for the satisfaction of their needs. If these officials are gracious and eager to be helpful, the problems of living and working in a totalitarian atmosphere are lightened. If they are arrogant, overbearing, slow moving or obstructive, such problems can be multiplied.

We found that in the Soviet Union many of the Soviet officials who had been charged with the performance of certain tasks in the field of international affairs realized that the failure of the Soviet authorities to accord the diplomatic missions in Moscow the privileges and courteous treatment that international practice required was likely to make more difficult the successful carrying out of those tasks. These officials, therefore, particularly those in Narkomindel, tried in a timorous sort of way to be helpful to the embassy. They seemed to have a fairly free hand in handling matters that did not touch on problems of security. Since from the Soviet point of view most aspects of living and working in the Soviet Union involved questions of security, however, their ability to be of assistance to the embassy was limited.

On a few occasions I found that the officials responsible for maintaining security were also courteous and helpful. In general, however, they seemed to regard foreign diplomats as untrustworthy persons who should be closely watched. Some of them with whom we came in contact seemed to begrudge the necessity of giving us the special treatment that they were supposed to give to diplomats.

When the Torgsins, which did business in foreign currency, were abolished the embassy was compelled to depend more than ever on imports to satisfy its needs for food and other essentials. The customs officials were frequently far from cooperative. They seemed to delight in holding up perishable foodstuffs brought in from abroad until they were no longer edible. Shipments of tinned food and other supplies for the embassy commissary arriving by boat in Leningrad were often exposed to the weather and arrived in Moscow in a damaged condition.

The problem of taking one's effects out of the country was one of the most vexatious that members of the embassy faced. Dozens of representations, oral and written, were sent to Narkomindel, and many complaints were made by members of the Department of State in Washington to the Soviet embassy on the subject. Soviet officials took the position at times that no article could be taken out of the country by a member of the embassy without payment of export duties unless the owner could prove to the satisfaction of the customs authorities that he had not acquired it in the Soviet Union. When Captain Nimmer, our naval attaché, for instance, left the Soviet Union in 1935, the customs authorities insisted that he pay customs duties on the books of his small library, including even the textbooks that he had used while in the Naval Academy. Furthermore, the customs authorities examined the personal effects of departing diplomats in a leisurely manner. Sometimes they spent weeks going through the effects of a three-room apartment. They also insisted on the payment of fees for the cost of the inspection, a new kind of tax to which the State Department objected.

The embassy spent many weeks in the spring of 1938 getting the effects of Ambassador Davies out of the country preparatory to his departure. He was touring the Black Sea area at the time on Mrs. Davies's yacht and was happily unaware of the struggle that we were having over his effects with the Soviet customs authorities, who were demanding the payment of thousands of dollars for examination and appraisal fees. Only after I had gone personally to top Soviet officials and pointed out to them that the U.S. government would never consent to the payment of such fees and that if the Soviet government would not permit his effects to leave the country there could be an international scandal, was it possible for us to prevail upon the customs authorities to withdraw their demands.

As the Great Purge increased in intensity, difficulties in obtaining entry and exit visas for members of the staff increased. A newly appointed clerk of the embassy might be required to wait for weeks before a visa would be granted him. Diplomatic and consular officers traveling over the Trans-Siberian Railway between Europe and the Far East were frequently required to subject their baggage to customs examination. Any books that they may have with them were studied by customs authorities with a scanty command of English in order to ascertain whether or not they might contain subversive material.

During the height of the purge, the isolation of the embassy became more complete. The guards at the doors became increasingly active in ascertaining the identity of all persons entering or leaving the embassy. There was a decline in the number of Soviet nationals who were permitted to attend embassy functions. For that matter many, if not most, of those who in the past had been allowed to have social intercourse with members of the embassy had gradually and sometimes mysteriously disappeared.

Travel in the vicinity of Moscow and elsewhere in the Soviet Union became increasingly restricted. In our trips by car to the beautiful countryside away from the depressing atmosphere of Moscow we more and more frequently ran into sentinels who informed us that the area had been closed.

One by one the more valuable Soviet members of our staff had been arrested. Many of the other diplomatic missions reported from time to time the discovery of microphones in their living and working quarters. It was not until 1937 that we discovered a microphone in the wall of the office of Ambassador Davies. We considered this discovery sufficiently important to report it to the State Department by telegram. By the middle of the century the practice of bugging diplomatic missions had become so common that the discovery of microphones in one's office or residence was regarded as a routine matter.

One of the more disagreeable practices of Soviet officials was their efforts to compromise members of the embassy in such a way as to make them subject to blackmail. I can recall the distressed look on Colonel Faymonville's face when one morning he brought into my office—I was chargé d'affaires at the time—a frightened American member of his staff. The young man had just returned from a chat in the office of the secret police to which he had been summoned. It seemed that on the preceding evening after a drunken party with some of his Soviet friends who, of course, were secret police agents, he had been photographed while engaging in a homosexual act. The police had shown him the photograph, had informed him that he had broken a Soviet law, that his position in the military attaché's office did not exempt him from prosecution, and that unless within three days he would bring them for photographing the code books of the military attaché, he would be arrested, sentenced to prison, and disgraced for life.

The colonel, who took pride in his apparently friendly relations with his Soviet counterparts, was stunned. It was difficult for him to believe that they had set about to trap one of his own men. He was particularly upset because of the Soviet desire to gain possession of his secret codes. "What," he asked, "can we do? It would be disastrous if this affair should become public." I said that a member of the embassy staff was leaving on the following morning for Helsinki in the capacity of a courier. We would immediately apply to Narkomindel on an urgent basis for an exit visa that would permit the young man in trouble to accompany the courier as a second courier. On occasions when we had important documents in the courier pouches we sent couriers out in tandem. Since time was of the essence we moved quickly. It was necessary to get the young man out of the country before the police could take steps to bar his departure. Luckily there was no delay in Narkomindel. Within a few hours we had his travel documents and the next afternoon he crossed the border safely into Finland.

This young man applied at the State Department for a clerkship in the Foreign Service following his return to the United States, and felt wronged when he learned that his application had been turned down because I was unwilling to recommend him to the department. He wrote me a letter pointing out that by reporting the affair to Faymonville he had proved himself to be a loyal and courageous U.S. citizen. I replied that so long as the Soviet police had in their possession the photograph he would be subject to blackmail regardless of where he might be working and that for his own good he should never again be employed in a confidential capacity by the U.S. government.

Some time later one of the embassy's American clerical employees who had been recruited in Europe came to me with a similar story. He had been informed by the Soviet police that they had compromising photographs of him and that they desired to have a talk with him. We also arranged for him to get immediately out of the country. Several other cases of blackmail involving affairs of members of the embassy with Soviet women also developed during my tour in Moscow. In order that our personnel would not be afraid to come to me, I warned them of the dangers of becoming compromised and urged them that if, as a result of an indiscretion, they found themselves in danger of being blackmailed, they should come to me at once so that I could do what was possible to help them.

Another means of bringing pressure on U.S. officials working in the area of Soviet-American relations was the stimulation of whispering or press campaigns against those officials who had assumed attitudes or taken positions that were particularly displeasing to the Soviet authorities. Officials in the Department of State who were working on matters pertaining to the Soviet Union or members of our embassy in Moscow might at any time become the target of a campaign of this kind. It was difficult for officers in the State Department handling Soviet affairs to draft memoranda relating to Soviet practices or to Soviet-American differences without indicating at times a lack of confidence in the trustworthiness of the Soviets or making other remarks of a critical character. Similarly, no member of the embassy could write honest, straightforward reports to the department regarding developments in the Soviet Union on problems in Soviet-American relations without engaging in a certain amount of criticism.

At different levels in the State Department as well as in other departments of the government and even in the White House, during that decade following the establishment of Soviet-American relations, there were persons emotionally sympathetic to the Soviet experiment who were shocked and angered when documents emanating from the embassy or the State Department would come to their attention that indicated a lack of confidence in Soviet good faith or tended to present the situation in the Soviet Union in an unfavorable light. Some of these persons sincerely believed that anyone who was suspicious of Soviet motives or was critical of Soviet conduct or accomplishments must be a fascist who should not be entrusted with the handling of matters pertaining to the Soviet Union. At dinner and cocktail parties these persons

would confide to like-minded friends that the writer of the critical document was "anti-Soviet" and should be removed from his position in the
State Department or the Foreign Service. The gossip thus generated
would eventually come to the attention of Soviet agents in the United
States, who, with the aid of their friends, the left-wing journalists, and
the more gullible liberals, would launch an organized campaign against
the writer. Sometimes these campaigns against members of the U.S.
embassy in Moscow would be generated by Soviet officials in Moscow,
who would hint to visiting Americans or to left-wing American journalists
residing in Moscow that the embassy or certain members of the embassy
were prejudiced against the Soviet Union. Eventually, the communist
press in the United States and the usual coterie of left-wing newspapers
and columnists would join in the hue and cry. Interesting enough, protracted campaigns of this character frequently succeeded in convincing a
large section of the American reading public that the person under attack
was a narrow-minded, rather stupid reactionary incapable of understanding the intellectual basis of communism. The period from 1933 to 1946
might well be called "the era of McCarthyism in reverse."

Officers in the embassy or in the Eastern European Division of the
State Department, aware of this situation, might well have been tempted
to write their reports, memoranda, instructions, and recommendations
in such a manner that they would not arouse the hostility of Soviet
authorities who might become acquainted with their contents. During my
first tour in Moscow no officers, so far as I know, succumbed to this
temptation. They reported situations and developments as they saw
them. Ambassador Davies was the only reporter in the embassy other
than Colonel Faymonville who, in preparing his dispatches and telegrams, usually tried to balance his critical comments with friendly explanations and rationalizations.

In a lengthy dispatch that I wrote on November 16, 1936, the third
anniversary of the establishment of diplomatic relations between the
United States and the Soviet Union, I devoted several paragraphs to the
Soviet practice of singling out for indirect attacks the U.S. governmental
institutions and officials with whom they were displeased. These paragraphs, written more than 30 years ago, read as follows:

> One of the most annoying of the practices of the Soviet Government is its
> attempts from time to time to bring pressure upon American govern-
> mental institutions or officials assisting in the conduct of Soviet-
> American relations by instigating or encouraging press or whispering
> campaigns against them either in the United States or among Americans
> living abroad. In engaging in this practice, the Soviet Government makes
> use of the following organizations or persons:

(a) Communist or so-called united front organizations in the United States;

(b) Certain groups of idealistic, well-intentioned American intellectuals or liberals who are dissatisfied with certain defects in American social conditions and are convinced that under the leadership of farsighted idealists the Soviet regime is working out a superior form of society. These persons are easily led to believe that the failure of the American Government to come to a full understanding with the Soviet Government on all points is the result of the machinations of prejudiced anti-Soviet American officials;

(c) American businessmen who hope by participating in a campaign agreeable to the Soviet Government to ingratiate themselves with that Government and to receive from it certain commercial concessions;

(d) Certain American intellectuals and journalists who are ambitious to be considered as authorities in the Russian field and hope to attain their ambition by gaining the gratitude of the Soviet Government to such an extent that it will grant them access to information not available to their colleagues; and

(e) Persons who for ideological, racial, or other reasons have become so antagonistic to one or more of the so-called fascist or militaristic countries, particularly Hitler-Germany or Japan, that they are inclined to judge American foreign policies in a somewhat emotional rather than an objective manner and are thus easily led into believing that the failure of the American Government to accede to the various desires of the Soviet Government, which they conceive to be the bulwark against fascism and militarism, is prompted by American officials who at heart are pro-fascist or pro-militarist.

During the years prior to recognition the Department of State was the chief target of the Moscow instigated campaign. Following the establishment of relations the State Department, particularly the Division of Eastern European Affairs of that Department, has continued to be one of the objects of indirect attack. A whispering campaign to the effect that the Eastern European Division and certain officials connected or formerly connected with the American Embassy in Moscow have been unfair in their treatment of the Soviet Union is being waged at the present time.

The line taken by such campaigns is usually that the tranquility of Soviet-American relations is being sabotaged by American officials who fail to present a true picture of the situation to their superiors. Various reasons are given for this failure, among which may be mentioned reactionary outlook, religious prejudice, personal pique or injured vanity, mediocre intelligence, careerism, and so forth.

Soviet officials in their efforts to break down the unity of this Mission and thus to undermine its effectiveness have on occasions gone so far as to endeavor to prejudice certain members of the Mission against persons serving with or under them and to intimate to other members that on account of their demonstrated friendliness towards the Soviet Government they were personally more *persona grata* than their fellow members.

In this respect American institutions and officials are the target for such attacks to no greater extent than those of other countries possessing democratic forms of government. British and French officials concerned with the handling of relations with the Soviet Union also find themselves from time to time subjected to Soviet-instigated criticism from their own countrymen.

It was amazing that the Division of Eastern European Affairs of the Department of State with the able Robert Kelley at its head weathered the attacks that were concentrated upon it for so many years. Left-wing columnists and newspapers had been attacking that division ever since its establishment in the early 1920s. Soviet officials never lost an opportunity to insinuate that the division was primarily responsible for the sad state of American-Soviet relations. As an example of their tactics, I quote Ambassador Davies's dispatch to the department on February 18, 1937, regarding a conversation he had during the course of a luncheon with Rosengolts, the people's commissar for foreign trade:

> Rosengolts also suggested that they had been informed that there was serious opposition to working out any agreement with Russia in certain quarters of the State Department and asked whether that was true. My reply was that I did not believe it to be true; that I had not found it to be the fact; that it might possibly be true "down below" just as it might possibly be true that "down below" in the Foreign Office of Russia there might be men who were bitterly hostile to the American Government as a representative of the hated capitalist order of society, but that I knew of no such attitude; and that I did know that such was not the fact so far as my President, the Secretary of State, Judge Moore or other responsible men in the Department, or I myself were concerned.

The left-wing American press was not so cautious in talking about those "down below"; neither was Litvinov in his private conversations with sympathetic U.S. visitors and officials. The main target in the State Department was of course the Division of Eastern European Affairs, the members of which collectively possessed more knowledge in depth regarding the Soviet Union than any institution in the United States. In June 1937, largely as the result of pressure exerted through influential persons in the White House, the Division of Eastern European Affairs was abolished. Most of its members were sent to the foreign field or to other areas in the department. Kelley, its chief, was assigned to Ankara as counselor of embassy; Orsen Nielsen, the assistant chief who had been handling Polish, Danzig, and Baltic affairs, was appointed assistant chief of the newly organized Division of European Affairs, in charge of the East European section of that division. The untransferred remnants of the Division of Eastern European Affairs remaining after the purge were incorporated in this section. The Russian library, which the division had built up during the course of more than fifteen years, was crated and sent to the Library of Congress; many of the valuable documents in the files of the division were mercilessly destroyed. Ray Murphy, one of the veterans of the division, was able secretly to salvage some of them and to keep them hidden until the mania to destroy had subsided.

The State Department henceforth did not have the personnel, the library, or the files to engage in any research work in depth relating to the Soviet Union. When a number of years later the department was criticized by members of the newly formed Office of Strategic Services for not having made more recent studies of developments in the Soviet Union, I told them what had happened to the Division of Eastern European Affairs. When they heard that the books, periodicals, and newspaper files of the library of the division had been transferred to the Library of Congress, they instituted a search for them in that library and finally discovered them in a storeroom in the crates in which they had been packed.

In August 1937 Kennan was transferred from the Moscow embassy to the State Department to assist Nielsen and remained there until shortly after I took over from Nielsen in the latter part of 1938.

As I have already indicated, one of the major difficulties experienced by the embassy in Moscow was its inability to convince the administrative areas of the Department of State that in view of the peculiarities of the Soviet system and of conditions in the Soviet Union, the embassy should be accorded special treatment by the department, the Bureau of the Budget, and the appropriate congressional committees. The Division of Foreign Service Personnel, in particular, could not understand why the embassy needed so many Soviet employees (translators, interpreters, doormen, messengers, chauffeurs, telephone operators, librarians), why we should have a commissary and a motor pool, and why we should be so insistent upon having only highly qualified American clerical employees.

Since Assistant Secretary Carr, the top administrative officer of the State Department, had confidence in the judgment of the members of the Division of Foreign Service Personnel, he had a tendency to back them rather than the members of the Division of Eastern European Affairs who understood our problems and tried to explain them to him. Carr, I may add, was personally not happy about the demands that the embassy was continually making on the department. In attempting to meet some of them in the past he had subjected himself to criticism by members of the Bureau of the Budget and of Congress.

In the latter part of 1936 I sent a series of telegrams, dispatches, and letters asking the department to transfer several of our clerks who had served more than two years in Moscow and to replace them with stenographers, since we were in urgent need of additional stenographic assistance. When I learned that Ambassador Davies would arrive in Moscow in January, I pleaded with the department to have in Moscow before his arrival at least one additional stenographer for his use.

When Mr. Davies arrived in Moscow and discovered how handicapped the embassy was because of the shortage of stenographers, he dictated a stinging telegram to the secretary of state. Although I was able to persuade him to tone down his language, the telegram that went out was nevertheless so strong that it provoked violent reaction in the State Department. The secretary personally called Carr to his office and asked for an explanation. The Division of Foreign Service Personnel in defending itself insisted that the embassy was well staffed and that its internal difficulties must be the result of poor administration. Kelley, representing the Eastern European Division, manfully defended the embassy. In any event, additional stenographers were sent and, in order to ascertain what the situation really was, Carr decided to send also to Moscow one of his most trusted inspectors, Klahr Huddle, to make a thorough inspection.

Huddle was known as a taciturn disciplinarian, an excellent administrator, and a fair-minded, considerate person. He arrived in Moscow early in 1937 just as Ambassador Davies was leaving for one of his extended tours in Western Europe. I was, therefore, in charge of the embassy while the inspection was taking place. For the first two weeks after his arrival in Moscow Huddle refused all social invitations extended by members of the embassy, including myself. He was courteous in his dealings with us but impersonal and withdrawn. He spent long hours going methodically through our files. He quizzed every American member of the staff regarding his duties. His last interview was with me; it lasted four hours. His questions were searching and to the point. He did not indicate whether he was displeased or pleased with what he found. At the close of the interview he said he was prepared to begin writing his inspection report and asked for a stenographer who could be trusted. I assigned one to him and saw little of him for the next three or four days.

Toward the end of his third week with us Huddle came into my office smiling and relaxed. He said that he would be glad now to meet members of the staff on a social basis; it was his practice not to establish informal friendly relations with members of an embassy that he was inspecting until he was sure that his report on the work of the embassy would be favorable. He had found that it was most embarrassing to be writing critical reports of a mission while he was enjoying the hospitality of its members. I was astonished when this man of few words then went on to speak in the most complimentary of terms of the embassy, of the ability it had shown to meet novel and difficult situations, of the high quality of its reports to the State Department, of its effective organization and efficient operation, and of the excellence of the morale of its members.

I believe that Huddle's inspection reports represented one of the turning points in my whole career. It gave me a clean bill of health with members of the administrative area of the State Department who in that period were accustomed to regard with suspicion the administrative abilities of officers whose departmental experience had been confined to one or more of the political-oriented geographic offices. The reports, furthermore, helped to clear the atmosphere between the embassy and the Division of Foreign Service Personnel. It also strengthened my position with Ambassador George Messersmith when the latter succeeded Carr in June 1937.

Messersmith took a deep and personal interest in the work and problems of our embassy. He studied our dispatches and from time to time called upon George Kennan, following the latter's transfer to the State Department in the fall of 1937, to fill him in on details. He took upon himself personally to discuss with Oumansky, the Soviet chargé d'affaires at the time, the problems of an administrative character that the embassy was encountering. The personal correspondence regarding the work and problems of the embassy between Messersmith and me during the twelve months following his assignment to the department was voluminous. He was particularly concerned at the strain that the cost of the maintenance of the embassy was exerting on the limited appropriations of the department and wrote me a number of letters in the early spring of 1938 on the subject.

I had heard informally that there was a strong sentiment in certain areas of the State Department that a convenient and relatively painless way of cutting the costs of the embassy was not to send a successor to Ambassador Davies when he left Moscow—it was understood that the ambassador had asked to be relieved in the spring of 1938—and to leave the embassy under the supervision of a chargé d'affaires for an indefinite period. It was my understanding that the advocates of this method of economizing were arguing that, although an ambassador had an opportunity to chat from time to time with the top officials of the Soviet government and to exchange hospitality with them, he was not able, regardless of his ability and energy, to exert any appreciable influence on Soviet foreign policies or on Soviet activities affecting the United States. Such information as he might obtain from his conversations with these officials was merely of the kind that they would like him to have and was of little value to the U.S. government. It was estimated that the cost of the embassy during the next fiscal year would amount to nearly $200,000—a staggering amount in the 1930s—of which amount more than $60,000 would represent the cost of maintaining an ambassador. The embassy could, therefore, save nearly a third of its operational costs by eliminating an ambassador and could function just as effectively under an able and experienced chargé d'affaires.

I was distressed at hearing that there was thinking of this kind in the department and took occasion in a letter to Messersmith, dated February 2, 1938, to give my personal views on the subject. I quote an excerpt from this letter:

> I would not be astonished, in view of the manner in which Ambassadors are treated in the Soviet Union by the Soviet authorities, to learn that there is a strong feeling in Washington that it is not only a waste of governmental funds but incompatible with our national dignity to support an Ambassador in Moscow and that it would be more in keeping with our relations with the Soviet Union to leave the Mission in the hands of a Chargé d'Affaires.
>
> With regard to the political aspects of the case, I think that it is hardly necessary for me to point out to you that:
>
> 1. Although the presence of an Ambassador in Moscow may yield few tangible results of a positive nature, nevertheless the failure of the American Government to appoint an Ambassador to succeed Mr. Davies might tend to increase world tension and might even lend encouragement to the aggressive elements of certain countries in need of raw materials and additional territory;
>
> 2. The failure of the American Government to appoint an Ambassador to succeed Mr. Davies would be certain to stir up criticism in more or less influential circles in the United States; in case war should break out within the near future between the Soviet Union and Japan or Germany, the Administration would in all probability be charged by these circles with a certain responsibility therefor on the ground that by its attitude it had strengthened anti-Soviet elements in Europe and Asia;
>
> 3. The Soviet Government would welcome an undemonstrative

sharp cut in the personnel and activities of this Mission, but would be annoyed at the decision of the Government to appoint no successor to Mr. Davies and might express its annoyance by taking steps to handicap still further the activities of the Mission.

With regard to the economic and political aspects of the question, it should be borne in mind that:

1. Thousands of dollars have been spent by the Government and by Mr. Bullitt and Mr. Davies personally to improve the representation possibilities of the Spaso House. If the Spaso House should be given up, it is doubtful if an equally suitable place would be placed at our disposal by the Soviet Government in case we later wanted to send an Ambassador to Moscow. Even if an acceptable house could be found, it would probably cost the American Government a large sum to make it suitable for representation purposes;

2. There is a considerable amount of expensive furniture, including specially-made curtains, in the Spaso House. In case the house is vacated much of the furniture must necessarily be packed and shipped abroad for use in other Missions or be stored since there are no appropriate storage facilities in Moscow. Some of this furniture could of course be used to supplement that which has been provided for the living quarters of the officers in the Mokhovaya Building. It is estimated that the cost of packing and shipping would amount to several thousand dollars;

3. In view of the costs which the closing of the Spaso House and the subsequent opening of a new residence would entail, it is doubted if any great saving would be effected by abandoning the house, unless a period of at least three years should elapse before the appointment of a new Ambassador;

4. If the Ambassador's residence were to be abandoned and the costs of the maintenance of the Mission correspondingly reduced, and at a later date it should be found advisable to appoint a new Ambassador to Moscow, it might be more difficult to obtain increased appropriations from Congress than to maintain present appropriations at their existing level.

On February 24 Messersmith wrote me a reassuring letter stating that the State Department had no intention of crippling the embassy or of giving up the ambassador's residence. Nevertheless, there were still strong sentiments in certain areas of the department in favor of not filling the vacancy to be created by the departure of Ambassador Davies. A member of the department, for instance, on March 24, 1938, sent to Messersmith a strong memorandum suggesting that the post of ambassador to Moscow might be left vacant for a while on the departure of Ambassador Davies. In his memorandum of reply, dated March 28, the assistant secretary stated that he appreciated the reasons that prompted the suggestion but he thought there were other reasons that outweighed them. He added that "in view of the general situation in Europe, I feel that the balance is in favor of sending a chief of mission to that post."

In spite of the views thus expressed by Messersmith, more than a year elapsed between the departure of Ambassador Davies from Moscow in June 1938 and the arrival of his successor in the summer of 1939. The savings thus effected were the ambassador's salary, travel costs, and so forth. We retained the Spaso House, the rental and upkeep of which was high.

CHAPTER 38

THE DIPLOMATIC CORPS IN MOSCOW AND THE PROBLEMS OF SOME OF ITS MEMBERS

IN VIEW OF THE CLOSE TIES that existed among the members of the diplomatic corps in Moscow and the frequency with which they met one another and exchanged information, no account of my experiences while in the Soviet Union would be complete unless it contained at least a brief discussion of the members of other diplomatic missions with whom the members of our embassy, including myself, had had more or less close association. Until I became chargé d'affaires in November 1935, I usually met chiefs of other missions only while making protocol calls upon them or at social functions.

During my early months in Moscow Ambassador Bullitt and John Wiley maintained close contacts with ambassadors and ministers while my associations were primarily with counselors, secretaries, and attachés. At that time the second ranking man of an embassy usually had the title of counselor or, if there were no counselor, of first secretary; the title of minister was reserved for the chiefs of legations; there was no such title as minister-counselor, which in later years is being given to many deputy chiefs of missions. During 1936–1937 and a portion of 1938, when for most of that time I was in charge of our embassy, it was necessary for me to keep in close touch with the chiefs of other missions. My associations with these ambassadors, ministers, chargés d'affaires, and members of their staffs resulted in friendships that during the next quarter of a century added to the richness of my life and proved helpful to me in connection with the carrying out of my duties at other posts.

In every post I subsequently served and at almost every diplomatic conference I have since attended, I have met friends with whom I had been associated in Moscow. Similarly, during my details to the Department of State there have usually been members of the diplomatic corps in Washington who had been my diplomatic colleagues in the Soviet Union. In looking through the old diplomatic lists recently I noted that no less than 30 of the counselors and secretaries whom I had known in Moscow have subsequently represented their countries in other parts of the world as chiefs of diplomatic mission. Among the ambassadors and ministers who were in Moscow with me, several eventually became prime ministers or foreign ministers of their respective countries.

THE MORALE OF THE DIPLOMATIC CORPS SAGS AS THE INTERNATIONAL SITUATION BECOMES PROGRESSIVELY MORE GLOOMY

During my last two years in Moscow, as the war clouds became darker and as such phrases as "our policy of peace" and "peace-loving nations" became progressively more inapplicable to some of the nations that were most prone to use them, an atmosphere of foreboding gradually enveloped the whole diplomatic corps. No one could be sure what would happen to his own country. In such an atmosphere even I began to have serious concerns about what might take place in my own country. I had not been in the United States for more than four years. Such information as I was able to obtain regarding the developing situation in it came from studies of the U.S. press and from conversations with Americans who had been there recently.

It seemed to me that there was a growing intolerance and arrogance among the more extreme left-wing New Dealers, some of whom appeared to hold positions of influence. There was an increasing tendency also among the columnists and editorial writers to label as fascist or nazi persons who did not agree with their left-wing views. Attacks on the "reactionary" State Department and the Foreign Service, which in my opinion were doing their best to keep the ship of state steady, were becoming more frequent and sharp. Some of the closest advisers of the president were openly expressing their contempt for the professionals who were trying to carry on in the area of foreign affairs. I had the feeling that the values I had been taught to cherish were in danger of being swept away, that the old virtues, which in my opinion had served to make the

United States great, were being gradually replaced by bright new concepts of individual and mass behavior. Most of these concepts I did not regard as new. To me they seemed similar to concepts that were in vogue among a series of decadent civilizations.

During the spring of 1938, as the international situation became increasingly gloomy, as the Communists in the United States seemed to be achieving successes in drawing an increasing number of persons and groups into their united front, and as attacks on the State Department and the Foreign Service became more and more shrill, it was difficult for me to maintain the morale of the American members of the embassy on my own. I was particularly depressed by the fact that not a single leader of the administration was lifting a voice in defense of the hundreds of conscientious persons who were working long hours under tremendous strain in the State Department and in our diplomatic missions and consular offices in all parts of the world.

A letter that I addressed to Milton Shy, one of my nephews, on May 3, 1938, in answer to a question from him as to whether or not in my opinion it would be advisable for him while in the university to prepare for a career in the Foreign Service, reflected my frame of mind at that time. An extract from this letter reads as follows:

> In my opinion it would be a mistake for you to prepare for the Diplomatic Service... With the world as it is, the future of persons specializing in political-economic fields is extremely uncertain. A sudden drastic change in our outlook with respect to the form of government most suitable to the United States, or the sudden rise to power of some political party which may have the view that everything that the American Government has done in recent years is wrong, is likely to result in the reorganization of the whole diplomatic service and of replacing the men in it with political appointees or partisans... Suppose that after you have spent fifteen years in the diplomatic service you should suddenly find yourself turned loose on the world. In that service you would have learned little that would fit you for other fields of work and you at middle age would be without a profession.

I made it clear to my nephew that I had no regrets at having entered the service, that I liked it and had no desire to do anything else, but that in the present uncertain world it was my opinion that if he had any ability in scientific or technical fields it would be preferable for him to attempt to develop it. "If you once have acquired a good technical training," I wrote, "and if you continue to keep yourself at the top by strict application, you have gained something which no revolution or no change in the social order can take from you."

Incidentally my nephew followed my advice. He decided to study medicine. Although he had a rich and satisfying life as a physician, he once confided to me that at times he had pangs of regret that he could not also have had a career in the Foreign Service. My advice to him, however, might not have been so bad. During the late 1960s, when youth had become exceptionally intolerant of their elders, many of the most distinguished members of the Foreign Service, whose ages were similar to that of my nephew, were being mercilessly ejected from the Foreign Service in order to satisfy the organized clamor of some of the young and ambitious members who regarded themselves as the exponents of the "new diplomacy" and who were demanding that those above them be pushed out in order that they might move more quickly up the career ladder of the Foreign Service.

The forebodings of disaster that troubled most members of the diplomatic corps turned out to be justified. Of the twenty-six countries that were diplomatically represented in Moscow in the early part of 1938, twenty-two became involved in a bloody war within the next four years; the territories of twenty were subjected to armed invasion or occupation; eleven lost their independence temporarily, and seven either lost their independence permanently or were reduced to the status of satellites. Of the ambassadors and ministers with whom we were accustomed to exchange views, one was executed by Hitler; one was seized while still in Moscow and was presumably executed; one committed suicide; one was imprisoned temporarily and in my opinion unjustly as a war criminal; and seven were doomed to permanent exile. Similar tragedies awaited many of the more junior members of the corps.

CHAPTER 39

THE CONTRAST BETWEEN
TWO AMBASSADORS

THE DESCRIPTION OF THE ACTIVITIES and problems of our embassy in Moscow during the years 1934–1938 would be incomplete if it should ignore the differences in the personalities and outlooks of the two ambassadors to the Soviet Union during that period, Ambassador Bullitt and Ambassador Davies.

WILLIAM C. BULLITT: THE FIRST U.S. AMBASSADOR
TO THE SOVIET UNION, DECEMBER 1933–SEPTEMBER 1936

Bullitt was not a stickler for the conventions in private life; traces of the Bohemianism that had characterized his youth remained with him as he became more mature. He had very strong conventional ideas, however, regarding the relations that should prevail among governments and states, between an official and his government, and between a private citizen and his country.

In passing judgments on people and actions Bullitt was prone to see the world in black and white. Gray areas to him represented weakness, opportunism, lack of courage, or a tendency to appease. He despised deceit and evasions and had no respect for those who in his opinion were not keeping their word or in some other way were failing to act in what he considered to be an honorable manner.

He was so confident that the principles of international intercourse on which he based his own thoughts and actions were correct that he was inclined to be intolerant of persons who in his opinion were not supporting or living up to them. His intolerance was not always of a passive character. At times he assumed an almost vindictive attitude toward persons and institutions that happened to differ with him on matters he deemed to be important. He was not inclined to forgive or forget actions or attitudes that he regarded as unworthy or as a betrayal of trust. He could be, as President Wilson discovered, a formidable enemy. Although I respected the firmness of his adherence to his convictions, I felt that at times he was not quite fair to those who had other convictions and were trying honorably and courageously to live up to them.

Bullitt had a loathing for persons who were aggressively on the make and for those whom he regarded as social climbers. Nevertheless, he had certain ambitions of his own.

From childhood he had had an abhorrence of war and his dream was of a world in which war could be effectively outlawed. In particular, he did not want the United States to be involved in another devastating war.

He was an intense patriot. He was proud of being a U.S. citizen and could not forgive, or associate with, any American who in his opinion by acts of commission or omission was damaging the United States or injuring its reputation.

Such tolerance as he had displayed toward the Russian revolution prior to 1934 had been based primarily on his belief that it would give the oppressed Russian masses a chance to lead better lives. He had thought that hidden in the totalitarianism and manifest cruelties of the Soviet regime there was a core of idealism. He had believed at the time of the establishment of relations between the United States and the Soviet Union that the Soviet leaders desired U.S. friendship and that for the sake of that friendship, as well as for that of their international reputation, they would live up to the promises that Litvinov had made to Roosevelt. For this reason he desired that those promises deal with all problems that might, if not solved in advance, cause friction between the two countries. He considered it important that such commitments as might be made be explicit and of a kind that could not easily be misinterpreted.

While still in his early forties, he arrived in Moscow in March 1934 to establish the first embassy of the United States to the Soviet Union. He possessed the confidence of the president of the United States and seemed to be popular in the Soviet Union. He had high hopes that he might succeed where others had failed and that he might be able to prevail upon the Kremlin to adopt policies that would enable the Soviet Union to become a respected and trusted member of the community of nations. He believed that if the Soviet government failed to live up to Litvinov's promises to the president, particularly the promise that the Soviet Union would not interfere in the internal affairs of the United States, any talk of sincere friendly relations between the two countries would be mere mockery. I am convinced that if his hopes had been realized there would not have been a Second World War.

During most of the period from March 1934 to August 1935 Bullitt concentrated on efforts to persuade—by cajolery, promises of fruitful friendship, and forceful language—the Soviet leaders that it was in their interest to live up to the promises made by Litvinov. With the exception of the matter of debts and claims, in return for the settlement of which the United States was prepared to extend large credits to the Soviet Union, he had little to offer the Soviet leaders in return for keeping the promises made by Litvinov except U.S. friendship and cooperation. At a time when the United States was trying to remain aloof from international politics, its friendship and cooperation were not likely to yield the kind of fruit the Soviet Union was looking for.

As it became progressively clearer that the Soviet leaders under various pretexts were relieving themselves of the promises made by Litvinov, Bullitt became more and more disillusioned and bitter. When, in spite of his vehement protests and warnings, the Seventh All-World Congress of the Communist International took place in Moscow, Bullitt in effect abandoned as hopeless his efforts to promote friendship and close relations between the two countries. He departed for the United States in the latter part of 1935 and returned near the end of February 1936 only to depart in April, never to return.

The failure of the Soviet government to carry out the promises made by Litvinov was not the only reason that prompted a change in Bullitt's attitude toward the Soviet Union. As he gradually became aware of the kind of life that the average Soviet citizen was leading and of the methods employed by the Soviet leaders to subject them to control, as he became better acquainted with codes that governed the conduct and ways of thinking of the Soviet leaders, and as he saw the manner in which these leaders were treating the tens of millions of people who were at their mercy, he lost such sympathy as he had had for an experiment that had been going on for so many years. He began to doubt that the product of the brutality, inhumanity, and deceit that he witnessed on every side would be a society that could loyally cooperate with the countries of what he regarded as the civilized world. Shortly before his final departure from the Soviet Union he wrote a dispatch, dated April 20, 1936, which we in the embassy referred to as his "swan song." In this dispatch he submitted his "views as to the policies the United States should follow with respect to the Soviet Union and Communism." Some of the excerpts that I quote below from this dispatch should assist the reader in understanding the kind of feelings Bullitt had toward the Soviet Union and communism after having served there for more than two and a half years as ambassador.

> Today Stalin considers it sound strategy to support democratic forms of government in countries in which communism is still weak; but the meaning of that support was displayed by Dimitrov at the Comintern Congress in August 1935, when he pointed out that at the moment the cause of communism could be promoted best by the use of the tactics of the Trojan horse and warned his communist comrades that they were not good communists if they felt that it was indecent or unduly hypocritical to become the collaborators and pretended friends of democrats in order the better eventually to lead those democrats to the firing squad.

> The problem of relations with the Government of the Soviet Union is, therefore, a subordinate part of the problem presented by communism as a militant faith determined to produce world revolution and the "liquidation" (that is to say, murder), of all non-believers.

> There is no doubt whatsoever that all orthodox communist parties in all countries, including the United States, believe in mass murder. Moreover, the loyalty of a believing communist is not to the nation of which he is technically a citizen but to his faith and to the Caliph of that faith. To such men the most traitorous betrayals are the highest virtues...

> It must be recognized that communists are agents of a foreign power whose aim is not only to destroy the institutions and liberties of our country, but also to kill millions of Americans. Our relations with the Soviet Union, therefore, involve questions of domestic policy which can not be answered except on the basis of a careful estimate of the strength of world communism and the reality or unreality of its threat to our liberties and lives...

> Russia has always been a police state. It is a police state today. The authority of the Kremlin rests on the strength of its army and the omnipresence of its secret police, no less than on the fervor of the convinced communists.

> The secret police and the army are better fed, housed, and entertained than any other portion of the population. Their loyalty to the Soviet regime is unquestionable. And there is no longer reasonable doubt as to the strength of the Red Army. It numbers today nearly a million and a half men. Its material equipment in artillery, airplanes, and tanks is abundant in quantity though deficient in quality. It cannot undertake offensive operations due to the fact that the railroads are still inadequate for the peace time needs of the country and to the equally important fact that there are literally no modern highways in the entire

Soviet Union. But on the defensive, the Red Army would fight hard, well and long...

What then should be the policy of the United States with regard to the Soviet Government and the world communist movement?

We should not cherish for a moment the illusion that it is possible to establish really friendly relations with the Soviet Government or with any communist party or communist individual.

We should maintain diplomatic relations with the Soviet Union because it is now one of the Greatest Powers and its relations with Europe, China, and Japan are so important that we can not conduct our foreign relations intelligently if we do not know what is happening in Moscow. Moreover, in spite of all efforts to conceal the truth from foreigners, it is possible to obtain in Moscow considerable information as to the Soviet Union and the world communist movement...

We should attempt to promote our trade with the Soviet Union by direct bargaining of the sort involved in our agreement of July 13, 1935. But we should have no illusion that our trade with the Soviet Union may ever be stable or permanent. It may be cut off for political reasons at any minute. Therefore, we should not make loans or give long-term credits to the Soviet Union and should advise American industrialists against putting in expensive machinery to produce for the Soviet market...

Our Federal Government should inform itself as to the membership of the Communist Party in the United States and as to the relations between the American communists, the Soviet Diplomatic and Consular Representatives, and the other agents of the Soviet Government and the Communist Party in the United States: Amtorg, Intourist, Voks, International Red Aid, etc.

In our domestic policies, we should act on the realization that there is one fatal blow which can be struck at communism not only in the United States but also in every other country in the world. The final argument of the believing communist is invariably that all battle, murder, and sudden death, all the spies, exiles, and firing squads are justified because communist dictatorship is the only method which permits a modern economic machine to run at full speed and to find always an unsatisfied buying power, whereas the maldistribution of the national income in our system causes inevitably recurrent crises and unemployment...If we can achieve such continuous increases in the buying power of the masses of our population that our fullest possible production may find demand, the single effective plea of the communists will disappear. To turn a much greater proportion of our national income each year into the pockets of those who have little so that there may be effective demand for the products of our fields and factories is, therefore, not only the moral obligation of a democratic people but also the most certain method of destroying the single intellectual justification of the Communist Faith.

The keynote of our immediate relations with the Soviet Union should be patience. The communist movement in the United States today constitutes a potential danger but not an actual threat. We do not need to get excited about it. Our political relations with the Soviet Union are negative; but our trade is increasing. It is difficult to conduct conversations with the Soviet Foreign Office because in that institution the lie is normal and the truth abnormal and one's intelligence is insulted by the happy assumption that one believes the lie. But patience and diplomats exist for just that sort of difficulty.

We should neither expect too much nor despair of getting anything at all. We should be as steady in our attitude as the Soviet Union is fickle. We should take what we can get when the atmosphere is favorable and do our best to hold on to it when the wind blows the other way. We should remain unimpressed in the face of slights and underhand opposition. We should make the weight of our influence felt steadily over a long period of time in the directions which best suit our interests. We should never threaten. We should act and allow the Bolsheviks to draw their own conclusions as to the causes of our acts.

Above all, we should guard the reputation of Americans for businesslike efficiency, sincerity, and straightforwardness. We should never send a spy to the Soviet Union. There is no weapon at once so disarming and effective in relations with the communists as sheer honesty. They know very little about it.

I may add that Bullitt was as hostile to nazism as he was to communism. As ambassador to France from 1936 to 1939, he did his best to keep the State Department informed of the dangers to world peace inherent in both Soviet communism and German nazism. When following the fall of France he was unable to obtain a position in the U.S. government that would enable him personally to engage in the struggle against Hitler-Germany, he entered the French Army and participated in the liberation of France.

Joseph E. Davies: The Second U.S. Ambassador to the Soviet Union, January 1937–June 1938

In the latter part of 1936, under instructions from the State Department, I presented to Litvinov an abbreviated biography of the life of Joseph E. Davies and asked for an agrément for him as United States ambassador to the Soviet Union. Although the commissar made a few sarcastic remarks about politicians with a lot of money who wanted to be ambassadors—remarks that I ignored—I was notified almost immediately that the agrément had been granted. Following the announcement that accompanied the submission of Davies's name to the Senate, the

Soviets instituted both in the United States and in the Soviet Union what I have referred to as the "bygones campaign." Let me describe this campaign by giving illustrations:

In early January 1937 Boris Steiger, the Soviet official whom the Kremlin was accustomed to use in sending messages to the embassy through channels other than Narkomindel, told me that he had an oral message for me. I incorporated the statements he made to me in a memorandum, a copy of which I handed the ambassador several days later when I met him at the Soviet-Polish border. The memorandum read in part as follows:

> The Kremlin has issued a directive to Mr. Litvinov to the effect that the People's Commissariat for Foreign Affairs shall treat Mr. Davies, the new Ambassador, with the utmost consideration and courtesy and that it shall endeavor to see that he receives similar treatment from Soviet officials with whom he may come in contact who are not in that Commissariat. Any irritations which may have arisen during the past three years are to be forgotten and a new book in the relations between the Embassy and the Soviet Government is to be opened.
>
> The Soviet Government is glad that the American Government has named as Ambassador to the Soviet Union someone who, it is understood, will approach his work in an objective spirit. It is difficult to say which is worse—an Ambassador who comes to the Soviet Union with a feeling of antagonism or one who does so full of sentimental friendliness. Probably the former is better since he will not be expecting exceptional treatment or personal favors and can be dealt with on a strictly business basis. Almost without an exception Ambassadors or Ministers who have come to the Soviet Union with an attitude of sentimental friendliness have in the end become embittered when they have discovered that such an attitude is embarrassing to the Soviet authorities who can not afford to treat them in a manner markedly different from the manner in which it treats other Chiefs of Mission.
>
> I hope that you will make two suggestions to the new Ambassador:
>
> 1. That he will not take seriously the critical remarks which the members of the Diplomatic Corps are certain to make to him regarding the Soviet Union; and
>
> 2. That he approach his tasks in a quiet and unobtrusive manner and not permit small irritations to influence him against the Soviet Union until he may have had time to form balanced opinions for himself.

Before the new ambassador left Washington, Ambassador Troyanovsky had given him similar counsel. Davies reported that:

The second point which Ambassador Troyanovsky made (and it seemed to me quite pointed in view of previous talks) was that he felt that the best opportunity for the development of friendly relations now lay in the interchange of visits by prominent persons of each country and that it would be best to let bygones be bygones in so far as controversial matters were concerned.

There can be no doubt that the "bygones campaign" made a lasting impression on Ambassador Davies. During the period that he was ambassador in Moscow he was careful not to enter into acrimonious discussions regarding the violation by the Soviet government of the various pledges made at the time of the establishment of relations. He, wisely, in my opinion, did not engage in arguments relating to continued Soviet interference in the internal affairs of the United States; it was only during his last days in the Soviet Union that he had a brief and amiable chat with Soviet leaders regarding the problems of debts, claims, and credits—a chat that did not result in progress toward their solution.

My first contact with Ambassador Davies took place at the Polish–Soviet border station on the night of January 18, 1937, where I had gone to meet him and his party, including Mrs. Davies, and to accompany them to Moscow. The new ambassador at the time was 60 years of age, of medium height, sturdily built with thinning gray hair and a mobile aquiline face, the most striking feature of which was his flashing, probing eyes. He was immaculately dressed and carried a walking stick with a heavy round gold head.

Mrs. Davies, who was to celebrate her fiftieth birthday within the next few days, appeared exceptionally young for her years. In spite of the long tiresome trip from Berlin she did not look at all travel worn. Mrs. Davies was one of the world's wealthiest women, and she did not hesitate to make use of her wealth to keep herself in good physical condition and to retain the beauty of her youth. She had brought with her to Moscow a staff to look after her, including her own hairdresser and masseur.

The ambassador had sent to me in advance for distribution to interested persons a short biographical sketch of himself. Following his election, Woodrow Wilson appointed Davies chairman of the Federal Trade Commission, where he would have an opportunity to make many important contacts. In 1918, with the backing of his relatives and friends in Wisconsin, he ran for the U.S. Senate but was defeated. When President Wilson offered him the ambassadorship to Russia, he declined the honor. He turned to the practice of law in Washington. In view of his experience in the Federal Trade Commission and of his many contacts in governmental and business circles he was not lacking in clients. He had represented the governments of Holland, Mexico, Greece, and the Dominican Republic. In fact, the first time that I had heard of him was in the early 1930s when he was visiting various desks in the State Department in his efforts to prevail upon the United States to recognize the government that Trujillo had set up in the Dominican Republic.

His law firm had also handled a number of famous cases, several of which had gone up to the Supreme Court. He was the author of two or three books of a legal character, including one that dealt with trust laws and unfair competition. He apparently had the idea that the word "diplomat" connoted an insincere and untrustworthy person. In any event it was customary for him to assure Soviet officials that he was not a diplomat. When I introduced him to Litvinov he told the commissar that he had held high offices of public trust and that he was a jurist, an author, and a businessman, but not a diplomat. On hearing this Litvinov turned to me in mock surprise and said "There must be some misunderstanding; I thought that you were presenting to me the new American ambassador, but our visitor denies that he is a diplomat."

During the eighteen months that I worked with Ambassador Davies I noted many differences between him and Ambassador Bullitt. Both were highly gifted, both had agreeable personalities, and both had the ability to speak and write persuasively. Davies, however, unlike Bullitt, tended to admire men because they had succeeded in amassing enormous wealth or accumulating great power. He cultivated them and liked to associate with them. Bullitt would become depressed when he saw mud-covered, weary, half-starved-appearing women waiting in line for an overcrowded streetcar or bus. These waiting lines did not appear unduly to disturb Davies. His eyes were directed to the people at the top. He did not seem to be particularly interested in the manner in which the Soviet leaders had been able to reach the pinnacles of power; he was a pragmatist in the sense that the mere fact that they had reached such pinnacles was to him proof that they were great men. When Soviet leaders whom he had been cultivating—like Rosengolts, the commissar for foreign trade; Krestinsky, the assistant commissar for foreign affairs; or Marshal Tukhachevsky—were toppled or executed, he did not display concern.

The ambassador and Mrs. Davies, his second wife whom he had married only a few months before his appointment to the Soviet Union, were apparently devoted to each other. They met the frustrations of Moscow gallantly and seemed to enjoy becoming acquainted with the Soviet leaders and mingling with members of the diplomatic corps. They were considerate of the staff of the embassy and frequently went out of their way to show courtesies to the American members of the embassy and their families. The impulsive Bullitt sometimes lost his temper, but Davies, when displeased, was likely to be coldly suave.

Bullitt was intimately acquainted with the international problems of Europe, the Far East, and the Middle East. Davies looked to his staff when he was in need of information of an international political character. He considered that friendly exchanges of views between himself and the Soviet leaders were evidence of progress in the direction of friendly relations between the United States and the Soviet Union. Bullitt believed that such exchanges were sterile unless they were accompanied by acts or were preludes to acts that would contribute to the removal of the basic causes of friction between the two countries.

It became evident immediately following the arrival of Ambassador Davies in Moscow that it was his intention to do his utmost to convince the Soviet leaders with whom he was to come in contact of his admiration for them, for their objectives, and for the good things that there were doing. The first official call that he made was on Krestinsky, the assistant commissar for foreign affairs who, in the absence from the Soviet Union of Litvinov, was in charge of the commissariat. After I had presented Davies he began at once to praise what he had seen in the Soviet Union. He said that he was particularly impressed with the appearance of the Soviet people whom he had met on the train and seen on the streets and he dwelt on the enormous amount of construction that was going on everywhere. He talked in a similar way during the other calls that we made.

It was to be expected that in conversations with Soviet leaders the subject of the differences that had developed between the two governments would arise. During discussions of this kind the ambassador played the temperate role of the seasoned statesman who was above the scene of struggle.

By keeping conversations touching on differences between the two governments on a highly noncontroversial level; by assuring Soviet leaders with whom he talked of the desire of himself and of his principals in the United States for closer friendly cooperation between the United States and the Soviet Union; by praising, whenever occasion offered, the objectives and accomplishments of the Soviet regime; by softening such criticisms of Soviet conditions and developments as were contained in his reports to the State Department by setting forth extenuating circumstances; and by refraining from making remarks critical of the Soviet Union in discussions with other members of the diplomatic corps, journalists, and visiting Americans, the ambassador succeeded in building up for himself both in the United States and the Soviet Union a reputation of being a friend and an admirer of the Soviet Union and its leaders.

In the course of his reporting the ambassador did not hesitate at times to present forthrightly the unpleasant aspects of the Soviet Union in strong language. In stating the extenuating circumstances he did not go so far as to defend what was going on. His rationalizations were usually confined to explanations of the circumstances or motives responsible for the actions or the situations that he was describing. For instance, in a dispatch to the State Department dated April 1, 1938, in referring to the Great Purge, he said:

> The Terror here is a horrifying fact. There are many evidences here in Moscow that there is a terrifying fear that reaches down into and haunts all sections of the community. No household, however humble, apparently but what lives in constant fear of a nocturnal raid by the Secret Police (usually between one and three in the early morning). Once the person is taken away, nothing of him or her is known for months—and many times—never thereafter. Evidences of these conditions come from many sources...
>
> It is commonly alleged that the Secret Police of this Proletarian Dictatorship are as ruthless and as cruel as any during the old Tsarist regimes. It seems to be an old Russian custom. This particular purge is undoubtedly political. From expressions that I have heard from some of the leaders of the Government it is deliberately projected by the Party leaders, who themselves regretted the necessity for it, but who nevertheless will not permit themselves to be sentimental or weak in the performance of what they regard as their duty. They believe that great revolutions cannot be projected by spraying perfume; that previous movements in the interests of the proletariat have been destroyed by weakness and false sentimentality. They recognize and regret that there must needs be many innocent who suffer in this situation, but they take the position that they must do this to save their cause, which is supreme and that the successful elevation of the condition of life of the proletariat will, in historical perspective, justify their present course. They wrap themselves about in the mantle of the angels to serve the devil. They are undoubtedly a strong, able group of ruthless idealists. But tyranny is tyranny, whatever be its government.

An excerpt from the ambassador's dispatch of June 6, 1938, reads as follows:

> As for ourselves—this system is a tyranny, clothed in horror. While a dictatorship of the most ruthless and cruel type exists here, it appears to differ from a fascist dictatorship, at least in one respect. Dictatorship is apologized for here. It is justified on the ground that it is a realistic expedient, resorted to only to protect the masses of the people, until they

can themselves rule under a system where ideologically the individual and not the state shall be supreme. Moreover, there is no doubt of the present sincerity of this regime in its desire to maintain Peace.

It seemed to me that the essential difference between the tactics pursued by Bullitt and those by Davies was that the former took the position that, unless the Kremlin would demonstrate that it was prepared to abide by the promises given at the time of the establishment of diplomatic relations, particularly the promise relating to non-interference in internal affairs, there could be no genuinely friendly relations between the United States and the Soviet Union; whereas Davies took the position that, in spite of the differences between the two countries, they could have friendly cooperative relations and that in keeping with the spirit of such relations they should be able to iron out their major differences, or at least to work together for their mutual benefit in spite of the existence of differences. The tactics of Davies included convincing the Soviet authorities that he was personally their sincere friend and that in his search for ways of eliminating or relegating to the background such differences as existed between the United States and the Soviet Union he was working for the good of both countries. There could be no doubt that the leaders in the Kremlin preferred Davies's tactics.

The ambassador did not like to pollute the friendly atmosphere that existed between him and Litvinov by becoming involved in discussions of unpleasant topics. He, therefore, left to his staff to the extent possible the responsibility of arguing with the Soviet authorities regarding such matters as the arrest and treatment of U.S. citizens; the inability of Soviet wives of U.S. citizens to obtain exit visas; the difficulties encountered by members of the embassy in taking their effects out of the country; delays in the procurement of visas for the entrance into the Soviet Union of Americans appointed to serve in the embassy; and the arrests of Soviet employees of the embassy. When under instructions from the State Department, or because it would be unsuitable for him as the chief of mission to remain silent, he did on occasions take up matters of this kind with Litvinov. He did so, however, in an apologetic manner as though he were asking a personal favor.

Since it was the understanding of the members of the embassy that the president and the State Department desired the embassy to report frankly on Soviet conditions and developments as they saw them, they continued to do so. The ambassador frequently toned down the criticisms contained in such reports prepared for his signature or merely failed to sign them and incorporated such of the data contained in them that appealed to him in reports of his own. During the period that he was in

Moscow he was an active reporter and kept the political and economic sections, and at times even the consular section, preparing studies for his use. He did not seem happy at some of the reports that were sent to the department during his frequent and protracted absences, but since they were for the most part factual he did not remonstrate regarding their contents. I was at times puzzled by his attitude. He seemed to desire the embassy, in reporting to the department, to present Soviet conditions and developments in a favorable light; nevertheless, he did not issue instructions to that effect. Neither did he indicate to me that we were to follow any particular line in his absence.

I found a partial explanation of the ambassador's attitude only a couple of weeks prior to his final departure from the Soviet Union. On June 5, 1938, as I was making final preparations for a trip that I had been planning to take to the Arctic Regions of central Siberia, I received a summons from him to come at once to his residence. When I arrived at the Spaso House I found him for the first time since his arrival in Moscow in a state of intense excitement. He said, "I have seen him; I have finally had a talk with him; he is really a fine, upstanding, great man!" He then told me in some detail that when he had made his farewell call on Molotov, who at the time held a position equivalent to that of prime minister, Stalin had entered the room. He thus had been able to talk to the real leader of the Soviet Union for more than two hours. He said that among the matters touched upon were the related problems of debts, claims, and credits and that he would like to discuss these problems again with Stalin and Molotov before his departure and would be appreciative if I would at once prepare a memorandum setting forth the main points at issue. He told me that this was one of the great days of his life, that the president had instructed him that his main mission in Moscow was to win the confidence of Stalin, to be able to talk over Soviet-American relations frankly and personally with Stalin, that he had been striving ever since his arrival in Moscow to carry out this mission, and that just on the eve of his departure he had finally succeeded. He was convinced that he had gained the confidence of both Stalin and Molotov. He felt that he had already won that of Litvinov. He would now, even though no longer stationed in Moscow, be in a position to act as a private pipeline between the White House and the Kremlin.

In his dispatch of June 9, 1938, the ambassador described his surprise meeting with Stalin as follows:

> I broke the ice by stating that I had returned to Russia because of a desire, on the occasion of my departure, to express my respects formally to President Kalinin and Premier Molotov, and to express my appreciation

of the courtesies that this Government and its officials had extended to me. Meeting Mr. Stalin, I then said, was a great surprise, and that I was very much gratified to have this opportunity. I then went on to say that I had personally inspected typical plants of practically all of the heavy industries of the Soviet Union, as well as the great hydraulic developments of the country; that these extraordinary achievements, which had been conceived and projected in the short period of ten years, had commanded my great admiration; that I had heard it said that history would record Stalin as the man who was responsible for this achievement and that he would be recorded as a greater builder than Peter the Great, or Catherine; that I was honored by meeting the man who had built for the practical benefit of common men.

To this, Stalin demurred and stated that the credit was not his; that the plan had been conceived and projected by Lenin, who had projected the original Dnieperstroi Dam project; that the ten-year plan was not his work; that it was due to the three thousand able men who had planned this work and those others of his associates; and above all that it was the "Russian People" who were responsible, and that he disclaimed any personal credit therefor. He gave me the impression of being sincerely modest.

Fortunately I had completed the preparations for my trip to Siberia and was able, therefore, to devote myself during the following 36 hours to the drafting of the memorandum to which I added a few suggestions that I thought might be helpful. The ambassador, despite requests on his part, was not able to see Stalin again. He did, however, talk again to Molotov who gave him a memorandum regarding the basis on which the problem of debts, claims, and credits might be discussed. When the ambassador had examined this memorandum he was disappointed since he knew that the basis suggested would be unacceptable to Washington. Following his return to the United States he had, with the consent of the White House, some further desultory conversations regarding this problem outside the usual channels but nothing ever came of them.

Although the meeting between Ambassador Davies and Stalin did not, as Ambassador Troyanovsky indicated to Mr. Hull on June 7, 1938, prove to be a "real turning point in the relations between our two countries, the clearing up of certain debt questions, as well as other minor matters...which have operated to keep up friction between our two Governments," it did represent a feather in Ambassador Davies's cap and increased his prestige among wide circles in the United States. The ambassador was able to bring out of the Soviet Union as trophies of his tour in Moscow the autographed photographs of Stalin, Molotov, and Litvinov—photographs that until his death he kept in prominent places in his library. As the "special friend of Stalin" he never hesitated during the last years of President Roosevelt's administration and the early years of that of President Truman to go to the White House from time to time to give advice with regard to the policies that we should pursue toward the Soviet Union.

Although I had no doubt that Stalin was pleased to have an opportunity to show his appreciation of the attitude that Davies had taken with respect to the Soviet Union during the latter's tour as ambassador, I came to the realization when reading Davies's description of the conversation of June 5 that Stalin had desired to have a talk with the ambassador on a subject that was close to his heart. The Soviet Union was trying feverishly to strengthen its armed forces. In particular, it was eager to have a powerful modern navy at the earliest possible moment. It, therefore, desired to purchase from abroad battleships of all classes, heavy naval guns, submarines, planes, heavy steel armor, and so forth. The United States seemed to be the only country that might be able to supply the Soviet naval and military needs. For several months the Soviet government had been trying to arrange for the purchase of a modern, fully equipped super-battleship. Negotiations with regard to the sale of a battleship and other types of arms were lagging.

I noted from the description of the conversation prepared by Ambassador Davies that just as soon as he and Stalin had concluded their exchange of amenities and Stalin had answered in a general way a question regarding the international situation put to him by Davies, Stalin had asked if the ambassador "was familiar with the pending negotiations which the Soviet Government was having with the Government of the United States in connection with the proposed contract for the construction of a Soviet battleship by an American firm." During the ensuing discussion it was clear that Stalin was trying to enlist the support of the ambassador in the expediting of the negotiations. Thus, it developed that in spite of the studied indifference that Litvinov had displayed regarding the deterioration of Soviet-American relations, the Soviet leaders had discovered that since there were certain things that the Soviet Union desired urgently to obtain from the United States, they were in need of American cooperation.

DAVIES ENDEAVORS TO KEEP THE PRESIDENT INFORMED REGARDING THE EUROPEAN SITUATION

While Ambassador Davies was stationed in Moscow, he had interests that embraced more than the Soviet Union. At the time of his appointment he had come to an understanding with the president that he might from time to time visit other countries in Europe and advise the president regarding the conditions that he found in them.

In order to facilitate their travels Mrs. Davies arranged for her yacht, the *Sea Cloud*, to be anchored during the warm months of the year in the harbor of Leningrad. The *Sea Cloud* was one of the largest, most beautiful, and most luxuriously furnished yachts in the world. With its complement of more than 50 men it could navigate either by steam or sail. The ambassador and Mrs. Davies made use of it in visiting ports on the Baltic Sea: Helsinki, Tallinn, Riga, Danzig, Copenhagen, Stockholm, and others. They also made a leisurely trip through the North Sea, the English Channel, Gibraltar, the Mediterranean, and the Dardanelles to the Black Sea, stopping at various ports, including those on the French Riviera, en route. Using the *Sea Cloud*, anchored at Odessa, as a base, the ambassador visited some of the great hydraulic and industrial projects of southern Russia. They also toured Central and Western Europe by train and automobile during those seasons that were not suitable for yachting. During these tours the ambassador made a point of calling on U.S. embassies and legations and exchanging views with our ambassadors and ministers who headed them.

At the request of the ambassador I prepared and gave him a brief memorandum containing the salient facts regarding each of the countries that he was planning to visit. Most of the data contained in these memoranda were taken from the current edition of *The Statesman's Yearbook* supplemented by such knowledge as I had acquired during my years in the service. On the basis of these memoranda and of such information that he himself had picked up during his travels, the ambassador prepared a report for the president and the secretary of state, setting forth his findings on each country that he visited. As a matter of courtesy, he was accustomed to send a copy of his report on each country visited by him to the U.S. ambassador or minister accredited to that country. These ambassadors and ministers almost unanimously took the position that he was infringing on their territory, that it was their responsibility to keep the president and the Department of State informed regarding the situation in the countries to which they had been appointed, and that they had received no instructions indicating that the ambassador to the Soviet Union was a sort of satrap of the president for all of Europe. Some of them contended, furthermore, that Davies lacked the background and experience required for preparing reports of any real value regarding their respective countries.

The "Swan Song" of Ambassador Davies

On the eve of his departure from Moscow Ambassador Davies also wrote his "swan song" in the form of a dispatch, dated June 6, 1938. In this dispatch he gave a detailed account of the current internal and external policies of the Soviet Union as he understood them and of conditions prevailing in the Soviet Union as he viewed them. He, like Bullitt, also prophesied that the Soviet Union with its enormous national wealth and extensive territories was destined to develop into an extremely great power. He pointed out that the present Soviet strength "is found in the resolute, bold, ruthless, and able leadership of Stalin," that "the military strength of the U.S.S.R. is impressive," and that the government "is supremely confident that it could successfully resist simultaneous attack by Japan and Germany."

The ambassador added in this dispatch that he expected to see the Soviet government, "while professing devotion to Communism, move constantly more to the right, in practice, just as it has for the past eight years . . . It may evolve into a type of Fabian socialism, with large industry in the hands of the State, with, however, the agricultural and smaller businesses and traders working under capitalistic property and profit principles."

He devoted considerable space to analyzing the differences that continued to exist between the United States and the Soviet Union and to de-emphasizing their importance. He repeated what he had said in previous dispatches, namely, that the Soviet Union was more friendly to the United States than to any other power, and maintained that the United States "has received more consideration and favor from this Government during the past year than has any other foreign state . . . A common ground between the United States and the U.S.S.R. and one that will obtain for a long time, in my opinion, lies in the fact that both are sincere advocates of peace."

In recommending what our future policies to the Soviet Union should be he said:

> In view of the extraordinary economic and political potentialities which exist here and which will undoubtedly continue to have an increasing effect upon both economic and political conditions of Europe as well as of the world, and particularly in view of the Japanese attitude in the Pacific, it would appear unwise to change the present status or to consider the discontinuance of diplomatic relations except under some severe provocation.

On the assumption that the United States decides to maintain diplomatic relations here, it is, in my opinion, advisable that the conduct of this Mission should be projected and maintained in as friendly and harmonious a spirit as is possible, consistent with the strict adherence to the performance of all obligations under the agreements between the two countries. The integrity of our democratic system and our requirement of strict performance of Soviet promises should, of course, always be maintained with vigor; but the methods employed in connection with current matters of relatively smaller importance and, in fact, methods employed in all matters should be based not upon a critical and intolerant attitude that induces irritations, but upon an attitude of tolerant understanding of the difficulties under which the officials here are laboring. It should not be an attitude that would induce suspicion and hostility directed against us. We should not, by reason of our conduct, be classed among "enemy powers."

Such a policy does not involve approving in any manner the ideological concepts of this Government. It does, however, recognize the right of self-determination. It is interpretative of the high-minded and Christian-like declarations of the foreign policy of the United States as expressed by the President of the United States and the Secretary of State in connection with foreign affairs. It is a "Good Neighbor Policy," and one consistent with the best traditions of our diplomatic history.

There is no doubt of the sincerity and the friendliness of the U.S.S.R. toward the Government of the United States, in marked contrast and to a greater degree than to any other nation. It has been my experience here, that where matters are projected as between the two countries in a spirit of tolerance, understanding, and friendliness, there has been a prompt and generous response on the part of this Government to try to accommodate itself to a reasonable agreement.

I had never previously worked closely with a successful "man of the world" of the kind that Ambassador Davies represented. Although we did not see eye to eye on many things I profited from our association and developed a real affection for him. I did my best to serve him loyally even though our approaches to, and evaluations of, problems and situations were sometimes widely at variance. Whenever he showed an interest in having my opinion I gave it frankly even though I was aware that it might not be in accord with views expressed by him. At times when I believed that the interests of the United States or his personal interests were involved I did not hesitate to give him advice even though not invited to do so. As the senior Foreign Service officer of the embassy I considered it to be my duty to remind some of the junior officers, when they showed signs of restiveness, that regardless of what their innermost feelings might be, they should constantly bear in mind that the ethics of the service required that the members of an embassy be loyal to their ambassador, that while serving under him they should not indicate by word, gesture, or even facial expression a lack of respect for him, and that they should endeavor to strengthen his prestige in the country to which he was accredited.

My friendly relationship with Ambassadors Bullitt and Davies did not terminate when they relinquished their respective ambassadorships to the Soviet Union. I was to keep in touch with both of them on a friendly basis so long as they lived. References to them will be found in subsequent portions of my narrative. In the late 1950s I served as one of the pallbearers when the body of Ambassador Davies was laid to rest in the National Cathedral in Washington, and in the early part of 1967 I made a sad journey to Philadelphia to attend the funeral of Ambassador Bullitt.

CHAPTER 40

THE GREAT PURGE

DURING 1934 unheralded but perceptible changes, which I had an opportunity to observe firsthand, were taking place in the attitude of many of the Muscovites. Some of them seemed to be losing their fear of being accused of bourgeois mannerisms. Articles were beginning to appear in the Soviet press suggesting that there was no reason why members of the proletariat should not take pride in their personal appearance. Some of these articles went so far as to intimate that it might be a good idea for men to shave more regularly and for women to take a more active interest in how they looked. Razors began to be offered for sale in some of the shops, and Madame Molotov, the wife of the prime minister, began personally to push the production, sale, and distribution of cosmetics. At the opera now and then I could spot persons or groups who were quite well groomed.

The members of the armed forces began to spruce up. The officers began to carry themselves as officers, and the soldiers began to be required to salute them. Official social functions began to be attended by leaders from different walks of life; frequently husband and wife began to appear in public together. At these functions the stiffness and self-consciousness tended to diminish and conversations began to liven in a more relaxed atmosphere.

In one of my letters to Robert Kelley of the Eastern European

Division of the State Department, I said that it was beginning to look to me that a new cosmopolitan society was being formed in Moscow—a society composed of the elite from the political, artistic, literary, scientific, and industrial sectors. Prominent members of the Communist Party, high civilian and military officials, well-known authors, leading journalists, composers and musicians, ballerinas and actors, engineers, and executives were beginning to mingle and to take interest in the activities and accomplishments of one another. I emphasized that, although such a society had not as yet crystalized, it seemed to me that it was in the process of forming.

In 1934 it also became apparent that the Kremlin had decided that, although world revolution should continue to be the cause for which the Soviet people should be taught to live or die, patriotism was still too useful a tool in maintaining control over the masses to be ignored. Measures were therefore taken to arouse feelings of patriotism and veneration of country. The Soviet press, the theater, the cinema, and other media began to be used to emphasize that the accomplishments of the Russian people and other peoples of the USSR in the fields of literature, music, art, science, inventions, and so forth were equal, if not superior, to those of any other peoples. Even some of the long-dead tsarist generals who had defeated the enemies of the old Russian empire began to be regarded as heroes and much space was given in Soviet publications to the fighting qualities of the pro-revolutionary Russian soldier and sailor.

I also noted, however, certain trends in the opposite direction. Ambitious and fanatical communist youth who in the universities had been steeped in communist theory and jargon and who had not as yet made their mark in the communist world regarded these tendencies toward forming a society of the successful, in which they had not as yet earned the right to participate, as dangerous and unbolshevik. They had been taught since childhood that if communism was to conquer the world one's whole life should be devoted to transforming the Soviet Union into an irresistible mechanism for its propagation. This was not the time, they seemed to think, for those who had achieved a degree of personal success to relax and enjoy the fruits thereof. It was my understanding that among the older Bolsheviks, those who had made sacrifices for the cause of the revolution during the tsarist days and had participated in the hardships of the early years of the Soviet state, there were also some who looked with suspicion on what they regarded as the discarding of the garments of proletarianism.

In the late spring of 1934 Ambassador Bullitt invited me to luncheon with Bukharin, the editor of *Izvestiia*; Radek, the most famous of Soviet journalists; and himself. Bukharin, it will be recalled, was a leader of the right wing of the Communist Party in the 1920s. He was also one of the persons responsible for the new economic policy of the early 1920s. He had taken the position in those years that a prosperous countryside was essential for the economic progress of Russia. It was he who had coined the slogan "Peasants enrich yourselves." He was one of Lenin's favorites and during Lenin's time had been regarded as one of the leading theorists of the party. Although he had always supported the concept of world revolution, he also believed like Stalin that the development of a powerful Soviet state was needed to serve as the basis for international revolutionary activity.

Radek had gained worldwide renown as a revolutionary as well as a journalist. At one time he had been charged by the party to promote a communist revolution in Germany. In spite of his failure, he continued to be one of the most influential leaders of the left wing of the party. As a left-winger it was natural that he would not be happy at any movement in the direction of nationalism. Nevertheless, in his position as a writer for the party he was compelled to follow the party line.

During luncheon I was amused by the interplay between these two famous revolutionaries representing opposite ends of the Communist Party's political spectrum. Although both of them had suffered setbacks in their party careers, they apparently had no concern about their future. Bukharin and Radek, who were apparently on intimate friendly terms, seemed to enjoy bantering one another during the luncheon. For instance, Bukharin remarked that he was surprised that Radek in one of his recent columns had used the word *rodina* (fatherland) in referring to the Soviet Union. Was it possible that Radek was also becoming a nationalist? Radek grinned at this sally and turned the conversation to other channels.

When Bullitt referred to the fact that both of them had from time to time been in tsarist prisons, Radek said that in his opinion the old tsarist police were unbelievably stupid. They arrested Bolshevik leaders again and again only eventually to release them or allow them to escape. Bukharin agreed. He said, "Yes, our Stalin was arrested several times yet he lived to destroy the police who had failed to destroy him." Radek continued, "But we Bolsheviks are not so stupid. When we arrest enemies of the state we either execute them or we put them away so that no one ever hears of them again." Bukharin again agreed. Neither one of them apparently had any idea that within the next three years Bukharin would be executed and Radek would be sentenced to ten years in prison.

On December 1, 1934, an event took place in Leningrad that brought to a gradual halt the development of what might be called a social relationship among the Bolshevik elite. At 4:30 in the afternoon a popular and powerful young Bolshevik, who was busily engaged in preparing a speech that he was to give later in the day to the active Communist Party workers of Leningrad, left his desk for a moment to step into his reception room. As he was returning to his private office a figure slipped into the room behind him and fired a pistol. The young man fell to the floor shot through the neck and his assailant was said to have shot himself. This young Bolshevik was none other than Sergey Mironovich Kirov, secretary of the Central and Leningrad Committees of the All-Union Communist Party and member of the Presidium of the Central Executive Committee of the Soviet Union. He was Stalin's right-hand man, the second most powerful man in the Soviet Union and a man who was regarded as the heir apparent to Stalin. The assailant was Leonid Vasilivitch Nikolaiev, a disgruntled minor Soviet official. Kirov died almost instantly.

The veil of secrecy surrounding the end of Nikolaiev was so heavy that we never learned precisely the time and circumstances of his death. The most reliable information that came to us was that he died either at once or in a few days without regaining consciousness.

When the news hit the Kremlin, the four leaders of the party and government—Stalin, Molotov, Voroshilov, and Zhdanov—accompanied by a flock of secret police agents rushed to Leningrad by special train to investigate the tragedy on the spot. On the same evening the Central Executive Committee of the USSR (the parliamentary organ of the state) issued a decree, signed by Kalinin, its president, and Yenukidze, its secretary, authorizing the summary trial and execution of persons connected with terroristic organizations or with terroristic acts. This decree provided for investigations to be completed within ten days, for the indictments to be delivered to the accused twenty-four hours before the trial, for the trials to be held without the participation of the accused, for no appeals from sentences or for clemency to be admitted, and for the sentence of death to be carried out immediately after pronouncement.

The members of the embassy were shocked at the death of Kirov, whom we regarded as one of the more moderate and able Soviet leaders. We did not at first, however, realize the extent of the impact that the murder might have on life in the Soviet Union. On the afternoon of December 3 or 4, while a number of us were in Durbrow's apartment in the Mokhovaya Building listening to a foreign news broadcast, John Wiley, who was chargé d'affaires at the time, entered the room accompanied by George Andreytchine, a vice president of Intourist. Andreytchine had formed a friendship with Bullitt many years previously when he, a young Bulgarian radical in exile, was living in the United States. Because of that friendship he had been assigned by the Kremlin to keep in close touch with Bullitt and the members of the embassy. Andreytchine, who was usually debonair in demeanor and optimistic in outlook, was visibly under strain. He told us that the death of Kirov, in his opinion, could have far-reaching ramifications and that an act of terror of this kind at this particular moment could trigger acts of repression on the part of the Soviet regime that would make even the collectivization campaign of 1930 look mild. He said that for some time Stalin had been angered at the latent opposition to his policies that existed in various quarters. The murder of his closest co-worker might well bring an end to such restraint as Stalin had hitherto shown in dealing with his critics and opponents. He added that the decrees of December 1 issued within several hours of the murder, which in effect gave the Commissariat for Internal Affairs a free hand in investigating activities, was an indication of what might be expected.

Andreytchine's dismal prophesies turned out to be true. During the ensuing months literally thousands of persons were arrested on charges that they were connected in some way or other with the killing of Kirov. In making arrests the officials of the NKVD, under the general direction of Stalin and the leadership of Yagoda, their commissar, used a shotgun approach.

The political section of the embassy, headed by Wiley, tried to keep the State Department informed of the developments. It reported, for instance, the announcement appearing in the Soviet press on December 6, 1934, of the arrest in Leningrad of 39 persons, of whom 37 had already been shot, and of the arrest in Moscow of 32, of whom 29 had been shot. Several days later it reported an announcement issued on December 12 that 9 of 12 persons arrested in White Russia had been shot and that 37 had been arrested in the Soviet Ukraine. These arrests were merely a prologue to what was to take place during the next three years.

Who was really responsible for the murder? Was it merely an act of personal vengeance on the part of Nikolaiev or was he acting as the agent of some group? The Soviet press, following the lead of the Soviet government, took it for granted from the moment that the report of the assassination reached Moscow that it was a political murder—that Nikolaiev was a member of a widespread conspiracy. The press appeared to be confused, however, regarding the membership of this conspiracy. Some reports indicated rather vaguely that so-called white guardists and reactionaries in Leningrad were responsible; others said that groups coming in from abroad through Poland, Latvia, and Estonia were participators; others indicated that Zinoviev, Kamenev, and other Trotskyites were in the plot; still others charged that the Latvian consul in Leningrad, George Bissenieks, was implicated. The Soviet government, maintaining that it had evidence that Bissenieks had paid large sums of money to Nikolaiev, demanded his withdrawal. The Latvian government, although insisting on Bissenieks's innocence, withdrew him.

Among the rumors that were circulated among the diplomatic corps were those to the effect that the secret police themselves were involved. Our embassy gave some credence to stories that the murder of Kirov represented an attack on the government by leftists who were known to be resentful at what they considered to be the movement of Stalin and his followers toward the right—a movement highlighted internally by growing differences between the wages paid to technicians, engineers, and administrators and those paid to common workers and by wider differences in scales of living, and externally by the decision of the Soviet Union to join the League of Nations and by the apparent willingness of the Soviet government to effect mutual assistance alliances with capitalistic countries. Much later, suspicions began to be expressed by foreign observers and by some Soviet nationals that the assassination had been engineered by Stalin personally in order to rid himself of Kirov, of whom he had become jealous, and at the same time to provide a pretext for eliminating both the overt and covert opposition by which he had been plagued for so many years.

The belief that Stalin planned the crime and then took pains to eradicate all who were aware of the part that he always played has been strengthened over the years by a mass of circumstantial evidence. The fact has been pointed out, for instance, that all of the members of the Commissariat for Internal Affairs, including Commissar Yagoda, and the secret police charged with the protection of Kirov, who might have been aware of Stalin's complicity, were subsequently executed. The circumstance that the decree of the Central Executive Committee could have been issued so shortly after the crime has also been advanced as evidence that it had been carefully prepared beforehand. Yenukidze, the secretary of the committee who drafted the decree for Kalinin's signature and then countersigned it, was one of the early victims of the purge. The story of Stalin's involvement included the conjecture that Nikolaiev had been assured by the secret police that he would be allowed to escape and would be rewarded for his act but that they had shot him immediately after the assassination.

Although I have no doubt that Stalin did arrange for the murder of a number of his colleagues and although I have a high respect for some of the Soviet experts who incline to the opinion that Stalin was responsible for Kirov's assassination, I still believe, as I did in 1934, that Stalin was not responsible for the murder, that Kirov was assassinated for personal reasons, and that Stalin made use of the murder to exterminate those elements in the state and party structures that, in his opinion, had been or might in the future be disloyal to him personally or that at some time or another might not be willing to follow unquestioningly his leadership.

I was inclined to believe, in essence, the story that Baltrusaitis, the Lithuanian minister, told to Ambassador Bullitt following the latter's return from the United States, partly because I had considerable confidence in Baltrusaitis as a person, and partly because I happened to know that he had contacts in certain Soviet circles in Leningrad, the members of which would at times tell him things that they would not dare to tell one another.

The story told by Baltrusaitis, in brief, is as follows: Kirov had become infatuated with the beautiful wife of Nikolaiev, a Soviet official working under his direction, and with Nikolaiev's knowledge had become involved with her. Nikolaiev had hoped that in view of his acquiescence, he would be advanced in the Soviet bureaucracy. When, however, he found that instead of being given a promotion he was in danger of losing his job, he felt double-crossed. In his anger he shot Kirov and then killed himself. The maiden name of Nikolaiev's wife was Milda Drauge. She was a Latvian by origin and had moved frequently among Soviet nationals of Latvian and Lithuanian origin. Among her friends was Madame Bissenieks, the wife of the Latvian consul who, during tsarist days, had been a well-known member of the Leningrad Ballet. It was Madame Bissenieks's friendship with Madame Nikolaiev that resulted in the request of the Soviet government for the withdrawal from the Soviet Union of the Latvian consul. Incidentally I might add that, while on duty in Riga during the latter 1920s, I had seen Madame Bissenieks perform many times with the Riga Ballet of which she was a member while her husband was attached to the Latvian Foreign Office.

During the last few days of December 1934 and throughout most of 1935 the movement that later became known as the Great Purge continued to gain breadth, depth, and momentum. In its early stages the charges against most of its victims were the employment of terror for the purpose of wrecking the Soviet Union politically and economically. Comparatively little emphasis was placed on espionage or on collusion with foreigners, although immediately after the assassination there were, as I have already indicated, pointed references to conspirators entering the Soviet Union through Poland, Latvia, and Finland. The antiforeign aspect of the purge did not come to the fore until 1936.

Official announcements appearing in the Soviet press in December 1934 indicated that the first two targets of the purge were the so-called white guardists and the members of the Zinoviev opposition. The white guardists, from such information as the embassy was able to obtain, were the remnants of the old Russian nobility, of high tsarist civil and military officials, and of former leading industrialists, merchants, and estate owners and members of their families, who were still living in Leningrad.

Although they represented an aging, disorganized, spiritless group without political, cultural, or economic influence, Stalin was uneasy at their presence. Wiley stated, in one of his reports written in the last part of March, that he had learned from a reliable source that among the arrests in Leningrad were 41 former princes, 33 former counts, 76 former barons, 35 former big manufacturers, 68 former big landlords, 19 former big merchants, 142 former high tsarist officials, 547 former high officers of the tsarist and White armies, and 113 former officials of the tsarist gendarmerie and secret police. To me, the surprising feature of this information was that so many persons belonging to these categories had contrived to survive the revolutions, massacres, and abject poverty of the preceding eighteen years.

A communiqué of the Commissariat of Internal Affairs published in the *Izvestiia* of December 22 announced that Nikolaiev was acting for a group of Zinoviev oppositionists known as the "Leningrad Center," whose aim was "to disorganize the leadership of the Soviet government by means of terroristic acts directed against the Soviet Union in the spirit of the Zinoviev-Trotsky platform." The communiqué listed the names of fourteen persons belonging to this group (including Nikolaiev who was supposed to be still alive at the time) who had been turned over for trial to the Military Collegium of the Supreme Court.

Several days later the embassy reported that it had reliable information that wholesale and indiscriminate arrests were being made throughout the Soviet Union. On December 24 Wiley sent another telegram to the State Department stating that he had been informed "privately" by a high Soviet official that the Soviet leaders had decided upon "a policy of combating terrorism with terrorism." In the same telegram he included a message to Ambassador Bullitt who was then in Washington to the effect that Bullitt's friend, Andreytchine, "was scared blue and in great danger of losing his job."* In the latter part of March Wiley informed the department that he had received reports from observers indicating that the arrests and deportation from Leningrad had reached figures ranging from sixty to a hundred thousand.

When Ambassador Bullitt returned to Moscow in April 1935 he began talking to those Soviet leaders who were willing to meet him, with colleagues of the diplomatic corps, and with American and other foreign journalists regarding the situation. His primary aim in conferring with

---

* Andreytchine was subsequently arrested and sent to a forced labor camp in northern Russia. He was released some seven years later and I met him again in the Soviet Union in 1942.

the Soviet leaders was to impress upon them how serious it would be if the congress of the Communist International scheduled for the latter part of the summer would be attended by U.S. delegates and if such a congress would issue instructions regarding the carrying on of revolutionary activities in the United States. During these conversations, however, he also tried to obtain as much information as possible regarding the developing purge.

On the basis of information that he had obtained from a variety of sources, the ambassador sent a dispatch to the State Department on June 8, 1935, stating that he had been informed by four reliable authorities that the Kremlin was at present in a state of apprehension and suspicion. He added that "it is difficult to exaggerate the fear which now exists among members of the Communist Party in Moscow." He reported that the forced dissolution on May 25 of the Society of Bolsheviks and the arrests of a number of members of that formerly revered society had been a severe shock to the historic leaders of the party. The Society of Bolsheviks was a prestigious organization, the membership of which consisted of prominent leaders of the Bolshevik revolution of 1917.

During 1935 it became progressively more difficult for foreigners to meet or talk with Soviet nationals. By the beginning of the summer so many of the Soviet officials who in the past had been permitted to mingle with foreigners had been arrested that those who survived seemed to feel that it would be wiser to stay away from them. Nevertheless, so far as the embassy could determine, no blanket warnings against associations with foreigners had been issued.

It seemed to me that the antiforeign aspects of the purge developed along with a gradual shift in Soviet foreign policies. As early as January 1936 the members of the embassy gained the impression from statements made by Soviet leaders, from articles published in the press, and from private conversations with the few Soviet officials who were willing to talk with us that the Kremlin was gradually abandoning the hope of effecting a dependable collective security arrangement with the Western powers against either Germany or Japan.

During the early part of 1936 the embassy detected evidence of increasing skepticism on the part of Soviet officials and the press regarding the willingness of France and Great Britain, unless themselves attacked, militarily to oppose German aggression. The failure of France to take military action in March 1936 when the Nazis calmly marched in and took over the Rhineland made the pact with France look like mockery. If France could supinely permit the Germans to take the Rhineland, how could one expect it to take armed action if Germany should make moves in the direction of Eastern Europe? An increase in attacks in the Soviet press on the Trotskyists and other deviationists made it appear that Stalin was under the impression that what was regarded in certain circles as the bankruptcy of his foreign policy was being used to weaken him by those who had no confidence in his leadership. As the press attacks became more shrill they began to hint of some kind of cooperation between the Trotskyites and the reactionary enemies of the Soviet state.

The members of the embassy who were trying to assess Soviet foreign and internal policies noted these trends with puzzlement. It was almost inconceivable to us that the Trotskyites could find a platform for cooperation with the anti-Semitic Hitler. In the middle of August 1936, therefore, we in the embassy were caught by surprise when an announcement appeared in the press that Zinoviev, Kamenev, and fourteen other members of the "Trotskyite terrorist center" were being brought to public trial on August 19 before the Military Collegium of the Supreme Court for implication in terrorist plots. I applied at once to Narkomindel for two tickets of admission to the trial, one for myself as chargé d'affaires and the other for one of our Russian-language officers. To my disappointment I was informed that in view of the lack of space no foreign diplomats other than chiefs of mission would be admitted and, therefore, only one ticket was sent to the embassy. I learned later that I was fortunate in obtaining even the one ticket since only six seats had been reserved for members of the diplomatic corps.

During the next 30 years much was to be written about this trial and the two great trials that followed it. There had been much speculation regarding Stalin's purpose in having such a trial held at this particular time, regarding the degree, if any, to which the accused were guilty of the crimes charged, and regarding the methods by which they had been induced to confess. As history unrolls it is frequently much easier to assess and interpret past events than it is to do so at the moment of their occurrence. Instead of trying to describe this trial from the vantage point of many years later, it might be more interesting for my readers to know what our little group in the embassy had to say about it in the summer of 1936. I say "our little group" because, although I wrote the reports, I did so only after many discussions with my fellow Foreign Service officers serving in the embassy.

On August 27, following the conclusion of the trial, I sent a long telegram to the State Department in reply to a telegram from it asking me for interpretive reports on the event. Excerpts from my telegram I quote below:

> The few foreign journalists and diplomats permitted to attend the trial of Zinoviev, Kamenev and others were puzzled and astonished at the

manner in which the defendants denounced themselves and Trotsky and dragged in the names of other prominent Soviet leaders who in the past had been opposed to Stalin.

It is difficult to state with any degree of certainty the extent to which the accused were guilty of the crimes to which they confessed or to explain the motives prompting their behavior at the trial.

Most of the foreigners present during the proceedings were of the opinion that:

(a) Zinoviev, Kamenev and other prominent defendants have had conversations regarding the advisability of assassinating Stalin and regarding their course of action in case of his death.

(b) The prominent defendants may have come into contact at times with some of the less well known so-called terrorists who stood trial with them.

Many such observers were not convinced however, that:

(c) Zinoviev, Kamenev and other prominent defendants had entered into a concrete plot to assassinate Kirov, Stalin or any other persons.

(d) Trotsky had sent instructions as alleged to the accused to engage in terroristic acts.

(e) The German police were involved.

The other Secretaries of the Embassy and I believe (a) and (b) and disbelieve (c), (d), and (e).

It is the opinion of the Embassy, based on its own analysis of the situation, that the trial was staged at the present time:

(1) To prevent expression being given to a wave of dissatisfaction with the Kremlin policy which has recently welled up in certain Party circles. There is a growing fear that Stalin is leading them away from Communism in the direction of state capitalism. The growing differentiation of wages which is becoming more pronounced with the raising of production norms; the tendency to organize collective farms along capitalistic lines; the steady growth in influence of the so-called new intelligentsia, technicians, high state officials, and even persons connected with the former *bourgeoisie*; the encouragement by Party and State of patriotism; and similar trends have caused some alarm among the old or ideologically inclined Party members. This alarm has been sharpened by the belief that the Kremlin is not sufficiently supporting the Spanish proletariat and as a result of passivity is losing hegemony over the revolutionary movement.

(2) To correct the mistaken impression obtained by some members

or former members of the Party that the announcement of the new constitution signifies the beginning of a new era in which they may safely criticize certain of Stalin's policies to which they may be opposed.

(3) To eliminate or nullify the influence of former leaders whom Stalin distrusts.

(4) To render it possible to ascribe certain failures in the realization of economic and financial plans to the sabotage of Trotsky and his adherents.

(5) By branding Trotsky as an ally of the German Fascists to endeavor to kill the influence of himself and his adherents in the united front and in the international revolutionary movement as a whole. It is understood that Trotsky's organizations which employ tactics similar to those used by the branches of the Communist International in seeking leadership are seriously hampering the efforts of the Kremlin to obtain domination over the united front.

(6) Incidentally still further to increase the hatred of foreign Soviet sympathizers for German Fascists.

It is also the belief of the Embassy that the prisoners testified as they did with the hope of escaping torture or obtaining commutation of sentence or from fear that failure so to testify would result in harm to members of their families or friends.

The opinions expressed above are shared by a number of the better informed foreigners in Moscow.

It is understood that hundreds of active or former Party members are being arrested and that discontented whispers in Party circles have been effectively hushed.

A usually well-informed Soviet official states in confidence that Bukharin, Pyatakov, Radek and Rykov will probably be exonerated to varying degrees from complicity in terroristic plots but that the stigma which has been attached to them will render them politically harmless for years to come.

I was present during all sessions of the trial and will report my personal impressions by despatch.

It will be noted that the "usually well-informed Soviet official" who told me that Bukharin, Pyatakov, Radek, and Rykov would probably be exonerated to varying degrees proved to be wrong. During the next two years all of them were tried and all except Radek, who was sentenced to ten years imprisonment, were shot. The well-informed official, by the way, was also shot in 1938.

I followed up this telegram with a dispatch dated September 1, 1936, in which I described the trial in more detail. This dispatch read in part as follows:

> The small former ballroom of the former Noblemen's Gathering Place (now the House of the Labor Unions), in which the trial was held, was so arranged as to seat precisely 400 spectators. Three rows of seats in the center of the portion of the hall allotted to spectators was reserved for correspondents. These rows on the right of the aisle bisecting the center of the hall were given over to Soviet correspondents, and those to the left to foreign correspondents. Altogether 30 seats were reserved for "foreign correspondents." Of these seats, five were occupied by Soviet officials, six by members of the diplomatic corps, two by Soviet citizens taking notes for the American correspondents, four by foreign visitors who for some reason or another were given tickets of admission, and the remainder by the correspondents themselves. During the intermissions three of the Soviet officials present, who were members of the Press Section of the People's Commissariat for Foreign Affairs, were busily engaged in trying to convince the foreign correspondents that the trial was *bona fide* and the Chief of the Protocol Section of the same Commissariat was usually occupied in talking along the same line to the diplomats. Assisting the members of the Press Section in endeavoring to influence the outgoing stories of the journalists were Mr. Kunits, an American citizen and member of the American Communist Party, who represents the NEW MASSES in the Soviet Union; Mr. D. E. Vendrov, formerly an American citizen but now a Soviet citizen, who represents THE JEWISH TELEGRAPH AGENCY; and Samuel Rodman, an American citizen who represents the London NEWS CHRONICLE and several American newspapers. Louis Fisher, the representative in Moscow of THE NATION and the BALTIMORE SUN . . . could not be present since he was engaged in conducting a group of tourists through southern Russia . . .
>
> The trial was beautifully staged. The three judges and their alternates, clad in uniform, sat behind tables on a high platform facing the audience. To their left on a platform enclosed with a fence and guarded by soldiers armed with rifles sat the 16 prisoners. To their right, facing the prisoners, the State's Attorney, or Procurer, as he is called in the Soviet Union, sat behind a desk also on a high platform.
>
> The trial was conducted with dignity despite the fact that at times little witticisms on the part of the prisoners or of the other actors in the drama caused the audience, the judges, the Procurer, and even the prisoners themselves, to laugh. In spite of the scathing names applied to them by the Procurer, and the sarcastic remarks made from time to time by the Presiding Judge, the accused were in general treated with courtesy and consideration by the court officials. With the possible exception of Zinoviev, who appeared to be under considerable physical strain, they

seemed to be in good condition physically. They wore better clothes than the average Muscovite, some of them being almost nattily dressed. The Procurer, Mr. Vyshinski, was exceedingly well-groomed and highly theatrical in manner. He reminded one of Lionel Barrymore acting in one of his favorite roles as a criminal lawyer.

The way in which the Procurer dominated the prisoners was impressive. They arose in turn and gave with only a few promptings from him the testimony apparently expected of them. His attitude was at times helpful, at times almost threatening. The prisoners when testifying were apparently extremely careful not to enter into a dispute with him. They showed hesitation in answering some of his questions, as though they were not sure as to the nature of the reply expected. When such occasions arose he usually assisted them by reframing his question in such a manner that the reply to be expected was obvious.

As I observed the performance day after day I began to feel that I was looking at a circus director putting a group of well-trained seals through a series of difficult acts. The manner in which the prisoners, while testifying, anxiously watched the face of the Procurer in order apparently to assure themselves from its expression that they were making no mistakes and the way in which they hastened to correct themselves when they felt that they were not saying the proper thing were convincing evidence to me that they were under the absolute domination of the latter. The foreign correspondents and diplomats present who had never witnessed a Soviet trial sat astounded as the various prisoners eloquently endeavored to convince their hearers not only that they were guilty of conspiracy to murder Stalin, Kirov, Voroshilov, and other prominent Party leaders, but also that they themselves were despicable, irredeemable characters, that they had acted under the instructions of Trotski, who was a traitor to the working classes of the world and an ally of the German Fascists, that the German Fascists, with whom they had cooperated, were the vilest of reptiles, that Stalin had always been right and that the population of the Soviet Union and the world proletariat in general should never in the future doubt the wisdom of his policies, and that the Soviet Union as a truly socialist state was making wonderful progress in the direction of bringing happiness and prosperity to its inhabitants.

All the prisoners were more or less accomplished public speakers and their confessions were apparently in the nature of carefully memorized orations. Kamenev was the dominating personality of the group and by far the most effective orator. His calm intellectual face and his gray-white hair and well-trimmed beard, as well as his dignity of manner, reminded one somewhat of Chief Justice Hughes of the United States Supreme Court. Even while delivering his "last word," that is, the farewell address which each of the accused was permitted to make before the passage of the sentence, he maintained his composure and distinguished bearing. Although the effect of his oratory and presence was such as to cause a number of the foreign correspondents and even several of the apparently hostile Soviet audience to weep during his farewell address, his own voice broke only once, and then but slightly, when he referred to his three sons serving as Soviet aviators and expressed the hope that they would live to redeem the name of their father. Zinoviev, although apparently crushed and unnerved, also proved to be an effective orator in spite of the fact that he was handicapped by lack of personality and by a high-pitched and almost whining voice.

In delivering their farewell addresses some of the accused did not maintain the high rhetorical level attained during their previous speeches. A number of them, including Zinoviev, Kamenev, Reingold, M. Lure, Pikel, and Olberg talked for from thirty minutes to an hour and a half with all the fervor of collegians engaging in an oratorical contest. Ter-Vagaryan, the Armenian, had difficulty in finishing his last speech. He was apparently suffering from nervous contractions of the throat which were only slightly remedied by the consumption of glass after glass of water.

The accused apparently expected the sentence of death. I was examining their faces carefully when it was passed and failed to note a sign of emotion on any of them. I am convinced, however, that at least some of them expected clemency in view of past services rendered to the cause of revolution or as a reward for the manner in which they had cooperated with the State in denouncing Trotski and the other accused.

It is extremely difficult for persons accustomed to the Anglo-Saxon methods of criminal procedure to accept as entirely *bona fide* trials of the type under discussion. It has been the belief for hundreds of years in countries accepting the Anglo-Saxon principles of law that to endeavor to determine the innocence or guilt of persons accused of crime by means of the extraction of admissions is likely to result in the obtaining by inquisitorial methods of statements of guilt from innocent persons. It is usually a custom in such countries, therefore, not to base the prosecution upon confessions extracted from the accused before the trial or to require the accused to testify against himself, but to determine his guilt largely upon the strength of evidence furnished by other persons. The Soviet criminal procedure system, judging from the more important public trials of recent years, appears, in practice at least, still to be based upon obtaining admissions of guilt from the accused before the case comes to trial and of confining most of the testimony to an oral restatement by the accused of confessions already made in writing. Since under a dictatorship of the type existing in the Soviet Union there are numerous effective devices for prevailing upon accused persons to confess to crimes of which they are not guilty, it is not difficult to understand why persons accustomed to Anglo-Saxon legal procedure should be somewhat shocked at what seems to them to be medieval methods of determining guilt, particularly when the accused are known to have given offense to the dictator himself.

As stated in my telegram under reference, I have not been convinced from what I saw at the trial or from a careful study of the evidence presented that the accused were really implicated in a specific plot to kill Stalin, Kirov, or other prominent Soviet leaders, that Trotski ever gave instructions to his adherents to assassinate Stalin, or that the German police had connections with any of the defendants. . . .

The views expressed by myself are those of all the foreign diplomats present at the trial, as well as of the other Secretaries of this Mission and of the foreign journalists whom I consider to be most competent to judge matters pertaining to the Soviet Union. The Minister of Norway, who attended certain sessions of the trial and whose opinion is of particular interest since he is the representative of the country in which Trotski is now residing, has informed me that he considers the trial to be a farce and that in his opinion the charges that Trotski had participated in a plot to kill Soviet leaders had not been substantiated.

From such contacts as the Embassy has among the Russian population, it would appear that many Soviet citizens are also inclined to look upon the trial with skepticism. They are, naturally, careful not to reveal their true feelings except to persons in whom they have explicit confidence and at places where they are sure that they will not be overheard.

It is reported to the Embassy from sources believed to be reliable that hundreds of persons have been arrested on charges of disloyalty to Stalin and the Party and that some of them are being tried in secret at the present time. The announcement of the execution of all sixteen of the condemned men within 24 hours of the passing of the sentence has made a profound impression, and a wave of fear, almost equal to that noticeable following the assassination of Kirov in December 1934, is said to be sweeping over the country. It is understood that members and former members of the Communist Party who at some time may have been on friendly terms with persons now branded as adherents of Trotski or with any of the persons accused or mentioned in the trial are now terror-stricken. The effect upon that section of Soviet officialdom charged with dealing with foreigners is particularly marked. Foreigners have noted that many Soviet officials who a few weeks ago spoke to them with an air of self-confidence are now most diffident and are apparently afraid to come to any decisions without protracted consultations with their superiors.

I was not satisfied with the reports regarding the trial that we had sent to the State Department during August and September. It was my belief that a trial of this kind involving several of the foremost leaders of the Bolshevik revolution would be a matter of international interest for many years. Only a handful of foreigners would be able to write about it as eye-witnesses. So far as I was aware, no photographs had been taken and no sound recordings of the proceedings had been made.

While observing the proceedings, I had jotted down my impressions of the courtroom, the defendants, the prosecutors, the judges, the audience, and the prevailing atmosphere. It was my intention to make use at once of these notes in preparing a supplementary report. The pressures of the current work of the embassy, however, were so heavy that it was not until December 31, 1936, when with the aid of Charlie Thayer, who at the time was assisting in the political section of the embassy, I was able to sign the supplementary dispatch regarding the trial and place it with its eight attached enclosures in the diplomatic pouch. I shall not undertake here to quote from that dispatch or its enclosures. Any of my readers who are interested in making a study of the trial might, however, profit from an examination of the dispatch and its enclosures, a copy of which is in the National Archives in Washington [Call number NA 861.00/11652].

I was sitting directly behind Radek when his name was first mentioned by one of the defendants and noted the red flush that crept up the back of his neck. I was surprised at the sensitivity of an old Bolshevik who in my opinion should have been hardened during more than 25 years of rough-and-tumble party strife. Two of the officials of the press section of Narkomindel whom I knew to be close friends of Radek were also visibly agitated at the mention of his name and exchanged whispers. They were among the many members of Narkomindel who were purged during the next few months.

The manner in which the Zinoviev-Kamenev trial was conducted and the hasty execution of the death sentence came as a shock to many communists and other leftists everywhere. Both Kamenev and Zinoviev had been very close to Lenin. In fact, Lenin, Trotsky, Kamenev, and Zinoviev had been names for communists throughout the world to conjure during the early years of the revolution when relatively few persons had even heard of Stalin. Many of the liberals and the leftists in the United States who had consistently defended the purge that had thus far taken place in the Soviet Union were given pause. They found it difficult to justify the execution of historic communist leaders like Zinoviev and Kamenev after a "show trial" of the kind given and yet they did not wish to criticize Stalin and his colleagues.

As I have already pointed out in previous chapters of my narrative many of the more leftist liberals in the West during the late 1930s were convinced that criticism of the Kremlin must ipso facto be evidence of conscious or subconscious pro-Nazi tendencies.

The Zinoviev-Kamenev trial and each of the two great public trials that followed—the trial of the group of seventeen including Radek and Pyatakov, held in January 1937, and that of the group including Bukharin and Yagoda that took place in March 1938—attracted worldwide attention. Ambassador Davies was in Moscow when the latter two trials were held and was, therefore, the observer for our embassy. He was accompanied by Kennan during the Radek-Pyatakov trial and by Bohlen during the Bukharin-Yagoda trial who, with their excellent knowledge of the Russian language, tried to help him understand what was going on. During 1936, 1937, and 1938 thousands of small unannounced trials were taking place throughout the Soviet Union about which few people, even members of the families of persons on trial, knew anything. Other trials, although held in private, were considered by the Soviet authorities to be of sufficient importance to merit announcements.

The most sensational of the nonpublic trials, which was allegedly held in June 1937, was that of Marshal Tukhachevsky and other high ranking officers of the Red Army. I use the word "allegedly" because there has been a lingering doubt as to whether or not these generals were actually given a formal trial. There were stories in Moscow that could not be altogether disregarded that some of them had been shot immediately after arrest, that at least one of them had been shot while resisting arrest, and that one or more had committed suicide.

Norris Chipman, his wife, my wife, and I had taken advantage of a long weekend, which happened to include Decoration Day 1937, to make a short relaxing boat trip down the upper Volga from Kostroma to Gorki. Upon our return to Moscow after a three-day absence, I discovered that the Great Purge was beginning to move into the armed forces. Statements had been published in the press announcing the demotions or transfers of top-ranking officers of the Red Army and the suicide of General Gamarnik, the first assistant commissar for defense and chief of the political administration of the Red Army. It was not until June 8 that the embassy had sufficient information in its possession to justify a report to the State Department. On that day I sent a telegraphic report, which read in part as follows:

> The demotion of Marshal Tukhachevsky and the suicide of Gamarnik who, as head of the political work of the army, has held rank almost equivalent to that of a marshal, have been reported in the Soviet press.
>
> The Soviet press has also announced the revival of the institution of Military Political Commissars by establishment of military Soviets each composed of three members in the various military districts, in the Far Eastern Army, and in various naval units. It appears that the composition of each Soviet will include the ranking military or naval officer and the ranking political officer. It is not as yet clear who the third member will be.
>
> Although not yet announced there seems little doubt that Tukha-

chevsky has been arrested and that the following persons have been arrested or at least removed in disgrace from their posts: Army Commander Kork, Head of the Frunze Academy (the equivalent of which in the United States is the Army War College); Corps Commander Eideman, Head of Civilian Defense Work and Chief of the organization Osoaviakhim; Corps Commander Gorbatchev, Assistant Commander and in active charge of the Moscow Military District; Corps Commander Gekher who until recently was Chief of the Foreign Relations Section of the People's Commissariat for Defense; Muklevitch, a newly appointed Assistant Commissar for Defense Industry who since the revolution has held various important military positions including the post of Commander of the Soviet Navy and Air Forces.

It appears that many officers more junior in rank including protégés of some of the general commanders mentioned above have also been arrested.

The Embassy agrees with the view of a number of competent foreign observers in Moscow that the arrests and shifting of army personnel and the changes which are being made in the army structure are prompted by a lack of confidence on the part of Stalin and the little Party group around him in the absolute loyalty to themselves of certain sections of the Red Army. Whether the Kremlin will go so far as to charge that there has been a gigantic Red Army plot will remain to be seen. If so it is likely that the utterances of charges will be of espionage, treason to the Fatherland, and Trotskyism rather than of anti-Stalinism. The press is already commencing to charge Gamarnik with Fascist espionage and treachery, the usual synonyms for lack of enthusiasm over Stalin's leadership.

It seems likely that the system of Military Soviets may adversely affect the efficiency of the army in that it is contrary to the principle of individual command and responsibility and will probably result in a diminishing of the respect of officers and men for their superiors. It is thought that at least one member of each Soviet will be chosen because of his proven loyalty to Stalin and will exercise vigilance in checking any order or movement which might threaten the power or prestige of the dictator. Stalin evidently prefers an army upon which he can personally rely to one which while perhaps more efficient technically is inclined to consider itself something of a professional autonomous organization which can afford to take an attitude of neutrality towards the internal political struggles which are now taking place. It would seem that the test of loyalty in the Red Army in the future will be its attitude toward Stalin and his henchmen rather than towards the Soviet State, the Communist Party, Communism and so forth.

On June 11 I sent a supplementary telegram reporting that, according to an announcement in *Pravda* of the same date, Marshal Tukhachevsky and General Officers Yakir, Uborevich, Kork, Eideman, Feldman, Primakov, and Putna had been arrested and charged with "violation of their military obligations (oath of allegiance), treason to the Fatherland, treason to the peoples of the U.S.S.R., and treason to the workers and peasants Red Army." In this telegram I quoted the following excerpt from the announcement:

> The investigation has established that the accused, and also Gamarnik, who committed suicide, participated in anti-State connections with leading military circles of a certain foreign nation which follows an unfriendly policy in regard to the U.S.S.R. Being in the military secret service of this nation, the accused systematically supplied the military circles of this nation with espionage information concerning the condition of the Red Army, conducted wrecking work designed to weaken the Red Army, and endeavored to prepare the defeat of the Red Army in case of an armed attack upon the U.S.S.R., and it was their purpose to facilitate the restoration of power of the landowners and capitalists in the U.S.S.R.
>
> All of the accused have pleaded guilty in the fullest measure to the charges brought against them.
>
> The hearing of the case will take place today, June 11, at a closed special judicial session of the Supreme Court of the U.S.S.R., consisting of the Chairman V. Ulrich, Chief of the Military Collegium of the Supreme Court, and the following members of the court.

The announcement carried the names of eight Red Army officers of general rank who were to be members of the court under Ulrich (who, as chief of the Military Collegium of the Supreme Court, was the presiding judge of the Supreme Court at the more important trials of the Great Purge.)

The eight officers who had been appointed to serve as judges under Ulrich were among the best known general officers of the Red Army. Budenny, for instance, was one of the senior marshals of the Soviet Union. He had won fame as a cavalry officer fighting the White armies following the Bolshevik revolution and was a colorful figure, popular among the masses, with his great mustache and his cavalry swagger. Bleucher had won fame fighting in the Far East. Alksnis, a Latvian by origin, had succeeded in making important improvements in the Soviet Air Force in spite of the shortage of technical skills. The officers had undoubtedly been named as judges in order to give credence to the findings of the court.

In March 1937 Ambassador Davies had given a stag dinner for the high-ranking members of the Soviet armed forces at which many of the accused and the judges were present. Following the dinner, which had been a lively affair, the ambassador had expressed great admiration for his guests, particularly Tukhachevsky. When reading the announcement in *Pravda* I wondered what the ambassador would say on his return to the Soviet Union at this development.

On June 12 I reported that the morning's press had announced that the death sentences had been pronounced on Tukhachevsky and the other defendants and added that:

> The PRAVDA in its editorial comment makes it clear that Germany was the country with which these men are supposed to have plotted. . .
>
> During the last week or two the emphasis on the danger of espionage in the Soviet Union has increased to such an extent as to indicate actual lack of mental balance on the part of persons responsible therefore. For days the entire feuilleton space of the Moscow PRAVDA has been devoted to the installments of a translation of R. Rowan's book on espionage. Other Soviet papers have been running material with the same key note. Articles written and speeches made by agents of the Commissariat for Internal Affairs describe the despicable methods used by foreign espionage services to entangle unsuspecting Soviet citizens in their meshes. The suggestion has even been advanced in the PRAVDA that every Soviet citizen should consider himself a secret service agent. One of the workers' resolutions is carried in the PRAVDA under the headline "we are all voluntary workers for the People's Commissariat for Internal Affairs."

On the following day I telegraphed that *Pravda* had carried the announcement that the death sentences on Tukhachevsky and his colleagues had been carried out on June 12 and added the following comment:

> It should be borne in mind that the value of the views of the Embassy regarding the extent if any of the guilt of the condemned officers is limited by the fact that it is in possession of no information regarding the nature of the evidence advanced during the investigations and the trial. The Embassy's opinions therefore are based merely upon its observations of the events which have unrolled here during the last 6 months, its own estimation of the officers in question, some of whom were personally known to members of the staff, the reputation of these officers, the foreign observers and Soviet citizens for whose views it has respect.
>
> It is the opinion of the Embassy that
>
>> (a) There is some truth in the reports which have circulated for years to the effect that the feelings toward Germany of many of

the higher officers of the Red Army are friendlier than those held by those responsible for the present Soviet foreign policy.

(b) Most if not all of the condemned (except Putna who has served as Military Attaché in Berlin) were trained in the German General Staff College when German-Soviet relations were in the Rapallo stage and there acquired a respect for the efficiency and fighting power of the Reichswehr and considerable admiration for German military traditions.

(c) Most if not all of the accused would have liked to have seen better relations established between Germany and the Soviet Union under conditions which necessarily would have included certain alterations in Hitler's own policies. They have been known to express their feelings of friendliness for Germany in public. At a farewell party given at the German Embassy 2 year ago for the departing German Counselor, Tukhachevski in the presence of other guests frankly stated that it was too bad that "the politicians were disturbing German-Soviet relations." Voroshilov is reported to have made similar remarks at a farewell dinner several years ago for von Dirksen. No one has attached great significance to statements of this kind since army officers have been accustomed in a bluff way to bemoan the manner in which "politicians" spoil good relations between the Soviet Union and other countries. They have on occasions even made remarks of this nature with respect to Soviet-American relations . . .

(d) It is the practice of the Kremlin to stretch into heinous crimes certain known views of persons whom it has decided to destroy. So in the present instance the Embassy believes that it distorted the known friendly feelings for Germany shared by the condemned officers into treason.

(e) The character and reputation for professional integrity of the condemned are such that it does not seem possible that all of them could have been guilty of the crimes for which they have been condemned. Their intelligence and experience made them extremely valuable and their loss is a severe blow to the efficiency and morale of the Red Army.

(f) It seems more likely that the real reason for their downfall was that Stalin had become suspicious of them; that he had been led to feel that they and other army officers were becoming too independent in their attitude and that he could not be sure of their unconditional loyalty to himself.

(g) There is reason to believe that Tukhachevski and at least most of the other condemned had acquired while in Germany a tendency to regard an army as a professional organization standing above politics and untouched by all but the most profound political changes, that they had therefore systematically endeavored to resist the penetration into the army of the agents and *provocateurs* of the Commissariat for Internal Affairs and had tried to prevent the officers and men of the army from taking part in party squabbles, even those involving Stalin. They may even have further annoyed Stalin by showing disapproval of some of his present intemperate policies. At any rate Stalin must have decided once and for all to demonstrate to the army its full dependence upon himself.

(h) Some credence should be given to the rumors prevalent in Moscow that Bleucher, Budenny, et cetera, did not pass upon the guilt of their former colleagues and friends at a formal secret trial but that they were merely shown the alleged confessions and commanded to sign the verdict.

There is a rumor among the Soviet population that the intelligence service of the French Army first discovered that the Red Army officers were involved in a conspiracy with agents of the German Government to overthrow Stalin and communicated their findings to the Soviet Government. The Embassy is not in a position to state whether there is any foundation for this rumor, which is ridiculed by the French Embassy here. Even though the French military intelligence service may have found cause to be concerned at friendly relations existing between certain Soviet and German officers and the prevalence of friendly feelings for Germany among the higher officers of the Red Army, the Embassy nevertheless is not convinced that the condemned men were guilty of the crimes attributed to them.

Although Germany and German nationals in the Soviet Union continued to be the main villains, the campaign against them widened during the spring of 1937 to include all capitalistic countries and all foreigners in the Soviet Union. In reporting on the development of the antiforeigner campaign I wrote a dispatch, dated May 14, 1937, as excerpted below:

At the present time practically all Soviet citizens who have had occasion during recent years to have relations with members of foreign diplomatic missions or with foreigners who keep in touch with their diplomatic missions appear to be in constant fear of being arrested on charges of espionage or terrorism. This alarm extends apparently even to those Soviet citizens who, as agents for the People's Commissariat for Internal Affairs, have been specially authorized to maintain contacts with foreigners.

There is hardly a diplomatic mission in Moscow which does not have some story to relate regarding efforts of the Soviet Government to eliminate still further the various channels with which in the past it has come into contact with Soviet life...

In view of the increased displeasure with which the Soviet Government appears to be looking upon Soviet citizens who have relations with foreigners, the American members of the staff of this Embassy hesitate to continue or to develop such contacts as they already have since they do not wish to be instrumental in causing misfortune to innocent persons.

In the late spring of 1937 the phenomenon that is now known as the Great Purge had reached such devastating proportions that the members of the embassy came to the opinion that for the use of the State Department and for the benefit of future historians they should prepare a comprehensive dispatch describing how the purge looked to them at that time. With the cooperation of my colleagues in the embassy I wrote on June 13, 1937, therefore, a detailed dispatch, which read in part as follows:

According to such information as this Mission is able to obtain, the rate at which Soviet and Party officials are being removed from office and arrested has of late been showing a tendency to increase rather than decrease. There appears to be no field in Soviet politics, government, education, science, literature, fine arts, and so forth, in which prominent persons have not been disgraced or arrested in recent months.

Since it is only in exceptional cases that the names of disgraced or arrested persons are given to the public, and since the developments which are taking place are enshrouded with secrecy, it is difficult to ascertain precisely just who is under arrest and who has been ejected from public life as untrustworthy...

The dismissals from office or the arrests of various People's Commissars or Assistant Commissars do not by any means give a full picture of what is taking place. In some instances whole commissariats are being ripped to pieces by dismissals and arrests of important officials below the rank of commissar. It would appear, for instance, that literally hundreds of outstanding officials of the Commissariat for Internal Affairs, the organ of the Soviet Government which itself is charged with making arrests of persons charged with political crimes, have fallen into disgrace and have been sent to prison, if not executed. It is typical of this era in Soviet internal politics that agents of the Administration of State Security, the Section of the People's Commissariat for Internal Affairs which before the formation of that Commissariat was known as the O.G.P.U. (Combined State Political Administration) should proceed so energetically to arrest one another.

The purging of the Red Army, which began several weeks ago, affords a similar spectacle of officers turning apparently with enthusiasm upon their former colleagues and comrades at arms. No one knows as yet how far the rending of the military structure will go. There seems little doubt, however, that scores of general officers are in disgrace or under arrest and that hundreds of officers of lower rank have dropped completely out of sight.

Some of the officials of the People's Commissariat for Foreign Affairs are so patently in abject terror that one must pity them. They fear to talk on almost any subject and apparently dread meeting foreign visitors, particularly those from the local Diplomatic Corps. It is rumored that Karakhan, former Soviet Ambassador to Turkey and previously Ambassador to China; Stern, the Chief of the Second Western Political Division (which handles German affairs); and Mironov, Acting Chief of the Press Section, are among the officials of this Commissariat who are under arrest. The Embassy doubts that Mironov is actually arrested. He has not been seen on duty for the last week and his colleagues are somewhat vague as to his whereabouts. Both he and Stern are understood to have been close friends of Krestinski, the former Assistant Commissar and Ambassador to Berlin, who undoubtedly is in disgrace and probably under arrest...

The theatrical world has not been overlooked by the agents of the Commissariat for Internal Affairs. The directors of the Bolshoi Theater (the Moscow Opera House), of the First Art Theater, and of the Jewish Theater have been removed from their posts. At least one of them, Mutnikh of the Bolshoi Theater, is under arrest. The works of some of the best known composers and playwrights have been banned and the authors disgraced if not arrested.

Two questions are certain to present themselves:

(a) What is the true reason for the great number of demotions, arrests, and dismissals from office; and

(b) What effect is the purging process having on the country in general?

With respect to the reasons for the attack which is being made upon so many prominent persons active in all phases of Soviet political, economic, professional, and cultural life, it may be stated:

1. The arrests appear to be inspired initially by Stalin himself, acting under the advice of, and in conjunction with, his closest and most trusted advisers, particularly Ezhov, the new People's Commissar for Internal Affairs.

2. Stalin, in spite of having many really great qualities and a calm exterior, is reputed...to be extraordinarily vain, loving of flattery, vengeful and unforgetful of real or fancied slights, jealous, suspicious, crafty, hot-tempered and capricious. During the long

conflict between Stalin and the clever and glib Trotski both before and after Lenin's death, Trotski easily showed himself to be Stalin's superior in abstract thinking and doctrinaire argumentation. On some occasions, it is said, Trotski succeeded in making his slower-witted opponent appear ridiculous. Although Stalin eventually defeated Trotski, his victory was not a sweet one since, according to those who knew Stalin, he had the consciousness that he had not triumphed through personal brilliance or as a result of intellectual prowess, but merely because of his superior organizational ability. The struggle with Trotski is said to have left two deep imprints upon Stalin, namely, an intense hatred for his opponent mixed with fear which is said to be increasing as the years go by, and a suspicion and fear of persons who tend to think in the abstract and whose intellectual processes he is unable to follow and comprehend.

3. The serious endeavors of the Trotskyists outside of the Soviet Union in the summer of 1936 to reestablish even though on a modest scale an international revolutionary organization in competition with the Communist International infuriated and frightened Stalin to such an extent that he threw off the restraint which had been exercised upon him by his advisers for many years and attempted to humiliate his old enemy in the eyes of the revolutionary world by demonstrating that the latter was merely an agent of Hitler. The Zinoviev-Kamenev trial was primarily staged in order to discredit Trotsky once for all in the eyes of the world international revolutionaries and to place him in revolutionary history not as an exiled martyr but as a traitor and double-dealer. It was also useful in helping Stalin to rid himself of a number of old Bolshevik rivals who, although confined in prison, still had enough former followers faithful to them to cause him some unrest. The Zinoviev-Kamenev trial, instead of ruining Trotsky, however, made him again a prominent world revolutionary figure. The unexpected result of the trial is said to have increased still further Stalin's exasperation and fear. In a spirit of revenge he began to seek out all means in his control to hurt his rival. He caused one of Trotsky's sons who still lived in the Soviet Union to be arrested and, it is reported, had lists made of Trotsky's former allies and friends. One by one, the persons whose names appeared on these lists were disgraced and usually arrested. Not only were Trotsky's former friends disgraced, but friends of his former friends, and even friends of friends of his former friends. It is said that a number of Stalin's advisers endeavored to persuade him to curb his vengeful instincts. Instead of showing gratitude, Stalin accused them of having Trotskyist sympathies and ruined or disgraced them and their friends. Stalin not only turned against those of his advisers who openly counseled restraint but also against the former promi-

nent Party leaders who would not approve of his program of revenge. It would appear that this program was broadened to include all persons against whom he bore political grudges as well as their friends. Although he disposed of another group of former Trotsky adherents in the Radek-Sokolnikov trial of last January, he apparently decided not to stage an open trial for such former right opponents as Bukharin and Rykov.*

4. During the last ten years there has sprung up in Moscow a circle of persons representing all phases of Soviet life who intellectually are somewhat in advance of their environment. In this circle are those to whom the Soviet regime has given special pecuniary and educational advantages, such as army officers, members of the organization formerly known as the O.G.P.U., professional men, writers, artists, musicians, educators, and men who hold high positions in the Government, Party, or various Soviet organizations because of talent of technical ability. On a less brilliant scale the counterparts of these circles have sprung up in many localities throughout the country. These circles are not organized; the members belonging to them have merely gravitated toward one another socially. The Soviet press is accustomed to refer to them with pride from time to time as the "new intelligentsia."

The "new intelligentsia" is the only class, if it may be called a class, in the Soviet Union which has what can be described as a public opinion. Its members are able more or less to reason for themselves and are not inclined to adopt as dogmatic conclusions which may appear in the censored Soviet press or in Party resolutions. They are in general loyal to the State and, in theory at least, to the principles of the world revolution. They are inclined nevertheless in varying degrees to consider themselves as adults who can think for themselves and to look with a somewhat amused and indulgent attitude upon the methods by which the Kremlin endeavors to control, and retain the support of, the masses of workers and peasants. There is no doubt that the members of the new intelligentsia for the most part took a somewhat cynical attitude toward the trials and even made the mistake of exchanging whispers of disapproval of the trials and of the numerous arrests which were taking place. Although these circles were Stalin's own product, many of them seemed to feel that they had outgrown their creator intellectually. Every now and then some of the new intelligentsia are said, without reproof from their fellows, to have made remarks which might be interpreted as ridicule of the dictator. The attitude of these circles is reported to have reached Stalin and to

---

* He did this, however, eight months later.

have stirred anew in him resentment and distrust of the intelligentsia, regardless of brand. According to such information as
the Embassy is able to obtain, he has given orders that every
person, no matter how highly placed, however gifted, or however
useful to the regime, who by word or deed has failed to show
proper respect to him shall, together with friends and adherents,
be disgraced. It has been reported that the agents of the Commissariat for Internal Affairs, in their eagerness to carry out Stalin's
orders, are not overly careful in obtaining definite proof of the guilt
of many of the arrested persons. Definite proof is difficult to obtain
and apparently many persons, therefore, are being condemned on
hearsay.

It is in keeping with the spirit of the times in the Soviet Union
that advantage is taken of the situation by unscrupulous persons to
pay off old grudges and cause the ruin of rivals and enemies. How
far the inroads upon the members of the new intelligentsia will
continue cannot as yet be determined.

5. In addition to the "new intelligentsia," there is another
body of persons in the Soviet Union which is accustomed to think
for itself. I refer to certain sincere theoretical and practicing communists who are burning with hatred for the so-called capitalists
and exploiters and who desire a greater degree of equality of
opportunity and living levels within the Soviet Union and the
adoption of more energetic measures on the part of the Kremlin for
the purpose of speeding up the development of the world revolution in other countries. For purposes of convenience these persons
might be referred to as "leftists."

It would be a mistake to think that all "leftists" are old
Bolsheviks. Many of them have been steeped in communistic
theories in the classroom and the "Red Corners," i.e., the propaganda sections of workers' clubs, and so forth. It would also be
erroneous to believe that all of them have considered Stalin as a
deliberate betrayer of the revolution. Many of them felt that although he was a sincere revolutionist he was following incorrect
tactics and had become so deeply interested in building up a
strong Soviet State that he was overlooking the fact that the State,
constructed in accordance with his plans, may itself develop into
an arch enemy of the world revolution.

It is understood that during recent years more and more
leftists have begun to believe that perhaps after all Trotsky was
right ten years ago when he charged that Stalin eventually would
betray the revolution. For a number of years Stalin has emphasized
less and less the world revolutionary aims of the Soviet State and to
all appearances has given much less attention than previously to
the activities of the Communist International and kindred organizations. He furthermore has openly admitted the existence of

inequalities in living standards of various categories of the Soviet population and has endeavored to justify them by pointing out that in the stage of socialism such inequalities must necessarily exist. More recently he has taken other steps which the leftists feel are not in the direction of communism, such as steps to strengthen the family unit, to give more regard to private property rights, to abolish the privileged position of the industrial workers, and so forth. It is quite possible that Stalin plans to take other steps in the immediate future that also may be displeasing to the leftists. At any rate the mutual distrust between Stalin and the leftists has become acute. Distrust for Stalin was of course heightened by the Zinoviev-Kamenev trial which most leftists considered to be a farce and still more recently by the Radek-Pyatakov trial.

In so far as can be ascertained, leftists have had no formal organization; in view of the manner of work of the agents of the People's Commissariat for Internal Affairs it is extremely dangerous for persons, particularly Party members, to exchange views critical of the Kremlin, and it is therefore frequently impossible for one leftist to identify another. Nevertheless, it seems probable that in some way or another a number of the leftists in the Party have contrived to cooperate with one another to an extent that has attracted the attention of the Kremlin and caused anxiety and irritation to Stalin and his advisers. The wave of arrests which is taking place is at present engulfing the more prominent, and in some cases the less prominent, leftist leaders who survived the arrests of 1936.

6. The publication in the spring of 1936 of the draft of the new "democratic Constitution" of the Soviet Union and the simultaneous announcements in the Soviet press to the effect that genuine democracy was about to be established in the Soviet Union had a considerable effect upon wide circles of Soviet citizens, particularly those who disagreed in many respects with various policies of the Kremlin. It revived in many breasts the desire for more freedom, and in numerous cases persons who formerly had not dared to criticize governmental or Party policies began to express their opinions openly. The temerity of these persons was soon checked but the seeds of a desire for more liberal treatment had already been planted and they began to germinate.

The wave of arrests which began early in July and has since continued to swell tended to cause thousands of thinking persons, including the new intelligentsia, the leftists, the surviving admirers, friends, and adherents of those who have been destroyed, and even some of the old bourgeoisie who had gradually reconciled themselves to the Soviet regime to feel revulsion at what is taking place and seriously to consider whether or not the time had not come to work for a more democratic and liberal regime. The

Kremlin could not remain unaware of the murmurings of these advocates of a liberal democracy and has of course not failed to include in the program of arrests those who were most outspoken.

7. An important factor which should not be overlooked . . . is the fear of assassination which Stalin seems to have entertained ever since the murder of Kirov in December 1934. It will be recalled that immediately following the assassination he was almost in a frenzy. He first had shot a large number of members of the old aristocracy and bourgeoisie who were being held in prison. A short time later a number of other persons allegedly sent into the country from abroad to bring about the overthrow of the regime were executed. Nearly two years afterwards Kamenev and Zinoviev were charged with being implicated in a Trotsky plot which resulted in the death of Kirov.

Regardless of whether a single person or a group was responsible for the shooting of Kirov his death seems to have convinced Stalin that no matter what safeguards he or any other Soviet leader may place around himself it is always possible for an assassin to break through them. This realization appears to have preyed upon him and to have resulted in an accentuation of the suspicious qualities of his nature . . .

Although as already pointed out the Embassy is not in a position to state categorically what effect the purging process is having upon the country as a whole it nevertheless feels that it should give the Department the benefit of such information relating to this subject as it is able to ascertain:

(1) The great masses of the peasantry have not as yet been fully awakened from their age-old political apathy. They are still only dimly interested in matters which do not promise to have a direct and immediate effect upon their ability to obtain the necessities of life. They have never been overly fond of the somewhat noisy and bothersome Soviet officials who from time to time have invaded their lives and who they vaguely feel are a set of crooks. When they hear that some of these officials are in trouble the peasantry is inclined to feel that the grafters are getting their just deserts.

(2) The young and ignorant industrial workers who have only recently arrived in the factories from the villages and who have not as yet grown cynical are said in general to believe most of what is told them by their political educators and what they read in the Soviet press. These workers, it is reported to the Embassy, are inclined to condemn those who have been disgraced or arrested as traitors and saboteurs.

(3) The seasoned industrial workers who have suffered consider-

able disappointment during recent years and who with resentment have seen the rift of living standards growing greater between themselves and the specialists, Stakhanovites, engineers, and the bureaucracy are reported to have little sympathy for their superiors who have been arrested. They do not appear to be particularly interested in answering the academic question of whether their superiors are actually guilty or not but are taking the opportunity to express their discontent and their jealousy for specialists, engineers, and white collar workers, whose prestige and authority have taken a sharp drop.

(4) The bureaucracy, engineers, technicians, and so forth, are, for the most part, in a panic. There is hardly one of them who at some unguarded moment has not made a remark which might now be used to show his disloyalty to Stalin or his disapproval of the events which recently have been taking place. They are so frightened that in general they do not want to attract attention to themselves. Accordingly they dodge responsibility and endeavor to pass along to one another the duty of making decisions. They are faced from below with lack of respect and discipline on the part of the workers and from above with officials who themselves would not hestitate to pass on to them any blame which may arise from shortcomings in work.

(5) In the universities and intermediate schools, professors and instructors in many instances are afraid to face their classes. Their histories have been condemned, their philosophical textbooks have been found wanting, their legal textbooks have been banned. Students are inclined to show their teachers less respect than hitherto, and in some cases to take advantage of old grudges to report statements made in lecture rooms which may be interpreted as treacherous.

(6) The theaters are just as brilliant as ever, but it is understood that when Stalin and his suite appear at any performance everyone connected with it, including the playwrights, the directors, the actors, and the managers are in a fright until a verdict has been rendered.

(7) The members of the new as well as the old intelligentsia are both frightened and resentful. Many of them not only fear for their own personal safety, but are resentful at having been deprived of the right of freedom of discussion on almost any subject, regardless of whether or not that subject appears to be connected with politics.

(8) The prestige of the Red Army has suffered tremendously. Only a few months ago it was considered as the bulwark of Soviet power. Its officers and men were accorded special treatment.

Discipline was good. It was said that it was freer of internal dissension than the armies of capitalist countries. In a comparatively brief period officers and men have been given to understand that the superiors in whom they had confidence are untrustworthy. The feeling is prevalent among all ranks that the new political commissars are being sent out to spy on the officers. The officers have lost confidence in themselves and the full respect of their men. It is understood that at the present time the same fear to take responsibility now exists in the Army as in civil life. A considerable period must elapse before the Army can recover from the blow which it has received.

(9) The uncertainty which pervades Soviet internal affairs has to a degree been extended into the field of foreign relations. During the last two days representatives of several diplomatic missions have informed the Embassy that negotiations in progress between themselves and the People's Commissariat for Foreign Affairs have been temporarily suspended. The Foreign Office has suggested to the German, Polish, and Japanese Embassies that the number of consular officers maintained in the Soviet Union by the countries which these Embassies represent be curtailed. Most of the few foreigners still resident in the country are being requested to leave. The newspapers are full of warnings to the population to be careful of foreign spies in artful disguises. Foreigners, regardless of political complexion, are being avoided to an extent said to be unprecedented in the history of the Soviet Union.

As I had anticipated, Ambassador Davies was shocked when he read in the press while outside the Soviet Union of the trial and execution of the officers whom he had so recently entertained and of whom he had spoken so highly. Following his return to Moscow in the latter part of June he went over the pile of translations from the Soviet press we had saved for him and copies of our various reports. It seemed to me that he was much less concerned about the trials, the executions, and the terror than he was at the thought that the way in which the purge was developing might mar the picture of Stalin as a benign, idealistic person that he had been trying to paint for the benefit of the president, the Department of State, and the other readers of his reports. He, therefore, wrote a number of reports and personal letters defending Stalin, with whom for six months he had been trying to arrange a meeting. On July 28, 1937, for instance, he wrote a dispatch to the department in which, after referring to rumors to the effect that Stalin's mental or physical health was declining, he said:

The "sick man of the Kremlin" theory is quite universally discounted. Stalin has had some heart trouble, as most of these men in the Government have had; but he has been seen on numerous occasions, and only recently by the writer, at very close range, and he looks strong, solid, healthy, and normal.

Moreover, generally speaking, in diplomatic circles here responsibility for these executions, in a strictly personal sense, is not attributed to Stalin. He commands a great deal of respect, outside of these terrible happenings. He is generally considered to be a clean-living, modest, retiring, single-purposed man, with a one-track mind, devoted to communism and the elevation of the proletariat. The responsibility is generally attributed to the "action of the Party" through its Party leaders. Of course, in that connection, it is generally considered that Stalin is by far the strongest character, and he is what we might term the type of "easy Boss," who permits it to appear that his associates have made their own decisions.

As to the alleged guilt of these Army Generals of overt acts—actual conspiracy with the German Government—the general opinion is here that the charge is not justified, although it should be said that two very well-informed Ambassadors, with whom I have discussed the matter, have stated it to be their belief that there was probably some truth in the allegations.

The Great Purge, including the antiforeigner campaign, continued to claim tens of thousands of victims during the latter part of 1937 and the whole of 1938. It abated in the spring of 1939 to the level of trials, executions, and disappearances that had been maintained before the murder of Kirov.

The trial of the members of the so-called "Trotskyist bloc" involving Bukharin and other former leaders of the party or former high government officials, which was held in March 1938, was the last of the three great public trials. The members of this "rightist" group were charged with working under the instructions of British, German, Polish, and Japanese intelligence services and with conspiring under Trotsky's leadership to murder and to sabotage for the purpose of overthrowing the Soviet government, dismembering the Soviet Union, and restoring capitalism. They were accused of having plotted to kill Stalin, Voroshilov, and others, and of having succeeded in murdering Gorki, the great writer; Menzhinsky, the former chief of the OGPU; and Kuibyshev, former director of the State Planning Commission. Of the twenty-one defendants all except two pleaded guilty, all were found guilty, and all except three who were sentenced to long terms of imprisonment, were executed. Among the defendants, as Ambassador Davies, who was the U.S. observer at the trial, pointed out in his report to the State Department, were, in addition to Bukharin, a former premier, six former cabinet officers, a former ambassador to England and France, and one of the most famous Soviet physicians.

The ambassador, in reporting on this trial in a telegram dated March 13, 1938, stated that:

> Despite a prejudice arising because of confession evidence and a prejudice against a system which affords practically no protection for the accused, after daily observation of the witnesses, their most awkward testifying, the unconscious corroborations which developed, and other facts in the course of the trial, together with others of which judicial notice could be taken, but as far as the political defendants are concerned sufficient crimes under Soviet law, among those charged in the indictment, were established by the proof and beyond a reasonable doubt to justify the verdict of guilt of treason and the adjudication of the punishment provided by Soviet criminal statutes. As to the doctors defendants I have reservations. Despite exaggerations induced by possible paranoia and other possible psychological influences among the political defendants and despite the obvious over-zealousness of the prosection in over-proving the case, my opinion is that not all charges as alleged were proved but that sufficient facts were established to prove that these defendants had plotted to overthrow the present Soviet Government, and were willing to use any means available to overthrow the Union, and were therefore guilty of treason under Soviet law. The opinion of those diplomats who attended the trial most regularly was generally that the case had established the fact of a formidable political opposition and an exceedingly serious plot which explained to them many of the hitherto unexplained developments of the last 6 months here. The only difference of opinion that seemed to exist was the degree to which the plot had been implemented by different defendants and the degree to which the conspiracy had become centralized.
>
> Aside from the natural horror instilled by this exhibition of intense drama and human tragedy the trial affords a shocking realization that there does exist still a modern system of jurisprudence which affords so little protection to the accused and to the rights of the individual.

The ambassador also wrote a series of letters to a number of friends in the United States, including politicians and jurists, informing them that in his opinion most of the defendants had been guilty of treason and the sentences that had been pronounced on them were justified.

The Deportation of Ethnic Minorities

One of the more brutal practices on the Soviet government from 1936 to 1939, a practice which reflected a mentality similar to that responsible for the purge, was the uprooting and deporting of families residing near the Soviet frontier who had ethnic kinship with peoples of other countries. Thousands of families of Polish blood, for instance, were shipped like cattle from areas near the Polish frontier to the wilds of Central Asia and Siberia. Thousands of ethnically Greek families, many of which had resided in southern Russia near the Black Sea for centuries, were either deported en masse to Greece or herded into Central Asia.

From the Soviet Caucasus Persian families who had lived in that area since it was a part of the Persian empire were dumped across the border into Persia or sent into the wild hinterlands of Soviet Asia. There were similar deportations of Afghans, Chinese, and Volga Germans. The deported families were usually replaced by retired veterans of the Red Army or by other carefully selected Russian families.

As I have already pointed out while discussing individual members of the diplomatic corps in Moscow and their problems, deportations of this kind frequently led to protests by the diplomatic representatives of the countries concerned. Such protests, however, were brushed aside by the Soviet government and served merely to increase the suspicions of Soviet officials of the loyalty of the deportees to the Soviet Union.

SOME LATER THOUGHTS ABOUT THE GREAT PURGE

As I now, in the mid-1960s, review the reports on the Great Purge that I made to the State Department while it was still in progress, I ask myself whether, if I had had the benefit of hindsight or had had the ability to foresee the future, I would have written as I did. I believe that I would at least have used different phrasing; I would have placed more emphasis on certain factors and less on others.

If, for instance, when I had written my telegram of August 27, 1936, regarding the Zinoviev-Kamenev trial I had had the knowledge and experience that I now possess, I would probably not have expressed so strongly the belief that "the persons testified as they did with the hope of escaping torture, obtaining commutation of sentence or from fear that failure so to testify would result in harm to members of their families and friends." I still believe that that hope might have been one of the factors that, consciously or unconsciously, influenced them, but I now consider it possible that their willingness to testify as they did was not always based merely on a lack of physical or moral courage. In some instances they might have had a desire by their abject confessions and breast-beating to contribute to the unity of the Communist Party and to the strengthening of the Soviet state. They might have been persuaded that, by their allegations of wrongdoing and by their praise of Stalin, they would be promoting the cause of international communism to which most of them, despite their differences, had dedicated their lives.

Similarly, if some 30 years later I were listing, as I tried to do in my telegram of June 13, 1937, the factors responsible for Stalin's decision to rid himself of Tukhachevsky and other top officers of the Red Army, I would have placed more emphasis on possible differences between Stalin and his officers regarding the strategies to be employed in case of the outbreak of a major war in Western Europe. I would have suggested that perhaps Tukhachevsky and other members of the general staff might have insisted too strongly that the preparations for the defense of the Soviet Union be concentrated on strengthening to the maximum its borders as they had existed in 1936 and that Soviet strategy be based on a gradual retreat from strong positions along the frontier to a series of fall-back positions so that the enemy, after advancing with heavy losses, would find himself in hostile territory facing a succession of strong, heavily fortified positions while his own lines of communication were becoming progressively longer.

Stalin, however, had announced on several occasions that if the Soviet Union should become involved in a war, the fighting would not take place on Soviet territory. Subsequent developments caused me to believe that as early as 1936 Stalin was already contemplating the occupation of Finland, the Baltic states, and portions of Poland and Romania in case France and Great Britain, or France by itself, should become involved in a war with Germany.

It seemed to me quite possible that Stalin may have been instructing his military advisers to draw up plans to be carried out if Germany should become involved in a war with the West, to be prepared to move quickly into the areas lying between Germany and the Soviet Union, and to construct in them fortified lines against possible German aggression.

On the evening of November 7, 1936, the nineteenth anniversary of the Bolshevik revolution, the Kremlin gave its annual reception and dinner to which members of the diplomatic corps were invited. At this particular dinner the chiefs of diplomatic missions were distributed among small tables at each of which an important Soviet official acted as host. Since I was only a chargé d'affaires I was seated at one of the lower tables with a host who was not of cabinet rank. My host was Marshal Tukhachevsky. He was a gregarious sort of person much less reserved than most Soviet officials with whom I have had the opportunity to chat. During the course of the evening I took occasion to refer to the manner in which the Russian armies had dealt with Napoleon's invasion of Russia, an account of which I had just been rereading, and asked Tukhachevsky why, in his opinion, similar tactics had not been employed by the Russians in 1914. Tukhachevsky replied with what to me was a surprising show of feeling that if the Russians in 1914 had not been so foolish as to invade Germany and thus expose themselves in an unfriendly terrain, the history of the war might have been different. He emphasized that if the Russians, instead of leaving their own country, had stoutly defended it in a series of strong positions always withdrawing in good order when necessary to retreat, they could, with their superior numbers, have gradually weakened the invading enemy. The Russian soldier, he said, was a superb fighter when he felt himself to be defending Russian soil against a foreign enemy.

It was not until the spring of 1939 when Stalin, in negotiating with the British and French, was seeking for a free hand in dealing with the countries to the west of the Soviet Union, that it occurred to me that his desire to establish front military positions beyond the existing borders of the Soviet Union might have met firm resistance from his military advisers—the kind of resistance that might have shown a lack of respect for his judgment and that might well have caused him to lose confidence in them.

During the years that I was working in the State Department, in the Baltic states, and in Moscow on matters pertaining to the Soviet Union I never found reason to doubt that Stalin was a sincere believer in, and promoter of, the world revolution. Even while witnessing the cruel excesses of the Great Purge, I did not doubt his devotion to the cause of the revolution. In my opinion he was convinced that his ultimate objective of achieving a communist world could be realized only if the communist movement would continue to be of a monolithic nature and if by maneuver, terror, or sheer force, it could maintain hegemony over other left-wing revolutionary movements. Any deviation that might lead to a splintering of the communist front should, therefore, be dealt with mercilessly.

As early as 1929 Stalin, it seemed to me, had begun to regard himself as the world revolution personified and to consider that any movement that might tend to undermine his authority was a threat to the revolution and should, therefore, be stopped immediately. It was, and still is, my belief that his distrust of those around him was based on his thought that they, like himself, adhered to the ethical philosophy of the revolution—a philosophy that junked many of the values on which a stable society is based and that considered deceit, trickery, the betrayal of friends, and even murder to be not only permissible but mandatory if they were for the good of the revolution. Since he could never be sure that some of his associates, friends, and even relatives might not come to believe that his liquidation would be in the interest of the revolution, he was distrustful in varying degrees of nearly all of them. As a result of this distrust he did not hesitate to sacrifice millions of his fellow countrymen, including some of his closest and most loyal friends, in the belief that in so doing he was safeguarding his own personal position and, therefore, preserving the monolithic quality of the revolution.

In my opinion Stalin was one of the most strongly history-conscious leaders of this century. If the revolution was to move along the paths charted by him, future generations, he thought, should depend upon accounts prepared under his direction of what had taken place in Soviet Russia during his era. Otherwise, following his death, deviationists, basing themselves on mischievous historical accounts, could spring up like weeds in a rose garden.

Stalin was dissatisfied with descriptions written by sympathetic and non-Russian writers of the Bolshevik revolution and of what had taken place in Soviet Russia during the years immediately following the revolution. Some of these descriptions did not place him at the right hand of Lenin. He therefore banned the distribution of these books in the Soviet Union and caused all of them that could be collected to be destroyed. Similarly, he gave orders for the destruction of the early volumes of the great *Bolshoi Encyclopedia* and caused the encyclopedia to be rewritten in a manner that would play down or ignore his rivals and give him more credit for Soviet successes. He apparently did not like the thought that old Bolsheviks, who had been close to Lenin and who would be in a position to write a version different from his of the revolution and its aftermath, should survive him. He set out, therefore, to eliminate them one by one. He was particularly disturbed at the thought that Trotsky in his exile was in a position to write historical accounts that did not agree with his. He, therefore, went to extremes to destroy Trotsky physically and historically.

Stalin was apparently also fearful that those to whom he had entrusted the carrying out of the Great Purge might later divulge certain facts of general knowledge, which in his opinion might be harmful to his memory and to the revolution. The two commissars for internal affairs, who, under Stalin's direction, had been the general conductors of the purge, first Yagoda and later Ezhov, were therefore executed. Similarly, hundreds of the assistants to these commissars who had played important roles in making arrests or in extracting confessions, were shot. Of the eight generals, for instance, who were alleged to have been members of the court that had found Tukhachevsky and his associates guilty, all except three became themselves victims of the purge. The real story, therefore, of the Great Purge will probably never be known.

CHAPTER 41

THE FOREIGN POLICIES
OF THE KREMLIN, 1934–1938

THE EMBASSY FOUND IT DIFFICULT to assess the twists and turns of Soviet foreign policies during the years 1934-1938. These difficulties were due in part to the fact that the Soviet government was merely one of several instruments through which the Kremlin was carrying on its foreign policies and that the pronouncements on foreign policies made by spokesmen of the government were frequently at variance with those made by spokesmen for the other instruments, including the All-Union Communist Party, the Communist International, and the Red International Labor Unions, to each of which the Kremlin was allotting the performance of certain specific tasks.

What were the underlying policies of the Kremlin during those years? It seemed to me, and I believe also to most members of the embassy at that time, that those basic policies continued to be the development of the Soviet Union—with its magnificent stretch of territory, its resources unexcelled in richness, and its virile population—into a powerful country that would be able not only to defend itself from foreign attacks but also to serve as a base for the promotion of a worldwide communist revolution. Among the more immediate tasks assigned to the government in the international field, in my opinion, were those of protecting by diplomacy and by the use or threat of armed force the integrity of the territory already under the control of the Soviet government and of making plans for taking advantage of changes in the international situation for expanding that territory. Among the current tasks of the Communist International and its associated organizations were those of propagating communism in noncommunist countries and of trying to gain and maintain control of the leftist revolutionary movements in various parts of the world.

It appeared to me that the Kremlin was attempting to coordinate the activities of the instruments under its control in order to make sure that all of them were performing with enthusiasm the tasks assigned to them as well as moving toward the common objectives of an impregnable Soviet Union and of world revolution. Its coordination also included the curbing of excessive zeal on the part of any one of its instruments in the performing of the functions assigned to it—a zeal that might nullify the work of one or more of the other instruments.

It was my belief that since leaders of the Kremlin were intending to contribute eventually to the violent overthrow of all the countries with which the Soviet Union maintained relations, they considered Soviet relations with every country to be of a temporary or transitional character, subject to change at any moment.

The career staff of the embassy in preparing dispatches for our ambassadors tried conscientiously to ascertain and report on the current trends of Soviet foreign policy and on such shifts in tactics as seemed to them to be taking place or likely to take place. Frequently, however, as I have already pointed out, the Soviet leaders and the Kremlin-controlled press engaged in double-talk. Also, the actions of the Soviet government were often not in harmony with statements made by its responsible officials. In such circumstances the foreign observer, even though he might be cognizant of the permanent basic policies of the Kremlin, might well fail to assess accurately the Soviet foreign policies of the moment.

For instance, on January 10, 1936, Molotov delivered a speech at the Second Session of the All-Union Central Executive Committee that, on the one hand, attacked all capitalist states and then on the other, stressed that *rapprochement* between the USSR and the United States had "enormous significance from the point of view of the preservation of general peace." The officer preparing a report on this speech, unless he was conscious of what the basic policies of the Kremlin were, might well wonder what the speaker had in mind. As another example, in Washington Troyanovsky, the Soviet ambassador, was assuring the secretary of state of the friendliness of his government to the United States at a time when the post offices in the Soviet Union were using a cancellation stamp on correspondence going abroad that displayed a fictitious lynching scene in the United States. It was therefore natural that there should be some doubt in our embassy regarding the nature of such friendliness. Similarly, when Ambassador Davies was listening to expressions of friendship for the United States from Soviet leaders while the Kremlin was issuing instructions to American Communists regarding the tactics that they should employ in endeavoring to undermine U.S. institutions and to promote revolution, doubts were likely to arise in the embassy regarding the sincerity of those expressions.

In its day-to-day reporting on Soviet foreign policies the embassy did not make a practice of stressing that the current policies of the Soviet government were actually established by the supervising Kremlin. Nevertheless, from time to time the embassy in its reports did remind its readers in Washington that underlying the current policies of the Soviet government were the basic policies of the Kremlin. Ambassador Bullitt, for instance, in his dispatch of July 19, 1935, wrote:

> Contrary to the comforting belief which the French now cherish it is my conviction that there has been no decrease in the determination of the Soviet Government to produce world revolution. Diplomatic relations with friendly states are not regarded by the Soviet Government as normal friendly relations but "armistice" relations and it is the conviction of the leaders of the Soviet Union that this "armistice" can not possibly be ended by a definite peace but only by a renewal of battle. The Soviet Union genuinely desires peace on all fronts at the present time but this peace is looked upon merely as a happy respite in which future wars may be prepared.
>
> If this basic postulate of the Soviet Government is understood, there is little or nothing in Soviet domestic or foreign policy that is not clear.
>
> I feel sure that the Department must have received many reports that the Soviet Government has abandoned the idea of world revolution and that the convictions I have expressed above may seem ill-founded. I can only say that my own observations, without exception, have convinced me of the accuracy of my statements. I have yet to converse with a single leader of the Soviet Union who has not expressed his belief in the necessity of world revolution.
>
> For example, a few evenings ago I said to Karl Radek that I hoped his communist friends at the meeting of the Third International would not behave in such a way as to break Litvinov's pledge to the President and make the continuance of diplomatic relations between our countries impossible. Radek leaped to his feet with the most violent anger and shouted, "We have lived without the United States in the past and we shall never permit you or anyone else to dictate to us what we shall do in Moscow." Upon his departure, Mikhailsky, one of the oldest of the Bolsheviks, who overheard Radek's remarks, said, "You must understand that world revolution is our religion and there is not one of us who

would not in the final analysis oppose even Stalin himself if we should feel that he was abandoning the cause of world revolution."

I touched on what I called the "ultimate objective of Soviet foreign policy" as well as on the more "immediate objectives" in a long dispatch regarding three years of Soviet-American relations, which I wrote on November 16, 1936, the third anniversary of the establishment of diplomatic relations between the United States and the Soviet Union. Several excerpts from that dispatch are set forth below:

> Persons interested in the conduct of American foreign relations who happen to read this despatch may obtain the impression that the points at issue and the sources of irritation do not appear to be of a really serious nature and may wonder if after all there is not a possibility, in case a sincere effort is made by both sides, to bring about mutually satisfactory relations between the two Governments without imposing upon either too great sacrifices in interests or principles. They may feel that if each of the two Governments would show a somewhat more tolerant attitude towards the other and if each would be willing to relax somewhat its demands upon the other they should be able to work together in harmony.
>
> It is my feeling, based particularly upon almost three years of experience in Moscow, that most of the differences between the two Governments go much deeper than might first appear to the casual observer. In my opinion, the relations between the American and Soviet Governments are not likely to be what might be regarded as cordial unless at least one of them displays a willingness to make several radical shifts in its general foreign policies and to abandon certain principles to which it has thus far steadfastly adhered.
>
> It seems to me that the Soviet Government in general pursues much more a progressively aggressive foreign policy than do most Powers which are endeavoring by peaceful means to satisfy their international ambitions. In my opinion, the aggressive characteristics of Soviet foreign policy are largely due to the fact that that policy, to a greater extent than the foreign policies of most other Powers, has before it a series of definite objectives, and that the work of Soviet officials responsible for the conduct of that policy is judged by the progress which those officials are able to make in the direction of these objectives.
>
> I am convinced, despite opinions to the contrary held by a number of persons who, I feel, are qualified to talk with a considerable degree of authority with respect to matters relating to the Soviet Union, that the establishment of a Union of World Soviet Socialist Republics is still the ultimate objective of Soviet foreign policy. Although this objective might be somewhat dimmer than it was a few years ago, and although the possibility persists that the Soviet leaders might eventually become so

engrossed in the accomplishment of their more immediate objectives that they will lose sight of it altogether, it is my belief, nevertheless, that this objective is a real one at the present time and is a factor not to be ignored in any discussion of Soviet-American relations. A much nearer but not an immediate objective, to my mind, is the establishment of Moscow as the capital of the foremost world Power and as the director in peace or war of the activities of the world revolutionary forces* in all countries.

The present immediate objective, as I see it, is that of warding off, without a sacrifice of basic principles, military attacks from without upon the Soviet Union until that country, as a result of its rapidly growing economic and military might, shall have become a great impregnable fortress.

Soviet officials usually refer to the Soviet policy of isolating the so-called aggressive Powers, such as Japan and Germany, as the "Soviet policy of peace", and frequently express the view that all nations which, like the United States, are anxious for the preservation of world peace should assist in the furtherance of that policy. In conversations with members of the Embassy staff and with American scholars and journalists, certain Soviet officials have taken the attitude that the Government of the United States, by adopting a policy of neutrality and by refusing to become involved in the struggle which they state is going on between the "peace-loving Powers" and the "aggressive Powers" in Europe and Asia, is failing to assume its share of responsibility for the maintenance of world peace.

It appears that they desire first of all that the "peace-loving Powers" of Europe, as well as the "aggressive Powers" be given definitely to understand that the Government of the United States sympathizes with what they are accustomed to refer to as "the efforts of the Soviet Government to preserve world peace". They seem to feel that this could be done by a series of statements and acts showing solidarity between the two Governments in matters relating to peace.

It seems quite clear, however, that such demonstrations of solidarity will not in themselves be sufficient. Some of these officials suggest that the American Government, as a next step, should give the "aggressive Powers" to understand that in case of an act of aggression the American Government would favor the injured party by furnishing financial and technical assistance and military and other supplies. It would, of course, be preferable, they point out, if the United States were to enter at once into definite treaties of mutual military assistance in case of unprovoked attack and thus greatly strengthen the whole collective security structure. They admit, however, that it would probably be necessary for a

---

* When speaking of "revolutionary forces" in this dispatch, I am of course referring to the "leftist" revolutionary forces.

considerable amount of preparatory educational work to be done in the United States before American public opinion would tolerate the assumption of obligations of so serious a nature.

It would appear that the Soviet demands upon the American Government for cooperation in the pursuance of the Soviet "policy of peace" are of a distinctly progressive nature. It seems to me that even the partial satisfying of them would involve radical changes in American foreign policy.

On numerous occasions in the past the Kremlin has shown that it prefers offending countries, the cooperation of which it stands sorely in need of, to severing the links (namely, various international organizations, including the Communist International) which connect the Soviet State with the discontented and revolutionary elements of those countries. In certain international situations the Kremlin has displayed a willingness temporarily to curtail or to make less noticeable the activities of these organizations. At the same time it seems always to have insisted that these organizations shall so conduct themselves as not to lose control over the more militant revolutionary forces abroad or to lose contact with those dissatisfied elements which look to Moscow for inspiration.

I wish to emphasize here that in my opinion the Kremlin is not demanding at the present time that the international organizations subordinate to it shall endeavor to stir up immediate revolution in all countries. The tasks which it imposes on these organizations vary with respect to particular conditions in, and the foreign policies of, the countries in which they are operating. There is one common task, however, which they are all called upon to perform, namely, to endeavor to organize the revolutionary-minded, the discontented, and even certain so-called liberals into compact well-disciplined groups willing unquestioningly to follow the lead of Moscow.

I am inclined to believe that the determination of the Kremlin to maintain control or at least influence over the revolutionary and potentially revolutionary forces of the world is due not only to the fact that it feels that the assistance of those forces is almost essential to the attainment of both immediate and less immediate objectives, but also to its fear that if it loses all guidance over those forces they are likely to develop into implacable foes of the Soviet Union and the Soviet system. That this fear is not without basis is demonstrated by the fact that revolutionary groups, such as the so-called Trotskyists, which no longer look to Moscow for inspiration, are now charging that the Soviet Union has become a nationalistic reactionary state in which the workers are being exploited for the benefit of the bureaucracy and a new bourgeoisie.

It is possible that in return for certain compensatory advantages the Kremlin might agree to keep under cover the activities in the United States of the international organization subordinate to it, but such an arrangement, in my opinion, is not likely to be of more than a temporary nature. There is even a possibility that if the international situation of the Soviet Union should become extremely precarious, the Kremlin might endeavor by establishing the ostensible headquarters of these international organizations in other countries to make less noticeable the fact that they are subordinate to Moscow. Nevertheless, I am convinced that unless the whole system of the Soviet State and the ideology of its leaders should undergo a complete change—and this does not seem likely in the foreseeable future—the Kremlin will continue to express certain of its foreign policies through the Communist International or similar organizations. It seems likely to me, therefore, that the question of interference in American internal affairs will continue to disturb American-Soviet relations as long as the Government of the United States is unwilling to close its eyes to the fact that the Kremlin is exercising control over certain revolutionary groups in the United States.

I have already pointed out that during my first tour in the Division of Eastern European Affairs (1925–1927) I had come to the opinion, after a two-year study of the Soviet Union, that it "was pursuing a policy of endeavoring to keep the countries of Europe at loggerheads." During my tour in the Soviet Union (1934–1938) I came to believe more strongly that one of the principal objectives of Soviet diplomacy, so far as Europe was concerned, was to prevent the countries of Western and Central Europe from working together in harmony.

In one of his most interesting dispatches, Ambassador Bullitt, on July 19, 1935, presented his views on the way in which the Kremlin was looking at the international situation in the summer of 1935.

The Soviet Union fears nothing so much as a general reconciliation of European hatreds, especially a reconciliation between Germany and France. The key to the desire of the Soviet Government to be present at all possible conferences and to have a finger in every pie is its desire to prevent any real agreement among the states of Europe. The reasons for this policy are two fold: (a) The Soviet Union fears that reconciliation in Europe may be based upon permission to Germany to obtain the economic outlets which she needs by acquisition of the Ukraine; (b) War in Europe is regarded as inevitable and ultimately desirable from the Communist point of view. The Soviet Government fears war in Europe at the present time because the Soviet Union is unprepared and it is feared that war this year or next in Europe would grow into world war with simultaneous attacks on the Soviet Union by Germany, Poland and Japan. But it is the conviction of the leaders of the Soviet Union that if war in Europe can be postponed until the Red Army is prepared and the railroads of the Soviet Union rebuilt, the Soviet Union will be able to intervene successfully in such a war, and will be able to protect and consolidate any communist government which may be set up as a result of war and ensuing revolution in any European state. To keep Europe divided and to postpone the war which will certainly come if Europe remains divided, is the substance of Russian policy in Europe.

The most conspicuous example of action proceeding from this policy was the conclusion of the Treaty of Mutual Assistance with France. The fundamental cause of the desire of the Soviet Government to conclude this Treaty was the fear that France might welcome reconciliation with Germany. To keep the flames of Franco-German hatred burning brightly is regarded as a vital interest of the Soviet Union.

The single nightmare of the Soviet Government is, of course, the fear that if Japan attacks in the Far East, Germany and Poland will attack in the west. The policies of the Soviet Union vis-à-vis Japan are also clear. They are: (1) to build up as large and effective a fighting force as possible in the Far East; (2) to avoid war so long as possible by making the minimum concessions necessary to make sure that Japan will not attack. It is the conviction of the Soviet Government that within ten years the Soviet Union will be so much more powerful than Japan that Japan for all future time will be as unable to attack the Soviet Union as Mexico is to attack the United States. But there is considerable doubt in the minds of the leaders of the Soviet Union that the Far Eastern Provinces of Siberia can be defended successfully against Japanese attack and today any necessary concessions will be made to Japan which do not involve the cession of Soviet territory...

It is, of course, the heartiest hope of the Soviet Government that the United States will become involved in war with Japan. If such a war should occur it would be the policy of the Soviet Union to remain outside the conflict and to gain whatever wealth might be acquired by supplying the United States with war materials via the west and supplying Japan with war materials in the east. To think of the Soviet Union as a possible ally of the United States in case of war with Japan is to allow the wish to be father to the thought. The Soviet Union would certainly attempt to avoid becoming an ally until Japan had been thoroughly defeated and would then merely use the opportunity to acquire Manchuria and Sovietize China.

The final conviction of the leaders of the Soviet Union with regard to the war they desire so ardently between the United States and Japan is that Japan would be defeated, that a Communist Government would then be set up in Japan, and Japan and the Soviet Union would then move happily hand in hand to establish communism in China...

To summarize: The aim of the Soviet Government is and will remain, to produce world revolution. The leaders of the Soviet Union believe that the first step toward this revolution must be to strengthen the defensive and offensive power of the Soviet Union. They believe that within ten years the defense position of the Soviet Union will be absolutely impregnable and that within 15 years the offensive power of the Soviet Union will be sufficient to enable it to consolidate by its assistance any communist government which may be set up in Europe. To maintain peace for the present, to keep the nations of Europe divided, to foster enmity between Japan and the United States, and to gain the blind devotion and obedience of the communists of all countries so that they will act against their own governments at the behest of the Communist Pope in the Kremlin, is the sum of Stalin's policy.

The Kremlin's endeavors by diplomacy to discourage Germany and Japan from attacking the Soviet Union were not limited to efforts to obtain promises from France to come to its assistance in case of a German attack or to maneuvering with the hope of increasing such animosity as already existed between the United States and Japan. Soviet diplomacy tried to set up in Europe during the mid-1930s a system of so-called collective security pacts directed against possible German aggression. It endeavored without success to persuade Great Britain and other countries to conclude a pact with it similar to its treaty with France. It brought particularly heavy pressure upon the smaller countries bordering the Soviet Union to enter into treaties which in effect would make the Soviet Union their protector. These countries had no illusions regarding what their fate would be if they should entrust their future to the Soviet Union and unanimously took the position that they preferred to remain neutral; they did not desire to become involved in struggles between the Soviet Union and Germany.

In the Far East the Kremlin, noting the desire of the United States not to become involved in an armed conflict with Japan, encouraged the Chinese to resist the demands that Japan was making upon them by covertly and indirectly giving the Chinese government the impression that if such resistance would lead to a Chinese-Japanese war, China could expect massive aid from the Soviet Union.

Neither Ambassador Bullitt nor the Foreign Service officers associated with him in the embassy believed that, regardless of what commitments it might make, the Soviet Union had any intention of going to war with Germany in case the latter should attack any other power unless it should be convinced at the time that such intervention would be in the interest of the Soviet Union or would contribute to the strengthening of the cause of international communism. It was our thought, for instance, that if Germany, as the result of a war with other powers, should become so weakened that, in the opinion of the rulers in the Kremlin, the Soviet Union with a minimum of risk to itself could finish it off and thus dispose of one of the powers that was blocking the western expansion of communism, they might well intervene and make use of their intervention to place additional territory under their control.

In our opinion, the Kremlin was convinced that in the aggressive mood that Hitler Germany was displaying the latter must eventually become involved in a war with one or more of its powerful neighbors. Kremlin diplomacy was therefore intent, first, on trying to effect a postponement of the outbreak of war for several years so that the Soviet Union would have time to develop further its military might and, second, on trying to assure that when war would come, it would be between Germany and Germany's western neighbors.

The shifts that were taking place in the mid-1930s in the diplomatic tactics of the Soviet government were accompanied by certain changes in the tactics of the other organizations that were operating under the direction of the Kremlin in the countries of the West. Just as in the sphere of diplomacy the Soviet Union was beginning to attempt to form a common front with Western noncommunist countries against Germany, so the Communist International and affiliated organizations began to form united fronts "against fascism," which would include the communist parties and noncommunist groups in the Western countries in which these parties were operating. The Kremlin desired that the communist parties in these countries would no longer openly fight other leftist groups for the control of the dissatisfied workers and youth and would no longer openly concentrate on attempts to undermine the noncommunist governments. The new line of the communist parties was to be that fascism was the most dangerous enemy, and that all leftists, liberals, and others dissatisfied with the status quo in their respective countries should join forces for the purpose of exterminating fascism.

Apparently one of the main reasons that the Kremlin called the Seventh All-World Congress of the Communist International that met in Moscow in the latter part of July 1935 was to give the leaders of the Comintern an opportunity to explain the new line to the delegates from the communist parties that were looking to Moscow for direction.

At this congress the social democrats and the other noncommunist groupings with whom the communists in various countries had been competing for the allegiance of the working people were not condemned as the principal villains as they had been at preceding congresses. The new villain was fascism, the extermination of which all the communist parties were called upon to concentrate. Although resolutions of the congress did not give a meaningful definition of fascism it was clear from the discussions that persons or groups who were anticommunist or who were opposing current policies of the Soviet Union were fascist or were at least displaying fascist tendencies. For instance, in one of his speeches Browder, the principal American delegate, characterized as "fascist" a group in the United States that had been organized for the purpose of fighting both fascism and communism.

It was evident at this congress that the Kremlin was trying to give as little cause for resentment as its basic policies would permit to countries with which it was trying to form a common front. It did not go so far in this respect, however, as to give the communist parties in those countries the discouraging impression that they were entirely to cease their revolutionary activities. These parties were instructed that in forming united fronts they were to retain their own organizational identity, they were to make use of their associations in such fronts to strengthen communism, they were to continue to base their decisions and actions on "concrete Marxist analysis," and they were to maintain close ties with the Communist International.

The result of the Kremlin's change in tactics was disappointing to Stalin and his colleagues. As I pointed out during my discussion of the Great Purge, the members of the embassy obtained the impression as early as January 1936 that the Kremlin was becoming disillusioned regarding the willingness of France to take a strong position against German aggression aimed at Central or Eastern Europe. It was also beginning to doubt the efficacy of collective security as a protective shield. In 1936, 1937, and 1938 the embassy noted and reported to the State Department what appeared to be a growing feeling on the part of the Soviet leaders that they were surrounded either by states that were aggressively hostile or by states that, although not necessarily hostile, had no intention of becoming involved in a war for the sake of the Soviet Union.

The weak stand taken by the League of Nations in the matter of Italian aggression against Ethiopia in 1935 and 1936, the vacillating policies of Great Britain and France with regard to the Spanish revolution during 1936 and 1937, the failure of France to take remedial action when German armed forces entered the Rhineland in March 1936, and the annexation of Austria by Hitler Germany in March 1938, were contributing to the Soviet belief that France and Great Britain had no intention of fighting Germany unless Hitler moved westward. The Kremlin, therefore, was reluctantly coming to the conclusion that it must depend primarily for its protection upon its own armed might although it would not discontinue its diplomatic maneuvering or abandon its efforts to make use of the united-front groupings that the Communist International set up in other countries in order to gain support for its foreign policies.

So far as we in the embassy were able to ascertain, the leaders in the Kremlin, in spite of the dangerous world situation developing in the middle and later 1930s, did not at any time consider abandoning their basic world-revolutionary aims in order to gain the confidence of, and closer and friendlier cooperation from, other great powers that were opposed to the aggressiveness of Hitler Germany and militaristic Japan. Neither did we find any evidence of willingness on their part to adhere to those principles of international intercourse that they had consistently flouted—principles that experience had shown were essential to the maintenance of truly friendly relations among nations. Instead, we noted among them a growing bitterness at the hesitation of the countries of the West to cooperate fully with them and an increasing distrust that at times seemed to approach hatred of all foreign countries and of all foreigners.

Although the Soviet Union continued during the remainder of my assignment to the embassy in Moscow—an assignment that terminated in early July 1938—to take an increasingly active interest in preparedness for war and to lay decreasing stress on cooperation with other nations, it did not entirely neglect diplomacy as an instrument of foreign policy. Soviet statesmen and the Soviet press during 1938 continued to make statements to the effect that the Soviet Union had done what it could to rally the "peace-loving" countries collectively to oppose aggression and that the failure of these countries to respond was moving the world inevitably toward war. It seemed to me that the purpose of some of these statements was to stir up opposition among the peoples in the countries of the West against their "reactionary governments" rather than to persuade these governments to cooperate with the Soviet government.

When in 1938 the Soviet Union was making increased efforts internally to strengthen its military might, it looked to its diplomatic apparatus to assist in obtaining from abroad supplies and equipment of which its armed forces were in sore need, including warships, airplanes, armor plates, and machinery especially designed to make instruments of war. Since the United States was in a better position than the countries of Western Europe to supply these needs, Soviet diplomacy during that year began to ascribe greater importance to its relations with the United States.

Ambassador Troyanovsky and special emissaries sent to the United States by the Kremlin did their best to persuade President Roosevelt and the top officials of the Departments of State, War, and Navy to take a sympathetic interest in Soviet military needs. Not only did Litvinov go out of his way to interest Ambassador Davies in the matter, but even Stalin and Molotov, during their farewell talk with Davies, after indulging in a number of complimentary remarks regarding his broad outlook, suggested that he use his influence in the United States to assist the Soviet Union in its efforts to purchase urgently needed military equipment. The special attention given personally to the president, to the responsible heads of the Departments of State, War, and Navy, and to Ambassador Davies was not accompanied by any noticeable relaxation of Soviet practices so far as the treatment of the U.S. embassy in Moscow and of most U.S. citizens in the Soviet Union was concerned. Nor was it accompanied by any fundamental changes in the Soviet attitude toward problems that were disturbing American-Soviet relations.

Although Soviet efforts through diplomacy to prevail upon the "peace-loving countries" to come to grips with the aggressors were disappointing, the Kremlin continued during 1938 to endeavor through the Communist International and kindred organizations to strengthen united fronts against fascism in those countries. These groups, once formed, did not limit their activities to denouncing or opposing fascism. Under communist prompting they turned their attention to bringing pressure upon their respective governments to follow the kind of internal and foreign policies that would tend to strengthen the Soviet Union and the cause of communism; they specialized in attacking specifically those groups or individuals who were actively opposed to communism.

Maintaining that anticommunism was merely a manifestation of sympathy for fascism, the united fronts sought and sometimes received the support of noncommunist liberals and other persons who were emotionally or intellectually opposed to Hitler and Hitlerian philosophies and actions. I learned when I took over my new duties in the Department of State in the autumn of 1938 that, in view of the revulsion throughout the country—particularly among the American liberals and certain types of intellectuals—against the aggressive acts of fascism, these campaigns had achieved considerable success in the United States.

CHAPTER 42

FAREWELL TO THE SOVIET UNION
AND RETURN TO THE UNITED STATES

DURING THE SIX DAYS that elapsed between my return to Moscow from the Siberian trip and my departure for the United States on July 2, 1938, I spent much time paying farewell calls and writing thank-you letters. My effects had been packed and sealed in a large van under the watchful eyes of a Soviet customs officer and my wife had already said her farewells and departed for Riga. Our plans were that she would join me later in Paris. The State Department had authorized me while en route to the United States to stop for short consultations with our legations in Helsinki, Tallinn, Riga, and Kaunas, with our consulate in Danzig and our embassy in Warsaw, and with our embassies in Berlin, Brussels (where I was briefly to visit Ambassador Davies), London, and Paris.

I said good-bye to Litvinov on the morning of my departure. He seemed to be in bad humor, which he vented by making several slighting remarks regarding Ambassador Davies—remarks that I particularly resented since the ambassador had always gone out of his way in his efforts to maintain cordial relations with Litvinov. He also complained about some statements that had recently appeared in the U.S. press critical of Soviet policy. Then he directed his attention to me and to the State Department. This portion of our conversation I summarized in a memorandum on July 2, 1938, which read as follows:

I called upon Mr. Litvinov today to tell him good-bye. During the course of the conversation, he told me that he had heard that I had been assigned to the Department of State and that while in Washington I would probably assist in the conduct of Soviet-American relations.

Mr. Litvinov said that it was his understanding that the Department of State played a very important role in the formulation and carrying out of American foreign policies; that most of the members of the State Department were reactionary, had fascist friends, were sympathetic to the fascist cause, and were antipathetic to the Soviet Union; that although the President of the United States was a great liberal and was anxious to further the cause of democracy and liberalism throughout the world, reactionaries in the State Department tried so to distort the policies laid down by the President as to give them an anti-Soviet and, sometimes, a pro-fascist bias. He added that he had received this information not from the Soviet Embassy in Washington but from American citizens. Some of his informants, he said, because of their position in the United States, were particularly well informed with respect to what was going on in Washington and were therefore worthy of credence.

I replied that I was certain that Mr. Litvinov's information with respect to the attitude of the personnel of the State Department both towards the policies of the President and towards international affairs in general was incorrect. I said that I had served on two different assignments in the State Department; that I personally knew many of the members of the Department; that I was convinced that the State Department was composed of conscientious, painstaking and able public servants who were endeavoring loyally to carry out such policies as might be outlined to them by the Administration. I added that in the United States there were various organized political and even racial groups which were much more interested in furthering one or more international movements than they were in advancing the interests of the United States; that these groups were extremely vociferous; and that one of the means of members of these groups of bringing pressure upon the American Government was to attack personally officials of the State Department, who, in the performance of their duties, were sometimes compelled to take steps which displeased such groups.

I said that in view of the fact that there was complete freedom of speech and of the press in the United States, it was extremely easy for disgruntled groups in that country to carry on campaigns against American administrative officials and that these campaigns frequently resulted in foreigners not acquainted with American life obtaining incorrect impressions regarding American officials and institutions.

Litvinov was the only Soviet official on whom I called who was disagreeable. I was not surprised since he had never forgiven me for having pressed the Commissariat of Foreign Affairs so hard on the cases of U.S. citizens who had been detained without trial in Soviet prisons and for the stand I had taken in respect to other differences that had arisen between our two governments. The other members of the Foreign Office with whom I had dealt were exceptionally cordial.

It was a wrench for me to leave Moscow, which had been my home for four years and four months. I was leaving many friends in our embassy, among other members of the diplomatic corps, among foreign journalists, and among other Americans and foreigners in Moscow. Although one did not dare for their sake to consider Soviet citizens as friends, I had also become quite fond of some of the Soviet officials with whom I had been dealing.

While serving in the embassy, I had had many worries and had been faced with many problems and frustrations. Nevertheless I had not had a dull moment. Almost daily there had been some kind of a challenge to be faced. In the Foreign Service challenges are usually welcome so long as one has the backing of his government, and I had had the feeling that despite periods of discouragement both the Department of State and the White House were convinced that I had been trying to carry out the policies of the administration even though within the department and other agencies of the government there had been sharp differences with regard to what our attitude toward the Soviet Union should be.

While on duty in Moscow I had been slowly moving up the career ladder of the Foreign Service. In October 1935 I had been promoted to FSO class 5, and in January 1938 to FSO class 4. As the result of the manner in which the Rogers Act had been administered, of the hump of young officers on the rounds immediately above me, and of the cessation of promotions during several depression years, it had taken me nearly sixteen years to reach a rung in the Foreign Service ladder that was still fourth down from the top.

During my visits to Finland, Estonia, Latvia, and Lithuania en route to Washington I had long discussions regarding the problems, both substantive and administrative, that they were facing and also regarding the situation in Eastern Europe from their respective points of view.

Most of the leaders of these countries were in a state of anxiety regarding what the ultimate effect on them might be of the clashing ambitions of Nazi-controlled Germany and the communist-controlled Soviet Union. They feared that if a war should break out much of the fighting would be on their territories and the freedom that their countries had been enjoying for nearly twenty years would be extinguished by the victor. These leaders were convinced that if their countries should place themselves in the Soviet camp by forming an alliance with the Soviet Union they would be either gradually absorbed by the Soviet Union under the pretext that it was taking steps to defend them or they would be subjected to attack by Germany for having taken sides with the enemy. Similarly, they believed that if they should enter into an alliance with Nazi Germany their countries would be devoured by the Nazis who would not hesitate to take advantage of the unequal partnership, or would be attacked as untrustworthy neighbors by the Soviet Union.

The Finns were more worried about the Soviet Union, with which Finland had common borders, than they were about Germany. Although the Estonians and Latvians also had no common borders with Germany, they feared that the Nazis would like to add them to the German Reich. The main concern of these three countries in July 1938, however, was the attitude of the Soviet Union, which by wheedling and threats was endeavoring to prevail upon them to enter into international commitments that would result in their entry into the Soviet camp. The chief worry of the Lithuanians, on the other hand, was the attitude of Nazi Germany, which had been making disagreeable noises about the Lithuanian port of Klaipėda (Memel). The Lithuanians were still resentful at what they regarded as the overbearing attitude displayed by Poland the preceding March, when the Poles through a threatening ultimatum had forced Lithuania, despite its twenty-year-old claim to Vilna, to open its borders to Poland and to enter into diplomatic relations.

These four countries, caught as they were between the jaws of the German-Soviet nutcracker and subjected to constant stresses and strains, had felt impelled, in order to maintain the internal unity that they considered essential to their continued independence, to drop many of the trappings of democracy. Their governments were not completely dictatorial; nevertheless, in varying degrees they approached dictatorships. I had become convinced from my previous experiences in the Baltic states and from what I learned while making this trip that a truly democratic form of government could not have effectively functioned in the atmosphere that at that time permeated Eastern Europe.

Moscow was infiltrating these countries with agents provided with ample funds to subvert newspapers, to employ journalists, and to appeal to minorities, particularly those who were desperately in fear of what might happen to them under the Nazis. Moreover, the Soviet radio vied with the German for control of the air of Eastern Europe. According to the communist dogma of those days any government opposed to communism must be, ipso facto, fascist or nazi. The communist press throughout the world was, therefore, accusing these countries of possessing fascist governments. Many liberals in the United States, revolted by what was going on in Germany and failing to see what was taking place elsewhere, naively swallowed this propaganda.

Moscow was not, of course, alone in applying internal pressures. Small but virulent nazi parties, nurtured by Berlin and cultivated by German minorities in these countries, were also threatening their internal unity. The main German pressure, however, was not of an internal nature; it consisted of threats of economic boycotts and of the use of armed force.

After leaving Kaunas I spent several days with Ambassador Anthony Biddle in Warsaw and a couple of days with Clark Kuykendall, our consul in Danzig. I obtained the impression that although the maneuvers of the Soviet Union and the irresponsible belligerence of Nazi Germany were giving rise to considerable tension, the Poles were apparently not so worried about the future of Poland as the Baltic peoples were about their countries. The Poles were, nevertheless, concerned about what Hitler might do with regard to the Polish Corridor. They seemed to realize that not only the German Nazis but the German people as a whole had never accepted as permanent a situation in which Germany was cut in two by a thin strip of Polish-owned territory extending from Poland proper to the Baltic Sea and in which the ancient German city of Danzig was separated from the German Reich.

The Polish government was faced with the fact that the relations between Poland and no less than four of its neighbors were not healthy: the existence of the Polish Corridor had embittered Polish relations with Germany; the Polish government had no doubt that the Kremlin was merely waiting for an opportunity to extend Soviet territory at the expense of Poland; the Polish-Lithuanian nineteen-year-old quarrel over Vilna had left unhealed wounds; and the Poles had deep feelings of resentment against Czechoslovakia, partly because at the time the Czechoslovak state had been put together following the First World War, Czech diplomacy had been successful in including in Czechoslovak territory the most valuable portions of the heavily Polish-populated district of Teschen, and partly because they were convinced that the Czechs were slyly trying to work out a plan that would provide for Soviet troops to cross Polish territory in order to render assistance to Czechoslovakia in case the latter should be attacked by Germany. One of the Polish leaders with whom I talked charged that Beneš seemed to be quite willing to sacrifice the independence of Poland for the benefit of Czechoslovakia.

One responsible Polish official told me in an almost apologetic tone that Poland had found it necessary to issue the ultimatum to Lithuania regarding Vilna and the opening of the Polish-Lithuanian borders. He pointed out that the League of Nations in awarding Memel to Lithuania had stipulated that Poland could also use that city as a port. In spite of this stipulation Lithuania had kept its borders closed to Polish traffic for more than eighteen years. In the meantime Polish territory in the north and west had been suffering from the lack of a convenient port. He also said that in view of the problems that Poland was facing from the Soviet Union to its east and from Germany to its west, it could no longer afford to continue facing an economic and political boycott on the part of Lithuania—a boycott that had been interfering seriously with normal communications between Poland and the Baltic states to the north of Lithuania.

I had the feeling that the Polish leaders, to a greater extent than the people of the Baltic, were relying on the League of Nations and on the Western powers to protect them from Soviet or German aggression. Nevertheless they were apparently trying, without permitting Poland to fall into the camp of either of its two powerful neighbors, to maintain as friendly relations with the Soviet Union and Germany as the circumstances would permit.

I spent several hours with Kuykendall, our consul in Danzig, discussing the problems of the Polish Corridor and Danzig. We agreed that these problems had potentials no less dangerous to the peace of Europe than problems connected with Czechoslovakia and Austria. The Nazis had already been entrenched for a number of years in Danzig and were creating many difficulties for the high commissioner and the other administrators of the area. During my visit in Danzig Kuykendall took me out to Gdynia, the port in the corridor that the Poles had developed during recent years in order to meet the Polish officials there. It was interesting to note that, although the amount of exports and imports through Danzig had tripled since Danzig had become a free city as a result of the Polish trade, the new port of Gdynia in 1938 was handling even more traffic than Danzig.

While in Berlin I found the members of our embassy full of resentment at the disdainful way in which they were being treated by Hitler and his Nazi officials. The career officers of the German Foreign Office had apparently been maintaining an attitude of personal friendliness toward the ambassador and the members of his staff and were doing what they could to be helpful. The Foreign Office, however, had been infiltrated with rabid Nazis who had taken over many of the policymaking positions and who seemed to take delight in being uncooperative. Although I sensed that Ambassador Hugh Wilson was becoming discouraged, he was nevertheless making special efforts to promote the embassy's morale. He told be that the Nazi leaders were so enraptured with their own ideas and so intoxicated with such successes as they had achieved that they were apparently not interested in what the outside world thought of them and not inclined to listen to suggestions from foreign diplomats.

The ambassador appeared to be particularly worried over the growing militancy of the German people. He said that Hitler seemed to be achieving considerable success in convincing them that the time was near at hand for them to redress, by force if necessary, the wrongs that Germany had been suffering during the last twenty years and to see that Germany in the future occupy its rightful place as the dominant power on the continent of Europe. The numerous parades that I witnessed during the few days that I spent in Berlin of smart-looking, high-stepping young soldiers in field uniforms and of marching columns of men, women, and children wearing Nazi insignia, carrying banners with Nazi slogans, and singing Nazi or patriotic songs, convinced me the ambassador had cause for concern.

Several of the U.S. army officers attached to our embassy told me that in their opinion the land and air armed forces of Germany were already superior to those of any other European country and that their strength was increasing daily.

It so happened that I was in Brussels on the day that Ambassador Davies presented his credentials to the Belgian king. Frances Willis, the first secretary of the embassy, had made arrangements for the ambassador to come from the presentation ceremony direct to a luncheon, which she was giving in honor of him and Mrs. Davies. To the luncheon she had invited the officers of the embassy and their wives. She had included me since I was a guest of the Davies. The ambassador arrived late. He explained that his tardiness was due to the fact that the king had detained him after the ceremony for a long chat. Davies was bubbling over with enthusiasm for the king and elated that he had been shown this special attention. His enthusiasm and the words and phrases that he used in describing the king brought me back to the scene in his office in Moscow in early June when he had shown so much enthusiasm for Stalin and had used similar words in expressing his admiration for the leader of the Soviet Union. At the ambassador's request I described my trip to Siberia and told him in detail the developments that had taken place in Moscow since his departure. I noted that although he seemed to like his new post, he was nevertheless continuing to take an active interest in the Soviet Union and in Soviet-American relations.

The British officials with whom I talked in London were frank in expressing the opinion that a war with Germany while Great Britain was in its current state of unpreparedness might well result in ruin for the United Kingdom and its empire. France, crouched behind its Maginot Line with no air fleet worthy of the name, was in no position to invade Germany; the Soviet Union could not be depended upon as an ally; Italy was likely to side with Germany; and the United States had made it clear that it did not intend to become involved in another European war.

Nevertheless, if France—in living up to its international commitments—should declare war on Germany, Great Britain could not afford to stand idly by while its closest ally was being destroyed. These officials were hoping, therefore, that an understanding could be reached with Germany that would insure peace on the European continent or at least postpone the outbreak of war until Great Britain was in a better position to fight.

From London I went to Paris where I spent several days consulting with members of our embassy and with French officials to whom they introduced me. My former chief in Moscow, Ambassador Bullitt, invited my wife, who had joined me in Paris, and me to have Sunday luncheon with him and his daughter Anne at the beautiful chateau where they were living in the environs of Paris. At the luncheon was another former member of our Moscow embassy, Elbridge Durbrow, as well as his bride of three days, the former Emily Moore, who had spent the spring in Moscow as the guest of one of the daughters of Ambassador Davies. It was natural, therefore, that much of the talk at the table should relate to our various experiences in the Soviet Union.

Following the luncheon the ambassador, Durbrow, and I had a long discussion regarding the European situation. The ambassador asked us many questions about the Soviet Union. I noted, however, that he had a deeper interest in the impressions that I had obtained during my recent visit to Berlin. I told him that Ambassador Wilson was not the only person who had expressed concern to me regarding the growing militancy of the German people and the manner in which the German armed forces had been strengthened. I said I had found similar concern among the British and French officials with whom I had since talked. The ambassador said many of the French political leaders with whom he was in close contact were also troubled about the present strength of the German armed forces. Several of them had expressed to him the opinion that although France might hold its own in a defensive war with Germany they doubted that France and Great Britain together, in view of their state of military unpreparedness, could successfully invade Germany.

In spite of his worries regarding the international situation, Ambassador Bullitt seemed to be in excellent spirits. He loved France and the French people. He apparently felt that he was succeeding in promoting good relations between France and the United States. His relations at the time with President Roosevelt and with top officials of the State Department, particularly with Judge Moore, were close. He continued to have frequent telephone conversations with the president even though the president had never fully forgiven him for having urged him not to try to pack the Supreme Court. I found Bullitt deeply concerned at developments in Germany. As I have already pointed out, it was his fear that if Hitler should continue to meet with success in his aggressive undertakings, Europe might again be plunged into a war that could well become almost universal.

It was in the first week of August 1938 that my wife and I arrived in the United States after an absence of more than four and a half years. It seemed to me that it might be a good idea, before allowing myself to be tied to a desk in the Department of State, to renew my acquaintance with my own country and to give my wife, who had never been further west than a few miles from Washington, D.C., an opportunity to see more of the United States. The department agreed with my idea and granted me a leave of sixty days. After reporting to the department for a week of briefing we, therefore, launched on an extensive tour by automobile. Among the places that we visited during our travels were Jefferson and Youngstown in Ohio where I had spent a portion of my boyhood; Northwestern University at Evanston, Illinois, including the fraternity house in which I had lived; Denver, Colorado Springs, and Trinidad in Colorado; Salt Lake City, San Francisco, Los Angeles, and Albuquerque, and the little valley in the Ozarks near Rogers, Arkansas, where I was born. While in Colorado Springs we visited my father, who had retired from the ministry, my stepmother, and other relatives. My younger brother and his wife took us on a fishing expedition high in the Rockies where my wife excitedly caught her first trout. In Albuquerque we visited my sister Zella, who was a principal of one of the schools in that city.

We had intended to visit Little Rock where I had attended grade school for six years but our trip was cut short by messages from the State Department. In the latter part of September it appeared for a few days almost certain that Hitler would seize Czechoslovakia and that France and Great Britain would, therefore, declare war on Germany. In view of the possibility of the outbreak of war, we altered our plans and returned from the Ozarks to Washington directly. En route we heard by radio of the conference that was taking place in Munich, and on October 1, when we were already in Maryland, we learned of the Munich Agreement signed on September 30 (although it was dated September 29), which at the expense of Czechoslovakia had averted war for the time being. Nevertheless, when on October 10 I assumed my duties as assistant chief of the Division of European Affairs charged with handling matters relating to Eastern Europe, the international situation, particularly the situation in the area on which I was to be working, was inauspicious.

PART X

Assistant Chief, Division of European Affairs, Department of State, Washington, D.C., October 1938–July 1942

CHAPTER 43

THE DEPARTMENT OF STATE, 1938–1942

IT WAS IN OCTOBER 1938 that I took over my desk as assistant chief, Division of European Affairs, in charge of the area that was handling matters pertaining to Eastern Europe. The office reserved for me was on the east corridor of the third floor of the old State, War and Navy Building overlooking the White House and its gardens—not more than 50 feet from the room that I had occupied when I was first assigned to the State Department in January 1925. During my absence of more than four and a half years there had been relatively few changes among the Civil Service personnel of the department. There had been a marked increase, however, in the number of political appointees at various levels and the normal shifting of Foreign Service officers between Washington and the foreign field had introduced new faces in the department. Changes had also taken place among the presidential appointees, that is, among officers of the department at the assistant secretary rank and above. The presidential appointees in October 1938 listed in ranking order were:

Cordell Hull, secretary
Sumner Welles, under secretary
R. Walton Moore, counselor
Francis B. Sayre, assistant secretary
George S. Messersmith, assistant secretary

Adolph Berle, assistant secretary
Green H. Hackworth, legal adviser

Welles and Moore, who in 1937 were assistant secretaries, had been rival candidates to succeed William Phillips as under secretary. The President and Mrs. Roosevelt had favored Welles, a former member of the Diplomatic Service with a Groton and Harvard background, and a friend since boyhood of the Roosevelt family. The secretary had supported the aged Moore, who had been one of his trusted colleagues in Congress. As a compromise Welles was appointed and Moore was elevated to the rank of counselor, an old State Department title resuscitated to meet the situation. With his new title Moore ranked with, but after, the under secretary.

Sayre was still handling economic, financial, tariff, and general trade questions. Messersmith, as I have pointed out previously, was a Foreign Service officer who in 1937 had succeeded Wilbur Carr as the principal administrative official of the department. Berle, a brilliant New York lawyer, was charged with working on such special problems as the secretary might assign to him.

During the next four years a number of changes occurred in this hierarchy. In 1939 Sayre left the State Department to become U.S. high commissioner to the Philippines. He was replaced by Henry F. Grady, an economist with a wide experience in academic and governmental activities.

In 1940 Messersmith was appointed ambassador to Cuba and was replaced by Breckenridge Long, a lawyer who had served as ambassador to Italy during the early Roosevelt years. In 1941 Moore, who had been helping the secretary in connection with the latter's relations with Congress, resigned because of ill health and for several years the position of counselor again fell in abeyance. Following Moore's resignation Long was transferred from the assistant secretaryship for administration to an assistant secretaryship established for maintaining liaison with the members of Congress. G. Howland Shaw, a Foreign Service officer who had been serving as chief of Foreign Service Personnel, succeeded Long as assistant secretary for administration.

In the early part of 1941 Henry Grady resigned and was replaced by Dean Acheson, among whose duties were those of handling matters of an economic and commercial character. In the meantime Berle, on the basis of seniority in tenure, had become the top-ranking assistant secretary of the State Department. Among the matters for which Berle had been given responsibility were those of a financial character. Since it was frequently impossible to disentangle financial questions from matters of an economic nature it proved at times difficult to decide which of the two assistant secretaries—Berle or Acheson—should handle certain specific problems.

During 1937 the secretary had created two new positions, the holders of which ranked immediately after the presidential appointees. James C. Dunn and Stanley K. Hornbeck were appointed to these positions and given the new title of "adviser on political relations." Dunn, a veteran Foreign Service officer who for several years had been chief of the Division of European Affairs, continued to take a deep interest in matters relating to Europe and worked closely and harmoniously with the chief of that division. Hornbeck was one of the outstanding authorities in the United States on matters pertaining to the Far East. For a number of years he had been chief of the Far Eastern Division. In his new position he continued to interest himself in Far Eastern affairs and to maintain close contacts with the members of that division. The secretary had created these positions because he desired to have these two highly experienced men, in whom he had great confidence, freed from the time-consuming work of administering an office in the State Department. He wanted them to be at his beck and call and to give him advice not only with regard to Europe and the Far East but with regard to any other matter that might require a decision on his part.

A number of new offices and divisions had also been established since my departure in February 1934. I shall not take up my reader's time by attempting to list all of them. I might, however, mention that Herbert Feis, who had been economic adviser to the State Department in 1934, had been placed in 1937 at the head of an important office and given the title of "adviser on international economic affairs," which placed him on a level with the two political advisers and above chiefs of division. Another new office of importance that had been set up in 1935 was that of Arms and Munitions Control. This office, which was headed by a veteran of the department, Joseph C. Green, was charged with controlling traffic in arms, ammunition, and implements of war and with assisting in the preparation of treaties and international agreements dealing with this subject. Another office, which was only three months of age in October 1938, was the Division of Cultural Relations headed by Ben M. Cherrington, a professor from the University of Denver who had long been interested in international cultural relations. Some of the old-timers of the State Department and Foreign Service, who tended to look with suspicion on innovations, doubted the appropriateness of a division devoted to culture in the Department of State. Cherrington and his two assistants who comprised the division continued, however, quietly to plant the seeds that germinated and developed into a giant organizational plant, the branches of which eventually extended into almost every corner of the globe.

As a result of the merger of the Divisions of Western and Eastern European Affairs into the Division of European Affairs, the number of so-called political or geographic divisions had been reduced to four: the Division of European Affairs, headed by Pierrepont Moffat; the Division of American Republics, headed by Laurance Duggan; the Division of Near Eastern Affairs, headed by Wallace Murray; and the Division of Far Eastern Affairs, headed by Maxwell Hamilton.

When I assumed my duties in the State Department in October 1938, I was the junior of four assistant chiefs of the Division of European Affairs. The other three, whose relative rank depended upon their length of service as assistant chief, were: John D. Hickerson, a former Foreign Service officer who had resigned from the Foreign Service to accept a permanent position in the department and who had held the rank of assistant chief since 1930; Paul T. Culbertson, a Civil Service officer who had held the rank of assistant chief since 1932; and Harold H. Tittmann, Jr., a Foreign Service officer who had been appointed assistant chief in 1937.

A number of changes occurred among the assistant chiefs of the division between October 1938 and August 1942, the month of my departure from the department. Tittmann was assigned in 1939 to Geneva as consul general and was succeeded by Robert T. Pell, a Civil Service officer who had had extensive foreign service experience in Western Europe. Hugh S. Cumming, also a Civil Service officer, who had been the administrative officer of the division while he was also handling north European affairs, was given the rank of assistant chief in 1942.

During the years that I was in the service I was fortunate in finding at every post to which I was assigned exceptionally able and cooperative colleagues. In the Division of European Affairs, for instance, the senior assistant chief, Jack Hickerson, never hesitated, when I turned to him for help, to give me the benefit of his counsel based on his long experience and, when needed, his whole-hearted support. During the period when the chief of the division was absent, I looked to Jack as my immediate chief. Jack continued to work in the European area of the State Department for many years before reverting to a Foreign Service status and taking another post abroad. In his quiet and unostentatious way he was to play a notable role in connection with the genesis and the carrying out of the Marshall Plan and in laying the basis for the United Nations and NATO. He retired in the early 1960s after several years of distinguished service abroad. His last post was ambassador to the Philippines.

Similarly, Harold Tittmann and Hugh Cumming, as well as Paul

Culbertson and Bob Pell, were helpful and cooperative. After his tour in Geneva, Tittmann served for a period as counselor of our embassy in Rome. In 1941 he had the interesting and novel assignment of assistant to the personal representative of the president to Pope Pius XII at Vatican City, an assignment that gave him an understanding equaled by few Americans of the diplomatic operations of the Vatican. In 1948 he was assigned to Peru where he served as ambassador for more than four years prior to his retirement. Hugh Cumming also had a colorful career subsequent to his detail to the Division of European Affairs. After being transferred from the Civil Service to the Foreign Service, he served at a number of interesting posts, including counselor at Stockholm, minister at Moscow, deputy secretary general of NATO for political affairs, and ambassador to Indonesia. He rounded out his career as the director for intelligence and research in the Department of State.

The merger in 1937 of the Western European and Eastern European Divisions had left the structure of the Western European Division relatively intact. It did, however, result in the breaking up of the Eastern European Division—the destruction of many of its valuable documents, the loss of its library, and a sharp reduction in its personnel. Those elements that had been opposed to the State Department engaging in research work other than that of a primarily historical character, which was being performed by the Division of Research and Publication, had won a temporary victory.

The personnel in the East European area of the European Division when I assumed charge consisted of: Waldemar J. Gallman, an experienced and capable Foreign Service officer whom I had known during my first tour in the State Department in the mid-1920s. He had served both in our legation to the Baltic states and in Danzig and was now concentrating on matters relating to Poland, the Baltic states, and Danzig; Edward Page, Jr., a Foreign Service officer and East European specialist who was working on matters pertaining to the Soviet Union; Raymond E. Murphy, a Civil Service officer who was observing the activities of international communism both in the United States and abroad and charged with certain responsibilities relating to our internal security; and a filing clerk.

In 1940 Moffat was appointed minister to Canada and was succeeded by Ray Atherton, one of the senior members of the Diplomatic Service, who served in an "acting" capacity since he was also retaining his title of minister to Denmark, where he could no longer serve since it had been overrun by the Nazis. Atherton, like Moffat, was a man of outstanding ability and rich experience. Following the untimely death of Moffat in 1943, Atherton was sent to Canada to succeed him.

There were also a number of personnel shifts within the East European section of the division. In the summer of 1941 Gallman, while continuing to handle matters pertaining to Poland, Danzig, and the Baltic states, was made an assistant chief, a position he held until his transfer to the embassy in London in 1942. While in London Gallman progressed from first secretary to counselor of embassy and then to minister. In 1948 he was appointed ambassador to Poland. Subsequently he served as ambassador to the Union of South Africa and Iraq. In January 1959 he became director general of the Foreign Service, a position which rendered it possible for the two of us again to work closely together.

In 1940 Francis B. Stevens, a Foreign Service officer and an East European specialist, was detailed to the area to work with Ray Murphy on the international aspects of both nazism and communism. In the same year Bartley Gordon, my former secretary in Moscow who had become a Foreign Service officer, was another welcome addition to our area. Frederick C. Barghoorn, who had specialized in the study of Soviet affairs while at Amherst and Harvard and who in June 1941 had received his Ph.D. from Harvard, joined us in September 1941. After a year in the department he was assigned to our embassy in the Soviet Union where he rendered valuable service for five years before returning to the United States to resume his career in the academic world. Page was sent back to Moscow in the early part of 1942 and was succeeded by Elbridge Durbrow. In June 1942 Bohlen, who had finally been released from his internment by the Japanese, was also assigned to the section.

During my first year in the division I felt keenly the lack of a secretary. There was a constant stream of diplomatic and other callers into my office. I was frequently compelled to answer the telephone and to carry on conversations over it in the presence of a caller, a discourteous and sometimes embarrassing practice, particularly if the caller happened to be a foreign ambassador or minister. Furthermore, although the assistants sent from the stenographic section were usually excellent stenographers and typists, it was a chore to be compelled to spell, while dictating, the names of foreign persons, places, and institutions with which they were not familiar. As the pressure of work on the East European section increased I finally rebelled and insisted that I be given a secretary. The administrative section of the division repeated what it had told me previously, that is, that assistant chiefs in the geographic divisions of the department did not rate a secretary. I thereupon wrote a strong memorandum describing my problem to the assistant secretary for administration—a memorandum that received the backing of Dunn. My memorandum brought results. When the other assistant chiefs of the Division of European Affairs and of the other geographic divisions learned of the success of my memorandum, they proceeded at once to request secretaries for themselves. It was typical of the State Department that most of these requests were granted. Some of my economy-minded, tax-paying readers may heave a sigh at this point and moan, "Henderson again demonstrates the validity of Parkinson's law." I have no apology to make in this respect. In my opinion, in view of the heavy load that the department was carrying during the war years, the addition of these secretaries had been long overdue.

One might obtain the impression from an examination of the organizational chart of the State Department that what remained of the former Eastern European Division had become an integral part of the Division of European Affairs. The East European area, in practice, however, was semiautonomous. Most of the problems facing the area were of a highly specialized character and Moffat and his successor, Atherton, who were heavily burdened with problems relating to the rest of Europe, exercised a minimum amount of supervision over its work. They trusted us to keep them informed regarding matters they should know about. They also gave us their support whenever the going became rough, as it did from time to time. On our part, we did not attempt to make important policy decisions. When faced with problems of significance we usually drafted recommendations regarding the kind of decisions that in our opinion should be made. At times these recommendations were considered to be of sufficient importance to warrant their escalation to the under secretary, the secretary, and even the White House.

It was one of the specific responsibilities of our section to serve as a backstop for our diplomatic missions and consular offices in Eastern Europe. We tried to serve them, help them, and give them guidance. In drafting departmental instructions to them we frequently consulted with other interested divisions of the State Department. In these instructions we sometimes asked them to furnish information that we thought the department or some other governmental agency would like to have. Some of our instructions merely supplied answers to questions they had raised; some praised them for outstanding work; some let them know if any of their actions or activities were not entirely satisfactory. In general the members of our section tried to make the personnel stationed in Eastern Europe feel that we understood their problems, that they had our friendly support, and that they could depend on us to be their spokesmen in the department.

Our section maintained close relations with the embassies and legations in Washington representing the countries of Eastern Europe. If a chief of a diplomatic mission desired to see higher officials of the State Department we usually tried to arrange an appointment for him. The secretary or the under secretary, when engaging in formal conversations with diplomatic representatives of the countries of Eastern Europe, frequently requested a member of our section to be present in order to furnish any background information that might be needed and to prepare the memorandum of conversation.

Our section was expected to keep other members of the Division of European Affairs, and for that matter the top officials of the department, informed regarding developments in Eastern Europe and to make suggestions, when occasion called for them. Members of our section were almost constantly required to participate in conferences within the State Department or conferences involving members of other departments. Fortunately, most members of our section were officers with a considerable amount of experience. They took their responsibilities seriously and did not hesitate to say what they thought, even though they were aware that their views might at times not be pleasing to some of their superiors or to representatives of other governmental agencies.

CHAPTER 44

INSTITUTIONS AND PERSONS WITH WHICH THE EAST EUROPEAN AREA OF THE DIVISION OF EUROPEAN AFFAIRS HAD FREQUENT DEALINGS, OCTOBER 1938–AUGUST 1942

IN THE DISCHARGE of its responsibilities the East European area of the Division of European Affairs of the Department of State maintained special relations with the Soviet and Polish embassies, the Latvian and Lithuanian legations, the Estonian consulate general in New York,* the U.S. embassies in Moscow and Warsaw, the U.S. legations in Tallinn, Riga, and Kaunas, the the U.S. consulate in Danzig.

THE SOVIET EMBASSY

The handsome building on Sixteenth Street several blocks from the White House, which before the Bolshevik revolution had served as the embassy successively of the tsarist and Kerensky governments, housed both the residence of the ambassador and the Soviet chancery.

Constantine A. Oumansky. In June 1938 the Soviet ambassador, Alexander Troyanovsky, went to the Soviet Union "on a vacation." He

---

* Because of the lack of funds, Estonia did not have a diplomatic mission in Washington during the 1930s. Relations between the United States and Estonia were, therefore, conducted through the Estonian consulate general in New York or the U.S. legation in Estonia.

never returned. Since neither he nor Ambassador Davies, who had left Moscow in the same month, were replaced until late in the spring of 1938, both our embassy in Moscow and the Soviet embassy in Washington were in the interim headed by a chargé d'affaires. The Soviet chargé d'affaires was Constantine A. Oumansky,* whom I had first met in Washington in November 1933 when he had accompanied Litvinov to the United States on the mission to establish diplomatic relations between the United States and the Soviet Union. At that time he was chief of the press section of the Commissariat for Foreign Affairs, the capacity in which he continued to serve until his appointment as counselor of embassy in Washington in 1936. While I was on duty in Moscow I had had occasion to meet him both officially and socially. We were, therefore, fairly well acquainted.

Oumansky was regarded both in Moscow and in Washington as a special favorite of Litvinov. In fact, it was believed in Moscow that Litvinov, who was not pleased with the performance in Washington of Ambassador Troyanovsky, had arranged for Oumansky's transfer to the embassy as counselor so that the latter could keep an eye on the ambassador.

The State Department's knowledge of Oumansky's background was limited. Like many high Soviet officials of the period he was restrained in discussing his past. It was our understanding, however, that he was of Ukrainian-Jewish origin, that although only about fifteen years of age at the time of the Bolshevik revolution he had thrown in his lot with the communists, and that by the time he had reached eighteen he had already become a competent journalist. In 1924, at the age of twenty-two, as a correspondent for TASS (the telegraph agency of the Soviet Union), he had had experience in representing that agency in Rome, Paris, and Geneva.

There were a number of rumors regarding Oumansky that we had not been able to verify. One of them was that while working for TASS he had also been serving the Soviet secret police. Another was that as a journalist he had demonstrated qualities that had so impressed Litvinov that the latter had invited him to become a member of his staff.

As chief of the press section of the Commissariat for Foreign Affairs Oumansky had been in charge of the relations of the Soviet government with the foreign journalists stationed in Moscow. His mental agility, his excellent knowledge of several foreign languages, including English, his

---

* Oumansky's name was spelled in different ways according to the manner in which it was transliterated from the Russian, i.e., Umansky, Umanski, or Oumanski.

ability to fence with newsmen in their own language, and his success in soothing or subduing them as the situation required, were assets that Litvinov valued. Litvinov, therefore, took Oumansky with him on many of his visits to foreign countries.

Oumansky's personal appearance was not particularly impressive. He was of medium height and given to stockiness in build. The most arresting feature of his clean-shaven, highly intelligent face was his smile, which revealed rows of gold teeth. His high-strung temperament was reflected in his nervous movements. He rarely seemed to be at ease.

In the three years that we served simultaneously in Washington I had scores of conversations with Oumansky, during which I became as well acquainted with him as a U.S. official is likely to become with a Soviet diplomat. He was by nature aggressive; his inclination was to push just as far as in his opinion the traffic would bear. His aggressiveness, however, usually had a veneer of ingratiating suavity. When frustrated he had difficulty in restraining himself, and in an emotional state he would sometimes talk or act in a manner that I was sure he later regretted. His addiction at times to sarcasm was a handicap since sarcasm has no place in diplomacy. He was well informed on current affairs and highly articulate. He seemed to revel in arguments during the course of which it was his practice to try to goad his opponent into making statements or admissions that he could report to Moscow or file away for possible future use.

Unlike his predecessor, Troyanovsky, who although formally a member of the Communist Party had not in my opinion entirely abandoned the ethics and values that the thoroughgoing Communists of the time branded as "bourgeois," Oumansky had been so steeped in communist morals and doctrines that insofar as I could ascertain he had no "bourgeois" scruples. What was good for the Soviet Union was good for the cause of the international revolution, and what was good for the cause of the international revolution was right. He conceived that his mission was to serve the Soviet Union and anything that he might do to make his mission a success was virtuous. If, for instance, in his opinion it would contribute to the success of his mission for him to tell an untruth, it would be sinful to tell the truth. Devotion to his family, a consuming personal ambition, and a streak of vanity, however, prevented him from being a model self-effacing Communist.

One of Oumansky's major weaknesses was his tendency to judge Americans and American institutions in the light of his own values and of his experience with Soviet institutions. He seemed to take it for granted, for instance, that U.S. officials told the truth only when they thought that the truth would be in the interest of the United States or of themselves personally. Similarly, he apparently believed that behind a façade of democracy the United States, like the Soviet Union, was in fact a dictatorship. He was convinced that the State Department, if it desired to do so, could either directly or through the president give orders to the U.S. courts, to members of Congress, to state and local officials, and to the American news media.

His inability to judge persons sometimes resulted in incidents of an unpleasant character. I shall give an instance of this inability, which happens to concern myself. It was, as I recall, in the spring of 1939 that Oumansky invited me, as he frequently did, to the embassy for luncheon. The other guest was Chip Bohlen, temporarily in Washington on leave from his post in Moscow. Bohlen was compelled to leave early in order to catch a train. Following his departure Oumansky, who seemed to be in especially good humor, invited me to have coffee with him in a small private sitting room. Over the coffee he steered our conversation into channels of a personal nature. He said that he was glad to have the opportunity for an intimate chat since I was one of the first U.S. officials with whom he had come in contact. He had enjoyed our association in Moscow and was appreciative of the consideration that I had been showing him while in the State Department. Although some of his American friends had been trying to convince him that I was not friendly to the Soviet Union he believed that I, like himself, desired close friendly relations between the Soviet Union and the United States. In view of this belief he was venturing to suggest that he and I enter into cooperation for the purpose of bringing our two countries closer together. His suggestion was that from time to time we meet privately for discussions and exchanges of views. These discussions would relate to matters of mutual interest. For instance, I could tell him for his strictly personal and confidential use the names, background, and attitudes of those U.S. officials with whom he might most advantageously deal and suggest what he might say or do in order to attain such objectives as his government might prescribe for him. I could also let him know the identity of the persons in the Department of State and other branches of the government who might be helpful to him or might become obstacles. He indicated that he was at present particularly disturbed at the difficulties the Soviet Union was encountering in obtaining from the United States industrial and military equipment and supplies of which it was in urgent need, and also at some of the articles unfriendly to the Soviet Union that were appearing in U.S. newspapers and magazines. He was confident that I was in a position to obtain information that could help him in struggling with these and other problems.

In return for my cooperation, Oumansky continued, he would use his influence with U.S. government officials in key positions and with important sections of the American press, including a number of well-known columnists, to advance my career. There was no reason, for instance, why, upon the completion of my present tour in the department, I should not be appointed ambassador to the Soviet Union. I would be amazed if I should know how many influential American friends he had who would be in a position to help me.

Since I suspected that microphones were recording our conversation I was careful in my reply. I told him that he was right in his belief that I desired close friendly relations between the United States and the Soviet Union. Ever since the establishment of diplomatic relations I had been hoping that a basis could be found on which mutual confidence, which was the necessary ingredient for really friendly relations, could be established. I had not abandoned this hope and would continue to strive for its realization. It would, however, be contrary to the ethics of the State Department or the Foreign Service for me to enter into any special cooperative arrangement with him or with any other foreign diplomat. It would also be unethical for me privately to discuss the attitudes and views of officials of the Department of State and other government agencies without authorization from my superiors.

Oumansky said that he could understand that the arrangement he had in mind might be unethical if it was likely to damage the United States, but since the international objectives of the United States and the Soviet Union were similar and since our cooperation could advance the attainment of these objectives he had ventured to make the suggestion.

In order to soften my rejection I assured Oumansky before taking my departure that within the framework of the policies of my government and in keeping with the trust that my superiors in the department had in me, I would continue to do what I properly could to cooperate with him and the other members of the Soviet embassy.

Upon my return to the State Department I immediately informed Adolph Berle, the assistant secretary of state who at the time was in charge of security matters, of the substance of the conversation. We agreed that behind Oumansky's proffer to arrange for friends in "key positions" to be helpful to me if I would give him the cooperation he desired, was an implied suggestion that if I failed to cooperate to his satisfaction his friends could be unhelpful.

My relations with Oumansky were not affected on the surface, at least, by my rejection of his proposal. He continued to call on me regularly, usually to register complaints of various kinds and to seek my assistance. His visits to the State Department were not limited to me; after conversations with me he frequently called on Moffat or Dunn and sometimes on Judge Moore, the assistant secretaries, Sumner Welles, and on Secretary Hull himself. The secretary, who was apparently irritated by Oumansky's mannerisms, was inclined to show him scant sympathy and at times was almost abrupt with him. During his tenure as chargé d'affaires, therefore, Oumansky's calls on the secretary were rare.

After he was elevated to the ambassadorship in June 1939 Oumansky gained in self-confidence and began more frequently to seek interviews with the top-ranking members of the State Department. He continued, however, to prefer to lay his major complaints before Welles rather than the secretary. During the latter part of 1940, the department decided to endeavor to relieve the strain on American-Soviet relations resulting largely from Soviet inability to obtain from the United States machinery, armament, and other supplies that it needed in order to carry out its program of strengthening the Soviet Union economically, industrially, and militarily. As a result of this decision Welles invited Oumansky to have a series of long conversations with him. During several of these talks, in addition to discussing the difficulties inherent in selling the Soviet Union everything that it desired, Welles tried without success to convince Oumansky that Hitler was planning to launch an attack on the Soviet Union in the not distant future. These conversations continued for a period of several months. I was present during most of them and incorporated in memoranda for the use of Welles the substance of the exchanges between Oumansky and himself.

In his public speeches Oumansky was careful not to make statements that could be offensive to the American people as a whole or to the U.S. government. In his off-the-record conversations, however, with individuals or with small groups of persons whom he considered to be discreet and sympathetic to his cause, he at times used bitter language in criticizing policies and attitudes of the U.S. government and U.S. officials and in denouncing the critics of the Soviet Union and of himself. He found sympathetic audiences among members of the faculties of several of our universities. Some of his listeners, however, incensed at his more extreme statements, passed them on to the State Department.

From October 1938 to June 1939, before he went to Moscow on leave and consultation, Oumansky was a frequent visitor at the National Press Club. He felt at ease with journalists and his chair or table in the club rooms was usually surrounded with members of the club who enjoyed the novelty of chatting with what at the time was a rarity—a talkative Soviet diplomat. Some members with leftist leanings tended to lionize him and to reward him for his willingness to talk with them by giving him tidbits of information in which they thought he might be interested. Some of the information that he picked up from his discussions with the journalists might have been helpful to him; much of it, however, was inaccurate and did not serve to keep him correctly informed of developments or thinking in the United States.

In the bull sessions at the Press Club in which Oumansky participated he was prone to attack and ridicule fascists of all hues, including Hitler and Mussolini, the "fascists" of Great Britain and France, and even those in the United States who were displaying a lack of confidence in the intentions of the Soviet Union and were not sympathetic with the activities of the Moscow-controlled "united fronts against fascism." He was accustomed to assure his listeners that persons who were circulating stories regarding the possibility of the Soviets coming to an understanding with Germany at the expense of the small countries of Europe were malicious slanderers. In early May, following the replacement of Litvinov by Molotov, Oumansky began to assume a mysterious air in discussing Soviet policies. While continuing to make sarcastic references to the "fascists" of the Western world, particularly to the members of the governments of Great Britain and France, he toned down his criticisms of Nazi Germany and Fascist Italy.

Fortunately for Oumansky's vanity he was in the Soviet Union in the latter part of August 1939 when the Soviet Union and Germany entered into the nonaggression pact, which by nature approached an alliance. He did not return to Washington until the middle of November by which time the initial shock of the change of Soviet policy had been absorbed. Nevertheless, he found the atmosphere of the National Press Club uncomfortable during the next eighteen months since many of its members believed that the Soviet Union shared responsibility with Germany for the launching of the Second World War. Only after the Germans in June 1941 invaded the Soviet Union and the Soviet Union, by the act of Hitler, was suddenly transformed into a "liberty-loving nation" fighting against aggression, did Oumansky again begin to consort with the members in the National Press Club.

I had mixed feelings of admiration, sympathy, and distrust for Oumansky during the period the Soviet Union was cooperating with Germany. My admiration did not stem from his effectiveness as a diplomat but from his pluck, from his staunchness in defending the policy of his government and in doing his utmost to carry out the thankless tasks that it was placing upon him. Behind the brazen, and at times jaunty, front that he assumed, I could sense that he was a most unhappy person smarting under the criticism that was being leveled almost constantly both at his government and at him personally. I have always regarded it as tasteless and, as a general rule, unfair for the news media of a country to launch personal attacks on a foreign diplomat accredited to it because of dislike for the policies of his government. Oumansky, by his tendency to talk too much and by his mannerisms, had undoubtedly invited a certain amount of personal criticism. Nevertheless, I sympathized with him in the distress that he so sturdily tried to conceal. Such sympathy as I had for Oumansky was tempered by my knowledge that, although he was the target for criticism by many columnists and radio commentators, he continued to be regarded as a hero by wide circles of left-wing Americans, Communists, fellow travelers, and intellectuals who would never allow shifts in the foreign policies of the Soviet Union to cause them to turn against it, and by many thousands of simple working people who had found life hard under a capitalist system during the years when jobs were difficult to find and hold and who were yearning for the kind of system that they were being told existed in the Soviet Union. The extent of the popularity of Oumansky as the personification of the Soviet Union among some of these discontented people had been brought home to me in the spring of 1939, when I went to New York to represent the secretary of state at the ceremonies accompanying the opening of the Soviet pavilion at the New York World's Fair. I was accompanied to New York by Lawrence Steinhardt who had been named by the president as our new ambassador to the Soviet Union and took advantage of the occasion to introduce him to Oumansky.

The ceremonies were open to the public. In addition to the guests who had been especially invited to attend the luncheon that was to follow the formal ceremonies, there were great throngs of people from many walks of life. I was not impressed by the well-dressed, sophisticated-appearing persons in the crowd whom I assumed to be communist leaders, fellow travelers, and enthusiastic left-leaning intellectuals. I was interested, however, in the hundreds of roughly-dressed men and women, many of them obviously foreign-born, who vied with one another in their efforts to meet the great representative from the land of the workers and toilers. I could see the adoring looks in the eyes of those who were lucky enough to be able to greet him personally and noted the awe with which they bowed before him or ventured to kiss his hand. This kind of homage apparently deeply affected Oumansky. It was one of the few occasions in which I saw his face glowing with unalloyed happiness.

Ruthless though Oumansky may have been in some ways he seemed to have an affectionate devotion, unfitting for a dedicated Communist, to his family. I had met his wife and daughter in Moscow in 1934 at the tennis courts of the Spiridonovka, the mansion that the Commissariat for Foreign Affairs used for entertainment purposes. During the summers of 1934 and 1935 the Soviet government had permitted members of our embassy to play tennis on these courts. The Oumanskys, who lived nearby, sometimes joined us. Their daughter, who at the time was a pretty well-behaved child perhaps of eight years of age, took delight in chasing tennis balls for us. When we appeared on the courts she would run out and place herself at our service. Oumansky and his wife doted on their daughter and made every effort to see that she received a good education and training. She was with them in the United States for a period but later returned to Moscow for her schooling. Mrs. Oumansky seemed to me to be a kind, self-effacing woman dedicated to taking care of her husband and child.

In September 1941 Oumansky returned to the Soviet Union where he served for a period as director of TASS. In May of 1943 he was appointed minister to Mexico with the personal rank of ambassador. Two days before the date that Oumansky, his wife, and daughter were scheduled to leave Moscow for Mexico City, a young Russian shot and killed the daughter, who at the time was about seventeen years of age, and then committed suicide. According to information that we received from Moscow the young man, the son of a high Soviet official, was so desperately in love with her that he preferred killing her and himself to being separated from her. We were also informed that since their transportation by plane across Siberia and the Pacific to the United States had already been arranged, the Soviet government had insisted that the ambassador and his wife depart as planned. After the hurried burial of their daughter, therefore, they set out for the United States. Several days after I had learned of this tragedy I received a long–distance telephone call from Oumansky. He told me that he and his wife had arrived in California and were meeting difficulties in obtaining transportation to Mexico. Could I not arrange for a special U.S. military plane to take them and their effects to Mexico City? I told him that in time of war it was not easy to divert a U.S. military plane to travel of this kind and asked if he could not arrange to go by a commercial airline. He replied in an agitated manner that he and his wife wished to travel by a plane that they could trust and that was why he was making the request. I promised to do what I could to help him and took occasion to say how grieved his friends in the State Department were at the death of their daughter. I passed his request through appropriate channels to the army which, as I recall, gave appropriate assistance to Oumansky and his wife on the last leg of their long journey.

On May 19, 1943, Chip Bohlen, at that time a member of the East European area of the Division of European Affairs, wrote a memorandum regarding the appointment of Oumansky to Mexico. This memorandum read as follows:

The appointment of Oumansky as Minister to Mexico appears to be more than merely a routine diplomatic assignment. Mr. Oumansky's personality, method of doing business, and general attitude towards the United States is sufficiently known to the Department to require no elaboration. He cannot under any circumstances be considered a friend of the United States.

His appointment to Mexico might be in connection with the fact that, according to available information, Mexico is the center for Comintern-directed activities in the Western Hemisphere and in particular for the Communist-controlled *émigré* political groups, such as the *Freies Deutschland* group.

Since his return to the Soviet Union, Oumansky, although still retaining a post in the Foreign Office, has been head of the TASS news agency and closely connected with the work of the Soviet Information Bureau. It may well be that his appointment as Minister to Mexico is more in connection with his recent work with Soviet publicity and propaganda institutions than with his past experience as a Soviet Diplomat.

He will undoubtedly while in Mexico utilize his left-wing contacts in the United States.

According to subsequent information coming into the State Department, Oumansky and his legation did in fact become the hub of communist propaganda and subversive activities throughout Latin America—activities that included efforts to promote hostility toward the United States.

Oumansky and his wife were killed on January 25, 1945, eighteen months after their arrival in Mexico, when a commercial plane on which they were traveling near Mexico City suddenly plummeted to the earth. There were no survivors. Thus was the whole Oumansky family extinguished.

As might be expected the tragedy that overtook the Oumanskys gave rise to a crop of rumors. Subsequent to their death, a person who was well acquainted with associates of the Oumanskys in Mexico City told me that from the moment of their arrival in that city they had lived in constant terror of assassination and that they were particularly reluctant to travel by plane. According to my informant they had been warned on their arrival in California en route to Mexico that a group of militant Trotskyites, who believed that Oumansky while stationed in Washington in 1940 had participated in the planning of Trotsky's murder in Mexico, had sworn to avenge the murder and that this warning had contributed to the Oumanskys' distrust of planes. On the other hand, another of my friends who had made a special study of the circumstances surrounding Trotsky's death scoffed at the idea that Trotskyites were in any way responsible for the death of the Oumanskys. He thought it more likely that Oumansky was one of the many Soviet officials liquidated by Stalin on the ground that they possessed knowledge of such a dangerous kind that they should not be permitted to live. So far as I know, no evidence has been adduced to support the view that the fall of the plane was due to sabotage.

Dimitry S. Chuvakhin. During the period June 1938 to June 1939 that Oumansky served as chargé d'affaires, the officer in the embassy next to him in rank was Dimitry S. Chuvakhin. While Oumansky was in Moscow on leave from July to November 1939, Chuvakhin acted as chargé d'affaires.

During the period of his assignment to Washington, Chuvakhin, in my opinion, had neither the personality nor the experience of the kind that a diplomat in his position should possess. His background was unknown but it seemed to us in the State Department that before coming to Washington in a diplomatic capacity he must have engaged in work in which roughness and rudeness were considered assets. He was a fairly young man, perhaps in his early thirties, with a low forehead and a swagger reminiscent of some of the Soviet secret police whom I had run across in the Soviet Union. His scanty knowledge of the English language was a handicap since when he tried to talk in English he used words and expressions that had no place in polite intercourse. He was inclined on occasions to be combative and argumentative, and at times seemed infuriated when I chose to ignore his provocative remarks and to continue my conversation with him as though I thought that he was trying to be polite.

As chargé d'affaires he was the host at the reception given by the Soviet embassy on November 7, 1939, on the occasion of the anniversary of the Bolshevik revolution. So unpopular was the Soviet Union at that time among official circles in Washington that I, despite my relatively junior position, was designated to represent the Department of State at the affair.

Chuvakhin returned to Moscow in 1942 in order to take the position of assistant chief of the division of the Commissariat for Foreign Affairs that was handling American affairs. I have no doubt that as he gained in experience and became accustomed to dealing with the representatives of foreign governments he developed both in the matter of personality and ability. In any event, he eventually advanced to the top level of the Soviet diplomatic service. As ambassador to Albania during the latter 1940s he assisted in establishing a communist government in that country and later served for a period as ambassador to Canada.

Andrey A. Gromyko. In the autumn of 1939 a former Soviet diplomat who had recently defected and fled to the United States told me that a rumor was circulating among Soviet diplomats that Oumansky upon his return from Moscow to the United States would bring with him a young man who was slated to succeed him. He said that according to the rumor the young man, whose name was Gromyko, had had little background and training in the field of foreign affairs, that he had been recommended, however, to Stalin as a trustworthy person who was not given to intrigue, and that Stalin after talking with him had taken a liking to him and had given orders that he be given important posts that would prepare him for top positions in Soviet diplomacy.

The name of Gromyko was familiar to me since through our embassy in Moscow I had already heard that a person by that name had been assigned in May 1939 to the Commissariat for Foreign Affairs as chief of the division that handled American affairs. In view of what the former Soviet official had told me I was particularly interested in this young man when Oumansky, in making a courtesy call following his return from Moscow in mid-November 1939, introduced Gromyko to me as the new counselor of embassy. I found myself shaking hands with a lanky man in ill-fitting clothes, about thirty years of age, a little above the average height, with dark hair and eyes and a face rather heavily lined for a person of his age. There was about him a sort of shy awkwardness—the kind of awkwardness of a rural schoolteacher upon his first visit to a large city. I noted in him a slowness of speech that gave the impression that he was weighing every word. I later discovered that this slowness was due in part to a lack of familiarity with the English language. As we looked at one another I had an intuitive feeling that he, like some of the Soviet officials whom I had met in the Commissariat for Foreign Affairs in Moscow, was the kind of person with whom I could deal with a certain amount of confidence.

According to the reply from the Soviet embassy to the State Department's request for Gromyko's background we learned that he was born in the little village of Starye Gromyke in the Gomel region of the White Russian Constituent Republic, that he had been educated in the Gomel Agricultural High School, the Borisov Pedagogical Institute, and the Minsk Institute of Agricultural Economics, and that from 1934 to 1939, before his assignment to the Commissariat for Foreign Affairs, he had been a senior member of the Institute of Economics of the Academy of the USSR.

During the ensuing two and a half years I saw much of Gromyko. In September 1941 Oumansky was recalled to Moscow and never returned. Gromyko, therefore, was in charge of the embassy until the arrival of the new ambassador, Litvinov, in early December. Both as counselor and as chargé d'affaires Gromyko had many matters to discuss with our East European area. While in Washington he was studying English assiduously and I noted during the course of our discussions that he was gaining steadily in assurance and in the ability to express himself.

In spite of the difficult and, at times, insoluble problems that Gromyko and I discussed, and of the frequent necessity for me to say "no" to requests made by him, he never seemed to become emotional or even impatient. His technique was similar to that which I had previously noted in dealing with Soviet diplomats in Moscow. When I would tell him that the U.S. government could not grant a request that he had made and would explain why it could not do so, he would listen patiently. After I had finished talking he would say that he understood there were difficulties but—and at this point he would painstakingly repeat his request. A day or two later he would call on me with the same request. After I had told him a number of times why his request could not be granted he would sometimes ask if I would object if he should discuss it with one of my superiors. I would, therefore, arrange for him to see Ray Atherton, who had become acting chief of the Division of European Affairs, Jimmie Dunn, or perhaps Sumner Welles, the under secretary. Even after one or several of my superiors had explained why the request could not be granted, he would make it again whenever a suitable occasion would arise. Interesting enough, these repeated requests would sometimes wear down the State Department to such an extent that at least some concession in the direction of acceding to them would be made.

Gromyko's wife, like Mrs. Oumansky, was a quiet, kind woman not given to ostentation, who was doing her best to be of assistance to her husband. The Gromykos were worried about the fate of members of their family living in White Russia when that constituent republic was overrun by the Germans, and I found myself sharing their worries. I was relieved when later they told me after the Germans had fallen back that their families had survived.

Gromyko as counselor of embassy concentrated on work connected with Soviet-American relations. He did not, so far as I could ascertain, try to ingratiate himself with American Communists and fellow travelers or attempt to bring pressure on the U.S. government either by the issuance of public statements or by making use of the services of pro-Soviet Americans. He was in fact almost self-effacing so far as the American public was concerned and did not, like Oumansky and Litvinov, try to ride the wave of Soviet popularity that followed the German attack on the Soviet Union.

In the spring of 1943 I went to New York to represent the secretary of state at a meeting of the society called "Friends of the Soviet Union." Honored guests at this meeting were Mrs. Litvinov and Gromyko who, in the temporary absence of Litvinov from the United States, was chargé d'affaires. I noted that the attention of those present at the meeting was concentrated on Mrs. Litvinov. The presence of Gromyko was almost ignored. The speakers uniformly began their talks with the formula "Madame Litvinov and Friends of the Soviet Union." I was the only speaker who began my short talk by saying "Mr. Chargé d'Affaires, Madame Litvinov, and Friends of the Soviet Union." Several weeks later I could understand the bewilderment and astonishment of the "Friends of the Soviet Union" when Litvinov, their great idol, was replaced as ambassador by this quiet young man of whom they had taken so little notice.

Gromyko's subsequent career is so well known that it would serve no useful purpose for me to enlarge upon it at this time. I will merely point out that after serving as ambassador to both the United States and Great Britain, after representing the Soviet Union before organs of the United Nations, after attending dozens of important international conferences, and after serving as vice commissar for foreign affairs, he became commissar for foreign affairs of the Soviet Union in 1957 and held that position for many years. I doubt that any other living diplomat in the mid-twentieth century has had experiences in international intercourse that can surpass those of Gromyko. The astonishing feature of his career is that for a period of more than 30 years he has maintained the confidence of the rulers of the Kremlin. During these years he has assisted diplomatically in depriving some small nations of their freedom, he has ably directed Soviet diplomacy in channels that run contrary to the interests of the United States and the aspirations of the American people, and he has frequently taken the lead in denouncing the United States and American policies. Nevertheless, I am inclined to believe from my early association with him that he has been doing what he conceived to be his duty, that is, carrying out the policies of his government—policies that over the long term are basically opposed to those of the United States and that have resulted in death or suffering to many millions of persons in various parts of the world.

Maxim M. Litvinov. On November 1, 1941, the State Department received from Steinhardt, our ambassador to the Soviet Union, a telegram stating that the Soviet government had requested an *agrément* for Litvinov as the new ambassador to the United States. In his telegram Steinhardt said, "I have little doubt that the principal purpose of Litvinov's mission would be to endeavor to persuade the President to speed and enlarge the program of American aid to the Soviet Union agreed upon at the Three-

Power Conference, as the Soviets regard Litvinov as having greater international stature than Oumansky."

The telegram instructing Steinhardt to inform the Soviet government that the appointment of Litvinov was agreeable to the U.S. government left the State Department within a few hours after the receipt of Steinhardt's telegram. Over the years Litvinov had gained the reputation in Western Europe and the United States of being a friend of the democracies of the West and a champion for cooperation between the Soviet Union and the West in opposing German and Italian aggression. His eloquent speeches in the League of Nations denouncing the Italian campaign against Ethiopia, his statements in support of the leftist loyalists in Spain, and his appeals during the middle 1930s to the countries of the West to join the Soviet Union in some kind of collective security arrangement to halt German aggression, had contributed to this reputation. His replacement in May 1939 as commissar for foreign affairs by Molotov had, therefore, sent a chill throughout the West. There was concern lest his removal might mean that the Soviet government was more interested in coming to an understanding with Hitler than in cooperating with Great Britain and France. The conclusion of the Molotov-Ribbentrop agreement (known as the German-Soviet nonaggression pact) less than four months later seemed to justify that concern, and Litvinov henceforth was regarded by many groups and persons in Great Britain, France, and the United States as a sort of martyr who had sacrificed himself on the altar of cooperation between the Soviet Union and the West.

The announcement in early November 1941 of the appointment of Litvinov to Washington was, therefore, warmly welcomed by the American press and public. Scores of adulatory telegrams were sent to him in Moscow by admirers in the United States. One of my former chiefs in Moscow, Ambassador Davies, for instance, sent a telegram on November 10 to Litvinov through the Department of State, which read as follows:

> None among your many friends found more satisfaction in your appointment to Washington than did we. We have found the greatest admiration and pride in the extraordinary effectiveness and magnificent heroism which the Soviet Union is displaying every day in this decisive battle for the preservation of civilization and freedom. Please give regards to Premier Stalin, Prime Minister Molotov, Ambassador Oumansky, Troyanovsky and our other friends. A warm welcome will be awaiting you here.

Litvinov arrived in Washington in November 1941 in a blaze of publicity that was almost as great and was even more flattering than that which had accompanied his arrival eight years previously, when he had come to the United States for the purpose of negotiating with President Roosevelt the establishment of diplomatic relations between the United States and the Soviet Union. It so happened that the day before he presented his Letters of Credence to the president the Japanese had made their attack on Pearl Harbor. Several days later Germany and Italy declared war on the United States. During Litvinov's tour as ambassador to the United States the Soviet Union and the United States were, therefore, at war with common enemies, Germany and Italy. Since the Soviet Union continued to maintain diplomatic relations with Japan, it was not, however, like the United States, fighting on two fronts. The fact that the United States and the Soviet Union were in effect allies as far as Europe was concerned tended, however, to strengthen Litvinov's position in Washington.

Litvinov lost no time in using his prestige to establish personal relations with the president and Mrs. Roosevelt and with officials and politicians close to the White House. During his first year in Washington he paid occasional calls on the secretary and the under secretary of state but he concentrated his attention on persons who, he thought, might be in the best position to influence the White House and American public opinion. During the last few months of his stay in Washington, however, he seemed to have found a sympathetic and influential listener in Welles, and they apparently began cooperating with one another. Ambassador Davies in a series of speeches and statements to the press proved to be one of Litvinov's more effective publicity agents during the whole of the latter's period of service as ambassador.

During his first year in Washington, Litvinov wielded a considerable amount of influence. Many influential Americans made a special effort to ingratiate themselves with him. During the height of his popularity, the Soviet embassy was frequented by U.S. officials who were hoping to gain his favor by performing services for him or passing along to him information of a kind in which he might be interested. Although the calls that he made on the State Department were not numerous he was kept well informed of what was taking place in it through a grapevine of U.S. officials and left-leaning correspondents. He did not hesitate to make use of his prestige in order to make life difficult for those officials whom he suspected of trying to thwart the attainment of some of his objectives.

After the presentation of his Letters of Credence, he made the customary calls on members of the State Department. Ray Atherton, who at the time was acting chief of the Division of European Affairs, brought him to my office so that he could meet the members of the area particularly concerned with East European affairs. Although he was formally polite when greeting me I could sense that he had not forgiven me for the stubborn way in which, while in charge of the U.S. embassy in Moscow, I had tried to protect U.S. citizens in trouble in the Soviet Union and U.S. interests in general. He rarely visited the Division of European Affairs after his initial call. When the Soviet embassy had problems to discuss with the division he usually sent Gromyko to act for him. When it was incumbent upon him personally to discuss matters with the State Department, he usually talked with Welles. He preferred, however, to have his ideas conveyed to the White House through leftist friends of Mrs. Roosevelt and the president.

Although I treated Litvinov with appropriate deference and courtesy, I could not admire him. During the four and a half years that I had served in Moscow subsequent to the establishment of diplomatic relations between the United States and the Soviet Union, I had had an opportunity to study his attitude, actions, and methods of operation at close range. I had come to regard him as a clever, ambitious, and intriguing opportunist whose duties included posing as pro-Western for the benefit of Westerners unacquainted with the situation in the Soviet Union. He knew enough about Western mores and ways of thinking to be able to hoodwink many U.S. visitors, including journalists, who felt flattered to receive attention from such a world figure. One of his ploys was to suggest that there were two conflicting schools of thinking in the Soviet Union. One school would like the country to move in the direction of democracy and friendly relations with the West. The other school was determined to follow the hard communist line of world revolution, to consider all noncommunist nations as ipso facto members of the enemy camp, and to be prepared, in the interest of the long-term success of the revolution, to cooperate on a short-term basis with fascist countries just as readily as with countries that considered themselves to be democratic. He would intimate that, in order to strengthen the former school, the countries of the West should be prepared to make concessions to the Soviet Union. In view of the nature of the Soviet government at the time, it was, in my opinion, impossible for Litvinov to drop suggestions of this kind without the knowledge and approval of the Kremlin. I believed, therefore, that he was assuming his pro-Western posture merely to lure naive Westerners into taking positions favorable to Soviet objectives. He seemed to enjoy this game and to regard with contempt those Westerners whom he was able to deceive and with suspicion those whose flattery of him was in his opinion insincere.

I found particularly offensive Litvinov's penchant for making slighting or cynical remarks in my presence regarding Americans whom I respected, some of whom considered themselves to be his friends. I was incensed, for instance, when on two occasions he referred in a sneering manner to Ambassador Davies, who had made every effort to establish friendly relations with him and who was losing no opportunity publicly and privately to praise him.

My distrust of Litvinov was also due in part to the role that he played in 1933 when, as commissar for foreign affairs, he had entered into a series of "gentlemen's agreements" with President Roosevelt that were to serve as the basis for the establishment of diplomatic relations between the United States and the Soviet Union. It had seemed to me that he must have known that the Soviet Union would not be able to live up to these agreements unless fundamental changes were made in the character and policies of the Soviet government and that there was no intention on the part of the Kremlin to make such changes. My distrust had been further strengthened when, while on duty in our embassy in Moscow, I had observed the cynical evasions and falsehoods to which he was resorting in meeting Ambassador Bullitt's insistence that the Soviet Union keep the commitments that he had made on its behalf. My respect for him was not increased by the fact that on several occasions during my own confrontations with him while I was in charge of the embassy in Moscow he had not hesitated while looking straight into my eyes to make statements that he knew that I knew could not be true.

Although I realized that Litvinov himself had not been the chief formulator of Soviet foreign policy, I was inclined to agree with our embassy in Moscow that his replacement by Molotov as commissar might have considerable international political significance. In a telegram dated May 4, 1939, Alexander Kirk, our chargé d'affaires in Moscow, had commented as follows:

> Although it is generally accepted here that Litvinov was little more than the instrument for the execution of such policy as had been decided on by Stalin and consequently powerless to pursue a personal policy, nevertheless his name has been so closely associated with the advocacy of the principle of collective security and resistance to Germany that any real or feigned departure from this policy that might be contemplated would be prejudiced by his remaining as Foreign Minister. It may likewise be that Litvinov desired to go farther in the direction of committing the Soviet Union to a definite agreement against Germany than the Kremlin considers desirable at the present time and consequently his elimination was determined upon. On the other hand the possibility cannot be excluded that the removal of Litvinov may be designed to produce, particularly in England, the impression of an imminent Soviet-German *rapprochement* with a view to accelerating a British decision in regard to the Soviet proposals which it is understood are still being discussed in London, and

that the appointment of Molotov may have been due to the Kremlin's dissatisfaction with Litvinov's conduct of these negotiations.

Litvinov never fully recovered from the humiliation that he suffered as a result of the loss of his position as commissar for foreign affairs. Although his appointment eighteen months later as ambassador to the United States and the deference shown him during his first months in the United States helped to heal his vanity, he continued to be full of bitterness during the whole of his stay in the United States.

During the latter part of 1942 and the spring of 1943 he seemed to be particularly irritated because of his lack of success in carrying out the most important task that his government had assigned to him—that of prevailing upon the United States to insist that Great Britain join it in immediately establishing a second front in Western Europe. His highly suspicious mind contributed to his belief that the delay in the establishment of such a front was due to political rather than to military considerations—that is, that reactionaries in the U.S. government did not want such a front established until the Germans had succeeded in mortally weakening the Soviet Union.

In my opinion Litvinov had come to the United States confident, in view of the successes that he had achieved during his visit in 1933, that he could prevail upon the president's advisers and upon the president himself to follow policies in the field of diplomacy and of military strategy that would be to the advantage of the Soviet Union. He became deeply disappointed, therefore, when he found that in spite of the adulation accorded him by certain sections of the American press and of the praise bestowed on him personally by many U.S. officials, U.S. political and military policies were too frequently not of the kind that he had been urging. In his disgruntlement he began to assume an almost querulous air in his discussions even with those U.S. officials who were most eager to be of maximum assistance to the Soviet Union. He was frequently overbearing and rude to members of the press and to representatives of other news media who desired to be friendly with persons in the United States representing the Soviet Union. As he became more acrimonious and resorted more and more to sarcasm, his friends gradually decreased in number. In some of his outbursts he went so far as to place the blame for his failures not only on the machinations of U.S. reactionaries but also on the attitudes and stupidities of his own government. He was apparently never able to forgive Molotov for succeeding him as commissar for foreign affairs and for replacing his favorites in the commissariat with officials in whom the new commissar could have confidence.

I noted the change that was coming over Litvinov as early as May

1942 when Molotov made a secret visit to Washington under the name of Mr. Brown. During the course of the visit Litvinov was especially sullen and uncommunicative, and I began to suspect that his sullenness might be due to jealousy of Molotov. Ray Atherton, the acting chief of the Division of European Affairs, and I were given the task of preparing an innocuous communiqué regarding Molotov's visit to be published after Molotov's departure and of obtaining Molotov's agreement to our draft. Since Litvinov was the Soviet ambassador, it seemed to me that it would be only courteous to obtain his views regarding the draft before showing it to Molotov. Atherton agreed, and I, therefore, telephoned Litvinov about ten o'clock in the evening in order to tell him that we had prepared the draft of a communiqué to be issued regarding Mr. Brown's visit and that we would like to show it to him before taking it to Mr. Brown. Instead of being appreciative, he said in a rude voice that he could not understand why we were disturbing him at his residence so late at night with regard to a matter of this kind. He had had nothing to do with the visit or with what had transpired during the visit and was not interested in looking over the draft.

Litvinov's sense of frustration and anger appeared to have reached a boiling point in March 1943. On March 4 he made a call upon Welles, who during the absence from Washington of Hull was acting secretary, in order to give vent to his feelings. After handing Welles a memorandum charging various U.S. governmental agencies with discriminating against the Soviet Union, he launched into a bitter oral attack on some "minor officials of the United States government" for their apparent intention "to prejudice relations between the Soviet Union and the United States." The ambassador also protested attacks made upon the Soviet Union by state and city officials.

Welles expressed regret that such attacks had been made and promised to have a survey made of the charges contained in Litvinov's memorandum.

Litvinov, apparently convinced that he had found a sympathetic listener in Welles, continued for the next two months to make calls on the latter during which he recounted some of the difficulties that he was facing in attempting to carry out his role of ambassador. On April 24, 1943, for instance, during one of his calls, Litvinov, in referring to a trip that he was planning to make to Moscow, said that he had no idea how long he would be away. He added that "his own situation here had become intolerable because of the fact that he had no information from his Government and no instructions and that he was consequently placed in a position where he was occupying an important post but was doing no real work." He indicated that he could not continue any longer to go on in such a way "and for that reason he would have to reach an understanding directly with his Government."

Litvinov was even more frank in criticizing his own government during his farewell call on Welles on May 7, 1943. He told Welles that he wanted to talk to him "completely off the record and asked that no official record be made of this conversation." The memorandum that Welles prepared of the ensuing conversation makes interesting reading. It is rare for an ambassador to attack the government that he represents in the presence of a representative of the government to which he is accredited in the manner and with the language used by Litvinov during this talk with the under secretary. He charged that Molotov had removed from the Foreign Commissariat "every important official who had any experience with the outside world and any personal knowledge of the United States or of the Western democracies." He said that he did not believe that his messages were being received by Stalin and he himself "was completely bereft of any information as to the policy or plans of his own Government . . . he had even been forbidden by his Government to appear in public or to make any public speeches."

Litvinov's success in winning the confidence and sympathy of the under secretary was surprising in view of the fact that over the years Welles had been one of the members of the State Department who had advocated taking a strong stand in dealing with the Soviet Union. During the spring of 1943 Welles inaugurated a campaign on Litvinov's behalf within the department, in the White House—where he had a potent ally in the person of Mrs. Roosevelt—and in conversations with members of the press. Word came to me through the journalistic grapevine that he was going so far in his private conversations with several journalists with whom he maintained close relations as to intimate that the secretary himself had little sympathy for the Soviet Union and had not been fair in his treatment of Litvinov.

I noted in the spring of 1943 that Welles was beginning to change not only with regard to his attitude toward the Soviet Union but in a number of other ways. He was no longer the person with whom I worked closely for so many years. He ceased to talk frankly regarding the international situation with other members of the State Department and no longer moved about with his usual air of self-confidence. When problems were laid before him he seemed indecisive. It was only in the latter part of August 1943 when I learned that he had submitted his resignation to the president that I realized that the change in him might to an extent have been accounted for by the fact that he was facing problems of a personal nature—the kind of problems that would place anyone under great strain.

Welles's ostentatious change of attitude with regard to the Soviet

Union during his last months in the Department of State indirectly led to an acerbic exchange between Secretary Hull and a well-known columnist who had been a close friend and confidant of the under secretary. The columnist in question aroused the ire of the secretary by indicating in one of his columns that Welles was leaving the Department of State because of differences of opinion in the department with regard to the Soviet Union and that with the departure of Welles there would be no one left in the department who would be interested in developing good relations with the Soviet Union.

The secretary called in Gromyko, the Soviet chargé d'affaires, on August 27 in order to brand the columnist's story as untrue, issued a statement to the press on August 30 denying that he and other high officials in the State Department were opposed to the Soviet government, and sent a strong telegram to our embassy in Moscow stating that the charges contained in the column were false and expressing the hope that Ambassador Standley could find an opportunity of denying them to Molotov.

In spite of the denials of the secretary, stories continued to circulate among certain types of liberals to the effect that he had never been really interested in the maintenance of close friendly relations with the Soviet Union. The secretary, who by nature was extremely sensitive, was conscious of the circulation of these stories, and from that time forth he was on the defensive so far as his attitude toward the Soviet Union was concerned.

THE POLISH EMBASSY

Count Jerzy Potocki.   When I took over my duties in Washington in October 1938 in the East European area of the Department of State, the Polish ambassador was Count Jerzy Potocki, a member of one of the great families of Poland.

Potocki was a fervent Polish patriot. He believed that the Polish armed forces, with the help of the British and the French, would be able to defend their country. He had a particular affection for the romantic Polish cavalry, which on so many occasions during Poland's long history had successfully repelled the enemy. He was by nature an optimist and was convinced until just a few weeks before the German attack that it would be possible to find an honorable way for Poland to remain at peace with its neighbors. He was heartbroken when, within a few days after the war had opened, German tanks had torn the Polish cavalry to pieces and Poland was hopelessly defeated. During the period immediately preceding the German attack and during the subsequent collapse of Poland, he made many appeals to the Department of State for assistance for his country. Although we sympathized with him in his anguish, there was little that the department could do for him and Poland at the time.

Following the invasion of eastern Poland by Soviet armed forces in the middle of September 1939, a couple of weeks after the German attack, left-wing groups in the United States who habitually sought to justify Soviet actions and policies began to argue that Poland, after all, was only a fascist country in which feudalism had still been tolerated and that the Soviets by their invasion were in fact liberating workers and peasants from the exploiters. In view of his background and family, Potocki was a vulnerable target for this type of propaganda. The Polish refugee government, which had been established in London, sensitive to this criticism, decided that Potocki should be replaced by an ambassador with a background and qualifications that might enable him to establish friendly relations with the left-oriented New Dealers who appeared to have more influence than officials of the State Department in the White House. Potocki was therefore retired and replaced by an ambassador who would be less vulnerable to leftist attacks.

Following his retirement Potocki went to Peru where he spent quietly most of the remaining years of his life.

Jan Ciechanowski. Jan Ciechanowski, the successor to Potocki, presented his Letters of Credence to President Roosevelt on March 6, 1941. Several days later, during the course of his calls at the State Department, he entered my room accompanied by Atherton, the acting chief of the Division of European Affairs. I had met Ciechanowski during my first tour in the department in the mid-1920s when he was the minister of Poland to the United States (at that time Poland was represented in Washington by a legation, not an embassy), but I had not seen him for more than fourteen years.

As we became better acquainted, I found that Ciechanowski was not, like Potocki, an extrovert. In his dealings with the State Department he was usually earnest and at times tense. His face had an almost constantly worried expression, as well it might in view of the tragedy for his country that was unfolding before his eyes.

Ciechanowski was not new to the ways of diplomacy. He had served Poland in a diplomatic capacity during the early days of the republic. He had been a member of the Polish delegation to the peace conference in Paris in 1919. During 1921 and 1922 he had been counselor of the Polish legation in London and for nearly seven years, 1922 to 1929, he had served as minister to the United States. In 1941 at the time of his appointment as ambassador to Washington, he had been occupying the position of secretary general of the Polish Foreign Office in London.

The primary tasks of his mission to the United States were to rally support and assistance for Poland and for the Poles in exile and to persuade the U.S. government to pursue policies that would be most likely to contribute to the restoration of an independent Poland following the war's conclusion. Since it was clear that the decisions of a foreign policy character were being made at the time in the White House instead of in the State Department, he concentrated on gaining friendship and support for Poland among those New Dealers in Washington who appeared to have the most influence in the White House. At the same time he did not fail to keep in close friendly touch with members of the department; nevertheless, he seemed to feel that most of them were already sympathetic to the maintenance of Polish independence.

Since he had had the reputation of being more to the left in the political spectrum than members of the more recent governments of Poland, and since his views on such matters as "social justice" and "democracy" were acceptable to the more moderate New Dealers, he met with considerable success in his efforts to win their friendship. When, however, it came to making choices between the ambitions of the Soviet Union for extension of territory under its control and the hopes of refugee Poles for an independent Poland, he found that most of the New Dealers who had influence in the White House, as well as President Roosevelt, were prone to yield to the insistence of the Soviet Union. Ciechanowski struggled tenaciously and courageously on behalf of his country. It was, however, a one-sided struggle. The power of the Soviet Union as represented by its huge armed forces and by the grim determination of its leaders prevailed. Finally, on July 5, 1945, after lengthy negotiations with the Soviets, the United States recognized *de jure* as the government of Poland a body of men selected by and subject to the control of Moscow, and Ciechanowski was relieved of his ambassadorship. Embittered and crushed as he observed the imprisonment, execution, or deportation to Siberia of his fellow countrymen in Poland who had been advocates of Polish independence, he wrote in 1946 a book, *Defeat in Victory*, describing his experiences in Washington during the war years. If Ciechanowski had returned to Poland following the conclusion of hostilities in Europe, he undoubtedly would have suffered the same fate as other Polish leaders who had favored the restoration of an independent Poland. He and his charming and devoted wife, therefore, continued after the war to live quietly in Washington.

His book has been read by relatively few Americans. Professors in our universities rarely place it on the prescribed reading lists of their students. In general, we Americans prefer to forget what happened to Poland, the country for the independence of which Great Britain and France allegedly went to war with Germany to defend. The book does not make pleasant reading for those who believe in the rights of peoples, which President Roosevelt and Churchill so eloquently proclaimed during the early years of the war, or who subscribe to the principles set forth in the charter of the United Nations. My main criticism of the book is the tendency of the author to place too much of the blame on members of the Department of State for the decisions that contributed to the failure of Poland to regain its independence. The members of the department of whom he was critical were not responsible for these decisions. They merely had the unpleasant duty of putting them into effect.

The American Embassy in Moscow

Alexander Kirk and staff. Following Mr. Hull's decision in the spring of 1938 that I was to be assigned to the State Department, Kirk was appointed to succeed me in Moscow. In June 1938 Ambassador Davies departed for his new post as ambassador to Belgium, and Kirk became chargé d'affaires, a position he held until early May 1939 when he was transferred to Berlin to serve as counselor of embassy. Shortly after his arrival in Berlin, Hugh Wilson, our ambassador to Germany, was recalled and Kirk became chargé d'affaires.

The embassy in Moscow never functioned better than it did during the ten months that Kirk was in charge. He was an experienced diplomat with a high degree of sensitivity regarding political trends and developments. His dispatches and telegrams to the State Department were clear and informative. He was fortunate in having on his staff several of the most able junior officers in the service. Stuart Grummon, the first secretary, was also a seasoned diplomat with a wealth of experience in Latin America, Europe, and the Far East. Grummon performed ably as chargé d'affaires during the three months that elapsed between the departure of Kirk and the arrival of Ambassador Steinhardt. Charles Bohlen, the second secretary, was particularly helpful to Kirk. Bohlen was a specialist in East European affairs and a trained Russian language officer. His previous experience in the Soviet Union enabled him to give Kirk guidance with regard to Soviet political developments. Norris Chipman, another able Soviet specialist with Russian language training, was in charge of the economic section of the embassy. And Angus Ward, who also spoke fluent Russian, continued to operate the administrative and consular sections.

Lawrence A. Steinhardt. Steinhardt was born in New York City in 1892 and was educated at Columbia University where he received A.B., M.A., and LL.B. degrees. After a brief period of service in the U.S. Army during the last year of the First World War and a year in the War Department as an associate counsel, he practiced law in New York for some thirteen years. Members of his family, including himself, participated in New York politics and were among the supporters of Franklin Roosevelt. In May 1933, in return for this support, Roosevelt named him minister to Sweden. In 1937 he was appointed ambassador to Peru, and on March 23, 1939, ambassador to the Soviet Union.

Steinhardt arrived in Moscow early in August, only three weeks before Germany began the invasion of Poland that constituted the beginning of the Second World War. He served as ambassador to the Soviet Union until November 1941. Following his return to the United States from the Soviet Union he was appointed on January 12, 1942, ambassador to Turkey, where he served for nearly three years. In December 1944 he was appointed ambassador to Czechoslovakia and in February 1948 ambassador to Canada. In 1950 a plane in which he was traveling from Ottawa to Washington for consultation with the State Department crashed, and he and all others on board were killed.

It will be observed that although Steinhardt was not a career diplomat he had been appointed chief of diplomatic mission at the age of 41 and during the ensuing seventeen years was either minister or ambassador to no less than six world capitals, a career that not one out of a thousand Americans who choose the Foreign Service as a career is able to achieve.

There have been strong differences of opinion among members of the State Department and of the Foreign Service whose work brought them in close contact with Steinhardt regarding the factors that contributed to his remarkable career. Some of them have insisted that he was appointed to post after post as a result of pressures brought by friends and relatives who were playing prominent roles in New York and national politics. Others have maintained that the president, after appointing him to Sweden for political reasons, became pleased with his performance at Stockholm and subsequent posts and, therefore, continued to make use of him. There was little doubt that President Roosevelt had a tendency to prefer experienced "political appointees" to professional Foreign Service officers.

Some of my friends who have served under Steinhardt had little respect for him and his ability; others have spoken of him in the highest terms. My own opinion of him, based on the fact that I was in a sense serving as his backstop in the State Department while he was in Moscow and also while he was in Turkey (during a portion of that period I was director for Near Eastern, African and South Asian Affairs), was that he was an energetic, shrewd ambassador who never hesitated to recommend to the department the policies that it should follow in meeting changing situations and who always tried with skill, courage, and determination to carry out the instructions of the White House and the department. He was by nature extremely sensitive and was inclined, sometimes with justification, to be suspicious of the loyalty to him of various members of his staff. When once convinced, however, that his subordinates were endeavoring sincerely to help him, he usually treated them with consideration, invited suggestions from them, and gave them due credit for such contributions as they might make to the mission.

Upon Steinhardt's arrival in Washington in the spring of 1939 from Peru, he consulted with members not only of the Department of State but also of other agencies of the government who had had experience in dealing with the Soviet Union. He had long talks with both Ambassador Davies and Ambassador Bullitt, whose advice, as can well be imagined, differed widely. He also had conferences with U.S. businessmen and journalists who had spent considerable time in the Soviet Union.

After several weeks of consultation and after listening to many conflicting stories, he told me that he had decided to adopt an attitude of friendly reserve in carrying out his duties as ambassador to the Soviet Union. He intended meticulously to refrain from engaging in gushing flattery in his dealings with Soviet officials. He had come to the conclusion that for him to set out to court them would result in a lessening of their respect for him; furthermore, it would lower his own self-respect. It was his intention to praise with due restraint when in his opinion praise was really due and to be courteously firm in defending the legitimate interests of the United States and of individual U.S. citizens. Even in trying circumstances he would not permit himself to engage in tirades or display loss of temper. He had become convinced that reciprocity should be our key to tolerable relations with the Soviet Union. A "tit-for-tat" policy might seem petty. Nevertheless, in view of the differences between the United States and the Soviet Union in systems of government, in procedures, and in objectives, he considered that such a policy was necessary if our relations were not to be of a lopsided character. He said that in telling me this he wanted to make it clear that he was not criticizing the tactics employed by any of his predecessors in the Soviet Union. Every chief of mission, in his opinion, should adopt a style of diplomacy that suited his own character and personality.

I was inclined to agree with the course upon which he had decided but suggested that before departing for Moscow it might be well for him to discuss it with the president and the secretary of state. Only after determining what his tactics as ambassador should be did Steinhardt begin to make contacts with Soviet officials in the United States. These officials were baffled, however, by his friendly yet restrained attitude in discussing matters of common interest. They noted the absence of flattering platitudes in his references to his hopes for friendlier relations between the two countries. After several conversations with him, Oumansky asked me privately what, in my opinion, were the ambassador's feelings with respect to the Soviet Union. I replied that in my opinion the ambassador was a sincere, undemonstrative sort of person who was hoping in a realistic manner to be able to contribute to the improvement of working relations between our two countries.

During the two years that Steinhardt served in the Soviet Union, he and I supplemented the formal official communications between the embassy and the State Department by the exchange of personal letters. There are many things that an ambassador would like officers in the department who are particularly concerned with the country in which he is serving to know—things that he cannot well discuss with complete frankness in telegrams and dispatches. Furthermore, the officers who are serving as an ambassador's backstops in the department frequently find that it would be helpful for them to have information of a kind that cannot be appropriately incorporated in the department's formal instructions. Exchanges of personal letters containing information and suggestions of a semiofficial character serve to promote understanding and teamwork between the State Department and the ambassador. It is my understanding that copies of some of the communications of a personal nature between Steinhardt and me were retained in his files, which since his death are in the possession of the Library of Congress.

It was my custom to discuss drafts of my letters to Steinhardt with the chief or the assistant chief of the Division of European Affairs and also with my associates in the East European area in order to obtain suggestions from them. When I thought that by doing so I could promote understanding between the ambassador and the State Department I would also show to appropriate members of the department his letters to me or excerpts from his letters.

From my vantage point in the State Department it seemed to me that Ambassador Steinhardt did an outstanding job in difficult circumstances during the period of his ambassadorship to the Soviet Union. He, like Kirk, was fortunate in the members of his staff, among whom I might mention Walter Thurston, the counselor, who arrived shortly after the ambassador; Llewellyn E. Thompson, who replaced Bohlen as second secretary in the latter part of 1940; Charles E. Dickerson, first secretary in charge of the economic section who arrived in Moscow early in 1940; Charles Thayer, who returned to Moscow early in 1940; and Angus Ward, first secretary and consul who continued to be in charge of the consular and administrative sections.

George S. Messersmith was a veteran Foreign Service officer whom the president appointed in 1937 to succeed Wilber Carr as assistant secretary of state for administration. Messersmith was what might be called a "hard line" administrator. He did not hesitate when, in his opinion, there was an occasion for sternness to state in strong language his disapproval of actions of, or suggestions from, members of the State Department that touched on administrative matters. I liked and respected Messersmith and as a rule saw eye to eye with him. I can recall only two occasions during our long association on which I received from him what I considered to be a reprimand. One of these occasions was connected with the assignment of Walter Thurston to Moscow as counselor of our embassy; the other had to do with the treatment that our government should accord to the non-American employees of our legations in the Baltic states in the autumn of 1939.

Prior to his appointment to Moscow in the spring of 1939, Thurston had served most of his long career (he had entered the service in 1914 at the age of nineteen) in Latin America. He had never been stationed in, or had any particular interest in, Eastern Europe. He was, therefore, surprised, as were most of us in the European area of the department, when he was assigned to Moscow to succeed Alexander Kirk. He came into my office shortly after his assignment was announced in a dejected frame of mind. He said that he did not believe that he possessed the qualifications that the senior Foreign Service officer in our embassy in Moscow should have and that he knew little about the Soviet Union and the Soviet governmental structure, about the methods employed by Soviet officials in dealing with foreign diplomats, and about the machinations of international communism. Furthermore, he had no acquaintance with the Russian language; he could not even decipher the letters of the Russian alphabet. I sympathized with him. I realized, in particular, how difficult it would be for him to administer our embassy in the Soviet Union unless he had some knowledge of the Russian language. It had long been my view that no officer should be sent to the Soviet Union who did not have at least a smattering of the language of the country. I had, therefore, with the approval of the department, made arrangements with the Slavic departments of several American universities whereby they would give Foreign Service officers who had been assigned to Moscow six weeks of intensive training in the Russian language. I suggested to Thurston that we might arrange for him to undergo such training at Harvard University before his departure.

Thurston was in a somewhat better frame of mind when he left my office. He returned the next day, however, even more downcast. He said that when he had mentioned to Messersmith the possibility of his spending six weeks at Harvard before his departure, the latter had said that the idea of his attempting to learn Russian was absurd; that if he did not wish to go to Moscow he should say so frankly and not try to find excuses for delaying his departure. I told Thurston that since it was I who had suggested that he undertake the study at Harvard, I would inform Messersmith at once that I, not Thurston, was responsible for the idea. Messersmith expressed astonishment when I told him this. He said he was surprised that a Foreign Service officer with my experience should not be aware that it would take years for anyone over 40 to acquire a truly useful knowledge of a foreign language. It would be a waste of time for Thurston to study Russian at Harvard or any other institution. I argued that one of my former chiefs, Dr. Hathaway, had learned to speak excellent German following his assignment at the age of 53 to Munich as consul general. Messersmith replied that he did not care to discuss this matter further with me, that he had had considerable experience in the educational field before entering the service, and that he knew whereof he spoke. Thurston, therefore, proceeded to Moscow innocent of any knowledge of the Russian language. His pride had been touched, however, and he spent many hours a day while in the Soviet Union studying Russian and had a good working knowledge of the language before he left in the latter part of 1942 to accept the position of minister to Salvador. Interesting enough, he was later—in 1946—to succeed Messersmith as ambassador to Mexico, one of the top posts in our Foreign Service.

William H. Standley. In the spring of 1943 the president appointed Admiral William H. Standley as ambassador to the Soviet Union to succeed Steinhardt. Standley had had an outstanding career in the U.S. Navy. He had served as an ensign in the Spanish-American War and had steadily moved upward until in 1933 he was appointed chief of naval operations, the top position of the navy. He retired in 1936 but was brought back to active duty as a four-star admiral in 1941.

Although 69 years of age when he undertook his ambassadorial duties, he was in my opinion—and I saw much of him—as alert, energetic, and active as most men of 50. Following his departure from the Soviet Union in 1943 he went into retirement. He and I, nevertheless, kept in friendly touch with one another up to the time of his death. I felt honored to be able to serve as one of his pallbearers when his body was laid to rest in Arlington Cemetery in the mid-1960s. An excellent account of his experiences as ambassador to the Soviet Union is to be found in a book entitled *Admiral-Ambassador,* written by one of his navy associates, Admiral A. Ageton.

THE AMERICAN EMBASSY IN POLAND

Anthony Joseph Drexel Biddle, Jr. Biddle had been appointed ambassador to Poland in 1937 after having served for nearly two years as minister to Norway. When the Germans moved on Warsaw in September 1939 he and his wife headed the American contingent of the caravan of foreign diplomats that moved slowly over roads clogged with refugees from Warsaw to Bucharest. As the war progressed Biddle served in London as U.S. ambassador to the refugee governments not only of Poland but also of Belgium, Norway, the Netherlands, Yugoslavia, Czechoslovakia, and Greece, as well as minister to the refugee government of Luxembourg. In 1944, when the allies began to establish fronts on the European continent, he resigned his ambassadorships in order to enter the U.S. Army. With the rank of colonel he served during the remainder of the war as liaison and protocol officer between the U.S. armed forces and military and civil officials of our allies. Biddle was easily the most colorful figure of all American diplomats during the period of the Second World War.

Among the members of the staff of our embassy in Warsaw, during the period that I was serving in the Division of European Affairs, were North Winship, the counselor, and Landreth Harrison, the second secretary. Winship, whose ancestral home was in Macon, Georgia, was a member of a well–known southern family. He was a gentleman of the old school, quiet and retiring by nature—an officer who performed his duties meticulously but who, during his 29 years in the service had never sought, or been in, the limelight. I had shared an apartment with Harrison in Riga when he was attached to the Riga consulate and I to the legation, and I knew him to be a resourceful and courageous officer.

Both Winship and Harrison distinguished themselves during the retreat of the members of the diplomatic corps and other foreigners from Warsaw as the Germans in the fall of 1939 shelled and moved into the city. Biddle turned over to them the task of organizing the retreat and maintaining the morale of the American contingent as the long line of automobiles moved slowly over roads that were being bombed by German planes. These two Foreign Service officers not only earned the gratitude of the Americans who were in the retreat but also that of refugees of other nationalities who were traveling in the caravan and to whom they rendered assistance. As reports of the conduct of these and other members of the Foreign Service during the period when the Germans were attacking Warsaw came to my desk, I was filled with pride in the service. Among the other members of the service who won the admiration of their fellows in the State Department was the little group of officers and clerical employees from our consulate in Warsaw who remained behind in order to be of assistance to those U.S. citizens who for various reasons could not leave the city.

CHAPTER 45

THE INTERNATIONAL SITUATION
AS OF OCTOBER 1938

THE MUDDLED EUROPEAN SITUATION

DURING THE FIRST FEW DAYS following my return to the State Department in October 1938, only ten days after the Munich Agreement, I tried to obtain as clear a picture of the European situation as the muddled condition of that continent permitted and simultaneously to gain a better understanding of what the policies of the United States were with respect to that situation.

In my endeavor I drew on my own experiences in Europe in 1919–1921, on what I had learned during the thirteen years that I had been specializing on Eastern Europe while in the Foreign Service, including the four and a half years spent in the Soviet Union, on what I had been able to pick up during my conversations in European capitals in the summer of 1938, and on the expressed views of members of the Department of State in whom I had confidence. I also pored over the telegrams and dispatches that had come from our representatives in Moscow and in other European capitals subsequent to my departure from Moscow on July 2, 1938.

I had observed the grim aftermath of war while serving with the American Red Cross in Western, Central, and Eastern Europe immediately following the First World War, and the thought of another great war was to me abhorrent. The situation in Europe was, therefore, depressing. As I looked at it I felt as though I were a spectator in a gigantic theater of the ancient Greeks, witnessing a play that must almost inevitably end in tragedy.

The atmosphere enveloping Europe was clouded with a mixture of excessive ambitions, fanatical dedication to militant ideologies, fears of war, intrigues, and mutual suspicions. The guiders of the destinies of two great European countries, Germany and the Soviet Union, were discontented with the current distribution of territory and power and with the prevalent social systems of Europe. The rulers of these two countries had no respect for what at the time were the generally accepted concepts of international law or the established conventions governing intercourse among nations. Neither did they feel themselves bound by any international commitments. They had quite different programs, however, for satisfying their respective ambitions—programs and ambitions that clashed sharply with one another.

Hitler seemed prepared to risk German involvement in war if it should become clear that only by force of arms could he bring about the changes he was determined to make—changes which if carried out would result in a Germany that not only dominated Europe but also possessed colonies in other parts of the world. He was apparently hoping to be able to move in the direction of his objectives by chicanery, deceit, maneuvering, threats backed by military power, and even war if he should come to the conclusion that he could not succeed by other methods.

Soviet foreign policies, as I assessed them in the State Department in October 1938, seemed to me to be a logical continuation of the policies that in my opinion Moscow had been following during the preceding four years.

Stalin, I thought, was no less determined than Hitler to effect changes in the face of Europe. His long-term ambitions included a communist Europe controlled by Moscow that could be used as a base for further communist conquests on a world scale. He was, however, more patient and cautious than Hitler. He did not want the Soviet Union in its unprepared state to become involved in a war. He subscribed to the communist dogma to which I have repeatedly referred that eventually an armed conflict between the communist and noncommunist world was inevitable and that it was the duty of the leaders of the communist world to do what they could to delay such a war until communist strength would be preponderant.

Pending a confrontation between the two worlds, in keeping with the communist theories that had been in vogue since the time of Lenin, Stalin was discreetly endeavoring by such means as were at his disposal, including diplomacy, disruptive propaganda, and subversion, to weaken the noncommunist world. He was trying to stimulate dissension within the noncommunist countries and to encourage them to quarrel with one another. It was his hope that while the strength of the noncommunist world was being sapped by bickering and even fighting, he could be rebuilding and strengthening the Soviet fighting machine that had been badly damaged by his own purges, strengthening Soviet economic might, and preparing to take advantage of such opportunities as might present themselves to expand the territory in Europe under communist control.

In view of what I believed to be Stalin's long-term objectives, I had no doubt that he was pleased at the existence of the rift between the Western powers and Germany. This rift served to prevent unity in the noncommunist world and also broadened his opportunities for maneuvering. He was troubled, however, lest Hitler, in trying to carry out his program for the domination of Europe, move toward the east with the aim of overthrowing the Soviet government and gaining control of at least part of the territory comprising the Soviet Union. Therefore, in addition to the longer-term objective of bringing Europe piecemeal into the communist world, Stalin had the more immediate objective of convincing Hitler that it would be unwise for Germany to engage in aggressive adventures that would threaten the integrity of the Soviet Union. In his endeavor to attain this objective he had been trying for several years to prevail upon the European powers, particularly Great Britain and France, to enter into a general collective security pact or a series of pacts of a nature that would cause Hitler to believe that if, because of aggressive action on the part of Germany, the Soviet Union and Germany would find themselves at war, the Western powers would come to the aid of the Soviet Union.

Serious difficulties had arisen in finding formulas for such a pact that would be acceptable to all parties. Great Britain and France, for instance, hesitated to enter into an agreement that would obligate them automatically to attack Germany in case war should develop between that country and the Soviet Union. They did not wish to give the Soviet Union the right to determine the timing and conditions that would plunge them into another great European war. A mutual assistance pact with the Soviet Union, furthermore, would not tend to promote the security of Great Britain and France unless it would obligate the Soviet Union to come to their aid if, as a result of Hitler aggression, they should become involved in a war with Germany. It was in this connection that one of the more serious obstacles to a mutually acceptable agreement had arisen. Since Germany and the Soviet Union had no common border, the Soviet Union could not render truly effective military aid to Great Britain and France in the event that the latter should become involved in war with Germany unless it could send troops against Germany through the Baltic states,

Poland, or Romania, the countries that separated the Soviet Union from Germany. These latter countries were making it clear, however, that they would not agree to permit Soviet troops to use them as corridors to Germany. They believed—justifiably, in my opinion—that Soviet troops, once admitted, would proceed to overthrow their governments and set up communist dictatorships subservient to Moscow. Furthermore, they feared that if they should enter into an agreement that would smack of an alliance against Germany, their stance of neutrality would be lost and the likelihood of an attack on them by Germany would be increased.

Great Britain and France, recognizing the cogency of these arguments, were unwilling to press these countries to take what the latter considered to be suicidal decisions. Since mutual assistance pacts of the kind under discussion would be of little value unless military plans for their implementation could be prepared in advance, and since in the absence of corridors between the Soviet Union and Germany no such plans could be made, negotiations between the Soviet Union and Great Britain and France were languishing when I took over my desk in the State Department in October 1938.

Stalin and his associates suspected that the primary reason for the reluctance of Great Britain and France to enter into the kind of a pact that they desired was hope on the part of the Western powers that Hitler, in order to satisfy his ambitions for German expansion, would decide to move against the Soviet Union. They surmised that these powers would be happy to see Germany and the Soviet Union destroying one another and that, in particular, these powers would be pleased if the communist government in Moscow, which had been a disturbing element in Europe for more than twenty years, would be overthrown. Stalin's suspicions had been strengthened by the manner in which Great Britain and France, without consulting the Soviet Union, had entered into an agreement with Hitler at Munich providing for the partition of Czechoslovakia. From his point of view, their unwillingness to come to a direct confrontation with Hitler over Czechoslovakia was an indication that they might well remain quiescent if Hitler should make moves threatening the security of the Soviet Union.

As his hopes of achieving an acceptable defensive understanding with the West had been gradually fading, Stalin had been shifting to another approach in his endeavors to keep the Soviet Union out of a war with Nazi Germany. In the early part of 1938 he and his associates, without discontinuing entirely their discussions with the West, had begun to try by double-talk and innuendoes to convey to Hitler the idea that the Soviet Union would be prepared to have friendly relations with

Germany if it could have adequate assurances that the latter had no intention of making moves that might adversely affect Soviet security.

There were differences of opinion both in Western Europe and the United States regarding Stalin's purpose in dropping these hints. Some observers believed that he was merely engaging in the classic communist game of playing opposing elements of the noncommunist world off against one another in the hope of obtaining advantages for the Soviet Union. Others thought that he was sincerely trying to persuade Hitler that it would be to the latter's advantage to have friendly relations with the Soviet Union. My belief in October 1938 was that Stalin was trying to induce Hitler to come to an understanding with him on a basis of mutual advantage and that he was hoping to convince Hitler that such an understanding would be preferable to a situation in which the Soviet Union, Great Britain, and France were allied against him.

I had no idea at the time, however, that Stalin might be willing to make with Hitler an agreement of a kind that would approach a treaty of alliance. It had seemed to me that for him to enter into such an agreement would be regarded as perfidy by friends and supporters of the Soviet Union everywhere—friends and supporters who regarded Hitler and his nazi-fascist ideology with burning hatred. Millions of Jews, for instance, throughout the world, although not communistically inclined, had been looking with friendly eyes on the Soviet Union primarily because of its opposition to Hitler. How would they feel if Stalin should become an ally of the deadly enemy of their people? The members of the "united fronts against fascism," which Stalin had set up in the countries of the West, had been conscientiously following orders from Moscow in denouncing fascism as the number-one enemy. How would they react if the Soviet Union should suddenly enter into a partnership with the world's leading fascist? Such a move on Stalin's part, it seemed to me, would not be viewed by the communists throughout the world as merely one of the temporary twists and turns they were permitted to take from time to time. It would be looked upon as a betrayal of the world revolution. It was my belief at the time that Stalin would prefer going down in history as a hero who had perished fighting for the revolution to being regarded as a turncoat who had betrayed the revolution for the short-term benefit of the Soviet state.

There was no doubt in my mind that the leaders of Great Britain and France regarded the Soviet Union with distrust. Most of them were fully aware that Stalin and his associates had dedicated their lives to a course that included the eventual overthrow by force of the governments of their countries. Some of them were also painfully conscious of the fact that even while they were carrying on conversations with the Soviet Union, groups of their own nationals, who were members of the Moscow-directed united fronts, were trying under orders from the Kremlin to undermine them personally. They also knew that the rulers of the Soviet Union, in order to attain either their short-term or long-term objectives, would not hesitate to break their written or oral promises if in their opinion they would thus be serving the cause of the revolution.

Undoubtedly there were certain elements in both Great Britain and France that would have been pleased to see Germany and the Soviet Union fighting one another while their own countries remained neutral. I could well understand that many groups in Great Britain and France would not be averse to seeing these two great powers dedicated to the conquest of their own countries weakening themselves by fighting one another. I did not believe, however, that the more responsible British and French leaders were trying to promote war between the Soviet Union and Germany.

I was, of course, not in a position to know precisely what these responsible leaders were thinking and hoping. It was my impression, however, based on numerous conversations and the reading of such documents as were available at the time, that they were planning for their countries to come to the aid of the Soviet Union if it should become involved in a war with Germany as the result of German aggressiveness. They were not planning to do so, in my opinion, because of any predilection for the regime in control of the Soviet Union but because of their fear that in case of a Soviet defeat, which in their opinion would be certain if they should remain neutral, Germany would gain control of vast areas of Soviet territory—areas capable of producing foodstuffs and raw materials that would greatly increase its war potentials.

I regarded the decisions taken by Great Britain and France at Munich in September 1938 as a prelude to further aggressive acts by Hitler. I was not, however, so critical of the British and French as were the American press and public at large. As a result of the conversations that I had had during the course of my visits at capitals in Eastern, Central, and Western Europe during the summer of 1938, I had obtained the impression that the armed forces of Germany were formidable. I could, therefore, understand the hesitation of the British and French leaders at Munich to take steps in the direction of a war that could be disastrous for them. Large sections of the U.S. press and public seemed to be taking it for granted that if the representatives of Great Britain and France had stood firm at Munich, Hitler would have capitulated. These representatives were being castigated as "milktoasts" and "timid souls" for their failure to "call Hitler's bluff."

As of October 1938 Stalin had shared major responsibility for at least a hundred times as much human suffering as Hitler who, although denouncing and persecuting Jews, whom he considered to be the irreconcilable enemies of a Nazi Germany, had not as yet launched his campaign of mass physical extermination. Both dictators had ambitions of an aggressive character and both were dedicated to ideologies that had little in common with the values most Americans had been taught to cherish. Why, then, at that time was the hatred of Hitler in many wide and influential circles in the United States so great that it almost obliterated the black marks against Stalin? Why did millions of noncommunist Americans regard Hitler as the devil incarnate while they looked upon Stalin as a potential savior?

One of the reasons that, rightly or wrongly, I ascribed for this phenomenon was that the Communists were at least professing to be seeking a goal that many Americans regarded as highly idealistic even though perhaps unrealistic: a governmentless, classless society to which each contributed in accordance with his ability and from which each received in accordance with his needs. The goal of the Nazis, on the other hand, seemed to be a society in which a people who considered themselves as racially and ethnically superior would conquer and dominate peoples whom they regarded as inferior.

Another reason seemed to stem from the attitude of Hitler toward the Jews. Stalin and his associates during recent years had imprisoned, tortured, banished to Siberia, or executed many thousands of Jews. Since Trotsky, the archenemy of Stalin at the time, was a Jew, Jews in general were suspect. They had not been persecuted, however, on the ground of their Jewishness. They, along with millions of non-Jews who had met similar fates, had been charged with political and other crimes. Hitler, however, had been singling out for persecution the Jews in the territory under his control and was denouncing Jews in general. It was shocking to the American public that the leader of a country that had contributed so much in the past to Western culture and civilization should embark on a campaign of persecution of persons merely because they happened to have Jewish blood. Millions of American Jews who had relatives and friends in Central or Eastern Europe were particularly concerned and these Jews, as well as millions of non-Jews who had been aroused by Hitler's treatment of the Jews of Central Europe, set about through the press, the radio, and other means of communication to concentrate the attention of the American public on what Hitler was saying and doing.

It was not difficult for the American public to learn to hate Hitler. His hysterical, malicious mouthings, his bellicose and frenzied threats, and his overbearing and vulgar behavior contributed to the hostility toward him of the peoples in Western Europe and the United States. Further-more, the threat that he represented to world peace seemed more imme-diate and, therefore, more alarming than the longer-term and more vague threat represented by Stalin. The fact that he was denouncing commu-nism, the Soviet Union, and the Soviet leaders tended to increase the prestige of Stalin in the United States and to add to the effectiveness of communist-directed organizations in the United States.

The dislike of Hitler and of the ideology that he represented had become so deep that in the autumn of 1938 there was a reluctance on the part of large sections of the American public to believe that he had been successful in creating a Germany militarily more powerful, for the mo-ment at least, than France and Great Britain combined. Officers in our military intelligence who had dared to stress the current military strength of Germany were being accused of bias in favor of Germany and of having fascist tendencies. The united-front organizations in the United States with their communist cores were seizing the opportunity to condemn Great Britain and France, to praise the Soviet Union, and to attack on a personal basis as Nazi sympathizers U.S. officials and institutions that were particularly obnoxious to the communists. In this they were joined by many so-called liberals and liberal organizations.

In my opinion, based on my conversations during the summer in the European capitals and from an examination of the communications that the State Department had received from our embassies in Eastern, Central, and Western Europe, the alternatives that faced the British and French representatives in Munich had been grim. These representatives had believed, and I thought they were justified in their belief, that Hitler was not bluffing, and that unless the Czechoslovak government would be willing to consent to the cession to Germany of the Sudeten areas of Czechoslovakia that were heavily populated with Germans, Hitler would march into Czechoslovakia and take these areas over by force. They had also believed that if a German army should invade Czechoslovakia, France, in keeping with the terms of its treaty with Czechoslovakia, as a matter of honor would declare war on Germany and that Great Britain would have no choice other than to enter the war in support of France.

Thus Great Britain and France, both of which were in a state of unpreparedness, would find themselves at war with a country that was ready to fight. The British and French leaders had been convinced, in my opinion, that there was little likelihood that such forces as Great Britain and France could muster would be strong enough to penetrate Germany and save Czechoslovakia from destruction. They had had no hope that they would receive any material assistance from the Soviet Union if the conference at Munich had ended in war. It was their belief that the Soviet

Union would move against Germany only if the Kremlin should come to the conclusion that Germany had become so weakened from fighting the West that it would not have the strength to put up a strong resistance to an attack from the East. In any event these leaders realized that the Soviet Union would not be able to help them without first committing aggression against one or more countries friendly to the West that separated it from Germany. Neither could they expect help from the United States, which appeared determined to remain neutral in accordance with its existing neutrality legislation.

Furthermore, it seemed to me that the British and French representatives in Munich were not entirely convinced that they would be justified in going to war with Germany in an attempt, which offered little chance of success, to assist Czechoslovakia in retaining the Sudeten area, an area in which the majority of the inhabitants were Germans who had for years objected strenuously to being under Czech rule.

The question that the British and French representatives were compelled to answer at Munich, therefore, was: Should they endeavor to persuade Czechoslovakia to accede to Hitler's demands or should they support Czechoslovakia in standing firm and go to war with Germany when Czechoslovakia was invaded? In deciding to bring pressure on Czechoslovakia to yield to Hitler's demands they were aware that they were leading their countries into one of the greatest diplomatic defeats in history. In spite of the promises that Hitler made at Munich, most of these representatives were far from being convinced that they would not in the future be facing other crises resulting from aggressive adventures on Hitler's part; nevertheless, in their opinion, they were gaining time that could be used to build up the armed strength of Great Britain and France.

It seemed to me in October 1938 that the British and French representatives at Munich should be pitied rather than reviled. They were the victims of history: of shortsighted and, over the long term, unworkable provisions of the Treaty of Versailles; of the failure of the British and French governments to take energetic action when the Germans, contrary to the provisions of the treaty, had begun to arm and when German troops had entered the Rhineland and Austria; and of the apathy of the British and French people in the face of growing German irredentism. The existence of a government in Russia that none of its neighbors could trust also had contributed to the difficulties of Great Britain and France in their endeavors through diplomacy to deal with Hitler.

It was to me inconceivable that Hitler, now that he had gained control of Austria and in essence of Czechoslovakia, would rest quietly regardless of his promises made at Munich so long as Germany remained cut in two by the Polish Corridor. Neither could I envision Poland peacefully giving up the corridor. A clash between Poland and Germany, therefore, seemed inevitable. The conquest of Poland by Hitler would open an avenue for Germany into the Soviet Union or vice versa. What would Great Britain and France do if Hitler attacked? Would the Soviet Union remain quiescent while the Germans moved through Poland toward its borders? These were to me important questions to which I had no ready answers.

It seemed to me that, although the countries caught between the jaws of an aggressive Germany and of an acquisitive Soviet Union had been relieved when the decision in Munich had for the time being averted war, they were continuing to look to the future with misgiving. I was disgusted, however, at the attitude displayed by Poland during and immediately after the Munich conference. Instead of remaining neutral and holding itself meticulously aloof from the great power struggle over Czechoslovakia, Poland played what in my opinion was the role of a vulture by demanding for itself a piece of Czechoslovak territory. The Poles in defense of their actions argued that the inhabitants of Teschen, the district that they insisted on annexing, were for the most part of Polish blood and that the district was so strategically placed that if it were to be a part of the German-controlled truncated Czechoslovakia of the future, it would serve to strengthen the grip of Germany on Poland. They also pointed out in informal conversations that in taking over this small but vulnerable chunk of territory they were not turning against a friendly neighbor and that for several years Czechoslovakia, instead of being a friend, had been trying to persuade Great Britain and France to enter into an arrangement with the Soviet Union, which, if carried out, would mean the sacrifice of the integrity and independence of Poland for the sake of the security of Czechoslovakia. The Poles were referring to an arrangement that would sanction the dispatch of Soviet armed forces across Poland for the purpose of aiding Czechoslovakia in case the latter should be attacked by Germany. Although these arguments served at least partially to explain Polish motives in participating in the mutilation of Czechoslovakia, they did not satisfy wide circles in the West. The Poles, by their ill-considered action in respect to Czechoslovakia, therefore, estranged many persons in Western Europe and the United States who had previously been ardent friends and well-wishers of Poland.

CURRENT U.S. FOREIGN POLICY

It was important for me to know what the U.S. policies were with respect to the European situation, particularly with respect to the Soviet

Union. Without such knowledge I could not move with confidence in making spot decisions on minor matters relating to Eastern Europe or in making recommendations on more important matters touching on that area. In keeping with the sentiments of the country as expressed through Congress and with public statements made by the White House and the State Department, our policy with regard to the struggles that were taking place in Europe was formally one of neutrality. Furthermore, our neutrality laws of the time offered little encouragement either to the aggressor or to those opposing aggression.

In spite of our official stance of neutrality, it was clear to me that our officials—from the president down to the lower echelons of the Department of State—had been in sympathy with the efforts of Great Britain and France to curb Hitler. The president certainly did not wish to see Europe plunged into a war. During the month of September 1938, without trying to pass judgment on the dispute between Germany and Czechoslovakia, he had sent a number of messages to the parties involved urging that their differences be settled by diplomacy rather than force. He had been careful in his public statements not to criticize the British and French representatives at Munich for what they had done. Nevertheless, it was apparent to me that he did not want a European peace based on conditions prescribed by Hitler and that he feared that the decisions taken at Munich might be laying the foundations for just such a peace.

So far as I could ascertain the president did not at the time have a fixed attitude with regard to the Soviet Union. During the almost five years that had elapsed since the establishment of American-Soviet diplomatic relations, he had managed to hold himself aloof from the disputes and bickering that had been one of the features of those relations. Although the U.S. officials who had been on the front lines in our relations with the Soviets had been acting under general or specific instructions that had emanated from the president, he had rarely allowed them to use his name. When our embassy in Moscow had delivered to the Soviet government notes of a kind that the latter did not relish, the embassy had usually indicated that it was doing so under instructions from the U.S. government or from the secretary of state. When it had seemed necessary for unpleasant things to be said to the diplomatic representatives of the Soviet Union in Washington, the secretary of state or one of his subordinates usually performed the task. The impression had gradually been created among Soviet officials and among sympathizers of the Soviet Union in the United States that the president personally was friendly toward the Soviet Union and that his desire for closer and more cordial relations was being undermined by the bureaucracy in the State Department and in other governmental agencies.

In the few discussions that the president had had with Soviet diplomatic representatives he had shown an inclination to be expansively agreeable and to avoid unpleasant topics. From time to time these representatives had taken advantage of his genial attitude to obtain promises or semipromises from him that more mature consideration caused him to regret. For instance, one of the embarrassing dossiers that I found on my desk when I arrived in the State Department related to a promise that the president had made in one of his expansive moments to assist the Soviet Union in building a powerful modern battleship. At the time our shipyards were working day and night in an effort to strengthen our own defenses. Furthermore, we were prevented by law and treaty obligations from constructing and turning over to the Soviet government some of the weapons that they desired for this battleship. The navy, with the president's reluctant acquiescence, had for some time been advancing various reasons, most of them sound, for not carrying out what the Soviets considered to be the president's promise.

My own conclusion was that as of October 1938 the president was fully aware that the Soviet Union had not lived up to the commitments that Litvinov had given him at the time of the establishment of relations in November 1933 and that he had little, if any, confidence in Soviet promises. He liked to believe, however, that in spite of the friction that existed between the two governments he, as an exception, was regarded with veneration and respect by the leaders of the Soviet Union. He had been pleased, therefore, when he had read the flattering dispatches and telegrams Ambassador Davies had sent informing him of the special position that he held in the affections of those leaders.

It seemed to me that the president, despite his distrust of Stalin and his associates, desired them to believe that he personally was friendly toward them and that he would be working more closely with them were it not for the attitude of Congress and of the American public in general. I did not attribute this desire so much to vanity as to his thought that at some time in the future the belief on their part that he was friendly toward them might help him in persuading the leaders of the Soviet Union to follow courses of action beneficial to the United States. The belief that he personally was inclined to be more friendly toward the Soviet Union and more sympathetic to the aspirations of its leaders than members of the State Department and other "old line" government agencies, such as the Departments of War and Navy, also strengthened him in his dealings with the left-wing members of the New Deal, some of whom held high government positions and wielded a tremendous amount of influence.

I was given to understand that in the day-to-day relations with the representatives of the Soviet Union, the president expected the members of the State Department to be scrupulous in protecting and promoting the interests of the United States and of individual U.S. citizens, that he believed that if the United States were to have the respect of Soviet leaders, its representatives should never show lack of courage, and that it was his desire that those of us who were working on matters pertaining to Soviet-American relations should be courteous, fair, and firm in our dealings with Soviet representatives. In my opinion, these views of the president were shared by Secretary Hull, Under Secretary Welles, and my more immediate superiors in the Department of State.

There was nothing ambiguous about the attitude of the president toward Nazi Germany and its leaders. Although he used restraint in his public utterances relating to them, he made no secret of the loathing that he had for the Nazi leaders and of the disgust that he felt at their behavior.

THE SOVIET UNION AND THE UNITED STATES IN THE FAR EAST

Just as the ambitions of the Soviet Union with respect to Europe were clashing with those of Nazi Germany, so were its ambitions with respect to the Far East in sharp conflict with those of Japan. Japan, which at the time was dominated by the militarists, was attempting to obtain control of China by force of arms while the Soviet Union was trying to do so with the help of the militarily well-organized and powerful Chinese Communist Party by infiltration, subversion, and internal insurrection. The Soviet Union was supplying the Chinese government with military equipment in amounts that would encourage it to continue its struggle against the Japanese armed forces. It was careful, however, not to render military assistance in such large quantities as to provoke Japan into a war.

One of the nightmares of the Soviet leaders for several years had been that the Soviet Union might be attacked simultaneously by Germany and Japan. They were, therefore, hoping that Japan would become so bogged down as the result of its war with China and of its ventures in countries to the south of China that it would not wish to add the Soviet Union to its list of enemies. Since the early 1930s these leaders had also been hoping that conflicts of interest in the Far East between Japan and the United States would eventually lead to a Japanese-American war, which would seriously weaken the two great powers most likely to try to prevent the realization of Soviet plans for the Pacific. An armed conflict among the noncommunist powers in Europe accompanied by an American-Japanese war in Asia would have, in my opinion, fulfilled the fondest hopes of the Kremlin.

Although our government was aware of Soviet long-term ambitions in the Far East, its first concern in that area was the short-term ambitions and the overtly aggressive actions of Japan. Just as Germany in the autumn of 1938 was looked upon in the United States as the most dangerous nation in Europe, so was militaristic Japan regarded as the arch-villain of the Pacific. Such dangers as the Soviet Union might present in the future to world peace were, in comparison with the immediate dangers offered by Germany and Japan, so remote that there was a tendency to downplay them.

CHAPTER 46

SOVIET FOREIGN POLICIES, PARTICULARLY THOSE RELATING TO EUROPE, BETWEEN THE MUNICH AGREEMENT AND THE OUTBREAK OF THE SECOND WORLD WAR

NO EVIDENCE OF ABANDONMENT BY THE SOVIET UNION OF ITS LONG-TERM BASIC FOREIGN POLICIES

WHILE THE WHITE HOUSE and the higher echelons of the Department of State were concerning themselves with broad problems of peace and war, we in the East European area, during the period between the Munich Agreement (September 29, 1938) and the outbreak of the Second World War (September 1, 1939), were engaging in the more modest tasks of attempting to keep ourselves informed with regard to what was taking place in the countries of Eastern Europe, of passing along our views on East European developments to other areas of the department and other agencies of the government, and of assisting in the conduct of day-to-day relations between the United States and the countries of Eastern Europe.

An important function of our area was that of endeavoring, in cooperation with our embassy in Moscow, to gauge the foreign policies, attitudes, intentions, and actions of the Soviet Union. The highly qualified personnel in our embassy in Moscow furnished us translations or summaries of statements appearing in the Soviet press, including pronouncements of responsible Soviet leaders relating to international developments, summaries of their conversations with Soviet and other officials, and their own views regarding trends in Soviet foreign policies. Although subsequent studies caused me to believe that, during the months following the Munich Agreement, certain shifts were taking place in Soviet short-term policies and tactics to meet changes that were occurring in the international situation, I did not find convincing evidence that the Soviet Union was abandoning any of its long-term objectives or basic foreign policies.

Moscow Continues to Adhere to Its Program of Communist World Revolution

It seemed to me that if the Kremlin sincerely desired to obtain the cooperation of the West in maintaining peace in Europe, it might have been willing to shelve at least temporarily attempts to promote revolution in the countries of the West; it might have sought to obtain the confidence of the leaders of those countries by ceasing to encourage the Moscow–controlled united fronts in the West to attack these leaders and their policies. The fact was that, while Soviet spokesmen during the period between the Munich Agreement and the outbreak of the Second World War were pursuing their tactics of double-talk, so far as Germany and the Western powers were concerned, they were simultaneously boasting of the success of the international revolutionary activities that were being carried on through the All-Union Communist Party, the Communist International, and kindred organizations. It was difficult for me to understand how so many noncommunists in the United States could maintain that the basic long-term objectives of the Soviet Union were changing, and that the Soviet Union was becoming a "liberty loving nation" interested only in opposing aggression and preserving the peace. It seemed to me that even the most rabid left–leaning wishful thinkers would have had some second thoughts if they had gone to the pains of learning what the Soviet press and Soviet leaders were saying.

The Moscow newspapers, for instance, on the fifteenth anniversary of Lenin's death gloried in the revolutionary achievements and aims of Stalin. In a dispatch dated January 30, 1939, our embassy in Moscow reported that:

> In its leading editorial of January 21, *Pravda* states in part as follows: "...During the past 15 years the world communist movement has grown into a tremendous force...At present, the communists of all nations are aiming their blows at the primary enemy of the toilers—at fascism. The communists are mobilizing all forces capable of fighting in the ranks of the people's front against fascism. *The Party is putting into effect Lenin's directions regarding the necessity of utilizing the internal contradictions between imperialistic plunderers in the interests of the Soviet people and in the interests of the international proletariat...*"

In a full-page dissertation on Lenin's testament and Stalin's pledges, published in *Pravda* of January 21, Emelyan Yaroslavski, one of the Party's leading theoreticians and historians, concludes with the following statement: "We keep in our hearts, and we are carrying out in practice, the pledge that Stalin made ('We swear, Comrade Lenin, that we will spare not even our lives to strengthen and broaden the union of the toilers of the whole world—the Communist International'). *The time is not distant when the crimson banner of Marx-Engels, Lenin-Stalin will flow over the entire world, for the great truth of bolshevism and the tremendous force of Marxian-Leninist ideas are irresistible"* . . .

An article . . . by D. Manuilski (a member of the Executive Committee of the Comintern and one of its principal leaders) . . . contains the following passages referring to the Comintern: "Under the direct influence of Leninist-Stalinist doctrines the Communist Party of France has grown into a first-rate political force. Also growing into a serious political factor is the Communist Party of the United States, which has become stronger in its fight against fascism and in its efforts to develop the democratic front. It is drawing into its ranks more and more of the best people in the American labor movement."

I have emphasized several of the passages in the above excerpts from the embassy's dispatch because I regard them as particularly significant from the point of view of Soviet policies and intentions.

The Views of the U.S. Embassy in Moscow with Regard to the Post-Munich Agreement Foreign Policies of the Kremlin

In the fall of 1938 we received a telegram from Moscow, dated October 31, in which our embassy described what it regarded as the "general tenor of Soviet opinion on foreign affairs since the Munich agreement." We found ourselves in general accord with the views expressed in this telegram, which read in part as follows:

The recent developments in connection with the Czechoslovak crisis have confronted the Soviet Union with the threat of isolation and, although a favored theme of published utterances here is the ability of the country to stand alone on the strength of its own resources and the adequacy of its own defenses, the weight of evidence at present points to a disinclination on the part of the Soviet Government to maintain a position of isolation as regards other countries and to a readiness to join in any movement of international concern which would enhance the prestige of the Soviet Government without incurring too great a risk. The impression prevails, however, that for the moment at least the Kremlin is inclined to await the course of further developments abroad to assist it in determining its policy in relation to other countries, either singly or collectively, and to refrain from any definite commitment in policy until these developments are more clearly defined. In the meantime it is believed the Soviet Government is continuing the program of armaments especially as regards the air force and the navy even in spite of the sacrifice which the concentration on heavy industries imposes upon the population. It is also believed that an added impetus may be given to the activities abroad of the Comintern and certain indications have become apparent of an attempt in this way to accentuate the class struggle and the differences between government factions in certain countries.

I have underscored the words "without incurring too great a risk" because I consider them to possess particular significance. They tended to confirm our belief that the Soviet government, while continuing to encourage movements of "international concern," had no intention of placing itself in a position in which it would become involved in a war with any great power unless the Soviet Union itself should become the object of attack or should be seriously menaced. The telegram also gave support to our belief that the current policy of the Kremlin continued to be (1) to discourage possible aggression against it by building up Soviet armed forces with all speed, and (2) simultaneously, with the aid of the united fronts operating in the West under the direction of the Communist International, to bring pressure upon the governments of the West to adopt foreign policies that would tend to make the West, rather than the Soviet Union, the chief antagonist of Nazi Germany.

The Soviet Union Does Not Envisage Cordial Relations with Any Noncommunist Country Except on a Temporary Basis of Expediency

Hidden away at the end of a dispatch from the embassy dated November 25, 1938, was a passage that we in the East European area regarded as sufficiently important to justify our bringing it to the attention of those members of the State Department who still looked upon the Soviet Union as a country with which a noncommunist state could have stable, normal relations. That passage read as follows:

The normal process of cooperation between countries in conformity with the established principles which govern the relations of the United States with friendly governments does not appear to constitute a basic factor in

Soviet foreign policy and, if the repeated utterances of Soviet leaders are considered, it may be assumed that the Kremlin does not envisage cordial relations with capitalist governments on any permanent basis but rather as a temporary expedient dictated by the more immediate objectives of Soviet policy.

This passage was the more significant because the dispatch in which it was incorporated had been prepared by three of the political officers of the embassy: Kirk, the chargé d'affaires; Grummon, the first secretary; and Bohlen, the second secretary. When I drew this passage to the attention of Moffat, the chief of the European Division, on December 21, 1938, he attached to the dispatch a memorandum in which he stated that the officers in the embassy "seem to feel that no foreign government mapping out its foreign policies should place any dependence upon sustained Soviet cooperation or should consider Soviet gestures of friendship as other than opportunistic moves taken in order to meet some international exigency." I had personally been convinced from years of observation that no amount of wishful thinking, flattery, cajolery, or concessions could alter the basic foreign policy of the Soviet Union with respect to noncommunist countries. There were still at the time many Americans in high positions and also many foreigners who thought they might be able to persuade the Soviet government to change its policies.

The attitude of the Soviet Union in the spring of 1939 seemed to be in general similar to its attitude in October 1938: observing developments; criticizing the actions, nonactions, and foreign policies of governments of noncommunist countries, including those of France, Great Britain, Germany, and at times even the United States; and refraining from taking a position that would place it irrevocably in the camp of either the "Western imperialists" or the "Fascist aggressors." The tendency that had been noted since even before the Munich Agreement of lumping together as members of the hostile capitalistic camp all noncommunist countries seemed to have become somewhat more pronounced. There was also a growing inclination to place more blame for the existing dangerous situation in Europe on Great Britain and France than on Germany and Italy.

SOVIET RESPECT FOR DYNAMIC FASCIST POWERS INCREASES AS COUNTRIES OF WEST DISPLAY TIMIDITY AND VACILLATION

Judging from articles appearing in the Soviet press and the pronouncements of Soviet leaders, there was a growing respect for the dynamic fascist powers and an increasing contempt for the vacillating and timid countries of the West. Since all recent German moves had been in an eastern direction, it seemed to us that the Soviet Union should have had grounds for concern. Soviet spokesmen, however, were assuming an attitude of confidence. They were maintaining that the Soviet Union had nothing to fear from Germany and that German moves during March and April 1939 were merely preparations for more important moves to be made later toward the west. Furthermore, they were pointing out, the Soviet Union was sufficiently powerful to beat back successfully any move that might be made against Soviet vital interests.

It was our opinion, however, that behind their façade of unconcern Soviet leaders were worried. They could not be sure what Hitler's intentions might be with regard to the Soviet Union. This worry, we believed, was responsible in part for an increase in Soviet efforts to strengthen the Red Army and Soviet Air Force. Another factor contributing to the Soviet drive to build up rapidly its armed strength was, in our opinion, the desire of the Soviet leaders to have the military capability, in case a war should break out between the countries of the West and Germany, to take advantage of any opportunity that might present itself to promote their long-term policy of world revolution by increasing the territory in Europe under communist control.

A telegram that the State Department received from our embassy in Moscow on April 6, 1939, caused us to believe that the views of our officers on duty in the embassy with regard to current Soviet attitudes were in general similar to our own. In that telegram the embassy indicated that, in the face of the recent developments in the West, Soviet foreign policy "can be described as merely negative in character and distinctly cautious in its application." It pointed out that during recent months "England and France were singled out for special condemnation as wreckers of the policy of collective security through the medium of which the Soviet Government had hoped to charge other countries with the brunt of impeding the expansion of Nazi Germany." It stressed that the violent campaign that the Soviet press had been carrying on against Germany had slackened and that "symptoms have even been detected of a possible inclination on the part of the Soviet Government to reduce the element of friction in its relations with Germany."

The telegram indicated that at the time of the Munich Agreement the "crisis circumstances" were such that Soviet Russia could envisage a war in which it need take no part on an extensive scale. Although it had declared itself ready to discharge the obligation to which it had committed itself, it had not during that period projected "itself as a dominating factor in influencing the course of events and, in spite of assertions to the contrary, no proof" had been "forthcoming that the Soviet Government succeeded in convincing the democratic powers that it could or would lend assistance commensurate with the strength of which it boasted."

The embassy expressed the view in this telegram that the European situation as of early April 1939 was quite different from that in September 1938: "The fate of Czechoslovakia and Memel, the threat to Danzig with attendant repercussions in Poland, and the economic hold in Rumania purported to be a trend which might eventually menace Soviet territory." Nevertheless, in spite of the changed situation, the embassy stated, "insofar as may be judged from public expressions, Soviet opinion does not consider that these moves actually constitute the pursuit on the part of Hitler of a policy of expansion to the east but may be regarded as merely preparatory to action in the west, or in the southeast, which would not necessarily constitute a menace to the Union."

The telegram expressed the view that despite the "vast expenditures of effort as well as of human and material resources" there was no proof that "the Soviet Union has as yet succeeded in developing a military force of superior power as an offensive weapon or produced a nation capable of the sustained effort which a war would entail." The knowledge, which it was to be assumed the Soviet government had of its military shortcomings combined with the fear of a war on two fronts, had contributed, in the opinion of the writers of the telegram, to a Soviet foreign policy "based primarily on considerations of defense."

In view of the impression that the last paragraph of the telegram of April 6 made on the State Department, I quote it below in full:

These, therefore, are the tests which Stalin may be expected to apply in determining Soviet policy in any situation precipitated by the conduct of aggressor states and these tests may be regarded as applicable not only in his relations in the West but also in the Far East. With the foregoing considerations in view, he is exercising and will continue to exercise extreme caution in his relations with all foreign countries. He will await developments abroad and will gauge those developments on the basis of the actual threat to Soviet security which he regards as inherent therein. He will avoid any commitments which might seriously restrict his freedom of action or embroil the country in conflicts in which its immediate interests are not involved, and even in the presence of commitments he will pursue a realistic policy in varying, according to the shifting demands of those interests, the manifestations of attitude toward foreign countries. He may promote divergencies among other nations which might tend to divert or lessen the menace of attack but he will refrain from provocative acts which increase that menace. Finally, in the face of a menace that seems imminent, he will endeavor to extend the system of collective action and to align himself therewith in order to lessen the danger to Russian frontiers on all sides. If, in spite of all precautions, a war should develop which in Stalin's opinion would threaten the security of the Soviet Union it must be assumed that he will fight. Even then, however, it is believed that he will limit the military efforts of the Soviet Union to the exigency of defensive operations and while reducing to the minimum the strain on the capacities of the country and of the regime which a war would entail, will in the end look to the advantages which may be derived from internal upheavals in other countries resulting from the strain to which they will be subjected in the process thereof. The Communist state, as based on the principle of revolution, has evolved into a dictatorship as based on the personal power of Stalin, but the Soviet state still professes irreconcilable hostility towards the capitalist world, and, in the last analysis, Stalin, in mobilizing the forces of the Soviet Union to the service of his dictatorship, need not be expected to ignore that factor both as a defensive and offensive weapon for the safety and profit of his regime.

SOVIET DETERMINATION TO OBTAIN HEGEMONY OVER THE COUNTRIES OF EASTERN EUROPE IS A STUMBLING BLOCK IN NEGOTIATIONS WITH FRANCE AND BRITAIN

I thought that the Soviet Union was, during the spring of 1939, taking advantage of negotiations with Great Britain and France in order to achieve one of its longer-term objectives, that is, attaining hegemony over the countries bordering it to the west. If it could prevail upon Great Britain and France to agree to give it a free hand in Eastern Europe there would be no great power to which Finland, Estonia, Latvia, Poland, and Romania could turn in their efforts to escape Soviet pressure except Germany, which would be just as dangerous to their integrity and independence as the Soviet Union. It might make it much easier for the Soviet Union to gain hegemony over the smaller countries of Eastern Europe if the peoples of those countries would be given to understand that the democratic powers of the West had made an agreement with the Soviet Union to support the latter in taking any action with respect to them that it considered to be in the interest of its security.

In the late spring of 1939 Welles, the under secretary of state, having noted the telegrams from Moscow regarding the progress of the Soviet-German conversations, called Moffat and me into his office to discuss some of the obstacles that seemed to be blocking the successful conclusion of the conversations between the Soviet Union and the British and French. Following our discussion he asked us to send him a memorandum on the subject. On June 2, therefore, I wrote a memorandum giving special attention to the problem of the Baltic states that had come to the fore in the latest exchange betewen the British and the Soviets. I pointed out that an examination of the text of what appeared to be the latest British proposal to the Soviet government indicated that Great Britain and France were not prepared to agree to support the Soviet Union in case that country should become involved in a war with Germany as a result of an invasion of the Baltic states by Soviet troops, unless the Baltic states, threatened by German aggression, had requested Soviet assistance. I added:

> It would appear, therefore, that the main point of the dispute... is whether or not the Soviet Union, with the support of Great Britain and France, may invade Latvia, Estonia, or Finland when it comes to the conclusion that the independence of these countries is being seriously threatened by Germany.
>
> The... Baltic countries fear that Great Britain may accede to the Soviet demands. They apparently feel that the granting of these demands will in effect mean the granting of a Soviet overlordship of the Baltic States and the according of a position to the Soviet Government which will enable it to exert external or internal pressure upon them at will. There is evidently a fear that the Soviet Government might take advantage of such a position in order to bring about communist revolutions in these countries, or at least to reduce them to satellites of the Soviet Union.
>
> The Soviet Government undoubtedly realizes that the British Government, in view of all the international considerations involved, would be extremely reluctant and possibly even unwilling to accede to its demands. The question, therefore, presents itself as to whether the demands are made merely for the purpose of gaining greater security or in order to effect a breakdown in the negotiations which would result in the Soviet Union being able, for an indefinite period, to play off the so-called democratic block against the Axis.

CHAPTER 47

EUROPE DRIFTING TOWARD WAR

PRESIDENT ROOSEVELT'S DEMARCHE OF APRIL 14, 1939

AS THE GERMAN AND ITALIAN ATTITUDE toward their neighbors in Eastern and southeastern Europe became increasingly threatening, President Roosevelt, on April 14, made a move that he apparently hoped would relieve world tensions. It took the form of identical notes addressed to Hitler and Mussolini. These notes, which were couched in friendly language, stressed the fears of the people of the world of a new war or a series of wars. In the notes the president emphasized that wars could be disastrous both to the victors and the vanquished and expressed his conviction that the cause of world peace would be advanced if the nations of the world could obtain a frank statement relating to the "present and future policy of governments." More specifically, he asked:

> Are you willing to give assurance that your armed forces will not attack or invade the territory or possessions of the following independent nations: Finland, Estonia, Latvia, Lithuania, Sweden, Norway, Denmark, The Netherlands, Belgium, Great Britain and Ireland, France, Portugal, Spain, Switzerland, Liechtenstein, Luxembourg, Poland, Hungary, Rumania, Yugoslavia, Russia, Bulgaria, Greece, Turkey, Iraq, the Arabias, Syria, Palestine and Iran?

Such assurances, the president indicated, should cover a period of not less than ten years or a quarter of a century—if one dared look that far ahead. He promised to transmit the assurances, if given, to the appropriate governments who, he was reasonably sure, would give assurances of a reciprocal nature so that the world would be granted a measure of relief.

The president added that if assurances of the kind suggested could be exchanged, the United States would be prepared to participate in discussions regarding the manner in which the peoples of the world could obtain progressive relief from the crushing burden of armament and regarding the manner in which avenues of international trade could be opened up so that every nation would be able to buy and sell on equal terms in the world market.

Copies of these telegrams were sent by the State Department to our diplomatic missions in the countries mentioned in them for delivery to the respective governments.

According to my recollection, the members of the State Department, including the secretary, were not particularly happy over these telegrams. It was our understanding that the idea of sending them had generated in the White House and that the first draft of them had been prepared by the president himself. He had, however, submitted it to the department for comment and Welles and several other members of the department had prepared a counterdraft in a secretive manner. The president was proud of his own draft and although he accepted several suggestions from the department, he had insisted on using his own ideas and language to the maximum extent. From a technical point of view the draft that he finally approved left much to be desired. There were, for instance, at that time no such "independent nations" as "Great Britain and Ireland," "the Arabias," "Russia," or "Palestine."

Some of us were also puzzled regarding the purpose of these telegrams. Past performance had shown that no reliance could be placed upon promises made by Hitler and Mussolini. Nevertheless, an inference might well be drawn from the contents of these messages that the president believed that additional assurances from these two dictators would be of value. In our opinion a reply from Hitler and Mussolini containing the assurances requested might well have given many of the optimistic lovers of peace a false impression that the danger of war was being averted. Nevertheless, the telegrams coming into the White House and the State Department from many of the governments that had been sent copies of the president's messages expressed warm praise for his action. Some of them in referring to his messages used such phrases as "statesmanlike step" and a "noble initiative." Kalinin, for instance, after congratulating the president on his "noble appeal" said: "You may be sure that your initiative finds the warmest response in the hearts of the peoples of the Soviet Socialist Union who are sincerely interested in the preservation of universal peace."

Telegrams received by the State Department during the next two days indicated that Hitler was furious when he read the president's telegram and that his first impulse was to send an angry reply. Instead of yielding to this impulse, however, he instructed his diplomatic representatives in most of the countries mentioned in the message to inquire of the governments to which they were accredited whether they considered their countries to be in danger of a German attack. Most of the governments of those states that were most vulnerable to German attack were careful to give answers to the German inquiries that would not be offensive to Hitler. Hitler was, therefore, in a position to maintain that the president's message had been based on fears that did not exist and that it had been sent for purposes other than the promotion of peace.

GREAT BRITAIN AND FRANCE STRIVE TO OBTAIN THE COOPERATION OF THE SOVIET UNION

As the British and French governments continued to pursue their new policy of containing Hitler by constructing around Germany a wall consisting of a series of defense agreements with Germany's neighbors, many influential political leaders in France and particularly in Great Britain began to agitate in favor of including the Soviet Union in this wall. If we go to war with Germany, these leaders insisted, a strong eastern front against Germany will be necessary. Only the Soviet Union can provide such a front. Furthermore, they argued, the successful conclusion of a defensive alliance with the Soviet Union might well give Hitler pause. This agitation was so appealing that in April 1939, yielding to internal pressure, the British and French governments, not without hesitation, began negotiations with the Soviet government in the hope that some kind of military alliance might be worked out that would be acceptable to Great Britain, France, the Soviet Union, and the other countries of Eastern Europe.

These negotiations were just starting when early on the morning of May 4, 1939, the announcement was made in Moscow that Litvinov had been relieved at his own request of his duties as commissar for foreign affairs and that his place would be taken by Molotov, who would continue as chairman of the Soviet of People's Commissars (a position corresponding to that of prime minister in the countries of Western Europe). Since Litvinov was widely looked upon in the West as an advocate of cooperation between the West and the Soviet Union, this announcement gave rise to fears that his dismissal might indicate a change in the foreign policies of the Soviet Union—a change in the direction of establishing closer relations with Germany.

So far as I could ascertain the substitution of Molotov for Litvinov did not seriously affect the conduct of the negotiations between the Soviet Union and the two Western powers, Great Britain and France. Since Molotov was more forthright and less evasive than Litvinov, it seemed to me that there was some advantage in his acting as the chief spokesman for the Soviet negotiators. Both the Soviet Union and Poland were among the countries for which the East European area of the State Department had special responsibilities. We were able to obtain only a general idea of what was going on, since many of the details became known only much later. I shall limit myself to touching on those aspects of the negotiations that impressed me most deeply in 1939.

It was not surprising to me that the British and French negotiators should immediately run into the same difficulties they had encountered during the negotiations with the Soviets prior to Munich. They came again face to face with the same old question: "How could Soviet troops enter Germany without crossing the territory of a power that would regard such a crossing as a violation of its sovereignty?" Not a single country, with the exception of Czechoslovakia—which lay between Germany and the Soviet Union although it had no common borders with the Soviet Union—alarmed though it might be at the threats presented by Hitler, was willing to agree to the passage through it of Soviet troops. Every European country bordering on the Soviet Union distrusted its eastern neighbor as much as, if not more than, it distrusted Germany. For twenty years these countries had been leading a more or less precarious existence under the shadow of a gigantic entity, which through its communist agents, its well–organized propaganda media, and its huge resources had been systematically trying to gain control over them. They were aware that Communists throughout the world had been taught to regard the Soviet Union as the power base for the promotion of the international communist revolution and they knew that it would be contrary to the concepts of Leninism and Stalinism for the Soviet Union not to take advantage of the presence of Soviet armed forces in neighboring countries in order to set up in them communist or united-front governments subservient to Moscow. The public announcements and the treaty commitments that Soviet officials had made over the years to the effect that the Soviet Union would respect the independence of its neighbors had been belied too often by utterances and actions of communist groups and persons under the control of the Kremlin.

During the negotiations in the spring and summer of 1939 the British and French tried to convince the Soviets that the guarantees that Great Britain and France had extended to Poland and Romania were in effect contributing to Soviet security since those guarantees had given the Germans to understand that they could not pass through Poland and Romania for the purpose of attacking the Soviet Union without going to war with Great Britain and France. Germany would find it exceedingly difficult, the allied representatives argued, to conquer the Soviet Union if its only means of access by land into the Soviet Union would be through Lithuania, Latvia, and Estonia. The Soviet negotiators, however, continued to insist that Germany through "indirect aggression" might gain control of the Baltic states and Finland and prepare in them an armed base for attacks on the Soviet Union. They demanded, therefore, that any agreement reached should include a provision that Great Britain and France and the Soviet Union guarantee all European countries bordering on the Soviet Union—Finland, Estonia, Latvia, Poland, and Romania— against both direct and indirect aggression. It was clear not only to the British and French but also to the governments of the bordering countries that the Soviet Union was trying to maneuver itself into a position that would enable it unilaterally to decide whether any of the countries lying between it and Germany, particularly the Baltic states, were in serious danger of being taken over by Germany. If the Soviet government should decide that any country was in such danger, it could, under the arrangements it was seeking, automatically move its forces into that country without awaiting the approval of Great Britain and France or of that country's government.

As the negotiations progressed, Finland, Estonia, and Latvia became more and more concerned lest Great Britain and France yield to the Soviet demands. They were convinced that if by silence they should fail to denounce an arrangement under which the Soviet Union would be free to "come to their assistance," they would be sacrificing what they considered to be one of the basic principles of their continued existence as independent nations—the principle of neutrality. It would also mean, they believed, that the Soviet government, once it had assumed the role of their protector, would begin to try to exercise suzerainty over them— suzerainty that would eventually lead to their absorption.

Early in June, therefore, Finland, Latvia, and Estonia publicly announced their determination to remain neutral and reject any unsought guarantee. On June 7, 1939, in order to demonstrate their neutrality, Estonia and Latvia entered into nonaggression pacts with Germany— pacts similar in nature to those they already had with the Soviet Union.

The difficulties of the negotiations were compounded by the Soviet manner of negotiating. Again and again when the British and French had succeeded in working out formulas that in their opinion should satisfy certain Soviet demands, the Soviet negotiators would raise additional objections or lay down new conditions.

In the middle of July, even though major differences had not been eliminated, the Soviet government suggested that an Anglo-Franco military mission come to Moscow for discussions with a group of Soviet military leaders regarding the manner in which any political agreement that might be reached could be supplemented by military plans and dispositions. The British and French, hoping that this suggestion indicated that the Soviet Union was really interested in reaching an agreement, acquiesced.

The Allied military mission arrived in Moscow on August 11 and met with the Soviet military leaders on the following day. During the ensuing week both the political and the military discussions bogged down. Among the differences that appeared to be almost insoluble was the unwillingness of the Soviets to consider any military plans that did not provide for troops to be sent into eastern Poland and the continued unwillingness of the Poles to agree, prior to the actual outbreak of war, to the presence of Soviet troops on Polish soil.

CHAPTER 48

GERMAN-SOVIET TRADE RELATIONS AND THE NONAGGRESSION PACT

GERMANY AND THE SOVIET UNION BEGIN EXCHANGE OF VIEWS REGARDING TRADE RELATIONS

WHILE FROM THE VANTAGE POINT of the State Department we were attempting to keep ourselves informed regarding the progress of British-French-Soviet negotiations, we were also studying a series of telegrams in early 1939 from our embassy in Moscow regarding developments in German-Soviet relations. In view of the confidential nature of the source of information in them, these telegrams were highly classified and their distribution strictly limited. Those of us who had access to them were enjoined not to discuss them in the presence of anyone who was not on the distribution list.

Several of these telegrams indicated that discussions were taking place between representatives of the German and Soviet governments looking toward the conclusion of a commercial agreement. These discussions seemed to taper off during March and April. In a telegram from our embassy dated May 20, however, we were informed that the German ambassador to the Soviet Union, Graf von der Schulenburg, had had a long discussion in Berlin in the middle of May with Ribbentrop, the German foreign minister, regarding German-Soviet relations, during the course of which Ribbentrop had told the ambassador that, in the opinion of the German government, communism had ceased to exist in the Soviet Union, that the Communist International was no longer a factor of importance in Soviet foreign relations, and that consequently it was felt that no real ideological barrier remained between Germany and Russia. "Under the circumstances," according to the embassy's informant, Ribbentrop had continued, "it was desired that the Ambasador return to Moscow to convey very discreetly to the Soviet Government the impression that Germany entertained no animosity toward it and to endeavor to ascertain the present Soviet attitude toward German-Soviet relations." This telegram strengthened our belief that the hint that Stalin and other Soviet spokesmen had been dropping of their willingness to have friendly relations with Germany had been stirring the interest of the German government.

GERMAN-SOVIET TRADE TALKS
BEGIN TO BROADEN INTO POLITICAL DISCUSSIONS

In a telegram dated May 22, 1939, the embassy reported that, according to one of its reliable sources, the German ambassador upon his return to Moscow had had a long talk with Molotov during which they had touched upon German-Soviet relations. The German ambassador had told Molotov that he had found the attitude in Berlin regarding the Soviet Union to be more favorable and inquired whether it might not now be possible to continue the economic conversations that had been in abeyance for several months. Molotov, apparently quick to sense that the ambassador was exploring the possibility of an improvement of German-Soviet political as well as economic relations, had expressed doubt regarding the feasibility of any improvement in economic relations in the absence of a "political basis" and had asked the ambassador what he thought. The ambassador, who had already done his part by cautiously veering the conversation into political channels, had replied that as an ambassador he was not a policymaker and was, therefore, not in a position to give an authoritative opinion on a matter of this kind. He had suggested, however, that it might be helpful if Molotov as prime minister could explain what the Soviet government envisaged as a "political basis." Molotov, who was apparently determined that if there were to be any talks of a political character between the Soviets and the Germans, they should be undertaken at German initiative, had countered that this was a matter that needed further consideration. Thus, this little friendly exploratory bout ended in a draw.

Grummon, who as chargé d'affaires had signed the telegram, added that the U.S. embassy's German informant had stated that the ambassador had obtained the impression that the reserve shown by Molotov during this conversation had been due to the unwillingness of the Soviet government to give consideration to any German proposal that was not of a specific character.

The Germans apparently kept the Soviets waiting for over a month before authorizing further conversations between Schulenburg and Molotov. During that period, however, Schulenburg had not been entirely idle. He had been gently and cautiously prodding his government not to let the possibility pass by of coming to an understanding with the Soviet government, which seemed to be willing to talk.

In a telegram dated June 29, 1939, our embassy in Moscow reported that it had learned from one of its sources that Schulenburg, while in Berlin during the latter part of June, had been informed by Ribbentrop that "Germany had no aggressive intentions in regard to the Soviet Union" but that Ribbentrop had stressed that the ambassador was not authorized to convey his remark as a statement of German policy to the Soviet government. Apparently the German government was waiting for the Soviet government to approach it before making an authoritative statement of its attitude toward the Soviet Union. According to our embassy's German sources, however, Schulenburg before leaving Berlin had on his own initiative informed Astakhov, the Soviet chargé d'affaires, that "Germany had no intention of attacking the Soviet Union and that consequently it would be a pity were the Soviet Union to become involved in the 'encirclement' policy of other states."

On July 1, 1939, our embassy in Moscow sent us another telegram describing a conversation on June 29 between Schulenburg and Molotov during which the ambassador had apparently again exceeded his instructions in connection with his efforts to promote Soviet-German friendship. In this telegram the embassy reported that according to its informant:

> The Ambassador told Molotov that, following his visit to Berlin, he could assure him that Germany entertained no aggressive designs against the Soviet Union and in confirmation thereof pointed out that the German press had ceased entirely the publication of any anti-Soviet views or articles; that acquiescence in the Hungarian annexation of Ruthenia could be regarded as proof that Germany entertained no designs on the Ukraine and that furthermore the conclusion of nonaggression pacts with the Baltic countries was additional proof of the absence of any German intention to attack the Soviet Union. In respect of the nonaggression pacts with the Baltic States, Molotov remarked that these treaties were with third countries and not with the Soviet Union. The Ambassador thereupon inquired whether the Soviet Government desired a similar treaty with Germany. Molotov evaded the question. The Ambassador then remarked that the nonaggression treaty of [1925]

between Germany and the Soviet Union was still in existence. To this Molotov replied that he was interested to hear the Ambassador say so inasmuch as the Soviet Government had had certain doubts as to the continued validity of that treaty in view of subsequent agreements entered into by the German Government. The Ambassador said that if Molotov referred to the German-Italian alliance* he could assure him that this in no way affected the treaty. Molotov then stated that the denunciation of the nonaggression treaty with Poland had raised doubts as to the value of such treaties at the present time, to which the Ambassador replied that the situation in respect of Poland was somewhat different, in that the German Government felt that Poland by joining the "encirclement" policy of Great Britain had in fact contravened the nonaggression pact with Germany.

After this cautious exchange, the German ambassador brought up the economic negotiations between Germany and the Soviet Union that had been recently renewed, but this subject was not discussed since Molotov stated that he was not familiar with the details of the negotiations. The ambassador before departing, however, put to Molotov the question that had clearly been on the minds of both but that had thus far been skirted. He asked whether "he was correct in assuming that the Soviet Union desired normal relations with all countries which did not transgress Soviet interests and whether that was equally applicable to Germany," and, according to the embassy's informant, "Molotov replied in the affirmative." It seemed to us that Molotov was beginning to thaw.

The Soviet Union Moves Cautiously in Determining Its Course of Action Between the Countries of the West and Germany

During the next five weeks such information as the State Department was receiving from our embassies in Moscow and Berlin caused us to believe that although the commercial or economic negotiations between Germany and the Soviet Union were progressing slowly but satisfactorily, the political conversations were at a standstill. I began to think that perhaps in view of their mutual distrust and of the desire of both Germany and the Soviet Union to maintain a high degree of flexibility in the fluid European situation, both parties were shying away from making any formal commitments that might limit their ability to maneuver.

---

* Molotov was apparently referring to the treaty of friendship and military alliance that Germany had signed with Italy on May 20, 1939.

During these weeks there were intermittent outbursts of what we considered to be naive optimism on the part of many columnists, commentators, and intellectuals of the West regarding the outcome of the British-French-Soviet negotiations. We, on our part, did not believe that the Soviets had any desire to hurry these negotiations to a successful conclusion. We thought that they were preferring to carry on two parallel sets of conversations in the hope that developments would eventually take place that would permit them to assume a neutral role in Europe while the noncommunist powers were tearing one another to pieces.

It was my custom while in the East European area of the State Department to address memoranda from time to time to my superiors setting forth the views of our area regarding current Soviet foreign policies and tactics. Many of these memoranda came back to our area files and were eventually destroyed. A few of them, however, found their way into the permanent archives of the department. Among those that have survived was one prepared by me on July 22, 1939. It was addressed to Dunn, adviser to the secretary on political relations, and to Jack Hickerson, who was acting chief of the Division for European Affairs. It read in part as follows:

> Numerous articles relating to Soviet foreign policies have lately appeared in the press which in my opinion must have been written by persons who have little knowledge or understanding of the mentality of the present rulers of Russia. In fact, there seems to me to be a complete lack of understanding, at least in the American press, of Soviet foreign policies.
>
> I am setting forth below a number of statements regarding what I conceive to be the guiding principles of Soviet foreign policy and the effect which recent international events have had upon the application of these principles:
>
> (1) The present rulers of Russia are still dominated by a spirit of aggressiveness, that is, they have not departed from the ultimate aim to enlarge the Soviet Union and to include under the Soviet system additional peoples and territories.
>
> (2) They are convinced, however, that their present tactics should be:
>
>   (a) To hold intact the territory already under their control; and
>
>   (b) To increase as rapidly as possible the economic and military might of that territory.
>
> (3) Ever since its establishment the rulers of the Soviet Union have been convinced that it will eventually be the target of attack from so-called capitalist powers, either because such powers are greedy for the great undeveloped wealth of Russia or because they have become convinced that eventually they must destroy the Soviet Union if the Soviet Union, ever increasing in strength, is not to destroy them.

(4) During recent years the Soviet leaders have been particularly apprehensive of a number of foreign hostile combinations, of which the following may be mentioned:

(a) Germany, together with Poland, and possibly with the assistance of Japan.

(b) The four great Locarno Powers: Great Britain, Germany, Italy, France (The Soviet leaders since 1918 have been convinced that if these four great Powers ever reach an understanding they will eventually turn against the Soviet Union).

(c) Japan alone with such aid as Germany and the European border states may render short of actually entering the conflict (during recent years the Soviet leaders have become convinced that if no third parties intervene they are now sufficiently strong to hold off Japan—a war with Japan, however, would result in great economic loss which they wish to avoid).

(5) So long as Germany and Poland were collaborating and there appeared to be a possibility that they might join in an attack upon the Soviet Union, the Soviet foreign policy with regard to Europe was based upon Soviet demands for so-called collective security, which in essence would have meant a Europe divided into two camps, in one of which the Soviet Union would have been playing a leading role.

(6) The break which took place between Poland and Germany last March, followed by British guarantees to Poland and Rumania, have changed the whole international outlook so far as the Soviet Union is concerned. At present for the first time the Soviet leaders are in no immediate dread of either a German-Polish combination or of a great four–Power European settlement.

(7) As a result of this change the Soviet Union has no longer any deep interest in the policy of collective security. It feels itself relatively safe from a dangerous European attack so long as Poland, supported by Great Britain, is at loggerheads with Germany. It is not anxious to enter into any European arrangement at the present time which may restrict its ability to maneuver. If it does come to terms with Great Britain, it will do so only on a basis which will give it what amounts to hegemony over Eastern Europe, and which will render impossible for at least many years to come a united Western Europe.

I realize that the above represents an over-simplification of a very complicated situation. You will notice that I have not even referred to the Communist International or to the attitude which the Soviet Union might take in case of the outbreak of a war in the near future between Poland and Germany. It is my feeling, however, that the points which I have brought out above should be considered whenever an attempt is made to understand the Soviet foreign policies.

I may have been wrong in indicating that the Soviet Union was "not anxious to enter into any European arrangement at the present time which may restrict its ability to maneuver." Regardless of what its attitude might have been on July 22, 32 days after I wrote those words, it did sign a treaty with a European power that sharply curtailed its political flexibility.

GERMANY AND SOVIET UNION SIGN A COMMERCIAL CREDIT AGREEMENT ON AUGUST 19, 1939

On the morning of August 21, 1939, we received a telegram from Steinhardt in which he reported that according to TASS a commercial credit agreement had been signed between the Soviet Union and Germany on August 19. He said that both *Pravda* and *Izvestiia* of August 21 had devoted their leading editorials to the new agreement and had stressed that in view of the strained political relations between the two countries the negotiations leading to the agreement had been difficult and had met with success only because both sides desired an improvement in their commercial relations. The *Pravda* editorial, he reported, had concluded with the following words: "The new commercial credit agreement between the Soviet Union and Germany which was born in an atmosphere of strained political relations is summoned to relieve this atmosphere. It may represent a serious step in the matter of the further improvement of not only the economic but also the political relations between the Soviet Union and Germany."

Once the ice was broken, developments in the relations between Germany and the Soviet Union—developments that were making profound changes in the European situation—moved with breath-taking speed.

In the morning of August 23 we received another telegram from Steinhardt stating that Ribbentrop had arrived by plane in Moscow at one o'clock that day (Moscow time) and was to see Molotov at three o'clock.

MOLOTOV AND RIBBENTROP SIGN NONAGGRESSION PACT OF AUGUST 23, 1939*

On August 24 Steinhardt sent the State Department a telegram, which read as follows:

---

* Although the pact was signed in the early morning hours of August 24, 1939, it carried the date of August 23, 1939.

Preliminary treaty was signed early this morning in the Kremlin by Molotov and Ribbentrop. Stalin was present at the final conference. The pact consists of seven articles, of which the following is a brief summary:

The two countries agree:

(1) to commit no act of aggression direct or indirect against each other.

(2) to refrain from supporting in any way any country at war with the other.

(3) to consult with each other on questions of mutual interest.

(4) to refrain mutually from associating with any group of powers aimed directly or indirectly against the interests of the other.

(5) to settle any differences which might arise between the two countries by excusively peaceful means.

(6) The treaty shall last for ten years, renewable for another five; and,

(7) The treaty shall be ratified within the shortest possible time by both Governments but will enter into force from the moment of signature.

The information contained in the above telegram, we learned later, came as we had surmised from the unnamed informants who had been furnishing the embassy information regarding developments to German-Soviet relations.

We in the East European area of the State Department who had been following the series of telegrams from our embassy in Moscow describing the conversations that had been taking place between Schulenburg and Molotov could not believe that the Soviet Union would agree to the signing of a treaty of nonaggression with Germany unless it had received from the German government the kind of assurances upon which Molotov had been insisting. I refer, in particular, to assurances with regard to the future of the Baltic states, Poland, and other countries of Eastern Europe, as well as those with regard to German policies in the Far East. It seemed to us, therefore, that in addition to the clauses summarized in Steinhardt's telegram of the morning of August 24, there must be an additional agreement of a secret nature.

The Secret Protocol to the Nonaggression Pact

We were not surprised, therefore, when a few hours after the receipt of that telegram another telegram came from Steinhardt, dated noon,

August 24, in which he reported that he had learned from his secret source that attached to the treaty was a secret agreement, the provisions of which seemed to meet the demands that Molotov had been making. The telegram read in part as follows:

> I am informed in strict confidence that a full "understanding" was reached last night between the Soviet and German Governments in reference to territorial questions in Eastern Europe whereby Estonia, Latvia, Eastern Poland, and Bessarabia are recognized as spheres of Soviet vital interest. Apparently Finland was not mentioned. My informant added that article 4, which prohibits the contracting parties from joining any group of powers directed against the other, in addition to precluding Soviet adherence to any Anglo-French alliance will also preclude any German-Japanese collaboration. I am informed that the negotiations were conducted personally by Stalin who did not disguise from Ribbentrop that he had long been in favor of a Soviet-German *rapprochement*. When the treaty was concluded Stalin drank a toast to Hitler and to "the revival of the traditional German-Russian friendship." As a result of the discussions dealing with territorial questions involving countries lying between Germany and the Soviet Union I am informed that there was a tacit agreement to the effect that the Soviet Union would be given territorial compensation, if it so desired, for both* territorial changes which might be introduced by Germany in those regions.

Comparison of Documents in Berlin Archives with Information Obtained by U.S. Embassy in Moscow During 1939 Regarding Soviet-German Negotiations

A volume entitled *Nazi-Soviet Relations, 1939–1941* contains translations of some of the reports found in the files of the German Foreign Office after the war from Ambassador Schulenburg to his government covering the series of his secret conversations with Molotov that led up to the conclusion of the nonaggression pact. These translations compare quite favorably with the accounts of the conversations received from our embassy in Moscow. There are, however, several differences in detail. In my opinion the accounts given by the secret informants of the embassy may in some instances be more dependable than those contained in the reports written by the ambassador for the benefit of his government. I say this because I knew Schulenburg well enough to realize that although he personally had a deep distrust for both Hitler and Ribbentrop and had no

---

* This was apparently a garble; undoubtedly *both* should have been *such* or *any*.

sympathy for the Nazi movement, he was at the same time a highly patriotic German devoted to promoting what he considered to be the interests of his country. He had told me on a number of occasions that in his opinion war between the Soviet Union and Germany would be disastrous for both countries and would not be in the interest of world peace. It is my belief, therefore, that he sometimes tailored his reports and conducted his conversations with Molotov in a manner that in his opinion would be most likely to lead to a German-Soviet *rapprochement*. Some of the differences between the accounts as reported by our embassy and those found in the files of the German Foreign Office might also be explained by mistakes made on the part of our embassy's informants or by failure on the part of the representatives of our embassy to understand or to recall precisely what the informants had told them. One of the major inaccuracies in the accounts as reported by our embassy was the statement contained in Steinhardt's telegram of August 24, noon, to the effect that Finland was not mentioned in the secret protocol. In any event the manner in which our embassy contrived to keep the State Department so well informed on the Molotov-Schulenburg conversations reflected, in my opinion, great credit on the embassy, particularly on Bohlen and other members of the embassy staff who had been successful in winning the confidence of key members of the German embassy and in keeping communication channels with them open.

We were puzzled to note that the telegram from Steinhardt summarizing the secret protocol did not include Lithuania among the states assigned to the sphere of Soviet influence ("Soviet vital interest"). Although Lithuania had no common boundaries with the Soviet Union, Soviet spokesmen had frequently shown keen interest in the future of that country. We had been surprised, therefore, that Stalin had not insisted that Lithuania be included in the Soviet sphere. The only explanation for this omission that seemed logical to us was that both Germany and the Soviet Union might prefer to be separated by a pair of buffer states composed of a German-oriented Lithuania and the small portion of Poland that had not as yet been assigned. Whether or not our assumption was correct I do not know. In any event more than a month later, on September 28, a supplementary German-Soviet agreement added Lithuania to the Soviet sphere and gave the unassigned portion of Poland to Germany.

Concern and Puzzlement in the Department of State Regarding Significance of Soviet-German Nonaggression Pact

Although we in the area of Eastern European Affairs had been reading the series of telegrams from our embassy in Moscow regarding the Nazi-Soviet negotiations, we were nevertheless surprised and shocked at the cold-blooded manner in which Germany and the Soviet Union were dividing Eastern Europe into their respective spheres of "vital interest." We could not be sure of what the signatories to the protocol had precisely in mind in using the expression, "sphere of vital interest." Was it their intention that each party should be free, so far as the other was concerned, to dispose as it pleased of the territory lying in its sphere? Would the Soviet Union, for instance, feel quite free to annex Estonia, Latvia, the eastern portion of Poland, and the Bessarabian province of Romania? Would Germany feel free to annex the sections of Poland that had apparently been assigned to its sphere? If such were the intentions of the parties to the protocol, how were Germany and the Soviet Union planning to carry them out? Obviously Poland could be divided only through war and Estonia and Latvia could be brought under Soviet control only through military action or the threat of such action. Such knowledge as I had gained over the years of the Soviet Union under Stalin caused me to believe that he would not permit any small country in the Soviet sphere of influence long to remain truly independent. I thought that he would consider it his duty as a Communist to add that country, as soon as the international situation might make it safe for him to do so, to the territory of the Soviet Union, or at least to place over it a government under the control of a communist party, which in turn would be taking its orders from the Kremlin.

Other members of the State Department, including the secretary and the under secretary, were also deeply concerned about the significance of the German-Soviet treaties from the point of view of the peace of Europe. Almost immediately after the announcement of the signing of the nonaggression pact of August 23, Under Secretary Welles sent for me and requested that the East European area prepare for the use of the State Department a memorandum summarizing such information as the department had in its possession regarding the possibility of a German-Soviet *rapprochement* and the significance of the newly signed German-Soviet treaties.

During the following week members of the East European area worked many hours combing the files of the State Department and preparing the memorandum. Once finished, we sent copies of it to the secretary, the under secretary, Dunn, Moffat, Berle, and Hornbeck on August 31, the day before Germany launched its attack on Poland.

DID CONCLUSION OF GERMAN-SOVIET NONAGGRESSION PACT MEAN THAT STALIN HAD ABANDONED THE OBJECTIVE OF WORLD REVOLUTION?

Stalin's apparent willingness to divide with Hitler the territories of Eastern Europe into respective spheres of interest and otherwise to cooperate with him caused me to take another look at my long-held convictions and beliefs. Were they still valid? By consummating what was in essence an alliance with Hitler, Stalin seemed to me to be displaying contempt for the opinion of Communists, fellow travelers, and Hitler-hating "liberals" throughout the world. Could it be possible that he was on the point of abandoning the struggle for what I had regarded for many years as his ultimate goal, that is, a communist world?

I began to wonder whether, in order to escape the danger of a war with Germany and simultaneously to expand the territory under his control, Stalin had decided to junk the Communist International and what it stood for and, in cooperation with Hitler, to draw up new territorial lines for Europe and perhaps for the Middle East. If he had made such a decision, there was no basis for predicting what his next moves might be. My uncertainty was heightened by a speech made by Molotov on August 31, a translation of which was given to me on September 1, 1939, by the Soviet chargé d'affaires. In this speech Molotov outlined the history of the Soviet negotiations with the French and British from the Soviet point of view, defended the Soviet decision to sign the nonaggression pact with Hitler as a measure to maintain peace between the Soviet Union and Germany, and castigated Great Britain and France as imperialistic instigators of war. He made no reference, direct or indirect, in his speech to the cause of the world revolution or to that of the world proletariat. He indicated or dwelt on what was good for the Soviet Union without any mention of what was good for international communism. He was blunt in asking the rhetorical question: "Is it really difficult to understand that the USSR is pursuing, and will continue to pursue, its own independent policy, based on the interest of the people of the USSR and only their interests?"

As could be anticipated, the announcement of the German-Soviet nonaggression pact came as a shock to large numbers of liberals and noncommunist fellow travelers in the United States who had been regarding the Soviet Union as a bulwark against fascism. Many members of the united-front groups against fascism, particularly the Jewish members, were disillusioned. Most members of the communist hard cores of these groups, however, soon recovered from their initial shock and continued loyally to follow the lines laid down by Moscow. They argued that by coming to an agreement with Germany, the Soviet Union had in fact advanced the cause of world communism, that it had foiled a plot of the imperialists to instigate a German-Soviet war, that if Europe plunged into an imperialist war, it would be the fault of Great Britain and France, and that the United States, like the Soviet Union, should not become involved in such a war.

Within two weeks after the conclusion of the German-Soviet treaty I had recovered from my state of uncertainty. The lines of policy, discreet though they were, pursued by the Soviet Union with respect to various parts of the world, the positions taken by the communist parties that were members of the Communist International, and the tone of the Soviet press caused me to believe that Stalin's decision to collaborate with Hitler did not indicate an abandonment of the Soviet struggle for the expansion of communism. It was merely a change in tactics—a change that in Stalin's opinion would result in strengthening and expanding the Soviet Union and in weakening the forces opposed to communism.

Following the publication of the nonaggression pact in Moscow and Berlin, there was speculation in the American press and elsewhere regarding the possibility that it might be accompanied by a secret, unpublished agreement containing clauses providing for the redistribution of territories in Eastern Europe. So far as I knew, however, the information sent to us by our embassy in Moscow was the only confirmation of an authoritative character received by the U.S. government, or by any other government not a party to the treaty, of the existence of any such secret agreement. So carefully was the secret protocol guarded that only a limited number of offcials of the German and Soviet government were informed of it. The members of the Lithuanian delegation to Moscow were informed, however, by the Soviet negotiators in the autumn of 1939 that there existed an understanding between the German and Soviet governments regarding spheres of influence in Eastern Europe. They were not told, however, so far as I could learn, that this understanding was in the nature of a formal protocol.

The inability of those of us in the Department of State who had been given access to the series of telegrams regarding the German-Soviet political conversations and, in particular, to the telegram summarizing the contents of the secret protocol, to discuss the contents of these telegrams or even to mention their existence to persons to whom they had not circulated was a source of considerable embarrassment to us. Some of our colleagues in the department and also members of other agencies of the government regarded us as being unduly suspicious of Soviet foreign policies and intentions and particularly of Soviet insistence that it was merely playing the role of a neutral country. A number of members of the academic community and left-leaning columnists and commentators who refused to believe that the Soviet government was secretly collaborating with Nazi Germany were, for a time, outspokenly critical of the Department of State for its apparent attitude of distrust of the Soviet Union.

CHAPTER 49

THE LAST DAYS OF PEACE

FOR SEVERAL DAYS following the announcement of the signing of the nonaggression pact, the members of the Anglo-Franco military mission, puzzled regarding the effect that the signing of the pact might have on their own negotiations, remained in Moscow. On August 25, however, after making a call on Voroshilov, the Soviet commissar for defense, the members of the mission decided that further conversations would be useless and departed from the country. The publication on August 24 of the nonconfidential portions of the Molotov-Ribbentrop agreement of August 23 added to the fear throughout Europe and the United States that war was just around the corner.

PRESIDENT ROOSEVELT'S DEMARCHE OF AUGUST 24, 1939

President Roosevelt, disturbed at the increasing tensions in Europe, sent telegrams on August 24 to Hitler and to President Moscicki, urging that the governments of Germany and Poland agree to refrain from any positive act of hostility for a reasonable and stipulated period and that they agree by common accord to solve the controversies that had arisen between them by direct negotiation or by submission of these controversies to impartial arbitration or that they agree to their solution through the procedure of conciliation. Copies of these telegrams were sent to the king of Italy.

Hitler acknowledged the receipt of the telegram addressed to him only on August 31, only a few hours prior to the outbreak of war, through a note addressed to the secretary of state by Thomsen, the German chargé d'affaires in Washington. This note, after expressing appreciation of the "kind intermediary" of the president, stated that the German fuehrer had "left nothing untried for the purpose of settling the dispute between Germany and Poland in a friendly manner . . . Owing to the attitude of the Polish Government, however, all these endeavors have been without result."

The king of Italy on August 30 in a direct telegram to the president expressed his gratitude for the president's interest and stated that he had transmitted the president's message to his government. The king added that everything "possible to bring about peace with justice" had been and was being done.

President Moscicki through Ambassador Biddle in Warsaw answered the president on August 25. In his message he stated that the Polish government had always considered direct negotiations between governments as the most appropriate methods of solving difficulties. It also considered the methods of conciliation through a third disinterested and impartial party, such as President Roosevelt, as a just and equitable method in the solution of controversies arising between nations. He added that Poland agreed to refrain from any positive act of hostility provided the other party would also agree to refrain from any such act direct or indirect.

THE LAST WEEK OF PEACE, AUGUST 25–31, 1939

The president on August 25 sent a second telegram to Hitler in which he quoted Moscicki's reply and stated that if Hitler would agree to the pacific means of settlement suggested by the government of Poland, thousands of lives could be saved. Although Hitler did not respond immediately to the president's two messages, telegrams coming into the State Department from London, Paris, and Berlin indicated that his attitude had not softened. On August 25, according to some of these telegrams, Hitler engaged in several conversations with the British and French ambassadors to Germany in which he made it clear to them that he intended to resort to force if Poland continued to reject his demands. He also indicated during these conversations that if Poland should remain intractible and if Great Britain and France should come to Poland's aid, a war would ensue that would be worse than the war of 1914–1918. He informed the French ambassador that Germany would expect to win such a war since its agreement with the Soviet Union was "a positive one."

During the next few days the State Department was flooded with telegrams from our missions in Warsaw, Paris, Berlin, and London describing exchanges that were taking place as the British and French were making last-minute efforts to forestall a German attack on Poland. Spokesmen for the British and the French appealed both to Germany and Poland to enter into conversations for the purpose of settling their differences by direct negotiations. They were apparently hoping for some kind of compromise that would not seriously undermine Poland's independence and territorial integrity. They were not, however, so far as I could ascertain, bringing pressure on the Poles to make a contribution to world peace by yielding to all of Hitler's demands, which seemed to become more exorbitant daily.

Hitler, apparently to strengthen the hands of the influential British and French groups opposed to Great Britain and France going to war over Poland and to make Poland appear to be responsible for the war that was sure to come, told the British and French that he was prepared to enter into negotiations with the Poles if they would send at once to Berlin an emissary with plenipotentiary powers.

The telegrams coming in to the State Department at this juncture became so confusing that we were unable to fathom the exact nature of what Hitler really wanted from Poland. It was clear to us, however, that it was his intention to make demands on the Poles of such an exorbitant nature that the latter would not be able to accept them as a basis for negotiations and he would, therefore, be in a position to tell the world that it was not he but the Poles who had proved intransigent.

It was impossible during the last days of August 1939 for the State Department to keep fully abreast of developments that were taking place in Berlin. The members of our embassy in that city under the leadership of our able chargé d'affaires, Alexander Kirk, were doing their best by discussions with the British, French, and Polish embassies to ascertain just what was going on. The information that they obtained, however, was not always accurate. Kirk began one of his telegrams written on September 1 with the statement that "The events of yesterday have produced complete confusion among foreign representatives here and up to the present no clear explanation is available which covers the various developments."

It appeared to us in the department, however, from the telegrams pouring in from our interested embassies in Europe that, even though the demands that Hitler was planning to make were likely to be unacceptable, the Polish government under pressure from the British and French had authorized Lipski, the Polish ambassador to Germany, on August 31 to inform the German Foreign Office that it was willing to enter into negotiations; that Lipski, therefore, had called upon a high-ranking member of the Foreign Office early in the afternoon on August 31 and on Ribbentrop early in the evening of the same day; and that he had left with Ribbentrop a document that the Germans had interpreted as an expression of the unwillingness of Poland to negotiate on the basis of Hitler's demands. Immediately after Lipski's talk with Ribbentrop, the German government announced over the radio the text of sixteen demands on Poland.

Ambassador Bullitt from Paris, in a telegram sent to the State Department at midnight of August 31 commenting on these demands, stated:

> I have discussed the trend of events tonight with Bonnet, Paul Reynaud, and the Polish Ambassador... There is not the slightest disposition in either Poland or France or, so far as I can learn, England to submit to these demands... It is expected therefore that Hitler will attack Poland in the near future. France and England will fulfill their obligations and fight to assist Poland.
>
> Since Germany has replied to the official statement by the Polish Ambassador of Poland's readiness to negotiate direcly with Germany by this public announcement of inacceptable demands I do not believe that any appeal will stop Hitler from attacking if he has the courage to face a general European war. I feel however that a statement by the President might make the moral issue clearer and might increase Hitler's reluctance to begin the conflict.

THE SECOND WORLD WAR BEGINS, SEPTEMBER 1, 1939

Early on the morning of September 1, Kirk sent from Berlin a telegram to the effect that the German government had just issued a proclamation announcing that Poland had rejected a peaceful solution of the problem of neighborly relations with Germany. After listing the offenses committed by Poland against German rights and territory the proclamation, according to Kirk, stated that "force must be met by force and that the battle will be fought in defense of German territory and honor." Kirk reported in the same telegram that the announcement of the annexation of Danzig by the Reich had also been declared.

Shortly after my arrival in the department on the morning of September 1, a telegram came to my desk from my friend Kuykendall, our consul in Danzig, stating that he had been "notified officially by the

Senate at 7:30 this morning that state of war between Germany and Poland exists since 4:45 this morning," and that Foster, the Nazi leader of Danzig, had announced that as of "today's date" Danzig was a part of the Reich.

This telegram caused considerable excitement in the State Department since, although it was already known that German troops were entering Poland, from no other source had we as yet been informed that there was a "state of war" between Germany and Poland. We drafted therefore an urgent telegram to Kuykendall asking him to check the accuracy of the Senate's notification. In his reply he said that the notification had been given to him orally and that the emissary who had made it was now denying that he had used the expression "state of war."

Nevertheless, September 1 was the fateful day. Germany seized Danzig, and German troops began their invasion of Poland. In spite of frenzied British and French warnings and ultimatums the Germans continued to move forward into Poland. On September 3, therefore, both Great Britain and France declared war on Germany, and the Second World War, which was to change the face not only of Europe but of the world, began.

My Deep Dejection

September 1 represented one of the dark days of my life. I had no doubt when the news reached the State Department of the German attack on Poland that a new world war was opening—a war that, regardless of its outcome, would reduce Europe to ruins, would permanently weaken Europe's position in world affairs, and would undermine Western civilization. I was convinced that, despite the desire of the American people to avoid being involved in such a war, we would eventually be drawn into it. This conviction was based on my belief that the Western powers were not strong enough to defeat Germany without U.S. assistance and that the U.S. government, seeing that without our armed help the war would end with the Nazis and Fascists in control of Europe, would find some way to aid the Western powers. There was also a danger, I thought, that while the noncommunist nations of the West were tearing one another to pieces, the Soviet Union could be strengthening itself internally, expanding internationally, and preparing itself to become the master of Europe.

Index

The documents reproduced in this series (unless otherwise indicated) are deposited in the archives of the Hoover Institution on War, Revolution and Peace at Stanford University. The purpose of their publication is to shed new light on some important events concerning the United States or the general history of the twentieth century.

HERBERT HOOVER AND POLAND: A DOCUMENTARY HISTORY OF A FRIENDSHIP, FOREWORD BY SEN. MARK O. HATFIELD
George J. Lerski, compiler

NEGOTIATING WHILE FIGHTING: THE DIARY OF ADMIRAL C. TURNER JOY AT THE KOREAN ARMISTICE CONFERENCE, FOREWORD BY GEN. MATTHEW B. RIDGWAY
Allan E. Goodman, editor

PATRIOT OR TRAITOR: THE CASE OF GENERAL MIHAILOVICH, FOREWORD BY HON. FRANK J. LAUSCHE
David Martin, compiler

BEHIND CLOSED DOORS: SECRET PAPERS ON THE FAILURE OF ROMANIAN-SOVIET NEGOTIATIONS, 1931–1932
Walter M. Bacon, Jr., translator and compiler

THE DIPLOMACY OF FRUSTRATION: THE MANCHURIAN CRISIS OF 1931–1933 AS REVEALED IN THE PAPERS OF STANLEY K. HORNBECK
Justus D. Doenecke, compiler

WAR THROUGH CHILDREN'S EYES: THE SOVIET OCCUPATION OF POLAND AND THE DEPORTATIONS, 1939–1941, FOREWORD BY BRUNO BETTELHEIM
Irena Grudzinska-Gross and Jan Tomasz Gross, editors and compilers

BERLIN ALERT: THE MEMOIRS AND REPORTS OF TRUMAN SMITH, FOREWORD BY GEN. A.C. WEDEMEYER
Robert Hessen, editor

LENIN AND THE TWENTIETH CENTURY: A BERTRAM D. WOLFE RETROSPECTIVE, FOREWORD BY ALAIN BESANÇON
Lennard Gerson, compiler

A QUESTION OF TRUST: THE ORIGINS OF U.S.-SOVIET DIPLOMATIC RELATIONS; THE MEMOIRS OF LOY W. HENDERSON
George W. Baer, editor